THE GREENWOOD DICTIONARY OF

World History

JOHN J. BUTT

GREENWOOD PRESS
Westport, Connecticut • London

Library of Congress Cataloging-in-Publication Data

Butt, John J.
    The Greenwood dictionary of world history / John J. Butt.
        p. cm.
    Includes bibliographical references and index.
    ISBN 0–313–32765–3 (alk. paper)
    1. History—Dictionaries. I. Title. II. Title: Dictionary of world history.
D9.B87   2006
903—dc22   2005020918

British Library Cataloguing in Publication Data is available.

Library of Congress Catalog Card Number: 2005020918
ISBN: 0–313–32765–3

First published in 2006

Greenwood Press, 88 Post Road West, Westport, CT 06881
An imprint of Greenwood Publishing Group, Inc.
www.greenwood.com

Printed in the United States of America

∞™

The paper used in this book complies with the
Permanent Paper Standard issued by the National
Information Standards Organization (Z39.48–1984).

10 9 8 7 6 5 4 3 2 1

TABLE OF CONTENTS

INTRODUCTION TO THE GREENWOOD DICTIONARY OF WORLD HISTORY

The *Greenwood Dictionary of World History* is for high school and college students. It is not comprehensive (that would be impossible and cumbersome in the attempt) but, rather, includes entries that might be of use to students. Entries were selected based on the guidelines and recommendations of organizations and agencies such as the National Council for History Education, the National Center for History in the Schools, the World History Association, the College Board World History Advanced Placement Test, and many state standards for history education. The entries are truly global in range and chronologically span prehistory to the present day. The content of the definitions has been kept brief and concise to provide fundamental facts rather than encyclopedic information. Spellings follow the most current usage, and foreign words and names follow modern standards. Common variant spellings of foreign names are shown in parentheses.

The existence of separate entries is noted within definitions through the use of **boldface**. The Topical List of Entries is intended to provide some assistance in locating entries related to a particular region of the world or era. However, many entries cross the boundaries. Breaking the categories into smaller units might make some sense, but that process would be endless. The maps are intended for reference along with the entries, and they too are also not intended to be comprehensive. The same is true for the list of Web sites. Web sites are additionally ephemeral. The URLs are good as of the publication of this dictionary, but they can change at any time. These supplemental instruments should help students and teachers to flesh out their understanding of world history.

ACKNOWLEDGMENTS

I WOULD LIKE TO THANK my present and past students for assistance of various kinds with this work, especially Sarah Doyle, my apprentice, as well as Christine Contrada, Alison Thrasher, Andrea Friesen, Allison Abbott, and Jeff Brothers. I thank G. Wright Doyle, M.Div., Ph.D., for his assistance on Christianity and Judaism. I would also like to thank my colleagues for their assistance in writing entries or for providing consultation on specific fields of study: Dr. Lee Congdon, eastern Europe and intellectualism; Dr. Steve Guerrier, United States; Dr. Shah Hanifi, Central Asia and the Middle East; Dr. Kevin Hardwick, United States; Dr. Louise Loe, Russia; Dr. Richard Meixsel, military affairs; Dr. Henry Myers, the ancient world and intellectualism; Dr. David Owusu-Ansah, Africa; and Dr. Philip Riley, Europe. I especially want to thank Dr. Michael Seth, without whose help on Asia and world the dictionary would have taken much, much longer.

I also want to thank and dedicate this book to my wife, Julia, and my daughters, Bergen and Evan, for their patience and forbearance.

ALPHABETICAL LIST OF ENTRIES

TOPICAL LIST OF ENTRIES

AFRICA

ASIA

Vedas
Vedic
Viet Cong
Viet Minh
Vietnam War
Vijayanagar
Vishnu
Vo Nguyen Giap
Wang Anshi
Wang Jingwei (Wang Ching-wei)
Wang Mang
Warlords
Warring States Period
Wayang
White Lotus Rebellion
Wudi (*see* Han Wudi [Wu-Ti])
Wu Zhao (Wu Chao)
Xia
Xi'an (Hsi-an)
Xi'an Incident
Xingjiang (Hsin-chiang)
Xiongnu (Hsiung-nu)
Xuanzang (Hsuan-tsang)
Xunzi (Hsun-tzu)
Yamagata Aritomo
Yamato
Yangban
Yang Guifei (Yang Kuei-fei)

Yangshao Culture
Yangzi River (Yangtze River or Chang Jiang)
Yayoi
Yellow River (Huang He)
Yi Dynasty
Yin-Yang
Yi Song-gye
Yi Sun-sin
Yoga
Yongle (Yung-le)
Yongzheng
Yosano Akiko
Yoshida, Shigeru
Yuan
Yuan Shih-kai
Yurt
Zaibatsu
Zen
Zeng Guofan (Tseng Kuo-fan)
Zhang Qian (Chang Ch'ien)
Zhang Xueliang (Chang Hsüeh-liang)
Zheng He (Cheng Ho)
Zhou (Chou) Period
Zhou Enlai (Chou En-lai)
Zhuangzi (Chuang-tzu)
Zhu Xi (Chu Hsi)

EUROPE—ANCIENT TO 500

Academy
Acropolis
Actium, Battle of
Adrianople, Battle of
Aegean City-States
Aeneid, The
Aeolian Greeks
Aeschylus
Agamemnon
Agora
Alexander III, "the Great"
Alexandria
Alphabet, Phoenician
Antigone (*see* Sophocles)
Antigonid Dynasty

Antony, Mark
Aphrodite
Apollo
Apollo Oracle at Delphi
Appian Way
Apulia
Aqueduct
Arch
Archimedes
Arete
Aristophanes
Aristotle
Assembly (Rome)
Athena
Athens

MEDIEVAL: 500–1500

MODERN: 1500–PRESENT

LATIN AMERICA

López, Francisco Solano
Machu Picchu
Madero, Francisco
Mayan Calendar
Mayan Civilization
Mesoamerica
Mestizos
Mexican Revolution
Mita
Mixtec
Moctezuma II
Monte Alban
Montezuma (*see* Moctezuma II)
NAFTA (*see* North American Free Trade
   Agreement [NAFTA])
Nazca
Neoliberalism
North American Free Trade Agreement
   (NAFTA)
OAS (*see* Organization of American
   States [OAS])
Oaxaca
O'Higgins, Bernardo
Olmec Civilization
Organization of American States (OAS)
Pachacutec (Pachacuti)
Pacific, War of the
Palenque
Panama, Isthmus of
Panama Canal

Perón, Eva
Perón, Juan
Pinochet, Augusto
Popol Vuh
Pyramid of the Sun
Quetzalcóatl
Quipu
Royal Commentaries of the Inca
Sandinista
San Martin, José de
Sendero Luminoso
Shining Path (*see* Sendero Luminoso)
Strait of Magellan
Tenochtitlán
Teotihuacán
Texcoco
Tierra del Fuego
Toltec Civilization
Topu Inca
Toussaint L'Ouverture, François
   Dominique
Tupac Amaru II
Vargas, Getúlio
Villa, Pancho
Vuh (*see* Popol Vuh)
Wars of Independence, Latin American
Zapata, Emiliano
Zapatista Uprising
Zapotec Civilization

MIDDLE EAST (INCLUDING EGYPT)

Abbasid Caliphate
Abdullah ibn Hussein
Abraham
Abu al-Abbas
Abu Bakr
Achaemenids
Aden
Afghanistan, Twentieth-Century
Akhenaton (*see* Amenhotep IV
   [Akhenaton])
Akkadians
Alhambra
Ali

Allah
Alp-Arslan
Amenhotep IV (Akhenaton)
Amir
Amon-Re
Amorites
Amos
Anglo-Afghan Wars
Antigonid Dynasty
Arabia
Arab-Israeli War, 1967
Arab-Israeli War, 1973
Arab League

NORTH AMERICA

OTHER

LIST OF MAPS

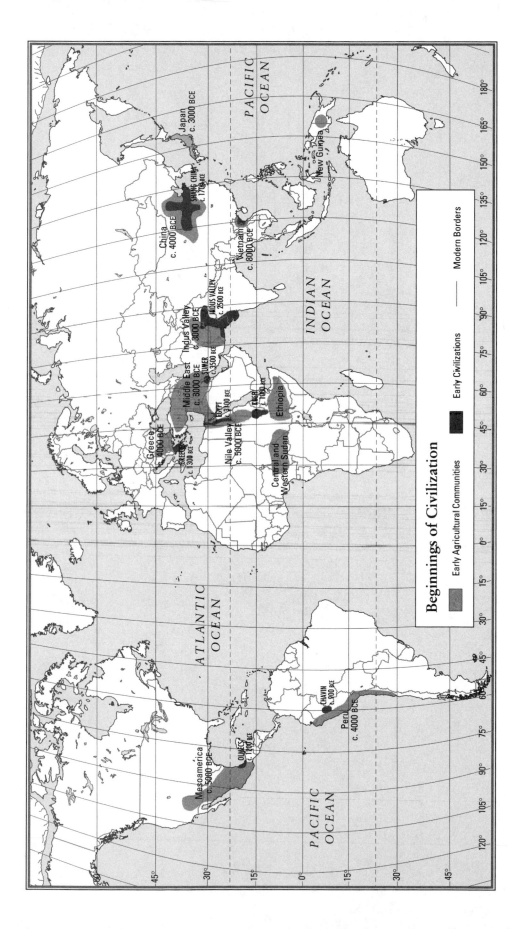

Beginnings of Civilization

Early Agricultural Communities

Early Civilizations

Modern Borders

China
c. 4000 BCE

SHANG CHINA
c. 1700 BCE

Japan
c. 3000 BCE

New Guinea

Vietnam
c. 8000 BCE

Indus Valley
c. 3000 BCE

INDUS VALLEY
c. 2500 BCE

Middle East
c. 3000 BCE

SUMER
c. 3500 BCE

EGYPT
c. 3100 BCE

Ethiopia

KUSH
c. 1000 BCE

Greece
c. 4000 BCE

GREECE
c. 1300 BCE

Nile Valley
c. 5000 BCE

Central and
Western Sudan

PACIFIC
OCEAN

PACIFIC
OCEAN

ATLANTIC
OCEAN

INDIAN
OCEAN

Mesoamerica
c. 5000 BCE

OLMEC
c. 1700 BCE

CHAVIN
c. 900 BCE

Peru
c. 4000 BCE

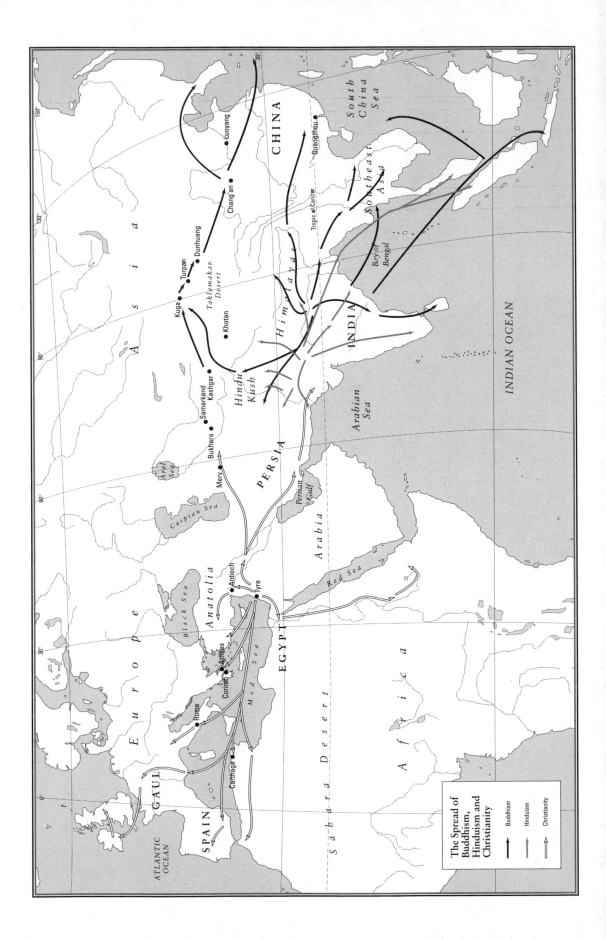

The Spread of Buddhism, Hinduism and Christianity

Buddhism

Hinduism

Christianity

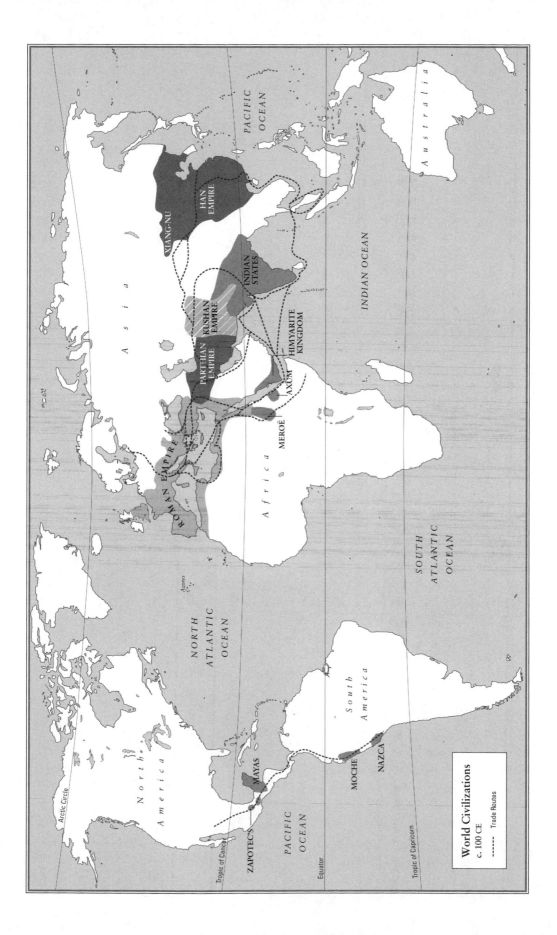

World Civilizations
c. 100 CE
------ Trade Routes

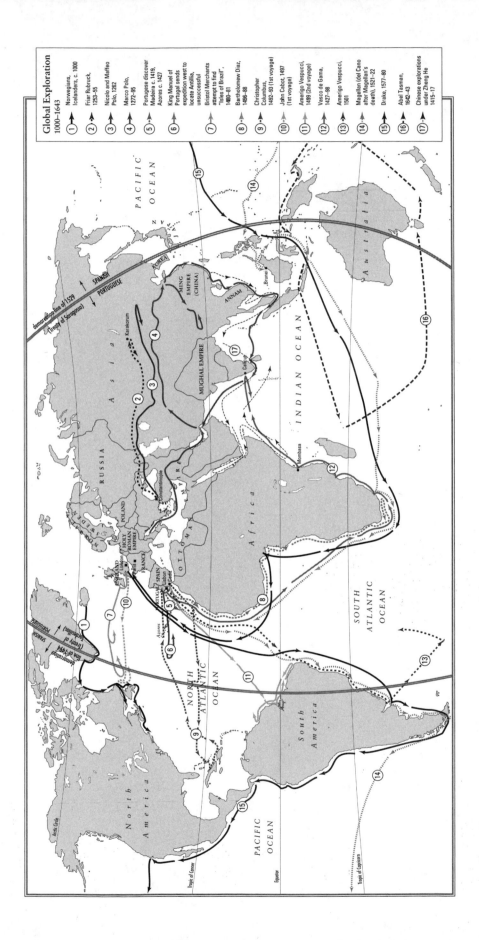

Global Exploration
1000–1643

1. Norwegians, Icelanders, c. 1000
2. Friar Rubruck, 1253–55
3. Nicolo and Maffeo Polo, 1282
4. Marco Polo, 1272–95
5. Portuguese discover Madeira c. 1419, Azores c. 1427
6. King Manuel of Portugal sends expedition west to locate Antilia, unsuccessful
7. Bristol Merchants attempt to find "Isles of Brazil", 1480–81
8. Bartholomew Diaz, 1486–88
9. Christopher Columbus, 1492–93 (1st voyage)
10. John Cabot, 1497
11. Amerigo Vespucci, 1499 (2nd voyage)
12. Vasco de Gama, 1427–98
13. Amerigo Vespucci, 1501
14. Magellan (del Cano after Magellan's death), 1521–22
15. Drake, 1577–80
16. Abel Tasman, 1642–43
17. Chinese explorations under Zheng He 1415–17

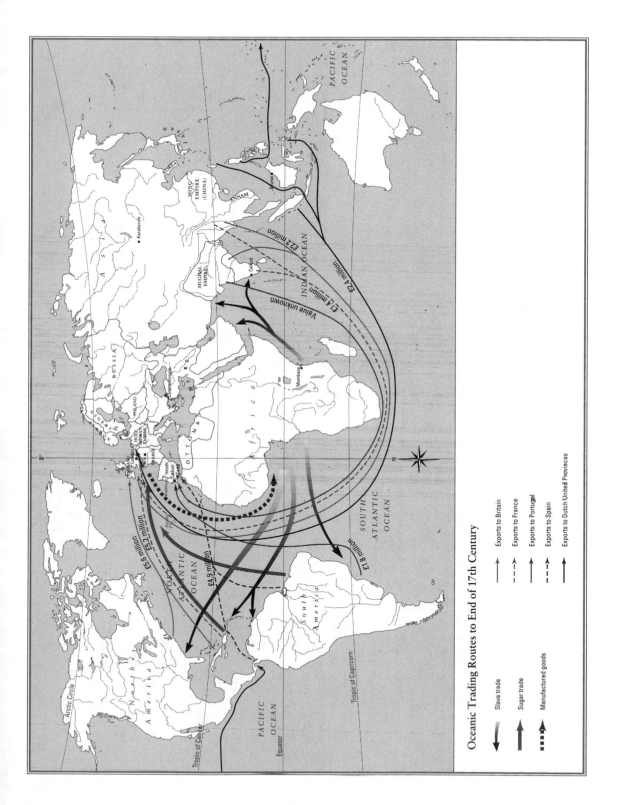

Oceanic Trading Routes to End of 17th Century

Slave trade
Sugar trade
Manufactured goods

Exports to Britain
Exports to France
Exports to Portugal
Exports to Spain
Exports to Dutch United Provinces

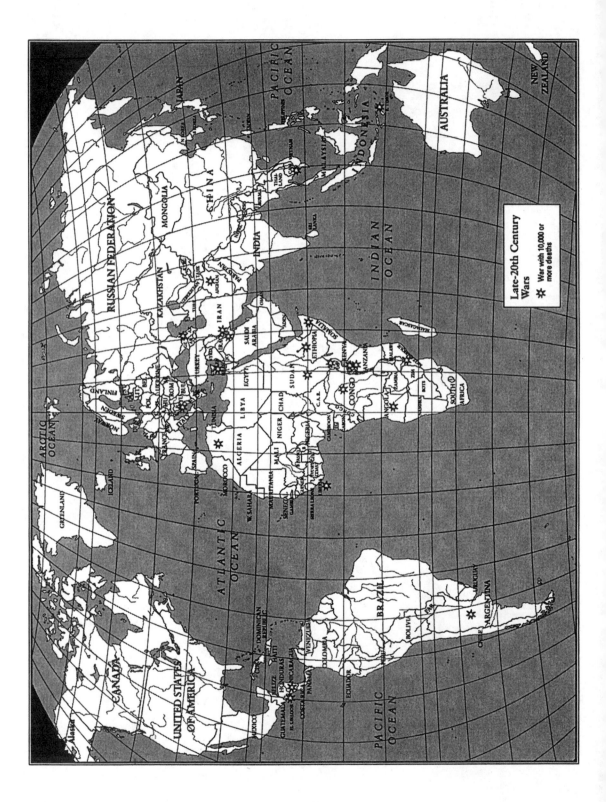

Late-20th Century Wars

✳ War with 10,000 or more deaths

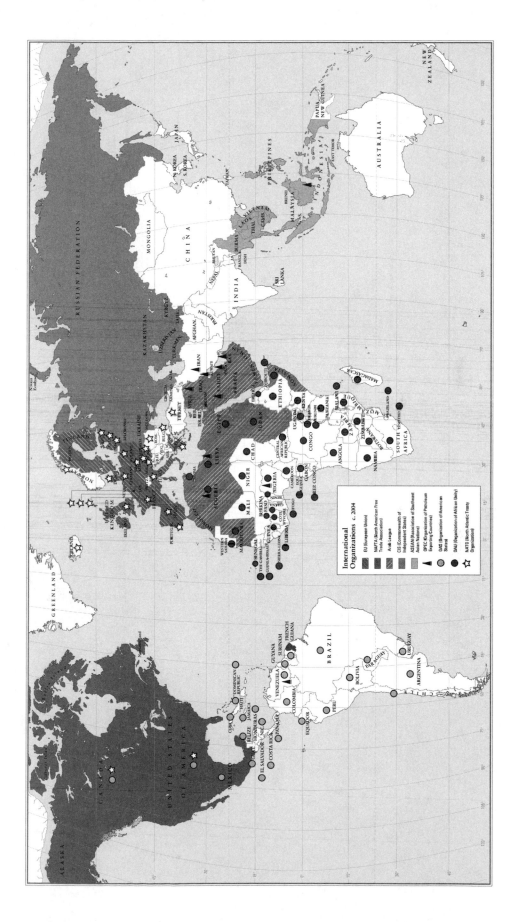

International
Organizations c. 2004

EU (European Union)

NAFTA (North American Free
Trade Association)

Arab League

CIS (Commonwealth of
Independent States)

ASEAN (Association of Southeast
Asian Nations)

OPEC (Organization of Petroleum
Exporting Countries)

OAS (Organization of American
States)

OAU (Organization of African Unity)

NATO (North Atlantic Treaty
Organization)

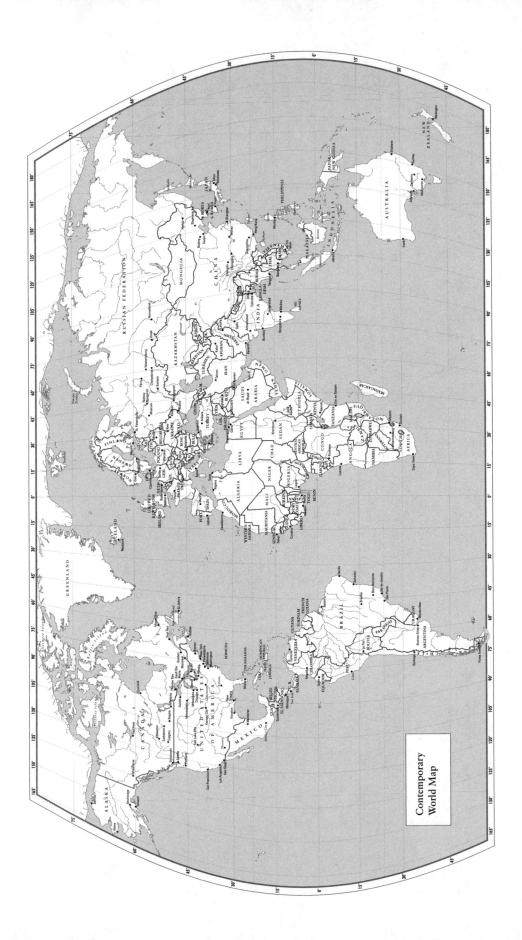

Contemporary
World Map

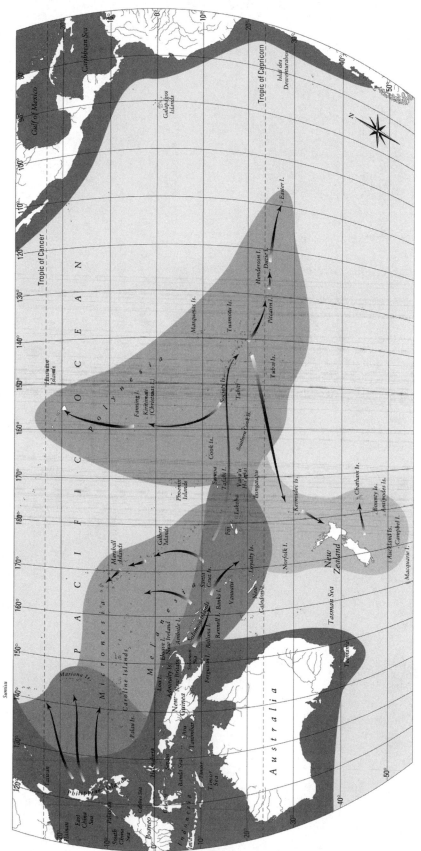

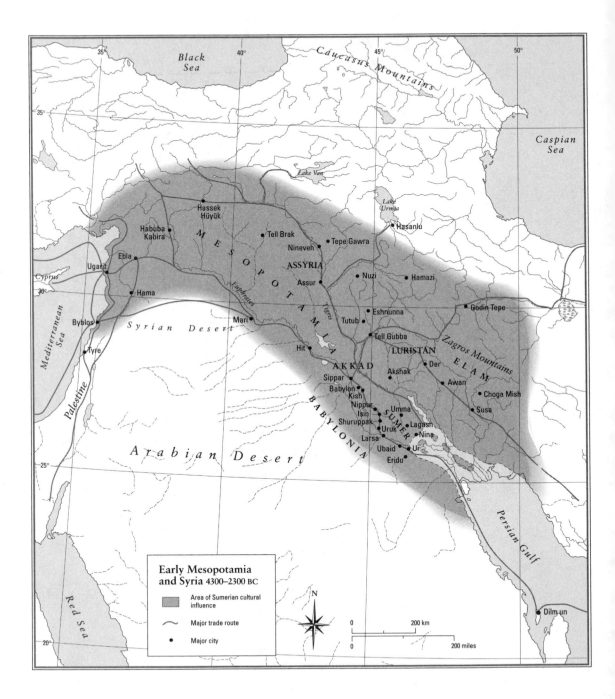

Black
Sea

Caucasus Mountains

Caspian
Sea

35°   40°   45°   50°

35°

Lake Van

*Lake
Urmia*

Hassek
Hüyük

•Hasanlu

Habuba
Kabira   •Tell Brak

M E S O P O T A M I A

Tepe Gawra

Nineveh

ASSYRIA

Ebla

Ugarit

Nuzi   •Hamazi

Cyprus

Assur

30°

Hama

Euphrates

Tigris

Eshnunna   Godin Tepe

Mediterranean
Sea

Byblos

Syrian Desert   Mari

Tutub

Tell Gubba

Zagros Mountains

Tyre

Hit

AKKAD

LURISTAN   E L A M

Akshak   •Der

Palestine

Sippar

Babylon

Kish

Awan

Choga Mish

Nippur

Umma

•Susa

A r a b i a n   D e s e r t

Isin

B A B Y L O N I A   Shuruppak

SUMER

Lagash

Uruk   •Nina

25°

Larsa

Ubaid

Ur

Eridu

Persian Gulf

Red
Sea

**Early Mesopotamia
and Syria 4300–2300 BC**

Area of Sumerian cultural
influence

Major trade route

N

0   200 km

•   Major city

0   200 miles

Dilmun

20°

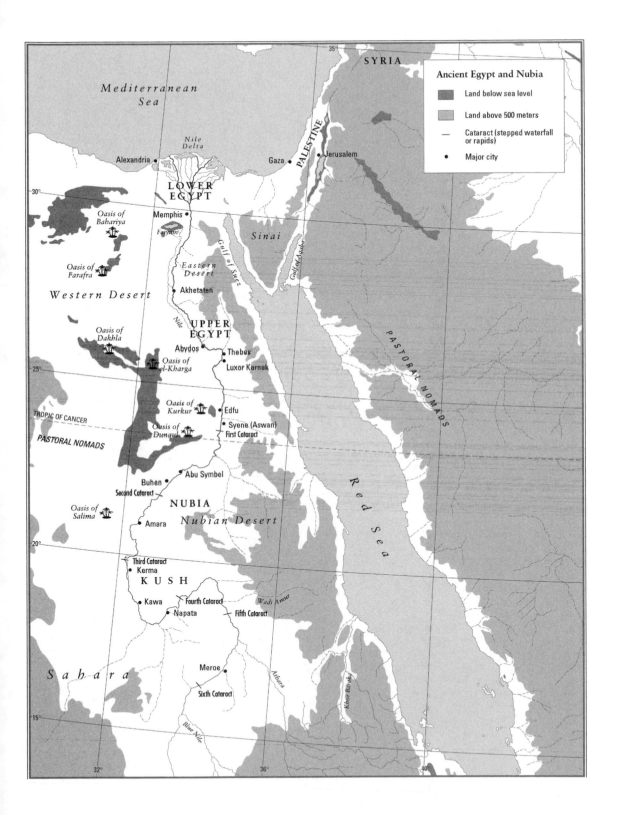

Ancient Egypt and Nubia

■ Land below sea level

■ Land above 500 meters

— Cataract (stepped waterfall or rapids)

• Major city

SYRIA

Mediterranean Sea

Nile Delta

Alexandria

Gaza

PALESTINE

Jerusalem

LOWER EGYPT

Memphis

Sinai

Fayum

Gulf of Suez

Gulf of Aqaba

Eastern Desert

Akhetaten

Western Desert

Oasis of Bahariya

Oasis of Farafra

UPPER EGYPT

Oasis of Dakhla

Abydos

Thebes

Oasis of el-Kharga

Luxor Karnak

TROPIC OF CANCER

Oasis of Kurkur

Edfu

Syene (Aswan)

First Cataract

Oasis of Dunqul

PASTORAL NOMADS

PASTORAL NOMADS

Red Sea

Abu Symbel

Buhen

Second Cataract

Oasis of Salima

NUBIA

Nubian Desert

Amara

Third Cataract

Kerma

KUSH

Kawa

Fourth Cataract

Wadi Amur

Napata

Fifth Cataract

Sahara

Meroe

Sixth Cataract

Atbara

Khor Baraka

Blue Nile

Nile

32°

36°

40°

35°

30°

25°

20°

15°

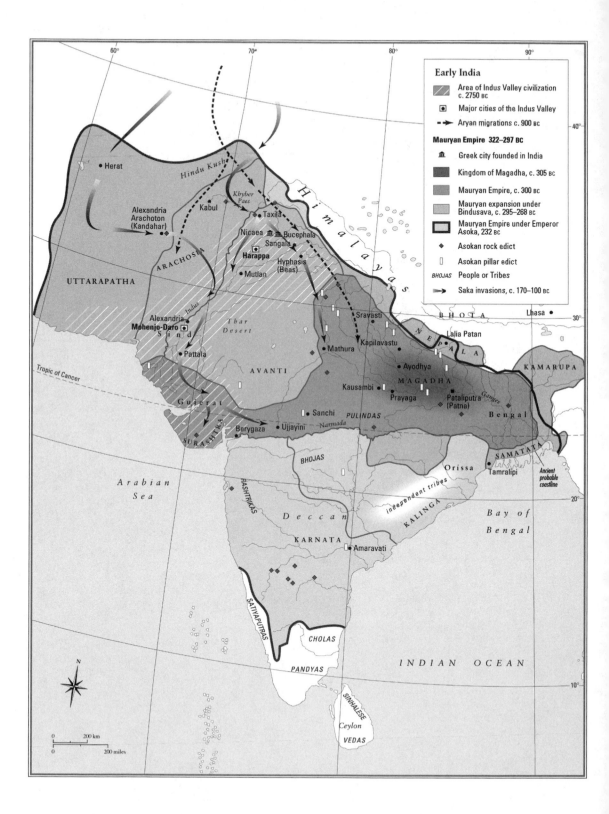

Early India

▨ Area of Indus Valley civilization c. 2750 BC

⊡ Major cities of the Indus Valley

▪- -→ Aryan migrations c. 900 BC

Mauryan Empire 322–297 BC

🏛 Greek city founded in India

Kingdom of Magadha, c. 305 BC

Mauryan Empire, c. 300 BC

Mauryan expansion under Bindusava, c. 295–268 BC

Mauryan Empire under Emperor Asoka, 232 BC

◆ Asokan rock edict

▯ Asokan pillar edict

BHOJAS People or Tribes

➤ Saka invasions, c. 170–100 BC

• Herat

Hindu Kush

Himalayas

Alexandria Arachoton (Kandahar)

• Kabul

Khyber Pass

• Taxila

Nicaea 🏛 🏛 Bucephala
Sangala •
Harappa
Hyphasis (Beas)
• Mutlan

ARACHOSIA

UTTARAPATHA

Sravasti •

B H O T A Lhasa •

N E P A L A

Lalia Patan •

Alexandria
Mohenjo-Daro ⊡
Sind

Thar Desert

• Mathura
Kapilavastu •

KAMARUPA

Tropic of Cancer

• Pattala

AVANTI

• Ayodhya

MAGADHA

Kausambi • • Prayaga
Pataliputra (Patna)

Ganges

Bengal

Gujerat

• Sanchi *PULINDAS*

Barygaza • Ujjayini *Narmada*

SURASHTRA

BHOJAS

Orissa

SAMATATA

Tamralipi •

Ancient probable coastline

Arabian Sea

RASHTRIKAS

independent tribes

KALINGA

Bay of Bengal

Deccan

KARNATA

• Amaravati

SATIYAPUTRAS

INDIAN OCEAN

N

CHOLAS

PANDYAS

SINHALESE

Ceylon

VEDAS

0   200 km
0   200 miles

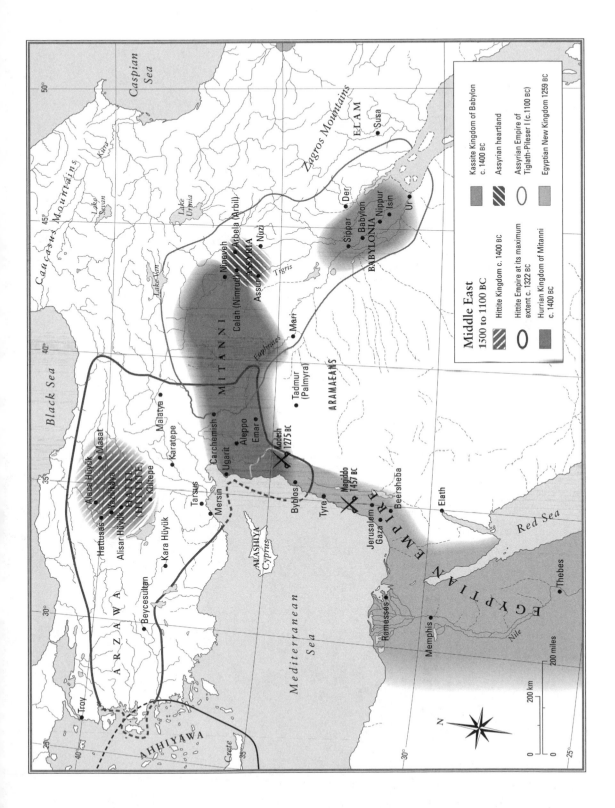

Caspian Sea

Caucasus Mountains

Black Sea

Lake Sevan

Lake Urmia

ELAM

• Susa

Zagros Mountains

Der •

Sippar • Babylon Nippur • Isin
BABYLONIA Ur

Nineveh • Arbela (Arbil)
Calah (Nimrud) • ASSYRIA Nuzi •
Assur

Tigris

Mari •

M I T A N N I

Euphrates

Tadmur (Palmyra) •

ARAMAEANS

Malatya •
Karatepe •
Carchemish • Aleppo •
Ugarit • Emar • Kadesh 1275 BC

Alaca Hüyük
Masat •
Hattusas • Bogazköy
Alisar Hüyük • Kültepe
H A T T I

Kara Hüyük •

Tarsus •

Mersin •

Beycesultan •

A R Z A W A

Troy •

Byblos • Megiddo 1457 BC
Tyre • Beersheba •

Elath •

Jerusalem •
Gaza • E G Y P T I A N   E M P I R E

ALASHIYA Cyprus

Mediterranean Sea

Memphis •

Ramesses •

Thebes •

Nile

Red Sea

AHHIYAWA

Crete

N

Middle East
1500 to 1100 BC

	Kassite Kingdom of Babylon c. 1400 BC
	Assyrian heartland
	Assyrian Empire of Tiglath-Pileser I (c.1100 BC)
	Egyptian New Kingdom 1259 BC
	Hittite Kingdom c. 1400 BC
	Hittite Empire at its maximum extent c. 1322 BC
	Hurrian Kingdom of Mitanni c. 1400 BC

N

0   200 km
0   200 miles

50°
45°
40°
35°
30°
25°

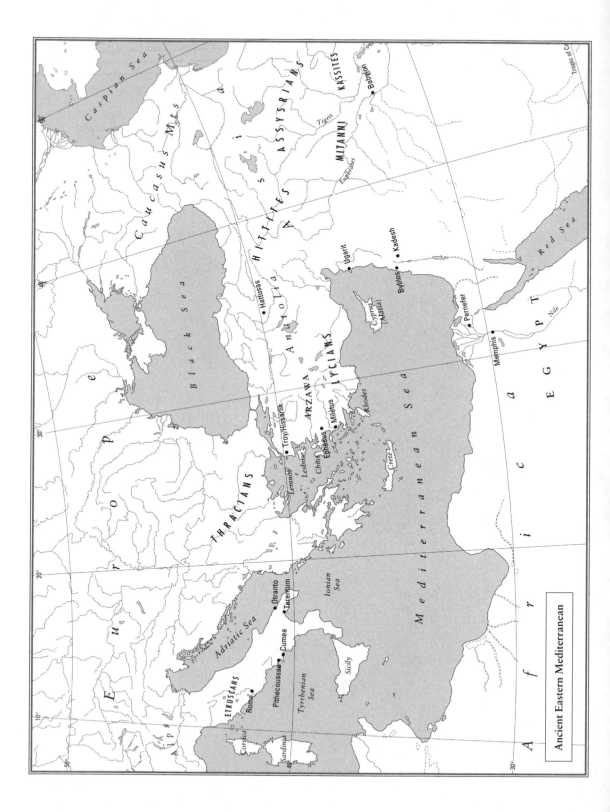

Ancient Eastern Mediterranean

Ancient Greece
c. 500 BC

ILLYRIA

*Black
Sea*

*Lake
Ohrid*

*Lake
Prespa*

T H R A C E

Ergene

Byzantium
Chalcedon

Axios

M A C E D O N I A

Nestos

Abdera

*Sea of
Marmara*

Pella

Amphipolis

Stagira

Thasos

Samothrace

Chersonese

Cyzicus

Daskylion

Methone

CHALCIDICE

Gorkceada

Abydos
Lampsacus

EPIRUS

Potidea

▲ *Mt. Olympus*

Lemnos

Ilium
(Troy)

MYSIA

Scione

Axiakmon

Dodona

THESSALY

Evstratios

*Aegean
Sea*

Pergamum

PHRYGIA

PERSIAN EMPIRE

Sesklo Dimini

Pharsalus   Iolkos

Nisvia

Lesbos
Mytilene

Arginusae

LYDIA

Ambracia

Argos

Sciathos

Skopelos

Skyros

Smyrna

Sardis

Leukas

AETOLIA

*Ionian
Sea*

PHOCIS

Thermopylae

Naupactus   Delphi

Gla

Euboea

Chios

IONIA

Teos

Kephallenia

Chalkis

Thebes
BOEOTIA

Patrae

Gulf of Corinth

ACHAEA

Megara

Deceleia

ATTICA

Athens
Piraeus

Ephesus

Aphrodisias

Andros

Elis

ARCADIA

Corinth

Samos

Miletus

Mycenae

ELIS

Zakynthos

Olympia

Argos
ARGOLIS
Troizen

Tegea

Ceos

Tenos

Icaria

Caria

Iasos

CARIA

Bassae

Peloponnese

Hydrea

Cythnos

Myconos

Patmos

Leros

Halicarnassus

MESSENIA

Pylos

LACONIA

Sparta

C y c l a d e s

Serifos

Syros

Dodecanese

Kabyminos

Cos

Ciphnos

Paros

Naxos

Amorgos

Cnidos

Nisyros

Syme

Cimolos

Sicinos

Ios

Astypalaea

Tilos

Melos

Pholegandros

Thera

Anaphi

Khalki

Rhodes

Cythera

Sea of Crete

Karpathos

Kasos

Knossos

Mallia

Crete

Kato Zakro

Haghia Triada

Phaistos

M e d i t e r r a n e a n   S e a

N

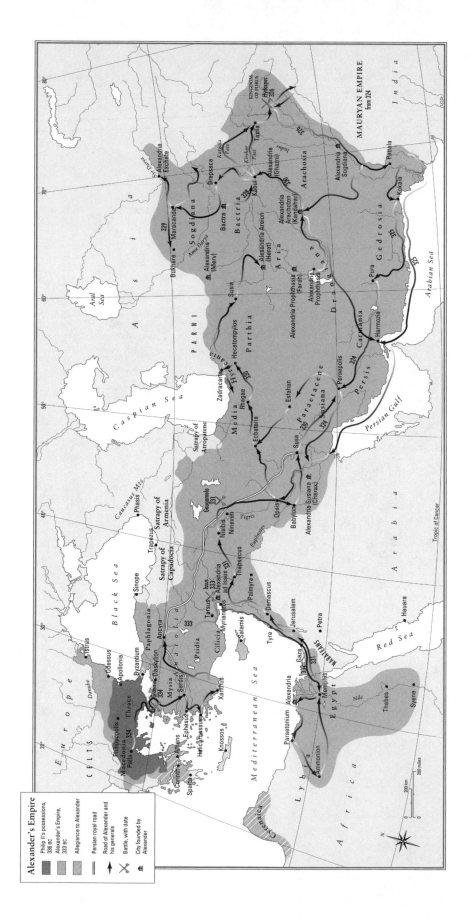

Alexander's Empire

Philip II's possessions, 336 BC

Alexander's Empire, 323 BC

Allegiance to Alexander

Persian royal road

Road of Alexander and his generals

Battle, with date

City founded by Alexander

MAURYAN EMPIRE from 324

KINGDOM OF PORUS

Hydaspes 326

India

Arabian Sea

Alexandria Eschate

Bukhara 329 Maracanda

Drapsaca

Taxila

Katigala

Khyber Pass

Kabul

Alexandria (Merv)

Bactra

Alexandria Arachoton (Kandahar)

Alexandria Areion (Herat)

Alexandria Prophthasia (Farah)

Alexandria (Ghazni)

Arachosia

Aria

Bactria

Sogdiana

Alexandria Sogdiana

Kotala

Alexandria Prophthasia

Pura

Gedrosia

Pattala

Drangiana

Carmania

Harmozia

Susia

Hecatompylos

Parthia

PARNI

Zadracarta

Hyrcania

Persis

Persepolis

Aral Sea

Asia

Amu Darya

Syr Darya

Caspian Sea

Satrapy of Atropatene

Media

Rhagae

Ecbatana

Esfahan

Paraetacene

Susiana

Susa

Alexandria Susiana (Charax)

Babylon

Opsis

Gaugamela 331

Nisibis

Nineveh

Tigris

Euphrates

Thapsacus

Palmyra

Damascus

Caucasus Mts.

Phasis

Trapezus

Satrapy of Armenia

Satrapy of Cappadocia

Sinope

Black Sea

Paphlagonia

Ancyra

Daskylion

Byzantium

Apollonia

Odessus

Istrus

Danube

CELTS

Europe

Thrace

Philippopolis

Macedonia

Pella 334

Corinth

Athens

Sparta

Ephesus

Sardis

Mysia

Lydia

Halicarnassus

Knossos

Pisidia

Cilicia

Tarsus

Issus 333

Alexandria ad Issus 333

Myriandrus

Salamis

Tyre

Jerusalem

Petra

Gaza 332

NABATEANS

Damascus

Hauara

Red Sea

Arabia

Tropic of Cancer

Alexandria

Paraetonium

Memphis 332/331

Ammonion

Nile

Libya

Thebes

Syene

Africa

Cyrenaica

Mediterranean Sea

Xanthos

N

0   200 km
0   200 miles

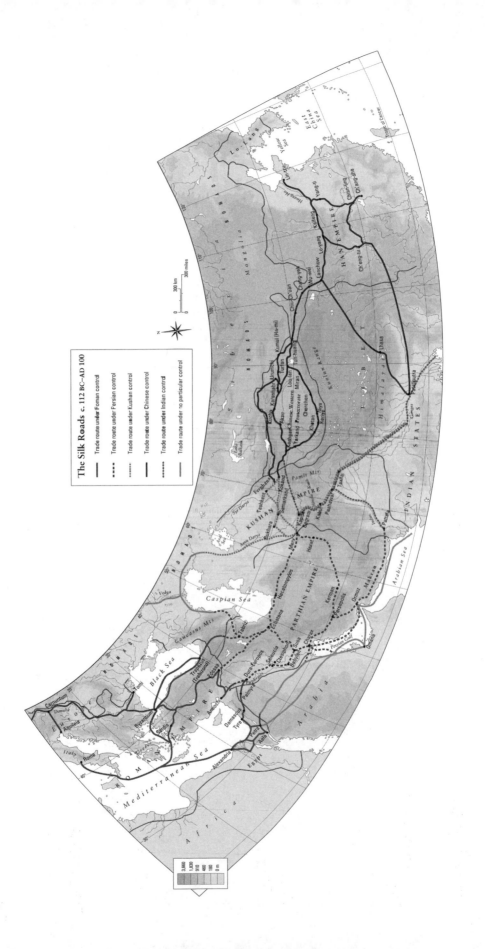

The Silk Roads c. 112 BC–AD 100

Trade route under Roman control
Trade route under Persian control
Trade route under Kushan control
Trade route under Chinese control
Trade route under Indian control
Trade route under no particular control

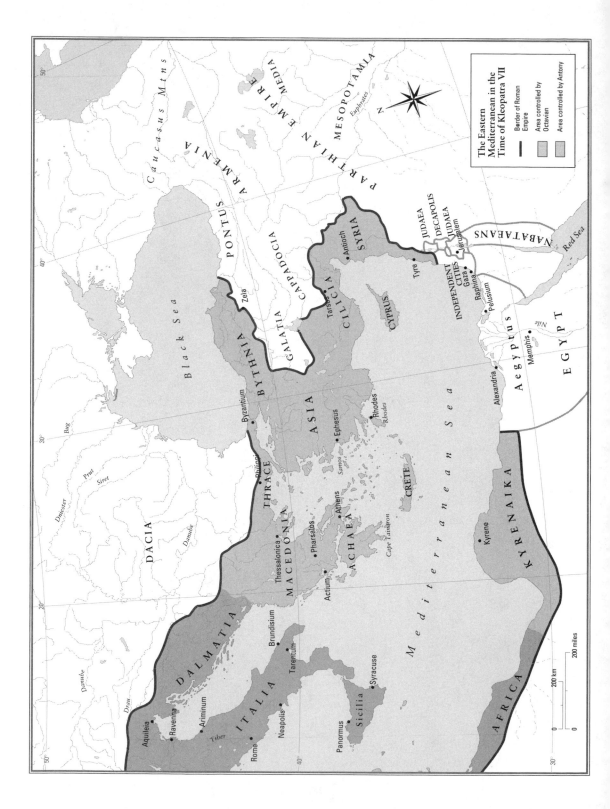

The Eastern
Mediterranean in the
Time of Kleopatra VII

Border of Roman
Empire

Area controlled by
Octavian

Area controlled by Antony

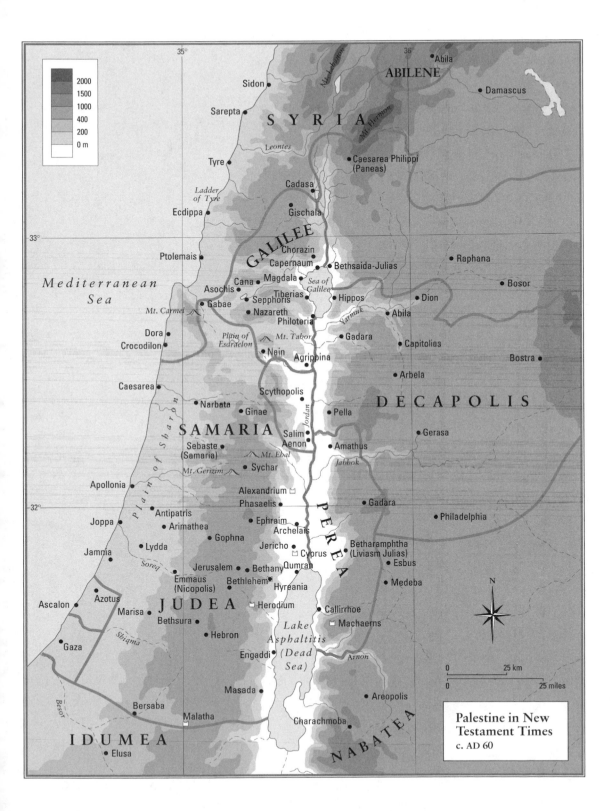

Palestine in New Testament Times
c. AD 60

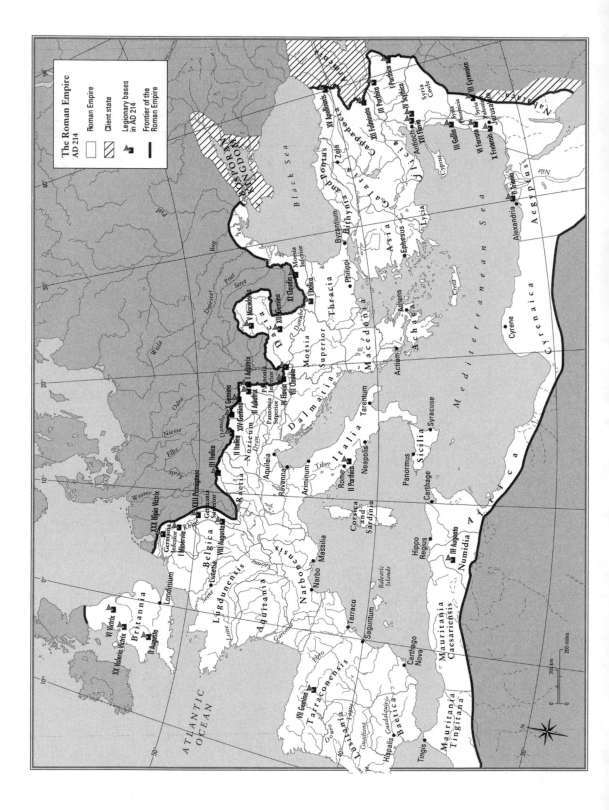

The Roman Empire
AD 214

Roman Empire

Client state

Legionary bases
in AD 214 ▲

Frontier of the
Roman Empire

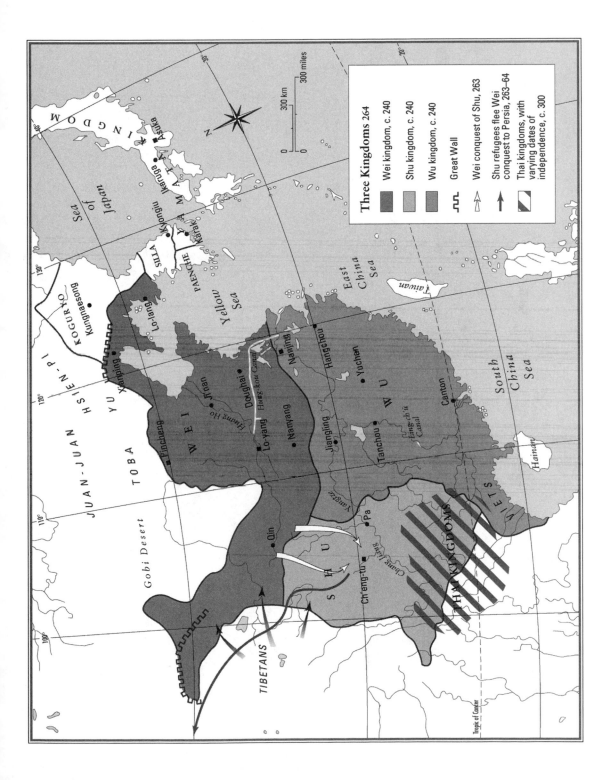

Three Kingdoms 264

Wei kingdom, c. 240

Shu kingdom, c. 240

Wu kingdom, c. 240

Great Wall

Wei conquest of Shu, 263

Shu refugees flee Wei
conquest to Persia, 263–64

Thai kingdoms, with
varying dates of
independence, c. 300

KOGURYO

Kungnaesong

JUAN-JUAN

TOBA

HSIEN-PI

YU

Xianping

Pincheng

WEI

Juan

Lo-lang

SILLA

PAENCHE

Karak

Khongiu

MATO

Ikaruga

Asuka

KINGDOM

Sea
of
Japan

Gobi Desert

Qin

Lo-yang

Doughai

Hang-kou Canal

Huang Ho

Nanyang

Yellow
Sea

Nanjing

Shanghai

Jiangling

Hangzhou

Yuchan

East
China
Sea

Taiwan

TIBETANS

SHU

Pa

Ch'eng-tu

Chang Jiang

Yangtze

Tanchou

Hang-ch'u
Canal

WU

Canton

South
China
Sea

Hainan

VIETS

THAI KINGDOMS

Tropic of Cancer

300 miles

300 km

N

110°

120°

120°

110°

100°

40°

40°

30°

30°

20°

20°

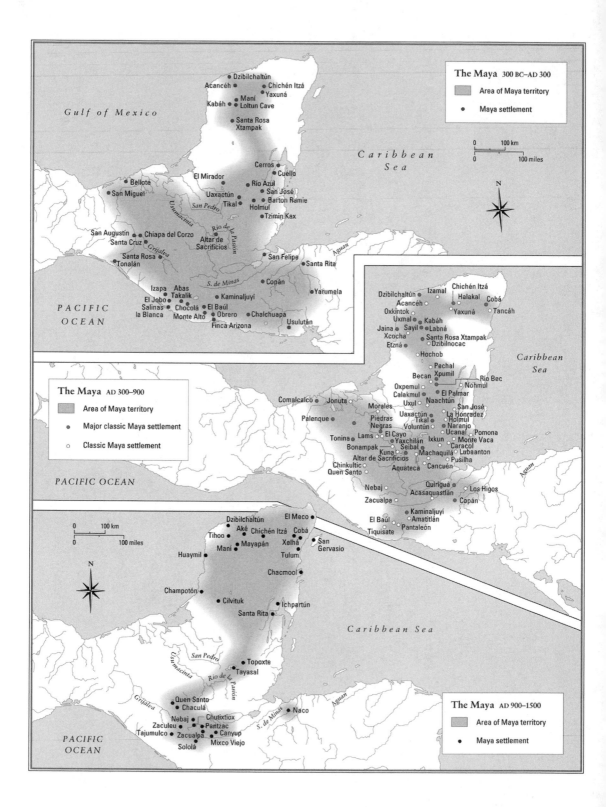

The Maya 300 BC–AD 300

- Area of Maya territory
- Maya settlement

Gulf of Mexico

Caribbean Sea

0   100 km
0   100 miles

N

Dzibilchaltún
Acancéh
Chichén Itzá
Yaxuná
Maní
Kabáh
Loltun Cave
Santa Rosa Xtampak

Cerros
Cuello
Bellote
El Mirador
Río Azul
San José
San Miguel
Uaxactún
Barton Ramie
Tikal
Holmul
San Pedro
Tzimin Kax

San Augustín
Chiapa del Corzo
Santa Cruz
Altar de Sacrificios
Santa Rosa
Grijalva
Tonalán
Rio de la Pasion
San Felipe
Santa Rita

Aguan

S. de Minas
Copán
Izapa
Abas
Takalik
Kaminaljuyú
Yarumela
El Jobo
Salinas
la Blanca
Chocolá
El Baúl
Monte Alto
Obrero
Chalchuapa
Finca Arizona
Usulután

PACIFIC OCEAN

The Maya AD 300–900

- Area of Maya territory
- ● Major classic Maya settlement
- ○ Classic Maya settlement

PACIFIC OCEAN

Dzibilchaltún
Izamal
Chichén Itzá
Halakal
Cobá
Acancéh
Oxkintok
Yaxuná
Tancáh
Uxmal
Kabáh
Jaina
Sayil
Labná
Xcocha
Santa Rosa Xtampak
Etzná
Dzibilnocac
Hochob
Caribbean Sea
Pechal
Becan
Xpumil
Río Bec
Nohmul
Oxpemul
El Palmar
Comalcalco
Jonuta
Calakmúl
Uxul
Naachtún
San José
Morales
La Hondadez
Palenque
Piedras
Uaxactún
Holmul
Negras
Tikal
Naranjo
Voluntún
Ucanal
Pomona
Tonina
Lams
El Cayo
Ixkun
Monte Vaca
Yaxchilán
Seibal
Caracol
Bonampak
Machaquilá
Lubaanton
Kuna
Pusilha
Altar de Sacrificios
Cancuén
Chinkultic
Aguateca
Quen Santo
Nebaj
Quiriguá
Los Higos
Zacualpa
Acasaquastlán
Copán
Kaminaljuyú
Amatitlán
El Baúl
Pantaleón
Tiquisate

Aguan

0   100 km
0   100 miles

N

The Maya AD 900–1500

- Area of Maya territory
- Maya settlement

Dzibilchaltún
Aké
Chichén Itzá
Cobá
El Meco
Tihoo
Maní
Mayapán
Xelhá
San Gervasio
Huaymil
Tulum
Chacmool
Champotón
Cilvituk
Ichpartún
Santa Rita

Caribbean Sea

San Pedro
Usumacinta
Rio de la Pasion
Topoxte
Tayasal
Grijalva
Aguan
Quen Santo
Chaculá
Naco
Nebaj
Chutixtiox
Zaculeu
Pantzac
S. de Minas
Tajumulco
Zacualpa
Canyup
Sololá
Mixco Viejo

PACIFIC OCEAN

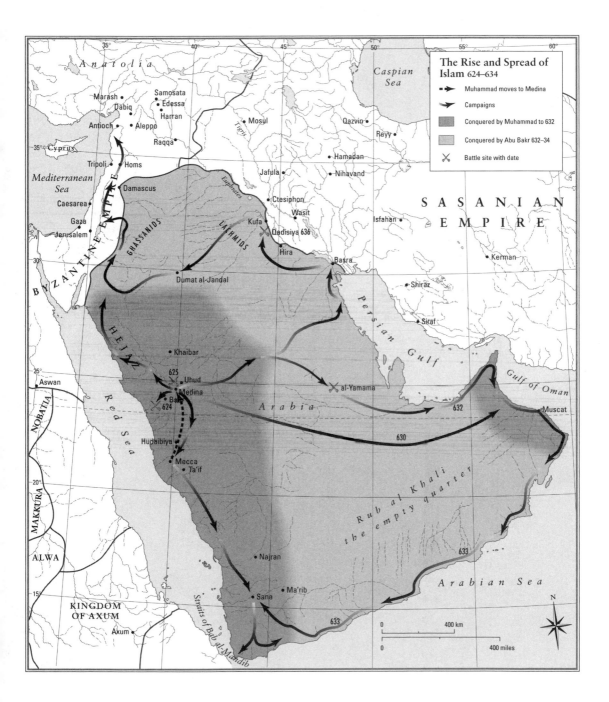

The Rise and Spread of
Islam 624–634

- ▪▪▶ Muhammad moves to Medina
- ──▶ Campaigns
- ▨ Conquered by Muhammad to 632
- ▨ Conquered by Abu Bakr 632–34
- ✕ Battle site with date

Anatolia

*Caspian
Sea*

Marash •
Samosata •
Dabiq • • Edessa
Harran •
Antioch • • Aleppo
Raqqa •

Qazvin •

Rayy •

35° — *Cyprus*

Tripoli • • Homs

Hamadan •

*Mediterranean
Sea*

Damascus •
Jafula •
Nihavand •

Caesarea •
Euphrates
• Ctesiphon

BYZANTINE EMPIRE
• Wasit

Gaza •
Isfahan •

• Jerusalem

Kufa
✕ Qadisiya 636

GHASSANIDS
LACHMIDS

30° —
Hira •

Basra •

Dumat al-Jandal •

*S A S A N I A N
E M P I R E*

• Kerman

• Shiraz

*Persian
Gulf*

• Siraf

HEJAZ

Khaibar •

Gulf of Oman

Aswan •

625
Uhud •

NOBATIA

Medina •
Badr •
624

Muscat •

Red Sea

Hudaibiya •

al-Yamama ✕

632

Arabia

630

• Mecca
• Ta'if

MAKKURA

*Rub al Khali
the empty quarter*

ALWA

633

Najran •

• Ma'rib

Arabian Sea

• Sana

633

15° —

*KINGDOM
OF AXUM*

Straits of Bab al-Mandib

N

Akum •

| 0 | | 400 km |
| 0 | | 400 miles |

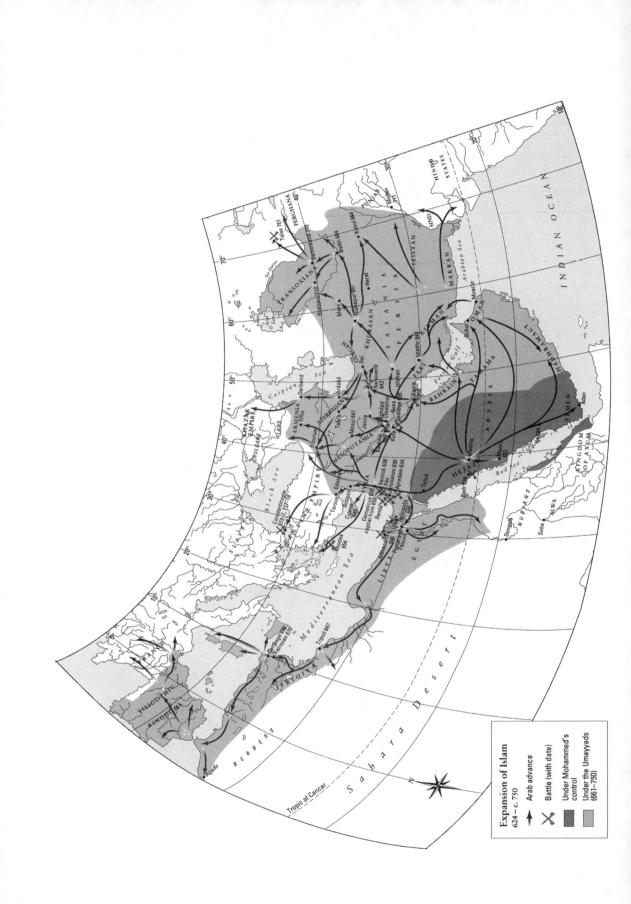

Expansion of Islam
624 – c. 750

→ Arab advance

✗ Battle (with date)

■ Under Mohammed's control

□ Under the Umayyads (661–750)

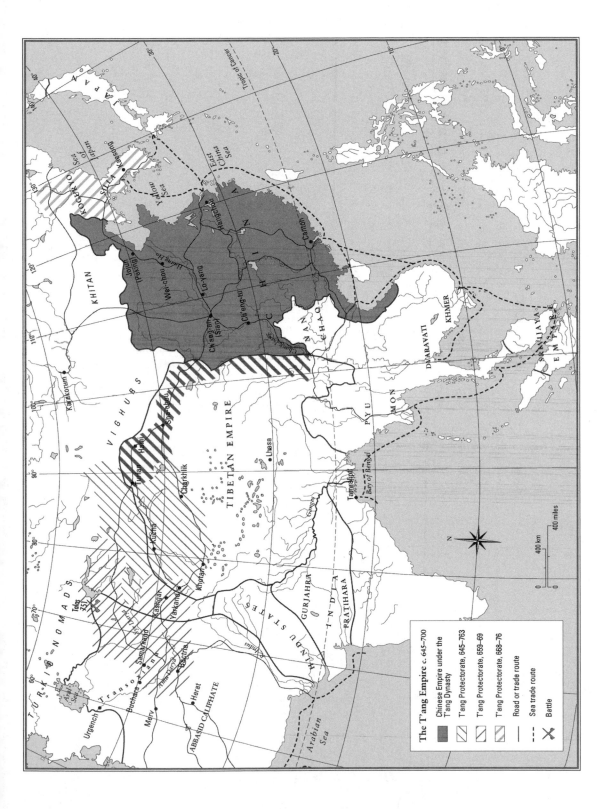

The T'ang Empire c. 645–700

Chinese Empire under the T'ang Dynasty

T'ang Protectorate, 645–763

T'ang Protectorate, 659–69

T'ang Protectorate, 668–76

Road or trade route

Sea trade route

Battle

TURKISH NOMADS

KHITAN

KOGURYO

SILLA

Sea of Japan

Yellow Sea

East China Sea

Tropic of Cancer

Karakorum

Ch'ang-an (Sian)

Cheng-tu

Loyang

Wei-chou

Chi-lin (Peking)

Hwang Ho

Yangtze

C H I N A

N A N

Hangchow

Canton

NAN CHAO

KHMER

DVARAVATI

MON

PYU

SRIVIJAYA

EMPIRE

TIBETAN EMPIRE

Lhasa

Tamralipti

Bay of Bengal

VIGHURS

Chu-khlik

Kucha

Khotan

Yarkand

Kashgar

Samarkand

Bukhara

Merv

Bactra

Herat

Urgench

Transoxiana

Amu Darya

Syr Darya

Aral Sea

Arabian Sea

ABBASID CALIPHATE

GURJAHRA PRATIHARA

HINDU STATES

I N D I A

Ganges

Indus

Talas 751

Herat

Balkh

Syr-khoul

400 km

400 miles

N

Temple mound builders

Hunter
gatherers

Maize
farmers

*Gulf of
Mexico*

C a r i b   f a r m e r s

**TOLTEC
EMPIRE**

**MAYA
CITY STATES**

City states
and Chiefdoms

Maya Chiefdoms

Caribbean Sea

*ATLANTIC
OCEAN*

Local Chiefdoms

Hunter gatherers

Amazonian Chiefdoms

**CHIMU
EMPIRE**

Manioc farmers

**HUARI
EMPIRE**

*PACIFIC
OCEAN*

Savanna and Highland farmers

**TIAHUANACO
EMPIRE**

Tropic of Capricorn

Hunter gatherers

Hunter gatherers

Tropic of Cancer

South and Mesoamerica
c. 900 CE

- States or Empires
- Chiefdoms-farming societies
- Farmers – with some hunter gatherers
- Hunter gatherers

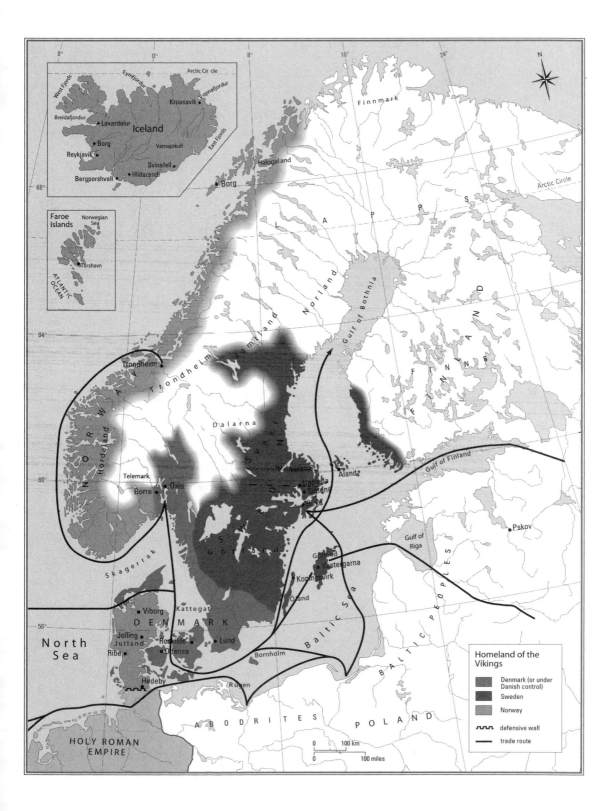

Homeland of the Vikings

Denmark (or under Danish control)
Sweden
Norway
defensive wall
trade route

0   100 km
0   100 miles

Viking Attacks, Trade and Settlement c. 910

→ Viking invasions

ICELAND

Norwegian Sea

Arctic Circle

FINNIC PEOPLES

NORWAY

Hladir

Kaupang

SWEDEN

Uppsala
Birka

Staraya Ladoga
(Aldeigjuborg)
Novgorod
(Holmgard)

KIEVAN RUS

North Sea

DENMARK

Roskilde   Lund

Hedeby

Baltic Sea

BALTIC PEOPLES

SLAVS

Kiev

IRISH KINGDOMS

Dublin

Cork

NORTHUMBERLAND

York

Dane Law

WELSH STATES

WESSEX

London

Bremen

Aachen   Cologne

Frankfurt

EAST FRANKISH KINGDOM (GERMANY)

Lorch

Cracow

HUNGARY

Nitrava

Mosapurc

PECHENEGS

Black Sea

Normandy

Paris

Orléans

WEST FRANKISH KINGDOM (FRANCE)

Besançon

UPPER BURGUNDY

LOWER BURGUNDY

Lyon

Milan

Venice

CROATIA

Serbia

R. Danube

Presov

BULGARIA

Philippopolis

Adrianople

Constantinople

ATLANTIC OCEAN

Corunna

Oporto

Bayonne

Bordeaux

Avignon

NAVARRE

ARAGON

Nice

Fraxinetum

Genoa

KINGDOM OF ITALY

Adriatic Sea

Nish

LEON

Barcelona

Tarragona

Corsica

Rome

PAPAL STATES

Barium

Thessalonica

Aegean Sea

Smyrna

MUSLIM STATES

Belansiyah

Sardinia

Pr. of Benevento

Naples

B Y Z A N T I N E   E M P I R E

Toledo

EMIRATE OF CORDOBA

Ishbiliyah

Ibn Hafsun (autonomous)

Cartagena

Balearic Is.

Panormus

Sicily

Crete

Chandax

M e d i t e r r a n e a n   S e a

Sétif

Tunis

Malta

Tripoli

Kairawan

IDRISIDS

RUSTAMIDS

ABBASIDS (AGHLABIDS)

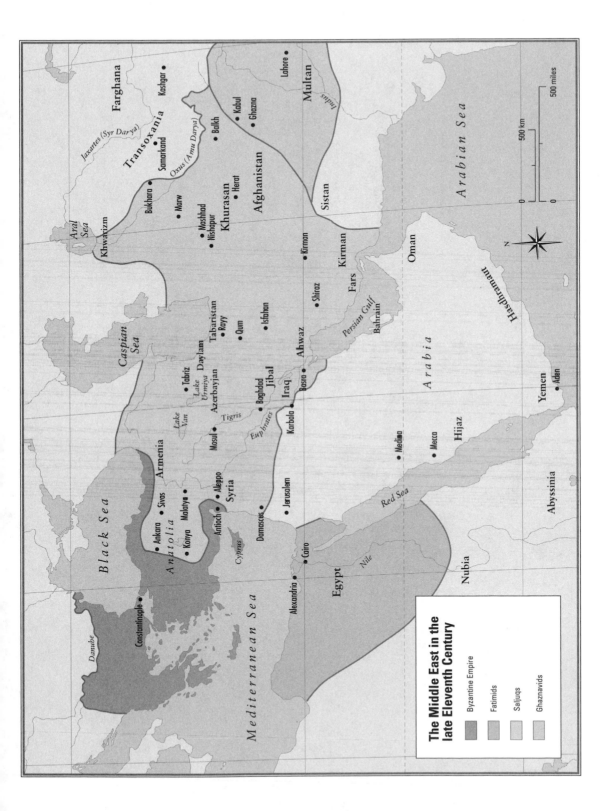

The Middle East in the
late Eleventh Century

Byzantine Empire
Fatimids
Saljuqs
Ghaznavids

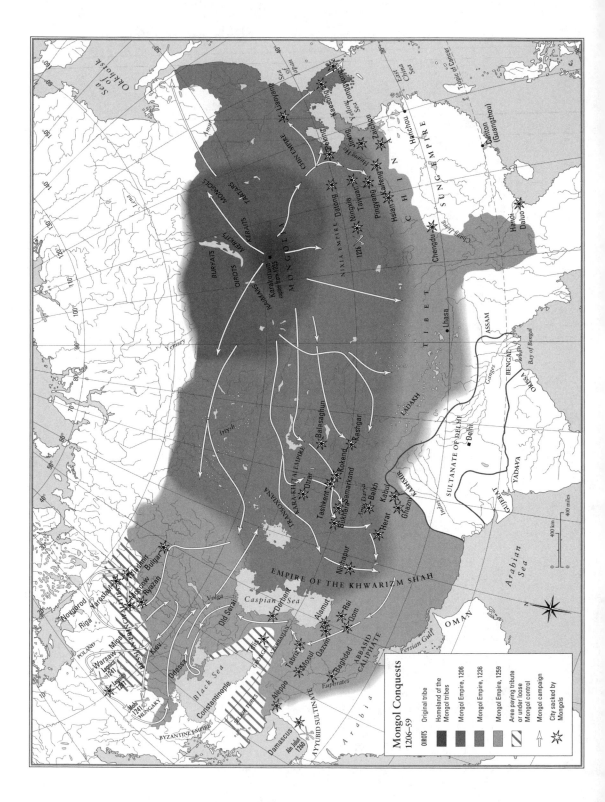

Mongol Conquests
1206–59

OIROTS Original tribe

Homeland of the
Mongol tribes

Mongol Empire, 1206

Mongol Empire, 1236

Mongol Empire, 1259

Area paying tribute
or under loose
Mongol control

Mongol campaign

City sacked by
Mongols

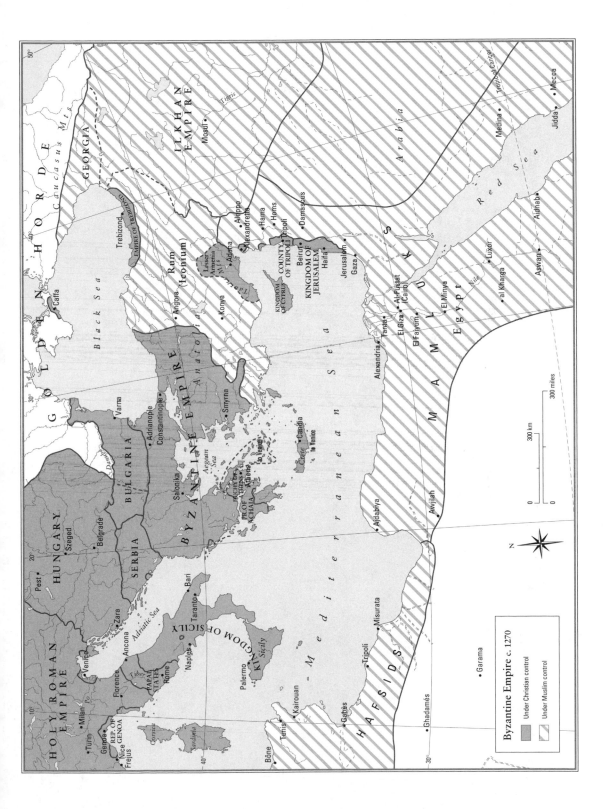

GOLDEN HORDE

Caucasus Mts.

GEORGIA

ILKHAN EMPIRE

Tigris

Mosul

Arabia

Red Sea

Medina

Tropic of Cancer

Jidda

Mecca

EMPIRE OF TREBIZOND

Trebizond

Rum (Iconium)

Aleppo

Hama

Homs

Damascus

Alexandretta

Adana

Lesser Armenia

Angora

Taurus Mts.

Konya

KINGDOM OF CYPRUS

Beirut

COUNTY OF TRIPOLI

Tripoli

Jerusalem

Gaza

KINGDOM OF JERUSALEM

Haifa

Al-Fustat (Cairo)

El Giza

El Faiyûm

Tanta

El Minya

Asyut

Luxor

al Kharga

Aswan

Caffa

Black Sea

Varna

Adrianople

Constantinople

BULGARIA

Salonika

Anatolia

BYZANTINE EMPIRE

Smyrna

Aegean Sea

DUCHY OF ATHENS

Athens

PR. OF ACHAIA

Chios

Candia

Crete

Venice

Alexandria

Ajdabîya

Awjilah

M A M L U K

Egypt

Nile

HOLY ROMAN EMPIRE

Pest

HUNGARY

Szeged

Belgrade

SERBIA

Danube

Po

Milan

Turin

Genoa

Nice

Fréjus

REP. OF GENOA

Venice

Zara

Ancona

Florence

Tiber

PAPAL STATES

Rome

Corsica

Sardinia

Adriatic Sea

Bari

Taranto

Naples

KINGDOM OF SICILY

Palermo

Sicily

Tunis

Kairouan

Bône

Gabès

Tripoli

Misurata

Mediterranean Sea

HAFSIDS

Ghadamés

Garama

Kingdom

Byzantine Empire c. 1270

Under Christian control

Under Muslim control

300 km

300 miles

N

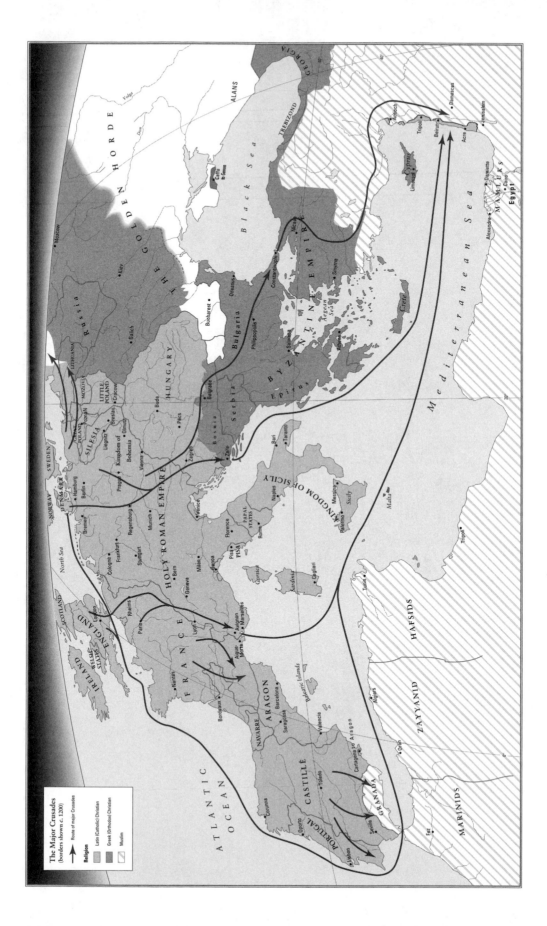

The Major Crusades
(borders shown c. 1200)

Route of major Crusades

Religion

Latin (Catholic) Christian

Greek (Orthodox) Christian

Muslim

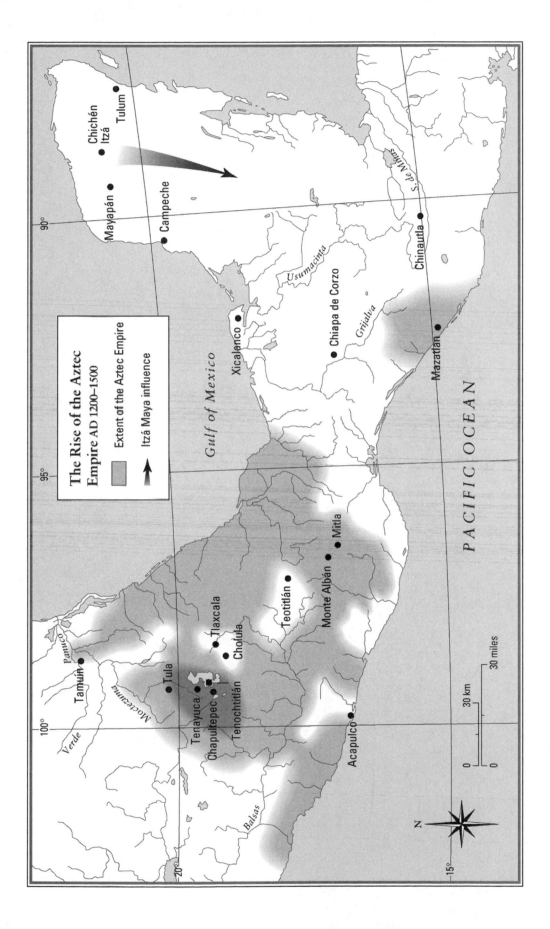

The Rise of the Aztec Empire AD 1200–1500

Extent of the Aztec Empire

Itzá Maya influence

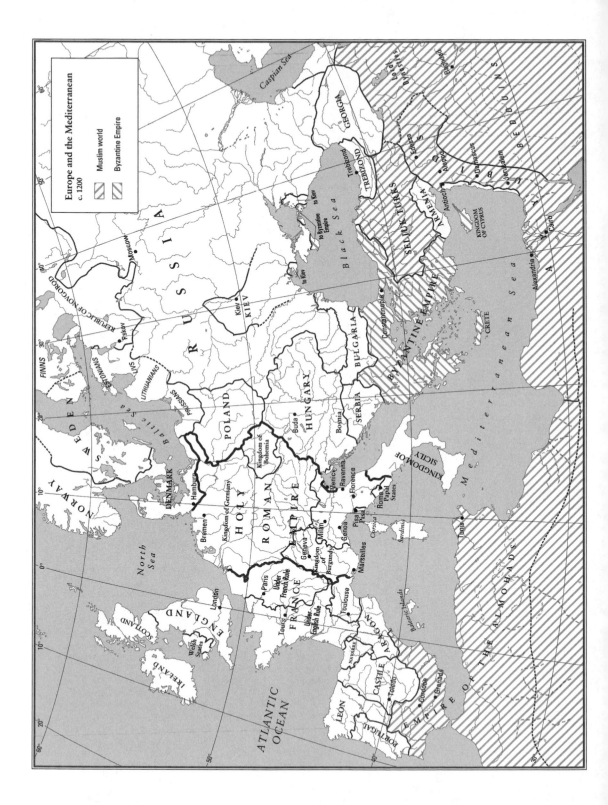

Europe and the Mediterranean
c. 1200

Muslim world

Byzantine Empire

Europe c. 1330

Arctic Circle

ICELAND
To Norway

Norwegian Sea

To Norway

To Norway

To Norway

LAPPS

NOVGOROD

Novgorod

NORWAY

SWEDEN

Oslo

Stockholm

To Denmark

To Denmark

Baltic Sea

SCOTLAND

North Sea

Edinburgh

DENMARK

Roskilde

TEUTONIC ORDER

LITHUANIA

Ireland
Dublin

York

MAZOVIA

POLAND

Kiev

ENGLAND

Bremen

RUSSIAN PRINCIPALITIES

London

Cologne

Craców

Aachen

Frankfurt

HOLY
ROMAN
EMPIRE

Bayeux

Nitra

GOLDEN
HORDE

Paris

Lorch

Orleans

HUNGARY

*ATLANTIC
OCEAN*

FRANCE

Besançon

Lyon

Bordeaux
To England
Bayonne

Avignon

Milan

Danube

Genoa

Venice

Nice

NAVARRE

PAPAL STATE

Adriatic Sea

Nish

Constantinople

SERBIA

BULGARIA

Corunna

Corsica

Rome

Pr. of Benevento

Philippopolis

Oporto

Salamanca

ARAGON

Barcelona

Barium

Thessalonica

BYZANTINE EMPIRE

TURKS

PORTUGAL

Tarragona

Naples

*Aegean
Sea*

Smyrna

CASTILE

Valencia

Sardinia

D. of
ATHENS

Balearic Is.

Seville

GRANADA

Cartagena

Mediterranean

Palermo

Sicily

To Venice

Tunis

Crete

Malta

Sea

MARINIDS

ZAYYANIDS

HAFSIDS

Tripoli

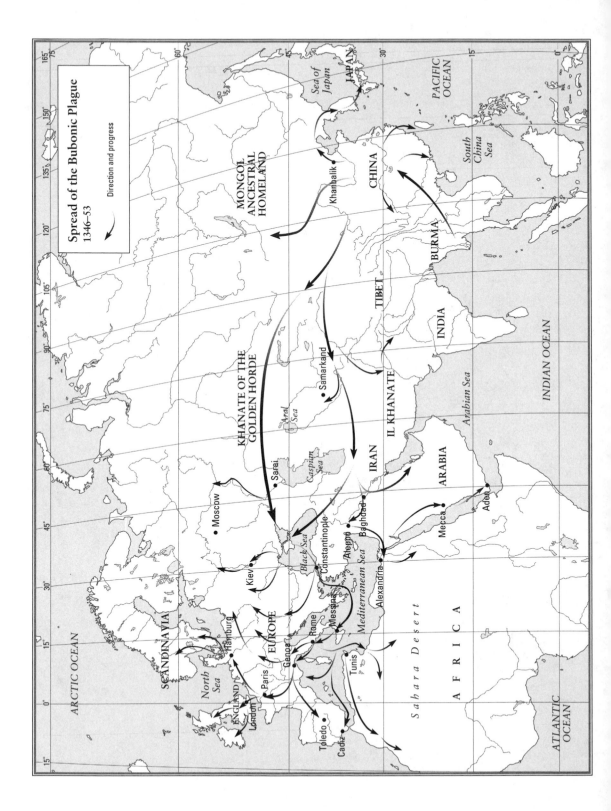

Spread of the Bubonic Plague
1346–53

Direction and progress

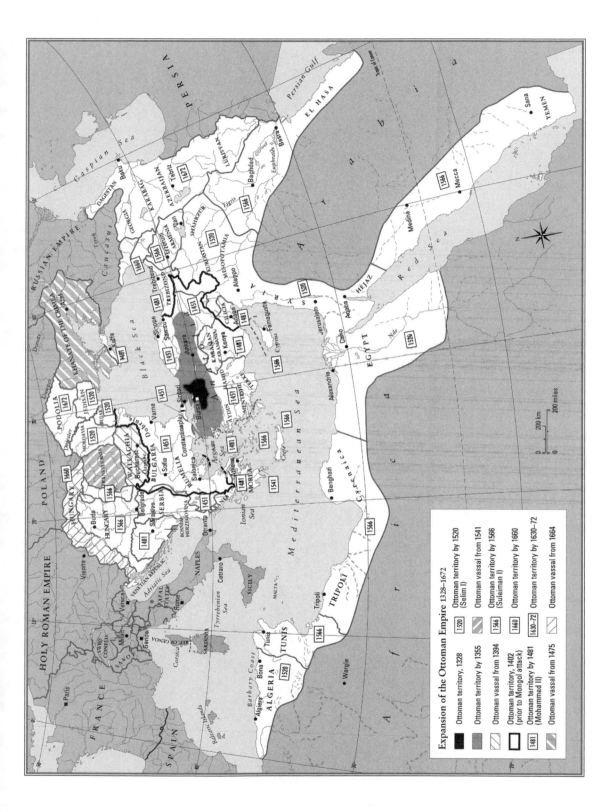

Expansion of the Ottoman Empire 1328–1672

	Ottoman territory, 1328	1520	Ottoman territory by 1520 (Selim I)		Ottoman vassal from 1541
	Ottoman territory by 1355	1566	Ottoman territory by 1566 (Suleiman I)		Ottoman territory by 1566 (Suleiman I)
	Ottoman vassal from 1394	1660	Ottoman territory by 1660		Ottoman territory by 1660
	Ottoman territory, 1402 (prior to Mongol attack)	1481		1630–72	Ottoman territory by 1630–72
	Ottoman territory by 1481 (Mohammed II)				Ottoman vassal from 1664
	Ottoman vassal from 1475				

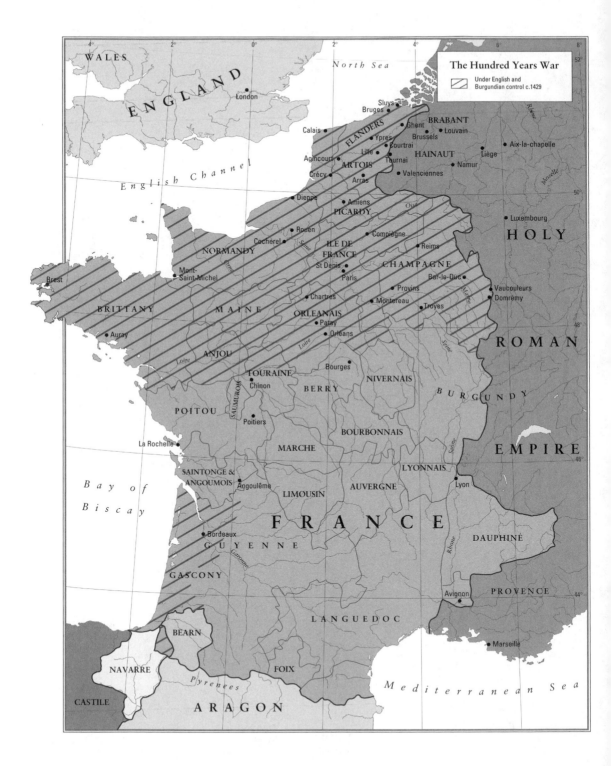

The Hundred Years War

Under English and
Burgundian control c.1429

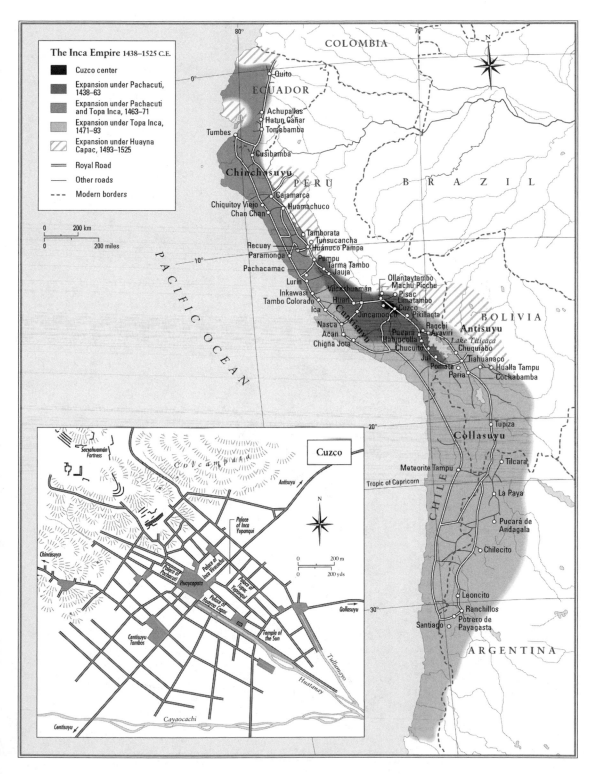

The Inca Empire 1438–1525 C.E.

- ■ Cuzco center
- ■ Expansion under Pachacuti, 1438–63
- ■ Expansion under Pachacuti and Topa Inca, 1463–71
- ■ Expansion under Topa Inca, 1471–93
- ▨ Expansion under Huayna Capac, 1493–1525
- ═ Royal Road
- — Other roads
- --- Modern borders

0   200 km
0   200 miles

COLOMBIA

ECUADOR

Quito

Achupallas
Hatun Cañar
Tomebamba

Tumbes

Cusibamba

Chinchasuyu

PERU

Cajamarca
Chiquitoy Viejo   Huamachuco
Chan Chan

Tamborata
Recuay   Tunsucancha
Paramonga   Huánuco Pampa
Pumpu
Pachacamac   Tarma Tambo
Jauja
Lurin   Ollantaytambo
Inkawasi   Machu Picchu
Tambo Colorado   Vilcashuamán   Pisac
Huari   Limatambo
Ica   Jincamoco   Cuzco
Nasca   Pikillaqta
Acan   Pucará   Raqchi
Chigna Jota   Hatuncolla   Ayaviri
Chucuito   Chuquiabo
Juli   Tiahuanaco
Pomata   Hualla Tampu
Paria   Cochabamba

Cuntisuyu

BRAZIL

BOLIVIA

Antisuyu

Lake Titicaca

Tupiza

Collasuyu

Meteorite Tampu   Tilcara

Tropic of Capricorn

La Paya

Pucará de
Andagala

Chilecito

Leoncito

Ranchillos
Santiago   Potrero de
Payagasta

ARGENTINA

PACIFIC OCEAN

CHILE

Cuzco

Sacsahuamán
Fortress

Colcampata

Antisuyu

Chincasuyu

Palace of
Inca Yupanqui
Palace of
Pachacuti   Palace of
Huaycapata   Inca Viracocha
Palace of
Tupac Yupanqui
Palace of
Huayna Capac
Centisuyu
Tambos   Temple of
the Sun

Qallasuyu

0   200 m
0   200 yds

Huatanay

Tullumayo

Cayaocachi

Centisuyu

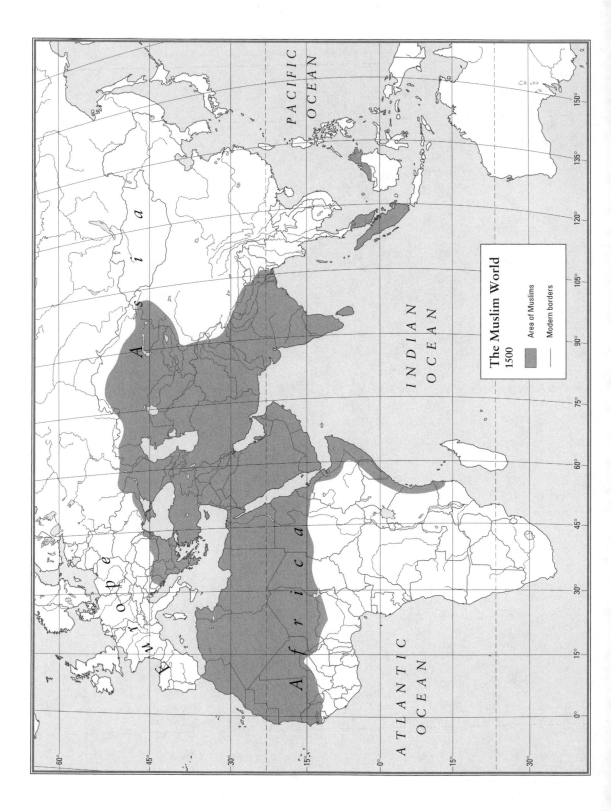

The Muslim World
1500

Area of Muslims

Modern borders

GENEVA

HOLY ROMAN EMPIRE

DUCHY OF SAVOY

DUCHY OF MILAN

REPUBLIC OF VENICE

FRANCE

Turin

Asti

SALUZZO

MONFERRATO

Milan

Mantua MANTUA

Genoa

REPUBLIC OF GENOA

DUCHY OF MODENA

Ferrara DUCHY OF FERRARA

Venice

ISTRIA (Venetian)

KINGDOM OF HUNGARY

DALMATIA (Venetian)

OTTOMAN EMPIRE

REPUBLIC OF LUCCA

Lucca

Pisa

REPUBLIC OF FLORENCE

Florence

Arno

SAN MARINO

Urbino

A
d
r
i
a
t
i
c

S
e
a

Siena

REPUBLIC OF SIENA

PAPAL STATES

A
p
e
n
n
i
n
e
s

Tiber

Rome

REPUBLIC OF RAGUSA

SARDINIA (Spanish)

Naples

Amalfi

Bari

KINGDOM OF NAPLES (Spanish)

Taranto

Tyrrhenian Sea

N

Palermo

KINGDOM OF SICILY (Spanish)

Mediterranean Sea

Renaissance Italy
c. 1500

Border of the Holy Roman Empire

0   100 km

0   100 miles

8°

12°

16°

46°

42°

38°

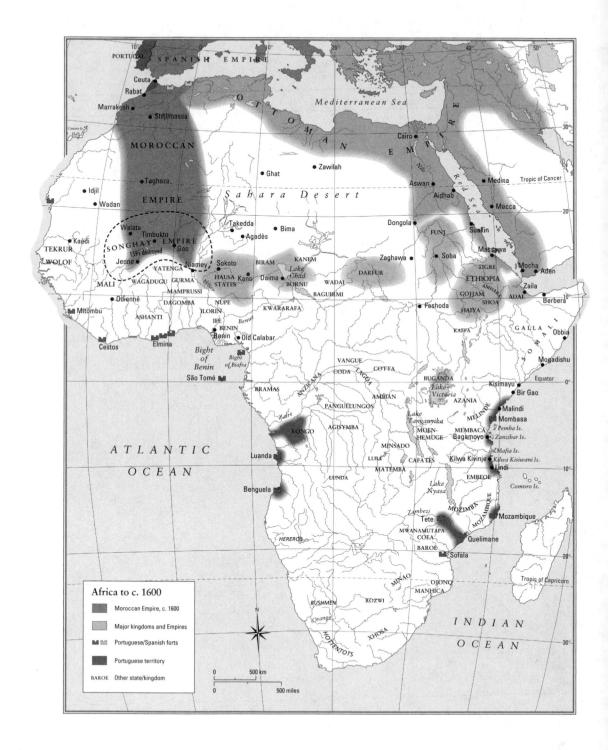

Africa to c. 1600

Moroccan Empire, c. 1600

Major kingdoms and Empires

Portuguese/Spanish forts

Portuguese territory

BAROE   Other state/kingdom

PORTUGAL   SPANISH   EMPIRE
Ceuta
Rabat
Marrakesh
Sidjilmassa
MOROCCAN
Taghaza
EMPIRE
Idjil
Wadan
Walata   Timbuktu
TEKRUR   SONGHAY   EMPIRE
Kaédi   1591 destroyed
WOLOF   Jenne   Gao
YATENGA   Niamey
MALI   WAGADUGU   GURMA   Sokoto   BIRAM
Odienné   MAMPRUSSI   HAUSA   Kano
Mitombu   DAGOMBA   NUPE   STATES   Daima
ASHANTI   ILORIN   BORNU
IFÈ   KWARARAFA
Cestos   Elmina   BENIN   BAGUIRMI
Benin   Old Calabar
Bight   Bight
of   of Biafra
Benin   São Tomé

Mediterranean Sea
OTTOMAN   EMPIRE
Ghat   Zawilah
Sahara   Desert
Cairo
Aswan   Medina   Tropic of Cancer
Aidhab
Takedda   Bima   Dongola   Mecca
Agadès   FUNJ   Suakin
KANEM   Zaghawa   Soba   Massawa   Mocha
Lake   WADAI   DARFUR   TIGRE   Aden
Chad   ETHIOPIA   Zaila
AMHARA   ADAL
GOJJAM   Berbera
Feshoda   SHOA
HAIYA   GALLA
KAFFA   Obbia
SOMALI
Mogadishu

VANGUE
CODA   COFFA   BUGANDA   Equator
ANZICANA   LAGOA   Lake   Kisimayu
BRAMAS   AMBIAN   Victoria   Bir Gao
PANGUELUNGOS   AZANIA   Malindi
Zaire   MELINDE   Mombasa
KONGO   AGISYMBA   Lake   MEMBACA   Pemba Is.
Tanganyika   Bagamoyo   Zanzibar Is.
MOEN-
HEMUGE   Mafia Is.
Luanda   MINSADO   CAFATES   Kilwa Kivinje   Kilwa Kisiwani Is.
LUBA   Lindi
MATEMBA   EMBEOE
LUNDA   Lake   Comoro Is.
Nyasa   MOZIMBA
Benguela   MOZAMBIQUE
Zambezi   Mozambique
Tete
HEREROS   MWANAMUTAPA
COEA
BAROE   Quelimane
Sofala
MINAO
OIONO
MANHICA   Tropic of Capricorn
ROZWI
BUSHMEN   INDIAN
Orange   OCEAN
HOFFENTOTS   XHOSA

ATLANTIC
OCEAN

0   500 km

0   500 miles

Canary Is.

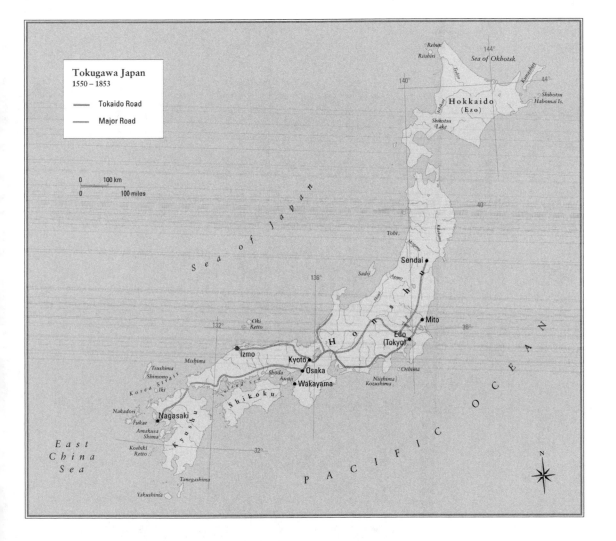

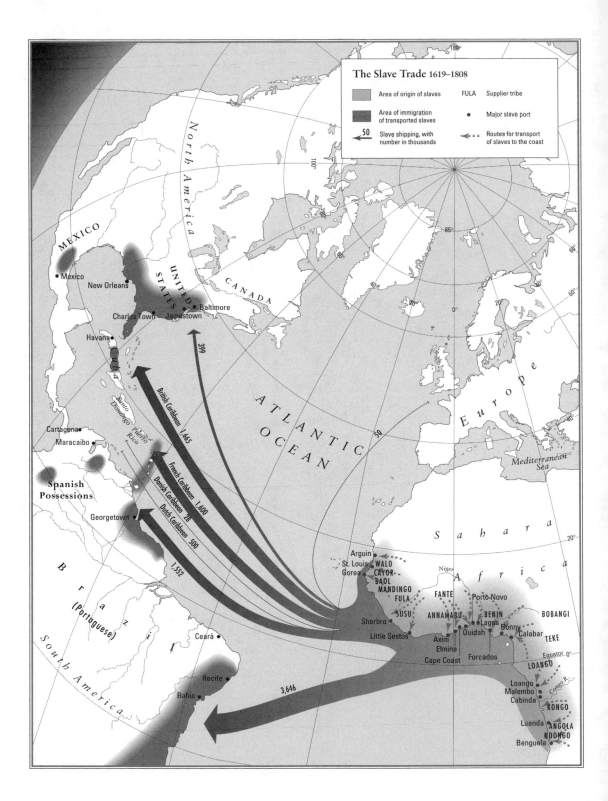

The Slave Trade 1619–1808

	Area of origin of slaves	FULA	Supplier tribe
	Area of immigration of transported slaves	•	Major slave port
50 ←	Slave shipping, with number in thousands	◄┄┄	Routes for transport of slaves to the coast

North America

MEXICO

ATLANTIC OCEAN

Europe

Mediterranean Sea

CANADA

UNITED STATES

• Mexico
New Orleans
• Baltimore
Charles Town • Jamestown
Havana •
Cuba

Santo Domingo
Puerto Rico

Cartagena •
Maracaibo •

Spanish Possessions

Georgetown •

B r a z i l (Portuguese)

Ceará •

Recife •
Bahia •

South America

399

British Caribbean 1,665
French Caribbean 1,600
Danish Caribbean 28
Dutch Caribbean 500
1,552

3,646

S a h a r a

A f r i c a

Arguin
St. Louis • WALO
Gorea • CAYOR
BAOL
MANDINGO
FULA
SUSU
Sherbro •
Little Sestos
Axim
Elmina
Cape Coast

Niger

FANTE
ANNAMABU
Porto-Novo
BENIN
Lagos
Ouidah
Forcados

Bonny
Calabar
BOBANGI
TEKE

Equator 0°
LOANGO

Loango •
Malembo •
Cabinda •
Congo R.
KONGO

Luanda •
ANGOLA
NDONGO
Benguela •

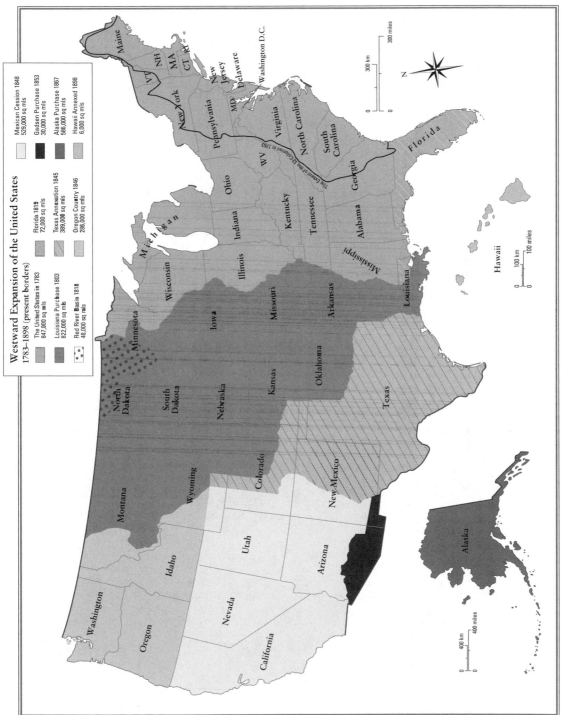

Westward Expansion of the United States
1783–1898 (present borders)

Mexican Cession 1848
529,000 sq mls

Gadsen Purchase 1853
30,000 sq mls

Alaska Purchase 1867
586,000 sq mls

Hawaii Annexed 1898
6,000 sq mls

The United States in 1783
847,000 sq mls

Florida 1819
72,000 sq mls

Texas Annexation 1845
389,000 sq mls

Oregon Country 1846
286,000 sq mls

Louisiana Purchase 1803
822,000 sq mls

Red River Basin 1818
48,000 sq mls

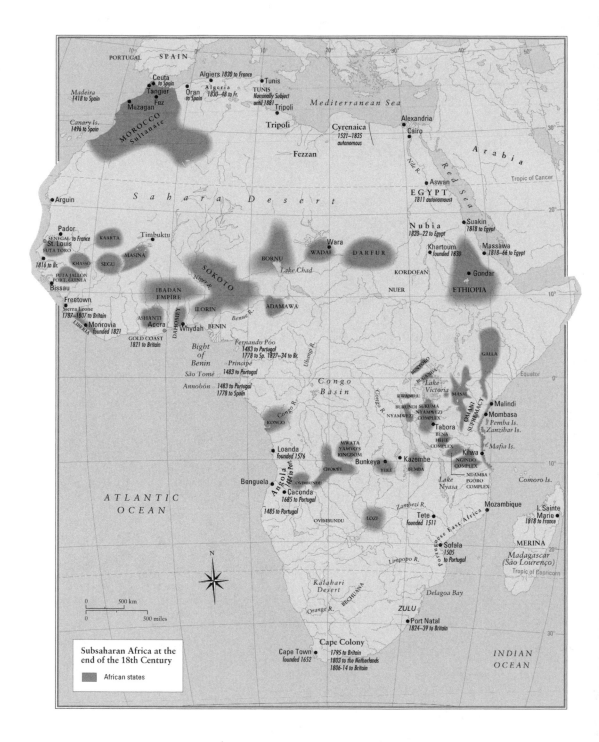

PORTUGAL   SPAIN

Madeira
1418 to Spain

Ceuta
to Spain
Tangier
Oran
to Spain
Fez
Mazagan
MOROCCO
Sultanate

Canary Is.
1496 to Spain

Algiers *1830 to France*   Tunis
Algeria
1830–48 to Fr.   TUNIS
Tripoli

Tripoli

Mediterranean Sea

Alexandria
Cairo

Arabia

Cyrenaica
*1521–1835
autonomous*

Fezzan

Tropic of Cancer

Arguin

Sahara   Desert

Nile R.

Aswan

EGYPT
1811 autonomoust

Red Sea

30°

20°

Pador

Timbuktu

SENEGAL *to France*
St. Louis
FUTA TORO

1816 to Br.

KAARTA

MASINA

Wara
WADAI   DARFUR

Nubia
1820–22 to Egypt

Suakin
1818 to Egypt

Khartoum
founded 1830

Massawa
1818–66 to Egypt

KHASSO
SEGU

BORNU

Lake Chad

KORDOFAN

Gondar

FUTA JALLON
PORT. GUINEA
Bissau

SOKOTO

Niger R.

Freetown
Sierra Leone
1787–1807 to Britain
LIBERIA   Monrovia
founded 1821

IBADAN
EMPIRE

ASHANTI   Accra
GOLD COAST
1821 to Britain

ILORIN

Benue R.
ADAMAWA

NUER

ETHIOPIA

10°

Bight
of
Benin

São Tomé

DAHOMEY
Whydah   BENIN

Fernando Póo
*1483 to Portugal
1778 to Sp. 1827–34 to Br.*
Príncipe
1483 to Portugal

Ubangi R.

Congo R.

*Congo
Basin*

Lake
Victoria

RWANDA
BURUNDI SUKUMA
NYAMWEZI
NYAMWEZI COMPLEX

MASAI

GALLA

Equator

Malindi
Mombasa
Pemba Is.
Zanzibar Is.

0°

Annobón   *1483 to Portugal
1778 to Spain*

KONGO   Congo R.

Loanda
founded 1576

Benguela

Angola
1484 to Port.
OVIMBUNDU

Caconda
1685 to Portugal

1485 to Portugal   OVIMBUNDU

*ATLANTIC
OCEAN*

MWATA
YAMVO'S
KINGDOM

CHOKWE   Bunkeya

Tabora

BENA
HEHE
COMPLEX

Kazembe

YEKE   BEMBA

LOZI

Lake
Nyasa

Zambezi R.

Limpopo R.

OMANI
SUPREMACY

Kilwa
NGINDO
COMPLEX

NDAMBA
PGÖRO
COMPLEX

Mafia Is.

Mozambique

Tete
founded 1511

Portuguese East Africa

Sofala
*1505
to Portugal*

Comoro Is.

I. Sainte
Marie
1818 to France

MERINA

Madagascar
(São Lourenço)

Tropic of Capricorn

10°

20°

N

0   500 km

0   500 miles

*Kalahari
Desert*

BECHUANA
Orange R.

Delagoa Bay

ZULU

Port Natal
1824–39 to Britain

*INDIAN
OCEAN*

30°

Cape Colony
Cape Town
founded 1652
*1795 to Britain
1803 to the Netherlands
1806-14 to Britain*

Subsaharan Africa at the
end of the 18th Century

African states

10°   20°   30°   40°   50°

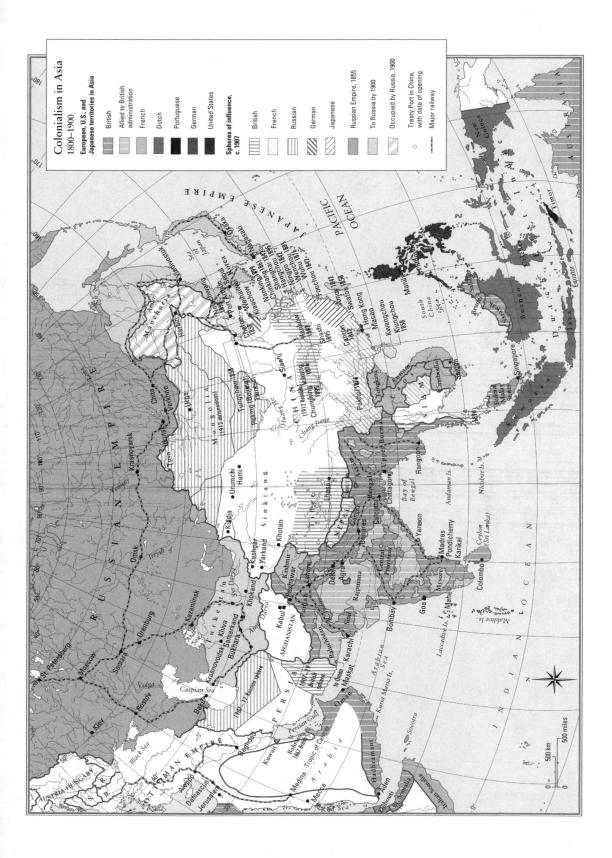

Colonialism in Asia
1800–1900

European, U.S., and
Japanese territories in Asia

British
Allied to British
administration
French
Dutch
Portuguese
German
United States

Spheres of influence,
c. 1907

British
French
Russian
German
Japanese

Russian Empire, 1855
To Russia by 1900
Occupied by Russia, 1900

○   Treaty Port in China,
with date of opening

━━━   Major railway

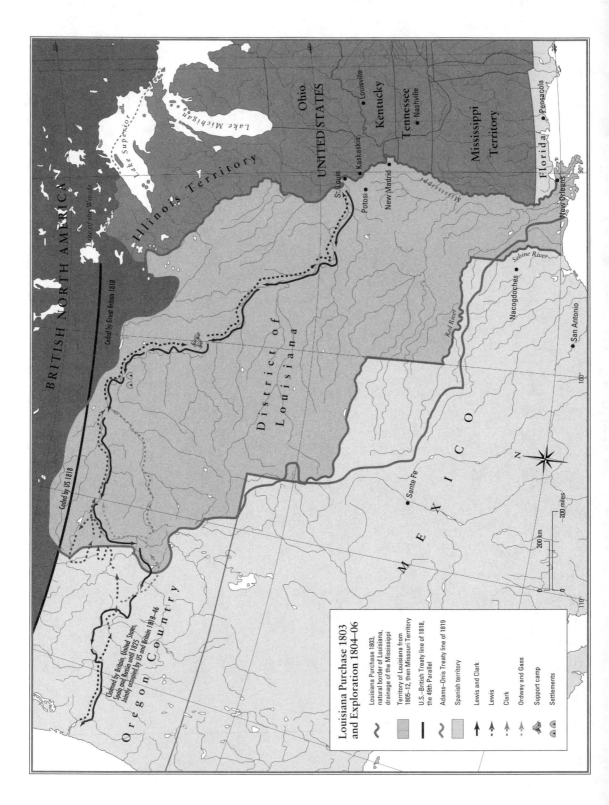

Louisiana Purchase 1803 and Exploration 1804–06

Louisiana Purchase 1803, natural border of Louisiana, drainage of the Mississippi

Territory of Louisiana from 1805–12, then Missouri Territory

U.S.–British Treaty line of 1818, the 49th Parallel

Adams–Onis Treaty line of 1819

Spanish territory

Lewis and Clark

Lewis

Clark

Ordway and Gass

Support camp

Settlements

BRITISH NORTH AMERICA

Lake Superior

Lake Michigan

Lake of the Woods

Ceded by Great Britain 1818

Ceded by US 1818

Illinois Territory

Ohio

UNITED STATES

Kentucky
• Louisville

Tennessee
• Nashville

Mississippi Territory

Florida • Pensacola

St. Louis

• Kaskaskia

Potosi •

• New Madrid

Mississippi

New Orleans

District of Louisiana

M E X I C O

• Santa Fe

Red River

Sabine River

• Nacogdoches

• San Antonio

Oregon Country

Claimed by Britain, United States, Spain and Russia until 1825. Jointly occupied by US and Britain 1818–46

N

200 miles

200 km

Europe in 1815 After
the Treaty of Vienna

▬▬ German Confederation

Iceland
to Denmark

Norwegian
Sea

Finland

Faeroe Islands
to Denmark

United until
1905

St Petersburg

Christiania

Stockholm

North
Sea

Scotland

Edinburgh

Baltic Sea

RUSSIAN
EMPIRE

Copenhagen

DENMARK

IRELAND

Dublin

GREAT

BRITAIN

Hamburg

HANNOVER

PRUSSIA

England

Amsterdam

London

Berlin

Warsaw

REPUBLIC OF
CRACOW

Brussels

NETHERLANDS

PRUSSIA

Prague

Cracow

ATLANTIC
OCEAN

Paris

BADEN

BAVARIA

Stuttgart

WÜRTTEMBERG

Vienna

Hungary

Buda

Pest

AUSTRIAN EMPIRE

Moldavia

Transylvania

NEUCHATEL

SWITZERLAND

FRANCE

SARDINIA

LOMBARDY
VENETIA

Wallachia

Bucharest

PARMA

Genoa

MODENA

Zara

Adriatic Sea

OTTOMAN EMPIRE

MASSA AND
CARRARA

Florence
TUSCANY

PAPAL
STATES

Montenegro

ANDORRA

LUCCA

Corsica

Rome

Oporto

PORT.

Madrid

Naples

Aegean
Sea

Lisbon

SPAIN

Balearic Is.

SARDINIA

KINGDOM OF THE
TWO SICILIES

Ionian Islands
to Great Britain

Athens

Mediterranean

Gibraltar
to Great Britain

Algiers

Tunis

Sicily

Sea

Crete

MOROCCO

ALGERIA

TUNIS

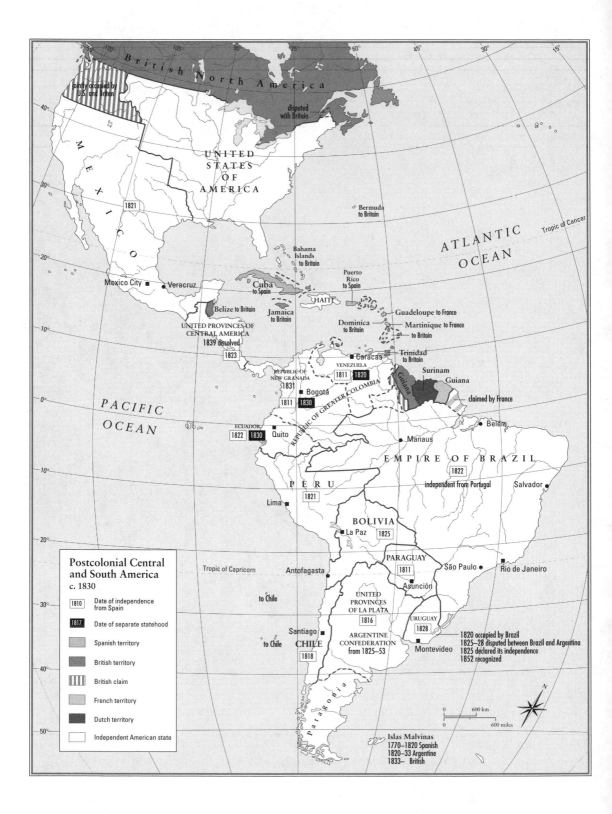

Postcolonial Central and South America c. 1830

British North America

disputed with Britain

jointly occupied by U.S. and Britain

UNITED STATES OF AMERICA

M E X I C O

1821

Mexico City   Veracruz

Bermuda to Britain

ATLANTIC OCEAN   Tropic of Cancer

Bahama Islands to Britain

Cuba to Spain

Puerto Rico to Spain

HAITI

Belize to Britain   Jamaica to Britain

Guadeloupe to France

Dominica to Britain   Martinique to France

UNITED PROVINCES OF CENTRAL AMERICA 1839 dissolved

1823

to Britain

Trinidad to Britain

Caracas

VENEZUELA

REPUBLIC OF NEW GRANADA

1811   1820

Guiana   Surinam   Guiana

1831

Bogotá

1811   1830

REPUBLIC OF GREATER COLOMBIA

claimed by France

PACIFIC OCEAN

ECUADOR

1822   1830   Quito

Belém

Manaus

E M P I R E   O F   B R A Z I L

1822

independent from Portugal

Salvador

P E R U

1821   Lima

BOLIVIA

La Paz   1825

Tropic of Capricorn

Antofagasta

to Chile

PARAGUAY

1811

Asunción

São Paulo

Rio de Janeiro

UNITED PROVINCES OF LA PLATA

1816

URUGUAY

1828

Santiago   CHILE

to Chile   1818

ARGENTINE CONFEDERATION from 1825–53

Montevideo

1820 occupied by Brazil
1825–28 disputed between Brazil and Argentina
1825 declared its independence
1852 recognized

Patagonia

Islas Malvinas
1770–1820 Spanish
1820–33 Argentine
1833– British

600 km

600 miles

N

Postcolonial Central and South America c. 1830

1810	Date of independence from Spain
1817	Date of separate statehood
	Spanish territory
	British territory
	British claim
	French territory
	Dutch territory
	Independent American state

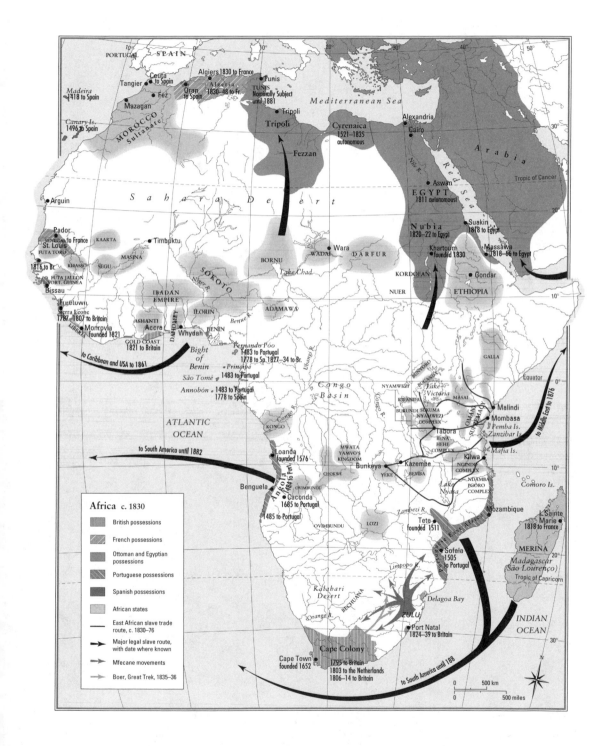

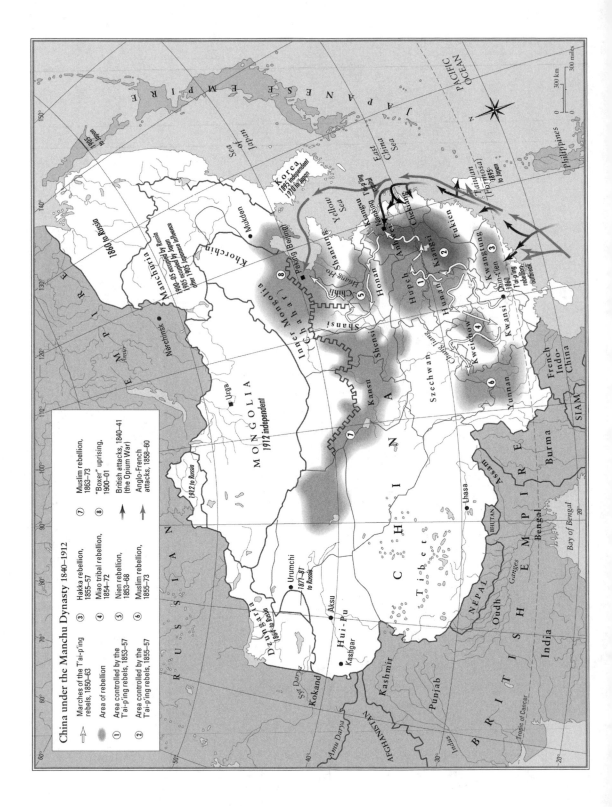

China under the Manchu Dynasty 1840–1912

Marches of the T'ai-p'ing rebels, 1850–63

Area of rebellion

① Area controlled by the T'ai-p'ing rebels, 1853–57

② Area controlled by the T'ai-p'ing rebels, 1855–57

③ Hakka rebellion, 1855–57

④ Miao tribal rebellion, 1854–72

⑤ Nien rebellion, 1853–68

⑥ Muslim rebellion, 1855–73

⑦ Muslim rebellion, 1863–73

⑧ "Boxer" uprising, 1900–01

British attacks, 1840–41 (the Opium War)

Anglo-French attacks, 1858–60

JAPANESE EMPIRE

PACIFIC OCEAN

Philippines

Sea of Japan

1905 to Japan

Korea 1895 independent 1910 to Japan

East China Sea

Taiwan (Formosa) 1895 to Japan

Mukden

Manchuria 1900–05 occupied by Russia 1905 occupied by Japan under 1905 Japanese influence

Khorchin

Yellow Sea

Peking (Beijing)

Kiangsu

T'ai-p'ing

Nanking T'ai-p'ing capital

Chekiang

Fukien

Kwangtung

Hwang Ho

Chihli

Shantung

Honan

Anhwei

Hupeh

Kiangsi

Kwangsi

Chin-tien 1860 T'ai-p'ing rebellion outbreak

Shansi

Shensi

Kansu

Szechwan

Hunan

Kweichow

Yunnan

Yangtze Kiang

French Indo-China

R U S S I A N   E M P I R E

1860 to Russia

Nerchinsk

Amur

Urga

M O N G O L I A
1912 independent

Inner Mongolia (Chahar)

① ⑧ ⑤ ① ② ③ ④ ⑥ ⑦

1912 to Russia

C H I N A

T i b e t

Lhasa

BHUTAN

NEPAL

Assam

Burma

SIAM

Bengal

Bay of Bengal

Ganges

India

B R I T I S H   E M P I R E

Oudh

Kashmir

Punjab

Indus

Dzungaria 1860 to Russia

Urumchi 1871–81 to Russia

Aksu

Hui-Pu

Kashgar

Kokand

Syr Darya

Amu Darya

AFGHANISTAN

Tropic of Cancer

300 km

300 miles

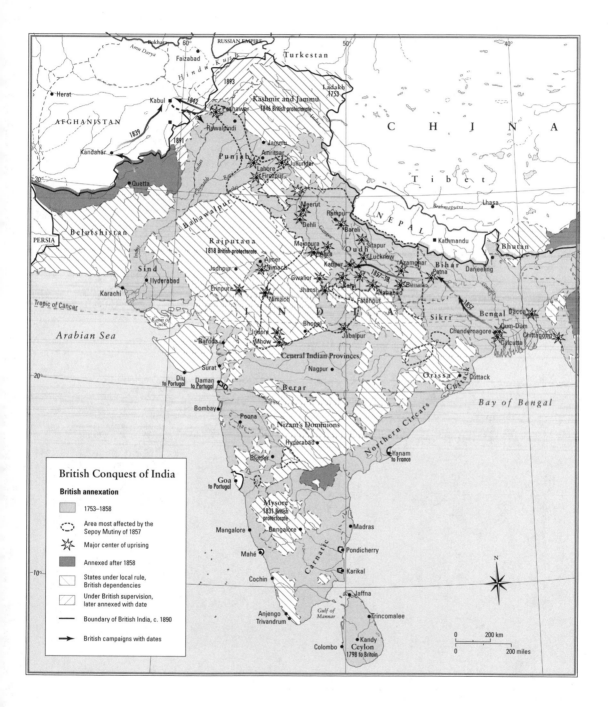

British Conquest of India

British annexation

	1753–1858
⊂⊃	Area most affected by the Sepoy Mutiny of 1857
✶	Major center of uprising
▓	Annexed after 1858
⧄	States under local rule, British dependencies
⧄	Under British supervision, later annexed with date
—	Boundary of British India, c. 1890
→	British campaigns with dates

RUSSIAN EMPIRE

Bukhara
Faizabad
Turkestan
Amu Darya
60°
50°
40°
Hindu Kush
1893
Ladakh 1753
Herat
AFGHANISTAN
Kabul 1842
Peshawar
Kashmir and Jammu
1846 British protectorate
C H I N A
1839
Rawalpindi
1891
Kandahar
Jammu
T i b e t
Quetta
Punjab
Amritsar
Jullunder
Lahore
Firozpur
Lhasa
Belutshistan
Bahawalpur
Meerut
Rampur
N E P A L
Brahmaputra
PERSIA
Rajputana
1818 British protectorate
Dehli
Bareli
Sitapur
Oudh
Lucknow
Kathmandu
Bhutan
Sind
Jodhpur
Ajmer
Nimach
Mainpura
Agra
Kanpur
Azamgar
Bihar
Darjeeling
Hyderabad
Gwalior
1857–58
Benares
Patna
Karachi
Erinpura
Nimach
Jhansi
Kalpi
Allahabad
1857
Tropic of Cancer
Rann of Cuch
I N D I A
Fatehpur
Sikri
Bengal
Dacca
Arabian Sea
Indore
Bhopal
Jabalpur
Orissa
Dum-Dum
Chittagong
Barda
Mhow
Chandernagore
Calcutta
Surat
Central Indian Provinces
Nagpur
Cuttack
Diu to Portugal
Daman to Portugal
20°
Berar
Godavari
Bay of Bengal
Bombay
Poona
Nizam's Dominions
Northern Circars
Hyderabad
Yanam to France
Bijapur
Goa to Portugal
Mysore
1831 British protectorate
Mangalore
Bangalore
Madras
Mahé
Pondicherry
10°
Cochin
Karikal
Carnatic
Jaffna
Anjengo
Trivandrum
Gulf of Mannar
Trincomalee
Colombo
Kandy
Ceylon
1798 to Britain

| 0 | 200 km |
| 0 | 200 miles |

N

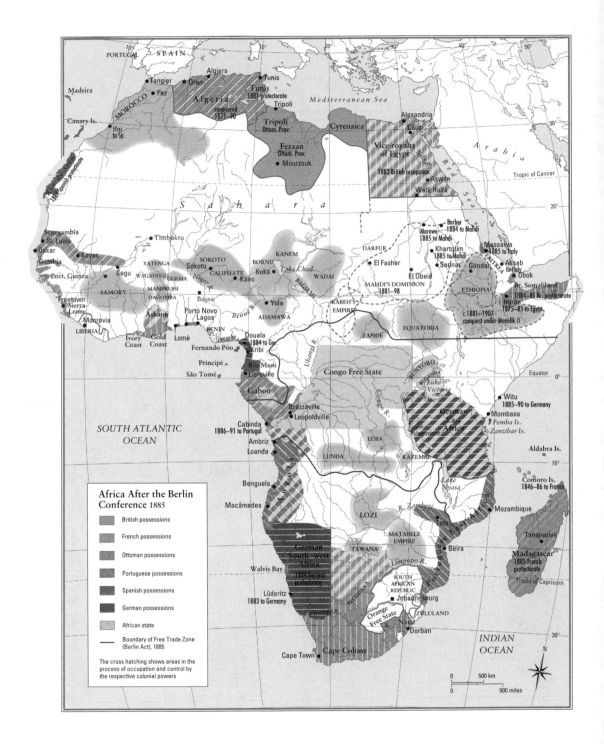

Africa After the Berlin Conference 1885

Legend:
- British possessions
- French possessions
- Ottoman possessions
- Portuguese possessions
- Spanish possessions
- German possessions
- African state
- Boundary of Free Trade Zone (Berlin Act), 1885

The cross hatching shows areas in the process of occupation and control by the respective colonial powers

SPAIN

PORTUGAL

Madeira

Canary Is.

Mediterranean Sea

Tangier
Fez
Oran
Algiers
Tunis
Tunis 1881 protectorate
Tripoli
MOROCCO
Algeria conquered 1871–90
Ifni to Sp.
Tripoli Ottom. Prov.
Cyrenaica
Alexandria
Cairo
Vice-royalty of Egypt
1882 British occupation
Aswan
Wadi Halfa
Fezzan Ottom. Prov.
Mourzouk

S a h a r a

Tropic of Cancer

Arabia

Red Sea

Senegambia
St. Louis
Dakar
Gambia
Kayes
Port. Guinea
Segu
Timbuktu
YATENGA
WAGADUGU
GURMA
MAMPRUSSI
DAGOMBA
SAMORY
SOKOTO
Sokoto
CALIPHATE
Kano
Kuka
Lake Chad
BORNU
KANEM
WADAI
BAGIRMI
DARFUR
El Fasher
El Obeid
Sennar
Khartûm
Berber 1884 to Mahdi
Marewe 1885 to Mahdi
1885 to Mahdi
MAHDI'S DOMINION 1881–98
Massawa 1885 to Italy
Gondar
ERITREA
Assab to Italy
Obok
ETHIOPIA
c 1881–1907 conquest under Menelik II
Br. Somaliland 1884–85 Br. protectorate
Harar 1875–85 to Egypt

Freetown
Sierra Leone
Monrovia
LIBERIA
Ivory Coast
Gold Coast
Lomé
Ashanti
Porto Novo
Lagos
BENIN
Bussa
Yola
ADAMAWA
RABEH'S EMPIRE
ZANDE
EQUATORIA

Benue
Niger

Douala
1884 to Ger.
Kribi
Fernando Póo
Principé
São Tomé
Rio Muni
Libreville
GABON
Brazzaville
Leopoldville
Cabinda 1886–91 to Portugal
Ambriz
Loanda

Congo Free State

Ubangi R.

Congo R.

BUNYORO
Lake Victoria
German East Africa
Witu 1885–90 to Germany
Mombasa
Pemba Is.
Zanzibar Is.
Lake Tanganyika

LUBA
LUNDA
KAZEMBE
Benguela
Macâmedes

SOUTH ATLANTIC OCEAN

Aldabra Is.

Comoro Is. 1846–86 to France

Equator

LOZI
Lake Nyasa
R. Zambezi
Tete
MATABELE EMPIRE
Beira
Mozambique

German South-west Africa
1884 German protectorate
Walvis Bay
Lüderitz 1883 to Germany
TAWANA
BECHUANA
Limpopo R.
SOUTH AFRICAN REPUBLIC
Johannesburg
Orange Free State
ZULULAND
Natal
Durban
Tananarive
Madagascar 1885 French protectorate
Tropic of Capricorn

Cape Town
Cape Colony

INDIAN OCEAN

0   500 km
0   500 miles

Latin America 1892

Land over 1000 ft
Land over 5000 ft

Caribbean Sea

PANAMA

VENEZUELA
Llanos
Caracas

BRITISH
GUIANA

DUTCH GUIANA

FRENCH GUIANA

UNITED STATES
OF COLOMBIA

Bogatá

Quito

EQUADOR

Negro

Manaus

Amazon

Belém

Fortaleza

Natal

A m a z o n i a

B R A Z I L

Recife

PERU

Lima

A

La Paz

BOLIVIA

Mato Grosso

Xingu

Araguaia

San Francisco

Salvador

Arica

n

d

Gran Chaco

Paraná

PARAGUAY

São Paulo

Rio de Janeiro

Asunción

Tropic of Capricorn

PACIFIC
OCEAN

e

s

ARGENTINA

Pampas

Porto Alegre

CHILE

URAGUAY

Juan
Fernandez
(Chile)

Santiago
Valparaiso

Buenos Aires

Montevideo

La Plata

ATLANTIC
OCEAN

Bahia Blaca

Patagonia

Falkland
Islands
(British)

Tierra
de Fuego

Europe on the Eve of War 1914

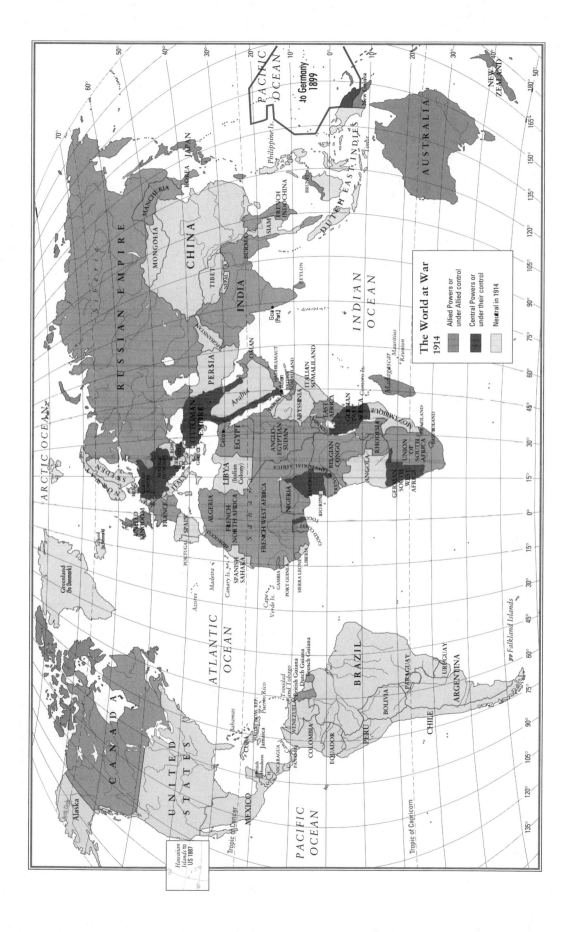

The World at War
1914

Allied Powers or
under Allied control

Central Powers or
under their control

Neutral in 1914

ARCTIC OCEAN

RUSSIAN EMPIRE

Siberia

MONGOLIA

MANCHURIA

CHINA

KOREA

JAPAN

TIBET

NEPAL

BHUTAN

INDIA

BURMA

SIAM

FRENCH
INDOCHINA

PHILIPPINE Is.

BRUNEI

DUTCH EAST INDIES

Timor (Port.)

New Guinea

to Germany
1899

PACIFIC
OCEAN

AUSTRALIA

NEW
ZEALAND

PACIFIC
OCEAN

CEYLON

INDIAN
OCEAN

Mauritius

Réunion

Comoro Is.

Madagascar

PERSIA

OMAN

Arabia

OTTOMAN
EMPIRE

CYPRUS

Cairo

EGYPT

ANGLO-
EGYPTIAN
SUDAN

ABYSSINIA

ADEN

HADHRAMAUT

BRITISH
SOMALILAND

ITALIAN
SOMALILAND

UGANDA

GERMAN
EAST
AFRICA

RHODESIA

MOZAMBIQUE

BELGIAN
CONGO

EQUATORIAL AFRICA

ANGOLA

GERMAN
SOUTH
WEST
AFRICA

UNION
OF
SOUTH
AFRICA

NYASALAND

BASUTOLAND

CAMEROON

NIGERIA

TOGO

GOLD COAST

RIO MUNI

Sahara

LIBYA
(Italian
Colony)

ALGERIA

FRENCH
NORTH AFRICA

MOROCCO

TUNIS

ITALY

GREECE

ROM.

SERB.

BULG.

MONT.

AUSTRIA
HUNGARY

GERMANY

FRANCE

SPAIN

PORTUGAL

UNITED
KINGDOM

NORWAY

SWEDEN

DENMARK

NETH.

BELG.

SWITZ.

ALB.

SPANISH
SAHARA

FRENCH WEST AFRICA

SIERRA LEONE

LIBERIA

GAMBIA

PORT. GUINEA

Cape
Verde Is.

Azores

Madeira

Canary Is.

Goa
(Port.)

BALUCHISTAN

AFGHANISTAN

Iceland

Greenland
(to Denmark)

ATLANTIC
OCEAN

CANADA

Alaska

UNITED
STATES

MEXICO

Tropic of Cancer

British
Honduras

GUATEMALA

HONDURAS

NICARAGUA

COSTA RICA

PANAMA

Panama Canal

Bahamas

CUBA

Jamaica

Puerto Rico

Trinidad
and Tobago

DOM. REP.
or HAITI

VENEZUELA

COLOMBIA

EQUADOR

PERU

BRAZIL

BOLIVIA

PARAGUAY

CHILE

ARGENTINA

URUGUAY

British Guiana

Dutch Guiana

French Guiana

Falkland Islands

Tropic of Capricorn

PACIFIC
OCEAN

Hawaiian
Islands to
US 1887

Europe
Post-WWI

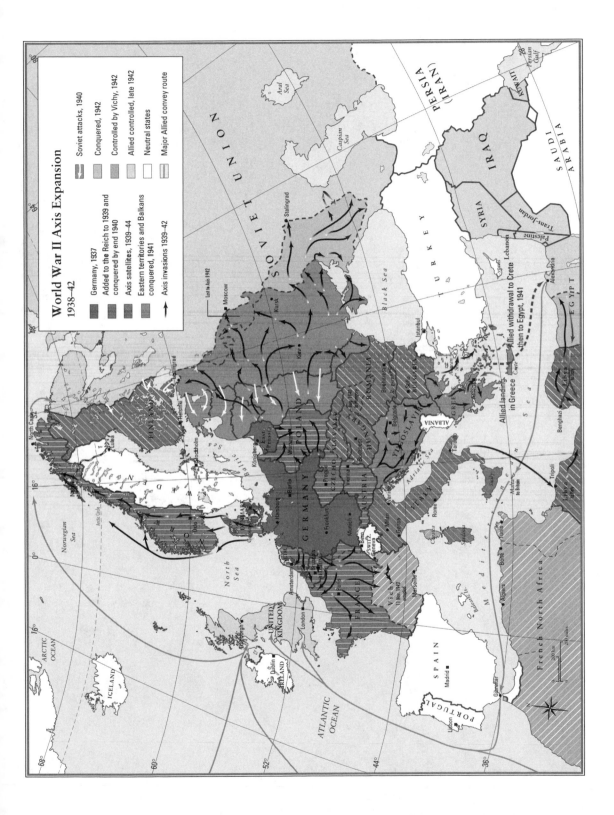

World War II Axis Expansion
1938–42

Germany, 1937

Added to the Reich to 1939 and
conquered by end 1940

Axis satellites, 1939–44

Eastern territories and Balkans
conquered, 1941

Axis invasions 1939–42

Soviet attacks, 1940

Conquered, 1942

Controlled by Vichy, 1942

Allied controlled, late 1942

Neutral states

Major Allied convey route

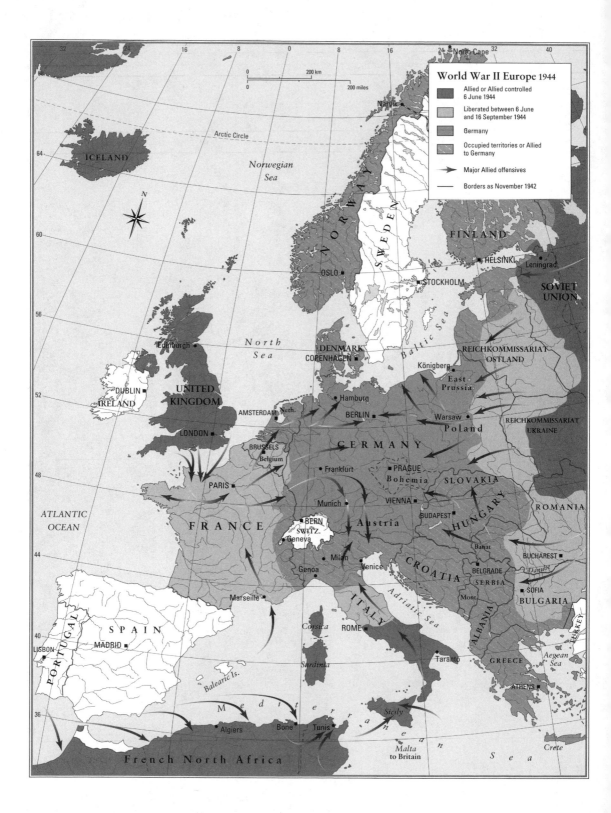

World War II Europe 1944

- Allied or Allied controlled 6 June 1944
- Liberated between 6 June and 16 September 1944
- Germany
- Occupied territories or Allied to Germany
- Major Allied offensives
- Borders as November 1942

200 km
200 miles

ICELAND

Norwegian Sea

Arctic Circle

North Cape

NORWAY

SWEDEN

FINLAND

Narvik

OSLO

STOCKHOLM

HELSINKI

Leningrad

SOVIET UNION

North Sea

Baltic Sea

REICHKOMMISSARIAT OSTLAND

Edinburgh

UNITED KINGDOM

DUBLIN

IRELAND

LONDON

DENMARK

COPENHAGEN

Hamburg

BERLIN

Königberg

East Prussia

Warsaw

Poland

REICHKOMMISSARIAT UKRAINE

AMSTERDAM Neth.

BRUSSELS

Belgium

GERMANY

Frankfurt

PRAGUE

Bohemia

SLOVAKIA

PARIS

Munich

VIENNA

ROMANIA

ATLANTIC OCEAN

FRANCE

BERN

SWITZ.

Geneva

Austria

BUDAPEST

HUNGARY

Milan

Venice

CROATIA

BUCHAREST

Genoa

BELGRADE

SERBIA

Danube

Banat

Marseille

ITALY

Adriatic Sea

Mont

SOFIA

BULGARIA

PORTUGAL

SPAIN

MADRID

Corsica

ROME

Aegean Sea

LISBON

Sardinia

Taranto

ALBANIA

GREECE

ATHENS

Balearic Is.

M e d i t e r

Sicily

TURKEY

Algiers

Bone

Tunis

Malta to Britain

Crete

French North Africa

r a n e a n   S e a

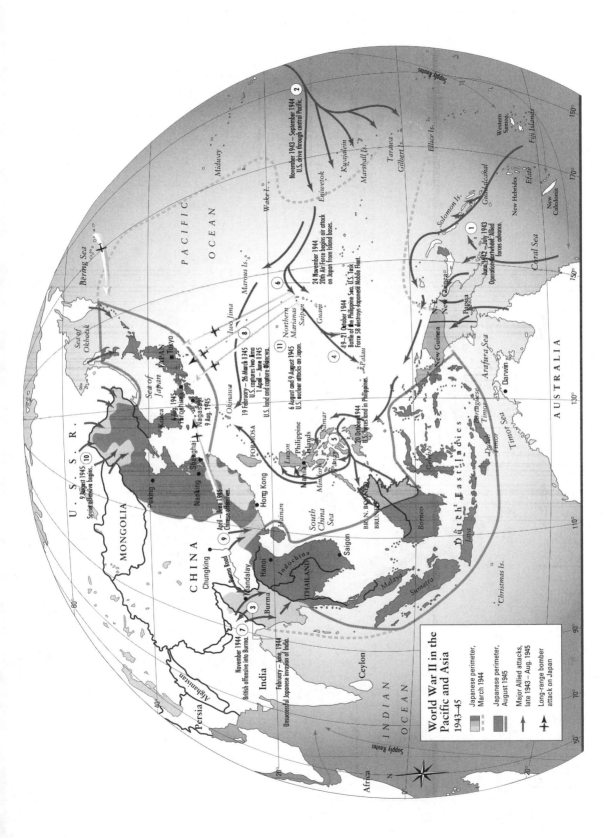

World War II in the
Pacific and Asia
1943–45

Japanese perimeter, March 1944

Japanese perimeter, August 1945

Major Allied attacks, late 1943 – Aug. 1945

Long-range bomber attack on Japan

① June 1942 – July 1943
Operation Cartwheel: Allied forces advance.

② November 1943 – September 1944
U.S. drive through central Pacific.

③ November 1944
British offensive into Burma.

④ 19–21 October 1944
Battle of the Philippine Sea. U.S. Task Force 58 destroys Japanese Mobile Fleet.

⑤ 20 October 1944
U.S. forces land in Philippines.

⑥ 24 November 1944
20th Air Force begins air attack on Japan from island bases.

⑦ February – June 1944
Unsuccessful Japanese invasion of India.

⑧ 19 February – 26 March 1945
U.S. captures Iwo Jima
1 April – June 1945
U.S. land and capture Okinawa.

⑨ April – June 1945
Chinese offensive.

⑩ 9 August 1945
Soviet offensive begins.

⑪ 6 August and 9 August 1945
U.S. nuclear attacks on Japan.

Africa

INDIAN OCEAN

Persia

Afghanistan

U.S.S.R.

MONGOLIA

CHINA

Chungking

Peking

Nanking

Shanghai

Burma Road

Burma

Mandalay

Hanoi

THAILAND

Indochina

Saigon

Malaya

Sumatra

Hainan

Hong Kong

South China Sea

FORMOSA

Luzon

Manila

Mindoro

Philippine Islands

Samar

Leyte

Palawan

BR. N. BORNEO

BRUNEI

Borneo

Celebes

Dutch East Indies

Java

Dutch Timor

Portuguese Timor

Timor Sea

Arafura Sea

Darwin

AUSTRALIA

New Guinea

Papua

N.E. New Guinea

Coral Sea

Solomon Is.

Guadalcanal

New Hebrides

Efaté

New Caledonia

Fiji Islands

Western Samoa

Ellice Is.

Gilbert Is.

Tarawa

Marshall Is.

Kwajalein

Eniwetok

Guam

Saipan

Northern Marianas

Palau

Marcus Is.

Iwo Jima

Wake I.

Midway

PACIFIC OCEAN

Sea of Okhotsk

Bering Sea

Sea of Japan

JAPAN

Tokyo

Hiroshima
6 Aug. 1945

Nagasaki
9 Aug. 1945

Korea

Okinawa

Christmas Is.

Ceylon

India

Supply Routes

Supply Routes

50° 70° 90° 110° 130° 150° 170°

20° 40° 60°

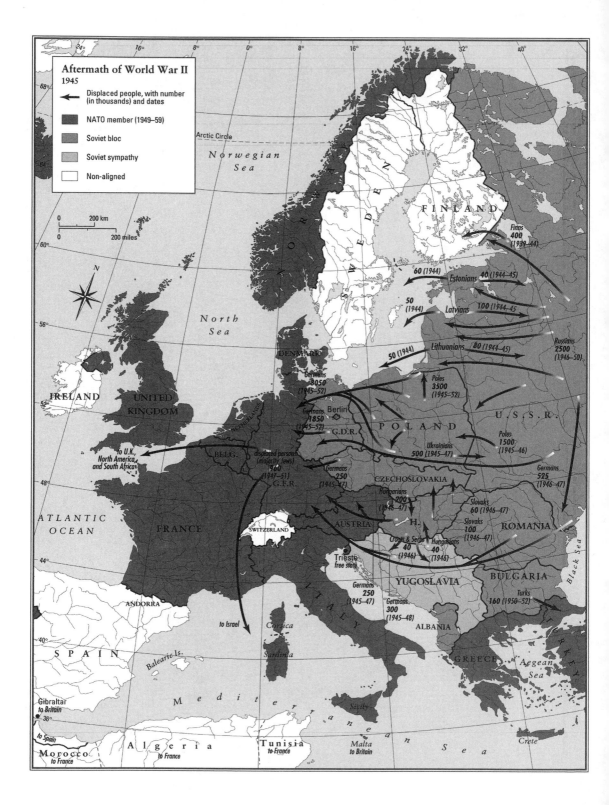

Aftermath of World War II
1945

← Displaced people, with number (in thousands) and dates

NATO member (1949–59)

Soviet bloc

Soviet sympathy

Non-aligned

0   200 km
0   200 miles

N

Arctic Circle

Norwegian Sea

North Sea

ATLANTIC OCEAN

IRELAND

UNITED KINGDOM

DENMARK

NETHERLANDS

BELG.

FRANCE

SWITZERLAND

ANDORRA

SPAIN

Gibraltar to Britain

to Spain

Morocco to France

Algeria to France

Tunisia to France

Balearic Is.

Corsica

Sardinia

ITALY

Sicily

Malta to Britain

Mediterranean Sea

SWEDEN

NORWAY

FINLAND

Finns 400 (1939–44)

60 (1944)

Estonians 40 (1944–45)

50 (1944)

Latvians 100 (1944–45)

Russians 2500 (1946–50)

50 (1944)

Lithuanians 80 (1944–45)

Poles 3500 (1945–52)

Germans 8050 (1945–52)

Germans 1850 (1945–52)

Berlin

G.D.R.

POLAND

U.S.S.R.

Poles 1500 (1945–46)

displaced persons (majority Jews) 960 (1947–51)

G.F.R.

Germans 250 (1945–47)

Ukrainians 500 (1945–47)

Germans 525 (1946–47)

to U.K., North America, and South Africa

CZECHOSLOVAKIA

Hungarians 200 (1946–47)

Slovaks 60 (1946–47)

Slovaks 100 (1946–47)

ROMANIA

AUSTRIA

H.

Croats & Serbs 40 (1946)

Hungarians 40 (1946)

BULGARIA

Trieste free state

Germans 250 (1945–47)

Germans 300 (1945–48)

YUGOSLAVIA

ALBANIA

Turks 160 (1950–52)

Black Sea

TURKEY

GREECE

Aegean Sea

Crete

to Israel

to Israel

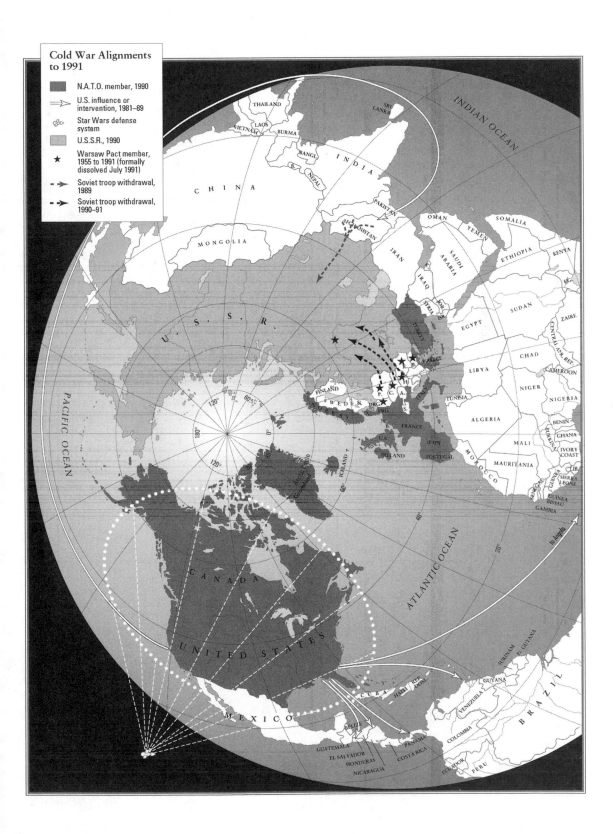

Cold War Alignments
to 1991

N.A.T.O. member, 1990

U.S. influence or
intervention, 1981–89

Star Wars defense
system

U.S.S.R., 1990

Warsaw Pact member,
1955 to 1991 (formally
dissolved July 1991)

Soviet troop withdrawal,
1989

Soviet troop withdrawal,
1990–91

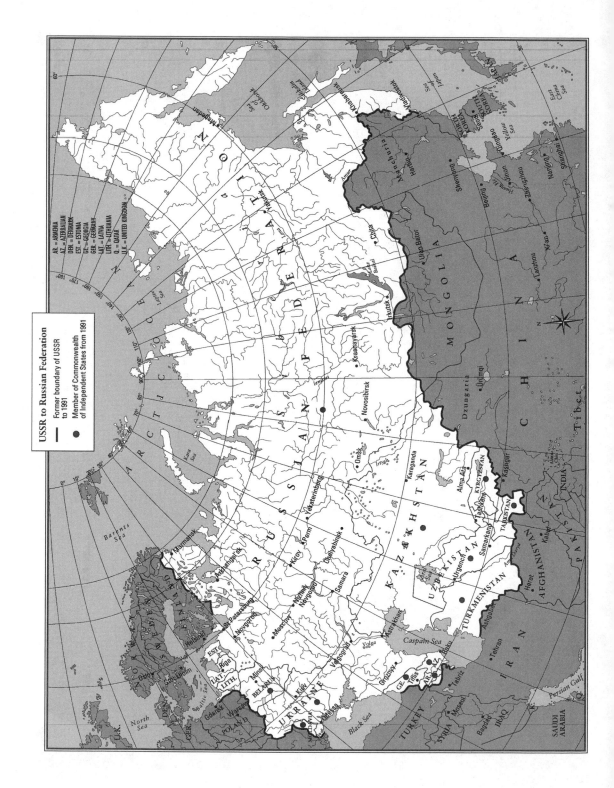

USSR to Russian Federation

— Former boundary of USSR to 1991

● Member of Commonwealth of Independent States from 1991

AR. = ARMENIA
AZ. = AZERBAIJAN
DEN. = DENMARK
EST. = ESTONIA
GE. = GEORGIA
GER. = GERMANY
LAT. = LATVIA
LITH. = LITHUANIA
Q. = QATAR
U.K. = UNITED KINGDOM

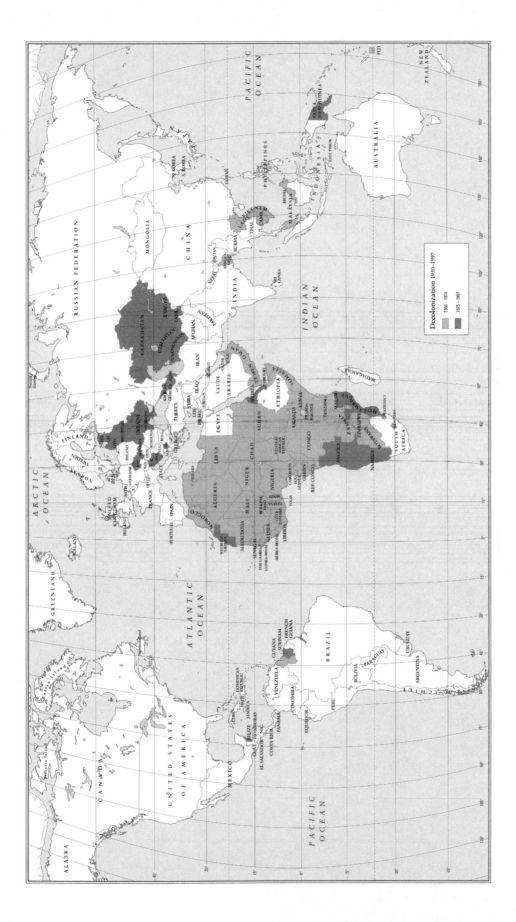

Aachen

Charlemagne's capital in northern Germany. Charlemagne established his permanent court here around 790. It became a town by eighth-century standards. Charlemagne built a beautiful chapel and library and brought together some of the greatest scholars of Europe in what has become known as the Aachen, or court school.

Abbasid Caliphate (750–1258)

Muslim dynasty centered in **Baghdad** during the so-called Golden Age of **Islam**, with brilliant culture and arts. In 750 Abu Muslim led a revolt in the area of modern day Iraq against the **Umayyad Caliphate** and established a new dynasty. Abu al-Abbas was proclaimed its first caliph.

Abdul Hamid (1842–1918)

Last sultan of Turkey. He promulgated the first constitution of Turkey in 1876. At his accession Abdul Hamid was suspiciously regarded as too liberal, but he soon showed himself as a despot and was known as "the Great Assassin" for his attacks on enemies and, especially, for his massacres of Christian Armenians (1894–1896). Abdul Hamid was deposed after the revolt of the **Young Turks**.

Abdullah ibn Hussein (1882–1951)

First king of Jordan (1946–1951). Hussein was **amir** of Transjordan (1921–1946) under British protection. When Jordan was declared independent in 1946, Hussein was made king. He was assassinated five years later.

Abelard, Peter (1079–1142)

French medieval scholar and philosopher noted for rational inquiry and a love affair. In 1115 Abelard was made canon and master of **Notre Dame Cathedral** and attracted students from all over Europe. Abelard was one of the most influential, albeit controversial, teachers in the **Middle Ages**, but in Paris he began a love affair with a woman, Héloise. Abelard was subsequently castrated, retreated to a monastery, and continued his controversial teachings. Abelard and Héloise were buried together in Paris, and their love letters were later collected and published.

Abolitionists

Advocates of the abolition of slavery in the eighteenth and nineteenth centuries in Europe and the United States. In Britain individuals such as **John Wesley**, John Newton, **Olaudah Equiano**, and William Wilberforce led the way to the abolition of the slave trade in 1807 and the abolition of slavery in the British Empire in 1833. The movement in the United States was especially strong from 1830 to 1861, leading to the start of the **American Civil War** in 1861. Abolitionists used the press, lectures, church pulpits, petitions, and even riots and assaults to promote their view. Some leaders of the U.S. abolitionist movement were William Lloyd Garrison, **Harriet**

Beecher Stowe, Wendell Phillips, ex-slave Frederick Douglass, and John Brown.

Aborigine
A term meaning "original inhabitants." Originally used to describe a mythical people of Italy, it later referred to any original inhabitants of a region and has come to be particularly associated with the native peoples of Australia, several physically distinct groups who are all dark-skinned hunter-gatherers.

Abraham
Traditional founder of Judaism and prophet of Islam, viewed as the founder of monotheism and revered by Jews, Christians, and Muslims. Abraham was a Semitic herder living in the Fertile Crescent around 1750 B.C.E. who traveled across Mesopotamia and the Levant. According to tradition, he made a covenant with Yahweh, the god that made all, that his people would revere only Yahweh (monotheism) and would receive Yahweh's favor. In the Jewish tradition Abraham's descendants became known as Hebrews ("wanderers").

Absolutism
Doctrine of power without limitation held by monarchs of the sixteenth and seventeenth centuries in Europe. These monarchs often claimed divine right and tried to rule without sharing power with any legislative body. Louis XIV of France was one of the most successful absolute monarchs in western Europe, while Maria Theresa of Austria is a prime example of an absolute monarch in eastern Europe.

Abu al-Abbas
Descendant of Muhammad's uncle and caliph of the Abbasid caliphate (750). The caliphate was centered in Baghdad after overthrowing the Umayyad caliphate and was destroyed by the Mongols in 1258.

Abu Bakr (c. 573–634)
Successor to Muhammad at his death in 632. Muhammad left no sons and no chosen successor so his closest followers selected Abu Bakr, Muhammad's father-in-law and one of his first supporters, as the first caliph ("successor") of Islam. Abu Bakr, who led from 632 to 634, was successful at unifying the movement and directing its expansion, by means of the jihad, toward neighboring peoples. Some Muslims believed that Muhammad's successor should be his closest male relative, hence the split between Sunni Muslims (who followed Abu Bakr) and Shia Muslims (who supported Ali, Muhammad's son-in-law).

Academy
Athenian school of philosophy founded by Plato between 390 and 380 B.C.E. Plato taught many students at the Academy, the most famous of whom was Aristotle, who later became tutor to Alexander the Great. The Academy as Plato created it survived until Cicero (106–43 B.C.E.), and in some form continued until it was closed by Justinian in 529 C.E.

Achaemenids
Persian Empire, 549 to 330 B.C.E. Founded by Cyrus the Great, who built an empire that extended from North Africa and Greece to the Indus River. Cyrus was followed by Darius I and Xerxes I, both of whom attempted unsuccessfully to conquer the Greeks in the fifth century B.C.E. Darius built a capital at Persepolis whose remains provide a glimpse of the empire's glory. The Achaemenids were very open to influence from abroad and incorporated Vedic and Persian cultures and religions. Alexander the Great invaded and conquered the empire in 334 B.C.E.

Achebe, Chinua (1930–)
Nigerian author who writes in English. The best-known African writer of the late

twentieth and early twenty-first centuries wrote *Things Fall Apart* in 1958 as an attempt to counter western distortions of Africans as simple and childlike. It describes the corruption brought from the West and the complexity and dilemmas of African culture and society. His later works include *Anthills of the Savannah* (1987).

Acheson, Dean (1893–1971)

U.S. Secretary of State (1949–1953) and adviser to four U.S. presidents. Acheson contributed much to U.S. foreign policy during the **Cold War**. His focus was on the European sector of the Cold War problem, especially during the **Korean War**; he feared that expanding the United States' influence in Asia would threaten U.S. interests in Europe.

Acropolis

A citadel or fortified part of an ancient Greek city, usually just outside the city and often raised up on a mountainside for defensive purposes. Each Greek **polis** had an acropolis for the defense of the entire community. **Athens**'s acropolis was destroyed by the Persians in 480 B.C.E. but was rebuilt, including the Parthenon.

Actium, Battle of (31 B.C.E.)

Roman naval battle in which **Octavian** defeated **Mark Antony** and **Cleopatra** in western Greece. Marcus Agrippa led the fleet for Octavian at Actium. Mark Antony and Cleopatra both committed suicide after the defeat. Octavian thereby eliminated all competitors and became ruler of **Rome** and in 27 B.C.E. was declared **princeps** and named Augustus ("Revered One").

Act of Union. *See* Union, Act of

Adams, John (1735–1826)

Second president of the United States (1797–1801); a prominent figure in the American struggle for independence and in the early years as a nation. Adams had a major role in the **Continental Congress** (1774–1777); wrote the constitution of the State of Massachusetts; was a signer of the 1783 **Treaty of Paris**, ending the war with Britain; and was the nation's first vice president (to **George Washington**). His presidency was troubled by feuding with other members of his party, the Federalists, and by the backlash against the Alien and Sedition Acts.

Adams, John Quincy (1767–1848)

Sixth president of the United States (1825–1829). The eldest son of president John Adams (a Federalist), John Quincy Adams (a Republican) was, before his own presidency, a great American diplomat. He developed what came to be known as the **Monroe Doctrine**. Adams had less success as a president than as a diplomat. Lacking tact, he had difficulty getting popular support for many of his proposals. After his presidency, Adams played a prominent role in the campaign to end slavery.

Aden

City in Yemen that was an important trading port for thousands of years. Aden is named in the **Old Testament**. It was a major terminus in the **spice trade** from Asia to the Middle East. In the nineteenth century the British made Aden a strategic base and a coaling station on the route to India. In 1937 Aden became a British crown colony. It became part of South Arabia in 1963 and the capital of South Yemen in 1968. With the merger of South Yemen and North Yemen in 1990 Aden was no longer a capital, but it remains an important port for long-distance trade.

Adenauer, Konrad (1876–1967)

German statesman and first chancellor of the Federal Republic of Germany

(1949–1963). Adenauer led the political and economic transformation of Germany after **World War II** and helped in the building of good relations with the United States and with other Western European countries.

Adowa, Battle of (1896)

Stunning Ethiopian defeat of an Italian army. As late-nineteenth-century European imperialism swept through Africa, Italy established a protectorate in Ethiopia in 1882. At Adowa an Italian army of 10,000–15,000 soldiers was soundly defeated by an Ethiopian army of more than 40,000 armed with modern weapons. The Italians lost more than 4,500 men. It was the worst European defeat in Africa and led to Ethiopia's continued independence and Italy's humiliation.

Adrianople, Battle of (378)

Roman Empire defeat by a **Goth** army. The Goths were in flight from the **Huns** when they met a **Byzantine** (Eastern Roman) army under Emperor Valens at Adrianople, west of **Constantinople**, and soundly defeated it. It was a serious blow to Roman attempts to control the Germanic tribes entering the empire.

Aegean City-States

Political units of ancient **Greece**. Between 1000 and 800 B.C.E. cities and their surrounding countryside of the southern Greek peninsula and Aegean Sea islands formed independent sovereign states. They were generally ruled by monarchies or oligarchies, although in the late sixth century B.C.E. **Athens** experimented with **democracy**. Because the Aegean city-states (in Greek, **polis**) were small and they were unsuccessful at forming permanent federations, they fell to larger powers such as the Macedonians and, later, the **Roman Empire**.

Aeneid, The

Poem by **Virgil** in twelve books begun around 30 B.C.E. and still incomplete at his death in 19 B.C.E. In his will Virgil ordered the poem to be burned, but his request was ignored. Written under the patronage of the emperor **Octavian**, who used the poem as a patriotic propaganda piece to trumpet the glory of Rome, it traces the journey of the Trojan hero Aeneas, who fled the city after it was destroyed by the Greeks. Aeneas was the embodiment of many Roman virtues like piety. Based on the Greek model of **Homer**'s **Odyssey** and **Iliad**, *The Aeneid* narrates Aeneas's trip across the Mediterranean and his flight from Troy to the Elysian fields and, eventually, **Latium**.

Aeolian Greeks

Greeks of the western part of **Asia Minor**. Greek civilization expanded from the late **Mycenaean** period from the southern, or Peloponnesian, part of the Greek peninsula to the lands around the Aegean Sea. Those who settled in the western part of **Asia Minor** became known as Aeolian and Ionian Greeks.

Aeschylus (525–456 B.C.E.)

Ancient Greek playwright and one of the three major authors of tragedy, along with **Sophocles** and **Euripedes**. Aeschylus wrote around ninety plays, of which only seven survive. He founded the school of Greek tragedy that incorporated a chorus and a plot with dialogue between two or more actors. His plays include *The Seven Against Thebes* (407 B.C.E.) and *Oresteia* (458 B.C.E.; includes *Agamemnon*, *The Libation Bearers*, and *The Eumendies*).

Afghanistan, Twentieth-Century

Country in **Central Asia**. Afghanistan gained full independence from Britain as a result of the Third **Anglo-Afghan War** in

1919. Victory in the war gave King Amanullah the domestic leverage to embark on an extensive modernization program. Amanullah's reign and the reforms characterizing it ended in 1929 with a tribal rebellion led by mullahs active in rural areas. Afghanistan remained neutral in **World War II**, as it had in **World War I**. Repeated disputes with Pakistan over the status of the Pashtun tribes straddling the Afghanistan-Pakistan border were the most significant foreign relations issues for the country from the 1940s through the 1960s. Muhammad Daoud was perhaps the dominant political personality from the early 1950s to the late 1970s. In 1978 a coup/revolution brought a socialist government to power, and in 1979 the **Union of Soviet Socialist Republics** (Soviet Union) invaded Afghanistan to support that government. The Soviet Union withdrew its military from Afghanistan in 1989. The United States conducted the largest covert operation in its own and world history to fund the **Islamic fundamentalist** mujahideen who claimed control of Kabul in 1992 but whose excesses led to their removal from the capital city and most provinces by the even more reactionary Taliban in 1996. The Taliban were removed from power by the United States' invasion and occupation of Afghanistan in 2001 but remained active in the country in 2005.

African Charter on Human and People's Rights

Charter adopted in 1981 by the **Organization of African Unity** (OAU) affirming the need to eliminate colonialism and racism and build economic and cultural rights for all people in Africa. The charter established a commission to examine human rights violations in Africa; however, such violations remain a major issue for many African states.

African Colonialism

European exercise of power in Africa, especially in the late nineteenth century. Europeans established trading bases along the African coast in the fifteenth and sixteenth centuries and ravaged Africa in the slave trade of the seventeenth and eighteenth centuries. After the decline of the slave trade and the rise of European industrialization in the nineteenth century, invasions of traders, missionaries, settlers, and administrators descended upon Africa and came into conflict with established African kingdoms. Superior weapons enabled Europeans to conquer large tracts of Africa. The **Congress of Berlin** (1884–1885) divided much of Africa into colonies of the European states. After **World War I** laws and policies in many of the colonies were defined. Shortly after **World War II** African colonies began the process of **African decolonization** and became independent countries but were often left with economies and social structures in ruin.

African Decolonization

Transfer of political power in Africa from colonial European rulers to independent indigenous governments during the twentieth century. Most of Africa had been conquered in the nineteenth century in the process of **African Colonialism**. With the exception of Egyptian independence in 1922, **World War II**'s pressures and exposure of European weakness brought on a wave of independence movements, especially Ghana's 1957 independence, which triggered a wave of African nationalism and independence throughout the 1960s. In 1963 thirty-two new African states formed the **Organization of African Unity** (OAU). By 1965 most African territory was free of European colonial domination.

African Diaspora
Dispersion of African peoples to other continents, often forcibly. The **Atlantic slave trade** by Europeans in the sixteenth to nineteenth centuries was the greatest influence on the African Diaspora. Africans were transported by ship to North and South America, the Caribbean, and Asia. Africans had dispersed to foreign lands voluntarily and involuntarily long before the sixteenth century, but European discovery of sea routes around the world internationalized the slave trade and increased the numbers of slaves greatly. An estimated 10 million Africans were in the Americas by 1800, 2 million of them in the United States.

African Imperialism. *See* African Colonialism

African National Congress (ANC)
South African nationalist organization that opposed white minority rule. In 1912 the South African Native National Congress was founded and led by **Mohandas K. Gandhi**. It used passive resistance and racial equality, as opposed to the **Pan-African Congress**. The ANC issued the Freedom Charter in 1956 and was outlawed in 1960. The ANC began some armed struggle but used international diplomacy and internal economic pressure to bring about change. In 1990 the ANC was made legal and under **Nelson Mandela** negotiated a transition to democracy in South Africa. In 1994 it won the first open elections and Mandela became president. In 1999 Thabo Mbeki became president of South Africa as leader of the ANC.

African Union
The name taken in July 2000 by the former **Organization of African Unity (OAU)**. Originally formed in 1963 with thirty-two states, the African Union charter in 2000 had fifty-three participant states.

Afrika Corps
A German **World War II** army of two divisions in North Africa under the command of General Erwin Rommel. Originally sent to support Italian forces, the Afrika Corps proved very effective against the British army in Egypt and Libya.

Afrikaners
Descendants of Dutch invaders and settlers who arrived in 1652 in the southern African Cape Colony. The settlement was first made by the **Dutch East India Company** and was augmented by immigrants from France and Germany, but those who were subsequently born in Africa became known as Afrikaners or Boers (*boer* is Dutch for "farmer"). They moved inland and founded independent colonies that became the Orange Free State and, later, the South African Republic. In the second **Anglo-Boer War** (1899–1902) the Afrikaners put up a fierce resistance to the British army as Britain took control of the region. Afrikaners remained the dominant group politically until the dismantling of the white South African government in 1994.

Agamemnon
King of Mycenae and Argos, according to tradition. Agamemnon married Clytemnestra and his brother Menelaus married Clytemnestra's sister Helen, daughters of the king of Sparta. Helen was stolen by (or ran away with) Paris, and Agamemnon was chosen to raise a fleet and army to retrieve Helen from Troy. The Achaeans (Greeks) raised a large force and besieged Troy. Archaeological evidence indicates there was a siege of Troy around 1250 B.C.E. Agamemnon fought bravely but quarreled with Achilles, the Achaeans' greatest warrior. After the siege it was foretold by Cassandra (daughter of Priam of Troy) that Agamemnon would be killed by his wife. He ignored this

warning, returned home with Cassandra and Clytemnestra, and was eventually murdered by Clytemnestra's lover. Agamemnon's son Orestes avenged him.

See also Greece, Mycenaean

Age of Enlightenment. *See* Enlightenment

Age of Exploration

Era when Europeans influenced by the **Renaissance** (and its focus on classical texts, including those on geography) and by the rising threat of the **Ottoman Turks,** who cut off access to the East via the **Silk Roads** and markets around the Black Sea, began to explore the west coast of Africa. After a successful attack on the North African city of Ceuta in 1415 provided a foothold, the Portuguese slowly and methodically began in 1419 to explore southward along the coast of Africa under **Prince Henry, "the Navigator."** As they explored they accumulated empirical evidence, altered ship design, and developed navigational technology. In 1487 the Portuguese **Bartolomeu Dias** rounded the tip of Africa; in 1498 **Vasco Da Gama** sailed to India. In 1492 the Genoese mapmaker **Christopher Columbus,** who had worked in Lisbon, Portugal, fulfilled his idea of sailing west to get to the East for the queen and king of Spain. In 1519–1522 **Ferdinand Magellan** led an expedition to circumnavigate the globe sailing west. He was killed in the East Indies, but a small group of men under Juan Sebastián de Elcano made it back to Europe. Within approximately 100 years Europe had opened access to the entire world, encountering new continents, peoples, animals, and diseases. This was the beginning of the West's domination of much of the world.

Agincourt, Battle of (1415)

Battle between England and France in the **Hundred Years War** (1338–1453). The French army, ignoring their disastrous defeats at the similar **Battles of Crécy** (1346) and **Poitiers** (1356), charged mounted cavalry against English archers using **longbows,** pikemen, and dismounted knights. The heavily outnumbered English decisively defeated the French. The French lost 5,000–7,000 men while the English lost 300.

Agitational Propaganda (Agitprop)

Political "guerilla theatre" of the avant-garde, which used short plays to protest during the 1960s and 1970s. These plays were performed on streets and in city parks to spread political protest ideals to the communities and people who did not attend theater plays. Some examples are the San Francisco Mime Troupe and playwrights David Rabe and Sam Shepard.

Agora

Ancient Greek community assembly space, usually in the center of a town. The agora was also used as a marketplace. The significance of the agora is that most ancient civilizations took care to ensure that the common people could not meet, whereas the Greeks ensured that they could. This did not mean the people had political power but that the will of the people mattered, an important factor eventually leading to **democracy.**

Agrarian Society

Term for a culture that moved to cultivation and livestock rearing from hunting and gathering. The process of developing agrarian society took place during the **Neolithic agricultural revolution.** Agrarian society requires enormous outlays of work but can support a larger population than hunting and gathering. Agrarian society made it possible to develop civilizations with cities and advanced social organizations.

Agricultural Revolution, Modern

Revolution of the seventeenth to nineteenth centuries in which the use of nitrogen-inducing forage crops (alfalfa, clover) increased the area under cultivation and thus the number of livestock. There was also an increase in the use of machines, new crops such as turnips and potatoes, and a "scientific" study of agriculture. This broke the closed circuit of medieval agriculture, which could not move beyond subsistence, and increased food production dramatically, making the growth of Europe and the **Industrial Revolution** possible.

Agricultural Revolution, Neolithic

Generic term for the period when a region moved from hunting and gathering into cultivation and livestock rearing. The term *agricultural revolution* is misleading in that the process of moving to dependence upon agriculture took centuries, even millennia. Agricultural activity dates from 10,000 to 8,000 B.C.E., and by 5,000 B.C.E. agriculture had become well established in southwest Asia, Southeast Asia, the Americas, and Europe. As large game was increasingly hunted into extinction and populations outgrew the natural supplies of food, agriculture spread as a necessity. The agricultural revolution made possible a dramatic increase in population that led to more complex social organization and the development of cities.

Aguinaldo, Emilio (1869–1964)

Filipino independence fighter against the Spanish and the Americans. A local government official, Aguinaldo was a leader of the 1897 Philippine rebellion against the Spanish and cooperated with the United States during the Spanish-American War. Disappointed by the U.S. failure to recognize Philippine independence, he led a guerilla war against the Americans (the Philippine-American War, 1898–1902). His capture in 1901 help to bring about the end of the conflict.

AIDS (Acquired Immunodeficiency Syndrome)

Disease caused by the human immunodeficiency virus (HIV), which attacks a person's immune system leaving him or her susceptible to other normally harmless diseases. Cases of AIDS were found as early as 1959; the number drastically increased during the 1970s. By the end of the twentieth century it was a worldwide epidemic most severely affecting Africa, where about three-quarters of the world's infected people live. Drugs to help delay the progress of the disease are expensive and unavailable in many areas, leaving some third world countries with no treatment alternatives. The problem of AIDS affects the governmental, social, and economic policies of countries.

Ainu

Race of Caucasoid-like people indigenous to Japan. Culturally related to the shamanist people of northeast Asia, they worship the bear and lead nomadic hunting and gathering lives. Since the 1880s the Ainu have been protected by the Japanese government as an aboriginal people. They maintain their culture in the northern Japanese island of Hokkaido.

Aix-la-Chapelle, Treaty of (1748)

Treaty that ended the War of the Austrian Succession. The terms of the treaty, drawn up by France and Britain, were accepted by **Maria Teresa** of Austria and restored most lands to their original owners. The treaty also provided a temporary truce between France and Britain in their ongoing conflicts in North America and India and established Prussia as a European power.

Akbar (1542–1605)
Third **Mughal** emperor (r. 1556–1605) who expanded his empire to include most of northern India and eastern Afghanistan. Akbar was an able administrator who laid much of the foundation that made the Mughal Empire the dominant state in the Indian subcontinent for two centuries. A **Muslim** from **Central Asia**, he was noted for his tolerance and brought Indian Muslims and Hindus into his administration. In an effort to bring harmony to the religiously diverse empire he created his own religious practice, *din-i-ilahi* ("religion of God"), which sought to harmonize all faiths. Akbar also sponsored works of art and literature that blended Indian and Persian cultural traditions.

Akhenaton. *See* Amenhotep IV (Akhenaton)

Akkadians
People of the Semitic empire established by Sargon I around 2350 B.C.E. along the **Euphrates River** (present-day Iraq). The Akkadians conquered the cities of **Sumer** and established one of the earliest true states with a powerful king and large army. Around 2200 B.C.E. the Akkadians were overthrown and a neo-Sumerian society was reestablished. The Akkadian language, one of the oldest recorded languages and spoken by the Assyrians and the Babylonians, existed in the **Middle East** for 2,000 years.

Aksum. *See* Axum (Aksum)

Alamein, Battle of el- (1942–1943)
World War II battle in North Africa. Britain's General Bernard Law Montgomery launched an attack on October 23, 1942, against Erwin Rommel's German army in el-Alamein, northern Egypt. The British outnumbered the German forces and tanks, but Rommel put up strong resistance. The Germans were pushed westward through Egypt and Libya all the way to Tunisia by mid-January 1943. This was the first decisive victory for the **Allies** in World War II.

Alamo
Mission church where Texans fought the Mexican army. In 1836 Texas declared itself independent from Mexico as the Republic of Texas. Mexican general Antonio López de Santa Anna, then dictator of Mexico, led a military expedition to suppress the rebellion. At San Antonio, Texans made a stand at the Alamo. All 187 Texas defenders were killed and the Mexicans lost more than 1,500 men. The loss at the Alamo inflamed Texans and Americans, who, under General Sam Houston, overwhelmed the Mexican army to the rallying cry "Remember the Alamo."

Alaska Purchase (1867)
Territory of Alaska, acquired by the United States in 1867. President Andrew Johnson's Secretary of State, William H. Seward, purchased the land from Russia for 7.2 million dollars, or about two cents an acre. With this new territory the United States added 586,412 square miles (1,518,690 sq km) to its area.

Albert, Prince (1819–1861)
Husband of British **Queen Victoria**. Albert was first cousin to the queen and prince of Saxe-Coburg-Gotha. He played a very strong role in Victoria's monarchy although the British government never gave him an official position. Together Albert and Victoria provided stability and a model of harmonious family life for Britain. Albert helped bring about the **Great Exhibition of 1851**, which also led to the development of South Kensington, its Victorian and Albert Museum, and the Royal Albert Hall. Albert's death from

typhoid fever was a shock from which Victoria never completely recovered, causing her to retreat from public life.

Alberti, Leone Battista (1404–1472)
Italian Renaissance architect and scholar of architecture. He first wrote treatises on architecture and studied the works of ancient **Rome** and upon **Filippo Brunelleschi**'s death became the leading Renaissance architect. Alberti designed the Palazzo Rucellai (1446–1451) in **Florence** and the church of S. Andrea (1470) in Mantua among others.

Albigensians
Members of a medieval sect who attempted to live a pure Christian life by rejecting the material world. Located in southern France, the movement became popular. The Albigensian view of a duality known as Catharism (God created good; something else created the evil in the world) was declared heretical by the **Roman Catholic Church** and condemned in 1119, 1179, and 1215. In their attempt to live pure lives Albigensians remained celibate and renounced all desires of the flesh. An Albigensian Crusade in 1208–1229 destroyed the Albigensians by executions and confiscations of their property.

Albuquerque, Alfonso de (1453–1515)
Portuguese admiral and conqueror in the East Indies. Albuquerque conquered **Goa** in India, Ceylon, the Sundra Islands, **Malacca** in the East Indies, and the island of Hormuz in the Persian Gulf. Goa became the center of the Portuguese overseas empire. Albuquerque, although often brutal, was known for his justice, but court intrigue destroyed him and he died returning to Portugal.

Alcuin (c. 735–804)
English scholar at **Charlemagne**'s court. Alcuin was the head of the palace school

at **Aachen** that brought together scholars from all over Europe and created the Carolingian renaissance, or cultural revival, that saved much of classical Roman art and literature.

Alexander I (1777–1825)
Tsar of **Russia** (1801–1825) and early in his rule a reformer. Alexander attempted to reform education and serfdom but was resisted by the aristocracy. Alexander's Russia fought against **Napoléon Bonaparte**, but with defeat Russia supported France against Britain. Russia later joined **Prussia** and Britain to defeat Napoléon. Alexander formed the Holy Alliance to defend Christianity and in his later years suppressed liberal movements.

Alexander II (1818–1881)
Tsar of Russia (1855–1881), known as the "Tsar Liberator" for emancipating millions of serfs in 1861. He also reformed the administration and the military and extended Russia's borders in the **Caucasus**, **Central Asia**, and the Far East, although he sold Alaska to the United States in the 1867 **Alaska Purchase**. Secret revolutionary societies in Russia attempted his assassination in 1862 and succeeded in 1881.

Alexander III (1845–1894)
Tsar of Russia (1881–1894) whose conservative suppression of liberal ideas and groups strengthened their resolve. Although interested in reforms of administration, taxes, and attitudes toward trade unions, Alexander was repressive toward nihilist and populist secret societies because they had assassinated his father in 1881. This stance strengthened the secret societies and weakened the hold of the state going into the twentieth century.

Alexander III, "the Great" (356–323 B.C.E.)
Macedonian king and general. King at age twenty when his father, **Philip II**, was

assassinated, Alexander forged one of the largest but shortest-lived empires in world history. In 334 B.C.E. Alexander crossed the Hellespont into **Asia Minor** with approximately 35,000 men to conquer Persia, leading the cavalry himself. His father had planned the project but died before he was able to carry it out. Alexander was noted for his tactical genius and fearless leadership. Eventually he conquered Syria, Egypt, most of the **Middle East**, Persia, **Bactria** (modern-day Afghanistan), and northwestern India. Alexander wanted to consolidate the empire, build roads and infrastructure, and unify the government, but he died of fever at age thirty-three. Often recognized as one of the world's greatest generals, Alexander built one of the world's largest empires with a vibrant economy and established dozens of new cities. His conquests began the spread of **Hellenistic Greek** culture throughout the Middle East and into India.

Alexander VI (c. 1430–1503)

Pope (1492–1503) and member of the Spanish Borgia family who mediated disputes between Portugal and Spain after the discovery of the New World and condemned **Girolamo Savonarola** to death in 1498. Alexander VI settled the dispute of ownership of lands around the world with The **Treaty of Tordesillas** of 1494, dividing the world into eastern and western spheres for Portugal and Spain, respectively.

Alexandria

City founded by **Alexander the Great** in 332 B.C.E. on the Mediterranean coast of Egypt. Alexander intended the city as the capital of his conquests. Alexandria became an important commercial center and transshipment point between Asia and Europe and was equally famous for its schools and its library, one of the great repositories of classical learning. Alexandria

was a major center of both Hellenistic and Jewish culture from 500 to 1500 C.E. Off the coast of Alexandria was the Pharos lighthouse, one of the seven wonders of the ancient world.

Alfred "the Great" (849–899)

Anglo-Saxon king of England. Alfred expanded the area of England under control of the king by pushing back Danish **Viking** invaders. He was noted for three innovations: Alfred divided his army into two units that would each serve six months; he built a navy of faster and longer ships to challenge the Vikings on the seas; and he built fortified settlements so that everyone was within a day's walk of protection. Considered a great warrior, Alfred was also known as a scholar and a brilliant administrator.

Alhambra

Muslim palace in Spain. Constructed between 1238 and 1358, the palace-fortress was part of a Muslim royal city of **Granada**. After the expulsion of the Muslims in 1492, much of the interior of Alhambra was ruined, and it was further destroyed and rebuilt in other styles over the centuries. The Citadel remains in the Moorish style.

Ali (c. 600–661 C.E.)

Son-in-law and son of an uncle of **Muhammad** and fourth **caliph** (656–661). Muhammad, at his death in 632, left no instructions as to a successor and no sons. Some of his followers selected **Abu Bakr** as caliph (successor) while others claimed that Muhammad had stated at Ghadir Qumm that Ali was his successor. The dispute arose over how to understand the term *successor*. Because Ali was the son of Muhammad's uncle and the husband of Muhammad's sole living daughter, Fatima, Ali was followed as the successor. Ali was murdered by one of his own disgruntled followers.

Alighieri, Dante (1265–1321)

Late medieval Florentine author best known for his masterpiece *The Divine Comedy*. Dante wrote this Christian epic poem in the Italian vernacular (everyday spoken) language, not in Latin. The journey of the narrator through hell, purgatory, and paradise illustrates both the religious ideas of the **Middle Ages** and the worldly concerns of the incipient **Renaissance**, as well as renewed interest in antiquity. Dante, often called the "creator" of the modern Italian language, died in political exile from **Florence**. By his example he inspired later poets such as **Petrarch** (1304–1374) and **Geoffrey Chaucer** (c. 1340–1400) to write in the vernacular.

Allah

Arabic for "the God." Allah is the god of the shared monotheistic tradition of **Judaism**, **Christianity**, and **Islam**. In Islam Allah is said to be the one and only god, all powerful but merciful and compassionate. Allah will bring his judgment on the world, rewarding the righteous and punishing the wicked.

Allende Gossens, Salvador (1908–1973)

Chilean statesman and president (1970–1973). Allende, a Marxist, vowed to push through socialist reforms in Chile after his election in 1970. The U.S. government ordered the **Central Intelligence Agency** to orchestrate a coup to overthrow Allende, but the coup failed. Allende's socialist direction antagonized the Chilean military, the Chilean elite, and the United States. Led by General Augusto Pinochet, the Chilean military, with U.S. support, toppled Allende, who was killed in the fighting in 1973.

Alliance for Progress

John F. Kennedy administration program of U.S. and international economic assistance to Latin America. Begun in 1961, the ten-year program sought to increase rates of economic development, foster social justice, and promote democracy throughout the region in order to undercut the appeal of revolutionary movements inspired by the Cuban Revolution. It is generally considered to have been a failure due to an inadequate commitment of resources and the unwillingness of many regional governments to undertake reform. It was easier for the United States to arm Latin American militaries than to generate an inclusive economic development program.

Allies (1939–1945)

Nations opposed to Germany, Italy, and Japan during **World War II**. The principal Allied Powers were Britain, France, China, the Soviet Union, and the United States. Twenty-one other nations were among the Allies.

All Quiet on the Western Front (1929)

Popular German novel dealing with **World War I** by Erich Maria Remarque. The novel is considered to be the most representative portrayal of life as a World War I soldier, dispelling illusions about the glamor of war. The author fought in the trenches of France during World War I.

Almeida, Francisco de (c. 1450–1510)

Portuguese admiral and first viceroy of Portuguese India (1505–1509). He sailed to India in 1503 and defeated the ruler of Calicut. As viceroy Almeida built fortifications and concluded alliances along the east coast of Africa and controlled the sea trade routes to India. He won a great naval victory against the Egyptians. Almeida was replaced by **Alfonso de Albuquerque**, and on Almeida's return to Portugal he was killed near the **Cape of Good Hope.**

Almohads (Al-Muwahidun)

Moroccan **Muslim** confederation that conquered much of Spain in the twelfth century and built a short-lived but brilliant empire. Inspired by a Muslim reformist leader, the Almohads attacked the **Almoravids** and in 1147 succeeded to the Almoravid territories in North Africa. By the end of the twelfth century most of Muslim Spain had been conquered by the Almohads. They unified all of Muslim Spain and temporarily halted the reconquest by the Christians. The Almohads defeated the king of Castile in 1195, which acted to stop inter-Christian warfare and unify the Christians against the Almohad threat. The Almohads were defeated by a Christian coalition in 1212, retreated to North Africa, and declined in the thirteenth century.

Almoravids (Al-Murabitun)

Mauritanian Berber **Muslims** who first unified the Maghreb (North Africa) and conquered most of Spain in the eleventh century. The Almoravids were originally invited to Spain by petty Muslim kings to help in their conflicts. They were temporarily repulsed by El Cid, but after his death in 1099 they progressively conquered eastern Spain as far north as Saragossa and controlled it until the mid-twelfth century. They were defeated by the **Almohads**, a Moroccan Muslim confederation.

Alp-Arslan (c. 1030–1072)

Second sultan of the **Seljuk Turks** (1063–1072). Alp-Arslan expanded the territory under Seljuk control, including Georgia and Armenia, taking these from the **Byzantine Empire**, which he defeated handily at Manzikert in 1071. He under-

took a successful expedition against the **Fatimid Dynasty** in Egypt on behalf of the **Abbasid caliphate** in Baghdad.

Alphabet, Phoenician

Alphabet of twenty-two symbols developed by the **Phoenicians**, who lived along the coast of the Mediterranean Sea around 1000 B.C.E. The Greeks borrowed from the Phoenicians the idea of individual sounds for each symbol but included some vowel sounds instead of just consonants. The **Etruscans** carried the Greek alphabet to Italy, where it was learned by the Romans and passed on to much of western Europe.

Amaterasu

Sun goddess of Japanese mythology. According to the myth recorded in the eighth-century works *Kojiki* and *Nihon Shoki*, Amaterasu's grandson Ninigi descended from heaven and his grandson Jimmu Tenno became the first emperor of Japan in 660 B.C.E. Later Japanese emperors used this myth to establish their antiquity and legitimacy, claiming an unbroken line of descent from the sun goddess. This was the basis for claiming a semidivine status for the emperor in Japan before 1945.

Ambedkar, Bhimrao Ramji (1893–1956)

Indian leader of the outcastes of **Hinduism** often called dalits or untouchables (**pariahs**). He was an ally of **Mohandas K. Gandhi** in the Indian independence movement, focusing on gaining constitutional rights for the pariahs. In 1934 Ambedkar and Gandhi agreed in the Poona Pact to reserve seats for them in the legislature. After Indian independence in 1947 Ambedkar was a major leader who continued to work for what became known as the scheduled classes. He also played a crucial role in the affirmative action policy for them.

Amenhotep IV (Akhenaton)
(r. c. 1364–1347 B.C.E.)
Ancient Egyptian pharaoh of the New Kingdom who changed the religion and capital of Egypt. Amenhotep renamed himself Akhenaton; introduced the worship of Aton, god of the sun disk, and closed the temples of other gods, especially **Amon-Re;** and moved the capital from Thebes to Akhenaton, a city newly created to lessen the influence of priests at Thebes. Amenhotep's reforms failed and his successor, **Tutankhamon** (r. 1347–1338), returned the capital to Thebes and restored the old gods.

American Anti-Slavery Society
(1833–1870)
Organization for the **abolition** of slavery in the United States. Founded in 1833 by William Lloyd Garrison, the American Anti-Slavery Society and its affiliated societies had membership of close to 200,000. They published articles and distributed information to spread the antislavery message. A split in 1839 created the less radical American and Foreign Anti-Slavery Society, but political pressures eventually led to the creation of the Republican Party in 1854. After the **American Civil War** and emancipation the American Anti-Slavery Society dissolved in 1870.

American Civil War (1861–1865)
U.S. war between northern and southern states fought over states' rights that acted as a major turning point in establishing national unity. Southern states wanting to maintain individual states' right to continue slavery seceded from the Union to form the **Confederate States of America.** Refusing those states the right to secede, the United States went to war with the Confederacy. The Confederacy had the advantages of a populace prepared for the rigors of war and fighting on their own

terrain. The Union had the advantage of a far larger population, far greater industry, and more money. More American lives were lost than in any other war. The Civil War, won by the Union, destroyed slavery in America, ended a semifeudal lifestyle in the South, and cemented the union of states and the authority of the federal government.

American Expeditionary Forces
(World War I)
Portion of the United States Army (about 2 million soldiers) that served in Europe during World War I. It was also known as the AEF. Under the command of General John J. "Black Jack" Pershing, the AEF held the southernmost third of the allied trench line in France and in the final offensives of the war provided the manpower edge that allowed the allies to defeat Germany.

American Federation of Labor (AFL)
Most powerful labor union of the late nineteenth century. The AFL was founded in 1886 by Samuel Gompers as a union for the workers in "skilled" trades. It had a reputation for practicality, moderation, and conservatism; most subsidiaries did not include women workers or minorities. At its height around the turn of the century, the AFL could boast roughly 1 million workers. By the mid-1930s, the influence of the AFL was waning due to its avoidance of some of the major trades, such as automobiles and rubber. The rival Congress of Industrial Organizations (CIO), formed in 1935, merged with the AFL in 1955 to form the AFL-CIO.

American Revolution (1775–1783)
Conflict in which American colonies won independence from Britain and created the United States of America. After the British won the **Seven Years' War** (French and Indian War) in 1763 they began to

assert more authority over the North American colonies through direct taxation with the **Stamp Act** (1765), the Townshend Acts (1767), and the Intolerable Acts (in response to the **Boston Tea Party** in 1773). The British refused to bend to colonial demands and war broke out in 1775 at the **Battles of Lexington** and **Concord**, although many colonists, called Loyalists, did not support independence from England. The early phase of the war (1775–1776) was fought in New England; the next phase (1776–1779), in the mid-Atlantic colonies; and the final stage (1779–1781) played out in the West and the South, where American forces (supported by the French navy) forced the British general **Charles Cornwallis** to surrender at Yorktown, Virginia. The **Treaty of Paris** (1783) declared American autonomy. Born of the **Enlightenment**, the American Revolution concluded with the formation of a government based on the sovereignty of the people, separation of church and state, a written constitution, and checks and balances. The **United States Constitution**, ratified by the states in 1788, would serve as ideological inspiration for the **French Revolution**.

Amerindians

Native American peoples. Amerindians of various types and cultures ranged from highly civilized urban dwellers in Central and South America such as the **Maya**, the **Incas**, and the **Aztecs** to the North American hunters and gatherers. Some, such as the **Iroquois**, developed sophisticated political organizations. The **Hopi**, the **Anasazi**, and the **Apache** left significant elements of culture.

Amherst, Lord Jeffery (1717–1797)

English general who won Canada from the French for Britain. Louisbourg was surrendered to Amherst in 1758, Ticonderoga in 1759, and Montreal in 1760. For his success Amherst was made governor-general of British North America.

Amin, Dada Idi (c. 1927–2003)

Ugandan military leader and head of state (1971–1979). With limited education Idi Amin rose from enlisted soldier to become one of Africa's most notorious leaders. At the independence of Uganda in 1962 Amin was commander of the army and an ally of President Milton Obote. In 1971 Amin led a coup against Obote and became head of state. Under his leadership Ugandan violence and corruption increased and the country's economy was nearly destroyed. During his reign an estimated 300,000 Ugandans were murdered. An invasion by Tanzanian forces united with Ugandan rebels drove Amin out of Uganda in 1979. He died in Saudi Arabia in 2003.

Amir

Title for high-ranking military officials in the Islamic world that became increasingly common after the **Abbasid caliphate** (750–945 C.E.). As a result of their military skill many amirs became political elites in their own right, at some times relying on caliphal, or state, patronage and at other times dispensing such patronage in state-like fashion on their own.

Amon-Re

Most powerful ancient Egyptian god before **Amenhotep IV**'s reign. Amon-Re was a combination of Amon of Thebes and Re of Heliopolis (the sun god). By the fourteenth century B.C.E. the two gods had been combined into Amon-Re, making this god more important and powerful than any other in a prelude to **monotheism**. When Amenhotep (renamed Akhenaton) came to the Egyptian throne he substituted a sun-cult god, Aton, for Amon-Re.

Amorites

Semitic group that unified **Mesopotamia** in the early eighteenth century B.C.E. Possibly originating in Arabia, the Amorites are believed to have helped bring about the collapse of **Ur**'s Third Dynasty (c. 2112 B.C.E.–c. 2004 B.C.E.) The most famous Amorite king was **Hammurabi** (c. 1792–1750 B.C.E.). The Amorites unified the Sumerian and Semitic groups in the region under the **Code of Hammurabi**.

Amos (Eighth Century B.C.E.)

Hebrew prophet who the Hebrews believe spoke for God and demanded social justice among the Hebrew people. The Book of Amos is the thirtieth book of the **Old Testament** and Amos is the third of the twelve minor prophets. The book focuses on Amos's foretelling of God's judgment on the northern kingdom of Israel for its people's turning their worship from God to other, foreign gods. Amos, originally from the town of Toccoa, was active during the reign of Israelite king Jeroboam II.

Amur River

River forming a 1,100-mile (1,800-km) boundary between Russia and the Manchurian region of China and flowing into the Pacific Ocean. As the Russians expanded in the Far East they established the Amur—known to the Chinese as the Black Dragon River (Heilongjiang)—as the border in the 1858 Treaty of Aigun.

Anabaptists

Followers of the **Reformation** movement of a more radical wing of Protestantism often viewed by Anabaptists themselves as outside Catholicism and Protestantism. The name, meaning "rebaptizers," was given to them by their opponents. During the sixteenth-century Reformation the Anabaptists were widely scattered individuals who believed in following the New Testament closely in matters such as adult baptism, nonresistance (nonviolence), and nonparticipation in worldly governance and the military. Anabaptist groups appeared first in Switzerland in 1525 and soon after in the Netherlands and southern Germany. They were persecuted by all other religious groups and all governments. **Mennonites**, Amish, and Brethren are examples of contemporary Anabaptist groups.

Analects

A compilation of **Confucius**'s thoughts from ancient China. The Analects are a human-centered philosophy that views politics as an ethical problem and provides guidance for individual morality. Confucius (b. c. 551 B.C.E.) believed that knowledge led to virtue. The Analects emphasize benevolence, love, compassion, and sympathy toward one's fellow human. The gentleman (*junzi*) plays a key role as a moral exemplar, and practicing ritual (*li*) encourages humaneness (*ren*). They also emphasize authority, order, and propriety. The Analects are human constructs and therefore **Confucianism** is a philosophy, not a religion.

Anarchy

A state of society with no laws, government, or supreme power. In the nineteenth century some Europeans believed that all government is evil and that anarchism is the only way.

Anasazi

Amerindians who lived as cliff dwellers in the southwestern United States from about the first century C.E. to about 1300 C.E. After about 700 the Anasazi are known as **Pueblos** from their multistoried, multiroomed mud-and-sandstone dwellings called pueblos. The Anasazi culture reached its peak circa 1000–1300.

ANC. *See* African National Congress (ANC)

Ancestor Worship

East Asian worship of ancestors; common in many cultures. In China the emphasis on lineage and family included rites to previous generations. The practice goes back to at least **Shang** times, when the kings honored their direct ancestors. People held annual ceremonies for family ancestors and often maintained ancestral tombs for their lineage. Tomb-Sweeping Day, the fourth day of the fourth month, was a time to return and perform ceremonies at the ancestral tomb or memorial in Korea. Japanese and Vietnamese also had rites honoring family ancestors.

Andrada e Silva, José Bonifácio de (1763–1838)

Brazilian statesman and scientist. Andrada e Silva is known as the "architect of Brazilian independence" for guiding Brazil to independence from Portugal in 1822. He was also a renowned metallurgist who studied in Portugal, France, Germany, Norway, Switzerland, and Britain.

Andropov, Yuri (1914–1984)

Head of the Soviet Union's **KGB** (state security apparatus) (1967–1982), general secretary of the Soviet Communist Party Central Committee (1982–1984), and Soviet president (1983–1984). He became a member of the Politburo in 1973. Andropov became ill in 1983 and died the following year.

Angkor

Name of Cambodian state and its capital from 802 to 1432. At its peak under Suryavarman II (r. 1113–1150) and Jayavarman VIII (r. 1181–1218), Angkor controlled much of what is now Cambodia, Laos, and Thailand and parts of Vietnam and Burma. Angkor Thom was the capital and Angkor's greatest city, covering 4 square miles (10.4 sq km) with a population of as many as 1 million people. Angkor is famous for its huge temple complexes, among the largest ever constructed. Greatly influenced by Indian culture, the temples were primarily Hindu, but the Angkor rulers also incorporated Buddhist and indigenous beliefs. The most famous temple is **Angkor Wat**. The prosperous state, based on an elaborate irrigation system, went into a decline after the twelfth century and relocated its capital to Phnom Penh in 1432, confining itself to the present-day territory of Cambodia.

Angkor Wat

Largest and most famous of the temple complexes built in the Cambodian capital of **Angkor**. Constructed by Suryavarman II (r. 1113–1150) as a Hindu temple dedicated to **Shiva**, **Brahma**, and **Vishnu**, it served as both a royal temple and an administrative center and covers nearly 1 square mile (2.6 sq km). It was later converted to a Buddhist temple and was abandoned in the fifteenth century. The temple is among the most magnificent in the world, vast in size and with many beautiful and skillfully rendered carvings of Hindu and Khmer scenes. Angkor Wat represents the wealth and high culture of the Angkor state. The ruins were rediscovered in the nineteenth century.

Anglo-Afghan Wars (1839–1842, 1878–1880, 1919)

Three conflicts in which Britain attempted to extend its control over Afghanistan. In 1839 Britain, already well established in India, sought to counter Russian interest in Afghanistan by replacing the Afghan leader with a pro-British king. After fairly easy conquest, an Afghan revolt in 1841 forced the British out. In 1878 the British again moved to exclude Russian influence by controlling Kabul, but after severe fighting the British were again driven out. In 1919 Afghanistan attacked British India and, although defeated, Afghanistan gained independence in the Treaty of Rawalpindi (1919).

Anglo-Boer Wars (1880–1881, 1899–1902)

Wars fought between Britain and the **Afrikaners**, also known as **Boers** (Dutch for farmers), of southern Africa. Dutch colonists had arrived in the southern African Cape Colony in 1652 and ruled native Africans. With the arrival of the British in the nineteenth century, Afrikaners left Cape Colony and refused to become part of a British colony. Afrikaners put up fierce resistance, and the first **Anglo-Boer War** ended in defeat of the British. In 1899 the British attempted to absorb the Afrikaners again, and war broke out. The Afrikaners were successful with their **guerrilla** techniques and their entrapment and sieges of the British at Ladysmith, Kimberley, and Mafeking. The Afrikaners won some independence in representative government, although British influence remained dominant in the Union of South Africa. The wars left the British questioning their military might but also left Britain with highly experienced troops who proved invaluable at the outbreak of **World War I**. The real losers of the Anglo-Boer War of 1899–1902 were the black South Africans.

Anglo-Burmese Wars

Series of wars between the British based in India and the kingdom of Burma (1824–1826, 1851–1851, 1885) that led to the British conquest of Burma (Myanmar). In the first war the British, reacting to a threatened Burmese invasion of Bengal, seized the Arakan and Tenasserim regions of Burma. In the second war the British responded to hostile treatment of their merchants by seizing Rangoon and southern Burma. In the third war the British captured the capital of Mandalay, sent King Thibaw into exile, and made Burma part of British India. Burma would not regain independence until 1948.

Anglo-Saxon Chronicle

Record chronicling Anglo-Saxon history annually from 1 to 1156 C.E. but written from circa 890 C.E. to the 1150s. Kept originally by monks, it has survived in seven copies. It is extremely valuable for study of the history of **Anglo-Saxon England** and the English language.

Anglo-Saxon England

Series of kingdoms developed by the Anglos, Saxons, and Jutes who settled in England between 400 and 600 C.E. There were seven major Anglo-Saxon kingdoms known as the Heptarchy: Northumbria, Mercia, East Anglia, Essex, Sussex, Kent, and Wessex. Egbert of Wessex unified much of England, but Danish **Viking** invasions disrupted the process. **Alfred the Great** defeated the Danes in 878 and continued the process of unification. Between 900 and 1066 Anglo-Saxon England became a unified, strong, commercial Christian state with a vibrant literature, documented in the **Anglo-Saxon Chronicle**. When the **Normans** invaded in 1066 Anglo-Saxon England was not inferior to the kingdoms of the continent but lost the conflict only by misfortune. The Normans intermarried with the Anglo-Saxons, and many of their traditions were absorbed into Anglo-Norman England.

Anglo-Zulu War (1879)

War between the Zulu of southern Africa and the British colonial army. Cetshwayo kaMpande (1832–1884), the last Zulu king, led a policy of friendship with the British until Britain moved to create a confederation of states in southern Africa. The Zulus fought defensively yet inflicted severe losses on the British army. Zululand was not annexed, and Cetshwayo was restored to the Zulu throne temporarily.

An Lushan (703–757)

Chinese general of Turkish background who led a revolt against the **Tang** in 755, proclaiming himself the emperor of a new dynasty. Although he was murdered by his son soon after, the rebellion he started continued until the Tang suppressed it in 763 with the help of the Uighurs. The An Lushan rebellion accelerated the decline of the Tang dynasty, resulting in the Chinese retreat from **Central Asia**, where China would not reestablish its authority until the **Qing,** and led to the emergence of the Uighurs as a major power in much of Central Asia.

Annam

Term (from the Chinese for "pacified south") used by the Chinese and sometimes by Westerners for Vietnam. From the late nineteenth century it was used by the French for the northern region of Vietnam. The term was never used by the Vietnamese.

Annan, Kofi (1938–)

Ghanaian international civil servant, secretary-general of the **United Nations Organization**, and recipient of the **Nobel Prize** for Peace in 2001. Educated in Ghana and the United States, Annan has served with the United States since 1962 except for two years. As undersecretary he won acclaim for his handling of the civil war in Bosnia, and since 1997 as secretary-general Annan has repaired relations between the United Nations and the United States. Kofi Annan and the United Nations were jointly awarded the Nobel Prize in 2001 for their commitment to world peace and human rights.

Anno Domini

Latin for "in the year of the Lord." The reckoning of years previously was by reigns of kings. The *Anno Domini* (abbreviated A.D.) system of reckoning is based on the work of Dionysius Exiguus (d. c. 550), although his calculations are inaccurate. The actual birth of Christ is believed to have taken place around 4 B.C.E. With the use of the more standardized dating of A.D. came the usage of B.C., "Before Christ." By the 1990s, the new terminology of C.E. ("Common Era") and B.C.E. ("Before the Common Era") became the norm, although they have the same dating value based on the Gregorian calendar.

Anschluss (meaning "annexation")

The March 1938 annexation of Austria into "Greater Germany" by **Adolf Hitler**. Although Austrians were a German-speaking people, the annexation was forced upon Austria in opposition to the **Versailles Treaty** and Hitler's own statements of two years earlier. That France and Britain took no action against the Anschluss encouraged Hitler to march into western Czechoslovakia's **Sudetenland** in March 1939, forcing Europe closer to **World War II.**

Anthony, Susan B. (1820–1906)

Early advocate for **woman's suffrage** in the United States. Anthony was also the founder (1890) and president (1892–1900) of the National American Woman Suffrage Association. Anthony did not live to see her goal accomplished, however, and suffered disappointment when, in 1869, Congress did not include a prohibition against sex discrimination in its amendments concerning race. The

Nineteenth Amendment, giving women the right to vote and owing much to the work of Anthony and her colleagues, was passed in 1920.

Antiballistic Missile Treaty. *See* SALT I (Strategic Arms Limitations Treaty)

Anti-Comintern Pact (1936)
A mutual agreement between Japan and Germany to unite against communist subversion. The pact was not an alliance, but it did contain secret provisos for exchange of information and consultation should either country be attacked by the Soviet Union. Italy signed the pact a year later, which added to the suspicions of American diplomats that Japan had allied itself with the fascist powers in Europe.

Antigone. See Sophocles

Antigonid Dynasty (306–168 B.C.E.)
Ancient Macedonian ruling house carved out of the remains of **Alexander the Great**'s empire. With control of most of the **Middle East** and conquests in the eastern Mediterranean, Antigonus I, a general of Alexander the Great, was proclaimed king in 306 B.C.E. He was attempting to re-establish Alexander's empire. In the fifth generation, Philip V of Macedonia came into conflict with **Rome** in 215. In 197 Rome defeated the Antigonids and relegated them to its control in Macedonia. Under Perseus they once again tried to free Greece from Rome, but their defeat in 168 was the end of the dynasty.

Anti-Semitism
Prejudice against Jews. Anti-Semitism is a misnomer because most Middle Eastern peoples are Semites, not only the Jews. Anti-Semitism developed from religious differences in Europe in the **Middle Ages**.

Christians blamed Jews for the death of **Jesus**, and during the years of the **Crusades** and the **Inquisitions** Jews were attacked and sometimes driven from entire countries. Anti-Semitism survived into early modern times, and in eastern Europe pogroms, widespread attacks on Jews, were often condoned and even organized by governments. In the twentieth century Anti-Semitism increased in Europe under the stresses of the **Great Depression**, and **Nazi** Germany developed a national policy of Anti-Semitism, exterminating millions of Jews. However, Germany was by no means the only country where Anti-Semitism was widespread.

Antony, Mark (80–30 B.C.E.)
Roman cavalry officer who rose to fame alongside **Julius Caesar**. After Caesar was assassinated in 44 B.C.E. Antony became part of a triumvirate with **Octavian** and Marcus Lepidus. Tensions with Octavian caused the triumvirate to break up, and the two faced off when Antony fought alongside **Cleopatra** (queen of Egypt) against the Roman navy in the **Battle of Actium**. Defeated, Mark Antony committed suicide in 30 B.C.E.

Apache
Native Americans inhabiting the North American Southwest until the end of the nineteenth century. The group had varying emphases (depending on the tribe) on hunting, gathering wild plants, farming, and raiding for subsistence. The Apache came into periodic conflict with Spain and, later, the United States until the late nineteenth century, when they were conquered and allowed to live on reservations within the United States.

Apartheid
Policy of racial separation predominant in South Africa until 1993. Whites had long

dominated blacks in South Africa, but after 1961, when the country withdrew from the British Commonwealth and became a republic, the **Afrikaners** built up their economic position and imposed a structure of separation of the races called apartheid. In 1993 President F. W. de Klerk struck down apartheid by introducing open democratic elections and majority rule. Black leader **Nelson Mandela** was elected president of South Africa in 1994.

Apennines

Mountain range traversing the entire Italian peninsula. The Apennine geography determined much of Italy's historical development with the division into Ligurian, Tuscan, and Umbrian Apennines and the creation of the major political divisions. The Apennines also give rise to the major rivers of Italy.

Aphrodite

Ancient Greek goddess of love, identified later with the Roman goddess Venus. Aphrodite and Venus play an important part in the literature of Greece and **Rome** and also the literature and art of the **Renaissance.**

Apollo

Ancient Greek god of manly youth and beauty, of poetry, music, and **oracles**. Apollo, the son of Jupiter and Latona and the twin of Artemis, was the god of the fine arts, music, poetry, and eloquence as well as of medicine or healing and was also known for his numerous affairs. Later Apollo was associated with the sun-god Helios.

Apollo Oracle at Delphi

Apollo, the Greek god, had several oracles associated with him, the most famous of them at Delphi, where people from all over Greece came to consult and make offerings. An oraculum was an answer of the gods to a question of humankind, and oracles were places or individuals where or through whom the gods could be consulted and answers provided, on both important and private matters. The Apollo oracle at Delphi was the most celebrated oracle in antiquity and claimed superiority over all others.

Appian Way (*Appia Via*)

Most famous Roman road, leading to lower Italy and constructed in 312 B.C.E. It was the major thoroughfare for commerce and the Roman armies and for contact between the city of Rome and the southern **Roman Republic** and, later, the **Roman Empire.** The Appian Way was once known as the queen of long-distance roads.

Apprenticeship (from the Latin for "to learn")

Arrangement whereby one individual is bound by agreement to serve another for a set period of time in order to learn a craft, trade, skill, or body of knowledge. An apprentice often lives with the master, typically for seven years, to learn not just the trade skills but also the social expectations of the field. In medieval Europe apprenticeship was very common. In all cultures and at all times apprenticeship has been used to train in fields such as crafts, music, law, and medicine.

Apulia

Region of Italy inhabited by the Apuli, a Samnite tribe, before it was conquered by the Romans. The **Appian Way** and the Trajana Way traversed Apulia. The region produced much grain, wine, and olives.

Aqueduct

Ancient Roman engineering and development of the rounded arch enabled the Romans to build bridges across ravines and valleys to bring water into Roman cities and supply the citizens with clean running water. One of the earliest Roman aqueducts was built by Appius Claudius Caecus (the builder of the **Appian Way**) in 312 B.C.E. The aqueducts often served as bridges for Roman roads, accelerating the movement of Roman troops and their supplies.

Aquinas, Saint Thomas (c. 1225–1274)

Most important medieval philosopher (whose philosophy is known as Thomism). A Dominican monk and a professor of theology at the University of Paris, Aquinas successfully synthesized classical Greek and Roman philosophy and Judaeo-Christian theology and attempted to merge faith and reason. *Summa Theologica* is often regarded as the most important of his many works. Aquinas was canonized in 1323.

Aquino, Corazon (1933–)

Political leader and president of the Philippines (1986–1992). She was the wife of political opposition leader Begnino Aquino, who was assassinated in 1983 as he returned from exile. After the incident Corazon Aquino emerged as the candidate against dictatorial President **Ferdinand Marcos** when he unexpectedly called for elections in early 1986. Officially, Marcos was reelected but Aquino's supporters contested the results, leading to mass demonstrations and the eventual ouster of Marcos and Aquino's assumption of the presidency. The first woman president of the Philippines, Aquino presided over the restoration of democracy but was less successful in curbing corruption and dealing with the nation's widespread poverty.

Arabia

Peninsula at the southwestern extremity of Asia bounded by the Red Sea, the Gulf of Aden, the Indian Ocean, the Gulf of Oman, and the Persian Gulf. Arabia is the site of the origin of numerous cultures, from the Semites of much of the Middle East to the kingdom of the **Queen of Sheba** circa 950 B.C.E. and the rise of Islam in the seventh century C.E.

Arab-Israeli War, 1967 (also called the Six-Day War or the June War)

The third of five wars between Israel and surrounding Arab states, fought from June 5 to June 11, 1967. After a surprise attack that crippled the Egyptian Air Force and launched the war, Israel also destroyed the air capabilities of both Syria and Jordan. This advantage translated into large territorial gains for Israel that came at the expense of the Arab nations: Israel took control of the Sinai Peninsula and the Gaza Strip from Egypt, the West Bank from Jordan, and the Golan Heights from Syria. On November 22, 1967, the **United Nations** issued Resolution 242, which called on Israel to return the territories taken in the war in exchange for peace from its neighbors and authorized a special representative to negotiate peace between Israel and its Arab neighbors.

Arab-Israeli War, 1973 (also called the Yom Kippur War, the October War, or the Ramadan War)

The fourth of five wars between Israel and its Arab neighbors. The war began on October 6 when Egypt and Syria launched a surprise attack on Israeli forces in territories occupied by Israel since the **1967 Arab-Israeli War**. Egypt and Syria, with small contributions from Iraq, Jordan, and other Arab states, sought to regain territory lost in the 1967 war. The **United Nations** issued Resolution 338, calling for a cease-fire. The cease-fire did not take effect, and involvement of the United States and the Soviet Union threatened to escalate the conflict. The war formally ended with a cease-fire in May 1974.

Arab League

Confederation of Arab states founded in 1945 to foster Arab unity. Originally head-quartered in Egypt, its headquarters was moved to Tunis, Tunisia, after the Egypt-Israeli peace treaty in 1979 and returned to Egypt in 1990. There are twenty-two member states.

Arab Nationalism in the Interwar Period

Nationalism in the Arab world between **World War I** and **World War II**. With the demise of the **Ottoman Empire** after World War I, Arab communities lost their traditional supralocal political struc-ture. Between World Wars I and II a **League of Nations**-sanctioned mandate system of European colonial domination emerged in key sectors of the Arab world. A number of political possibilities for these communities emerged under the heading of Arab nationalism during the mandate period that lasted through World War II. These possibilities included most of the nations of the contemporary Middle East and a number of unrealized alternatives such as Greater Syria and other pan-Arab and pan-Islamic national proposals. The distinguishing feature of each political agenda and framework was the contentious question of what the Arab nation would include and exclude.

Arafat, Yasser (1929–2004)

Palestinian leader. Born in Cairo to a Pal-estinian father with Egyptian ancestry and a Palestinian mother from Jerusalem, in 1955 Arafat received an engineering de-gree from a university in Cairo, Egypt. He served briefly as an engineer in the Egyp-tian army before moving to Kuwait to work for a private firm in 1956. In 1958 he and two associates formed FATAH, a Palestinian group dedicated to the liber-ation of **Palestine** through broad-based revolutionary struggle. In 1968 FATAH delegates joined the Palestine National Council that then elected Arafat chairman of the Executive Committee of the **Pales-tinian Liberation Organization** (**PLO**). The PLO militant strategy to escalate con-flict with Israel, resulting in Black Septem-ber 1970, in which clashes with Jordanian forces led to the expulsion of Arafat and the PLO from Jordan to Lebanon, where they began operating. In 1982 Israel's inva-sion of the PLO in Lebanon and inter-national pressure led to the PLO's exile to Tunisia. In 1994 Arafat and his forces were permitted to enter Gaza, and he became president of the Palestinian Authority and shared a **Nobel Prize** for Peace with Shimon Peres and **Yitzhak Rabin**. By 2000 Arafat as leader of the PLO was isolated and held almost in house arrest in his compound by Israeli forces. He died in December 2004.

Arbenz Guzman, Jacobo (1913–1971)

President of Guatemala (1951–1954) who focused on economic development and agrarian reform. He was eventually over-thrown because his nationalist economic policies antagonized the United States and Guatemalan landowners (all large landowners in Latin America have been es-sentially conservative). Arbenz's efforts to tax a U.S.–owned fruit company and expropriation of some of their land led to alarm in the U.S. government, and Ar-benz's friendly relations with communists were used against him. The U.S. **Central Intelligence Agency** helped organize an army that invaded Guatemala and forced Arbenz to resign. He went into exile, lived in Uruguay and Cuba, and eventually died in Mexico.

Arch

Construction of wedge-shaped blocks, each pointing toward the center and forming a strong and self-supporting frame upon which great pressure can be exerted (as opposed to post-and-lintel construction). Even though the arch was known in ancient **Egyptian Civilization**, **Mesopotamia**, and **Classical Greece**, it was not used extensively until the **Roman Empire**. Additionally, the Romans used concrete extensively, making the construction of the arch highly adaptable for large buildings and **aqueducts**.

Archimedes (287–212 B.C.E.)

Ancient Greek mathematician and inventor. His greatest achievements were in geometry, nearing the level of calculus. Archimedes reputedly thought of the idea of mass displacement of water as a means of measurement and the water-screw, now known as the Archimedes' screw.

Arete

Ancient Greek concept of all-around excellence in a human. Arete incorporates qualities such as courage and intelligence.

Arianism, Medieval

Christian belief declared heretical by the Christian church. Arianism originated with Arius (d. 336) of **Alexandria**. Arianism denied the coeternity of **Jesus** and his equality with God. Condemned by the church in 325, Arianism continued to spread. Several Roman emperors believed in and supported Arianism, and many of the Germanic tribes that entered the **Roman Empire**, such as the **Goths** and the **Vandals**, were converted to Arian Christianity. Arianism as a major movement was stamped out by 400.

Aristocracy (Greek for "rule by the best")

Form of government in which power is in the hands of a small privileged class, nobility, or a superior caste of humans.

Aristophanes (c. 448–385 B.C.E.)

Ancient Greek comic dramatist and poet of **Athens**. Wrote fifty-four comedies including *The Clouds*, *The Wasps*, *Lysistrata*, and *The Frogs*. Many of his plays criticized contemporary Athenian politics or society.

Aristotle (384–322 B.C.E.)

Philosopher and political thinker of ancient **Athens**. Aristotle was a student of **Plato** and emphasized empiricism (understanding based on the collection of evidence), or the scientific approach. He established the school Lyceum, teaching as he walked about; hence his students were called Peripatetics, from the Greek word for "tread." He wrote *History of Animals* based on investigation and treatises on astronomy that stood as the explanation of the universe for nearly 2,000 years. Aristotle was tutor to **Alexander the Great**.

Armada. *See* Spanish Armada

Arms Race (1945–)

Cold War–era competition between the United States and the **Union of Soviet Socialist Republics**, primarily concerning qualitative and quantitative increases in nuclear weapons capabilities. Following the United States' development of atomic weapons in 1945 and the failure of efforts at international control of those weapons in 1946, the Cold War competitors vied constantly for advantage over their rival. The Soviets developed an atomic bomb in 1949, prompting both sides to develop more powerful thermonuclear weapons (H-bombs) in the early 1950s. The 1950s also saw a greater diversity of nuclear weapons, with yields tailored to specific purposes such as tactical battlefield use. Similarly, competition emerged in the creation of more effective means of delivering nuclear weapons, leading to the development of intercontinental bombers and of missiles launched from ground, air, and sea of up to intercontinental range. By the 1960s both sides possessed nuclear stockpiles numbering in the tens of thousands and were attempting to develop various means of active defense against nuclear attack. Arms-control agreements have provided some limits on the nuclear competition, and stockpiles have been reduced since the **fall of the USSR**. However, all nuclear powers continue to seek qualitative improvements in their nuclear weapons. More broadly, the arms race includes efforts to obtain a qualitative or quantitative edge in all categories of weapons, nuclear and nonnuclear.

Armstrong, Louis (1901–1971)
Revolutionary jazz musician, trumpeter, soloist, singer, bandleader, and film star also known for incorporating humor into his work. Armstrong was nicknamed "Satchel Mouth" as a child, shortened to "Satchmo" as he became famous. Growing up in extreme poverty in New Orleans, Louisiana, he was influenced by the early jazz music that had its foundations in his hometown. World famous by 1929, he became the first great jazz soloist and toured the United States and Europe to perform throughout his career. As the premiere influence on the swing era he influenced all jazz horn players as well as singers like Bing Crosby and Billie Holiday. Armstrong had many movie, radio, and television roles as a comedic entertainer. Constantly successful throughout his career, Armstrong urbanized jazz music and made sure jazz would last past his lifetime.

Armstrong, Neil (1930–)
American astronaut and the first human to set foot on the moon (1969). In 1961 President **John F. Kennedy** committed the United States to landing a man on the moon by 1970. On July 21, 1969, Neil Armstrong, commander of the mission, walked on its surface.

Arouet, François-Marie. *See* Voltaire

Articles of Confederation (1781–1788)
American colonial document drafted in 1777 to provide a legal framework for coordinating the **American Revolution** and ratified in 1781. The document created a confederation in which ultimate sovereignty rested in the states. The Congress established by the articles provided a weak national government with treaty-making ability and diplomatic authority but no authority to levy taxes or regulate commerce.

Art of War (*Bingfa*)
Chinese classic of war and military strategy reputedly by **Sunzi (Sun-tzu)** (fl. early fourth century B.C.E.). Treasured as an important guide for generals and statesmen throughout Chinese history, it stressed the importance of taking political factors into consideration in war and in having a good knowledge of the enemy. Sunzi also advocated the use of deception to avoid battle until conditions favored the attacker. His ideas had great influence on Chinese and, more recently, Western military strategists.

Arusha Declaration (1967)
Socialist policy proposed by Tanzanian president **Julius Nyerere**. The first president of Tanganyika and, later, Tanzania, Nyerere proposed in the Arusha Declaration the creation of a socialist, egalitarian society where land would be collectively farmed. It also called for universal education, a mass literacy campaign, and economic growth to make Tanzania

independent of foreign aid. While the program did not result in rapid economic growth, it established the basis for Tanzania's political and cultural self-determination. The educational policies outlined in the Arusha Declaration succeeded in making Tanzania one of the most literate countries in Africa.

Aryans

Term for ancient tribes speaking **Indo-European** languages and, more narrowly, for Indo-European speakers who settled in India between 2000 and 1200 B.C.E. The religion of the Aryans, called Vedas and meaning the truths, later fused with indigenous Indian beliefs and practices to form **Hinduism**. Some historians believe that their attempts to maintain their ethnic distinctiveness and political dominance is the origin of the caste system. Most Indo-Aryan languages of northern and central subcontinent today, such as Hindi, Bengali, Punjabi, and Gujarati, evolved from the speech of the ancient Aryans. The term *Aryan* became discredited in the twentieth century when it was used by European ultranationalists, most notably the Nazis, to support ideas of racial superiority.

Asante (Ashanti)

African people of southern Ghana and adjacent Togo and Ivory Coast and the name of an important state in the eighteenth and nineteenth centuries. Asante alliances with other tribes formed the Asante Union around 1700. In the nineteenth century the British clashed with the Asante, defeated them, and annexed the state. Although the Asante Union was re-created in 1935, the state was not. Today the Asante, who number around 2 million, are primarily farmers of various religions including Christianity, Islam, and traditional religions.

Asceticism

Physical self-denial as used in many religions to cleanse oneself, to help in focusing on the supernatural, or to reach a higher state of spirituality. Certain groups in ancient Greece practiced asceticism, but its practice is best known in **Christianity**, **Hinduism**, **Buddhism**, and **Islam**. Asceticism within Christianity began with desert hermits in the **Middle East** in the third century C.E. and was transmitted to **monasteries and convents** in the West in the **Middle Ages**. Both Hinduism and Buddhism designed their means to gain the highest ends based on asceticism. Islam incorporates an entire month of asceticism each year, called **Ramadan**.

Ashanti. *See* Asante (Ashanti)

Ashikaga

Shogunate of Japan from 1339 to 1573 founded by the **shogun** Ashikaga Takauji, who overthrew the Kamakura shogunate. From 1392 the Ashikaga lived in the Muromachi district of Kyoto, hence the period of their rule from that date is often called the Muromachi period. The Ashikaga shoguns exerted control over vassals in a feudal-like system until 1466. After that they became nominal rulers and the regional warlords called **daimyo** rose to importance. The Ashikaga shoguns were great patrons of the arts, popularizing **No** theater and the **tea ceremony** and reestablishing trade with China, but they exercised little effective power over most of Japan, where real authority was in the hands of the daimyo. Fighting among rival warlords led to the rise of **Oda Nobunaga**, who brought the shogunate to an end.

Ashkenazic Jews

Adherents of **Judaism** who settled in German territories in the Middle Ages, as distinct from the **Sephardim**, who settled in the **Iberian Peninsula**, and Oriental Jews, who lived in the Middle East and Asia. The Ashkenazim migrated to eastern and western Europe and then, in the nineteenth and twentieth centuries, to other regions, especially the United States. Most spoke Yiddish, a type of medieval German with some Hebrew expressions, written in Hebraic script. After 1948 many moved to the new state of Israel.

Ashoka (r. c. 272–232 B.C.E.)

King of Magadha and third emperor of the **Maurya** dynasty of India. After carrying out a series of wars of conquest Ashoka converted to **Buddhism** and regretted the suffering his wars had caused. He issued a number of edicts inscribed on pillars and rocks, many of which survive today, in which he renounced killing. He built hospitals for humans and animals and sent missionaries to propagate Buddhism in other lands, most notably to Sri Lanka. Ashoka was important in making Buddhism a major world religion.

Asia Minor

Peninsula in western Asia between the Black Sea and the Mediterranean Sea. It is generally coterminous with Turkey and is usually considered synonymous with Anatolia.

Askia Muhammad. *See* Muhammad I Askia

Assassins

European name for a sect of **Muslims** founded in the eleventh century in Persia who employed executions to prevent ambitious men from rising to power. The movement spread to Egypt and Syria. The **Mongol Empire** destroyed the Persian Assassins in 1256, and the Egyptian Assassins were suppressed in 1272. The name came to be associated with any illegal political execution.

Assembly (Rome)

Part of the structure of government in the **Roman Republic**. When the Romans formed a republic it had a tripartite structure: chief magistrates (**consuls**), **Senate**, and Assembly. The Assembly was originally composed of **plebeian** representatives from each ward of **Rome** whose vote was determined by the majority within the ward, but the Assembly had little power. Gradually in the fifth century B.C.E. the plebeians formed their own body called the Tribal Assembly, with tribunes as members. The Tribal Assembly could obstruct passage of laws and continued into the **Roman Empire**.

Assembly Line

Production method developed in the United States by Henry Ford for efficient production. In 1913 it took Ford workers twelve and a half man-hours to assemble a Model T chassis. When Ford installed assembly lines in 1914 that moved the work to the workers, each chassis was assembled in one and a half hours. The moving assembly line made production efficient and therefore less costly, providing products at a lower price. The assembly line quickly spread to many other products.

Assyria

Mesopotamian state of the fourteenth to thirteenth and ninth to seventh centuries B.C.E. The early Assyria, in northern Mesopotamia on the **Tigris River**, was a dependency of **Babylon** until the fourteenth century B.C.E., when it became a major power in the **Middle East**. It declined in the twelfth to tenth centuries B.C.E. but reemerged in the ninth century under a series of powerful kings. From the ninth to the seventh centuries B.C.E. Assyria controlled most of the Middle East from Egypt to the Persian Gulf and nearly to the Black Sea. The Assyrians were renowned for their fighting ability and cruelty. Assyria was destroyed by the Medians in 609 B.C.E.

Aswan Dam

Egyptian dam on the Nile River, funding for which precipitated major international conflict. In 1955, with **Gamal Abdel Nasser** in power in Egypt, relations shaky with Britain and the United States, and continued Israeli military incursions, Egypt attempted to buy arms from the West unsuccessfully and so turned to Eastern Europe for arms. Then in 1956 Egypt tried to negotiate funding from the West to build the High Dam at Aswan. The United States withdrew its support and Nasser responded by declaring the **Suez Canal** in Egyptian hands, precipitating the **Suez Crisis** with Britain and France. Egypt turned to the Soviet Union for aid in building the dam. The shift from western to eastern Europe in Egyptian relations caused great concern in the **Cold War**. Construction of the second Aswan High Dam, four miles to the south of the first, began in 1960 and was substantially completed in 1971. The Aswan High Dam annually produces 10 million kilowatts of electricity and has a reservoir 310 miles long known as Lake Nasser that holds of 5,544 billion cubic feet (157 billion cubic meters) of water. It has been criticized for the ecological problems it has created such as silt buildup and downstream erosion.

Atatürk, Kemal (Kemal Pasha) (1881–1938)

Turkish president (1923–1938), general, and statesman born Mustafa Kemal. After **World War I** the **Ottoman Empire** was dissolved by treaty and the Anatolian peninsula was to be partitioned, but armed resistance commanded by Mustafa Kemal led to the Treaty of Lausanne and the 1923 establishment of the Republic of Turkey

with Mustafa Kemal as president. Forceful and dramatic modernization brought him the title *Atatürk* ("Father of the Turks"). Atatürk pushed Turkey to become a modern secular state and maintained a policy of neutrality between communist and Western democratic states.

Athena

Ancient Greek goddess of war and patron deity of **Athens**. Athena was daughter of **Zeus**, who swallowed her mother and had to be split open to birth Athena. Athena is usually depicted with her attributes as a war goddess, helmet, spear, and shield, but she was also patroness of women's household arts, especially spinning and weaving. In **Ovid**'s account Athena becomes the Roman goddess Minerva.

Athens

Capital of modern Greece and center of ancient Greek culture. Athens was a **polis** and a major city in ancient Hellas (Greece). The center of philosophy, arts, science, and mathematics, it marked the origin of **democracy** in 508 B.C.E. Athens defeated the Persians in a stunning upset in 480 B.C.E. that opened the classical period in ancient Greek history. In the late fifth century B.C.E. Athens was nearly ruined by the protracted **Peloponnesian War** with **Sparta**, which Athens eventually lost in 404 B.C.E.

Atlantic, Battle of the

Anglo-American effort during **World War II** to defeat the German submarine (U-boat) menace in the Atlantic Ocean. German success at sinking a substantial portion of Allied shipping—a sailor in the merchant marine was more likely to be killed in World War II than was a soldier in the navy, army, or air force—threatened the United States' ability to send war matériel, foodstuffs, and soldiers across the Atlantic to keep Britain fighting and to build up supplies for the invasion of Europe. By May 1943, however, a combination of improved detection technology, superior intelligence-gathering capability, long-range air patrols, and an increase in convoy-escort ships allowed British and U.S. forces to win the Battle of the Atlantic.

See also Ultra

Atlantic Slave Trade

Primarily the west African slave trade from the 1440s to the 1870s. Slaves have been traded in other regions of the world throughout history, but the Atlantic Slave Trade from the **Slave Coast** (**Congo** to Nigeria), the Ivory Coast (Ivory Coast), and Gold Coasts (**Ghana**), and Angola across the Atlantic to the Americas and the Caribbean between roughly 1650 and 1850 exported as many as 15 million people. Most were between fifteen and thirty years old. The slaves went in very large numbers to plantations supporting the Caribbean sugar and rum-production industries and to South American plantations and mines. Approximately 10–20 percent died in the four-to-six-week transportation across the Atlantic. The Atlantic slave trade declined in the nineteenth century as Britain outlawed it and other nations followed suit.

Atman

In **Hinduism**, the concept of a self, soul, or essential part of a person that transmigrates into another body upon death. First elaborated in the **Upanishads**, the ultimate goal for an individual should be to escape the cycle of births and rebirths, an event called *moksha*, and merge one's atman with the universal soul or essence, called **Brahman**.

Atomic Bomb, World War II

Nuclear bomb dropped on Japan to end **World War II**. Initially tested in July 1945, the atomic bomb was used by the United States to speed the end of the war and try to avoid a massive land invasion of Japan. The first bomb was dropped on **Hiroshima** August 6, 1945, instantly killing about 80,000 Japanese. A second bomb was dropped on **Nagasaki** three days later. Japan surrendered September 3, 1945. Debate continues on whether the use of the atomic bomb on Japan was justified.

Atomic Theory

Scientific understanding of the properties of the atom discovered in the twentieth century. Starting with the discovery of the electron at the end of the nineteenth century, rapid changes in understanding came about with **Albert Einstein**'s 1905 theory of relativity and Einstein and Max Planck's experimental and mathematical proofs of quanta. In 1939 Einstein wrote to President **Franklin D. Roosevelt** to explain that work by Enrico Fermi and Leo Szilard had raised the possibility of splitting atoms and releasing enormous amounts of energy in the form of a bomb. Six years later the Manhattan Project had produced such an **atomic bomb**, and the United States dropped it on **Hiroshima**.

Attica

The territory of ancient Greece often called **Athens** and with the city of Athens at its center. Attica, ruled from the city of Athens, became the most important **polis** in Hellas (Greece). Most leaders and intellectuals of Attica lived in Athens.

Attila (d. 453)

Fifth-century warrior-king of the **Huns**. Attila led the Huns from their homeland in **Central Asia** westward into Hungary and the Balkan region of the **Roman Empire** and invaded as far west as France and Italy. The Huns became an almost unstoppable military force, pushing Germanic groups such as the **Goths, Franks,** and **Vandals** into the middle of the Roman Empire, severely disturbing imperial order. At Attila's death the Hun influence disappeared.

Attlee, Clement, First Earl Attlee (1883–1967)

British Labour prime minister (1945–1951) following **Winston Churchill** at the end of **World War II**. His surprising landslide victory against Churchill enabled Attlee to enact legislation creating a modern welfare state in Britain and widespread nationalization of industries such as coal, gas, and electricity. Attlee also presided over the dismantling of the British Empire as colonies began to withdraw.

Augsburg, Peace of (1555)

Reformation resolution between Lutherans and Catholics. The Peace of Augsburg allowed princes and lords to choose to follow either the Lutheran Augsburg Confession (1530) or Catholicism and to determine the faith of their subjects. It was never fully accepted by either side but averted further violence for several decades.

Augustan Age

Movement in eighteenth-century English literature. Also called the Neoclassical Age, the Age of Reason, and the **Enlightenment,** it is called the Augustan Age because of the self-conscious imitation of the original Augustan writers **Virgil** and **Horace.** Major writers of the Augustan Age are Alexander Pope, **John Dryden**, Jonathan Swift, and Joseph Addison, all of whom strove for harmony and precision in their writing.

Augustine of Canterbury, Saint (d. c. 604)

Missionary to England and first archbishop of Canterbury. Pope **Gregory the Great** sent Augustine from Rome to England in 597 with some thirty monks to convert the Anglos and the Saxons. He established his headquarters at Canterbury and built Christ Church Cathedral and an abbey. England was simultaneously being converted to Christianity from Ireland by **Saint Columba of Iona** (d. 597), and Augustine failed to resolve differences with the Celtic Christian Church in England.

Augustine of Hippo, Saint (354–430)

Leading early theologian of the Christian church. Born in North Africa of a Christian mother and a pagan father, Augustine, after a restless life, settled on Christianity and became a voluminous writer of works including 500 sermons, hundreds of letters, and many treatises defending Christianity against heretical beliefs. Augustine believed that all truth is spiritual and derived from God, and that acceptance of truth is dependent upon God's grace. Within each person is a spark of the divine truth. His most famous work, *City of God*, is a struggle between believers and nonbelievers.

Augustus, Caesar. *See* Octavian, Julius Caesar

Aung San (1915–1947)

Leader of Burma's independence movement. Aung San's rise to leadership began when he led a student movement against the British in 1936. During **World War II** he formed the pro-Japanese Burmese Independence Army but then turned against the Japanese. At the end of the war he negotiated an agreement with Britain for Burmese independence in 1948, but he was assassinated the year before it. He is Burma's most revered national hero and the father of human rights leader **Aung San Suu Kyi.**

Aung San Suu Kyi (1945–)
Burmese opposition leader and daughter of the independence leader **Aung San**. Educated abroad, she returned to Burma (Myanmar) in 1988 and founded the political party National League for Democracy, which called for the end of Myanmar's repressive military government and the creation of a democratic society. Although she was placed under house arrest in 1989 her party won a sweeping victory in the 1990 parliamentary elections. The military refused to allow her and her party to take power. She was award the **Nobel Prize** in 1991 for her work for human rights.

Aurangzeb (1618–1707)
Mughal emperor. Son of Shah Jahan, who built the **Taj Mahal**, he became emperor in 1659 and ruled for nearly half a century until his death. Aurangzeb extended the Mughal Empire by conquering almost all of southern India, bringing virtually the entire Indian subcontinent under his rule. He was an orthodox **Muslim** and showed somewhat less tolerance for non-Muslims than some of his predecessors. Much of his reign involved an unsuccessful effort to put down Maratha rebels in the western Deccan.

Aurelius, Antoninus (called Caracalla) (188–217)
Roman emperor (198–217) and general. Originally named Septimius Bassianus, he was renamed after **Marcus Aurelius**. Aurelius commanded an army in Britain against the Caledonians (Picts in Scotland). He strengthened **Hadrian's Wall** as the frontier there again. He fought the Alamanni in Germany and moved eastward because of an obsession with **Alexander the Great**. He tried to marry a Parthian princess but was rejected. As he prepared a campaign against the East he was murdered.

Aurelius, Marcus (121–180)
Roman emperor (161–180), general, and writer. Favored by Emperor **Hadrian** and adopted by Hadrian's son, when Marcus became emperor he dealt with many problems on the Roman frontiers in Britain, Germany, along the Danube, and in the East. Germanic tribes were moving into the **Roman Empire** all along the frontier. Marcus is remembered as a wise ruler, partly for his famous writing *Meditations*, never known to his subjects, which records his reflections on life.

Auschwitz-Birkenau. *See* Death Camps, German

Ausgleich (1867)
Compromise establishing the dual monarchy of **Austria-Hungary**. The concord determined the relations between Austria and Hungary in the Austro-Hungarian Empire.

Australopithecine (Latin for "southern ape")
Fossils of hominids closely related to human beings. First discovered in 1924 in South Africa and later in several sites in southern, eastern, and northeastern Africa, the Australopithecines have been dated to about 8 million to 1.6 million years ago. The most spectacular find, "Lucy," was in the Afar Triangle of Ethiopia. It is clear that Australopithecine represents a step between apes and human beings. It is unclear if there was a single development of hominids from Australopithecine to Homo erectus and Homo sapiens or if various developmental lines evolved simultaneously.

Austria-Hungary
Central European country formed by the **Ausgleich**, or compromise of 1867. The **Habsburg** Empire (1806–1867) had a

problem of any dynastic empire—it contained many ethnic groups. In 1867 the compromise created a dual monarchy, with Austria containing Germans, Czechs, Poles, and Slovenians, and the Kingdom of Hungary containing Hungarians, Romanians, Slovaks, Croatians, and Serbs. The two countries had some autonomy over their internal affairs while the imperial government controlled foreign and economic affairs. This provided some solution to the internal problems, although the early twentieth century witnessed ethnic groups moved by nationalism alienated from Austria-Hungary. This situation, called the **Balkan Crisis**, was the catalyst for the outbreak of **World War I** and led to the **breakup of Austria-Hungary**.

Austria-Hungary, Breakup of

Dismemberment of **Austria-Hungary**. The country survived into the twentieth century as a multinational dynastic empire held together by allegiance to the Habsburg family, but dissent was growing inside its borders. In early-twentieth-century Europe **nationalism** led people to believe that each ethnic group has the right to its own country. Austria-Hungary resisted this until a palace revolt in the independent kingdom of Serbia replaced rulers sympathetic to the empire with ardent nationalists. Serbia's independence became a focal point for discontented Slavs in the southern part of the country. A terrorist organization, the Black Hand, was supported covertly by the Serbian government. On June 28, 1914, Gavrilo Princip, a member of the Black Hand, assassinated Archduke Francis Ferdinand, the heir to Austria-Hungary's throne, in Sarajevo, the capital of Bosnia. Austria-Hungary sent demands to Serbia, which met all but one of them. Austria-Hungary took the opportunity to declare war on Serbia. Germany, allied with Austria-Hungary, promised support.

Russia came in to defend its Slavic brethren and brought in its ally France. Britain also entered the war on the side of France and Russia after Germany invaded neutral Belgium. Thus Europe quickly became embroiled in **World War I**. The war went badly for Austria-Hungary, and during the war Emperor **Francis Joseph**, the source of imperial unity, died. At war's end in 1918, the victorious leaders President **Woodrow Wilson** of the United States, Prime Minister David Lloyd George of Britain, and Prime Minister Georges Clemenceau of France met in Paris, and in 1919 they drew up a peace settlement dividing Austria-Hungary into four nations, Austria, Hungary, Czechoslovakia, and **Yugoslavia**, and enlarged Romania.

Automobile

Personal vehicle first developed in the late nineteenth century and made common by Henry Ford in the early twentieth century. Karl Benz, a German engineer, invented the internal combustion engine that was used to power automobiles by the 1890s. In 1908 Ford produced the Model T, and in 1914 he began to manufacture the first mass-produced automobiles with an **assembly line**. By 1925 automobiles in the United States were affordable for the masses. Louis Renault followed this process in France. The automobile freed people from the constraints of rural life and from dependence on mass transportation. By the 1920s the automobile was viewed as a means to personal freedom, leading to the "car culture" and the creation of suburbia, which was only possible with the automobile.

Avars

Steppe people who ruled a loosely organized empire from the Black Sea to the edge of eastern Europe by 600 C.E. The Avars were extremely wealthy from conquests and were considered nearly invincible until the 790s when **Charlemagne** destroyed them, almost without a fight, and confiscated all their wealth.

Avignon

City in southern France where the **popes** resided from 1309 to 1377, rather than in **Rome**. In 1309 a French pope, Clement V, was elected and chose to remain in France at Avignon. Subsequent popes resided there, in the period sometimes called the Avignon Captivity (also known as the **Babylonian Captivity**), until the **Great Schism** of 1378, when a pope was elected who resided in Rome and then another was elected in opposition who resided in Avignon. In 1409 an attempt to resolve the schism led to the election of yet a third pope. The schism ended in 1417 with the election of one pope, who resided in Rome.

Awami League

Bangladeshi political party founded in 1949 in the region then called East Pakistan. Under the leadership of Sheikh Mujibur Rahman the Awami League won all but 2 of the 169 parliamentary seats allotted to East Pakistan in the 1970 elections, making it the largest party in the Pakistan National Assembly. The Pakistan military intervened, causing most of the leaders to flee to India, from where they led an independence revolt. When Bangladesh became independent following the **Indo-Pakistan War** of 1971 the Awami League was the ruling party. The league supported a secular state. After Rahman was assassinated in 1975 the league remained one of the two major political parties in Bangladesh under the leadership of his daughter Sheikh Hasina Wajad.

Axial Age

Term first used in the nineteenth century by German scholar Karl Jaspers for the period from 800 to 200 B.C.E. when many of the world's great religious and philosophical systems emerged. It was a period when ethical and reflective thought flourished independently in different parts of the Old World Afro-Asiatic belt of large, complex societies. Among the important religious thinkers and philosophical system builders from the Axial Age were **Confucius, Mencius, Laozi, Socrates, Plato,** Zoroaster, **Siddhartha Gautama, Mahavira,** and the major Hebrew prophets. They established the belief systems that framed most of the Eurasian civilizations, **Judaism, Hellenic philosophy, Zoroastrianism, Buddhism, Jainism, Confucianism,** and **Daoism,** and laid much of the basis for modern **Hinduism, Christianity,** and **Islam.** Many historians argue that this is merely coincidental and that there was no Axial Age.

Axis Powers

Alliance of Germany, Italy, and Japan during **World War II.** The original agreement was made between Germany and Italy with the claim of an "axis" binding Rome and Berlin in 1936, and Japan was added in the German-Japanese **Anti-Comintern Pact** of the same year. The Pact of Steel of 1939 bound Germany and Italy militarily, and the Tripartite Pact of 1940 strengthened the ties of the three nations. The Axis Powers opposed the Allied Powers, or **Allies,** during the war.

Axum

Wealthy African kingdom of the first to seventh centuries C.E. Axum was founded in what is now Ethiopia from the kingdom of Shaba (Sheba) across the Red Sea, and its rulers claimed descent from King **Solomon** and the **Queen of Sheba.** Axum owed its prosperity to its location as a trade crossroads between India and the Mediterranean and challenged the **Roman**

Empire for control of the region. Axum exported ivory, frankincense, myrrh, brass, and slaves. Axum became Christian in the fourth century and was renowned for the type of stele, or tower, erected to mark a royal tomb. Cut off from its trade by the advance of **Islam**, Axum declined in the eighth century and was bypassed commercially.

Ayatollah Khomeini. *See* Khomeini, Ayatollah Ruhollah

Ayudhya (Ayutthaya)

Thai state (1351–1767) that controlled most of what is now central Thailand. Founded by U Thong, the state was named after the capital city in the Menam Valley. It brought Khmer (Cambodian) dominance over much of Thailand to an end and in 1432 forced the Cambodians to abandoned their capital at **Angkor**. After a Burmese invasion in 1569, it went through several changes of name; the best known is Siam, which became the name by which Thailand was known to Westerners. After a second sacking by the Burmese in 1767 the capital was moved to Bangkok under a new dynasty.

Azikiwe, Benjamin Nnamdi

(1904–1996)

First Nigerian president (1963–1966) and author. Educated in the United States, Azikiwe became an editor of newspapers and leader of the National Convention of Nigeria Party. After serving in several political posts he was elected as the first president of the Federal Republic of Nigeria and ruled until displaced by military rule in 1966. He remained active when military rule was lifted until his retirement in 1986.

Aztecs (c. 1200–1521)

Mesoamerican civilization in the Valley of Mexico. People who called themselves Mexica built a great empire in central-southern Mexico with the capital at **Tenochtitlán** built in Lake Texcoco. Tenochtitlán had a population of 200,000–300,000 people with huge civic buildings of temples and palaces. In many ways the Aztecs were heirs to the **Toltec**, **Teotihuacán**, and **Olmec Civilizations**. The civilization was hierarchical and authoritarian. The Aztecs were a warring people who exacted tribute from those conquered, including human sacrifice on an enormous scale. Victims had their hearts cut out while alive. Many thousands, including children, were sacrificed each year to please **Huitzilopochtli**, the god of sun and war; to avoid disaster; and to keep the sun rising. In 1519 approximately 400 Spaniards under **Hernando Cortés** with alliances of Aztec enemies marched on Tenochtitlán, and by 1521 they had defeated the Aztecs.

B

Ba'athism

Pan-Arab political party known officially as the Arab Ba'ath Socialist Party. The party was formed in Damascus in 1954 from a combination of former Arab Ba'ath Party and Arab Socialist Party members. The party's founding principles were unity and freedom of the Arab nation within its homeland and a belief in the Arab nation's special mission of ending colonialism and promoting humanitarianism. There are Ba'ath parties in many Arab nations, with those in Iraq and Syria being the most prominent. The Ba'ath party was in power in Iraq until the 2003 U.S. invasion.

Babar. *See* Babur

Babel, Tower of. *See* Babylon

Babur (Babar) (1483–1530)

Founder of the **Mughal** Empire. Of mixed Mongol and Turkish descent and claiming descent from **Genghis Khan** and **Timur**, Babur led a **Central Asian** army into India, defeating the ruler of the Delhi Sultanate Ibrahim Lodi at the battle of Panipat in 1526 and proclaiming himself emperor that year. Although Babur died four years later the Mughal Empire, after being re-established by his successors, continued for over two centuries.

Babylon

One of the greatest cities of ancient **Mesopotamia**, on the banks of the **Euphrates River**. Babylon was an important trade center and the capital of numerous ancient kingdoms from 2000 B.C.E. on, from **Babylonia** to **Assyria** and Persia. Babylon had many large palaces and temples and the **ziggurat**, or Great Tower of Babylon (known in the **Old Testament** as the Tower of Babel). Babylon was also famous for its Hanging Gardens, which were described by the Greeks as one of the Seven Wonders of the World.

Babylonia

Ancient region of **Mesopotamia** between the **Tigris** and **Euphrates rivers**. Between 2700 and 500 B.C.E. Babylonia home to a great civilization that produced one of the first forms of writing, a set of laws under King **Hammurabi**, and studies in mathematics and astronomy. The great cities of Babylonia included **Ur** and **Babylon**. Babylonia was ruled as a kingdom at different times by Hammurabi, **Nebuchadnezzar II**, and **Alexander the Great** and was known as Sumer, Babylon, **Assyria**, Persia, or Macedonia.

Babylonian Captivity (B.C.E.)

The conquest and removal of the Hebrews from **Judah** in 587 B.C.E. Under the Chaldeans (625–538 B.C.E.) the Babylonian empire arose again. Their expansion brought them into contact with **Palestine**. In 604 B.C.E. and again in 597 B.C.E. **Nebuchadnezzar II**, king of **Babylon**, removed the treasures from the **Hebrew Temple** of Jerusalem, and then in 587 B.C.E. he destroyed the temple building and deported the Jews to Babylon. This Babylonian Captivity inspired the writings of Isaiah and a Jewish revival. A second temple was constructed in 515 B.C.E. after **Cyrus the Great** released the Jews from Persia.

Babylonian Captivity (C.E.)
Term (coined by **Petrarch**) for the papal residence in **Avignon** (1309–1377), in reference to the **Babylonian Captivity** of the Israelites in the sixth century B.C.E. The term implied that the **papacy**, having moved to Avignon from Rome, was corrupt and that the French cardinals were holding the church captive.

Bach, Johann Sebastian (1685–1750)
German music composer and organist. Bach studied predecessors such as Dietrich Buxtehude, Girolamo Frescobaldi, and Johann Pachelbel. He composed stunningly innovative cantatas, chorales, toccatas, concertos, arias, oratorios, and masses and was a renowned organist at Weimar and Leipzig. Bach composed for the organ and violin as well as for orchestral, choir, and chamber groups. Bach's work was rediscovered in the mid-nineteenth century, and he is considered among the most influential composers ever.

Bacon, Francis (1561–1626)
English philosopher, statesman, and scientist. A member of Parliament from 1584 and knighted by James VI and I in 1603, Bacon held numerous high offices including lord chancellor. In 1618, he became Lord Verulam and in 1621 became Viscount Saint Alban. Complaints of his acceptance of bribes brought about his downfall. Bacon encouraged a new approach to the natural world in which hypothesis would drive the collection of evidence in a systematic way with experimentation to verify facts. This method of science is laid out in his *Advancement of Learning* and

The Great Instauration. Baconian science as others followed it became more of an encyclopedic accumulation of facts. Bacon also wrote of a fictional land in *New Atlantis*, in the vein of **Sir Thomas More**'s *Utopia.* Bacon died impoverished.

Bactria
Historic **Central Asian** land between the Hindu Kush and the Amu Darya River (ancient Oxus River), with its capital Bactra, now part of Afghanistan, Uzbeskistan, and Tajikistan. In ancient times Bactria was a very important crossroads of trade, religion, and culture. Part of the Achaemenian empire of **Cyrus the Great** in the sixth century B.C.E., it was conquered by **Alexander the Great** in the fourth century B.C.E. After Alexander it became part of the **Seleucids**' empire, bringing strong Greek, or Hellenistic, influence to the region. Variously under the sway of the Tocharoi, Kushans, **Sasanids**, **Turks**, and (in the seventh century C.E.) **Muslims**, Bactria was a central part of the **Silk Road** trade between the East and the West.

Baganda. *See* Ganda

Baghdad
Capital of modern Iraq founded in 762 C.E. as the center of the **Abbasid caliphate**. Baghdad became a great cultural city and is the setting of the *Arabian Nights*. In 1258 the Mongols conquered Baghdad, but by the sixteenth century the city had become part of the **Ottoman Empire**.

Bahá'i Faith
Religion founded in Persia (Iran) in 1863. The Bahá'i Faith teaches that there is truth and unity in all revealed religions of the world and that Bahá' u' lláh (born Husayn Ali) was the latest in a long line of prophets that includes Moses, **Jesus of Nazareth**, and **Muhammad**. Bahá'i Faith also teaches

that there is one god and that humans should worship by serving humankind.

Ba Jin (b. 1904–)

Chinese writer best known for his trilogy novel *Family* (1931), which depicted the younger Chinese generation's break with tradition. Born Li Feigan, he became part of the anarchist movement and adopted the pseudonym Ba, Jin derived from the Chinese pronunciation of the names of anarchists (Mikhail) Bakunin and (Pyotr) Kropotkin. He was persecuted during the **Great Proletarian Cultural Revolution** (1966–1976), but the communist government has mostly honored Ba Jin.

Bakufu (literally "tent government")

Name given to the governments of the military samurai in Japan from the twelfth to the nineteenth centuries. There were three bakufu: the **Kamakura** (1192–1333), established by **Minamoto Yoritomo**; the Muromachi or **Ashikaga** (1339–1573); and the **Tokugawa** (1603–1868). Under the bakufu Japan had a dual government with an emperor and court in **Kyoto** and a separate military government that wielded actual authority. The military government was headed by a military hegemon known as the **shogun**, who ruled through great military lords who were his vassals in a system similar to European feudalism.

Balance of Power

Principle of international diplomacy established at the **Congress of Vienna** in 1815. The principle of balance of bower was that no one country in Europe would be powerful enough to overwhelm the others. By establishing counterbalancing countries with agreements to support weaker nations threatened by stronger ones, no country would be willing to go to war with another. Balance of power worked to some degree until 1914 and the outbreak of **World War I**, although the unification of Germany had upset the balance by 1870.

Balboa, Vasco Núñez de (1475–1519)

Spanish explorer and the first European to see the Pacific Ocean on the west coast of the **Isthmus of Panama**. Balboa commanded a Spanish settlement on Darien, on the isthmus, and in 1513 led a twenty-five-day march to the west coast, viewing the Pacific.

Balfour Declaration (1917)

Pledge to establish a national home for the Jewish people in **Palestine**. Briton Lord Balfour announced British support in a letter to Zionist Lord Lionel Walter Rothschild. At the same time, the British were encouraging Arab nationalism in the **Middle East** to destabilize the **Ottoman Empire** because of **World War I**. The Balfour Declaration forced Britain into a dilemma of maintaining these conflicting positions as the British mandate in the Middle East until 1947, when the **United Nations** voted to partition the Palestine mandate into two states, one Jewish and one Arab.

Balkans Crisis of World War I

Breakup of the **Ottoman Empire** in the Balkans that led to confrontations that triggered **World War I**. **Austria-Hungary** feared that the growth of nationalism, which was splintering the Ottoman Empire, would do the same to it. When Serbian nationalists assassinated Austrian archduke Francis Ferdinand in 1914, Austria-Hungary declared war on Serbia, forcing Russia to begin mobilizing its army and triggering Germany to declare war on **Russia** and France.

Bandaranaike, Sirimavo (1916–2000)

Sri Lankan stateswoman and prime minister (1960–1965, 1970–1977, 1994–2000).

She succeeded her husband, S. W. R. Bandaranaike, after his assassination to become the world's first woman prime minister in 1960. Her daughter Chandrika Bandaranaike Kumaratunga became prime minister and then president in 1994, being succeeded as prime minister by her mother.

Bangladesh War (1971)
Conflict between Pakistan and India that led to the creation of the independent Bangladesh nation. Known since the partition of India in 1947 as East Pakistan, the predominantly Muslim, Bengali-speaking region, one of the most densely populated in the world, suffered from poverty and political domination by the slightly less populous West Pakistan. In 1966 the **Awami League** demanded greater autonomy and won a sweeping victory in the 1970 elections. The demand for autonomy was denied by Pakistan's military government, leading to civil war. India aided the East Pakistan guerillas, which led to war between India and Pakistan in December 1971. The war ended with India's victory and the declaration of independence of East Pakistan, renamed Bangladesh.

Ban Gu (Pan Ku) (c. 32–92)
Chinese historian, author of *Han Shu* (*History of the Former Han Dynasty*), and literary figure. Ban Gu, after serving as a court official, spent a number of years writing the history begun by his father. It follows the work of **Sima Qian** but makes some innovations that became the model for the official dynastic histories that Chinese scholars compiled after each dynasty. Ban Gu also perfected a new literary genre, the rhapsody (*fu*). His brother was the distinguished general Ban Chao, who brought much of **Central Asia** under Chinese authority, and his sister **Ban Zhao**

was a noted writer and scholar who completed the history.

Bank of the United States
U.S. bank established in 1791 under a twenty-year charter to serve as a repository for federal funds. **Alexander Hamilton** proposed the bank as part of his "Hamiltonian program" to establish a strong commercial national economy. **Thomas Jefferson** and his followers opposed it because they feared it would be a source of corruption for republican institutions, and they succeeded in preventing the renewal of its charter in 1811.

Bank War (1832)
U.S. conflict between national bank advocates and anti–national bank forces led by President Andrew Jackson. Jackson vetoed the rechartering of the **Bank of the United States**, claiming that it represented the big-money business interests of the East and unduly consolidated the control of money in the hands of the federal government to the detriment of the states.

Bannerman
Military system developed by the **Manchus** in the early seventeenth century that enabled them to conquer China and, later, to maintain control under the **Qing** dynasty. The bannermen (in Chinese, *qibing*) were divided into eight (later expanded to twenty-four) companies, each with a distinctive banner. During peacetime the bannermen lived with their families but were called to duty when needed. They consisted of Manchu, Mongol, and Chinese banners. The system declined in effectiveness during the late Qing. In **Silla** Korea there was a similar type of military organization, called the "oath banner system."

Banpo
Village near modern-day **Xi'an** in the **Yellow River** basin of northern China that

is the site of a neolithic village discovered in 1952. Exploration of the site led to the further discovery of the **Yangshao culture**, a matriarchal society that flourished in China between 4500 and 3000 B.C.E. and is noted for its fine painted pottery. Banpo was the first Yangshao site to be excavated extensively.

Bantu

Term used for African languages and peoples. The Bantu are a group of over 150 million central and southern African peoples with related languages. There are about 600 Bantu languages or dialects, and speakers of each generally consider themselves to be a separate people, including the Zulu, the Swahili, and the Kikuyu. Although they share the same basic grammars and vocabularies, most dialects are not mutually intelligible. The Bantu peoples originated in what is now Cameroon and spread eastward and southward. Much of sub-Saharan Africa is populated with Bantu peoples, comprising perhaps one-third of the African population.

Bantustan

Ten former territories of white-dominated South Africa that were designated as black states, or homelands. Essentially, the Bantustan were enclaves for black South Africans so that most of the country could remain white controlled and blacks could be excluded from the political system, **apartheid**. None of the states was recognized by foreign governments. As early as 1913, black South Africans were placed on reserves; in 1959 the homelands were designated; and in 1970 residents of the Bantustan were forbidden South African citizenship and civil rights. In the 1970s and 1980s South Africa declared four of the states independent, although all remained entirely dependent upon South African aid. When apartheid was abolished in 1994 the Bantustan were all reincorporated into South Africa.

Ban Zhao (c. 45–115)

Distinguished Chinese poet, essayist, and historian. A young widow who never remarried, she devoted herself to writing and scholarship and completed the influential history *Han Shu* (*History of the Former Han Dynasty*) started by her brother **Ban Gu**. She also wrote the influential *Nüjue* (*Lessons for Women*), which promoted the ideal of an educated woman who was obedient to male superiors and devoted to her children.

Baojia

System for controlling the population of imperial China by combining ten households to form a *bao* and ten *bao* to form a *jia*. Heads appointed for each unit were made responsible for the conduct of the households under them. Developed in the **Song**, the *baojia* system came into widespread use under the **Ming** and **Qing** dynasties as a way of maintaining order with minimal use of officials. It created a sense of mutual surveillance and collective responsibility, especially in the countryside. It was also used for the administration of the corvée labor system.

Baptism, Christian

Symbolic washing away of sins in **Christianity**. The concept of baptism predated **Jesus of Nazareth** but became an integral part of Christianity with John the Baptist's immersion of Jesus in the river Jordan and Jesus's instructions for his disciples to baptize all nations. Baptism is central to all Christianity, making the baptized individual a participant in the religion. Catholicism had moved to infant baptism by the fourth or fifth century C.E. During the **Reformation** some groups returned to adult baptism because it was biblical.

Barbary Coast. *See* Barbary States

Barbary States
North coast of Africa from modern-day Morocco to Libya, known for its pirates from the sixteenth to the nineteenth centuries. Pirates would attack any shipping traversing the Mediterranean Sea. From 1795 to 1801 the United States paid the Barbary States to protect its ships from the pirates, and starting in 1801 the United States fought first Tripoli and then Algeria. In 1815 it gained promises to stop acts of piracy against U.S. ships.

Bardi and Peruzzi
Florentine banking companies of the fourteenth century. Each of these companies dwarfed the size of the later Medici bank, with branches or agents in many of the major trading towns of Europe. The Bardi was the most powerful. Enormous loans granted to English king **Edward III** to fight the **Hundred Years War** were defaulted upon in 1345, bankrupting the Bardi and Peruzzi banks.

Baroque-Rococo
Period of art, architecture, and literature from approximately 1600 to the mid-1700s. The baroque response to the **Reformation** in Europe was architecture by the **Roman Catholic Church** and, later, secular rulers that emphasized power through building in a grandiose style, to revive the grandeur of ancient **Rome**. The baroque also elaborated exteriors and interiors with organic-looking ornamentation as an expression of the mystery of the Catholic Church. Baroque sculpture emphasized extreme emotions. Great artists of the baroque include **Bernini**, Caravaggio, and Van Dyck. Secular rulers found the effect useful in the seventeenth-century attempt to establish order and stability. Rococo, meaning "pebbled" or "fretted," refers to a somewhat lighter and more playful variation of the baroque. Great rococo artists include Watteau, Fragonard, and Gainsborough.

Barrangay
A community of families under a local chieftain in the Philippines prior to the Spanish conquest. In the twentieth century the term was used for a local administrative unit.

Barth, Karl (1886–1968)
Swiss Protestant theologian and major critic of the twentieth century. Barth, writing after **World War I**, criticized the weak theology of the church, which had become more concerned with social ethics than with rightness between mankind and its god. His many writings include *The Word of God and the Word of Man* (1918) and *Against the Stream* (1954).

Bartók, Béla (1881–1945)
Hungarian pianist and music composer. Bartók was one of the leading composers of the twentieth century, and his works include string quartets, concertos, an opera, and hundreds of piano pieces. Bartók moved to New York City during **World War II** and taught at Columbia University.

Barton, Clara (1821–1912)
Founder of the American Red Cross. Barton nursed soldiers in the **American Civil War** (1861–1865); went to Switzerland in 1869; and served as a nurse in the **Franco-Prussian War** (1870–1871), where she observed the International Committee of the Red Cross. After returning to the United States, Barton founded the American Red Cross in 1881 and later convinced the Red Cross to provide relief in natural disasters as well as in wars.

Baseball

Sport played by two teams with bases, a ball, and a bat. The game developed in the nineteenth century in the United States, although it is similar to English cricket, where it is considered the national sport. It has spread to Canada, Japan, and much of Latin America, where baseball is taken very seriously. Many players in the U.S. major leagues come from Puerto Rico, Cuba, the Dominican Republic, Nicaragua, and Venezuela. Baseball is also played in the **Olympic Games**, when teams from around the world compete.

Basho, Matsuo (1644–1694)

Early and highly regarded master of the brief Japanese poetic form **haiku**. A former **bushi** (samurai), Basho wandered the country and composed a famous poetic account of one of his travels, *The Narrow Road to Oku*. His haiku are still popular in Japan.

Basilica

Early Christian church design modeled after the Roman imperial building of a rectangular nave with two rows of columns setting off aisles on either side. The basilica design also had a semicircular apse, usually at the eastern end. Basilicas had large clerestory windows and were roofed with wood.

Basques

Ancient northern Iberian (Spanish) people. The Basques preceded the Germanic invasions of **Goths** and **Franks**, neither of whom was able to dominate them. The Basques attacked **Charlemagne**'s rearguard army at Roncesvalles in 778, not the **Muslims**, as in *The Song of Roland*. The Basques have always seen themselves as separate from the rest of Spain. In the **Spanish Civil War** they were attacked particularly fiercely. In the late twentieth and the twenty-first centuries the Basque separatist movement has become violent.

Bastille

French royal fort in Paris, the storming of which opened the **French Revolution**. With the assembly meeting and royal troops surrounding Paris, citizens stormed the Bastille, thinking it contained political prisoners and weapons. Although it had neither, the symbol of the people taking a royal installation was a powerful inspiration for the revolution.

Battle of the Atlantic. *See* Atlantic, Battle of the

Bay of Pigs

A failed U.S. effort to depose Cuban leader **Fidel Castro**. Castro's 1959 communist overthrow of U.S.-backed dictator **Fulgencio Batista** in Cuba led to a U.S. embargo on Cuba and the **Union of Soviet Socialist Republic**'s aid to Cuba. Fearing a communist country ninety miles from Florida, the **Central Intelligence Agency** (CIA) under President **John F. Kennedy** organized the Bay of Pigs operation to oust Castro from power. The plan was to use trained Cuban refugees living in the United States to invade Cuba. The April 1961 operation failed miserably. Many refugees were killed or captured and the Cuban population did not rise up against Castro as the CIA had hoped. In some ways the Bay of Pigs debacle led to the **Cuban Missile Crisis**.

Beauvoir, Simone de (1908–1986)

French existentialist philosopher, novelist, and social activist. Beauvoir, often associated with her lifelong companion **Jean-Paul Sartre**, wrote of individual freedom and moral responsibility. Best known for her book *The Second Sex* (1949), Beauvoir asked, "What is it to be a woman and a human being?"

Becket, Thomas (1118–1170)
Chancellor of England (1154) and archbishop of Canterbury (1162) who stood for the church against the state. As Chancellor, Becket supported the young King **Henry II** of England, even against the church. He became chief advisor to and a close friend of the king. Henry assumed that as archbishop Becket would continue his support and act as a tool of the king, but instead Becket became a staunch defender of the rights of the church and defiant toward the king. The king set out the relations of church and state in the Constitution of Clarendon, but Becket refused to sign or observe it. Becket left England for France to avoid punishment. After papal pressure, King Henry recanted and Becket returned and attempted to dismiss all bishops who supported the king. Supporters of Henry murdered Becket.

Beckett, Samuel Barclay (1906–1989)
Irish-born writer most famous for the play *Waiting for Godot* (1952). Beckett was influenced by his friend the fellow Irishman James Joyce. Beckett moved to France in the 1930s, where he wrote in French and translated works into English. Beckett's works often show the absurdity and pathos of humankind.

Bede, "the Venerable" (673–735)
English scholar considered the father of English history. Bede was a monk at Jarrow in the north of England. He wrote about English saints and clerics and in 731 wrote the *Ecclesiastical History of the English People*, the first written account of the formation of Anglo-Saxon civilization.

Bedouin
Arabic-speaking nomads of North Africa and the **Middle East**. Well adapted to life in the desert, these nomadic pastoralists played a central role in Middle Eastern

history for millennia. Most Bedouins are herders of camels, goats, and sheep, and although currently sometimes settled and agrarian, they traditionally had no ties to any organization other than tribe. Many of the Bedouins were swept up by the Islamic expansion of the seventh and eighth centuries and became **Muslims**.

Beethoven, Ludwig van (1770–1827)
German music composer and musician. He wrote his first compositions at age thirteen. Beethoven studied under **Franz Joseph Haydn**. His work is divided into three periods and he composed in many forms, but he is renowned for his nine symphonies, the last of which is unusual in having a choral component. His works are emotional, dramatic, and powerful. Beethoven composed one symphony in honor of Napoléon Bonaparte, but after Napoléon became a megalomaniac Beethoven renamed it the *Emperor* symphony.

Begin, Menachem (1913–1992)
Prime minister (1977–1983) of Israel and **Nobel Prize** winner. As a guerrilla leader of the underground Irgun in the 1940s, Begin was considered a terrorist by the British, who put a price on his head. When he gained office, Begin took a hard line on holding the West Bank and the Gaza Strip, lands taken by Israel during the **Arab-Israeli War** of 1967. U.S. president **Jimmy Carter** convinced Begin to meet with Egyptian president **Anwar Sadat**, leading to the Camp David Accords (1978) and a peace treaty between Israel and Egypt. Begin and Sadat were awarded the **Nobel Prize** for Peace in 1978.

Beijing (Peking)
China's political capital and one of the world's major cities. The site was originally one of the five imperial capitals of

the Liao dynasty. It became the primary capital of the Jin dynasty as Zhongdu ("Central Capital"). The Mongols sacked Zhongdu in 1215, but **Khubilai Khan** established Dadu ("Great Capital") near the site as his imperial capital in 1274 and it served as the **Yuan** (Mongol) dynasty capital until 1368. In 1420 the Ming moved their capital from Nanjing to the site of present-day Beijing, because of its strategic location near the northern frontier, and gave it its present name. It has remained the capital since except for 1928–1949, when the **Guomindang** governed from Nanjing and Chongqing. Under the **Ming,** Beijing became a model of Chinese urban planning and architectural splendor. Many of its palaces and temples survived **Mao Zedong**'s destruction of the nation's heritage and are tourist attractions today. Beijing surrounds the **Forbidden City,** where the imperial palace is situated.

Bell, Alexander Graham (1847–1922)

Scottish-born American teacher, scientist, and inventor of the telephone in 1876. Bell was born and educated in Scotland and moved to Canada in 1870 and then the United States in 1871, were he trained teachers of hearing and speech-impaired students. Bell invented the telephone and exhibited it at the Centennial Exposition in Philadelphia in 1876.

Benares (Varanasi)

Holy city on the **Ganges River** in Uttar Pradesh state in northern India. An ancient city dating from at least the second millennium B.C.E., Benares was the capital of the Kasi kingdom at the time of **Siddhartha Gautama** (the Buddha), who gave his first sermon in the nearby town of Sarnath. A major center for Hindu worship, it is famed for the many ghats along the river where Hindus bathe and are cremated.

Benedict, Saint (c. 480–550)

Italian monk who outlined the most effective plan for **monasteries**. Benedict, born in Nursia, Italy, and hence called Benedict of Nursia, came from a middle-class family but spent a few years living as a hermit. Around 529 Benedict took some followers to Monte Cassino and built a monastery. Monte Cassino became famous for its order, the devotion of its monks, and its library. Benedict designed a plan, later known as the Benedictine Rule, to organized the lives of the monks at Monte Cassino. The rule was effective for its moderation, evenly distributing the activities of prayer, study, and work. The Benedictine Rule has guided most monastic orders ever since, especially the **Benedictines**.

Benedictines

An order of Christian monks and nuns who follow the Benedictine Rule of **Saint Benedict**. The first Benedictines were the monks at Monte Cassino who followed the rule set down by Saint Benedict (c. 480–550). Use of the rule spread across Europe in the centuries that followed. Benedictines became very influential in medieval political, economic, and intellectual affairs. Benedictines were sporadically accused of corruption or lack of spirituality, and new orders would then arise, such as the Cistercians, the **Dominicans**, and the **Franciscans**.

Benelux

Name given to the economic union of Belgium, the Netherlands, and Luxembourg formed in 1948. The union provided a common foreign-trade policy and open borders for the movement of goods, capital, and workers. A new treaty in 1958 (which took effect in 1961) created a single trading unit for trading beyond the three countries. Benelux set standards followed by the **European Economic Community** (now the **European Union**).

Ben-Gurion, David (1886–1973)

First prime minister of Israel and its minister of defense (1948–1953, 1955–1963). Born in **Russia**, Ben-Gurion settled in Palestine in 1906. As a Zionist leader, he worked for the creation of a Jewish state, and at the independence of **Israel** in 1948 he was made prime minister. Ben-Gurion directed the Israeli invasion of the Gaza Strip and the Sinai Peninsula during the **Suez Crisis**.

Benin, Kingdom of

Ancient African kingdom in the area of present-day southern Nigeria. Founded around 1000 c.e., the Kingdom of Benin achieved prominence in the region, with a hereditary monarchy and powerful hereditary chiefs below it. By the fifteenth century Benin begin to expand. Reaching its greatest extent and most centralized power around 1650, the kingdom was known for its crafters of wood, ivory, and brass. In 1485 the Kingdom of Benin was encountered by the Portuguese and began trade with the Europeans. Benin, however, was known for refusing to take part in the early slave trade.

Berbers

Peoples of North Africa, especially the Maghreb (Morocco, Algeria, and Tunisia) and the Sahara. The Berbers, an indigenous people, were conquered by **Muslim** Arabs in the seventh and eighth centuries and became **Sunni** Muslims. They established several dynasties of their own, such as the **Almohads** and the **Almoravids**. In the twenty-first century the Berbers continue to maintain much of their original culture and Berber languages, although fewer are nomadic herders. There are approximately 7 million Berbers, divided into more than 200 tribes.

Bergen-Belsen

German concentration camp of **World War II**. Part of the **Nazi** program to collect Jews, Gypsies, and other "undesirables," Bergen-Belsen, located near Hamburg, was not technically a **Death Camp**, or extermination center. When British troops liberated the camp in 1945, however, they found 10,000 unburied dead and 40,000 starving prisoners.

Berlin, Conference of (1884–1885)

A series of negotiations held in Berlin, Germany, in which the major European nations discussed questions concerning central Africa. Originally proposed by Germany and France because of conflicts with Portugal, the conference declared the Congo River basin to be neutral, established freedom of trade, forbade slave trade, and allowed for the creation of the Congo Free State. The Conference of Berlin allowed for an orderly carving up of Africa by major European nations including Germany, France, Britain, and Belgium.

Berlin, Congress of (1878)

Conference of major European powers to decide the fate of the **Ottoman Empire**. Chaired by German chancellor **Otto von Bismarck**, the Congress of Berlin limited Russian naval expansion; granted independence to Serbia, Montenegro, and Romania; granted **Bosnia-Herzegovina** to **Austria-Hungary**; reduced the size of Bulgaria; and placed Cyprus under British control. The congress left nearly all parties unhappy, creating dissatisfaction that contributed to **World War I**.

Berlin, Congress of (1884–1885). *See* Berlin, Conference of

Berlin, Division of

Division of the city of Berlin at the conclusion of **World War II**. Germany was split into the Federal Republic of Germany (West Germany), comprising British, French, and American zones, and the

German Democratic Republic (East Germany), consisting of the Soviet zone. Berlin, deep in the heart of East Germany, was also split into West Berlin and East Berlin. In 1948 **Joseph Stalin**'s **Union of Soviet Socialist Republics** cut off access to Berlin, hoping to use the city as a chip to balance power in Europe. A campaign led by the United States to airlift supplies to the city forced the Soviets to back down. In 1958 **Nikita Khrushchev** threatened to end Berlin's status as a free city inside communist East Germany. In 1961 Khrushchev had a wall constructed separating West and East Berlin to stop the flow of East Berliners into West Berlin. In 1989 the Berlin Wall was destroyed and Berlin reunited. In 1990 East and West Germany were reunited.

Berlin, Occupation of

The occupation and division of **Berlin** by the Soviet Union, the United States, Britain, and France at the end of **World War II**. Nearly destroyed by the war, Berlin was occupied by Soviet troops in May of 1945. American and British troops arrived in July; the French, in August. The **Division of Berlin** into four sectors, one for each of the occupying nations, led to disagreements and a long-term divide between Soviet East Berlin and Allied West Berlin.

Berlin Air Lift (1948)

The dispensing of supplies to blockaded West Berlin. After the Soviet invasion of Germany at the end of **World War II** and the USSR's subsequent prevention of land access to the western sector of a divided Berlin on June 24, 1948, the United States organized the airlift of supplies to the isolated sector of the city.

Berlin Wall

Wall between East Berlin and West Berlin constructed in 1961 to end movement to

West Berlin. At the end of **World War II** in 1945, troops of Russia, France, Britain, and the United States occupied the city of Berlin. The Allied zones were united as West Berlin, and the two sectors clashed over governance. The Soviets tried to drive the Allies out, but the 1948 **Berlin Airlift** foiled their plan. In 1958 the Soviets again tried to drive the Western powers from Berlin, but instead a steady exodus of East Germans to West Berlin caused Khrushchev to order the East German police to begin construction of a wall to seal exits. Eventually the Berlin War was ninety-six miles long, averaging twelve feet in height and surrounding West Berlin. The Berlin Wall became a **Cold War** symbol of communism's failure in having had to wall in its people. In November 1989 the wall was opened, and by the end of 1990 it had been torn down.

Bernard of Clairvaux, Saint (1090–1153) Cistercian monk, founder of Clairvaux, and church reformer. Bernard reinvigorated the Cistercian order, making it the most popular monastic order of the twelfth century, and founded Clairvaux and other **monasteries**. Bernard, a French Cistercian monk, was a friend and supporter of Abbot Suger, who built the Gothic Church of Saint-Denis near Paris. He was active in church reform, helping end a papal schism. Bernard preached support for the Second **Crusade**, attacked the scholar **Peter Abelard** for his rationalism, and helped found the Knights Templar.

Bernini, Lorenzo Giovanni (1598–1680) Prolific Italian **baroque** sculptor, painter, and architect. Bernini spent most of his life in Rome. He became a master of the baroque style, as evident in statues like the *Rape of Proserpina* (1621–1622), *David* (1623), and *Apollo and Daphne* (1622–1625). Their realism evokes movement and emotion, and they are designed with the viewer's perspective in mind. Bernini's dramatic *Ecstasy of Saint Teresa* (1645–1652) is a combination of sculpture, painting, and architecture, as is *Throne of Saint Peter* in Saint Peter's Cathedral. Bernini designed several fountains in Rome, including *The Fountain of the Four Rivers* (1648–1651) in Piazza Navona. The artist is best remembered for his tremendous bronze canopy (*baldachino*) over the high altar of Saint Peter's Basilica (1633) and for designing the colonnade in the piazza in front of the basilica, which symbolizes the "embracing arms of the Catholic Church."

Bessemer, Sir Henry (1813–1898)

English inventor of a process used to make steel on a large scale. The process, known as the Bessemer converter and invented in 1856, made steel by passing a blast of air through molten iron. The Bessemer converter greatly accelerated steel production and made the later nineteenth-century **Industrial Revolution** possible.

Bhagavad Gita (Sanskrit for "Song of the Lord")

Indian philosophical treatise incorporated in the Hindu epic **Mahabharata**. In the *Bhagavad Gita*, Krishna, in the guise of the warrior Arjuna's charioteer, instructs Arjuna in his **dharma** (duties) and explains the basic ethical teachings of **Hinduism**. It has become one of the most famous and popular religious texts in Hinduism.

Bhakti

Devotional **Hinduism** that usually focused worship on a personal deity who reciprocated the devotee's love. Bhakti, strongly influenced by South Indian traditions, emerged in the first millennium C.E. as an important aspect of Hinduism. Although **Shiva** and other gods were sometimes the object of devotion, most often bhakti centered around Rama or Krishna. The *bhakti-marga* ("way of devotion") contrasted with earlier Hinduism that focused on achieving salvation or liberation from the cycle of rebirths by rituals, study, or ascetic discipline. Some historians have pointed out the similarities of bhakti to **Mahayana Buddhism** and Christianity, which also center around the worship of a loving deity who promises salvation to followers.

Bhubaneswar

City in the eastern Indian province of Orissa famous for its Hindu temples. About 7,000 temples and shrines were reported to have been built between the third century B.C.E. and the sixteenth century C.E., of which about 500 survive. Among the best known is the Lingaraja Temple. They are excellent examples of Hindu architecture.

Bhutan

Predominantly Buddhist Himalayan kingdom between China to the north and India to the south. The state has existed since the seventeenth century, although not much is known about its early history. In the nineteenth century the British government in India recognized Bhutan as a self-governing state, with Britain in charge of its external affairs. Later a fully independent state, Bhutan has closely adhered to its traditional culture, retaining its monarchy and limiting outside access and cultural influence, but has suffered ethnic clashes as a result of an influx of Tibetan refugees and Nepalese immigrants after 1950.

Bhutto, Benazir (1953–)

Pakistani political leader and daughter of **Zulfikar Ali Bhutto**. After her father's execution in 1979 she succeeded him as leader of the Pakistan Peoples Party and served as Pakistan's prime minister

(1988–1990, 1993–1996). She campaigned for social reforms and political liberation, but despite considerable personal popularity she was unable to deal effectively with the nation's widespread poverty, political corruption, and the threats to the Pakistani political and social order posed by the rise of militant Islamism. After being dismissed from office in 1996, she lost in the elections of 1997. Bhutto now lives primarily in the United Kingdom.

Bhutto, Zulfikar Ali (1928–1979)

Pakistani statesman who formed the Pakistan Peoples Party in 1967 combining **Islam**, **democracy**, and populism. He became president in 1971 following Pakistan's defeat in the **Bangladesh War**, which discredited the military government. He stepped down as president to serve as prime minister in 1973 under a new constitution. In 1977 he was removed from power in a military coup, and he was hanged two years later by the military rulers on charges of complicity in a political murder. Although autocratic in his methods, he led the struggle for civilian rule in Pakistan. His daughter **Benazir Bhutto** succeeded him as leader of the Pakistan Peoples Party and served as Pakistan's prime minister.

Biafra

Country declared independent of Nigeria in 1967. A civil war followed in which Nigeria's army destroyed Biafra's army and ravaged the Biafran countryside. Extensive poverty and starvation shocked the world when scenes of emaciated children were disseminated by the media. By 1970 the state had ceased to exist.

Bible

Collection of sacred writings of the Judaeo-Christian tradition. The **Old Testament** is shared by both religions (known as the Hebrew Testament in **Judaism**), while the **New Testament** is fundamental for the religion of Christians. The **Bible** consists of seventy-three books (forty-six in the Old Testament and twenty-seven in the New Testament, though Protestants recognize sixty-six books, thirty-nine Old Testament and twenty-seven New Testament) written by various authors between roughly 1200 B.C.E. and 100 C.E.

Bill of Rights, United States (1791)

Amendments to the **United States Constitution** that provide specific guarantees of personal freedom. The original Constitution, adopted in 1789, did not provide personal guarantees, and many states demanded that they be added. The first eight amendments guarantee personal freedoms, while the ninth and tenth forbid Congress from infringing upon the others. The rights include freedom of religion, speech, press, assembly, and petition; the right to bear arms; protection against unreasonable search or seizure; protection against self-incrimination; the right to a speedy trial; the right to a trial by jury; and protection against unusual punishment.

Bishop

The **Roman Catholic Church**'s administrator of a diocese or district of the church. The term *bishop* means "overseer" or "inspector." The church viewed bishops are successors of the apostles and therefore its safe keeping was entrusted to the them. The **pope** is the Bishop of Rome. Any church where a bishop resides is considered a **cathedral**.

Bismarck, Otto von (1815–1898) (Prince of Bismarck, Duke of Lauenburg)

Prussian-German statesman and chancellor (1871–1890) of a newly united Germany, known as the "Iron Chancellor."

A war hero, Bismarck incited the Franco-Prussian War (1870–1871). He unified liberals, royalists, and socialists and instituted many social reforms, although he ensured that power continued to reside with the aristocracy and the emperor. Bismarck used shrewd manipulation in diplomacy and warfare to unite Germany and to increase its influence in Europe. He resigned in 1890 over a conflict with the emperor.

Black Death

Epidemic diseases of bubonic, pneumonic, and septicemic plagues that encircled the globe from the twelfth century through the sixteenth century encompassing much of the Inter-Communicating Zone, including large parts of Asia, Africa, the **Middle East**, and Europe. The Black Death (*Pasteurella pestis*) appeared in Europe in 1347 (some historians now believe that the medieval European plague was not bubonic). It swept across Europe, killing between one-third and one-half of the entire population within a few years. The bubonic plague (the most common type), carried by fleas on the black rat, caused fever and nausea and attacked the lymphatic system first, rupturing blood vessels and raising large black swellings (buboes). It then attacked the nervous system, causing death in 50–80 percent of cases within seven days. The pneumonic plague was passed via air, while the septicemic plague was an overwhelming infection of the bloodstream. Initially, the Black Death caused chaos because people at all levels of society died and there was no effective medical treatment. In Europe it led to the massacre of many Jewish communities as rumors spread that the Jews had poisoned wells. Eventually the Black Death brought about the decline of **feudalism** by reducing the available peasant workforce. It also reduced the power of the aristocracy, but in consolidating landholdings and raising wages it increased the wealth and power of the rising middle class. Bubonic plague existed before the **Middle Ages** and continues to exist today.

Black Friars. *See* Dominicans (Black Friars)

Black Hole of Calcutta (1756)

Place of imprisonment of British soldiers in India. In a 1756 conflict between the local ruler of Bengal and the British **East India Company**, the local ruler occupied Calcutta, a major trading center under British control. One hundred forty-six British men were arrested and imprisoned in a small, lightless room, and forty-three of them died of suffocation. Later, John Zephaniah Holwell, a British official, wrote an account of the event that brought on outrage in Britain and led to increasing British military involvement in India and, ultimately, Britain's domination of the entire Indian subcontinent.

Black Panthers (1966–1972)

Revolutionary black nationalist organization. Founded in 1966 in Oakland, California, by Bobby Seale and Huey P. Newton as a response to charges of police brutality, the Black Panthers became the leading black militant organization of the late 1960s. Cultivating a confrontational image that led to numerous violent clashes with local and federal authorities, the Black Panthers also sponsored self-help programs such as free clinics, schools, and food banks. Police attention and factional disputes led to the decline of the party after 1972.

Black Ships

Name the Japanese gave the eight ships of **Commodore Matthew Perry**'s fleet that arrived off the Japanese coast in 1853.

Perry's expedition sought to forcibly open Japan. The name (*Kurofune* in Japanese) is derived from the black color of the painted wooden vessels or from the black smoke from the steamships.

Blitzkrieg (German for "lightning war") War strategy used by **Nazi** Germany to move troops and equipment into position rapidly to take the enemy by surprise. The concept was used by Germany much earlier, including by **Otto von Bismarck** in the Franco-Prussian War and in **World War I**, but the term became associated with the later warfare after Germany's invasion of Poland in 1939. The Germans' successful combination of air power, mechanized armor forces (tanks, or panzers), paratroopers, and communications was dubbed blitzkrieg ("lightning war") by journalists who witnessed the rapidity with which German armies overran eastern and western Europe early in **World War II**.

Boadicea. *See* Boudicca (Boadicea)

Boccaccio, Giovanni (1313–1375) Prolific Italian author who wrote prose, verse, and nonfictional works. His acknowledged masterpiece *The Decameron* (1348–1351) consisted of a hundred stories told by ten Florentine men and women who fled the city to escape the **Black Death**. Boccaccio produced influential literary works in both Latin and Italian. Many of these focused on secular subjects. Like many early **Renaissance** figures he was a devout follower of Christianity fascinated by pagan mythology and the classical world. He strongly influenced **Geoffrey Chaucer**.

Bodhisattva
In **Mahayana Buddhism**, a heavenly being who voluntarily postpones his or her entry into **nirvana** in order to help others achieve salvation or to limit suffering. Originating in India during the first millennium C.E., the concept of bodhisattvas came to play a central role in most forms of **Buddhism** practiced in East Asia. Bodhisattvas became examples of compassion, mercy, and wisdom and were personal saviors assisting their followers in achieving Buddhahood or nirvana, roughly analogous to the saints of medieval **Christianity**. The most popular was Avalokiteshvara, known in China as Guanyin, originally a male but later a female bodhisattva. Worship of bodhisattvas did much to spread the popularity of Buddhism in East Asia.

Boers. *See* Afrikaners

Boer Wars. *See* Anglo-Boer Wars

Boethius, Ancius (c. 480–524)
Roman philosopher of the late **Roman Empire**. Boethius was a **consul** under and advisor to Emperor **Theodoric** the Ostrogoth. He wrote *The Consolation of Philosophy* on the comfort of philosophy, especially that of **Plato, Aristotle,** and others. Boethius was a Christian and began the merger of Christian and pagan philosophies that became the foundation of medieval European society.

Bolívar, Simón (1783–1830)
South American leader, statesman, and hero of the revolution that led to the independence from Spain of Venezuela, Colombia, Ecuador, Panama, Peru, and Bolivia. Bolívar became active in the revolution in 1806 and took part in more than 200 battles before the decisive victory ending Spanish domination in 1824. He signed those countries into independence but continued to lead armies to put down opposition and civil war. Bolívar also became the dictator of Bolivia, Colombia, and Peru. He died from tuberculosis in 1830.

Bologna University

Possibly the oldest **university** in the world. Founded around 1120, Bologna was renowned for its education in civil and canon law. Although Muslim, Confucian, and Buddhist academies existed earlier, Bologna was the first institution to provide higher learning in several nonreligious subjects. In 1870 the university was reestablished and is one of the great universities of Europe, located in Bologna, Italy.

Bolshevik Revolution

The **Russian Revolution**'s second stage. In March 1917 Russia was engaged in **World War I** and food riots broke out. Soon the riots turned into a full-scale revolution, and Tsar **Nicholas II** abdicated. Between March and October the provisional government was reorganized four times. The first All-Russian Congress of Soviets was dominated by socialist revolutionaries, Mensheviks, and **Bolsheviks**. In November 1917 the Bolsheviks, who had proclaimed a program of "peace, land, and bread" that gained great support from the populace, staged a coup, occupying government buildings and reconvening the Congress of Soviets, which approved the new government controlled by the Bolsheviks.

Bolsheviks

Russian revolutionaries during the **Russian Revolution**. The name *Bolshevik*, given the revolutionaries by **Vladimir Ilyich Lenin** in 1903, is Russian for "majority," even though they were not. Lenin's policy for the Bolsheviks revised **Karl Marx**'s ideology. Lenin believed that Russia could combine capitalist and socialist revolutions and that an elite corps of party members could lead the masses during the revolution, as opposed to Marx's idea of the revolution coming from the mass of people themselves. In November 1917 the Bolsheviks staged a coup, overthrowing Russia's provisional government and gaining control of the Congress of Soviets in what became known as the **Bolshevik Revolution**.

Bombay (Mumbai)

Capital of Maharashtra State and India's largest commercial and financial center. The Portuguese gained control of the port in 1534 and gave it the name *Bombay*, which is probably derived from the Portuguese for "good bay." It passed into British hands in 1661 and became India's most important seaport. After India's independence it continued as a major industrial and commercial center and the home of India's "Bollywood" movie industry. In the 1990s the name was officially changed to Mumbai, after Mumba, the local name for the **Hindu** goddess Parvati, consort of **Shiva**.

Bonaparte, Napoléon. *See* Napoléon Bonaparte

Book of Akbar

Chronicle of **Akbar** (1556–1605). Originally written in Persian by Abul Fazl Allami, the *Akbarnama* is the official year-by-year chronicle, or memoirs, of the **Mughal** king Akbar, who ruled northern India from 1556 to 1605. While recounting the events and activities of the ruler and his army and court, the *Akbarnama* was designed to establish a new form of political legitimacy for a Timurid dynastic line stretching from **Timur** (Tamerlane) and **Babur** to a divinely inspired Akbar and his descendants.

Book of Exodus

Second book of the Hebrew **Bible**, one of five attributed to Moses. The first nineteen chapters describe the slavery of Israelites in Egypt, the call of Moses to lead them to freedom, the ten plagues that convinced

Pharaoh to let the people go, the institution of the Passover meal, the crossing of the Red Sea, the provision of "bread from heaven" (manna), and the journey to Mount Sinai. Chapters 20–24 contain the Ten Commandments and various regulations for civil life. Chapters 25–40 include instructions for the ritual life of Israel, including the tabernacle, priesthood, and offerings.

Book of Odes (Shi Jing)

Also known as the *Book of Poetry*, a **Zhou** dynasty collection of 305 poems, reputedly edited by **Confucius** (551–479 B.C.E.) but dating from the early Zhou period. It became one of the "Five Classics" of ancient China and a model of poetic expression for later generations of Chinese.

Book of the Dead

Ancient Egyptian writings on **papyrus** that were placed in graves. The writings were to assist the dead in passing examinations that would take place to enable them to enter the afterlife. Collectively, the writings are known as the Book of the Dead.

Booth, John Wilkes (1838–1865)

Famous actor, Confederate sympathizer, and assassin of President **Abraham Lincoln**. Booth slipped into the presidential box and shot Lincoln at Ford's Theater in Washington DC on April 14, 1865.

Borges, Jorge Luis (1899–1986)

Argentine writer noted for his elaborate and complex stories that mix reality and fantasy in an intricate, mazelike ambiguity. Borges's *The Garden of Forking Paths* (1944) begins as a spy story but becomes a labyrinth of paths where the stories double back and reflect one another and reality is never clear.

Borgia, Cesare (c. 1475–1507)

Italian Renaissance duke and son of Pope **Alexander VI**. A master of political maneuvering, Cesare Borgia was used by **Niccolò Machiavelli** as an example of a new prince—one who allowed ends to justify means. With papal and French backing, Borgia was feared throughout Italy. He became a cardinal in 1493 and captain-general of the papal armies in 1499, controlling much of central Italy.

Bormann, Martin (1900–c. 1945)

German **Nazi** Party leader. Bormann became part of **Adolf Hitler**'s personal staff of storm troopers in 1928. In 1941 Bormann was appointed head of the administration of the Nazi Party, making him one of the most powerful men in Germany, controlling legislation, promotions, and access to Hitler. Bormann was one of the strongest advocates of the extermination of Jews and Slavs. He disappeared at the end of **World War II**, was presumed dead in 1945, and was declared dead in 1973 with the identification of his skeleton in Berlin. He was indicted for war crimes in absentia at the **Nürnberg Trials** in 1945.

Borobodur

Massive **Buddhist** temple in Java, Indonesia, about twenty-six miles (forty-two km) northwest of Yogyakarta. It was constructed between 778 and 850 C.E. by the Sailendra dynasty. The structure is meant to resemble the mythical Mount Meru of **Hinduism**, but the many relief carvings depict the story and lessons of the **Buddha**. Borobodur reflects the influence of **Gupta** and Indian culture on Javanese artistic traditions.

Bose, Subhas Chandra (1897–1945)

Indian nationalist who began his political career in Calcutta, serving as leader of the left wing of the Indian National Congress party. He was forced to resign as president of the party in 1939 after a dispute with **Mohandas K. Gandhi**. Jailed by the British for his **Axis** sympathies in **World War II**, he escaped in 1941 and fled to Germany. In 1943 he organized the Japanese-sponsored Indian National Army in Singapore. He attended the Japanese-sponsored Greater East Asia Co-Prosperity Sphere conference as the representative of Free India. He was killed in an airplane crash at the end of World War II, in 1945.

Bosnia-Herzegovina

Territory removed from the **Ottoman Empire** and granted to **Austria-Hungary** by the **Congress of Berlin** in 1878. As the Ottoman Empire deteriorated, nationalist movements spread through the Balkans. Serbia, Montenegro, and Bulgaria became independent. Bosnia-Herzegovina was declared a crown land under the protection of Austria-Hungary. In 1908 Austria-Hungary annexed Bosnia-Herzegovina, causing resentment. When the **Young Turks** took control of the Ottoman Empire in 1909 **Muslim** Bosnians were sympathetic. When the heir to the **Habsburg** throne of Austria-Hungary, Archduke Francis Ferdinand, traveled to Bosnia he was assassinated by Bosnian nationalists, sparking **World War I**.

Boston Tea Party (1773)

Attack by American colonial patriots opposed to British taxes. In 1773 the British **Parliament** enacted a tax on tea to bale out the bankrupt **East India Company** by granting it a monopoly on the tea trade. A party of men dressed as Native Americans boarded three ships, broke open casks containing 90,000 pounds of tea, and dumped the tea into Boston Harbor. This act proved to the British that the colonies were serious and caused Parliament to pass the Coercive Acts and close Boston Harbor.

Botha, Pieter Willem (P. W.) (1916–)

South African statesman, prime minister (1978–1984), and state president (1984–1989) who initiated limited reforms and a new constitution for South Africa. Botha's reforms angered many South African whites, and his resistance to more progressive reforms and support of **apartheid** lost him favor with the African majority.

Botticelli, Sandro (c. 1445–1510)

Italian Renaissance artist whose legacy is founded on his distinct style. He utilized bold lines; brilliant color; and graceful, fluid, representations of the flimsy garments that covered his subjects. This Florentine produced religious scenes such as *Adoration of the Magi* (1475) under the patronage of the **Medici** as well as pictures with mythological subjects like *The Birth of Venus* (1485) and *The Primavera* (1478), which show his interest in antiquity and Neoplatonist scholarship. Recognized as one of the leading artists of his day, Botticelli was called to Rome by Pope Sixtus IV in 1481 to be a painter of the **Sistine Chapel**.

Boudicca (Boadicea) (c. 20–62)

Briton queen of East Anglia who led a major rebellion against the Romans. When her husband, Prasutagus, king of the Iceni, died in 60, he left his kingdom to his daughters, but it was claimed by **Rome**. Boudicca protested and was flogged and her daughters raped by Roman soldiers. She raised a rebellion that nearly drove the Romans from Britain, destroying the Roman settlements at Camulodunum, London, and Verulamium. In a final battle, the Romans defeated the Britons and massacred as many as 80,000 men, women, and children.

Bourbon

Dynastic French family descended from a son of **Louis IX** and the female heir to the Bourbon lordship. Their son was the first Duke of Bourbon, Louis (1279–1341). The Bourbon title passed to other families several times. When the last **Valois** king died in 1589, a Bourbon became king as **Henry IV** (r. 1589–1610). His heirs ruled uninterrupted until 1792, when **Louis XVI** was overthrown during the **French Revolution**. After the **Napoleonic Wars** the Bourbons were restored in 1814 and ruled until 1848, when **Louis-Philippe**, the last of the Bourbons, died. The Bourbons have ruled Spain from 1700 to the present (excepting 1931–1975).

Bourgeois (meaning "burgess" or "townsman")

French term originally designating a person of the middle class, which included shopkeepers, later used by Marxist or socialist writers to designate a person with private-property interests. Often used in the form *bourgeoisie*, to indicate the middle class as a whole. Marxist theory claimed that the final class conflict would be between the bourgeoisie and the proletariat (the working class).

Boxer Rebellion (Boxer Uprising) (1899–1900)

Chinese populist anti-Western movement in the late nineteenth century. To resist western influence in China in the nineteenth century, a widespread secret society, Society of Harmonious Fists, or Boxers, arose. Its members were violently antiforeign and attacked Christian converts and missionaries. Supported by the **Manchu** officials, the Boxer movement became a full-scale uprising against foreigners in northern China. European troops seized Chinese sites to safeguard European interests. China declared war on all foreign powers, and several hundred Europeans were killed. European forces quickly put down the rebellion and established wider controls within China, further damaging the already shaky Manchu regime.

Boyle, Robert (1627–1691)

English chemist, mathematician, and inventor born in Ireland. Boyle advanced the field of chemistry and performed experiments with pumps, but he is best known for Boyle's Law, a statement of the relation between pressure and volume of a gas.

Brahe, Tycho (1546–1601) (most commonly known as Tycho only)

Danish astronomer of the **scientific revolution** who added observations to **Nicolaus Copernicus**'s mathematical theory of the sun-centered universe. Tycho was the most exact and active observer of the heavenly bodies of his day. He was not a great mathematician, but his accumulated observations helped to verify the mathematical theories of others. In many ways Tycho, like **Andreas Vesalius** in anatomy, established careful observation as a cornerstone of modern science.

Brahma

Creator god of **Hindu** mythology. Some Hindus taught that there was a trinity of gods: Brahma, the creator; **Vishnu**, the preserver; and **Shiva**, the destroyer. Brahma was more important in ancient India, and from medieval times most worship has focused on Vishnu and Shiva.

Brahman

In **Hinduism**, the absolute being or reality. In the **Upanishads**, written after the seventh century B.C.E., it was the goal of each person to unite his or her individual soul (atman) with the universal Brahman. Brahman has also been worshiped as a creator god, **Brahma**. Some Hindus taught that there is a trinity of gods: Brahma, the creator; **Vishnu**, the preserver; and **Shiva**, the destroyer.

Brahmin Caste (Brahman Caste)

The highest of the four **varna**, the major delineation of caste in the Hindu caste system. The Brahmins were the priests of **Hinduism**, with exclusive authority to carry out necessary religious rituals. In ancient India they were the scholars, and writing was primarily confined to their group. The high social status and special privileges of Brahmins was justified because they had earned good karma in previous lives. The Brahmins formed a distinctive social class in India by at least late **Vedic** times. They dominated Indian political leadership in the twentieth century, but after 1947 they no longer had legal privileges, and their political dominance has gradually eroded.

Brahmo Samaj (Sanskrit for "Society of God")

Indian religious movement founded in 1828 by Ram Mohan Roy to promote religious and social reform. Influenced by ideas of **monotheism** and Western secular thought, Roy and his successors wanted to remake **Hinduism** by rejecting **polytheism** and the caste system, prohibiting child marriage, and permitting widows to remarry. The movement never attracted numerous followers but had an important influence on Indian social thought. It was part of the effort to combine the Indian/Hindu inheritance with Western social concepts.

Brandenburg

City in eastern Germany, and formerly a state that became the core of **Prussia**. It became a strong state in the fifteenth century and expanded in the seventeenth century under **Frederick William** during the **Thirty Years' War** as it became Brandenburg-Prussia. When Elector Frederick III was granted the title King of Prussia, Brandenburg became a province of the Prussian kingdom. The city is now a major steel producer and has an inland shipyard that builds fishing boats.

Brandt, Willy (1913–1992)

German statesman, leader of the German Social Democratic Party (1964–1987), chancellor of the Federal Republic of Germany (1969–1974), and **Nobel Prize** winner (1971). During **World War II** Brandt's political activities forced him to flee Germany, first to Norway and then to Sweden. He achieved fame as mayor of West Berlin (1957–1966), resisting the Soviet Union's attempt to control the city. As chancellor of West Germany he concentrated on foreign affairs and, especially, on improving relations with communist Eastern bloc countries. For these efforts, especially the reconciliation between West Germany and East Germany, Brandt was awarded the Nobel Prize for Peace.

Bretton Woods Conference (1944)

Meeting in Bretton Woods, New Hampshire, to plan economic arrangements for the postwar world near the end of **World War II**. The resultant plan to provide economic stability and capital for the reconstruction of war-ravaged countries included the **International Monetary Fund** (IMF) and a world bank known as the International Bank for Reconstruction and Development (IBRD).

Brezhnev, Leonid (1906–1982)

Soviet statesman and Communist Party leader. A member of the Central Committee and the Politburo under **Joseph Stalin**, at Stalin's death Brezhnev lost his posts. Under **Khrushchev** he again rose to the

Central Committee and the Politburo. At Khrushchev's removal, Brezhnev and Alesksey Kosygin jointly led until Brezhnev emerged as the dominant figure. He controlled foreign affairs, establishing the **Brezhnev Doctrine**, and invaded Czechoslovakia in 1968. He attempted to ease international tensions through détente with the West, including the United States, yet he built up the Soviet military, especially nuclear weapons capabilities and the navy, and overtook the United States' space program. In 1977 Brezhnev became the first person to hold leadership of both the Communist Party and the **Union of Soviet Socialist Republics**. He attempted to suppress dissent in the Soviet Union and Poland and invaded Afghanistan in 1979. His foreign and military focus drained and stagnated the Soviet economy, leading to the country's gradual decline.

Brezhnev Doctrine

Western name for the Soviet policy devised under **Leonid Brezhnev** that asserted the right of the **Union of Soviet Socialist Republics** to intervene in foreign affairs in cases where the interests of socialist countries were threatened. It was used as justification for the invasions of Czechoslovakia in 1968 and Afghanistan in 1979 as well as for support of wars of national liberation in developing countries.

Bridgewater, Francis Egerton, Third Duke of (1736–1803)

Originator of the British canal system. He built the first great canal in modern Britain by 1761, from Worsley to Manchester, to move coal from his own estate. Between 1760 and 1800 there was a network of 3,000 miles of canals and 1,000 miles of navigable rivers throughout England, moving goods more cost-effectively than

overland transport until the coming of **railroads** in the 1840s.

Brinksmanship

Policy of nuclear threats by the United States implemented by Secretary of State **John Foster Dulles** during President **Dwight D. Eisenhower**'s administration (1953–1961). Brinksmanship used threats of nuclear attack to prevent the Soviets from continuing their aggressive expansionism. The threats were never acted upon.

Britain. *See* Great Britain

Britain, Battle of (1940)

World War II attempt by Germany to gain air superiority over Britain to enable Germany to invade in Operation Sea-Lion. In June 1940 France fell to Germany, and Britain stood alone in resistance. **Adolf Hitler** decided to prepare an invasion, but it required air superiority over the English Channel. As many as 1,800 German aircraft flew daily over Britain, bombing and strafing. London was bombed repeatedly. Outnumbered four to one, British fighter planes kept the Germans from gaining control of the channel and thwarted the invasion.

British East India Company. *See* East India Company (English)

British North American Act (1867)

Act of British **Parliament** uniting Quebec, Ontario, and the Maritime Provinces as well as, prospectively, the western provinces into the federal self-governing Dominion of Canada. It acted as Canada's constitution until 1982.

British Raj

Term for the British colonial government in India, derived from the Hindi *raj* ("rule"). British rule began gradually from the seventeenth century under the **East India Company.** The term *Raj*, however, is often more narrowly used for the period of direct rule that was established in 1858 after the **Sepoy Mutiny** and lasted to independence in 1947. At its peak the British ruled nearly the entire Indian subcontinent as well as Sri Lanka (Ceylon) and Burma. A viceroy appointed by the crown governed a huge bureaucracy, the Indian Civil Service, made up of British and Indian officials, and the Indian army, consisting mostly of Indian troops and British officers. Administration was direct over three-quarters of the country and indirect in about 500 princely states, where indigenous rulers were given autonomy over internal affairs. In 1877 **Queen Victoria** was named empress of India. In the first half of the twentieth century Indians successfully agitated for a greater role in governing India and eventually pressured the British to turn over complete control their subjects. In 1947 British India became the independent nations of India and Pakistan, and in 1948 Ceylon and Burma became independent.

Bronze Age

A period of history, varying from region to region, between 4000 and 1000 B.C.E., when humans learned to make implements out of metal instead of stone, especially using bronze (an alloy of copper and tin). Bronze can be cast into whatever shape is needed and is a hard metal, good for making weapons. It is a difficult metal to work with, however, and has limited tensile strength (ability to stress or flex). The wide-scale production of iron, when that metal became readily available, signaled the advent of the **Iron Age.**

Bronze Casting in Shang

Ancient Chinese artwork. During the **Shang** dynasty (1766–1122 B.C.E.), China produced a variety of splendid bronze works. The art of bronze casting may have been transmitted to China from western Asia, but the Shang casting was unique. The Chinese excelled all ancient peoples in their ability to cast large and intricate ritual vessels. The largest vessels and cauldrons weighted up to 1,500 pounds (680 kg) and were made in several sections from clay molds and then fitted together. Bronze weapons, armor, and chariot fittings were also produced.

Brown, John (1800–1859)

Abolitionist leader involved in antislavery violence in Kansas and a raid on the federal arsenal at Harper's Ferry, Virginia. After becoming involved in the abolitionist cause in the 1830s, Brown led an antislavery **guerrilla** force in the Kansas Territory in a series of violent confrontations with proslavery forces from 1855 to 1857. He later sought to sponsor a slave rebellion in the South. To obtain arms for this purpose, Brown led twenty-one followers in a raid on the federal arsenal at Harper's Ferry in October 1859. Captured after briefly holding the arsenal, Brown was quickly tried and hanged in December. The raid on Harper's Ferry further increased sectional tensions and made compromise between North and South less likely.

Bruegel, Pieter (1525–1569 C.E.)

Versatile artist from **Flanders** who painted landscapes, scenes of religious and allegorical subjects, and representations of peasant lifestyles. His technical style, use of humor, and portrayal of popular culture inspired by folk life were often imitated in the Netherlands and beyond.

Brunelleschi, Filippo (1377–1446)

Italian **Renaissance** architect best remembered for the egg-shaped dome on **Florence**'s cathedral (completed in 1436).

Brunelleschi was a leading Florentine engineer/architect whose innovative, crisp, classical designs utilized columns and **arches**. Brunelleschi was also the sculptor who lost a famous contest to design the bronze doors on Florence's baptistery to Lorenzo Ghiberti. Among his other architectural accomplishments in Florence are San Lorenzo (1419) and the Pazzi Chapel (1430).

Bruni, Leonardo (1369–1444)
Italian humanist who laid the intellectual foundation of the **Renaissance**. Bruni prescribed the *studia humanitatis* (the study of grammar, rhetoric, oration, history, moral philosophy, and poetry) as the foundation for an active civic life of political service to the Florentine Republic. Interested in the political and literary activities of **Cicero**, he wrote a biography of the Roman's life titled *New Cicero*.

Brutus, Marcus (Iunius) (85–42 B.C.E.)
Roman administrator, general, and writer. Brutus's father was murdered by **Pompey the Great**, and Brutus resisted Pompey's attempt to become a dictator. He was made a pontifex under **Julius Caesar** and governed part of **Gaul**. He led the conspiracy to assassinate Caesar and became one of the major opponents of **Octavian** and **Mark Antony**. Brutus raised a major army that defeated Octavian, but in a second battle Brutus was defeated and committed suicide. As a writer he was admired by **Cicero**, but none of his literary work has survived.

Bubonic Plague. *See* Black Death

Buddha. *See* Buddhism; Siddhartha Gautama

Buddhism
Major world religion that developed out of **Hinduism** through the teachings of **Siddhartha Gautama**, known as the Buddha ("Enlightened One") in the fifth century B.C.E. Buddhism offered a way to salvation from the miseries of life and the cycle of births and rebirth that did not rely on the caste system and the elaborate ritual of Hinduism. The key was understanding the **Four Noble Truths**: that all life is full of suffering; that the cause of suffering is desire; that the way to end desire is to end suffering; and that the way to end suffering to follow the **Eightfold Path**, which involved a moral and disciplined life, the practice of meditation, and self-reflection. With the conversion of Mauryan emperor **Ashoka** in the third century B.C.E., it became a major religious force carrying out missionary activity throughout most of Asia. Two basic forms of Buddhism were **Theravada** (or Hinayana), "Lesser Vehicle," which became the dominant religion of Sri Lanka, Burma, Thailand, Laos, and Cambodia, and **Mahayana**, "Greater Vehicle," which predominated in East Asia. By the end of the first millennium C.E. Buddhism had declined to a minor sect in India but was the most popular religion in most of East and Southeast Asia. Buddhism today is widespread in China, Japan, and Southeast Asia and is practiced throughout the world.

Bukhara
City in Uzbekistan located in the fertile Zerafshan Valley. From the early first millennium C.E. Bukhara was one of the major cities on the **Silk Road** and an important cultural center of **Central Asia**. As such, it attracted the attention of **Genghis Khan**, who captured it in 1220, and **Timur**, who seized it in 1370. In the sixteenth century it became the capital of the Uzbek Shaybani state, and later of the Khanate of Bukhara. It became part of **Russia**'s empire in the late nineteenth century.

Bulgars
Turkic people from **Turkestan** who settled in the Balkans in the sixth century. The

Bulgars overwhelmed the **Slavs** living in the region and in 681 were recognized as a Bulgar state by the **Byzantine** emperor. They became Christian in the ninth century, following the **Eastern Orthodox Church**. The Bulgars adopted the Slavic language and developed a brilliant culture in the early **Middle Ages**. In 1393 Bulgaria was absorbed into the **Ottoman Empire**.

Bulge, Battle of the (1944–1945)
World War II German offensive on the Western Front. After the Allied invasion of Europe in June 1944, the **Allies** moved rapidly through France and Belgium. In December 1944 the Germans surprised General **Dwight D. Eisenhower** and the Allied forces by counterattacking and forcing a huge bulge in the Allied lines around the Ardennes region of Belgium. The Germans hoped to retake the port of Antwerp. By early January 1945 the United States army made its own counteroffensive and forced the Germans to retreat. The Battle of the Bulge was the last major offensive that the German army was able to mount.

Bumiputra ("Sons of the Soil")
Name given to the indigenous ethnic Malay peoples of Malaysia. During British colonial rule many Chinese and Indian laborers came to work in the mines, timber camps, and commercial centers of the areas that became Malaysia. Upon its independence in 1957, the ethnic Malays feared being overwhelmed by these emigrants and their descendants. The Malaysian government provided preferences in government and industry for the Bumiputra to ensure their political domination of the country.

Bunraku Theater
Japanese puppet theater that emerged in the late sixteenth century and became a popular art and entertainment form during the **Tokugawa** period (1603–1868). Puppet theater was popular throughout East Asia, but in Japan it achieved a prestige and popularity that it had never attained in China or Korea. In the eighteenth century, **Chikamatsu Monzaeomon** (1653–1725), generally regarded as Japan's greatest playwright, wrote many plays for Bunraku.

Burckhardt, Jakob (1818–1897)
Swiss historian who established the study of the **Renaissance**. Educated in history and art at the University of Berlin from 1839 to 1843, Burckhardt emphasized the study of culture and the arts in history. In *The Civilization of the Renaissance in Italy* (1860) he labeled the Renaissance as a distinct cultural period born in Italy that was based on individualism, a revival of antiquity, and secular values. He played a large role in creating the concept of the Renaissance as the birthplace of the modern world.

Burgundy
Region of eastern France that has waxed and waned in importance in history. First established as a kingdom in the fifth century by the Burgundians, one of the Germanic tribes that infiltrated the **Roman Empire**, Burgundy was absorbed into the Carolingian empire and, later, the **Capetian** kingdom of France. In the eleventh century it was made a duchy, with the Duke of Burgundy the son of the king. Burgundy reached its greatest importance in the fourteenth and fifteenth centuries, when it was again enlarged. At that time the Duchy of Burgundy rivaled the French monarchy itself in wealth and influence. During the latter part of the **Hundred Years War**, in the fifteenth century, the Burgundians even sided with the English against the French crown.

Burial Mound

Artificial small hill or mound usually made of earth that marks a grave. Burial mounds are found in many parts of the world and generally indicate a fairly complex level of social organization—at least above a small family grouping because their construction entails considerable labor. Well-known burial mounds include mounds found in Europe that were constructed between 4000 B.C.E. and 600 C.E.; huge mounds constructed in Japan during the Tumulous Period (third to sixth centuries) and in Korea during the Three Kingdoms period (fourth to seventh centuries); and North American mounds constructed by the Hopewell and Adena cultures between 1000 B.C.E. and 700 C.E.

Burke, Edmund (1729–1797)

British statesman and conservative political writer. Best known for his attack on the **French Revolution** in *Reflections on the Revolution in France* (1790). Burke raised the fundamental question of the relationship of the citizen to the state. He recognized that times change but insisted that reforms must be gradual and well considered to avoid losing the good with the bad. He argued that the state was the product of a slow and complex process of historical and social development and that revolutionaries destroy all of this development in the hope of creating something better that is unproven. Burke also argued that a state governed by the masses rather than by the discerning would lead to disaster.

Bush, George H. W. (1924–)

Forty-first president of the United States. Following service as a Navy pilot in **World War II** and a career in the oil business, George H. W. Bush was elected to the House of Representatives as a Republican from Texas in 1966. After losing a U.S. Senate race in 1970, he served as ambassador to the **United Nations** and chair of the Republican National Committee under President **Richard M. Nixon**, and as a representative to China and **Central Intelligence Agency** director under President Gerald R. Ford. Losing the Republican presidential nomination in 1980 to **Ronald Reagan**, he served as Reagan's vice president. In 1988 Bush was elected president. Facing a Democratic-controlled Congress, Bush had few domestic successes apart from passage of the Americans with Disabilities Act (1990). His later reversal on a campaign pledge of "No new taxes" hurt his standing with voters. In foreign policy, he worked to maintain global stability during the collapse of the Soviet Union and organized a coalition of powers that ejected **Saddam Hussein**'s Iraqi military from recently conquered Kuwait in the **Iraq War** of 1991. He also mounted a successful invasion of Panama, leading to the arrest and conviction of Panamanian leader Manuel Noriega on drug-smuggling charges. Bush was defeated by Bill Clinton in the presidential election of 1992. He is the father of President **George W. Bush**.

Bush, George W. (1946–)

Forty-third president of the United States. The son of **George H. W. Bush**, the forty-first president of the United States, George W. Bush is a Republican and self-described "compassionate conservative." Before becoming president Bush attended Yale University and Harvard Business School. He was a co-owner of the Texas Rangers baseball team and the first governor of Texas to be elected for two consecutive terms (in 1994 and 1998). Taking office as U.S. president in 2001 after a contested election, Bush's first term is remembered for the September 11 terrorist attacks on the World Trade Center and the Pentagon as well as for naming and fighting the "War on Terror" by invading Afghanistan and Iraq. During his presidency record deficits plagued the economy. In 2004 Bush won reelection over Massachusetts senator John Kerry. Bush's second term started with commitments to deal with deficits in Medicare and Social Security, but by late 2005 was absorbed with continuing troubles in Iraq, the appointment of two Supreme Court justices, and the monumental natural disaster of hurricane Katrina devastating New Orleans.

Bushi

Warriors of Japan who grew from provincial warriors in the late **Heian** period to become the dominant class from the twelfth into the nineteenth centuries. The bushi, also known as samurai (warriors/retainers), developed an ethos that emphasized courage, loyalty, and discipline. Unlike the warrior class of feudal Europe, the elite bushi also valued learning and the arts, especially poetry. They were patrons of **Zen Buddhism** and the **tea ceremony**, as well as prizing skill with the sword. During the **Tokugawa** period (1603–1868), two centuries of peace made their warrior role obsolete, and many became civil servants and teachers. Because of their military training and their often broad learning, some bushi were swift to appreciate the need for sweeping reform in the face of the Western incursions in the mid-nineteenth century and led the **Meiji Restoration** in 1868. The new Meiji leaders abolished legal recognition of the class.

Bushido (meaning the "way of the warrior")

Japanese code of training and behavior for the ruling warrior class of Japan known as bushi, or samurai. It emphasized martial skills, especially swordplay; duty and loyalty to superiors; and a sense of personal honor symbolized in the practice of seppuku (ritual suicide, often incorrectly called hara-kiri). Bushido incorporated ideas from **Confucianism, Buddhism,** and **Shinto** and served as an ideal in during the **Tokugawa** period. Later, the ideals of bushido were borrowed and adapted by various modern Japanese, from pre–**World War II** ultranationalists to post–World War II businessmen.

Byron, Lord (George Gordon) (1788–1824)

English lord, Romantic poet, and hero-martyr for Greek independence. Byron was well known for his poetry when he left England in 1823 to fight for Greece in its struggle for independence from the **Ottoman Empire.** In 1824 he died from fever during a botched military assault at Missolonghi. Byron became a hero-martyr for Philhellenes (lovers of ancient Greek culture) throughout Europe, who sent money and volunteers to aid the Greeks. Byron's masterpieces include *The Vision of Judgment* and *Don Juan.*

Byzantine Empire

Eastern half of the **Roman Empire** after the collapse of the empire's western half. The **Eastern Roman Empire** continued after the western half collapsed under the pressure of Germanic invasions and became known as the Byzantine Empire to later historians (people in this region called themselves Romans). It flourished from 476 to 1453 C.E., with its capital at **Constantinople** (formerly Byzantium). Until the thirteenth century it enjoyed a period of imperial brilliance, synthesizing Greco-Roman and Christian culture. Emperor **Justinian** led a revival within the Byzantine Empire that consolidated power; expanded its boundaries; and extended codified law, the **Corpus Juris Civilis**. After 800 years of conflict with the Islamic world, in 1453 the remnants of the Byzantine Empire were conquered by the **Ottoman Turks**, who battered down Constantinople's renowned defensive walls with enormous **cannons**.

C

Cacao

Tree from which cocoa products and **chocolate** are derived; also, the name of the commodity. The tree is indigenous to Central America. In **Mesoamerica** cacao was so prevalent that it was used as currency. Europeans began to show interest in cacao in the sixteenth century, when contact between Europe and the New World was becoming more extensive. It is now cultivated chiefly in Brazil, Venezuela, and western Africa.

Caesar, Julius (c. 100–44 B.C.E.)

Roman general, statesman, and writer. A brilliant military commander and orator, Caesar rose to power through military prowess, political maneuvering, and the support of the common people. As a virtual dictator (47–44 B.C.E.) he implemented many reforms, including introducing the **Julian calendar**, expanding the **Roman Senate**, reducing the debt of the state, and limiting the distribution of free grain. He was assassinated on the Ides of March in 44 B.C.E. because republicans (like **Marcus Brutus** and **Gaius Cassius**) feared that he would make himself king. Caesar's grand-nephew and adopted son, **Octavian**, later rose to power and began the use of the name *Caesar* as a title.

Cairo

Capital city and commercial, financial, industrial, cultural, and educational center of Egypt. It is situated at the head of the Nile River delta. With at least 15 million inhabitants, it is the largest city in the **Middle East**. Cairo was founded in 969 C.E. by the **Fatimids**, a **Shia** Islamic dynasty from Tunis. By 1340, with approximately 500,000 people, it was probably the largest city anywhere outside China. Cairo was not only the gateway to the Nile but the link between East and West. Throughout the **Middle Ages** it was a major depot for the spice trade. By the sixteenth century Cairo had begun to decline in size and importance.

Caliph

Title of Islamic leaders; from the Arabic for "successor." The meaning of the term *successor* is unclear, however. The first caliph of **Islam** was **Abu Bakr** (632–634), successor to **Muhammad** at his death in 632. Muhammad left no sons and had no chosen successor. His closest followers selected Abu Bakr, Muhammad's father-in-law. Some Muslims believed that Muhammad had declared **Ali** his successor, the son of Muhammad's uncle and husband of Muhammad's sole living daughter, Fatima. Ali was selected as the fourth caliph in 656, but he was murdered by a disgruntled follower in 661. The contention over the interpretation of "successor" has led to a divide between **Sunni** (followers of the Abu Bakr line) and **Shia** Muslims (followers of the Ali line).

Caliphate

Leadership of **Islam** dating from **Muhammad**'s death in 632. **Abu Bakr** was chosen as **caliph** ("successor") at Muhammad's death. The first four caliphs are known as the Rashidun ("rightly guided") caliphs—Abu Bakr, **Umar**, Orthman, and **Ali**. The next was the **Umayyad Caliphate**, in Damascus, followed by the **Abbasid caliphate**, in Baghdad. One of the Umayyad caliphs founded the caliphate of Córdoba in Spain. The **Fatimid caliphate** was established in Egypt.

Calpulli (Calpullis)

Units of organization among all Nahuatl-speaking peoples of central, western, and eastern Mexico, including the **Aztec**. Calpullis were large kinship groups to which everyone belonged. They were sometimes used by the elite to organize the commoners to gather tribute to build public projects, such as temples. Each calpulli was a self-governing unit with an elected head and its own temples, schools, and common land.

Calvin, John (1509–1564)

French **Protestant** theologian of the **Reformation** and founder of **Calvinism**. Embracing the new reformed ideas of **Martin Luther** and of Christian **humanism**, Calvin fled persecution in France, going first to Basel then to Geneva in Switzerland. In 1536 he published *Institutes of the Christian Religion* (expanded several times). In Geneva from 1541 onward, Calvin forged a thoroughgoing reform of the state (sometimes called a theocracy, meaning "rule by the godly"). Although Calvin never held a political post, his theology determined the structure of the state. Calvin's influence on Protestant theology spread to Scotland, the Netherlands, and England.

Calvinism

Theology of **John Calvin** (1509–1564) that became one of the dominant strands of European **Protestantism**. Calvinism spread in Switzerland, Scotland (known as Presbyterianism), the Netherlands, and England (known as Puritanism). Calvinism in the form of Puritanism migrated to the North American colonies. Calvinism, like Lutheranism, promotes justification (salvation) by faith, not by works; in the priesthood of all believers; and in predestination, meaning that God decrees who will be saved (the elect) and who will be damned (the reprobate). Some followers of Calvinism looked for signs of "election" in themselves and lived cleanly and worked hard to show that they had God's favor, in what has been called the "Protestant work ethic."

Calvinists. *See* Puritans

Camus, Albert (1913–1960)

Algerian-born French existential philosopher, novelist, and playwright. Camus's philosophy pitted the logical man against the indifferent universe and found it absurd. Against this absurdity, Camus found, humankind rebels, but it is the acceptance of the absurdity that proves human existence. Camus was often in debate, and sometimes bitter feud, with **Jean-Paul Sartre**. Camus's works include the novels *The Stranger* (1942), *The Plague* (1947), and *The Fall* (1956).

Candide. See Voltaire

Cannon

Projectile-firing weapons first developed by Europeans in the early fourteenth century. **Gunpowder** was invented by the Chinese by the tenth century and was used in warfare as well as in fireworks. The Chinese seem to have developed the cannon by the fourteenth century too, possibly even in the thirteenth century, but it was Europeans who progressed in the refinement of cannons. The use of cannons spread to the **Middle East**, and the **Ottoman Turks** used German engineers to manufacture enormous cannon bombards to batter down the defensive walls of **Constantinople** in 1453. The largest fired a cannonball of 1,000 pounds (454 kg) using several hundred pounds of gunpowder. Europeans found that small, maneuverable cannons were much more effective. By the sixteenth century, warfare was heavily determined by cannons.

Canterbury Tales
A group of poems written by the English author **Geoffrey Chaucer** in the 1380s and 1390s. The poems, fictional tales of pilgrims told to one another on their way to the holy site of Canterbury, England, range from classic tragedy to raw sexual comedy. They criticize the clergy as well as all classes of society.

Canton (Guangzhou)
Chinese city in the southern Guandong province. Strategically located at the head of the Pearl River estuary, a city has existed on the site of Canton since at least the second millennium B.C.E. Under the **Tang**, Canton became a major port and a center of international commerce with a large foreign community of Arab and Southeast Asian merchants. From the sixteenth to the nineteenth centuries it was the principal port for trade with Western merchants. Discontent with the "Canton system," which restricted Westerners to the port and to trading with authorized Chinese merchant houses, led to the **Opium Wars**, which opened other ports. Canton remained one of China's most important commercial centers.

Cao Cao (Ts'ao Ts'ao) (155–220)
Chinese military commander who brought much of northern China under his control after the collapse of the **Han Dynasty**. His son established the Wei Dynasty, one of the Three Kingdoms. Later, Cao Cao and his military campaigns became the subject of plays, operas, and the classic novel *The Romance of the Three Kingdoms*.

Cao Dai
Vietnamese syncretic religion that draws from **Buddhism**, **Daoism**, **Christianity**, and other religious traditions. It was founded in 1926 by Ngo Van Chieu, a Vietnamese official in the French colonial government. It combines a belief in karma with a pantheon of saints that include **Jesus, Muhammad**, Victor Hugo, **Pericles**, and **Sun Yat-sen**. During **World War II** the Cao Dai organized an army to resist the Japanese. Although it never claimed more than 2 million adherents, it was a force in South Vietnamese politics up to 1975.

Cape of Good Hope
Promontory on the southern tip of Africa. The first European sighting was by the Portuguese sailor **Bartolomeu Dias** in 1488, as he returned from rounding Africa for the first time. Dias named it Cape of Storms for the severe weather he experienced. Portuguese king John II renamed it Cape of Good Hope for its good fortune in the Portuguese attempt to reach India. The name *Cape of Good Hope* was applied to the major province of southern and western South African, also known as Cape Province.

Capet, Hugh (r. 987–996)
King of France and founder of the **Capetian** dynasty. Very little is known of Hugh, but as founder of the Capetian line he holds great significance in French history.

Capetian
French dynastic line that ruled as kings of France from 987 to 1328. They include

Robert II (r. 996–1031); Philip I (r. 1060–1108); **Philip II**, "Augustus" (r. 1180–1223); **Saint Louis IX** (r. 1226–1270); and **Philip IV**, "the Fair" (r. 1285–1314).

Capitalism

Economic system based on private ownership of the means of production and distribution, free trade, open competition in both products and labor, and motivation by profit. Capitalism has existed throughout history, and regional elements of capitalism may have connected in a world economy in the thirteenth century spreading, from China to Europe. Capitalism became common in Italian cities in the fifteenth century during the **Renaissance**, and later spread with European hegemony. In capitalist systems, workers are paid a wage for their labor but do not own what they produce, and prices are based on supply and demand rather than being set by a political authority.

Caracalla. *See* Aurelius, Antoninus

Carafa, Giovanni Pietro (Pope Paul IV) (1476–1559)

Powerful **Renaissance pope**. Born into a noble Neapolitan family, he became a cardinal in 1536 and was elected pope of the **Roman Catholic Church** in 1555. Hot-tempered, Carafa gave church positions to relatives who often turned out to be incompetent and became involved in a disastrous war with **Philip II** of Spain. His legacy includes reforming the church to cut down expenses, and leading the harsh Roman **Inquisition** (1542) to combat heresy.

Cárdenas, Lázaro (1895–1970)

Mexican president (1934–1940) who implemented the ideals of the **Mexican Revolution**, including nationalizing industries, land reform, secularizing education, and offering loans to peasants. Cárdenas was a popular and successful Mexican politician. He was president of the National Revolutionary Party in 1930, minister of the interior in 1931, and minister of war and marine in 1933 before becoming Mexico's chief executive. He became the symbol of Mexican nationalism after his expropriation of U.S.- and British-owned petroleum firms in 1938. After his presidency he was made commander of Mexico's Pacific Coast forces during **World War II**.

Cardinals, College of

The **Roman Catholic Church**'s body that acts as assistants and advisers to the supreme pontiff, or pope, and selects the next pontiff. The College of Cardinals dates from the twelfth century, although there were cardinals even before then. The pope chooses cardinals from among the Catholic clergy.

Carnegie, Andrew (1835–1919)

American industrialist and philanthropist. Born in Dunfermline, Scotland, Carnegie's family emigrated to Pittsburgh, Pennsylvania, in 1848. Carnegie founded a steel company, Carnegie Steel (later, U.S. Steel) that became the largest in the world. He gave enormous amounts of money to institutions in the United States and Britain, ranging from public libraries and universities to peace institutes and educational foundations.

Carolingian. *See* Charlemagne (Charles the Great)

Carranza, Venustiano (1859–1920)

Mexican revolutionary and president of Mexico (1917–1920). Carranza played a major role in shaping both the **Mexican Revolution** after 1913 and the constitution of 1917. As a moderate president, Carranza angered the more radical **Emiliano Zapata** and **Pancho Villa**, who fought to overthrow him. Driven from office, Carranza was then assassinated.

Carter, Jimmy (1924–)

Thirty-ninth president of the United States (full name: James Earl Carter Jr.). Elected in 1976, Carter sought to restore trust to government following the Watergate scandal. His domestic accomplishments were few, and his programs suffered from a lagging economy. In foreign policy, Carter sought to emphasize human rights, returned the Canal Zone to Panama, brokered the Camp David Accords for the Middle East, and continued arms-control negotiations with the Soviet Union. His administration was crippled by the Iran hostage crisis, and it suffered further with the collapse of détente following the Soviet invasion of Afghanistan, both in 1979. He was defeated by **Ronald Reagan** in 1980. By the 1990s Jimmy Carter had established himself as a world statesman.

Carthage

Phoenician colony and, later, a major Roman city on the Mediterranean coast of North Africa. Founded probably in the eighth century B.C.E., Carthage became a very important trading center. By the sixth century B.C.E. it had its own ruling oligarchy and controlled mercenary armies, but, most importantly, Carthage controlled sea trade routes. It came to control Sardinia, parts of Sicily, and Spain. Carthage and **Rome** had treaties in 508 and 348 B.C.E. but came to blows in 264 B.C.E. in the first **Punic War**. The Punic Wars eventually brought the destruction of Carthage in 146 B.C.E. By the second century C.E. Carthage was the second city after Rome in the western Roman Empire.

Cassius, Gaius (c. 79–42 B.C.E.)

Roman military commander, politician, and leader of a conspiracy against **Julius Caesar**. Commander of part of the Roman navy, a magistrate, and imperial legate, Cassius led the conspirators who assassinated Caesar (44 B.C.E.). **Mark Antony**, in retaliation, defeated Cassius (42 B.C.E.), and Cassius ordered his own freed slaves to slay Antony.

Caste

A social ranking based on birth. In **Hinduism**, birth into a caste is based on the notion of reincarnation. Hindus maintain that a person is born into a caste because of good or bad deeds in an earlier life. Anthropologists refer to the notion of purity and pollution as the fundamental premise of a caste system.

Castiglione, Baldassare (1478–1529 C.E.)

Italian author of *The Courtier* (1528), one of the most influential writings of the **Renaissance**. Castiglione used his experience as diplomat to write this guide. Describing the "perfect" courtier and court lady, it was a popular guide for social relations. It illustrates a concern with outward appearance and reputation, offering a glimpse into the sixteenth-century Italian court of **Urbino**.

Castle

Fortified building occupied in most instances by a nobleman and his family. A royal castle was often a large building or a set of connected, fortified buildings including the central keep or donjon, a surrounding wall with defensive towers, and a courtyard, occupied by numerous knights and support staff. A castle provided a defense against almost any attack, enabling the nobleman to maintain control over a region of land.

Castro, Fidel (1927–)

Cuban revolutionary and communist leader of Cuba since 1959. Castro led a revolution that in 1958 drove out the corrupt dictator General Fulgencio Batista. He declared himself prime minister, a title he held until 1976, and then became president of the Council of State and the Council of Ministers. Castro transformed Cuba into one of the leading countries of Latin America in terms of health, education, and welfare and the first communist nation in the Western Hemisphere. Since coming to power Castro has been in conflict with the United States and its presidents from **John F. Kennedy** to **George W. Bush**, who refused to allow a socialist country in their backyard. Castro allied with the **Union of Soviet Socialist Republics** after the **Bay of Pigs** invasion of Cuba in 1961 and allowed missiles to be placed on Cuban soil, leading to the **Cuban Missile Crisis** in 1962. Since the collapse of the Soviet Union in 1990, Castro has led Cuba through severe economic crises. He has moved to embrace market forces at the beginning of the twenty-first century, as a way of forestalling national bankruptcy.

Çatal Hüyük (Çatal Hayük or Catalhuyuk)

Neolithic site in south-central Turkey, first excavated by British archaeologists (1961–1965). Dated circa 7250–6150 B.C.E., the town's as many as 8,000 inhabitants lived in brick houses, which were entered from the roof via ladders and contained ovens and sleeping and working platforms. The surrounding land supported an **agrarian society** cultivating plants and rearing livestock. The residents of Çatal Hüyük manufactured baskets, leather goods, metal tools, pots, and jewelry. They also produced refined wall paintings.

Catapult

Machine for throwing objects through the air in warfare. Catapults have been used since ancient times to throw stones, pieces of metal, arrows, or flammable or explosive matter. The Romans were very effective at catapult construction. Catapults have been used in most civilizations, often as siege machines to attack fortifications.

Cathedral

The church of a diocese in the **Roman Catholic Church**. Whatever church a **bishop** resides as administrator of the diocese is considered a cathedral. Therefore size does not make a church a cathedral; however, most diocesan churches would need to be large.

Catherine of Aragon (1485–1563)

Spanish princess, daughter of **Ferdinand of Aragon** and **Isabella** and the first wife of **Henry VIII** of England (1509). Married first to Henry's older brother Arthur, at Arthur's death the pope granted a dispensation to allow Catherine to marry Henry. Catherine bore Henry a daughter, the future **Mary I**, but no male heir. When she was beyond childbearing years, Henry sought to annul his marriage to Catherine on the grounds that he should not have married his brother's wife but in reality to gain a male heir. The ensuing conflict over the annulment (1533) led to the English church's split from the **Roman Catholic Church**.

Catherine of Siena, Saint (born Caterina Benincasa) (1347–1380)

Italian mystic and patron saint of Italy. A tertiary (member of a monastic order who takes simple vows but may remain outside a convent), Catherine of Siena gained a reputation for her holiness. She helped to resolve a conflict between the **papacy** and the city of **Florence** in 1376, played a role in resolving the conflict known as the **Avignon Captivity** (**Babylonian Captivity**) in 1378, and helped to reorganize the church under Pope **Urban VI**.

Catherine II, "the Great" (1729–1796)
Empress of **Russia** (1762–1796) and "Enlightened Despot." German-born Catherine organized the assassination of her husband, Tsar Peter III, and seized the throne. She was notorious for her sexual appetites and her ruthlessness. Oriented toward the West, Catherine read the **Enlightenment** writers and attempted social and political reform for Russia, mostly unsuccessfully. Two wars with Turkey, a Cossack rebellion, and entrenched aristocratic resistance ended her interest in reform. In Catherine's later life she banned Enlightenment writings in Russia.

Catholic Church. *See* Roman Catholic Church

Catholic Counter Reformation. *See* Catholic Reformation

Catholic Reformation
Movement to reform the **Roman Catholic Church** in the sixteenth century. The **Reformation** began with individuals within the church attempting to bring about reforms, with some of them breaking away from the Catholic Church to form **Protestant** churches. In response, or counter to the Protestant reforms (hence the alternative term **Counter Reformation**), and with the establishment of the **Society of Jesus** or Jesuits (1540), reforms within Catholicism gained momentum. The **Council of Trent** (1545–1563) corrected many of the problems of the Catholic Church. By the second half of the sixteenth century the Catholic Church had become reinvigorated and Catholic missionaries were active in reconverting Protestants in Europe and gaining new converts in Asia, Africa, and the New World.

Catullus (c. 87–54 B.C.E.) (Gaius Valerius Catullus)
Roman poet of the new school of poetry of the first century B.C.E. Catullus wrote polished verses of love, often very vivid poems about his girlfriend.

Caucasus
Geographic region between the Black and the Caspian seas that has produced many peoples and languages. Caucasian or Caucasoid peoples have spread throughout Europe, North Africa, the **Middle East**, and India. This is also the region from which the **Indo-European** languages may have originated and spread.

Caudillos
Latin American local strongmen from the nineteenth century onward who filled a vacuum left by the collapse of colonial authority. As countries became independent from Spain, these military strongmen seized power, took control of the state, and perpetuated their power by controlling the masses and protecting the power of the elites.

Cavour, Camillo, Conte di (1810–1861)
Italian statesman and leader of the unification of Italy. Cavour pushed for unification from the 1840s, founding the newspaper *Il Risorgimento*. He became premier of Piedmont and established an alliance with France, fighting in the Franco-Austrian War, all the while working for Italian unification. In 1861 Cavour became premier of a united Italy under the newly crowned king Victor Emmanuel.

Celts
Members of an **Indo-European** linguistic group widespread in western and central Europe in the first millennium B.C.E. Archaeological sites, like that in La Tène, Switzerland (c. 450–50 B.C.E.), give clues to the Celts' polytheistic mythology, skilled metalwork, and their village-based hierarchical society (headed by nobles and priests called Druids). The Celts did not

keep written records, so early literary accounts come from Greek and Roman writers (like **Julius Caesar**). Powerful enough in 390 B.C.E. to sack **Rome**, they were conquered by the Romans (who called them Gauls) and the **Germanic tribes** by the first century B.C.E. and pushed into Ireland, Brittany, Scotland, Wales, and Cornwall. The Celtic culture came to embrace and spread **Christianity**.

Central Asia

Term used to designate the central region of the Eurasian landmass, also called Inner Asia. The boundaries of Central Asia are vague, but the region is usually defined as including grassland **steppe** from the Urals to Manchuria, the **Gobi Desert**, and the deserts and river valleys of **Turkestan**. Some people include Afghanistan and the Tibetan Plateau as well. Some of the valleys are especially suitable for agriculture. Central Asia has been important as a crossroads linking the civilizations and cultures of Europe, the **Middle East**, and Asia. The **Silk Roads** traversed it. The region also gave birth to many formidable nomadic-warrior confederations. With the conquest of most of the region by Russia and China in the eighteenth and nineteenth centuries and the decline and disappearance of the overland caravan trade, Central Asia lost some of its former importance; however, as the Afghan War (2001–) demonstrated, it still is of strategic importance.

Central Intelligence Agency (CIA)

Principal U.S. intelligence agency in the period following **World War II**. The Central Intelligence Agency (CIA) was established by the National Security Act of 1947 to serve as a coordinating agency for all foreign intelligence–related activities of the U.S. government. Its creation was inspired by the intelligence failures leading to the attack on Pearl Harbor, the wartime experience of the Office of Strategic Services, and the growing need for intelligence that came with the onset of the **Cold War**. The CIA's principal role is to collect and assess intelligence in support of U.S. foreign policy, but it has also been involved in numerous covert operations against unfriendly governments, parties, and individuals. The exposure, failure, or questionable nature of a number of these covert operations led to congressional investigations in the 1970s and 1980s and sporadic criticism since then, which has often obscured the CIA's many analytical successes.

Centuriate Assembly

Originally a group of 100 within the Roman army, a unit of a legion composed of sixty centuries. The Centuriate Assembly, dating from the fifth century B.C.E., was made up of centuries of cavalry and foot-soldiers and some centuries of noncombatants. Reforms to the Centuriate Assembly in the third century B.C.E. left 193 century voting units.

Cervantes, Miguel de (1547–1616 C.E.)

Spanish writer best known for the novel *Don Quixote* (1605, 1615). This playwright, poet, and novelist produced innovative literature in sixteenth-century Spain. Cervantes used irony in his work to challenge the traditional values in Spain with **Renaissance** ideals.

Chaco War (1932–1935)

Conflict between Paraguay and Bolivia over the Chaco, a huge area of 250,000 square miles with a sparse population but with petroleum, which both countries claimed. Despite the Bolivian force's being larger and better-trained, the Paraguayans took advantage of their superior knowledge of the terrain and clever tactics to gain victory. A treaty was signed in 1938, with Paraguay receiving three-quarters of the Chaco and Bolivia the remaining one-quarter.

Chalukyas

Ruling dynasties in the **Deccan Plateau** of India from the mid-sixth to the mid-eighth century, and from 973 to the late twelfth century. In the seventh century, the Chalukyas under Pulakesin II (r. 608–662) checked the southern advance of **Harsha**'s empire. The backbone of the Chalukya states was the Western Ghats; their northern capital was visited by the Chinese Buddhist traveler **Xuanzang**. After suffering a defeat by **Chola** in 642 they were replaced by the Rashtrakutas as the dominant power in the Deccan, but a second Chalukya dynasty arose in the tenth century.

Chamberlain, Neville (1869–1940)

British prime minister (1937–1940) who signed the **Munich Pact** (1938) as a policy of appeasement toward **Nazi** Germany. Chamberlain traveled to Munich, Germany, to reach an agreement allowing **Adolf Hitler**'s Germany to gain control of western Czechoslovakia, the **Sudetenland**, in return for Hitler's halt to further expansion. He returned to Britain proclaiming "peace for our time," but only five months later German forces marched into the rest of Czechoslovakia. Chamberlain resigned when Germany invaded Belgium.

Champa

Kingdom in what is now the southern part of Vietnam established by the Chams, a people speaking a language related to Malay. Probably established in the second century C.E., Champa was conquered by Annam in the fifteenth century, although a small state survived until the seventeenth century. A center of trade, it was reputed to be the origin of "Champa rice," a quick-ripening variety that led to an increase in population growth and prosperity in southern China when introduced there in the eleventh century. Champa also played an important role in the South China sea trade.

Chandra Gupta (r. c. 320–330)

Third ruler of the **Gupta Empire**, who established it as the dominant power in northern India for two centuries.

Chandragupta Maurya (r. c. 325–297 B.C.E.)

Founder of the **Maurya Empire**, the first to extend its rule over most of the Indian subcontinent. He overthrew the Magadha kingdom in northeastern India and established his capital at Pataliputra (now Patna, in Bihar state) and extended his empire to the **Indus River** and Afghanistan.

Chandragupta II (r. c. 375–415)

Gupta emperor, son of Samudra Gupta and grandson of **Chandra Gupta**, whose reign marked the cultural apogee of the **Gupta Empire**. He extended the empire, adding Gujarat in the east and Malwa in the west. Reputed to be an able ruler, he earned the title Vikramaditya ("Sun of Valor"). His court in Ayodhya included the **Sanskrit** playwright **Kalidasa** and the Chinese pilgrim **Faxian**.

Chang'an. *See* Xi'an (Hsi-an)

Chanson de Geste

Song of praise of heroic deeds. A type of Old French epic poem of the twelfth century, the *Chanson de geste* was popular among the aristocracy in the **Middle Ages**. One of the earliest and greatest of the Chansons de geste is *Song of Roland* (*Chanson de Roland*).

Chanson de Roland. See *Song of Roland*

Charlemagne (Charles the Great)
(742–814)
King of the **Franks** and builder of a great
empire. Charles ruled jointly with his
brother Carloman in 768, but following
Carloman's death in 771 Charles ruled
alone until 814. On December 25, 800,
Charlemagne was crowned emperor of
the Romans by the **pope**, though what
this meant is not exactly clear because the
western **Roman Empire** no longer existed. Under Charlemagne, the Frankish
"empire" was expanded to incorporate
much of the old western Roman Empire. The capital was at **Aachen**, where
Charlemagne gathered scholars from all
over Europe. He instituted numerous reforms in what is known as the Carolingian
Renaissance, including legal reforms; the
spread of a new script (the Carolingian mi-
nuscule); church reforms; a new currency
of pounds, shillings, and pence; and, especially, intellectual reforms that invigorated
scholarship. Under his leadership books
were gathered and copied, libraries were
built up, great illuminated manuscripts
were produced, and great churches with
innovative new features were built. Charlemagne forged a strong alliance with the
papacy of the **Roman Catholic Church**.

Charles I (1600–1649)
King of England, Ireland, and Scotland
(1625–1649) whose conflicts with **Parliament** brought about the **English Civil War**.
Charles I's belief in the divine right of kings
and absolute monarchy ran up against the
growing authority of Parliament. War
broke out in 1642, and in 1649 Charles was
convicted of treason and beheaded.

Charles II (1630–1685)
King of England, Ireland, and Scotland
(acceded 1649, restored 1660–1685). Son

of **Charles I**, and a Stuart (royal family
from Scotland that ascended the throne of
England in 1603), he attempted to take the
crown by military force after his father's
execution but was defeated. At the fall of
the protectorate republic (after the execution of Charles I, England became a republic and in 1653 **Oliver Cromwell** was
made Lord Protector or virtual dictator),
Charles was invited to return as king in
1660. He supported the establishment of
the Royal Society, a scientific organization.
Following his death, his brother, **James
II**, ruled.

Charles V (1500–1558)
Holy Roman emperor (1519–1556), king
of Spain (as **Charles I**, 1516–1556), and
archduke of Austria (1519–1521). At-
taining the rule of the Netherlands at age
fifteen, Spain at sixteen, and the **Holy
Roman Empire** at nineteen, Charles ruled
over much of Europe as well as Spanish
America. He struggled against the rise of
Protestantism in the **Reformation**, antag-
onism in the west with France, and antago-
nism in the east with the **Ottoman Turks**.
Charles declared war on Protestantism, a
movement that after his death would
break up his empire in the Netherlands. In
1527 Charles's imperial troops opposed
France and marched into Italy against
the **pope**, sacking **Rome**. Charles tried to
reform the **Roman Catholic Church**,
and in 1545 the **Council of Trent** was
called, which eventually brought about reforms. Charles, worn out by conflicts and
wracked by physical pain, abdicated his
role in the Netherlands and Spain to his
son **Philip II** and his title of emperor to
his brother Ferdinand I. Charles retired
to a **monastery** in Spain for his last years.

Charles the Bold (1433–1477)
Duke of **Burgundy** (1467–1477). Charles
built Burgundy into a powerful dukedom,

expanding his territories into the Rhineland and nearly establishing a kingdom independent of France, aligning himself with the Holy Roman Emperor. Charles was killed in battle with the Swiss, and his dukedom was divided between the king of France and the emperor.

Charles the Great. *See* Charlemagne (Charles the Great)

Charon
Ancient Greek mythological boatman of the passage to the underworld. Charon (pronounced "KAY-run") ferried the dead across the River Styx to Hades. The dead had to pay with a copper coin, so in Greek burials a coin was put under the tongue of the dead. Otherwise, souls were forced to wander for years before Charon would ferry them across to their rest.

Chaucer, Geoffrey (c. 1342–1400)
English medieval writer, author of the poems the *Canterbury Tales*. Chaucer wrote in Middle English (related to modern English) at a time when vernacular English was beginning to replace Latin and French as the language of literature and of literate English people. He traveled to France and Italy, where he was influenced by the literature, especially **Giovanni Boccaccio**'s *The Decameron*. Chaucer wrote numerous other poems. *Canterbury Tales* satirizes many of the institutions of medieval society such as the church, clergy, knighthood, and marriage.

Chavín Culture
Early, highly developed culture in pre-Columbian Peru named after Chavín de Huántar, the archaeological site where most of the culture's religious iconography was found. The site, located in northern Peru, is one of several centers of Andean civilization that were unified for the first time by a common religion or culture. The estimated period during which Chavín culture flourished is 900–200 B.C.E.

Cheng Ho. *See* Zheng He (Cheng Ho)

Chiang Ching-kuo (Jiang Jingguo)
(1910–1988)
President of the Republic of China (Taiwan) from 1978 to 1988. The son of **Guomindang** (Nationalist Party) leader **Chiang Kai-shek**, he served in many positions in the government and became the party leader when his father died in 1975. Although a loyal supporter of his father, he carried out democratic reforms during his presidency and brought many Taiwanese into positions of power, including Lee Tung-hui, whom he made his successor.

Chiang Kai-shek (Jiang Jieshi)
(1887–1975)
Chinese leader who gained control of the **Guomindang** (Nationalist Party) in 1926 and headed it until his death forty-nine years later. From 1928 to 1937 his government in Nanjing established its rule over most of China. From 1937 to 1945 he led the nationalist resistance to the Japanese, but he was defeated by the communists in the civil war that followed and fled with the remnants of his regime to Taiwan in 1949. Although his rule on the Chinese mainland was ultimately a failure marred by corruption and brutality, in Taiwan he promoted reforms and presided over an impressive economic transformation of the island state. Until his death, he claimed that the Republic of China on Taiwan was the legitimate government of all China and that it would eventually return to oust the communists. His wife **Soong Mei-ling** was a prominent figure who helped him gain U.S. support for his regime on the mainland and Taiwan. He was succeeded as head of the Guomindang by his son **Chiang Ching-kuo.**

Chichén Itzá

One of the most prominent cities of the **Maya** during the postclassical era, located in the northern Yucatán Peninsula. The Itzá group founded the city in the early sixth century but abandoned it around 670. The city was rebuilt in the tenth century with the return of the Itzá, when it became a center of Maya culture. **Toltec** invaders ruled the city until roughly 1200, further developing the architecture and culture. By the time of the Spanish arrival in the early sixteenth century, however, the city had been abandoned for at least a hundred years.

Chikamatsu, Monzaemon (1653–1725)

Japanese literary figure of the **Tokugawa** period, generally regarded as Japan's greatest playwright. Chikamatsu transformed Japanese theater by developing both dramatic structure and characters portrayed with psychological insightfulness. Many of his themes dealt with historical episodes, but others dealt with the lives of middle-class townspeople. His plays, patronized by the commercial classes, were part of the vigorous urban cultural life of Tokugawa Japan.

Chimú

Powerful state in northern Peru from the twelfth to the fifteenth centuries. The Chimú civilization was agrarian, yet they built large irrigation systems and the capital, Chan, was an enormous city with rectangular city blocks, great walls, and pyramid temples. Chimú was conquered by the Incas by the 1470s.

China, Republic of. *See* Republic of China

Chinese Characters (*Hanzi*)

System of writing developed in China in the second millennium B.C.E. and still used today, the oldest continuously used system of writing in the world. *Hanzi* is an ideographic script, in which each symbol represents a word or an idea rather than a sound. The earliest surviving examples are on bones and tortoise shells from **Shang** and, perhaps, pre-Shang times. The script was adopted by the Vietnamese, Koreans, and Japanese and is still used, along with phonetic symbols, by the latter two.

Chinese Communist Party (CCP)

Chinese political party organized in Shanghai in 1921 by Li Dazhao and Chen Duxiu. Under the influence of the Comintern in Moscow, the party organized in Chinese cities but was severely repressed by the **Guomindang** (Nationalist Party) in 1927. After the CCP established bases in the countryside, first in Jiangxi in southern China, and then after the Long March (1934–1935), party leaders fled to the remote northwest and established their headquarters in Yanan. In 1935 **Mao Zedong** was elected party leader. Under Mao the party, based mainly on the peasantry, came to power in 1949 after a civil war and established the **People's Republic of China**. After Mao's death in 1976 the CCP deviated from its strict adherence to socialist ideas but remained the ruling and only legal party of China.

Chinggis Khan. *See* Genghis Khan (Chinggis Khan)

Chivalry

Code of behavior for warriors and the aristocracy in the **Middle Ages**. Chivalry was a mixture of Christian and military codes of ethics designed to rein in the lawlessness and brutality of the tenth and eleventh centuries. Chivalry set standards for knightly treatment of other warriors and treatment of women and by the thirteenth century was expressed in tournaments and general aristocratic attitudes. New orders such as the Knights Templar and Knights Hospitaller took chivalry to the **Crusades**.

Chocolate

Food native to Central America and introduced to Europe in the seventeenth century, made from **cacao**. **Aztec** warriors drank a concoction of chocolate before going into battle because it acted as a stimulant. It was considered a divine beverage and was forbidden to commoners. Not until the seventeenth century and its entry into Europe was chocolate mixed with milk and sugar. It became a very fashionable drink, along with **coffee** and tea, in seventeenth- and eighteenth-century Europe.

Chola (Cola)

Tamil dynasty and state that dominated much of southern India from the ninth to the thirteenth centuries. Based in what is now Tamil Nadu state in India, the Cholas ruled from at least the third century C.E. Under Rajaraja I (985–1018) and Rajendra I (1018–1048) they created a maritime as well as a continental empire that controlled many of the sea-lanes in the eastern Indian Ocean. Chola sponsored Tamil art and literature and contributed to the spread of Indian culture over much of Southeast Asia.

Chongqing (Chungking)

Chinese city in Sichuan Province in south-central China. Located at the confluence of the Jialing and **Yangzi** rivers, it has been an important city for centuries. During **World War II** it served as the capital of the **Chiang Kai-shek's Guomindang** (Nationalist Party) regime (1939–1945), selected because of its remoteness from the Japanese-controlled coastal areas. The Japanese bombed Chongqing many times but failed to capture it.

Choson

The name of an ancient Korean state and the name for Korea under the Yi Dynasty (1392–1910). It is derived from the Chinese *Chao Xian* ("Morning Freshness," sometimes translated as "Land of the Morning Calm"). Ancient Choson, sometimes called Old Choson, was located in northern Korea from at least the third century B.C.E. until its conquest by China in 108 B.C.E. The later Choson (Korea of the Yi Dynasty) was a period of increased influence of Chinese culture and, especially, of **Neo-Confucian** thought. Korea during the Choson period became East Asia's most **Confucianist** society and was a loyal tributary of **Ming** and, later, **Qing** China. It also pursued a policy of isolationism that earned it the epithet "the Hermit Kingdom" by Westerners until it was forcibly opened by Japan in 1876. After a period of unsuccessful reforms and foreign interventions, Korea was annexed by Japan in 1910.

Chou. *See* Zhou (Chou) Period

Christianity

Religion founded in the first century C.E. in the **Middle East** in the **Roman Empire**. Christianity came out of **Judaism** and maintains many similar beliefs: in one god, in ethical behavior, that God's expectations were transmitted through prophets. Additionally, Christians believe in **Jesus** Christ as the messiah, the son of God sent to wash sins from believers. Christianity was developed into an independent religion from Judaism by **Paul the Apostle** (formerly Saul of Tarsus). Christians were originally persecuted, but by the fourth century the religion was protected within the Roman Empire, and by the end of the fourth century it became the empire's official religion. Several **Germanic tribes** converted to Christianity in the fifth and sixth centuries, and when the **Franks** converted they began a long tradition of collaboration between church and state in Europe. In the eleventh century the **Eastern Orthodox** and western **Roman Catholic** churches split. In the sixteenth century European Christianity further divided during the **Reformation**. Christianity is found worldwide and along with **Islam** is one of the largest world religions.

Chulalongkorn (1853–1910)

King of Siam (Thailand) who reigned as Rama V from 1868–1910. After traveling abroad early in his reign, he pursued a number of modernizing reforms and appointed technical advisors from several Western countries. His most important achievement resulted from his astute diplomacy, which he used to play the colonial powers Britain and France against each other to preserve Thailand's independence. He was forced to cede some southern territory to the British in Malay and to surrender claims in Laos to France. In the process of consolidating his kingdom and making concessions to the colonial powers, Chulalongkorn established the present boundaries of Thailand.

Churchill, Sir Winston Leonard Spencer (1874–1965)

British statesman, prime minister, and author. Born at Blenheim Palace to Lord Randolph Churchill and Jeannete Jerome and educated at Harrow School and Sandhurst military academy, Churchill served in the military and as a civilian correspondent. During **World War I** Churchill served as first lord of the Admiralty. At the outbreak of **World War II** he was recalled to the Admiralty. Then, as the war began and Britain was in dire straits, Churchill was appointed prime minister by King George VI. Churchill's brilliant grasp of the English language rallied the British people to

continue fighting Germany and Italy. Churchill served as a member of Parliament almost continuously from 1901 to 1963.

Cicero, Marcus Tullius (106–43 B.C.E.)

Roman statesman, defender of the **Roman Republic**, and one of the greatest writers in Roman literature. Cicero refused to join the dominant political powers and turned to writing philosophy, political theory, and oratory. Nearly 1,000 of his letters survive. Cicero was condemned to death by **Octavian**, **Marc Antony**, and Marcus Lepidus and was assassinated for his support of **Julius Caesar**'s murder. Cicero's Latin prose style became the standard in Western literature.

Cincinnatus, Lucius Quinctius (c. 519–439 B.C.E.)

Roman statesman and general known for his willingness to take command of the Roman army, achieve victory, and then resign his post and return to his farm. In 458 B.C.E. Cincinnatus was commander in chief for sixteen days and upon completing his job stepped down.

Cinque Ports

Five medieval English port towns. Hastings, Dover, Sandwich, Romney, and Hythe were required to provide ships annually for the king in return for certain privileges. The Cinque Ports (pronounced "sink" ports) were essential to the defense of the English realm.

Ciompi Revolt (1378)

Revolt of the lowest cloth workers (*ciompi*) in **Florence**, Italy. The Ciompi Revolt was an indication that the social orders were shifting in the late **Middle Ages**, as also seen in the 1381 **Peasants' Revolt** in England. The immediate result was the establishment of a ciompi **guild** and a temporary sharing of municipal power.

Circus Maximus

Circus, or oval structure, used for races in ancient Rome. The Circus Maximus accommodated an audience of 250,000. Horse races and horse-and-chariot races were wildly popular, like the battles in the **Colosseum**. Every major Roman city had a circus and/or a stadium. This entertainment pacified the urban masses, providing order.

Cisalpine. *See* Gaul

City-State

Political unit in which a city controls or dominates surrounding territory as an autonomous country. The city-states of medieval and **Renaissance** Italy included **Venice**, **Florence**, and Genoa, where the cities politically and economically controlled large surrounding territories. The **Aegean City-State**, or **polis**, of ancient Greece was technically somewhat different because the city and the countryside were considered equal. With the rise of larger states in the sixteenth and seventeenth centuries, the small European city-states often were militarily defeated and gradually consolidated.

Civilization (from the Latin for "city")

Societies developed enough to have cities. Many cultures throughout global history were not civilizations. Beginning about 5,000–6,000 years ago, more complex ways of life began to appear, with irrigation used to increase agricultural production and systems that made it possible to support and organize larger populations. Early civilizations include the **Harappan**, Chinese **Shang**, **Egyptian**, **Mesoamerican**, and the **Mesopotamian** civilizations of **Sumer**, **Akkadia**, and **Babylonia**. The period in which these civilizations arose in the Old World is known as the **Bronze Age**. The Mesoamerican civilization had late developments in metallurgy but had monumental architecture similar to that of several other civilizations.

Civil Rights Act of 1964

Legislation that ended discrimination based on race, color, religion, or national origin in the United States. The legislation was brought before Congress in 1963 and was under debate when President **John F. Kennedy** was assassinated. The new president, **Lyndon B. Johnson**, worked to pass it. On February 10, 1964, the House of Representatives passed the bill 290–130. It was debated at great length in the **Senate**, and on July 2, 1964, Johnson signed the Civil Rights Act into law. It was the most significant piece of civil rights legislation in U.S. history. The act prohibited discrimination in public businesses and enterprises, including public accommodations like hotels, restaurants, gas stations, and places of entertainment. It demanded that employers provide equal employment opportunities and prohibited discrimination in any federally funded program. Segregated schools would no longer receive federal funds. This act essentially ended official racial segregation on every level of U.S. society.

Civil Rights Movement

Post–**World War II** effort to attain full social and political equality for African Americans and other minorities. The civil rights movement was a multifaceted undertaking including legal challenges to inequality, legislation, and mass political action. While there were limited accomplishments in the late 1940s and early 1950s, such as the desegregation of the armed forces and favorable rulings in some court challenges to segregation in graduate education, the mid-1950s saw the movement accelerate with the Supreme

Court ruling in *Brown v. Board of Education* (1954), the second *Brown* decision (1955), and a successful Montgomery, Alabama, bus boycott (1955–1956). In 1957, Dr. **Martin Luther King Jr.** formed the Southern Christian Leadership Conference (SCLC) to coordinate the mass movement; Congress passed a civil rights act; and President **Dwight D. Eisenhower** dispatched federal troops to Little Rock, Arkansas, to enforce school desegregation. Mass political action increased in the early 1960s, with lunch counter sit-ins in Greensboro, North Carolina, and elsewhere in 1960 and the formation of the more confrontational Student Non-Violent Coordinating Committee (SNCC). In 1961 "freedom rides" sponsored by the Congress of Racial Equality (CORE) sought desegregation of interstate transportation. The next two years saw mass marches in Albany, Georgia, and Birmingham, Alabama, as well as successful efforts to integrate the University of Mississippi and the University of Alabama. In many instances demonstrators were met with violence, often from local police. Media coverage helped sway public opinion outside the South in favor of the movement and compelled the administration of President **John F. Kennedy** to take action in support of the protesters. King led a massive rally in Washington, where he delivered his "I Have a Dream" speech in 1963. Following Kennedy's death, President **Lyndon B. Johnson** achieved passage of the **Civil Rights Act of 1964** and the Voting Rights Act of 1965, while northern activists led a "Freedom Summer" campaign to register black voters in Mississippi in 1964, amid much violence from local opponents. Other marches followed, including the 1965 Selma to Jackson march in Mississippi, again meeting a violent response. By the mid-1960s the frustration of rising expectations led to destructive riots in a number of cities, including Newark, New Jersey; Los Angeles, California; and Detroit, Michigan, while more radical black nationalist organizations, such as the **Black Panthers**, challenged the mainstream civil rights movement and its nonviolent tactics. In 1968 King attempted to broaden the objectives of the movement with an antipoverty campaign and support for striking black workers. King was assassinated in Memphis, Tennessee, on April 4, 1968, while helping to support a strike by sanitation workers. The mass-action phase of the movement largely ended with his death. Since 1968 the movement has focused on legal and legislative remedies, including affirmative action, school busing, economic opportunity, and the problem of de facto segregation, making additional progress toward the goal of full equality but thus far falling short of complete fulfillment.

Civil Service Examinations
Examinations for government positions. The use of civil service examinations as a way of selecting officials to serve a state originated in China as early as the **Han Dynasty** (202 B.C.E.–220 C.E.). The imperial government experimented with the practice, and beginning in the **Tang** Dynasty (618–907) it became a major and systematic method for recruiting the officialdom that administered the Chinese empire. A series of highly competitive exams screened out all but a few applicants for government posts. The system increased the prestige of officials and of the state they served, and it promoted literacy and **Confucianism** because mastery of the Confucian classics was an essential part of most exams. The system was adopted in Korea in 958. The use of civil service examinations attracted the attention of Europeans thinkers in the eighteenth century, contributing to the introduction of the

practice in Western countries in the nineteenth century.

Civil War, American. *See* American Civil War

Ci Xi. *See* Empress Dowager (Ci Xi)

Cleisthenes (c. 570–507 B.C.E.)
Ancient Greek founder of Athenian **democracy.** After a period of tyranny by **Peisistratus** and **Hippias,** civil war broke out in **Athens** in 510 B.C.E. The aristocracy tried to reestablish an oligarchy, but Cleisthenes, an aristocrat, opposed this plan. To gain support, he went to the Athenian people, known as the *demos.* In 508 Cleisthenes created an assembly of all male citizens that legislated for Athens; hence Athens became the first **democracy.**

Clement VII (1478–1534)
Roman Catholic pope (1523–1534) during the **Reformation.** Clement VII aligned himself with the French king **Francis I** and brought on the wrath of the Holy Roman emperor **Charles V.** Charles's imperial troops attacked and sacked **Rome** in 1527 and temporarily imprisoned Clement. Clement also refused to grant English king **Henry VIII** a divorce from **Catherine of Aragon,** which led to the English church splitting from Rome and the spread of the Reformation to England.

Cleopatra VII (69–30 B.C.E.)
Last **Ptolemy** ruler of Egypt. Cleopatra was joint ruler with Ptolemy XIII in 51 B.C.E., was driven from power in 48 B.C.E., and was restored by **Julius Caesar** in 47 B.C.E. She had a son by Caesar (by her claim) and accompanied him to **Rome.** Following his assassination in 44 B.C.E., Cleopatra returned to Egypt, met **Mark Antony** in 41 B.C.E., and gave birth to his twins. In 34 B.C.E. Antony and Cleopatra divided the

Eastern Roman Empire between her and her children, but **Octavian** declared war on her in 32 B.C.E. and at the **Battle of Actium** defeated the Egyptian forces and Roman forces under Antony. Cleopatra was taken prisoner, and in 30 B.C.E. committed suicide. Egypt became part of the **Roman Empire.**

Climatic Change
Scientifically noted changes in the earth's weather and temperature. The earth's climate is subject to periodic variations, some lasting many millennia and others lasting only centuries. These variations have had a profound impact on human history that is only beginning to be understood. Examples of climatic change in history are rainfall patterns from 6,000 years ago that led to the increasing aridity and expansion of the Sahara, and the "**Little Ice Age.**" Climatic change may have contributed to the decline of many civilizations and states.

Clive, Robert, First Baron Clive of Plassey (1725–1774)
British general and colonial administrator in India. In 1745 he joined the **East India Company** and fought against the French. He avenged the **Black Hole of Calcutta** incident and at the **Battle of Plassey** (1757) defeated a vastly superior Indian army largely by bribing Indian officers and soldiers to defect to the British side. After several years of rule in India, Clive returned to Britain, entered **Parliament,** and was made a baron (1762). In 1765 he returned to India to reform the civil service and the military, but his measures were so drastic that he was forced to return to Britain, where a government inquiry into his actions brought about his suicide in London.

Cloud Messenger
A work by the fourth-century Indian writer **Kalidasa,** considered one of the

masterpieces of **Sanskrit** literature. A poem of about 100 verses, it tells a romantic story of an exiled man who sends a message via a cloud to the wife he misses. The *Cloud Messenger* (*Meghaduta*) is one of the most popular Sanskrit poems.

Clovis I (c. 466–511)

First Christian **Merovingian** king of the **Franks** (481–511). Clovis established the Franks as a leading Germanic kingdom in the collapsing western **Roman Empire**. His conversion to Catholicism allied him with the **Roman Catholic Church**. The Merovingian kingdom survived for more than 200 years and was taken over by a Merovingian mayor, creating the Carolingian Dynasty.

Cluny

Medieval **monastery** in central France that led a reformation of Christianity in the tenth century. The Abbey of Cluny, founded in 909, attempted to reform and revive declining monasticism. Soon other monasteries attached themselves to Cluny, and the Cluniac order was created. The movement spread, and many **Benedictine** monasteries and convents accepted the reforms and adopted the Cluniac way of life as many new Cluniac houses were founded. By the middle of the twelfth century Cluny was the "motherhouse," or center, of an order of more than 300 monasteries or "daughter houses" and its influence was Europe-wide. The Cluniac order was the first true order or organization of monasteries and hence became the model for later orders such as the **Dominicans** and the **Jesuits**.

Coalbrookdale

Town in Shropshire, England, where **Abraham Darby I** founded iron-smelting works in 1709 using his new method of coke as the fuel source. This eliminated the need for wood as fuel and increased the production of iron and the need for coal. **Abraham Darby III** built the famous Coalbrookdale iron bridge across the Severn River, the first major iron bridge.

Code of Justinian. *See* Corpus Juris Civilis; Justinian (Justinian the Great)

Coffee

Drink consumed in Islamic civilizations by the fifteenth century and brought to Europe in the seventeenth century. Coffee was first introduced to **Muslims** centuries earlier, probably by Yemeni **Sufis**, but it was not popular before the fifteenth century. In the middle of the seventeenth century, coffee, along with tea, **chocolate**, and tobacco, entered the European mainstream, and by the eighteenth century coffee became very fashionable. Coffee cultivation spread from Yemen to tropical parts of the Americas and elsewhere to meet the demands of European and American consumption.

Cola. *See* Chola (Cola)

Colbert, Jean-Baptiste (1619–1683)

French controller-general of finance and chief minister to King **Louis XIV**. Colbert brought about economic, administrative, and naval reforms that made France the dominant power in Europe and made it possible for the king to rule as absolute monarch. However, the wars of Louis XIV drained the treasury, and Colbert spent his last years in disappointment.

Cold War

Competition between the United States and the **Union of Soviet Socialist Republics (USSR)** and their allies. The Cold War began almost immediately after **World War II** and ended with the collapse of Soviet-supported regimes in Eastern

Europe in 1989 and the USSR itself in 1991. It was both a great-power rivalry between the two superpowers and an ideological conflict between the market economy and liberal democratic ideals espoused by the United States and the communist system of the USSR. It was a called a "cold" war because, armed with nuclear weapons, the two powers were careful to avoid direct military conflict with each, Instead, they fought proxy wars between client states and by competing for influence, especially in the **third world**, through economic aid, military support, and propaganda. Many conflicts during this time, including the **Korean War**, the **Vietnam War**, and the first Afghan War, were part of the Cold War.

Colosseum

Roman amphitheater or stadium built 72–80 C.E. for sporting events. It seated 50,000 and had multicolored awnings to protect spectators from the elements. A great feat of engineering, the Colosseum had highly organized entrance and exit stairs to ensure a smooth flow of traffic. Entertainment included fights to the death between gladiators or between humans and animals. The Romans tried flooding the arena for mock naval battles, but it did not work well. The Colosseum was the stadium for the city of **Rome**, but most major cities had a stadium and a circus (such as Rome's **Circus Maximus**) for entertaining the urban masses.

Columba of Iona, Saint (d. 597)

Irish missionary to Scotland. Born to a noble Irish family, Columba established many **monasteries** in Ireland and Scotland. The most renowned was founded on the island of Iona in 563 off the west coast of Scotland. Columba founded the Celtic Christian church in Scotland, which spread to England and competed with the church founded in England by **Saint Augustine of Canterbury** (d. c. 604).

Columbian Exchange

Term for the global diffusion of plants, food crops, animals, human populations, and disease pathogens that took place after European contact with the Americas, starting with **Christopher Columbus's** 1492 voyage. Because the Americas were separated by oceans from the lands of the Old World, their flora and fauna were radically different. The biological exchange that took place was therefore dramatic. For thousands of years the various species of the Eastern Hemisphere, the Western Hemisphere, and Oceania had evolved separately. By linking these biological zones, the European voyages set up a round of biological exchange that permanently altered the world's human geography and natural environment.

Columbo Plan

Short name for the Colombo Plan for Co-operative Economic Development in South and Southeast Asia, an organization established at a meeting in Columbo, Sri Lanka, in 1950 to promote economic development in Asia. Originally intended for the British Commonwealth nations of the region, its membership grew to twenty-six, including many non-Commonwealth states. The United States and Japan were its principal financial contributors, in part as an effort to stem communist influence in the region.

Columbus, Christopher (1451–1506)

Explorer who discovered the New World for Europe. Born in Genoa (present-day Italy), by age twenty-four Columbus was a chart-maker in Lisbon, Portugal. He received sailing experience in Genoese and Portuguese fleets. In 1479 Columbus married Donã Felipa Perestrello e Moniz and received her father's maps and charts to the Madeira Islands off the coast of Europe. Around 1485 Columbus conceived the idea of sailing west to the Indies and proposed it to the Portuguese king John II. The idea was rejected and Columbus took it to the Spanish king **Ferdinand** and queen **Isabella**. Initially rejected, it was accepted and sponsored by the queen in 1491. On September 6, 1492, Columbus sailed westward from the Canary Islands with three ships—the *Niña*, the *Pinta*, and the flagship *Santa María*. By underestimating the circumference of the earth and overestimating the length of the Eurasian continent (both calculations accepted at the time), Columbus expected to hit land at about the meridian of modern-day Cuba. On October 12, 1492, land was sighted, probably in the Bahamas. Columbus returned to Spain believing he had reached Asia. Three subsequent trips were inconclusive in proving whether he had reached Asia or instead discovered new continents. Columbus's seamanship is generally considered remarkable.

Common Market. *See* European Economic Community (EEC)

Communism

Political and economic system in which property is owned by the state and wealth is equally shared by all members of the state, creating a classless society. The idea of communism was introduced by **Karl Marx** and Friedrich Engels in *The Communist Manifesto*. According to Marx and Engels, history is composed of constant struggles between the workers and the corrupt people who own the means of production. Eventually the workers will revolt and overthrow the corrupt owners, establishing a "dictatorship by the proletariat." This step, called **socialism**, will eventually lead to authentic communism, in which a society is completely without private property or class distinction. Marx and Engels's idea was adopted by **Vladimir Ilyich Lenin**, who thought that the working class needed encouragement from a powerful party; this led to the creation of the **Bolshevik** Party in Russia in the early twentieth century. Lenin's ideas were brought to fruition in the **Union of Soviet Socialist Republics** and adopted by **Joseph Stalin**, who added the role of an absolute dictator and rule through fear and violence to the idea of communism. Communism quickly spread from Russia and throughout eastern Europe to Bulgaria, Czechoslovakia, East Germany, Hungary, Poland, Romania, Yugoslavia, and Albania. In Asia, a communist regime was established in China in 1949 by revolutionary leader **Mao Zedong**. Communism spread through Asia to North and South Vietnam, North Korea, Laos, and Cambodia throughout the 1960s and 1970s. On the other side of the world, communism became Cuba's form of government in 1958. Several wars were fought over communism, including the **Korean War** and the **Vietnam War**. Communism began to crumble in the late 1980s largely because of Mikhail Gorbachev, then president of the Soviet Union. Communism, after the fall of the **Berlin Wall** in 1989, is considered moribund.

Compass

Instrument using a floating magnetic needle to point to magnetic north. The compass was known in Europe by the eleventh century, possibly introduced by Arabs who got the idea from the Chinese. Magnetic polarity was understood in China from the first century C.E. and was used as a compass on Chinese ships by at least the tenth century. The compass enabled sailors to find an absolute direction anywhere on the globe—especially useful on the open seas. In the twelfth century in Europe, the compass was made more useful by combining it with markings of directions (North, South, East, and West). To the superstitious, the mysterious movement of the compass needle suggested occult powers, and ship's pilots often had to hide their use of a compass. By the time of **Christopher Columbus** the compass was in common use.

Comprador

Term for Chinese merchants who worked with Western traders in the nineteenth and early twentieth centuries, derived from the Portuguese term meaning "to buy." Compradors played an important role in internationalizing China's economy but came to be viewed by Chinese communists and nationalists as collaborators with Western imperialists, and the word still has bad connotations to Chinese today. It is used by economic historians to refer to the "shop-keeping" or "bazaar" class anywhere.

Compurgation

Method of determining guilt or innocence employed throughout the **Middle Ages** in Germany and in ecclesiastical courts until the fourteenth century. The defendant swore an oath of innocence and then had compurgators, or "oath helpers," swear to the validity of the original oath.

Concord, Battle of (April 19, 1775)

Continuation of the first battle of the **American Revolution** begun at **Lexington**. American militia got word of the shots fired in Lexington and assembled at the nearby town of Concord. While three British companies searched for colonial arms and ammunition caches, three other companies encountered the colonial militia, armed with the very weapons being sought. The British retreated to Boston

after losing the fight. The early victory committed the colonies to an armed rebellion against Britain.

Confederate States of America

Eleven states that seceded from the United States of America before and during the **American Civil War**. The seceding states believed that the only way to protect their liberties was to leave the Union. The process began with six states (South Carolina, Mississippi, Florida, Alabama, Georgia, and Louisiana) declaring their withdrawal from the Union between December 20, 1860, and February 1, 1861, and organizing an autonomous government. They were followed by Texas, Virginia, Arkansas, Tennessee, and North Carolina. The president of the Confederate States of America was Jefferson Davis of Mississippi, with Alexander H. Stephens of Georgia as his vice president. The Confederate States of America ceased to exist in 1865.

Confucianism

Western term for the east Asian ethical, social, and political philosophy founded by **Confucius**. Confucianism placed emphasis on obligations to family and society and on the importance of each person carrying out his or her proper role in their relationship to others. Society ideally should be government by men of virtue who lead others by their moral example. The most important virtues were filial piety and loyalty to rulers. Subordinate members of society, such as children and subjects, were bound to be obedient and loyal, and parents and rulers were obligated to be benevolent and responsible. Confucianism viewed society as hierarchical, with the young subordinate to the old, women to men, and subjects to rulers. Most Confucianists valued learning, decorum, and the proper performance of rituals. Confucianism was promoted by the

Han Dynasty rulers and was officially sponsored by subsequent Chinese dynasties. It was adopted by Korea, Japan, and Vietnam and is still influential in East Asia today.

Confucius (551–479 B.C.E.)

Latinized form of name of the Chinese philosopher and moral teacher known as Kongzi. Long after his death he was known as Kongfuzi, westernized to Confucius. No writings by him exist, but after his death his followers collected his sayings in the Analects (*Lun*). Confucius, who lived during the **Warring States period**, was concerned about the need to establish an orderly and harmonious society. His main message was that this could be accomplished if people in positions of authority and responsibility, such as rulers, government ministers, and heads of households, would pursue virtue and lead by moral example. Confucius believed in moral standards, such as propriety, benevolence, and compassion, as the source of order. Confucius also believed that these qualities could be taught; hence education created a person who was concerned about what was right. He taught respect for authority and superiors as part of order and harmony. Confucius began a line of teachings (later elaborated upon by others such as **Mencius**) that eventually became the dominant system of thought about government, society, and ethics in East Asia, making him China's single most influential thinker and one of the world's most influential.

Congo

Name of a region and a river in central equatorial Africa. The river, including the Lualaba River, is 2,720 miles (4,377 km) long, the second longest in Africa. It drains 1,425,000 square miles (3,690,000 sq km) and is a great source of hydroelectric potential. Before the nineteenth century two kingdoms and several chiefdoms populated the region. In the fourteenth century the Bakongo established a powerful kingdom in central Africa known as the Kingdom of **Kongo**. When the Portuguese appeared along the coast, they traded with the Kingdom of Kongo. The Portuguese influenced a dynastic change in the sixteenth century and introduced Christianity and slavery. In the seventeenth century the Kingdom of Kongo disintegrated. Another kingdom, the Teke, arose in the fourteenth century and became major traders into the nineteenth century, using the Congo River as their main supply line. When Europeans arrived in the nineteenth century, the Congo was economically thriving but politically fragmented. The Congo was explored by **David Livingstone** and **Henry Stanley** in the middle to late nineteenth century. It was named Congo Free State in 1885 and renamed Belgian Congo in 1908. It became the Democratic Republic of Congo in 1960 and was again renamed, as **Zaïre**, in 1971. In 1997 the name was returned to Democratic Republic of Congo.

Congo Crisis (1960–1965)

Political and economic turmoil in the Democratic Republic of Congo after it became independent from Belgium in 1960. The Congo became a Belgian territory in 1885 and was named Belgian Congo in 1908. As the movement for colonial independence gained momentum after **World War II**, Belgium did little to provide for the Congo's self-governance. Pressure in 1959 led to Belgium's almost immediate withdrawal from the Congo in January 1960. Fighting erupted between rival tribes, and much of the economic infrastructure, built by Belgium, was destroyed. The government requested **United Nations** forces, which were sent, but a coup by Colonel **Sese Seko Mobutu** overthrew the prime minister in

1961, and in 1965 Mobutu and the army declared Mobutu president.

Congress, Indian National

Major political party in India. Founded in 1885 as means for western-educated Indians to gather and lobby for a greater role in the government of British India, after 1920 under the leadership of **Mohandas K. Gandhi** it became a centrally organized mass movement for Indian independence. Under the leadership of **Jawaharlal Nehru** and, later, his daughter **Indira Gandhi** and grandson Rajiv Gandhi, it was the ruling party of India for three decades. After its defeat to the Janata Party in 1977 it lost its dominance of Indian politics, but in 1980 the party regained power and continued to rule until 1989. In 1996 the party lost the election and was out of power for nearly a decade. In 2004 the Indian National Congress formed a new government in India.

Conquistadors

Spanish class of soldiers developed during the **Middle Ages** to fight for the reconquest of Spain from **Muslims** who turned into overseas adventurers in the sixteenth century. These soldiers were turned loose in the newly discovered lands of the Americas and in Asia. With their **gunpowder**, organization, and especially the diseases they carried, the conquistadors conquered many peoples and empires rather easily. **Hernando Cortés** conquered the powerful **Aztecs** of Mexico, and **Francisco Pizarro** conquered the **Incas** of Peru.

Conrad III (r. 1137–1152)

German king, duke of Franconia, and first Hohenstaufen king. Conrad joined Louis VII of France on the Second **Crusade** and lost most of his army to the **Seljuk Turks**. Conrad designated as his successor **Frederick I, "Barbarossa."**

Conservative Party, Great Britain

Political party. In the 1830s political parties became more formalized with the Tory and Whig parties. The Tory, or Conservative, Party generally stood for the rights of landowners, the Church of England, and the monarchy, patriotism, and existing laws. By the late nineteenth century the Tory Party embraced many social and political reforms in the face of the Liberal Party (founded 1859). Prominent Conservative Party prime ministers include **Benjamin Disraeli** and **Winston Churchill**. In 1979 **Margaret Thatcher** reinvigorated the Conservatives, who held power in **Parliament** until 1997.

Constantinople

Second capital of the **Roman Empire**. Built as the "New Rome" of the Roman Empire it became the capital of the **Byzantine Empire** and one of the most important cities of the **Middle Ages**. Originally the **polis** of Byzantium, the city was made the second capital of the Roman Empire by Emperor Constantine in 324. As the western Roman Empire fell to Germanic invaders, the eastern half of the empire survived as the Byzantine Empire. Constantinople withstood hundreds of years of attacks by the **Ottoman Turks**, but finally fell to continuous siege in 1453 and was renamed **Istanbul** by **Mehmet II**.

Constituent Assembly. *See* National Assembly

Constitution, United States. *See* United States Constitution

Consul

The **Roman Republic's** top executive office. The office consisted of two magistrates from the **patrician** class, elected to serve one-year terms (they could be reelected up to ten times) as consuls and share control over the military and civil issues. During the **Roman Empire** the consul was no longer elected because the emperor either served as consul himself or appointed a favorite to the post.

Consumer Society

Post–**World War II** mentality of materialism initiated by Western countries, especially the United States. The economy of capitalism in the West began to feed itself after the war. The more people bought, the more the economy grew. The more the economy grew, the more money people were paid, enabling them to buy more. Simultaneously, the growth of industry often lowered the price of manufactured goods, making it easier for people to buy them. Relentless advertising campaigns using various psychological techniques helped convince people to buy goods. Consumer society is the view that people in the twentieth and twenty-first centuries have become more interested in acquiring possessions than in more serious intellectual or spiritual pursuits.

Continental Army

American army organized by the Second **Continental Congress** to fight the British during the **American Revolution**. The army was placed under civilian control at the highest level, and the U.S. military has remained that way ever since. The initial force of fewer than 17,000, commanded by **George Washington**, eventually reached a height of about 35,000 in November 1778, but continually suffered from serious shortages of men and supplies. Army regulars were supplemented by local militias, but those forces faced issues of reliability and discipline and made forming an organized fighting force difficult. Nevertheless, the Continental Army, with the help of the French, was ultimately able to defeat the well-disciplined British army.

It was officially disbanded on November 2, 1783.

Continental Congress

American group of delegates sent by the colonies to Philadelphia and who made decisions during the time of the **American Revolution**. The First Continental Congress met in 1774 and discussed the colonial response to the Intolerable (Coercive) Acts passed by the British **Parliament**. Despite many varying opinions of the individual colonial representatives, it was generally agreed that the colonies desired affairs to return to the status quo of 1763 and did not seek open rebellion. By the time of the Second Continental Congress in 1775, however, the war had begun, and such a peaceable route was no longer possible. The congress, therefore, worked on war issues and the American **Declaration of Independence**. The Second Continental Congress met from 1775 to 1781.

Continental System

French Napoleonic attempt to control world trade. As **Napoléon Bonaparte** built his **Grand Empire**, controlling nearly all of Europe, he attempted in 1806 to close all ports of the empire to British commerce, both British ships and British goods on neutral ships. The British countered with their own blockade and attacks upon French ports and French shipping. Although the Continental System strained Britain, it did not break it. It was also impossible to enforce tightly.

Convention

French legislative body during the **French Revolution**. On June 17, 1789, the **National Assembly** formed from the **Estates General**. On July 7 the body changed its name to Constituent National Assembly, and from this point is often referred to as the Constituent Assembly, or simply

Constituent. The Constituent Assembly was dissolved on September 30, 1791, and replaced by the Legislative Assembly, which was in turn replaced by the Convention on September 21, 1792, the beginning of year I of the revolutionary calendar. It was the Convention that made the decisions to execute King **Louis XVI**, to declare war on Britain and other countries, to separate church and state, and to establish the Constitution of the Year III (1795). On October 26, 1795 the Convention was replaced by the Directory.

Convents. *See* Monasteries and Convents

Cook, James (1728–1779)
English naval captain and explorer. Cook became marine surveyor of the coast of Newfoundland and Labrador in 1759. In 1768 he was appointed to a geographical expedition to the South Pacific, where in 1769–1770 he "discovered" and charted New Zealand and then Australia, both of which he carefully surveyed and took possession of for Britain, but failed to find the great southern continent that was believed to exist. On a second voyage (1772–1775) Cook was the first explorer to cross the Antarctic Circle, but again without reaching Antarctica. Cook pioneered the care of sailors by developing a diet to combat scurvy. A later voyage (1776–1779) searched for the Northwest Passage going up the west coast of North America to the Bering Strait. He had discovered Hawaii earlier on this trip and returned to the islands, only to be engaged in a fight with islanders and stabbed to death.

Copernicus, Nicolaus (1473–1543)
Polish astronomer, discoverer of the sun-centered universe, and a founder of the **scientific revolution**. Copernicus's work *On the Revolution of the Heavenly Spheres* (1543), published on his deathbed, mathematically rearranged the heavenly bodies, suggesting a heliocentric (sun-centered) universe instead of the accepted Aristotelian or Ptolemaic earth-centered universe. Initially, Copernicus's ideas did not create much of a stir, but as other astronomers such as **Johannes Kepler**, **Galileo**, and **Isaac Newton** offered proof that they were correct, the sun-centered universe became one part of an entirely new view of the natural world.

Coptic Christians
Members of the Coptic Orthodox Church, the largest Christian body in Egypt. Their name comes from the Arabic translation of the Greek word for Egypt, because they stem from the original inhabitants of the land. Tracing its origin to the earliest days of **Christianity**—the church was purportedly founded by **Jesus**'s disciple Mark—the Coptic Orthodox Church comprises less than 5 percent of the population of Egypt. The Patriarch of Alexandria (who resides in Cairo) rules it with the help of bishops. When church leaders were declared heretical for their Monophysite view of the nature of Christ at the Council of Chalcedon in 451 C.E., they split from what became the **Eastern Orthodox Church**. Angry with the **Byzantine** emperor, who had tried to coerce them to accept the Chalcedonian decrees, Copts welcomed the Arabs when they conquered Egypt in 642 C.E. Some converted to **Islam**, but others remained Coptic Christians. Most worship is now conducted in Arabic.

Córdoba, Great Mosque at
Islamic mosque built in 784–786 in Cordoba, Spain. The Great Mosque of Córdoba was built under the **Umayyad** ruler Abd ar-Rahman I. With additions in the ninth century, the Great Mosque became the largest sacred building in the Islamic world. It was converted into a

Christian cathedral in the thirteenth century following the Castilian reconquest. The mosque remains one of the most celebrated examples of Spanish and Islamic architecture.

Corinthian Order
Architectural order of design in ancient Greece. The Corinthian Order followed the **Doric Order** and the **Ionic Order** and was characterized by an ornate capital with acanthus leaf design and a column on a complex base.

Corn
Grains such as wheat, oats, barley, rye, and **maize**. In the tenth century Europe moved to a heavily grain-oriented agriculture wherein most of the population was directed through **manorialism** to produce corn. Bread and ale became the dietary staples.

Corn Laws
British regulations of 1815 restricting the importation of grain, struck down in 1846. The Corn Laws were intended to increase domestic production and control prices, but in the nineteenth-century movement toward the abolition of trade restrictions in response to **Adam Smith**'s *Wealth of Nations*, the Corn Laws were seen as aristocratic misrule causing artificially high food prices. The Anti–Corn Law League pressed for repeal, but the Irish **potato famine** of 1845–1848 forced the issue of cheaper food, and the laws were repealed. The repeal of the Corn Laws became a symbol of free trade.

Cornwallis, Charles, First Marquis (1738–1805)
British general during the **American Revolution**. Lord Cornwallis was successful against the American rebels at Camden and Guildford Court House, defeating Nathanael Greene, but suffered great losses. Cornwallis had acted without consulting his superior, General Henry Clinton, and he was ordered to march his wrecked army to Virginia and attempted to recover in the safe location of Yorktown. The French fleet under Admiral François Joseph Paul Comte de Grasse trapped the British army, leaving it without prospect of relief by sea. General **George Washington** and the Comte de Rochambeau abandoned plans to take New York and brought the siege of the British that led to Cornwallis's surrender. The British sought peace terms with their former colonies, ending the American Revolution.

Corpus Juris Civilis
Codification of Roman law drawn up under Emperor **Justinian** (527–565). There were four parts to the law corpus, including enactments dating back to Emperor **Hadrian** (117–138), interpretations by jurists, an introductory law manual, and laws enacted during Justinian's reign.

Cortes
Spanish legislative assembly composed of nobles, clergy, and elected representatives. Similar to the English **Parliament**, the Cortes evolved in the various kingdoms that became Spain as early as the twelfth century. Convened when summoned by the king, it considered royal proposals and petitions brought forward from the representatives. Once proposals were accepted by the Cortes and signed by the king, they became law.

Cortés, Hernando (1485–1547)
Spanish conquistador who conquered the **Aztecs** of Mexico in 1521. Peacefully allowed entrance into **Tenochtitlán**, the capital of the Aztecs, Cortés, with a few hundred soldiers, captured the Aztec

emperor, **Moctezuma**, and with enemies of the Aztecs conquered the empire using gunpowder, organization, and disease and hunger as the capital, in Lake Texcoco, was cut off from the mainland. Cortés then established Mexico City, capital of New Spain, on the site of the old capital.

Cossack (meaning guerrillas)

Powerful military people, especially cavalry, often allied with the Russians against the **Turks** in the seventeenth through the nineteenth centuries. The Cossacks were an Orthodox Christian group who left Poland and Muscovy in the seventeenth century because of religious persecution by Roman Catholics and settled in southern **Russia**. There the Cossacks developed a tribal society and played a large role in Ukrainian history.

Cottage Industry

Seventeenth- and eighteenth-century European small-scale domestic manufacture method and forerunner of the **Industrial Revolution**. Increased population led many peasants to manufacture textiles and other products to supplement their agrarian incomes. In the eighteenth century middlemen began to organize the cottage industries into the putting-out system, whereby wool was delivered to weavers, collected, and delivered to other stages of the process. Increased production led to the idea of collecting workers into one site (a factory) and, eventually, to powering the looms or other machines by water and, later, steam.

Council of Pisa (1409)

Roman Catholic Church council to resolve the **Great Schism** that had divided the papacy in two since 1378. Previously, all attempts to resolve the division had

failed. In 1408 cardinals and bishops from both parties revolted. They met and called a general council, which convened in Pisa with four patriarchs; twenty-two cardinals; eighty bishops; and doctors of theology and canon law from the universities of Paris, **Oxford**, and Cologne. Both sitting popes, Gregory XII and Benedict XIII, were found doubtful, and a new pope was elected in their place, Alexander V. This resolved some of the division, but not all of it. Historians of the church claim that the council was improperly convoked and that its decisions therefore had no claim to represent the church.

Council of Trent (1545–1563)

Council of the full **Roman Catholic Church** in response to the **Protestant Reformation**. The reforming pope Paul III called a council to be held in the city of Trent, on the border between Italy and the **Holy Roman Empire**. The council met in three long sessions. Some major conclusions of the Council of Trent were that justification (salvation) is by faith and good works, hope, and love; that the church is based on scriptures and tradition; that the sacraments are seven; that mass would be in Latin, not the vernacular; and that priests would remain celibate. The Council of Trent gave an enormous boost to Catholicism, which began to regain support lost to the Protestant movement. It opened what is known as the **Catholic Reformation**.

Counter Reformation. *See* Catholic Reformation

Cranmer, Thomas (1489–1556)

English archbishop of Canterbury who initiated the **Protestant Reformation** in England. Cranmer was appointed archbishop by **Henry VIII** in 1532, and in 1533 he granted an annulment of the marriage of Henry and **Catherine of Aragon**. In 1534 the Act of Supremacy removed the English church from the control of Rome, and between 1536 and 1539 many monastic and church lands were confiscated by the crown. Reformed elements crept into the church until England was thrust into Protestantism under King Edward VI, with liturgical reforms including the English Prayer Book (1549). When **Mary I** came to the throne, Cranmer was tried for high treason and heresy and burned at the stake in Oxford.

Crazy Horse (c. 1849–1877)
Sioux chief who defeated Colonel George Custer at the Battle of Little Bighorn (1876). Leading 2,500 Sioux and Cheyenne warriors along with Chief Sitting Bull, Crazy Horse surrounded Custer's army of 265 and killed every one of them. This is known as Custer's Last Stand. In 1877 Crazy Horse surrendered to authorities and was killed in custody.

Crécy, Battle of (1346)
Battle between England and France in the **Hundred Years War** (1338–1453). English king **Edward III**'s army was cornered and outnumbered, but their longbowmen decimated the mounted French warriors. The victory enabled the English to take the port of Calais, which they held for two centuries.
See also Longbow

Crimean War (1854–56)
War fought by Britain and France against Russia in the Crimean Peninsula over Russian expansionism into the Black Sea region. Britain was attempting to halt Russia's expansion and the disintegration of the **Ottoman Empire**, which would disturb the balance of power in the Mediterranean and Britain's access to India. Famous Crimean War battles include

those at Balaclava and Sevastopol. Florence Nightingale pioneered nursing techniques during the war. The war was marked by military blunders on both sides, but the final defeat was of Russia, thwarting its expansion toward the Mediterranean and leading to the creation of Romania in the region.

Crockett, Davy (David) (1786–1836)
Frontiersman and U.S. congressman from Tennessee. He fought in Andrew Jackson's campaign against the Creek Indians in 1814 and died fighting for Texas's independence at the **Alamo** in 1836.

Croesus
Last king of Lydia (c. 560–546 B.C.E.). Croesus completed the subjugation of Greek cities in **Asia Minor** but had good relations with the Greeks. The rise of the **Persian Empire** under **Cyrus the Great** forced Croesus to look for help among the Greeks, but he was overthrown. According to tradition, Croesus then threw himself on a pyre, but was miraculously saved by **Apollo**.

Cro-Magnon
Prehistoric **Homo sapiens** from circa 33,000–8,000 B.C.E. Remains found in Cro-Magnon, France, in 1868 are difficult to place in human development. Cro-Magnon peoples settled, used tools and implements, buried their dead, and produced art. Cro-Magnon art includes small sculptures of animals and humans, often pregnant women, and cave paintings in southern France and in Spain. They also decorated their tools.

Cromwell, Oliver (1599–1658)
English general for the parliamentary forces during the **English Civil War**. Cromwell, a **Puritan**, organized the **New Model Army** that defeated the Royalist

army and then helped organize the execution of King **Charles I** in 1649. After the war Cromwell became lord protector of the Commonwealth from 1653 until his death in 1658 (he refused **Parliament**'s offer of the crown) as England became a republic. He was also known for his brutal suppression of Catholics in Ireland.

Crop Rotation

Agricultural method of leaving a portion of land fallow (unplanted) to renew itself and alternating crops planted from field to field. In two-field rotation, half the land is planted and half is left fallow. The next year the fields are switched. In three-field rotation, one-third is left fallow, one-third is planted in one crop, and one-third is planted in another crop. The next year the three fields are rotated. Crop rotation keeps the soil fertile, but one-third to one-half of the land is always out of use. By the seventeenth century the use of alfalfa or clover added nitrogen to the soil and overcame the need for leaving land fallow. Use of this method is known as the **agricultural revolution.**

Crossbow

Weapon of a short bow fixed horizontally on a wooden stock with a groove to hold a missile. The crossbow had a range of about 300 yards and was very powerful but inaccurate. At close range the crossbow was armor piercing. The crossbow's complexity made it difficult to construct and slow to fire, however. The **longbow** had the advantages of simplicity, accuracy, and rapid fire. The crossbow was used by the late twelfth century in Europe and may have been brought back from the **Crusades.**

Cross-Cultural Encounters

Term used to describe the historically significant encounters of peoples from different cultures. Cross-cultural encounters occur most commonly through trade, such as the famous **Silk Roads** or the **trans-Saharan trade** routes, but they also occur as a result of invasions, migrations, religious pilgrimages, and exploration. Cross-cultural encounters have taken place throughout history and continue to do so as people of various lands meet in various ways. They spread new ideas and technologies and are a major cause of historical change.

Crusades

Military expeditions from western Europe to the **Middle East** between 1095 and 1270 to drive the **Muslims** from the Holy Land of **Palestine**. In 1094 an appeal by the **Byzantine** emperor to Pope **Urban II** for assistance against the **Seljuk** Turks led to a papal call for a crusade in 1095. Additionally, pilgrimages from the West to the Holy Land had increased, and pilgrims were occasionally mistreated, so Europeans felt that something must be done. Consequently, the First Crusade reached **Constantinople** in 1096 and took Jerusalem in 1099. All subsequent crusades (the second through the eighth plus the Children's Crusade and the Peasant Crusade) were generally unsuccessful. The Crusades were a disaster for the Near Eastern economy, but they provided a stimulus to the economy and trade of Europe and between Europe and Byzantium. The Crusades fed the growth of many trade towns such as **Venice**, Genoa, and Pisa. They also brought about intellectual interaction between Europe and the Middle East and probably resulted in the transfer of devices such as **windmills** and possibly **paper**. Near Eastern Christians often suffered at the hands of their coreligionist Crusaders, but the Crusades strengthened the hold of the western Christian church, especially the **papacy**, in Europe. At the same time, the Crusades accelerated the development of royal powers in several countries.

Crystal Palace

British exhibition hall for the **Great Exhibition** of the Works of Industry of All Nations of 1851. This exhibition was the first world's fair, intended to show off Britain as the workshop of the world. The Crystal Palace was made of iron and glass and measured more than 1,800 feet (550 m) long and 400 feet (120 m) wide. It was tall enough to enclose tall elm trees in Hyde Park, London (where it was built), making it the largest enclosed space in the world at that time, yet it was planned and built within one year. It contained exhibits from around the world, especially of new mechanical inventions such as the telegraph and the sewing machine.

Cuban Missile Crisis

Confrontation between the United States and the **Union of Soviet Socialist Republics** over the introduction of nuclear missiles to Cuba. **Fidel Castro**'s 1959 communist overthrow of U.S.-backed dictator Fulgencio Batista in Cuba led to a U.S. embargo on Cuba and the Soviet Union's aid to Cuba. Fearing a communist country ninety miles from Florida, the **Central Intelligence Agency** under President **John F. Kennedy** organized the **Bay of Pigs** operation to oust Castro from power. The April 1961 operation failed miserably, but Castro wanted additional Soviet protection, and Premier Nikita Khrushchev obliged. In October 1962, U.S. spy planes photographed Soviet construction of missile-launching sites in Cuba, forcing Kennedy to take action. Many military advisors advocated the use of force, but Kennedy instead "quarantined" Cuba using a naval blockade to stop and search Soviet ships. Rather than confront the U.S. Navy, Khrushchev removed missiles from Cuba in exchange for the removal of U.S. missiles from Turkey.

Culloden, Battle of (1746)

Battle fought in northern Scotland that ended the uprising by Bonnie Prince Charlie in his attempt to regain the British crown for the Stuarts. In 1688 the **Glorious Revolution** drove the Stuart monarch out (he escaped to France) and replaced him with William and **Mary**. Charles Edward Stuart, heir to the family line, was encouraged to return and take the crown. In 1745 an uprising was mildly successful, but a lack of nerve drove Stuart back north to Scotland, where a British army led by the Duke of Cumberland pursued and caught the Scots at Culloden. The Scots were annihilated and Scotland's ability to rebel was ruthlessly destroyed as castles and Stuart supporters (Jacobites) were hunted and slaughtered. This was the last land battle in Britain.

Cultural Revolution. *See* Great Proletarian Cultural Revolution

Cuzco

Ancient capital and hub of the **Inca** empire in south-central Peru, and one of the oldest continuously inhabited cities in the Western Hemisphere. The city may have had a population as great as 200,000 by the time of **Francisco Pizarro**'s Spanish conquest in 1535. Much of the expertly crafted architecture and stonework of the Inca empire remains in Cuzco today.

Cyril of Jerusalem, Saint (c. 315–386)

Christian bishop who opposed **Arianism**. Cyril battled the Arian heresy at the Council of Constantinople in 381. His view of the Trinity became the accepted one within the **Roman Catholic Church**.

Cyrus the Great (r. 559–529 B.C.E.)
Founder of the Persian Empire. Cyrus led
an army against his grandfather, became
king of Media and Persia, and later conquered **Croesus** and **Babylon**. He allowed
the Jews to return to **Jerusalem** from their
Babylonian Captivity.

Czechoslovakia and Germany. *See*
Sudetenland

D

Dacca. *See* Dhaka (Dacca)

Da Gama, Vasco (c. 1469–1524)
Portuguese explorer who, in 1497, sailed from Portugal around Africa and on to India. Departing with four ships, Da Gama returned twenty-six months later with two ships and one-third of his crew, but with information on sailing to India that offered Portugal the possibility of breaking the **Muslim** trade monopoly with Africa and, especially, the Muslim monopoly in the **spice trade** with the East.

Dahomey
African kingdom on the continent's west coast, known as the **Slave Coast.** The kingdom of Dahomey developed in the seventeenth century, and in the eighteenth century it became important in the **Atlantic slave trade.** The king of Dahomey was an absolute monarch who required human sacrifices to demonstrate his power. Slavery began as captives were used to work the land locally, but later slaves were sold to Europeans. In the early seventeenth century the Oyo invaded; they came to dominate Dahomey and increased trade with the Europeans. Dahomey was at its peak in the 1750s and 1760s, controlling slave trade inland and with the Europeans. As slave trade declined in the early nineteenth century, so did Dahomey's economy. A coup overthrew the king in 1818, and expanded production of palm oil was encouraged to replace the lost slave trade, but the income from it was insufficient and Dahomey's standard of living and importance continued to decline. Conquered by the French, Dahomey ceased to exist in 1900.

Daimyo (Japanese for "great names")
Japanese regional feudal lords. The daimyo rose to power during the **Ashikaga** shogunate and fought one another for control of Japan. Under the **Tokugawa** shogunate the daimyo were allowed limited control over their individual fiefs, which occupied two-thirds of the country, although effective political power was in the hands of the central government in Edo. During the Tokugawa shogunate, the position of daimyo became a regular government institution. The "outer daimyo" in western Japan had more autonomy and became the centers of opposition to the shoguns in the crisis that followed the opening of Japan by **Commodore Matthew Perry**. After the **Meiji Restoration** the daimyo were abolished.

Daladier, Édouard (1884–1970)
French statesman and premier (1933–1934, 1938–1940). Daladier, along with Britain's **Neville Chamberlain,** appeased **Adolf Hitler** in his demand to annex the **Sudetenland** of Czechoslovakia in the **Munich Pact** (1938). Daladier was arrested, tried, and acquitted but imprisoned by the Vichy government. He was later elected to the government of France's Fourth Republic.

Dalai Lama

Title of the head monk of the Tibetan Yellow Hat sect of Buddhism. The title is Tibetan for "ocean of wisdom and compassion" and was created in the sixteenth century. Originally a purely religious position, in the seventeenth century the fifth Dalai Lama became the secular ruler of Tibet. Each Dalai Lama was succeeded by his reincarnation, generally found in a small child somewhere in Tibet. The fourteenth Dalai Lama, Tenzin Gyatso (1935–) was forced into exile in 1959 when China under **Mao Zedong** assumed direct control over Tibet. Since then he has led a Tibetan government in exile based in Dharamsala, India. In 1989 he was awarded the **Noble Prize** for Peace.

Damascus

The capital of modern Syria, with an estimated 6 million inhabitants in 2004. The ancient city was, at various times in its pre-Islamic past, home to Assyrians, Persians, Greeks, and Romans. Damascus served as the capital of the **Umayyad Caliphate** from 661 to 763 C.E., when a new **Abbasid Caliphate** transferred the Islamic **caliphate** to Baghdad. The Umayyad Mosque complex in Damascus (finished in 715) architecturally Islamized the renowned Church of Saint John the Baptist, which was built in the fourth century C.E. upon a Greek temple to Jupiter that may have been the original habitation of the site. In 1076 Damascus was captured by the **Seljuks** and in 1260 it fell to the **Mongols**. In 1401 it was sacked by **Timur**, and in 1516 it came under the control of the **Ottoman Turks**. Syria became an independent state with Damascus as its capital after **World War I**, although from 1920 to 1946 France claimed it as a mandate. From 1946 to the present day, Damascus has been the capital of Syria.

Dandin (fl. late sixth to early seventh century)

Poet of southern Indian origin considered one of the masters of **Sanskrit** literature. Although active after its decline, Dandin is often associated with the **Gupta's golden age** of literature and arts. The two works that are attributed to him with certainty are *The Adventures of Ten Princes* and *The Mirror of Poetry*, both romantic works in poetic form.

Dante. *See* Alighieri, Dante

Dao De Jing (Tao Te Ching)

Chinese Daoist classic text probably written in the third century B.C.E. but attributed to the fifth-century B.C.E. author **Laozi**.
    See also Daoism (Taoism)

Daoism (Taoism)

A Chinese system of philosophical thought and religion that emerged in later **Zhou** times. The reputed founder was **Laozi**, presumed to have been a contemporary of **Confucius**, but Daoism has no one founder and incorporates various philosophical and mystical traditions. The basic teachings include belief in living and acting in harmony with the "way" (*dao*) of nature, eschewing the artificial, avoiding unnecessary effort, and preferring simplicity and the natural. Daoist thinkers such as the third-century B.C.E. writer **Zhuangzi** and the author of the **Dao De Jing** avoided rigid logical categories and wrote in paradoxical, mystical, and often ironic styles. The natural way, the spontaneity, and the simplicity emphasized by Daoism had a considerable influence on Chinese culture and acted as a balance to the rigid formalism of **Confucianism**. Later, a religious Daoism emerged in China with temples, rituals, and priests patterned somewhat after **Buddhism** and emphasizing the search for immortality.

Darby, Abraham (1678–1717)
English entrepreneur who discovered how to smelt iron ore using coke in 1709. Darby developed this technique at **Coalbrookdale**, England, when a timber shortage necessitated finding another fuel for iron production. Coal produced too much smoke, but by heating coal, impurities were burned off, and the resulting coke was ideal for iron smelting. With the invention of the Newcomen steam engine, the demand for iron increased tremendously. The increased iron production and the demand for coal and alternate fuel started the **Industrial Revolution**.

Darby, Abraham, III (1750–1791)
English manufacturer and grandson of Abraham Darby I, who at **Coalbrookdale**, England, built the first large iron bridge. This bridge proved that iron could replace wood and stone.

Dar es Salaam
City and port in Tanzania. Dar es Salaam, founded in 1862 by the sultan of **Zanzibar**, remained a small town until German colonization of German East Africa in the nineteenth century. It then became the starting point of the German-built railroad and the capital of the colony. It remained the capital of Tanganyika and later was the capital of Tanzania until 1974, when Dodoma was designated the capital of Tanzania.

Darius I, "the Great" (c. 550–486 B.C.E.)
King of Persia (522–486 B.C.E.). Darius reorganized the **Persian Empire**, introduced standard currencies and measures, built an infrastructure of roads and canals, and expanded into the **Indus River** region of India. His rule inaugurated nearly two centuries of peace in Persia. Darius suppressed Greek revolts in Ionia (499–494 B.C.E.), and when **Athens** supported the Ionians, he moved to crush Athens but was defeated by the Athenians at the **Battle of Marathon**. His successor, **Xerxes I**, continued the conflict with the Greeks.

Darwin, Charles (1809–1882)
English naturalist, author of *Origins of the Species*, and architect of the theory of evolution. Educated at the universities of Edinburgh and Cambridge, Darwin was an experienced naturalist when he joined the ship *Beagle* (1831–1836) for a voyage around the world. The expedition visited Atlantic islands off Africa's coast, the coast of South America including the Galapagos Islands, and the South Pacific and South Atlantic. In 1859 Darwin published *On the Origins of the Species by Means of Natural Selection; or, The Preservation of Favored Races in the Struggle for Life*, proposing the theory of evolution that would become known as **Darwinism**.

Darwinism
The theory of evolution, an explanation of biological development as espoused by **Charles Darwin** in *On the Origins of the Species* (1859), and the social version of that theory, known as **social Darwinism**, espoused by Herbert Spencer. Darwinism says that species produce more offspring and variation than are necessary for numerical reproduction and that through natural selection those most suited to their environment survive. This produces change in species over time. Some species evolve into new forms while others become extinct.

Da Vinci, Leonardo (1452–1519)
Innovative, immensely influential, and well-known **Italian Renaissance** artist and scientist. He was an accomplished painter, sculptor, draftsman, theorist, architect, designer, and engineer. With his large range of interests, Leonardo, the first of the **High Renaissance** artists, sought to

understand the world around him via scientific investigation. He established a new era of classical monumentality with an ideal harmony and balance in works such as the *Last Supper* (1494–1498) and *Mona Lisa* (1503–1505). Leonardo's drawings confirm his scientific brilliance, with subjects including an embryo in the womb and a flying machine. His legacy includes written commentaries on art as well as artwork from many genres. Leonardo was also interested in experimental techniques, Renaissance classicism, and human anatomy.

Death Camps, German

German **Nazi** extermination camps. At the beginning of **World War II, Adolf Hitler** began almost immediately to create concentration camps such as **Bergen-Belsen** to incarcerate Jews, Gypsies, and any other "enemies of the state." Part of the "Final Solution" to eliminate all of these people was the building of death camps, extermination centers where approximately 6 million people were systematically murdered between 1942 and 1945. The death camps include Treblinka, Auschwitz-Birkenau, Dachau, Chelmno, Belzek, Majdanek, Sobibor, and others. Some, like Auschwitz and Majdanek, served first as concentration camps and then as extermination centers. Many methods of killing were used, including shooting and gassing.

Deccan Plateau

Large, triangular geologic plateau covering much of the interior of southern India. The name is derived from the **Sanskrit** word *daksina* ("south"). The region's low rainfall has made it poor and somewhat less densely populated than most of the subcontinent. Historically, it has been a difficult region for empire builders to control. It was the home of the last major Hindu state, the **Vijayanagar** empire (c. 1347–1565), and the home of the Hindu Marathas, who controlled much of the region until defeated by the British in the nineteenth century.

Declaration of Independence (1776)

Document declaring the independence of the American colonies from British rule. Written predominantly by **Thomas Jefferson**, the Declaration of Independence is an excellent example of **Enlightenment** thinking, declaring that humankind has natural rights and that humans are created equal and have the right to rule themselves. It declared abuses by **George III** and the right of the colonists to be free of those abuses and was signed by fifty-six of the leading colonial statesmen.

Declaration of Rights (England) (1689)

English statement protecting existing rights, primarily of the landed classes from the monarchy. After **James II** proved himself to be incompetent and married a Catholic, producing a Catholic son and heir, an assembly of peers and commons was called (only the king could call **Parliament**). The assembly agreed to remove James and replace him with Mary, the closest Protestant heir, and her husband William as dual monarchs. On February 13, 1689, William and Mary signed the Declaration of Rights, which listed previous abuses of the crown and thirteen "ancient rights and liberties," including Parliament's rights to exist and to execute law and levy taxes, limits on a standing army, subjects' rights to bear arms, and freedom of speech in Parliament. Many of those rights appear in the American **Declaration of Independence** and the U.S. **Bill of Rights**.

Declaration of the Rights of Man and Citizen (1789)

Preamble to the future constitution written by France's National Assembly at the opening of the **French Revolution** on August 27, 1789. The declaration codified the basic ideas of the eighteenth-century **Enlightenment**, such as liberty of conscience, property, and press and freedom from arbitrary imprisonment. The Declaration of the Rights of Man and Citizen effectively ended the ancien régime.

De Gaulle, Charles (1890–1970)
French general, leader of the French resistance in **World War II**, and president of France (1959–1969). General De Gaulle escaped to London at the fall of France to Germany in World War II and led the Free French armed forces. At the end of the war De Gaulle became interim president of the Fourth Republic but later resigned. He was elected president of the Fifth Republic in 1959 and 1965. De Gaulle withdrew France from Algeria and from the **North American Treaty Organization** (NATO) and blocked the United Kingdom's entry into the **European Economic Community** (EEC).

Deism
Belief in a god who created the universe but who exerts no influence on it. Deism existed in seventeenth- and eighteenth-century Europe among people who believed in the truths of the **scientific revolution** and the **Enlightenment** and saw no need for a god who interfered in physical actions of the universe. God was described as a "great clock-maker" who created the universe, wound it up, and let it run.

Delhi
Capital of India and one of its largest cities. Located on the Jumna River, Delhi has a strategic position on the northern part of the Gangetic Plain near the northern region of the subcontinent. For this reason it was chosen by **Muslim** rulers from the twelfth to the sixteenth century as the center of their rule. In 1905 the British moved their administrative center for India to Delhi from Calcutta. In 1947 Delhi became the capital of independent India.

Delhi Sultanate
A series of **Muslim** dynasties that governed much of northern India from **Delhi** during the twelfth to sixteenth centuries: the Ibaris (1206–1290), the Khaljis (1290–1320), the Tughluqs (1320–1414), the Sayyids (1414–1451), and the Lodis (1451–1526). All military regimes, they were established following Muhammad of Ghur's and his chief lieutenant Qutb uddin Aibek's victory over Hindu forces in 1192. The Delhi Sultanate was important for establishing Muslim rule and influence over much of India.

Delian League
Modern name for the Greek Athenian–led alliance formed in 478 B.C.E. against Persia. After Sparta pulled out of leadership of the eastern campaign, **Athens** took the lead and forged an alliance of Greek Peloponnesian poleis. The alliance's headquarters were established on the sacred island of Delos, hence the name *Delian League*, and Athens determined the share of participation of each **polis** with Athens in command. With the Delian League's success at driving the Persians out of Thrace and coastal regions, the league grew to include nearly 200 members, but Athens gradually forced it into becoming its empire. This eventually led to the **Peloponnesian War** between Athens and **Sparta** and the deterioration of the entire Greek civilization.

Democracy
From the Greek for "rule by the people" (*demos*). Greek democracy, first established in **Athens** in 508 B.C.E. by **Cleisthenes**, was a true democracy of direct

participation. Each citizen had equal rights to sit in the assembly, and all decisions were made by the assembly and considered to have been made by the people. With English democracy in the form of parliamentary government and since the founding of the United States and the French Revolution, democracy has spread around the world, mainly in the form of representative governments (republics) where citizens vote for representatives who then make the decisions.

Democracy Wall

Chinese wall of protest posters. In late 1978, inspired by hints of political change, students and others in **Beijing** began putting up posters in public places protesting the existing conditions in China and expressing their views on the **Great Proletarian Cultural Revolution**. The most radical posters were put on a wall near the Forbidden City that became known as Democracy Wall. Authorities shut down the wall fairly soon after postings began.

See also Imperial City

Demosthenes (384–322 B.C.E.)

Athenian statesman whose orations called for the defense of Athens against **Philip II** of Macedonia. Demosthenes attempted to unite the Greek poleis militarily, but the Greeks were defeated in battle by the Macedonians in 338. After a failed revolt by the Athenians, Demosthenes committed suicide.

Deng Xiaoping (Teng Hsiao-p'ing) (1904–1997)

Chinese communist leader who studied with **Zhou Enlai** in France in the early 1920s, participated in the **Long March**, and became an important official in the **People's Republic of China** after 1949. Deng became associated with the pragmatic wing of the **Chinese Communist Party** (CCP) that was critical of **Mao Zedong**'s **Great Leap Forward**. In the early 1960s he was one of the principal figures in trying to aid in China's recovery following that disastrous policy. Twice purged by Mao, he emerged shortly after Mao's death in 1976 as the preeminent leader of China. From 1978 to the early 1990s he was the single most influential leader in China, although often wielding power from behind the scenes. Deng pushed for an economic program known as the **Four Modernizations** that called for opening up China to foreign investment, privatizing agriculture, and allowing for private industries and businesses. Despite greater freedom of movement, travel, and economic decision making, he insisted on tight political control by the CCP and ordered the crackdown on students in Tiananmen Square in 1989. He spent his last years securing his policies of promoting economic growth through pragmatic economic policies and placing **Jiang Zemin** in power as his successor.

Depression, Great

Worldwide depression of the 1930s. After a post–**World War I** slump, the economy in the United States and parts of Europe picked up. In the United States, there was unprecedented prosperity from international trade and domestic development of industry. Growth produced unwarranted confidence, however. People bought stocks and products on credit, leading to speculation. In October 1929 the U.S. stock market collapsed, with a domino effect on the rest of the U.S. economy and on Europe's economy. Soon, banks failed, corporations halted production, and markets dried up. Unemployment soared and demoralization set in. The Great Depression lasted through the 1930s until **World War II** and led to extreme measures and, in several countries, extreme governments.

Descartes, René (1596–1650)
French mathematician, philosopher, and a founder of the **scientific revolution** and its mathematical understanding of the universe. Descartes believed truth can only be understood as that which is proved, therefore he began with the statement "I think, therefore I am." His philosophy is referred to as "Cartesian."

De Soto, Hernando (c. 1498–1542)
Spanish explorer and conquistador. De Soto participated in the Spanish conquests of Panama, Nicaragua, Honduras, and Peru. He was the first to discover the **Inca** civilization and led in its conquest. He was appointed governor of Cuba and explored Florida and the heartland of what would become the southern United States. The first European to see the Mississippi River, he traversed 4,000 miles (6,400 km) in a fruitless search for gold and silver. De Soto died near present-day Natchez, Mississippi.

De Valera, Eamon (1882–1975)
U.S.-born Irish statesman, president, and prime minister of Ireland. As an Irish nationalist, de Valera was one of the leaders of the 1916 Easter Rising. Sentenced to death, he was released and became leader of the **Sinn Fein** (1917–1926). From 1919 to 1922 de Valera served as president of the provisional Irish government. He opposed British negotiations and led the nationalist Fianna Fáil Party in the newly formed Dáil (parliament). De Valera served as president of the Irish Free State from 1932 to 1937 and then, as the new constitution restructured the country, as prime minister of Eire (1937–1948, 1951–1954, 1957–1959). He served as president of Ireland from 1959 to 1973.

Devanagari (from Sanskrit *deva*, "god," and *nagari*, "city"—"Divine City")
The script used to write Hindi, **Sanskrit**, and other northern Indian languages. Ultimately derived from the ancient Brahmi script of India, it came into use between the seventh and eleventh centuries. It is basically an alphabetic form of writing containing forty-eight letters—thirty-four consonants, and fourteen vowels—although in older forms the vowels were not always written. The letters in modern languages are usually joined with horizontal bars.

De Vega, Lope (1562–1645)
Spanish playwright of Spain's golden age. His plays are rich in invention and dialogue with gallant and courageous heroes and clever heroines. Lope de Vega's plays reflect Spain's glorious past more than the struggling times in which they were written.

Devshirme
Levy of special troops within the **Ottoman Empire**. The elite social structure of the Ottomans was comprised of several slave groups, including the older Turko-Islamic aristocracy and the newer devshirmes, for which young male prisoners of war and confiscated Christian boys were recruited by the imposition of a special tax. The youths, aged eight to eighteen, were sent to **Istanbul** and converted to **Islam**. The most promising were given special education to perform as administrators in government, and the less talented went into the military to become **Janissaries**, the elite military unit and core of the Ottoman army.

Dhaka (Dacca)
Largest city and capital of Bangladesh. The city served as the **Mughal** capital of Bengal and still contains a number of impressive buildings from that era. It later declined but in 1905 became the capital of East Bengal, losing that status in 1911 with the cancellation of the partition. Between 1947 and 1971 the city served as the capital of

East Pakistan. With Bangladesh's independence in 1971 it became the capital of that new nation.

Dharma

In **Hinduism**, right or proper conduct; in Buddhism, universal truth. In Hinduism, each caste follows its own dharma. If one's actions are in line with one's dharma, karma is increased, leading to reincarnation as a higher form or, ultimately, *moksha*, or release from earthly suffering. In Buddhism, dharma signifies the teaching of the Buddha and is one of the Three Jewels (Triratna).

Dhow

Ship type that plied the waters of the Mediterranean Sea, the Red Sea, the Persian Gulf, and the Indian Ocean during the **Middle Ages** and beyond. The dhow (from Swahili, *daw*) was a very effective commercial ship, double ended (pointed front and back), made of sewn teak or coconut wood, and having one or two masts and lateen sails. Dhows sailed from Africa to India.

Diamond Sutra

Popular short Buddhist sutra known as the Vajracchedika-sutra ("Diamond Cutting sutra") written in the form of a dialogue. Originally a **Sanskrit** work of Indian origin, it appeared in Chinese translation around 400 C.E. The Diamond sutra emphasizes the illusionary and transitory nature of existence. It was extremely influential in east Asian **Buddhism**, influencing the later development of **Zen** (Chan) Buddhism.

Dias, Bartolomeu (c. 1450–1500)

Portuguese explorer who rounded the southern tip of Africa in 1487. A storm blew Dias's three ships far out to sea, but on February 3, 1488, they landed after sailing up the east coast of Africa. They returned around the tip, naming it the Cape of Storms. (It was later renamed Cape of Good Hope by the Portuguese king John II.) Dias returned to Lisbon in December 1488.

Dickens, Charles (1812–1870)

English novelist and social critic. Dickens began writing sketches in monthly magazines, and his first major work was *Pickwick Papers* (1837), followed by *Oliver Twist* (1838) and then nearly yearly novels. Most of his novels were written as monthly installments in magazines. Dickens is known for his combination of humor, social satire, horror, and character portrayal.

Diderot, Denis (1713–1784)

French writer, author of the monumental *Encyclopedia* published from 1751 to 1772. It incorporated all the new knowledge of the **Enlightenment** world known to Diderot. The work was very contentious and was even suppressed by the French government in 1759, but it continued to influence thinking in France and elsewhere in Europe.

Dien Bien Phu

Viet Minh victory over French forces in 1954 that brought about the armistice ending the French Indo-China War. The Vietnamese, led by General **Vo Nguyen Giap** and equipped with Chinese-supplied artillery, forced a French garrison to surrender in May 1954. Two months later French rule in Vietnam ended.

Diesel, Rudolf (1858–1913)

German engineer and inventor of the diesel engine (1892). The first diesel engines were not really built until 1895 and were exhibited at the Munich Exhibition of 1898. The diesel engine's compression of air causes the fuel combustion and maintains constant pressure in the engine using no igniting mechanism. Diesel did not live to see the possibilities of his invention fulfilled.

Diffusion
Term for the process by which innovations such as ideas, technologies, food crops, and so forth begin in one place and then spread. Diffusion occurs with **cross-cultural encounters**. In the past, most historical changes, including the development of agriculture and the idea of civilization itself, were thought to have had one place of origin—southwestern Asia—from which they diffused, but now most historians recognize independent origins and developments for both.

Dingiswayo (c. 1770–1816)
African military and political leader who began the unification of chiefdoms into a military confederation that would become the powerful Zulus. Dingiswayo introduced a new structure to the military, organizing men into strong groups of comrades. When Dingiswayo was murdered by a rival, his military leader, **Shaka Zulu**, took power, united the confederation, and assumed the Zulu kingship.

Diocletian (245–313)
Roman emperor (284–305) who reformed the **Roman Empire**. Diocletian brought about extensive reforms, dividing the empire into east and west (286) and reformed the military, the economy, taxes, and the imperial succession that enabled the empire in the west to survive for another century. He was also noted for his persecution of Christians. Diocletian retired in 305.

Diodorus (c. 90–21 B.C.E.)
Roman historian. Born in Sicily and a contemporary of **Julius Caesar** and **Octavian**,

Diodorus wrote a history of the world in forty books, only part of which has survived. He wrote a famous description of **Alexander the Great**'s funeral procession.

Dionysus
Greek god of wine and festivals also called Bacchus. Dionysus was born of Zeus and a human mother. The importance of Dionysus is seen in **Euripides**' *The Bacchae*. The Dionysia were festivals in honor of the god where followers clothed themselves in fawn skins and ivy and carried musical instruments and phalli. Dionysian religion became important and were associated with fertility, with Dionysus representing the sap of life and the excitement of nature—the god of ecstasy.

Disraeli, Benjamin (1804–1881)
British prime minister (1868, 1874–1880), statesman, and author. Disraeli was a member of the **Conservative**, or Tory, Party, which represented primarily the landowners, the Church of England, and the preservation of existing rights. However, Disraeli was largely responsible numerous social reforms and for the Reform Act of 1867, which doubled the electorate. The electorate responded by electing his archrival, **William Gladstone**, prime minister. Disraeli was well liked by **Queen Victoria** and had her declared empress of India.

Divine Comedy, The
Dante Alighieri's epic poem. He wrote the *La Divina Commedia* (*The Divine Comedy*) (1307–1321) while in exile from the city of Florence. One hundred cantos (chapters) comprise the three "books" *Inferno, Purgatorio,* and *Paradisio,* which lead the reader on an imaginative journey through hell, purgatory, and heaven along with the pilgrim, who is led by **Virgil** and Beatrice, Dante's muse. Written in the vernacular (Italian), this poem is full of rich

classical, scriptural, and medieval symbolism.

Dome of the Rock (Qubbat al-Sakkrah)
Sacred Muslim shrine in **Jerusalem**. After capturing Jerusalem in 637 C.E., the **Muslims** built a mosque, al-Aqsa, and shrine, Dome of the Rock (692), on the site of the ancient **Hebrew Temple**, and Jerusalem became a holy site for adherents to **Islam**. The structure occupies a very large section of the Old City. Muslim tradition holds that **Muhammad** was divinely transported to Jerusalem and commissioned there, despite the lack of specific reference to this event in the **Quran**. Muhammad is also said to have ascended to heaven from this location. The first domed mosque, it contains a rock believed to be the place where **Abraham** offered his son as a sacrifice before God intervened (Genesis 22).

Dominicans (Black Friars)
Order of mendicant (begging) friars founded by Saint Dominic in 1216. The Dominicans were substantially different from the traditional **Benedictines** and the mendicant **Franciscans**. The Dominicans maintained the traditional prayer and liturgy of monasticism but added poverty, preaching, and teaching as emphasis. Consequently, the Dominicans emphasized education and became leaders in European education in the thirteenth century, with members such as **Thomas Aquinas**. The Dominicans also became active in the **Inquisition** as defenders of Christian orthodoxy.

Donatello (c. 1386–1466)
Italian sculptor (full name Donato di Niccolo di Betto di Bardi) of the early **Renaissance** who used a variety of materials including bronze, marble, terra-cotta, and wood to create works commissioned for secular and religious purposes. Donatello's art contained both elements of classical idealism and realistic depictions. Among his most influential works were the bronze *David* (1425), possibly the first free-standing bronze nude to be created since classical antiquity, and the harshly realistic wooden *Mary Magdalene* (1455).

Donne, John (1572–1631)
English poet and cleric. Donne, a contemporary of **William Shakespeare** (1564–1616) and Ben Jonson (1573–1637), wrote most of his best poetry before age twenty-five and went on to become one of the most famous and esteemed preachers and poets in England. One of the metaphysical poets, Donne is sometimes given his own category, as the "school of Donne." One of his better-known poems is "Death Be Not Proud."

Dorian Greeks
A division of classical Greeks. The four divisions—Dorians, Aeolians, Ionians, and Achaeans—populated the Peloponnese, the southern part of the Greek peninsula. The Dorians are usually considered conquerors of the earlier Greeks, the Ionians and the Achaeans.

Doric Order
Architectural order of design in ancient Greece. Doric is the earliest and simplest of the orders, followed by **Ionic Order** and **Corinthian Order**, and is characterized by a simple capital with a cushionlike design and a column without a complex base.

Douglass, Frederick (1818–1895)
Abolitionist leader, antilynching and woman's suffrage spokesperson, orator, editor, and writer. Douglass ranks as the most influential African American leader of the nineteenth century. He penned three important autobiographies describing slavery and race in the United States.

Dravidians

Speakers of the languages of the Dravidian family such as Tamil, Telugu, Malayalam, and Kannada. Dravidian speakers live primarily in southern India, where they predominate today. Historians believe that these languages were once spoken throughout most of the subcontinent prior to the coming of the Indo-European-speaking **Aryans** in the second millennium B.C.E. The builders of the **Indus Valley** civilizations were most likely Dravidians. **Hinduism** is an amalgam of Aryan and Dravidian religious beliefs and practices.

Dreadnaught, HMS (for "His Majesty's Ship")

British battleship developed in 1907. Completely revolutionizing naval warfare, it had ten twelve-inch guns (more than twice the firepower of any other ship), greater speed than other ships (its steam turbines ran on coal or oil), and heavy armor. The *Dreadnaught* made other ships obsolete. Its creation forced Germany to begin constructing similar battleships, followed by France and the United States and, eventually, Japan. Germany's greater steel-manufacturing capabilities gave it the edge and forced an arms race between Britain and Germany that contributed to the outbreak of **World War I.**

Dreyfus Affair

Accusation, trial, and imprisonment of Alfred Dreyfus (1859–1935) that caused a crisis in French society. Dreyfus, of Jewish descent, was falsely accused in 1894 of passing military secrets to Germany. In the wake of its defeat in the Franco-Prussian War, the French military wanted someone to blame. **Anti-Semitism** clashed with militarism and antimilitarism, exposing wide rifts in French society.

Druze

Middle Eastern religious sect. Located primarily in Lebanon, the Druze have maintained cohesion and loyalty with few conversions into or out of the sect and few intermarriages. The sect was founded in 1017 in Egypt as an offshoot of **Islam** and its members have held their sect under a cloak of secrecy. They believe their founder did not die but vanished and will one day return to inaugurate a **golden age.** The Druze played a prominent role in Lebanon into the twenty-first century.

Dryden, John (1631–1700)

English poet and dramatist. Writing in the Restoration period, Dryden was renowned for social and political statements in his literature, although many of his works were also extremely witty. His best-known work is the play *All for Love* (1677). As poet laureate Dryden defended **James II** and the church of England, but after the **Glorious Revolution** removed James and replaced him with William and Mary, Dryden lost favor with the crown.

Duarte, Juan Pablo (1813–1876)

Father of Dominican independence. In 1843 Duarte attempted to oust Haitian rule from the eastern part of the island of Hispaniola. Although he failed and fled, the revolt revived and succeeded in 1844, when the Dominican Republic proclaimed independence. Duarte returned, but when military dictator took power he was exiled to Venezuela.

Du Bois, W. E. B. (1868–1963)

African American writer and father of Pan-Africanism. W. E. B. (William Edward Burghardt) Du Bois earned a doctorate from Harvard in 1896. He became an advocate for equal rights for American blacks and founded the National Association for the Advancement of Colored People (NAACP) in 1909. Du Bois was opposed to Marcus Garvey's "back to Africa" movement and Booker T. Washington's willingness to accommodate to white society. Du Bois organized **Pan-African Congresses**, campaigned for recognition of all black peoples, and was a prolific writer on the subject. In later life Du Bois became a Marxist; was critical of American society; and moved to Ghana, where he died at age ninety-five.

Du Fu (Tu Fu) (712–770)

Chinese poet of the **Tang** dynasty considered one of China's greatest poets. A younger contemporary of Li Bo, the other great Tang poet, Du Fu celebrated the beauty of nature in his many poems. They are noted for their satire and compassion toward people in distress. In his own life, he suffered many hardships and saw his children die of starvation, but he later was admired and imitated by generations of east Asians.

Dulles, John Foster (1888–1959)

Lawyer and U.S. Secretary of State. After a distinguished career as a lawyer focusing on international issues in which he participated in the drafting of the **Versailles Treaty**, the United Nations Charter, and the Japanese Peace Treaty (1951), Dulles was named Secretary of State by President **Dwight D. Eisenhower**. A **Cold War** hardliner, Dulles advanced the concepts of massive nuclear retaliation, **brinksmanship**, and the liberation of Soviet-controlled Eastern Europe. He also oversaw covert operations by the **Central Intelligence Agency** (CIA), headed by his brother Allen, in Iran, Guatemala, Indonesia, Eastern Europe, and Cuba as well as the armistice in Korea (1953) and the expansion of U.S. involvement in Vietnam.

Dunkirk, Battle of (1940)

World War II battle. As German armies swept through the Netherlands, Belgium, and France and cornered the British Expeditionary Force (BEF) on the French coast of the English Channel 338,000 Allied troops (224,000 of them British) were rescued from the beaches by a flotilla of naval ships and private boats of all sorts. Nearly all weapons and ammunition were left behind. The battle was a colossal military disaster for the **Allies**, although **Winston Churchill** praised the valiant effort that evacuated the core of the British army.

Dupleix, Joseph-François (1697–1763)

French colonial administrator. Dupleix became governor-general of the French East India Company in 1741, and it began to rival the British **East India Company**, threatening British trade dominance in India. Dupleix hoped to found a French empire in India but was frustrated by **Robert Clive**. Dupleix was recalled in 1754.

Dürer, Albrecht (1471–1528)

German artist of the **northern Renaissance**. He was a painter, printmaker, draftsman, and theoretician. His influential woodcuts explored perspective and naturalism in complex arrangements using many different material surfaces, mathematical determinants of human proportion, and a variety of shading methods. His work was soon collected, and his style was copied (predominantly in Germany) during a period known as the Dürer Renaissance (1570–1620).

Dutch East India Company

Trading company established in the Netherlands in 1602. The Dutch East India Company was given monopoly trading privileges for the Far East. Headquartered in Batavia (now Jakarta), Indonesia, the company traded large quantities of pepper and other spices. The Dutch East India Company was a competitor of the British East India Company during the seventeenth century. The company was dissolved in 1798.

See also East India Company (English)

Dutch Republic (formally Republic of the United Netherlands) (1588–1795)
State of the northern Low Countries along the North Sea. Seven Netherlands provinces fought a war for independence from Spain known as the Dutch Revolt (1559–1609), and out of the Union of Utrecht (1579) they became the Dutch Republic in 1588. For the next two centuries the Dutch Republic was a major power in Europe with its **golden age** in the seventeenth century producing great wealth and brilliant arts. Long wars with England in the late seventeenth century and with France in the eighteenth century brought about a rapid decline, and in 1795 the republic collapsed in the wake of a French invasion during the **French Revolution** and the Napoleonic Wars.

Dyula
Mande-speaking people of western Africa in the **Congo** region. The Dyula were major gold traders during the ancient kingdoms of **Ghana** and **Mali**. They acted as a link between the gold-producing lands in the south and the trading routes to north Africa and the Mediterranean Sea. Although gold was its most distinctive trade commodity, the Dyula also traded in kola nuts. They were also known as expert crafters. Today, the Dyula live mostly in towns as merchants in Ivory Coast, Burkina Faso, Mali, and Ghana.

ε

Eastern Orthodox Church
Christian church of eastern Europe, **Russia**, Greece, and western Asia. The Eastern Orthodox Church split with the **Roman Catholic Church** in 1054 over a phrase in the Nicene-Constantinopolitan Creed (381) claiming that the Holy Spirit proceeds from the Father (the Eastern view) rather than from the Father and the Son (the Western view), and also over the pope's claim to authority over all churches. The patriarch of Constantinople holds the position of greatest honor but does not have authority over other churches. The Eastern Orthodox Church has seven major sacraments similar to Roman Catholicism.

Eastern Roman Empire
Eastern half of the **Roman Empire** ruled from Constantinople and after 476 referred to by historians as the **Byzantine Empire** (referring to themselves as Roman). The Roman Empire's expansion to the eastern Mediterranean in the first century B.C.E. added vast regions, including Greece, Egypt, and much of the **Middle East** (called Asia), that were markedly different from the west. Linguistically, the east spoke Greek instead of Latin as the universal language. In 330 Emperor Constantine established a second capital at Byzantium, called **Constantinople**, giving the empire two administrative centers. In the late fourth century, under Emperor Valentinian in the west and his brother Valens in the east, the empire was divided in two, with each maintaining its own court. The two halves of the empire became increasingly separate and different. With the decline of the western Roman Empire, Constantinople and the east became the bastion of the empire, with a flourishing economy and culture. As the west crumbled, the Eastern Roman Empire remained and became known as the Byzantine Empire. Under **Justinian**, in the sixth century it expanded into north Africa, Italy, and Spain. As the Byzantine Empire, the Eastern Roman Empire gradually declined under pressure from Islam until Constantinople fell to the **Ottoman Turks** in 1453.

East India Company (English)
English trading corporation for the Far East. Founded on the last day of 1600, England's Honorable East India Company was the greatest of the joint stock-trading firms formed to bring the wealth of Asia to Europe. Starting with a few trading posts established along the east and west coasts of India in the mid-1600s, by the end of the eighteenth century "John Company," as it was called, had effectively supplanted the Mughals and other competitors as rulers of the subcontinent.

East India Company, Dutch. *See* Dutch East India Company

East Timor
Formerly Portuguese Timor and now an independent state sharing the island of Timor with Indonesia. When the 450-year-old colony declared its independence

from Portugal in 1975, Indonesia invaded and annexed it as the province of Timor in 1976. The action by Indonesia, done with the implicit acceptance of the United States and Australia, began a long, bloody **guerilla** war with the FRETILIN (Revolutionary Front of Independent East Timor) in which as many as 200,000 died in a country of less than 1 million. In 1996 the **Nobel Prize** for Peace was award jointly to Jorge Ramos-Horta, a FRETILIN activist living in exile, and Bishop Carols Belo of East Timor for their efforts at freedom and human rights. After its forces committed a number of atrocities Indonesia withdrew, and East Timor achieved independence in 2002.

Edict of Milan. *See* Milan, Edict of

Edict of Nantes. *See* Nantes, Edict of

Edict of Worms. *See* Worms, Edict of

Edison, Thomas Alva (1847–1931)
American inventor. With almost no formal education, Edison invented many devises, mostly electrical, and is most famous for the phonograph (1877) and the electric light (1879). Edison built a workshop and laboratory in Menlo Park, New Jersey, and took out more than 1,000 patents. Edison's inventions have become some of the most important contributions to modern society.

Edo
Ancient Japanese name for the modern city of Tokyo. Centrally located in the agriculturally rich Kanto plain, it remained a small village until the Japanese warlord **Tokugawa** Ieyasu established his headquarters there in the late sixteenth century. In 1603, when he made himself **shogun**, it became the center of government. By the eighteenth century Edo was a great commercial and cultural center as well as the seat of the Tokugawa shogunate, with its population of 1 million making it perhaps the largest city in the world. In 1868 during the **Meiji Restoration** the emperor was moved from Kyoto to Edo, which was then renamed Tokyo ("Eastern Capital").

Edward I (1239–1307)
English king (1272–1307 who laid the administrative foundation of the English nation. Known as Edward "Longshanks," he strengthened the crown and government including **Parliament**. Parliament met with commoners for the first time in 1295. Edward subdued Wales and attempted to subdue Scotland, but at the Battle of Stirling Bridge (1297) William Wallace and the Scots defeated the English. Edward was noted for his administrative and judicial efficiency and reforms as well as his military prowess.

Edward III (1312–1377)
English king (1327–1377) at the opening of the **Hundred Years War** (1338–1453). Grandson of **Edward I**, **Edward III** followed his inept and weak father, Edward II. Edward III claimed the French throne but also wanted to regain Gasgony and its wine trade, leading to the war. Two of the great battles of the Hundred Years War were fought during Edward's reign—the **Battle of Crécy** (1346) and the **Battle of Poitiers** (1356). Also during Edward's reign, the **Black Death** (bubonic plague) broke out all across Europe. His descendants include members of the two noble houses of Lancaster and York who later fought for the throne in the Wars of the Roses, which took its name from the rose symbols of each house.

Egyptian Civilization
Ancient Middle Eastern civilization along the **Nile Valley**, known as Lower Egypt and

Upper Egypt. The history of ancient Egypt is divided into thirty-one dynasties that are grouped into five periods: Early Dynastic (c. 2925–2575 B.C.E.), Old Kingdom (c. 2575–2130 B.C.E.), Middle Kingdom (1938–1600 B.C.E.), New Kingdom (c. 1540–1075 B.C.E.), and Late Period (1075–525 B.C.E.). The Old Kingdom was a period of powerful pharaohs, prosperity, expansion, development of new technologies, and building of great monuments. Most of the construction of the **Pyramids of Giza** took place during the Old Kingdom. A period of fragmentation followed. During the Middle Kingdom, the gods of **Amon-Re** and **Osiris** and **Isis** were dominant. Around 1600 B.C.E. Egypt was invaded by the **Hyksos**, who quickly adopted Egyptian culture. In the New Kingdom, the pharaohs involved Egypt in international affairs (contrary to Egyptian tradition). The New Kingdom had several powerful queens. **Hatshepsut,** a queen who declared herself pharaoh, brought about expansion of the economy, trade, and administrative innovations. Nefertiti was the renowned and beautiful queen of **Amenhotep IV.** In 525 B.C.E. Egyptian civilization was conquered by the Persians. The Egyptian writing, in the form of **hieroglyphics,** was lost for centuries until deciphered with the use of the **Rosetta stone.**

Eightfold Path

In **Buddhism,** a path toward **nirvana.** There are **Four Noble Truths** in Buddhism, and the fourth—the course to follow—contains the Eightfold Path to the elimination of suffering. Its eight aspects are to hold, practice, and follow rightful views, aspirations, speech, conduct, livelihood, effort, mindfulness, and meditation. By following the Four Noble Truths, including the Eightfold Path, one may reach the goal of nirvana, or escape from suffering.

Einstein, Albert (1879–1955)

German-born U.S. physicist and **Nobel Prize**–winner for physics. Einstein published the special theory of relativity in 1905 and the general theory of relativity in 1915. These altered the previously held views of the relations of mass and energy and of the absolutes of time and space. Mass and time vary with velocity, while energy and mass are interchangeable. He won the Nobel Prize in 1921. A Jew, Einstein emigrated from **Adolf Hitler's Nazi** Germany to the United States in 1933. In 1939 he wrote to President **Franklin D. Roosevelt** to warn him of research being done in Germany on **atomic theory** that could lead to the production of an **atomic bomb.** Einstein spent the latter part of his life unsuccessfully searching for a unified field theory and speaking out in opposition to nuclear weapons.

Eiriksson, Leif (fl. c. 1000)

Scandinavian explorer who explored North America around 1000. Archaeological evidence in Newfoundland, Canada, has confirmed stories in the Vinland saga that tell of Leif, son of Eirik the Red, and his exploration from Greenland of the North American coast. There were numerous Norwegian colonies on Greenland from which sailing to North America would have been relatively easy.

Eisenhower, Dwight D. (1890–1969)

U.S. Army general and thirty-fourth president of the United States. A professional army officer, Eisenhower was chosen to command the successful Allied invasion of north Africa in 1942. Named supreme Allied commander in Europe, he oversaw the D-day invasion of France and the final defeat of Germany. After serving as **North Atlantic Treaty Organization** (NATO) commander, Eisenhower was elected U.S. president as a Republican in 1952 and was reelected in 1956. As president, Eisenhower did not fundamentally alter the expanded federal government he inherited from **Franklin D. Roosevelt** and **Harry S Truman**, although he opposed public power and aid to farmers. He later used federal troops to enforce the desegregation of pubic schools in Little Rock, Arkansas. In foreign policy, he obtained an armistice in Korea and generally stabilized relations with the **Union of Soviet Socialist Republics**. **Cold War** tensions increased at the end of his administration, with a renewed crisis over Berlin and the downing of a U-2 spy place over Soviet territory in 1960.

Ejidos

Spanish term for communally held village lands in Mexico. Land reforms of 1856 had the result of taking much of these lands away from small villages, especially indigenous villages, despite the fact that the intent of the reforms was to dissolve huge church estates. **Emiliano Zapata**, among others, fought in the **Mexican Revolution** to recover these ancestral lands. The constitution of 1917 restored the ejidos to landless villages. Ejidos comprised 55 percent of the cultivated land in Mexico in the 1980s, but their number has been shrinking yearly as a result of privatization.

Eleanor of Aquitaine (1122–1204)

Queen of France and wife of Louis VII from 1137 to 1151. She accompanied her husband on a crusade. Their marriage was annulled in 1151, and the same year she married Henry, Duke of Normandy and Anjou, who became **Henry II** of England. As queen of England Eleanor bore Henry three daughters and five sons, two of whom became kings of England: **Richard I** and **John I**. Eleanor was placed under house arrest from 1174 to 1189 for conspiring with her sons to revolt against her husband. Independently wealthy, Eleanor

was a patron of the arts and encouraged troubadours, poets, and artists at her court in Poitiers.

El Greco (Domenikos Theotocopoulos) (1541–1614)

Spanish artist of the mannerist movement. El Greco (Spanish for "the Greek") was born in Crete, studied in Italy, and moved to Spain during the 1570s to become a church painter in Toledo. Like other mannerists, his figures where elongated, contorted, and painted in unusual colors. The stormy backgrounds of his works reflects the religious tension and upheaval in Europe during the **Catholic Reformation**. El Greco produced not only religious works but also depicted psychological questions (*Cardinal-Inquisitor Fernando Nino de Guevara*); landscapes of Toledo; and mythological subjects, such as *Laocoon*, with spirituality and intense emotion. His style would influence abstract artists of the late nineteenth and twentieth centuries.

Elizabeth I (1533–1603)

English monarch. Born to King **Henry VIII** and Anne Boleyn, Elizabeth ascended the thrown in 1558 after her half brother Edward VI and half sister **Mary I** and ruled until her death in 1603. When she became queen England was in a sad state in the midst of religious turmoil and economic decline. Most held little hope for Elizabeth's leadership, but she turned out to be one of England's greatest monarchs. Elizabeth chose advisors very wisely. During her reign England became a world power and produced some of its greatest intellects and leaders: **William Shakespeare**, John Donne, Francis Bacon, Robert and William Cecil, Sir Francis Drake, **Sir Walter Raleigh**, and **Sir John Hawkins**. Elizabeth never married, but she used the prospect of marriage as a diplomatic tool. She died childless but left England secure. Her cousin Mary, Queen of Scots's son **James VI** of Scotland followed Elizabeth as **James I** of England.

Ellora, Rock Temples of

Thirty-four **Hindu, Buddhist,** and **Jain** cave temples carved out of rock in the Maharashtra state of India. They were carved between the mid-sixth and the tenth centuries. The most famous is the Kailasa temple, dedicated to **Shiva** and carved to look like a free-standing structure.

E-maki

Japanese horizontal handscrolls used for pictorial purposes. Derived originally from China, they were employed by the Japanese from at least the twelfth century to create a major art form that blended scenes to create a narrative. The most famous include the Genji Scrolls, telling the *Tale of Genji*, and the Heiji Scroll, depicting a conflict in 1159 between the Minamoto and Taira families.

Emerson, Ralph Waldo (1803–1882)

American poet and essayist. With a strong New England **Puritan** background, Emerson became a Unitarian minister. He was influenced by the Romantic poets and believed that God is in every person. Emerson became the central figure among a group of New England intellectuals known as the Transcendentalists that included Henry David Thoreau. They believed in a free, deep, harmonious life transcending the mundane and connecting each individual with God. Emerson became an ardent **abolitionist.**

Emile. See Rousseau, Jean-Jacques

Empress Dowager (Ci Xi) (1834–1908)

Mother of the Chinese emperor Tongzhi (r. 1862–1874) and regent for his successor, Emperor Guangxu (r. 1874–1908).

She remained the power behind the throne and regent for the remainder of the latter's reign. Generally regarded as capable and intelligent but ignorant of the changing world situation, she became associated with the conservatives at the **Qing** court, who opposed attempts at reform. After fleeing foreign forces in the **Boxer Rebellion** in 1900, she made some concessions to reformers but tried to delay the creation of a constitutional monarchy.

Encomienda

Spanish sixteenth-century colonial exploitation of native peoples. The encomienda system, as sanctioned by the Spanish crown, was taken from medieval practice: A group of Indians in the colonies was granted to a Spaniard, who had the right to use them as forced labor or to provide tribute. The Spaniard was supposed to protect his Indians, provide a priest, and defend the colony. The encomienda proved so devastating that native populations dwindled. The **repartimiento** was an extension of the encomienda in which Indians had to provide tribute or occasionally provide some work for shorter periods.

English Calvinists (Puritans). *See* Calvinism; Pilgrims; Puritans

English Civil War (1642–1649)

War fought between pro-Royalist forces, known as Cavaliers, and pro-parliamentary forces, known as Roundheads. Issues of the conflict were complex, including complaints against the king, **Charles I**; the role of the monarchy; and the role of **Parliament**, as well as social, economic, and religious differences. The Royalists tended to be aristocrats or other old, landed families or the peasantry, religiously conservative, and from the midlands or the north and west of England.

The Parliamentarians tended to be gentry (middling landowners) or of the merchant class, religiously **Calvinist** or **Puritan**, better educated, and from the south and east of England. The English Civil War ended with the defeat of the Royalists, the execution of Charles I, and the establishment of a republic headed by **Oliver Cromwell**, one of the generals of the army for the parliamentary forces. The republic lasted until 1660, when the monarchical line was returned with Charles I's son **Charles II** in the Restoration.

English Peasants' Revolt (1381)

Uprising by peasantry and some urban laborers. Tensions between landlords and tenants from changes brought on by the **Black Death** starting in 1348; the Statutes of Laborers of 1351, which froze wages; poll taxes imposed between 1377 and 1381; and losses in the **Hundred Years War** with France triggered a revolt in Essex and Kent that moved to London lasted scarcely a month. When the rebels reached London concessions were made to them, and they were then tricked, their leaders arrested and executed. The result was a long-lasting dread of peasant uprisings in England.

Enigma

German **World War II** code machine used to scramble messages sent to and from German U-boats. In a campaign known as **Ultra**, the British captured an Enigma machine and broke the code through painstaking work at Bletchley Park. Cracking the code enabled the British to know the position of U-boats and win the **Battle of the Atlantic**.

Enlightenment

Eighteenth-century movement attempting to understand humankind's social interactions and institutions in a scientific method. Immanuel Kant called the Enlightenment mankind's coming of age. Trying to understand human institutions in the same way that **Isaac Newton** had understood the physical universe, Enlightenment writers, primarily French and Scottish, established "natural laws" and principles by which humans think and form society. Important writers of the Enlightenment include Diderot, **Voltaire**, Baron Montesquieu, **David Hume**, and **Jean-Jacques Rousseau**. The Enlightenment ideas were put to political effect for the first time in the establishment of the United States and soon afterward in the **French Revolution**. The **Declaration of Independence** is a prime example of Enlightenment thinking.

Enuma Elish

Mesopotamian mythological cosmological text. The *Enuma Elish* describes the origins of the world as a watery chaos, of the sea and fresh water under ground. Out of the mingling of the waters were born the first gods: Lahmu and Lahamu, the gods of the silt, and Anshar and Kishar, the gods of the horizon. They created Anu, the god of heaven, and he created Ea, the god of fresh water. The *Enuma Elish* establishes human authority in monarchy as the source of order and stability on earth.

Epicurus (341–270 B.C.E.)

Greek philosopher. His philosophy, Epicurianism, emphasizes hedonism, or achieving pleasure and avoiding pain, although mental pleasure is more highly valued than physical pleasure. The ultimate pleasure is avoidance of anxiety, fear, and grief.

Equiano, Olaudah (Gustavus Vassa) (c. 1745–1797)

British **abolitionist** of African origins and author of *The Life of Olaudah Equiano*

(1789). Born in an area that is part of modern-day Nigeria, taken into slavery and transported to Barbados, and sold to a British ship captain, Equiano sailed around the world, learned English, was sold to an American ship captain, bought his freedom, sailed on an expedition to the Arctic and throughout the Mediterranean, and participated in the abolitionist movement in Britain and many of its most important causes. His autobiography is a classic that helped bring an end to slavery.

Erasmus, Desiderius (1466–1536)

Dutch-born monk and humanist who combined Christian theology with classical tradition in his prolific scholarship. One of his most influential works, *Education of a Christian Prince* (1516), offers views of Christian society and government. Although Erasmus was involved in **Reformation** debates between Catholics and Protestants, he did not advocate one side or support doctrinal changes, although he was a critic of church abuses. *The Praise of Folly* (1509) is his most celebrated and most controversial writing.

Erech. *See* Uruk

Ericsson, Leif. *See* Eiriksson, Leif

Essay Concerning Human Understanding. See Locke, John

Essenes

Religious sect in Palestine from the second century B.C.E. to the first century C.E. The Essenes lived in tightly controlled communities with communal property, abstaining from public life and often from women, and carefully following the Law of Moses. The Dead Sea Scrolls were probably written and stored by an Essene community in the caves of Qumran.

Estates General (States General)

Formal gathering of the three estates of a realm in medieval or early modern Europe. The three estates were clergy; aristocracy; and the Third Estate, which included everyone else. They were called by the king to provide him advice. In England this structure developed into **Parliament**, which became an essential part of government by the sixteenth and seventeenth centuries, while in France **Louis XIV** ruled without the Estates General as an absolute monarch during the seventeenth and eighteenth centuries. France's Estates General was not called from 1614 until 1789, when its reconstitution turned into the **National Assembly** and led to the **French Revolution**.

Eta Class

Hereditary outcaste group of Japan, of disputed origin but probably derived from criminals, captives in war, and hereditary groups whose occupations such as butchering or leatherwork were considered unclean by the predominantly Buddhist Japanese society. In **Tokugawa** times they were estimated to form about 2 percent of the population. In 1871 the eta (also known as *hinin* or *burakumin*) were given legal equality, but severe discrimination persisted. Members of the caste formed a number of organizations in the twentieth century to overcome the social barriers they faced, but despite some improvements discrimination against them still prevails in Japan.

Etruscans

Pre-Roman civilization of the Italian peninsula. The Etruscans, now believed to be indigenous, had developed a rich, artistic, and technologically advanced civilization by the eighth century B.C.E. In the seventh and sixth centuries B.C.E. the Etruscans, along with **Greece** and **Carthage**, were the major traders in the western Mediterranean. The Etruscans produced beautiful painted pottery, bronze work, and jewelry and also traded in olive oil and wine. The rise of the Romans in the sixth century B.C.E. brought about the decline of the Etruscan civilization, and by the end of the fourth century B.C.E. the Romans had absorbed the Etruscans into their civilization.

Eugène of Savoy (1663–1736)
French statesman and field marshal who worked in the employ of the Holy Roman Emperor. Rumored to be the illegitimate son of **Louis XIV**, Eugène, of the House of Savoy, left France for the service of Austrian Holy Roman Emperor Leopold I. Eugène proved himself one of the greatest strategists of his era, fighting the Turks in eastern Europe, freeing Hungary from the Turks, fighting France in the War of the Grand Alliance (1689–1697), and fighting in the War of the Spanish Succession (1701–1714) alongside the Duke of Marlborough at Blenheim. His greatest victory was at Belgrade (1718), where, against enormous odds, he annihilated the Turkish enemy and took the city. Eugène taught **Frederick the Great**.

Eunuch
A boy or man castrated or entirely emasculated for use as a singer or guardian of a **harem**. Many civilizations have castrated boys for specific purposes. In the West, boys were castrated to maintain their soprano voices for church choirs in place of women. The Vatican choirs still had eunuchs into the twentieth century. In the **Middle East** and in ancient China, eunuchs were used to guard harems because they would not sexually interfere with the women and could not become progenitors of competitive families of power or wealth. In China, eunuchs were normally surgically emasculated.

Euphrates River
River originating in the mountains of Turkey and running 1,700 miles to the Persian Gulf. The Euphrates and the **Tigris** rivers begin in the same mountains of Turkey, the Euphrates to the west of the Tigris, and travel parallel courses only 250 miles (400 km) apart at the widest and 30 miles (50 km) apart at the narrowest, near Baghdad, and they join together approximately 50 miles (80 km) before reaching the gulf. The region between the two is known as **Mesopotamia** ("land between the rivers"). The Euphrates, as well as the Tigris, enabled the development of some of the earliest civilizations in the world. For thousands of years the rivers were tapped for irrigation, and the **Sumerian**, **Babylonian**, and **Assyrian** cultures arose there.

Euripedes (c. 484–406 B.C.E.)
Ancient Greek playwright and one of the three major authors of tragedy along with **Aeschylus** and **Sophocles**. Euripedes wrote more than ninety plays of which nineteen survive, including *Medea* (431 B.C.E.), *Electra* (c. 413 B.C.E.), and *The Bacchae* (c. 406 B.C.E.; produced posthumously). It is said that Socrates admired Euripedes' plays.

Eurocentrism
A term that means viewing the world from a point where Europe is the center. It generally implies giving greater importance and value to European or Western culture. Eurocentrism reached a peak at the end of the nineteenth century and the beginning of the twentieth century as nineteenth-century **imperialism** expanded Europe's control and influence to its greatest heights, with vast empires around the world controlled from the European countries. The pseudoscientific racism of **Nazi** Germany and other movements also demonstrate Eurocentrism.

Critics of Eurocentrism argue that it has resulted in a false dichotomy between East and West that characterizes much thought about the world and exaggerates the importance of Europe and the West in world history while failing to recognize the achievements and influence of non-Western societies.

European Community (EC)

Organization of European countries established in 1967 out of the **European Economic Community** (EEC), the European Atomic Energy Commission, and the European Coal and Steel Community. The EC was committed to the economic and political union of its member states, Belgium, Germany, France, Italy, Luxembourg, and the Netherlands. In 1973 Denmark, Ireland, and the United Kingdom were added to the EC. In 1981 Greece joined, and in 1986, Portugal and Spain. In 1993 the EC became the **European Union** (EU).

European Economic Community (EEC)

Organization of six European countries established in 1957 by the Treaties of Rome. (The **European Union** claims a birth date of May 9, 1950, the date of the first talks of the six countries.) The six countries of the EEC were Belgium, Germany, France, Italy, Luxembourg, and the Netherlands. Their areas of cooperation were in agriculture, industry, and trade, with a goal of political union. In 1967 the functions of the EEC merged with two industrial oversight organizations to form the **European Community** (EC).

European Union (EU)

Political, legal, and economic organization of fifteen countries established in 1993. The EU replaced the former **European Community** (EC), which in turn had replaced the **European Economic Community** (EEC). The EU absorbed the European Parliament and moved beyond the EC in agreeing to share foreign policy and security. Trade barriers among members have been dropped, and in 1999 the euro replaced the individual currencies of eleven EU countries. The fifteen original member countries are Austria, Belgium, Denmark, Finland, France, Germany, Greece, Ireland, Italy, Luxembourg, Portugal, Spain, Sweden, the Netherlands, and the United Kingdom. In 2004 Cyprus, the Czech Republic, Estonia, Hungary, Latvia, Lithuania, Malta, Poland, Slovakia, and Slovenia were added to the EU, for a total of twenty-five countries.

Exodus. *See* Book of Exodus

Expressionism

Artistic movement of the early twentieth century. Expressionism stresses the artist's emotional attitude toward the world, shown through use of vibrant color and bold distortions of image. Some of the leading expressionist artists were Henri Matisse (1869–1954), Georges Rouault (1871–1958), and Wassily Kandinsky (1866–1944). After **World War I** several German artists followed the path of expressionism, including George Grosz (1893–1959) and Max Beckmann (1884–1950).

Eyck, Jan van (c. 1390–1441)

Northern **Renaissance** Flemish naturalistic painter. Van Eyck worked in Bruges (in modern-day Belgium) using the newly developed technique of oil painting, which allowed him to produce paintings of greater detail and subtlety. His best-known paintings include the *Ghent Altarpiece* (1432) and *Arnolfini Wedding* (1434). Van Eyck's paintings incorporate a great number of symbolic items and show great detail, such as individual stitches on clothing or reflections in a mirror.

Falklands War (1982)

War between the United Kingdom and Argentina over the South Atlantic Falkland Islands. Claimed by Britain since 1690 and inhabited by British citizens since 1833, the islands were also claimed by Argentina (as the Islas Malvinas), which invaded them in 1982. British forces sailed 8,000 miles, reinvaded, and retook the islands, capturing 11,000 Argentine troops. Prime Minister **Margaret Thatcher**'s popularity increased, and the "Falkland factor" played a significant role in the general election that she called in 1983.

Fan Kuan

Eleventh-century Chinese painter noted for his landscapes. Painting in the tradition of Li Cheng, Fan Kuan was one of the greatest masters of the northern **Song** landscape. He had a profound influence on later east Asian art. His one extant work, *Traveling among Streams and Mountains*, depicts the power, beauty, and mystery of nature.

Fanon, Frantz (1925–1961)

West Indian psychoanalyst, philosopher, and writer on national liberation. Educated in Martinique and France, Fanon served in the French army in **World War II** and later became a psychoanalyst in Algeria. He joined the Algerian liberation movement in 1954. In 1952 he wrote about racism, and in 1961 he published his most influential work, *The Wretched of the Earth*, which encouraged colonized

people to use violence to overthrow their European oppressors.

Fascism

Political ideology of the twentieth century that assumes perpetual emergency conditions that necessitate a strong state to control those conditions. Fascism believes that the individual is subordinate to the state, and the state should be ruled by a strong leader. The term *fascism* comes from the Latin *fasces*, for a bundle of sticks with an ax projecting out from it that symbolized strength through unity for ancient Rome. Fascism assumes the need for complete unity of power, dissolving opposition parties, and depends upon a police state to crush dissent. Fascism is highly nationalistic and identifies itself with the needs of the state, suppressing the needs of the individual and often creating national racism to encourage unity. To strengthen the state, the media, such as newspapers, radio, and television, are controlled, and fascism creates a military or paramilitary structure within the government. Fascism came to power in Italy in 1922 and in Germany in 1933. It was also strong in Spain, Portugal, Austria, and even existed in Britain in the first half of the twentieth century and continues to appear when emergency conditions threaten countries.

Fashoda

Incident during the Scramble for Africa in 1898. That summer, a French force under Jean-Baptiste Marchand, marching into the Sudan from Gabon, and a British force under H. H. Kitchener, moving up the Nile to recover Khartoum, met. The stand-off created tensions between the two colonial rivals that was resolved when Britain and France reached an agreement demarcating the Nile and **Congo** watersheds as their respective spheres of influence.

Fatimid Caliphate

Shia Islamic caliphate that ruled in eastern North Africa from 909 to 1171 C.E. The Fatimids claimed descent from the prophet **Muhammad**'s daughter Fatima, who was the wife of Ali, the fourth caliph. The Fatimids formed a rival Shia Islamic caliphate to the Sunni Abbasids, who were centered in Baghdad from 763 to 1258. The Fatimids conquered Cairo in 969 and built the al-Azhar mosque and madrassa (a center for Islamic education; in this case a university) complex that is a highly renowned locus of Islamic learning. They oversaw the growth of the **Nile Valley** as a major trans-hemispheric route between the Indian Ocean and the Mediterranean Sea and expanded the caliphate to Palestine, Syria, and Arabia. The Fatimids were themselves overthrown by **Saladin**.

Favelas

Poorly built shantytowns on the edges of Brazilian cities such as Rio de Janeiro and São Paulo. Uncontrolled population growth and **industrialization** from the 1940s saw the beginnings of favelas, but they expanded due to a huge population explosion in the 1960s and 1970s during the industrialization encouraged by the Brazilian military regime. They continue to be a problem today.

Faxian (Fa-hsien) (fl. 399–414)

Chinese Buddhist monk and pilgrim noted for his travel to India via Central Asia to study Buddhist sutras. His trip helped to encourage other Chinese as well as Korean and Japanese Buddhists to make the pilgrimage to India. He wrote an account of his travels that provides valuable information about conditions in India at that time and some information on Southeast Asia, through which he returned.

Fazenda

Large plantations in Brazil. In the sixteenth to eighteenth centuries plantations worked by slave and free labor were developed in Brazil, similar to the plantations of the United States. The owners were typically of Portuguese descent, and the slaves were typically black Africans. The crop most commonly produced in the sixteenth to eighteenth centuries was sugar, replaced by coffee in the nineteenth century.

Feltre, Vittorino de

Humanist and educator of the **Italian Renaissance**. The humanist vision of a classical education was exemplified in institutions such as the school founded by Vittorino de Feltre in fifteenth-century Italy. The liberal education of the Renaissance taught students a comprehensive intellectual curriculum, based on study of the humanities and the art of rhetoric and persuasion. Humanists believed in the ability of humans to be educated, and many intellectuals produced tracts discussing educational philosophy. When Feltre founded his school at Mantua in 1423, under the patronage of the Gonzaga family, it educated the elites of the small state based on the teachings of classical authors such as Cicero and Quintilian.

Feminist Movement

Women's rights movement of the 1960s and later. Commonly viewed as a reaction to the decreased economic opportunities available to women after the **World War II** demobilization and the conformity of the

1950s, and inspired by the struggle for **civil rights**, the feminist movement has sought equality for women in all aspects of American society. Often dated from the publication of Betty Friedan's *The Feminine Mystique* in 1963, the movement proceeded on several levels. Moderate feminists sought improving status through legislation, the courts, and regulatory action, or through organizations such as the National Organization for Women (NOW, formed in 1966). Much effort was devoted to the failed attempt to add the Equal Rights Amendment to the **U.S. Constitution**, and to abortion rights. In the late 1960s more radical feminists sought equality through the altering of the political-economic system by revolutionary action and by challenging traditional gender relationships. Radical feminism faded with a conservative backlash of the late 1970s and 1980s. Since then, the feminist movement has become more global in nature, with the **United Nations** holding four World Women's Conferences in the 1980s and 1990s, focusing on political empowerment, an end to violence against women, and an end to poverty. In the United States, the movement has operated largely within mainstream politics since the 1980s, making progress toward full equality but thus far falling short of its goals.

Ferdinand of Aragon (1452–1516)
King of a united Spain and initiator of the **Spanish Inquisition**. Ferdinand married **Isabella**, future monarch of Castile, in 1469; became king of Aragon in 1479; united Castile and Aragon in 1481; and became king of Castile at Isabella's death in 1504. He added Granada in 1492 and Navarre in 1515. In 1478 Ferdinand received a Bull from the **pope** authorizing a separate Spanish Inquisition to combat heresy. Ferdinand and Isabella funded **Christopher Columbus** on his explorations westward across the Atlantic. They had a son and three daughters, including Catherine of Aragon, who married **Henry VIII** of England and produced **Mary I** (Bloody Mary) of England.

Fertile Crescent
Region of the **Middle East** that produced some of the earliest civilizations. The arc, or crescent, of territory runs from the Nile delta through **Palestine** and the Levant westward into Anatolia and southeastward through **Mesopotamia** slightly east of the **Tigris River**. The Fertile Crescent produced the **Egyptian civilization** by 3000 B.C.E., the **Sumerian** by 2800 B.C.E., the **Akkadian** by 2300 B.C.E., and the **Hittite** by 1700 B.C.E., as well as the later **Babylonian**, **Assyrian**, and **Hebrew** civilizations. Although now mostly arid, the crescent once had plentiful rainfall and fertile, productive soil. The region had forests; the precursors of later cereal grains, such as wild barley and wheat, that became the first cultivated grains by 7000 B.C.E.; and wild sheep and goats that became domesticated.

Feudalism
The decentralization of power and authority into a severe hierarchy of nobility where the subordinate noble (**vassal**) owed military service to another noble (lord) in return for protection and land (a feud or **fief**). This is known as the lord-vassal relationship. Feudalism provides security and a structure for gathering a military force. Because of the many variations and nuances to the political, social, and economic relationships of medieval Europe, some historians no longer use the word *feudalism*, believing that it leads to simplistic views of a complex situation.

Ficino, Marsilio (1433–1499)
Italian Renaissance philosopher, theologian, and musician who played a major

role in the rediscovery of classical learning. Ficino translated the works of **Plato** from Greek to Latin. A **Neoplatonist**, he believed that philosophy and religion shared views of good, love, immortality, and humanity. Ficino, whose patrons were the **Medicis**, is credited with converting **Giovanni Pico della Mirandola** to Neoplatonic study. Fincino believed there was a hierarchy of beings in the universe. His 1482 work *Theologia Platonica* combined Platonic philosophy and Christian theology.

Fief

Land granted as the economic component within a **feudal** relationship, given by a lord for the military service of his **vassal**. In addition to the fief, the lord provided the vassal protection. The vassal was able to provide a living from the fief by renting out parcels of the land to serfs who worked it.

Filial Piety

One of the three cardinal virtues of the Confucian tradition of East Asia, the other two being loyalty between subject and ruler, and distinction between men and women. Of the three, filial piety is generally considered the most fundamental to a moral order. The bond between parent and child and the obligation of a person to a parent was central to ethical teachings and was often used as a metaphor for the ties of mutual obligation that held the larger society together. Duty to one's parents was reinforced in China, Korea, and Japan with elaborate mourning rituals.

Firearms. *See* Guns

Five Dynasties

Period of Chinese history from the fall of the **Tang** dynasty in 907 to the establishment of the **Song** dynasty in 960, named for the five brief dynasties that ruled northern China at this time. It is also known as the Ten Kingdoms period, after the small contemporary regional states that ruled southern China. Despite its political instability, the Five Dynasties period was a time of literary and artistic creativity, especially in poetry and painting.

Five Nations. *See* Iroquois; Iroquois, League of

Five Pillars of Islam. *See* Islam

Flanders

Region of Northern Europe with highly developed trade centers in the late **Middle Ages**. Flanders extends along the English Channel from present-day France through Belgium to the Netherlands. Its rich soils; wool and linen production; and trade, especially with England, made Flanders one of the leading trade centers and most densely populated areas of Europe in the fourteenth and fifteenth centuries, with major Flemish cities of Bruges, Ghent, Antwerp, and Ypres. Flanders's wealth produced a highly developed culture of Flemish art, music, architecture, and literature. Flanders was ruled by counts until absorbed into France by **Napoléon Bonaparte**.

Floating World (*Ukiyo*)

Name for the pleasure and entertainment quarters of the cities of Japan during the **Tokugawa** period (1603–1867). *Ukiyo* was a medieval Japanese Buddhist term describing the fleeting and sorrowful existence that is life, but it came to be used for the Yoshiwara district of **Edo** (Tokyo), the Shinmachi district of Osaka, and the Shimabara district of Kyoto, which bustled with brothels, theaters, teahouses, public baths, and restaurants. These districts became important centers for Japanese culture that produced the dramatic form kabuki and the paintings of urban scenes and geishas known as *ukiyo-e*, "floating world pictures."

Florence

Italian city that was prominent during the **Renaissance**. Florence reached its cultural, political, and economic apex between the thirteenth and sixteenth centuries. Although affected by civil strife between the Guelph and Ghibelline factions in the late thirteenth century and the devastating effects of the **Black Death** (1348), Florence flourished as a center of industry and trade. The **Medici** family were bankers who dominated the politics of the city, and eventually the entire region of Tuscany, as a dukedom for 300 years beginning with Cosimo de Medici in 1434. Considered the "cradle of Renaissance civilization," Florence was a center of artistic and intellectual creativity supporting such artists as **Michelangelo**, **Donatello**, and **Leonardo da Vinci** as well as great thinkers like **Niccolò Machiavelli**.

Florentine Council of Ten

Ruling council of **Renaissance** Florence. After the **Medici** were removed from power in Florence in the late fifteenth century, the republican government was administered by the Florentine Council of Ten. **Niccolò Machiavelli**, who served as its secretary in 1498, was sent on many diplomatic missions around Italy as well as to France and Germany to negotiate treaties and report military ideas and observations to the council. The council comprised an elite oligarchy (ruling power in the state was in the hands of a few powerful persons or families) that represented a small percentage of Florence's populous—only those who had citizenship. A rotation of short terms in office gave eligible men plenty of opportunity to serve a term on the council.

Flying Tigers

Corps of American civilian fighter pilots recruited by Colonel Claire L. Chenault to aid the Chinese in their resistance to the Japanese invaders in 1941–1942. Volunteers, they delivered supplies to the besieged Chinese regime in **Chongqing**, protected the vital Burma road supply link, and fought Japanese planes. With the entry of the United States into **World War II** many were absorbed into the U.S. Tenth Air Force.

Fontenelle, Bernard le Bovier, Sieur de (1657–1757)

French writer and scientist. A precursor to the **Enlightenment** and friend of **Montesquieu** and **Voltaire**, Fontenelle wrote treatises emulating the Roman writers and criticizing religions. His most famous work, *A Plurality of Worlds* (1688), supported the Copernican view of the universe, which was not yet fully accepted.

Foot Binding

Chinese practice of tightly wrapping strips of linen around the feet of young girls to restrict their growth. The custom resulted in very short feet in women, partially crippling them. Foot binding originated in the **Song** period among the wives and concubines of the elite and became widespread during **Ming** and **Qing** times, when all but the Hakka and **Manchu** minorities practiced it. However, the practice was relaxed among the lower classes, where women's labor was in greater demand. Foot binding reduced the freedom of women, emphasized their subordination and dependency on men, and represented their lowered status in late imperial Chinese time. It was banned in the early twentieth century.

Forbidden City. *See* Imperial City

Four Modernizations

Official program of China focusing on the need to modernize agriculture, industry, national defense, and science and technology. It was proclaimed by **Deng Xiaoping** after he secured power in 1978 and implied a rejection or at least a modification of **Mao Zedong**'s more ideologically rigid approach to development. Guided by the Four Modernizations, the Chinese government pursued a more pragmatic approach to development, encouraging foreign investment, privatizing agriculture, promoting technical training, and permitting private businesses and industries. These policies inaugurated a period of rapid economic growth in the 1980s and 1990s.

Four Noble Truths

Buddhist premises. In **Buddhism** there are four Noble Truths: (1) the problem—that all is bound up with pain and suffering; (2) analysis of the problem—ignorance of the fundamental nature of reality is the cause of suffering; (3) hope of overcoming the problem—control of the senses relieves one from the suffering of dying and being reborn to suffer again; and (4) the course to follow—the **Eightfold Path** to the elimination of suffering. The goal in accepting the Four Noble Truths is **nirvana**, or escape from suffering and reabsorption into the spiritual infinite.

Francesca, Piero della (c. 1420–1492)

Renaissance artist. He was inspired by the realism of classical style, and, unlike artists of the Florentine school, whose style accentuated sweet emotions, rich decoration, and fine detail, Piero focused on human dignity and the beauty of nature, which he depicted with a mathematically accurate perspective. He was popular in the courts of Rimini and Urbino, where he was commissioned to paint a portrait of the Duke and Duchess of **Urbino**, which painting of the same name depicted the realistic profiles of Federigo da Montefeltro

and his wife, Battista Sforza, against the landscape of their dukedom.

Franciscans (Friars Minor or Grey Friars) (f. 1209)

Religious order of Christian monks, originally evangelists, founded by **Saint Francis of Assisi**. The Franciscans, also known as Friars Minor or Grey Friars, wandered around Europe preaching a gospel of love, caring for the sick, and begging for their food. They avoided organization, hierarchy, and buildings of their own. However, the Franciscans were so popular that they were given money, lands, and buildings, making them much like other monastic orders. They became known for their scholarship, notably in the fields of theology and science.

Francis Joseph (Franz Josef) (1830–1916)

Emperor of Austria (1848–1916) and king of Hungary (1867–1916). He became emperor at age eighteen during the European revolutions of 1848 and worked to suppress growing nationalism within his realm. Defeated by the Prussians in 1866, he lost influence over Germany, established the dual monarchy of **Austria-Hungary** in 1867 to meet Hungarian nationalist demands, lost territories to Italy in its nationalist aspirations, and aroused Slav resentment in the Balkans. Francis Joseph opposed most social reforms within his country. The attack on Serbia after the assassination of the Austrian archduke Francis Ferdinand precipitated **World War I**.

Francis of Assisi, Saint (c. 1181–1226)

Religious leader and founder of the **Franciscans**. Francis was born into a wealthy family but gave up his wealth and dedicated himself to a life of poverty and service to the sick and poor, which brought him great honor and respect. In 1209 the **pope** approved the founding of the Franciscans, a monastic order committed to following the life of **Jesus of Nazareth** in service and simplicity. Francis's life of chosen simplicity created a legend of his friendship with animals. In 1228, only two years after his death, Francis was declared a saint.

Francis I (1494–1547)

French king (1515–1547) and authoritarian **Renaissance** ruler. During his rule France was frequently at war (often in contention with the Holy Roman Emperor **Charles V**). Francis was an avid patron of the arts, well illustrated by his support of **Leonardo da Vinci**'s move to France and his project to rebuild the Louvre in Paris. Much of his reign is also remembered for its excesses and heavy spending.

Franklin, Benjamin (1706–1790)

American diplomat and prominent figure in the **American Revolution**; also internationally known as a scientist, inventor, and author. Franklin's inventions include the lightning rod and bifocal lenses. His *Poor Richard's Almanac,* written under the pseudonym Richard Saunders, was extremely popular in America. Franklin's contributions as a statesman were also great; his relations with the French during the American Revolution had the result of securing France's financial and military assistance. He also was a member of the Second **Continental Congress**, a signer of the **Declaration of Independence**, and served as the first postmaster general of the United States.

Franks

Germanic tribe that moved into the **Roman Empire** and established an enduring kingdom. The Franks first moved into Gaul in the Roman Empire, between modern France and Germany, in the third century C.E. and were ruled by the **Merovingian** dynasty in the sixth and seventh centuries and by the **Carolingian** dynasty from the eighth century.

Franz Josef. *See* Francis Joseph (Franz Josef)

Frederick I, "Barbarossa" (c. 1123–1190)

German king (1152–1190), Holy Roman Emperor (1155), and leader of the Third **Crusade**, against **Saladin**. One of the greatest kings of Germany, Frederick Barbarossa ("Red Beard") was a Hohenstaufen through his father and a Guelf through his mother. He was designated to become king of Germany by **Conrad III** before his death. Frederick's reign was a constant struggle at home and abroad. He drowned during the Third Crusade.

Frederick II (1194–1250)

Holy Roman Emperor (1220–1250) and wonder of the world. Frederick II, grandson of **Frederick I, "Barbarossa,"** expanded the power of the **Holy Roman Empire** and led a **Crusade** (1228–1229) to the Holy Land that gained **Jerusalem**, Nazareth, and Bethlehem. A brilliant administrator and military leader, Frederick was in almost continuous conflict with the **papacy** and parts of Italy, and by the time of his death German states were in revolt. He left a legacy of disintegration.

Frederick II, "the Great" (1712–1786)

King of Prussia (1740–1786) and devotee of French culture. Frederick centralized government, promoted progress in agriculture and industry, and became known as an enlightened despot. He expanded Prussia through wars with Austria and allied with Britain and Hanover against France, Russia, Austria, Spain, Sweden, and Saxony in the **Seven Years' War** (1756–1763). Frederick, an intellectual, promoted religious toleration at home, although he ruled as absolute monarch. However, Frederick the Great did not believe in the divine right of kingship but, rather, in being the first servant of the state.

Frederick William (1620–1688)

The "Great Elector" (1640–1688) of **Brandenburg** who laid the foundations for the military greatness of **Prussia**. He came to power during the last eight years of the **Thirty Years' War**, fighting **Louis XIV** of France and Charles XI of Sweden. After the war he rebuilt ruined Brandenburg, improving its infrastructure and military. At his death his son became **Frederick William I**, king of a prosperous and well-run Prussia.

Frederick William I (1688–1740)

First king of Prussia (1713–1740) and builder of Prussian power. An absolute ruler, Frederick William I dominated an efficient government and a large, powerful, and well-trained military. Son of **Frederick William**, the "Great Elector," Frederick William I made Prussia a major military player in European politics.

Freemasons

Fraternal organization called the "Free and Accepted Masons." The Freemasons are known for their secrecy and elaborate rituals. Probably originating as a **guild** of free (independent) masons in the **Middle Ages**, by the seventeenth century the fraternity included "accepted" masons—individuals who had no training as masons. They were interested in **Neoplatonic** mysticism, which may have had ties to the Knights Templar or the Rosicrucians. The organization was influential during the **Enlightenment**. Four lodges in London merged in

1717 to form the Grand Lodge, and the Freemasons spread around the world. Many prominent men have been Freemasons, such as **George Washington** and **Benjamin Franklin**. Fear that the Freemasons were involved in the **American Revolution** and the **French Revolution** led to anti-Masonic movements in the nineteenth century.

French and Indian War. *See* Seven Years' War

French Revolution (1789–1815)

Revolution that began in France with the overthrow of the Bourbon monarchy and spread throughout Europe. Financial problems; conflict between the aristocracy and the crown for control of the *parlements* (courts); and the spread of **bourgeois** ideas of the **Enlightenment**, such as broadening the electorate, all put pressure on the crown. When the king called the **Estates General** in 1789, the failure to grant the Third Estate wider powers led to the establishment of the **National Assembly**. When people of Paris stormed the Bastille on July 14, 1789, the French Revolution had begun. Its motto became "Liberty, Equality, and Fraternity." In August the ancien régime was dismantled; in September **Louis XVI** was reduced to a constitutional officer; in 1790 church lands were confiscated; in 1791 a constitution was passed; and in 1792 France declared war on Austria and the **Reign of Terror** began, in which thousands were executed as enemies of the revolution. In 1793 the king was guillotined and France was ruled by the **Convention** and the **Committee of Public Safety** while the war against France expanded to include Austria, Prussia, Britain, Spain, and Portugal. In 1795 the Convention was dissolved and replaced by the Directory. In 1799 **Napoléon Bonaparte** made himself first consul of a three-man consulship, and the wars continued successfully for France. Between 1801 and 1803 there was peace, while in 1802 Napoléon declared himself first consul for life. In 1804 Napoléon crowned himself emperor of the French and defeated most of the European powers and built his **Grand Empire** with Napoleonic law and the **Continental System**. In 1812 Napoléon's French army invaded Russia, but the fierce winter thwarted them. In 1814 Napoléon was defeated and exiled to the island of Elba. In 1815 he escaped, returned to France, and raised an army that was defeated by a coalition army under the duke of Wellington at **Waterloo**. Napoléon was exiled for life to the south Atlantic island of Saint Helena. Historians now sometimes extend the French Revolution to include the revolutions of 1830 and 1848 because the 1789–1815 revolution failed to produce a republican government.

French Wars of Religion (1562–1598)
Series of civil conflicts between French **Huguenots** (**Calvinists**) and Catholics during the **Reformation**. The conflicts had as much to do with the possible successors to the French throne as with religion. In 1559 the French Calvinists met in their first general synod. Eventually the religion spread to 2,000 churches. In 1560 the new king, Charles IX, was only ten years old, and in 1562 he was unable to halt the country's slide into civil war. The Huguenots were outnumbered and losing battles but remained on the offensive. In the **Saint Bartholomew's Day Massacre** of 1572 Catholics throughout France killed thousands of Huguenots because of the fear of a Huguenot takeover of government. In 1594 the French king Henry IV converted to Catholicism, and in 1598 he issued the **Edict of Nantes**, a compromise allowing the Huguenots freedom of worship (except in Paris), but with the state remaining Catholic, thereby ending the **Wars of Religion**.

Freud, Sigmund (1856–1939)
Austrian physician, psychologist, and founder of psychoanalysis. Freud's view of the human psyche—of the id, ego, and superego—has influenced all subsequent psychology. His psychoanalysis created the understanding that humans can become ill psychologically, be treated with therapy, and be healed. He built his fame on the treatment of psychiatric disorders, especially on the belief that most behavior is the result of primitive desires such as sex. These desires in the id are mediated by the ego, which struggles to control the desires within the constraints of society. The struggle between the id and the ego can cause physical and mental problems. In recent years Freud's theories have been criticized, but his influence has changed the understanding of human nature and human interactions.

Friars
Term meaning "brothers" applied to the mendicant, or begging, orders of Christian monks. Materialism in the thirteenth century among traditional monastic orders led to the establishment of orders such as the **Franciscans**, **Dominicans**, Augustinians, and Carmelites who adopted the practice of poverty and begging for their food to renounce worldly possessions. This simplicity caused mendicants to be known as friars rather than as monks.

Froissart, Jean (c. 1337–1410)
French historian and poet. Author of *The Chronicles of France, England, Scotland, and Spain*, describing the period from 1325 to 1400. Froissart's firsthand and researched history of the **Hundred Years War** is still used by historians although often inaccurate. Froissart is best in his descriptions of personalities.

Frond (1648–1652)
Revolt of French nobles against the monarchy. Begun as a revolt of the **Parlement** (court) of Paris against tax policies, it was crushed in 1649 by the prince of Condé, who the next year led a new revolt of nobles. Stopped in 1652, the revolt led to an increased consolidation of power in the hands of the monarchy.

Fujiwara Period
Japanese period from the late ninth to the late twelfth century when an aristocratic family of ancient lineage held effective power. In 858 starting with Fujiwara Yoshifusa, the Fujiwara served as regents to the emperors, who were little more than puppets. Their source of power was kinship relations with the emperors because they married their daughters to them. The Fujiwara period saw important artistic and literary achievements; among the best known is Lady **Murasaki's** *Tale of Genji*, a novel set in the Fujiwara-dominated court. However, the period also saw a decline in central government institutions and the rise of regional warlords.

Fukuzawa Yukichi (1835–1901)
Leading popularizer of Western culture in nineteenth-century Japan. A **bushi** student of "Dutch Learning," he taught Dutch and English before traveling to the United States and Europe in the early 1860s. Fukuzawa's writings on Western politics and society were influential in spreading knowledge about the West and in shaping and gaining acceptance for the modernizing reforms of **Meiji Japan**. A strong proponent of modern education and women's rights, he established Keio University, one of Japan's leading institutes of higher education.

Fulani (Fulbe)
West African people who expanded from 1000 C.E. onward across much of the west African savanna and were instrumental in spreading **Islam**. Originally a pastoral and agricultural people in the Senegal River valley and Nigeria, some Fulani became urban by the twelfth century. During the course of the fifteenth to nineteenth centuries the Fulani adopted Islam. Already in the fifteenth century, Fulani were frequently clerics in Hausa towns. Their zeal in spreading Islam led to the creation of the Sokoto caliphate and the dominance of the **Hausa states**. Early in the nineteenth century the Fulani launched a **jihad** led by **Usman dan Fodio** that led to the defeat of the Hausa states.

Funan
Kingdom in the lower Mekong region occupying much of present-day Cambodia and parts of southern Vietnam that flourished in the first millennium C.E. Its port Oc Eo was an important center in the trade routes between the South China Sea and the Indian Ocean. Funan was strongly influenced by Indian culture; it rulers called themselves **rajas** and adopted many religious practices of **Hinduism**. Funan declined in the sixth century and was absorbed by the neighboring Khmer and Chams.

Funj
Dynasty of kings of northeastern Africa from the sixteenth to nineteenth century. The Funj capital of Sennar was founded in 1504 on the Blue Nile River when Arab **Muslim** immigrants and the Funj dynasty allied, creating the Funj sultanate. The sultanate reached its height of power in the seventeenth and eighteenth centuries, controlling a large region in central and southern Sudan. In the late eighteenth century the Funj declined because of internal dissension and in 1821 the Funj sultanate was conquered by the Ottoman ruler of Egypt.

G

Gagarin, Yuri (1934–1968)
Soviet astronaut and the first person to travel in space (1961). Gagarin orbited the earth only once, landing 108 minutes after blastoff. This feat pushed President **John F. Kennedy** to declare that the United States would land a man on the moon by the end of the decade. In 1968 Gagarin died test flying a jet fighter.

Galen (129–c. 200)
Physician of Pergamon and **Alexandria**, founder of experimental physiology, and author of the authoritative writings on medicine used throughout the **Middle Ages**. Galen saw disease as an imbalance between the four humors and established that the most important organs of the human body—the heart, brain, and liver—each had its own systems of nerves, arteries, and veins. Galen's authority on anatomy was finally overthrown by **Andreas Vesalius** in 1543.

Galilei, Galileo (1564–1642)
Italian astronomer, mathematician, scientist, and a founder of the **scientific revolution**. Galileo proved many of the astronomical theories of **Nicolaus Copernicus, Tycho Brahe**, and **Johannes Kepler** and advanced human understanding of the universe by mathematics and observation combined. Galileo built (but did not invent) a telescope by which he observed and verified mathematical reasoning. With it, he saw many more stars than by the naked eye, an irregular moon,

moons around Jupiter, and phases of Venus, all of which proved that the previously held view—that the universe was perfect and unchanging—was wrong. His *Starry Messenger* (1610) startled the intellectual community. Galileo's proof that the Copernican view of the universe (that the earth revolves around the sun, not the converse) was correct got him into trouble with the **Roman Catholic Church.** Galileo spent much of his later life under house arrest, still experimenting and writing about physics and astronomy.

Galileo. *See* Galilei, Galileo

Gamelan
Indigenous orchestral music of Java and Bali played with a variety of percussion instruments that perform to a melody often set by a bamboo flute or bow-string instrument. Gamelan was used in court ceremonies and to accompany **wayang** theater. An elaborate and highly refined music, it represented the rich cultural tradition of that region.

Ganda
Ethnic group of Uganda. A **Bantu**-speaking people, the Ganda were agriculturalists with a well-organized state by the nineteenth century, when the British entered Uganda. In present-day Uganda the Ganda are often viewed as the most numerous people and those who control the most valuable lands and are the most literate and prosperous.

Gandhi, Indira (1917–1984)
Prime minister of India (1966–1977, 1980–1984) and daughter of the leader of Indian independence movement **Jawaharlal Nehru**. Married to Feroze Gandhi (who was not related to **Mohandas K. Gandhi**), she was elected head of the ruling **Indian National Congress** but broke with the party's old guard soon after becoming prime minister to form the Congress Party–Indira, or Congress-I. Her slogan was *Garibi Hhatao* ("Abolish Poverty"), but she made little progress in doing so. Gandhi played a crucial role in adopting the U.S.-sponsored Green Revolution program to increase food productivity. Under her leadership India emerged victorious in the independence war with Bangladesh. In June 1975 she declared a state of emergency that continued to March 1977, and she arrested members of the opposition while adhering to the provisions of India's constitution. The emergency and accusations of forced sterilizations and other drastic measures to curb population growth were unpopular, but she returned to power in elections two year later. In 1984 she was assassinated by **Sikh** bodyguards in revenge for her crackdown on Sikh militants.

Gandhi, Mohandas Karamchand
(1869–1948) (known as Mahatma ["Great Soul"] Gandhi)
Indian nationalist leader and advocate of nonviolent protest. Son of the prime minister of Gujarat state, Gandhi was trained as a lawyer. During 1893–1915 he worked in South Africa to unite the diverse Indian community in an effort to end discrimination against it. Returning to India in 1915, he emerged as a leader of the **Indian National Congress** in 1920, helping to transform its appeal from a small elite to the masses. In his campaign for Indian independence from Britain he developed his technique of *satyagraha* ("truth-force"), a form of nonviolent resistance that framed the political movement in ethical terms. His most famous campaign was the Salt March to Dandi in 1930, which encouraged millions to make sea salt rather than accept the government's monopoly over salt production. He adopted a political style that involved dressing as a traditional holy man and making his own homespun cloth that appealed to ordinary Indians. He was, however, unable to prevent **Muslim** Indians' call for a separate state that led to the partition of India and Pakistan in 1947. Gandhi also worked for social reforms such as the end of discrimination against untouchables (**pariahs**), whom he called *harijan* ("children of god"). He was assassinated by a Hindu militant six months after India's independence, but his example of nonviolence continued to have a global influence.

Ganges River
1,550-mile (2,500-km) river starting in the Himalayas and flowing eastward to Bengal. A slow, broad river, the Ganges is regarded as sacred in **Hinduism** and worshiped as a goddess. The Gangetic Plain has since the first millennium B.C.E. formed the heartland of northern India and is one of the most densely populated areas of the world, with much of India's population living in the vast alluvial plain watered by the Ganges and its tributaries.

Gang of Four
Four ultraleftist Chinese communist leaders. **Mao Zedong**'s wife, Jiang Qing; Wang Hongwen; Yao Wenyuan; and Zhang Chungqiao rose to prominence during the **Great Proletarian Cultural Revolution** (1966–1976). After Mao's death in 1976 they were removed from power, put on trial, and convicted, a move that signaled

a rejection of the Cultural Revolution and Mao's more radical policies.

Gao

Capital city of the great kingdom of **Songhay** in the fifteenth and sixteenth centuries. An ancient settlement, Gao was one of the major centers of the western Sudan along with **Timbuktu**. The Songhay empire is sometimes referred to as the Empire of Gao. At its peak Gao had approximately 75,000 residents. The city was on a local trade network route that became a **trans-Saharan trade** route by the ninth century. Ivory, gold, and slaves were exported from Gao, and the city controlled the salt trade from the Sahara to much of the savanna and forest zones. By the eleventh century Gao was a major urban center.

García Márquez, Gabriel (1928–)

Colombian novelist and author of *One Hundred Years of Solitude* (1967). García Márquez is the most famous writer of the Latin American literary explosion of the 1960s and 1970s. His novels are known for their realism mixed with fantasy, called "magical realism," symbolizing in a mythic fashion Latin American culture and society including oppression, extremes of rich and poor, and dictatorial government. García Márquez won the **Nobel Prize** for Literature in 1982.

Gaul

Region of the **Roman Empire** comprising two areas: **Cisalpine** Gaul and **Transalpine** Gaul. Cisalpine Gaul was the region of modern-day northern Italy from the **Apennines** into the Alps. During the **Roman Republic** this region was not considered part of Italy but a land infiltrated by **Celts** from north of the Alps. Cisalpine Gaul was invaded and conquered by the Romans by 191 B.C.E. and settled by them. The region north of the Alps was Transal-

pine Gaul, covering most of modern France from the Alps and the Pyrenees to the English Channel. Transalpine Gaul became a Roman political unit in the first century B.C.E., known as Gaul because the Cisalpine had by this time been absorbed into Italy, and continued as such until **Octavian** divided Gaul into four provinces in the fifth century C.E. Later two more were added, and **Diocletian** subdivided them into thirteen provinces. By the fourth century C.E. Germanic tribes of **Franks** and Burgundians had moved into Gaul and settled there. The Franks would eventually form their own kingdom as the **Merovingians** and, later, the **Carolingians**.

Gautama Buddha. *See* Siddhartha Gautama

Geneva Accords. *See* Geneva Conference

Geneva Conference (1954)

A conference in Geneva, Switzerland that negotiated an end to the Indo-China War. Representatives of Cambodia, China, France, Laos, the Soviet Union, the United Kingdom, the United States, and the North Vietnamese people met to make arrangements for Korea and Indo-China. After the fall of the French at **Dien Bien Phu** a cease-fire was agreed upon by France, Vietnam, Laos, and Cambodia. The Geneva Conference worked out the details and drew the line at the seventeenth parallel, dividing Vietnam. The Final Declaration was left unsigned by all parties. The United States chose to support South Vietnam against **communism**.

Geneva Conventions

Series of international treaties between 1864 and 1977 for the purpose of improving the treatment of soldiers and civilians during war. The first Geneva Convention was initiated by Henri Dunant, founder of the Red Cross, in 1864. Subsequent conventions in 1907, 1929, and 1949 have been ratified by the majority of world states and other organizations, while the 1977 convention has been ratified by far fewer states (the United States has not ratified it). The Geneva Conventions address the treatment of prisoners of war and the protection of civilians and prohibit deportation, torture, hostage-taking, collective punishment, and the use of chemical or biological weapons.

Genghis Khan (Chinggis Khan)
(c. 1162–1227)
Warrior who united the Mongol and Turkic tribes and created the Mongol empire. Born Temuchin, in 1206 he was given the title *Genghis Khan* ("Universal Ruler") by a *kuriltai* ("assembly") of all the tribes. He then conquered the Xi Xia state in **Central Asia**, partially conquered the Jin in northern China by 1215, and by 1221 had brought Khorezm in Turkestan under his rule, thus ruling most of northern China and the eastern and central **steppe**. Genghis Khan was the greatest steppe empire builder up to his time and a master military strategist who made effective use of military intelligence and psychological terror to defeat his enemies. His success was also due to his remarkable organizational genius and his willingness to borrow and adapt skills and methods from his neighbors. He developed administrative and taxation systems partly based on Chinese models and employed Chinese siege devices. Genghis Khan established a system of laws and an alphabet for writing Mongolian. After he died his empire was divided into four khanates. Genghis's grandson **Khubilai Khan** conquered all of China in 1279.

Genji, Tale of
Japanese novel written around the year 1000 by Lady **Murasaki Shikibu**, a court

lady, that depicts life and mores in the **Heian** court of Japan. A work of great psychological subtlety, it has been considered by Japanese critics as Japan's greatest literary masterpiece and is one of the world's first novels. It represents and depicts the refinement of the small imperial court-centered elite in Japan at that time, and the unique role of women, who produced much of the best literature of the period.

Genro (Japanese for "Senior Councillors")
Seven Japanese advisors from Satsuma and Choshu who unofficially became the chief advisors to the Emperor Meiji and therefore were the power behind the throne. The Genro alternated as ministers in the first several cabinets (1890–1917). They include **Inoue Kaoru**, **Ito Hirobumi**, Kuroda Kiyotaka, Matsukata Masayoshi, Oyama Iwoa, Saigo Tsugumichi, and **Yamagata Aritomo**. They were joined by Katsura Taro and Saionji Kinmochi, who were called the Later Genro.

Geography/Topography
Important factor in shaping history. Some historians emphasize geographical determinism—the idea that geography is the single most important factor in shaping world history. Strict geographic determinists believe that "geography is destiny," but this extreme stance is no longer common. In recent years environmental geography (ecology or climate as single most important factor) and biogeography (physical geography plus germs and genes) have become more popular variants of geographical determinism.

George III (1738–1820)
King of the United Kingdom of Great Britain and Ireland during the **American Revolution**, the **French Revolution**, and the **Napoleonic Wars**. George was also

elector, and later king, of Hanover. English to the core, he tried to restore authority and respectability to the crown. The American Revolution was a blow to his hopes; however, the Napoleonic Wars proved Britain's naval might. Bouts of insanity hindered George's reign, and in 1810 the insanity became permanent. His son, the future George IV, was proclaimed prince regent in 1811.

Germania. *See* Tacitus, P. Cornelius

Germanic Tribes
Linguistically related tribes including the Alemmani, Angles, Saxons, Jutes, Burgundians, Franks, Ostrogoths, Visigoths, and Vandals who invaded the West. Germanic tribes began to enter the **Roman Empire** in the second and third centuries C.E., some being absorbed into the empire. By the fifth century the Germanic tribes had helped to break up the empire in the West, and several of them, such as the **Franks** and the Visigoths, had established their own kingdoms.

German Peasants' War. *See* Peasants' War

German Reunification
The uniting of East Germany and West Germany. On October 3, 1990, East and West Germany officially reunited after decades of existence as two separate nations, one communist and the other democratic. From the beginning, West Germany had a better economy than East Germany, and in the 1950s East Germans began leaving for the West by the thousands through divided **Berlin**. East Germany began building the **Berlin Wall** in 1961. This state of enforced separation lasted until 1989. That May Hungary opened its borders to Austria, and East Germans began moving to Hungary. By October millions of people were demonstrating in the streets of East Berlin. They wanted free access to information, the right to dissent with the government, the right to travel, and the right to affect politics. These demonstrations forced East Germany to open the wall on November 9, 1989. Chancellor Helmut Kohl of West Germany announced his Ten Points Plan for the eventual unification of Germany. In March 1990 East Germany held free elections. On July 1, 1990, East and West Germany formed a monetary, social, and political union and ended all travel restrictions. Reunified Germany continues to struggle with residual problems. Unemployment in eastern Germany is twice as high as unemployment in the west, and technology and education lag behind.

Ghana
Kingdom of the western Sudan grasslands of Africa in the sixth to thirteenth centuries. Ghana was to the north and west of the present-day state of Ghana (and unrelated historically). It was a major intermediary in the **trans-Saharan trade** route of gold and ivory from the upper Senegal–Niger region to the Mediterranean Sea. Its capital and major commercial center was Kumbi-Saleh. **Islam** was introduced to Ghana by the eleventh century, but traditional religions remained important. In 1076 the **Almoravids** invaded Ghana, sacked Kumbi-Saleh, and imposed control over the kingdom. This weakened Ghana, and as it declined it was replaced by the empire of **Mali** in the thirteenth century.

Ghazni, Kingdom of
Large but not well integrated medieval **Islamic** principality centered on the city of Ghazna (or Ghazni) in eastern Afghanistan. It originated with a Turkish slave garrison led by Sebuktegin (r. 976–997) that became independent of the Iranian Samanid dynasty. Sebuktegin's son Mahmud (r. 998–1030) was responsible for greatly

expanding the empire's boundaries and prestige by repeatedly invading north India. The wealth gained in these forays attracted a number of Persian literati to Ghazna, such as Firdawsi, who wrote the epic *Shahnama*. In addition to beginning the Islamization process in north India, the Ghaznavids bequeathed the Persian language as a means of cultural expression and bureaucratic recording, refined by later **Muslim** rulers in South Asia such as the **Mughals**.

Ghenghis Khan. *See* Genghis Khan (Chinggis Khan)

Ghent
Prominent medieval commercial city in **Flanders**. Ghent was the residence of the counts of Flanders and by the thirteenth century became the major textile center of Europe and one of the largest cities in northern Europe along with **Bruges** and **Antwerp**. In the fifteenth century Ghent's independence and commercial prominence were curtailed.

Gilbert, William (1540–1603)
English scientist of magnetism and a founder of experimental science. Gilbert believed that magnetism was one of the fundamental forces of nature, and in his book *On the Magnet* (1600) he outlined many experiments that proved factual points and refuted erroneously held beliefs about magnetism. Gilbert also investigated magnetism of the earth, although most geomagnetic experiments did not take place until the nineteenth century. Gilbert's own work and theories inspired others such as **Isaac Newton**.

Gilgamesh, Epic of (c. 2000 B.C.E.)
The oldest written story in the world. This Sumerian tale about a real person ruling from the city of Uruk in **Sumer** was written around 2000 B.C.E. Gilgamesh is the first hero in world literature. In the epic a great flood obliterates the human race except for a favored family who survive it by building an ark, similar to the biblical flood of Noah. As in the **Bible** story, this family is the source of all subsequent people. The *Epic of Gilgamesh*, although placed in history, is not a history of the time, but rather a symbolic or creation story.

Giotto (Giotto di Bondone) (1267/75–1337)
Tuscan painter and architect who was a student of Cimabue and contributed greatly to the artistic development of the early **Renaissance**. The naturalistic style Giotto used in his narrative cycles to depict human drama, emotion, realism, and perspective (by using architecture, color, and light) represented a milestone in regard to the stylistic changes that would come to define the art of the Renaissance period.

Giza, Pyramids of. *See* Pyramids of Giza (Egypt)

Gladiators
Roman combatants who originally fought at funerals to honor dead warriors. By **Julius Caesar**'s reign, 49–44 B.C.E., gladiator combat had become widespread entertainment along with beast fights. Very expensive to promote, **Octavian** and **Trajan** each provided games with 5,000 pairs of gladiators in combat. The main venue was the Roman Forum. There were four types of gladiators. Two of them were heavily armed, with oblong shield, helmet, and short sword; one fought with net and trident; and the fourth, Thracians, fought with a round shield and a scimitar. Prisoners of war and condemned criminals were compelled to fight as gladiators, but there were also professionals—often

slaves but sometimes volunteers—who were paid to fight.

Gladstone, William Ewart (1809–1898)
British prime minister (1868–1874, 1880–1885, 1886, and 1892–1894) and statesman. Gladstone was a member of the **Liberal Party** who occupied the office of prime minister for most of the late nineteenth century. His archrival was **Benjamin Disraeli**. Gladstone and the Liberals stood for the middle class and fought for social and political reforms including the introduction of elementary education. He pushed unsuccessfully for Irish Home Rule.

Glenn, John (1921–)
U.S. astronaut, the first American to orbit the earth (1962), and U.S. senator. After the Soviet Union orbited **Yuri Gagarin** in 1961, the United States worked frantically to catch up in its space program. Glenn gained great fame from his space mission and in 1974 was elected to the **U.S. Senate**. In 1998 Glenn once again flew as an astronaut in the U.S. space program, and in 1999 he retired from the Senate.

Globalism/Globalization
Term used by historians to refer to the increased interaction and interconnections among the various peoples and societies of the world that has characterized modern history. Some historians see globalism as leading to a cosmopolitan world society that will dominate or replace regional, national, and local cultures. Others see it as a hegemonic centralizing ideology that resembles a form of neocolonialism.

Glorious Revolution (1688–1689)
English revolution, sometimes called the Bloodless Revolution, achieved without a war. After the **English Civil War**, with its great loss of life, and the **Restoration** of the English monarchy, **Parliament** deposed

James II in 1688 and crowned his daughter Mary II and her husband William III, prince of Orange and stadholder of the Netherlands, as the joint monarchs William and Mary. James was a Catholic and William and Mary were Protestants. James fled to France, ending the Stuart monarchy. In 1689 the Bill of Rights was passed. It obligated the monarchy to govern with Parliament; prohibited the monarchy from arbitrarily taxing and from keeping a standing army; and provided for free speech, free elections, and regular meetings of **Parliament**—primarily rights of the nobility and upper class.

Goa
Former Arabian Sea port and later Portuguese colony (1510–1961), now an Indian state. During the heyday of the Portuguese seaborne empire in the sixteenth and seventeenth centuries, all Portuguese activity in Asia and East Africa was administered from Goa. In 1961 an Indian invasion ended Portuguese rule and incorporated Goa within India.

Gobi Desert
Vast arid and semiarid region of **Central Asia** stretching from the Altai Mountains in the west to the Greater Khingan range to the east, an area of approximately 500,000 square miles (1.3 million sq km). The Gobi covers the greater part of Outer Mongolia (the modern state of Mongolia) and parts of the Inner Mongolia Autonomous Region of China. Historically, the Gobi and the adjacent moister grasslands have been home to many nomad groups who created formidable confederations, such as the **Xiongnu** and the **Mongols**.

Godwin, Mary Wollstonecraft (1759–1797)
English social critic and writer. Her book *A Vindication of the Rights of Women* (1792)

argued for education and equality for women. Her ideas were radical for their time. She left England for France during the **French Revolution** because of its call for equality. She married William Godwin, an English social reformer.

Goebbels, Joseph (1897–1945)
German **Nazi** politician and head of propaganda for the Nazi government. Goebbels joined the Nazi Party in 1926 and became one of **Adolf Hitler**'s strongest supporters. He designed the means to spread the Nazi philosophy and to manipulate the masses into support for **anti-Semitism** and war. He and his wife killed their six children and then committed suicide in a bunker in Berlin in 1945.

Goering, Hermann Wilhelm (1893–1946)
German **Nazi** who was second in command to **Adolf Hitler**. Goering became Reich Marshal and commanded the **Luftwaffe** (the German air force) and the German armaments industry. He attempted to have the Luftwaffe subdue Britain in the **Battle of Britain** but failed, and he again failed in his attempt to thwart an invasion of the Continent by Allied forces. At the end of **World War II** Goering was found guilty of war crimes at the **Nürnberg Trials**, but he committed suicide with poison just before he was scheduled to be hanged.

Goethe, Johann Wolfgang von (1749–1832)
German writer and scientist. Goethe's play *Faust* (1832) is one of the most influential in modern literature. A brilliant poet, Goethe became a major writer of the German Romantic movement. His novel *The Sorrows of Young Werther* (1774) made him famous. He also completed studies of geology, botany, and zoology. A prolific writer, Goethe was Europe's most celebrated writer in the early nineteenth century.

Golden Age
An imagined period of ease and peaceful life in the distant past; or, a term meant to designate a historical peak. Both the Greeks and the Romans wrote of a golden age when people did not have to work for their food and lived together in harmony. The concept of a golden age was used to contrast with the struggle for existence in contemporary life and to suggest that if problems were solved the golden age could be regained. In historical literature, the term *golden age* indicates a period when a civilization or culture was at a peak, such as the seventeenth-century golden age of Dutch history.

Golden Horde
Mongol khanate of the western **Kipchaks** (1242–1480) who ruled the region from the lower Volga River to the Dnieper River and claimed control over all of Russia. The name is derived from the Mongol word *ordos* (meaning "army" or "camp"), and "golden" refers to the magnificent camp of the khanate's founder, Batu Khan. The nomadic-warrior state was governed by a mix of **Mongols** and Turkic-speaking Kipchaks and eventually established its headquarters at Sarai, on the Volga River. It required the princes of Russia to pay tribute until it was defeated by **Ivan III** of Moscow in 1480. The Russians refer to the period when they were forced to pay tribute to the Golden Horde as the "Tartar Yoke."

Gold Standard
Monetary system in which a fixed amount of gold is the standard by which other currencies are set. The gold standard was first used by Great Britain in 1821, followed

by France, Germany, and the United States in the 1870s. The gold standard can work when gold is relatively plentiful. The gold standard was dropped several times—during **World War I**, the **Great Depression**, and **World War II**—but re-established afterward. In the 1970s most countries moved away from the gold standard.

Gold Trade

The movement of gold from one region of the world to another. Often referring to the enormous movement of gold from the New World to Europe in the sixteenth and seventeenth centuries, the gold trade was also important throughout the **Middle Ages**, from western Africa in the south to the Mediterranean coast. European exploration in the fifteenth and sixteenth centuries was driven by the desire for gold. In Roman times the gold trade was from southern France and Spain to Italy until the first century, when most of the gold trade was from the Balkans. **Greece** was always short of gold, and much of its gold trade was from Macedonia. With the European exploration and conquest of the New World, the gold trade moved from the Western Hemisphere to Europe and Asia.

Good Emperors (96–180)

Roman emperors following the Flavians, known for their outstanding abilities. The emperors Nerva (96–98), **Trajan** (98–117), **Hadrian** (117–138), Antoninus (138–161), and **Marcus Aurelius** (161–180) were related as adopted sons, one after the other.

Gospel

From Old English *godspell* ("good news"), a translation of the Latin *evangelium*, itself a Greek word meaning "good news." (1) One of four books at the beginning of the New Testament written by **Jesus**'s disciples or their immediate followers between 60 and 90 C.E. The first three—Matthew, Mark, and Luke—are so similar that they are called "synoptic Gospels" because they can be viewed together. The gospel of John, though following the same general chronology, possesses a distinctive style and content. (2) The basic Christian message, centering on the life, teachings, death, and resurrection of Jesus of Nazareth and the offer of forgiveness and eternal life to those who believe in him.

Gothic Architecture

European medieval design begun in the twelfth century by Abbot Suger at Saint-Denis (1137–1144) near Paris; one of the great achievements of the **Middle Ages**. Gothic architecture incorporated ribbed vaulting, pointed (rather than rounded) arches, flying buttresses, and large stained glass windows. The buttressing supported the tall buildings and enabled the walls to be opened into windows that brought in more light. The total effect was of soaring inspiration—the eyes of a viewer move upward—suggesting an earthy manifestation of God's heaven. Even the exterior was symbolic of the heavenly realm, with soaring towers, spires, and pinnacles. By the thirteenth century Gothic design had spread to the rest of Europe, as seen in brilliant examples such as **Notre Dame Cathedral** (Paris), **Westminster Abbey** (London), and Cologne Cathedral. Many Gothic cathedrals took 50 to 100 years to build.

Goths

Germanic tribe that moved into the Black Sea region around 200 C.E. and in the third century C.E. moved to the edges of the **Roman Empire**. In the fourth century the Goths accepted **Arian** Christianity. They divided into East Goths (Ostrogoths), who settled in lower **Russia**, and West Goths (Visigoths). The Ostrogoths were overrun by the **Huns** in the late fourth century, but the Visigoths moved westward into the **Roman Empire**, destroying a Roman army in the Battle of Adrianople (378) in Dalmatia. The Visigoths, under King Alaric, sacked the city of **Rome** (410) and then moved westward and established a kingdom stretching from southern France through Spain. Shortly after 711 **Muslims** of the **Umayyad Caliphate** conquered the Visigothic kingdom in Spain.

Government/Politics

A basic subject of study by world historians. A government can be broadly defined as a system of authority of a people and territory not based entirely on kinship units. Politics is an activity related to the structure and distribution of power within a state. In recent decades historians have tended to focus more on nonpolitical subjects such as technology, economics, family, and gender but continue to be concerned with government and politics.

Granada

Province of southern Spain that was the last European region of Islam in the fifteenth century. As the Moorish kingdom of Granada, it was the final stronghold of the Moors in Spain, falling to the Catholic monarchs **Ferdinand II** and **Isabella** in 1492. When Granada fell, the reconquest of Spain for Catholicism was complete, and Ferdinand and Isabella could put their energies and money elsewhere. In that same year they supported the expedition by **Christopher Columbus** to attempt to reach the East by sailing west.

Grand Alliance, War of the (1689–1697)

The third major French war of **Louis XIV**. France's expansionist plans were blocked by an alliance of England, the United Provinces of the Netherlands, the Austrian **Habsburgs**, Sweden, Spain, Savoy, and several German principalities. The Netherlands stood in the way of French aggression, and in 1688 **William of Orange**, stadholder of the Netherlands, became King William III of England in the **Glorious Revolution**. He brought England into continental affairs by coalition with those states and thus began a protracted off-and-on struggle between France and England that would last for 125 years.

Grand Canal

1,100-mile (1,700-km) canal in China, the world's longest. The southern part of the canal was completed about 610 by the **Sui** dynasty rulers to transport grain from the fertile **Yangtze River** to their capitals of Kaifeng and Luoyang in the **Yellow River** basin. The northern section of the canal fell into disuse, but in the later thirteenth century the canal was extended to the **Yuan** (Mongol) capital of **Beijing**. The canal greatly facilitated interregional trade in China, contributing to what has become known by some historians as China's medieval "commercial revolution." It is still in use today.

Grand Empire

French Napoleonic empire after 1804. In 1804 the Empire of France was proclaimed and **Napoléon Bonaparte** made its emperor, with the crown to descend to male heirs. Having already annexed Tuscany, Piedmont, Genoa, and the Rhineland into France, Napoléon made his brother Louis king of Holland, his brother Jérôme king of Westphalia, his stepson Eugène Beauharnais king of Italy, and his brother Joseph king of Spain, and he granted the Grand Duchy of Warsaw to his ally the king of Saxony.

When Napoléon divorced Joséphine and in 1810 married the Austrian princess Marie-Louise, nearly all of Europe was in his grasp.

Great Awakening

An evangelical revival of religion, begun in England and which spread to America. In England the movement's leader was John Wesley, who founded Methodism out of the Anglican Church. One of the movement's greatest preachers was George Whitefield. They carried the movement to America, where in the 1730s and 1740s (the First Great Awakening) and the later nineteenth century (the Second Great Awakening) the Great Awakening transformed the religious climate. Starting with Jonathan Edwards and exploding with George Whitefield in 1739, evangelical "fire and brimstone" sermons were preached across the colonies with moving descriptions of damnation and God's grace. The First Great Awakening split the colonists between two religious camps, one based upon **Enlightenment** logic, and the new, evangelical one, on emotions. The Second Great Awakening started around 1800 and began at colleges in the eastern United States, such as Yale, and spread to the South and the West, The first camp meetings were held in Kentucky by Presbyterians and were soon imitated by Methodists and Baptists.

Great Britain

Name used for England and Scotland after the **Act of Union** in 1707. The two nations were amalgamated into the Kingdom of Great Britain, and the Union Jack (merging the flags of Saint George and Saint Andrew) became its flag. Ireland was added as a separate Act of Union in 1800 (and the flag of Saint Patrick was added to the Union Jack).

Great Depression. *See* Depression, Great

Great Exhibition of 1851

The first world's fair. The Great Exhibition of the Works of Industry of All Nations was held in Hyde Park, London, where the **Crystal Palace** was constructed to hold exhibits from around the world. The Great Exhibition was really held to show off Britain as the workshop of the world, although there was technology from many countries, such as the sewing machine from the United States. Britain did have more than half the 13,000 exhibits. The entire exhibition was planned and the enormous Crystal Palace erected of iron and glass within one year.

Great Fear

Mass hysteria in France after the start of the **French Revolution** on July 14, 1789. A rumor spread throughout much of France that "brigands" were coming as part of some counterrevolutionary plot to save the aristocracy and feudal order.

Great Leap Forward (1958–1961)

Name of China's failed five-year economic plan launched by **Mao Zedong** to rapidly develop the Chinese economy. It emphasized organizing the countryside into communes in which peasants would greatly increase agricultural production and would produce steel in backyard steel mills in both the countryside and cities. The policy attempted to rely on revolutionary fervor and socialist and nationalist ideals to achieve feats of production rather than on technical expertise. It was a disastrous failure that resulted in a famine in which an estimated 20–30 million people died, temporarily discrediting Mao's policies.

Great Potato Famine. *See* Potato Famine

Great Proletarian Cultural Revolution
(1966–1976)
Decade-long attempt by **Mao Zedong** to purify the **Chinese Communist Party** and Chinese society. Mao used the Cultural Revolution to remove leaders who he thought had nonrevolutionary tendencies. Schools were closed, and millions of young men and women were organized as **Red Guards**. Drilled in the ideas of Mao as presented in the *Little Red Book* of his selected quotations they attacked so-called bourgeois and revisionist elements in society. Mao apparently sought to recapture the fervor of the early years of the revolutions. The most violent phase ended in 1969, but the attempt to promote his radical policies continued to his death in 1976. His successors quickly abandoned the campaign, which had resulted in a setback in China's efforts at modernization and the loss of much of the nation's cultural heritage.

Great Pyramids of Giza. *See* Pyramids of Giza (Egypt)

Great Schism (1378–1415)
Division of the papacy of the **Roman Catholic Church** with two and even three popes concurrently. When **Urban VI** was elected pope in 1378 his actions were so abusive that they precipitated the **Great Schism** wherein a second pope was elected but Urban remained. Urban resided in Rome while the other pope was in Avignon, France. This continued until 1409, when a council met to resolve the situation and elected yet a third pope. In 1415 a council accepted the resignation of one pope, deposed the other two, and elected one new pope.

Great Wall
Term for the series of fortifications along the northern border of China built as a protection against warlike **Central Asian** tribal peoples. During the **Zhou** period a number of fortified walls were constructed by northern Chinese states. These were unified and extended by the Qin emperor **Shi Huangdi** in the late third century B.C.E. There was never a single wall, as widely believed, but elaborate fortifications and protective walls that were built and rebuilt by various dynasties over the next 2,000 years. Some dynasties did not use protective walls at all. The present Great Wall was largely constructed by the Ming rulers in the fifteenth and sixteenth centuries. After the expansion of the Chinese empire into Mongolia by the Qing rulers in the seventeenth and eighteenth centuries, the Great Wall ceased to have any useful function. It has served, perhaps inaccurately, as a symbol of China's isolation.

Great War. *See* World War I

Great Zimbabwe (1100–1450)
Capital of medieval Zimbabwe and largest **Iron Age** site in southern Africa. A huge enclosure, 31 feet (9.5 m) high and more than 800 feet (245 m) in circumference, of granite blocks is the most distinctive feature of Great Zimbabwe. The name *Zimbabwe* means "houses of stone." Stone towers, entrances, and numerous artifacts indicate a civilization of considerable importance. The economy included farming and cattle raising. Great Zimbabwe was an important part of the gold trade. Imported items from as far away as **Ming** China have been found there, indicating that Zimbabwe was connected with trade routes on the east coast of Africa. Great Zimbabwe was also a religious center. Other smaller complexes of stone buildings are scattered throughout the Zimbabwe plateau and surrounding areas. Great Zimbabwe, with a population of approximately 10,000, was occupied between the eleventh and fifteenth

centuries, although settlement there can be traced back as far as 200 B.C.E. It was abandoned due to a long drought, warfare, and an influx of and plundering by a war-like people.

Greece, Archaic (776–479 B.C.E.)
Period of ancient Greek revival. Homer wrote the *Iliad* and the *Odyssey* approximately 750 B.C.E., but 776 B.C.E. is the conventional date for the beginning of historical Greece, the date of the first **Olympic Games**. Around this time Greek **Iron Age** civilization began to recover and expand. Colonization spread Greeks throughout the Mediterranean region. Towns contained civic buildings, an **agora** (an open meeting place that doubled as a market), and an **acropolis** (a citadel for defense), all indicating the importance of the people of the community even though each **polis** (state) was ruled by an aristocracy. In archaic Greece wealthy commoners struggled for political participation. After a lengthy civil war (545–508) **Cleisthenes** established **democracy**.

Greece, Classical (480–323 B.C.E.)
High point of ancient Greek civilization. In 480 B.C.E., Persia, under **Xerxes I**, attacked **Athens** with an army of 150,000 transported in 700 ships. The Athenians raised a navy of 200 ships and an army of 9,000. With little chance of success, the Athenians outsmarted the Persians and won the **Persian War**. The Athenians rebuilt their city with great exuberance because of the new faith in humankind's ability to accomplish great things if people worked together and used their intelligence. Buildings were monumental, sculpture celebrated the glory of humankind (primarily men), and Athens exploded into a **golden age**. The Athenians' later conflict with Sparta would lead to the eventual deterioration of both **poleis** (states) ending the classical period in 338 B.C.E.

Greece, Dark Ages (c. 1100–776 B.C.E.)
Period after the collapse of **Mycenaean Greece**. The period witnessed a near collapse of Greek culture including literacy, hence the term *Dark Ages*. Writing as evidence of Greek civilization disappeared. However, during this period the population expanded with new settlements, and Greeks discovered the use of iron.

Greece, Hellenistic (323–31 B.C.E.)
Period of Greek history after the death of **Alexander the Great** and before rule by the Romans. It was not a unified period but was marked by a succession of rulers and empires. The **Ptolemies** and the **Seleucids** ruled for much of this period, until the Romans conquered the region in 146 B.C.E. and supervised Greece through governors of Macedonia.

Greece, Mycenaean (c. 1400–1100 B.C.E.)
Aristocratic, **Bronze Age** civilization in the southern Greek peninsula (Peloponnese) and Aegean Sea. The *Iliad* and the *Odyssey* of **Homer** tell stories of Mycenaean Greece (although written around 750 B.C.E.). The Mycenaean period was noted for its aristocratic society and warfare (as in the *Iliad*) and for its palace-fortresses. The Mycenaean era came to a fairly abrupt end from either internal warfare or invasions.

Greek and Persian Wars. *See* Persian Wars; Plataea, Battle of; Salamis, Battle of

Greek Orthodox. *See* Eastern Orthodox Church

Gregory of Tours (d. 594)
Bishop and author of a history of the **Franks**. Gregory helped to maintain the **Roman Catholic Church** during a difficult

time in European history. He wrote several works of history and on church functions and is renowned for his *History of the Franks*, about a period otherwise little documented.

Gregory I, "the Great" (540–604)

Pope (590–604), encourager of monasticism and missionary work, and reformer of the **Roman Catholic Church**. Gregory sent **Augustine of Canterbury** as a missionary to convert Britain, spread monasticism throughout Europe, and changed much of the liturgy of the church, which became the standard for the rest of the **Middle Ages**. Gregory also wrote several important books that served as guides for pastoral care and a history of the church. Gregory is known as one of the church fathers.

Guerrilla (Spanish for "little war")

A person fighting in irregular fashion, often independently, instead of in an organized massed army with traditional maneuvers; also, or the warfare of these people. The term was coined during the **Napoleonic War** in Spain (1807–1814), when the Spanish citizenry fought minor confrontations and harassed the French armies to keep them from gaining a complete victory. The technique was used before that time, but it later became a recognized form of warfare that was effective when fought on the guerrillas' home territory against an otherwise overpowering enemy.

Guevara, Ernesto "Che" (1928–1967)

Avid supporter of the Cuban revolutionary Left during the 1950s. In 1956 he joined **Fidel Castro** in his takeover of the Fulgencio Batista regime in Cuba. During the 1960s, Guevara created the Four-Year Plan, which called for **industrialization** of Cuba to diversify away from sugar, but the end goal was never accomplished. He also fought against capitalism and free markets. He tried to establish a common cause among peoples struggling against imperialism and wanted to influence the Cuban population to desire moral rather than material incentives. Due to the revolution's success in Cuba from the use of **guerrilla** tactics, Guevara hoped to spread the idea of revolution using the same type of strategies to other countries.

Guild (Gild)

Organization or grouping of individuals in a specific craft or for religious and social purposes. Guilds first developed in Europe in the thirteenth century and in Japan in the sixteenth century. Craft guilds set regulations, determined who could join by requiring apprenticeships, and required that to become a master a member had to complete a masterpiece. These regulations limited the number of members and ensured the quality of products so that incomes were protected. The larger the town, the more specialized the trades and the more guilds there were. Goldsmiths, weavers, dyers, fishmongers, brewers, and wheelwrights were typical guilds. Paris in the late **Middle Ages** had more than 120 guilds.

Guillotine

Execution device that decapitates; developed by Joseph Guillotin, a revolutionary during the **French Revolution** and a member of the **Constituent Assembly**. Although similar devices had been used in Scotland and elsewhere, the guillotine was adopted in France in 1791 as the most humane method of execution. After some initial problems, the guillotine became the most used instrument, including on King **Louis XVI**.

Gulf War. *See* Iraq War (1991)

Gunboat Diplomacy

Informal international policy used by Western powers in the nineteenth century. Nineteenth-century developments in Western technology such as rapid-fire, breech-loading, smokeless-powder **rifles**; steam-powered, iron-hulled (later, steel-hulled) **gunboats**; and **quinine** as a protective against malaria enabled Europeans to impose European-favorable trade conditions on much of Africa and Asia, or even to conquer parts of those continents. This was known as gunboat diplomacy because European states and the United States "influenced" peoples and states to accept their will by threatening them with gunboats.

See also Nanjing, Treaty of; Opium War

Gunboats

Small steam-powered, iron-hulled boats with a number of small cannons on board, developed in the 1830s to travel along coastal waters or up rivers to intimidate and influence local peoples with **gunboat diplomacy**. Used effectively by Europeans in Africa in the nineteenth and twentieth centuries.

Gunpowder

Explosive used for warfare. Traditionally claimed to have been developed by the Chinese for scaring demons, gunpowder was in fact used by the Chinese for warfare and fireworks by the tenth century and in **cannons** at least by the fourteenth century and possibly in the thirteenth century. The **Mongols** were responsible for the spreading use of gunpowder throughout Eurasia in the thirteenth century. It began to be used in cannons in Europe in the first decades of the fourteenth century. Gunpowder is a mixture of saltpeter, charcoal, and sulfur.

Gunpowder Empire

Thesis that views the establishment of strong empires across Africa and Eurasia in the fifteenth to seventeenth centuries as the result of the introduction of firearms. During this period the **Ottoman Empire** in the **Middle East** and North Africa, the **Safavid** dynasty in Persia, the **Mughal** empire in South Asia, the **Qing** and **Tokugawa** empires in East Asia, and the Moscovy state of Russia formed a belt of formidable empires across the Eastern Hemisphere. The rise of these central empires has been attributed in part to the use of gunpowder, especially artillery. Artillery was effective against warriors on horseback and fortifications including castles. But artillery was expensive to acquire and maintain, giving advantage to rulers who possessed considerable resources. The seaborne empires of Spain and Portugal and, later, the Netherlands, France, and England are among the gunpowder empires.

Guns

Weapons for sending projectiles with explosives. Gunpowder, developed by the Chinese by the tenth century, was used in cannons in China and in Europe by the early fourteenth century. Small arms developed in the sixteenth century. Muskets fired a round ball and were not accurate at long range. **Rifles** came into use in the eighteenth century. The nineteenth century saw rapid refinements including caps, oblong bullets; paper cartridges; breech-loading, repeater rifles; and Maxim guns.

Guo (Kuo)

Chinese term usually translated as "kingdom" or "country," such as in the Chinese name for China, Zhongguo (literally, "Middle Kingdom"). It may have referred originally to a walled or a fortified town. By the **Warring States period** (475–221

B.C.E.) it referred to the six or seven states that contended for power.

Guomindang (Kuomintang)
The Nationalist Party of China (also called the KMT) founded by **Sun Yat-sen** and Song Jiaoren in 1912. It replaced Sun's earlier Revolutionary Alliance. The party ideology was the Three People's Principles: nationalism, democracy, and "people's livelihood." After Sun Yat-sen died in 1925 his successor as party leader, **Chiang Kai-shek**, launched the Northern Expedition from the party's southern stronghold in 1926 and by 1928 had established a loose control over most of China. Following the Guomindang's defeat by the communists in 1949, Chiang Kai-shek and the Guomindang leaders fled to Taiwan, where they ruled until defeated in a presidential election in 2000.

Gupta Empire
Dynasty that ruled much northern India from the mid-fourth to the mid-sixth century. At its peak it had direct control over the Gangetic plain and some measure of control or dominion over much of central and eastern India. The Gupta empire experience a **golden age** of culture, with a number of great poets, playwrights such as **Kalidasa**, and philosophers flourishing. Advances were made in science and mathematics; for example, the zero may have come into use at this time. The dynasty declined in the sixth century.

Gustavus II (Adolphus) (1594–1632)
Swedish king and general who built Sweden into a major European power in the **Thirty Years' War**. Gustavus successfully ended wars with Denmark (1613) and **Russia**

(1617) and warred with Poland (1626–1629). In 1630 he led Lutheran Sweden into the Thirty Years' War in Germany, opposing the Catholic powers. His armies won a major victory at Breitenfeld, and Gustavus met and defeated General **Albrecht von Wallenstein** in the Battle of Lützen but was himself killed in battle. Gustavus, with his chancellor Oxenstierna, reformed Swedish politics and made Stockholm the capital of Sweden.

Gutenberg, Johannes (c. 1400–1468)
German credited with being the first European to print with a movable-type **printing press**, around 1445. Gutenberg cast type, or individual letters, in metal and arranged the letters in a case from which a page could be printed with a press. By 1455 he produced a spectacular **Bible**, known as the **Gutenberg Bible**, which looked handwritten.

Gutenberg Bible (c. 1455)
The first substantial printed book in the West, printed in the German city of Mainz by **Johannes Gutenberg**, who developed a printing press with movable type. The Gutenberg Bible was a two-volume Latin version of the **Bible**. About 180 copies were printed, and 48 whole copies survive today, some of which have been digitized by the museums or libraries that own them so that each page can be viewed on the World Wide Web. The printing industry spread rapidly across Europe, and the new availability of printed materials, which had previously been painstakingly copied by hand, had revolutionary effects on the European **Renaissance**. The new availability of texts promoted literacy, the exchange of scholarship, and commerce.

Habsburg

Aristocratic family that ruled much of central Europe from the fifteenth to the twentieth century. Rudolf IV, Count of Habsburg (pronounced and sometimes spelled "Hapsburg"), was elected king of Germany in 1273 and acquired Austria in 1282. In the fifteenth century the Habsburgs gained control of the Luxembourg lands; married into the lands of Burgundy; added the Netherlands, Artois, and Franche-Comté; and then in the sixteenth century added by marriage Castile, Aragon, all Spanish New World possessions, Naples, Sicily, Sardinia, Hungary, and Bohemia. **Charles V** (r. 1519–1556) ruled all these and was Holy Roman Emperor. While the direct Spanish line died out and the Spanish crown passed to the Bourbons, the Austrian line continued, including **Maria Theresa** (1717–1780) and her son **Joseph II** (1741–1790), but the Habsburgs lost the Austrian Netherlands and the title of Holy Roman Emperor in the Napoleonic Wars. The Habsburgs continued to rule **Austria-Hungary** through **World War I**, but the war and **nationalism** caused the empire to disintegrate, and the last Habsburg emperor, **Charles I** of Austria, renounced his title in 1918.

Hacienda

A large landed estate in Spain or in Spanish territories in the New World. The hacienda was the dominant agricultural and economic unit of Latin America from the seventeenth through the nineteenth century. This created a semifeudal social structure using Amerindian laborers, from which the poor fought to free themselves in the nineteenth and twentieth centuries throughout Latin America. The **Mexican Revolution** of 1910 was fought partly to break up the haciendas.

Hadith

Islamic collection of the sayings and art ascribed to the Prophet, **Muhammad**. The Hadith help to clarify and explain the principles of the **Quran** and is considered a revered source of religious law and guidance. In the ninth century **Muslim** scholars developed a system of classification of the Hadith.

Hadrian (76–138)

Roman emperor (117–138) and consolidator of the **Roman Empire**. **Trajan** (98–117) adopted Hadrian, who in turn adopted Antoninus (138–161). Trajan extended the Roman Empire to its greatest extent, and Hadrian consolidated and strengthened those gains. Hadrian was one of the most gifted administrators Rome ever had, and he even designed buildings, such as the Pantheon (126). **Hadrian's Wall**, in northern Britain, was built after he visited, as a means to keep out the fearsome Picts.

Hadrian's Wall

Defensive wall built by Romans in northern Britain (122–126). The Roman emperor **Hadrian** emphasized consolidation and defense of the **Roman Empire**, which had reached its greatest extent under **Trajan**, his predecessor. The farthest north the Roman Empire reached was northern Britain, where the Romans met the Picts, a fierce Celtic people. After visiting the area, Hadrian decided to have a large defensive wall with mile-castles (castles built into the wall every mile) and fortifications built to keep the Picts out of Roman territory. The wall, 73 miles (117 km) long, was largely ineffective and eventually was abandoned, in 383.

Hagia Sophia (Greek for "Holy Wisdom") Church in **Constantinople** (modern-day **Istanbul**, Turkey) built under **Justinian** 532–537 C.E. As a centerpiece of the eastern capital of the **Roman Empire**, the design was intended to both replicate and surpass the architecture of **Rome**. An architectural wonder with an enormous dome, Hagia Sophia became a mosque after the Turkish conquest of **Constantinople** in 1453.

Haiku
Poetic form popular in Japan during the **Tokugawa** period (1603–1868) that consists of three lines, the first of five syllables, the second of seven syllables, and the third again of five syllables. It developed in the seventeenth century from the initial line of a type of "short poem." Because of its brevity it had to be highly suggestive. Masters of haiku, the greatest being **Matsuo Bashō** (1644–1694), were admired for their skill. Haiku were especially popular among the urban middle class and represent the increasing cultural sophistication of that group during the prosperous Tokugawa period.

Haile Selassie. *See* Selassie, Haile

Hajj
Muslim pilgrimage. Of the Five Pillars of Islam, the fifth is that those who are able must undertake at least one pilgrimage to **Mecca** during their lifetime, expressed in the **Quran** and in the **sharia**, Islamic holy law. A pattern of pilgrimage rites was established by **Muhammad**, but many pilgrims to Mecca visit sites out of the proper order. The Hajj serves to unify Islam by bringing together Muslims of diverse backgrounds.

Hajra. *See* Hijra

Hamilton, Alexander (1755–1804)
Early American political figure. Hamilton, the New York delegate to the Constitutional Convention (1787), and a major contributor to the Federalist Papers, was chosen by **George Washington** to be the first secretary of the treasury for the United States (1789–1795). He is known as the main voice for a strong central government, opposing the Democratic Republicans' desire for decentralized power. Hamilton was killed in a duel with Aaron Burr on July 12, 1804.

Hammurabi (c. 1792–1750 B.C.E.)
King of **Babylon**. Hammurabi, an **Amorite**, was the first ruler to unify all of **Mesopotamia**, ruling **Sumer**, Babylon, **Nineveh**, Nimrod, and Mari. He established a code of law known as the **Code of Hammurabi**.

Hammurabi, Code of
Set of laws established by **Hammurabi**, king of **Babylon**, around 1770 B.C.E. Articles of the **Amorite** law code of 282 dealt with a wide range of issues including wages, fees, and social relations such as slavery and marriage. Hammurabi assembled the laws and had them carved on stones and placed at all temples, but he did not legislate or originate the laws.

Han (206 B.C.E.–221 C.E.)

Dynasty that ruled a large, prosperous Chinese empire that was roughly contemporary with the **Roman Empire** and comparable to it in size. The Han was founded by Liu Bang, who ruled as emperor Gaozu. The Han emperors turned away from the harsh rule of their **Qin** predecessors and promoted **Confucianism** and other schools of thought while retaining some of the useful autocratic features of **legalism**. Under **Wudi** (140–87 B.C.E.) the empire expanded to include parts of Central Asia, Korea, and Vietnam. The Chinese developed steel, the water mill, high quality stoneware (china), and paper under the Han.

Handel, George Frederick (1685–1759)

German late-baroque composer best known for his oratorio *The Messiah* (1741). Handel emigrated to England in 1711, where he produced many operas, oratorios, and other pieces such as *Royal Water Music* (1717). He died in 1759 in London.

Han Feizi (Han Fei-tzu) (c. 280–233 B.C.E.)

Chinese philosopher and one of the formulators of **legalism**. Han Feizi emphasized the need for the authority of the ruler and the power of the state to be asserted and strengthened in order to establish an orderly, peaceful society. His belief in the need for strict laws, regulations, and punishments had an important influence on the **Qin** state and on subsequent Chinese political thought.

Han Gaozu (Kao-tsu) (256–195 B.C.E.)

Born Liu Bang, Han Gaozu led a successful revolt against the tyrannical **Qin** dynasty and founded the **Han** dynasty (206 B.C.E.–220 C.E.). Of humble origin, he was as an able leader who reigned as emperor Gaozu (206–195). The dynasty he established endured for more than four centuries, laying a more solid foundation for Chinese unity than did the short-lived Qin dynasty.

Han'gul

The indigenous alphabet of Korea, created by a committee of scholars under the reign of King Sejong and officially proclaimed in 1443. The alphabet combines letters (originally twenty-eight) to form syllables. Sometimes declared to be the most scientific writing system in the world, it is strictly phonetic. Because of the prestige of Chinese characters it did not become the dominant system of writing in Korea until the twentieth century.

Hangzhou

Chinese city on Hangzhou Bay in the **Yangzi River** basin, capital of Zhejiang Province. It served as the capital of the Wu-Yue kingdom (907–978) during the **Five Dynasties** period. With the opening of the **Grand Canal** in 609 it was linked to the **Yellow River** to the north. It was the capital of the southern **Song** dynasty from 1126 to 1279. Hangzhou was probably the largest city in the world under the Song.

Hannibal (247–182 B.C.E.)

Carthaginian general who led the fight against **Rome** during the Second **Punic War** (218–201 B.C.E.). He invaded the Italian peninsula by coming across the Alps with elephants, an amazing military feat, and had some victories before he was defeated in 202 B.C.E. by the Roman general Scipio Africanus Major in North Africa at the Battle of Zama. Although he was at first allowed to remain in control of Carthage, his efforts to rebuild the city brought on renewed Roman attacks. Hannibal fled east and committed suicide rather than be taken by his Roman enemies.

Hanoi
Capital city of North Vietnam from 1954 to 1976 and of unified Vietnam since 1976. An ancient site at the apex of the Hong (Red) River delta, it became the capital of the Ly dynasty (1109–1225) in 1010 and remained the capital of Vietnam until 1802, when the Nguyen dynasty shifted its capital to Hue. The city was renamed several times and acquired the name Hanoi (meaning "city between the rivers") in 1831.

Hanoverians
Branch of the British royal family from the German territory of Hanover. When Queen Anne died without an heir in 1714, the Act of Succession of 1701 placed the crown on her closest Protestant relative, James I's great-grandson through his daughter's daughter Sophia. This was George, elector of Hanover, who became George I of Great Britain. George I, II, III, and IV and William IV were all rulers of both Britain and Hanover. Only with Queen Victoria were the two separated, although Victoria's son Edward VII was still known as of the House of Hanover. His son, George V, declared during **World War I** that the family was henceforth the House of Windsor.

Hansa. *See* Hanseatic League (Hansa)

Hanseatic League (Hansa)
Confederation of north German cities in the High and late **Middle Ages**. Banded together for trade and mutual protection, the Hanseatic League included many of the German cities along the North Sea and the Baltic Sea, such as Hamburg and Lübeck, although it changed configuration over time. From the thirteenth century until it gradually dissolved in the late Middle Ages, the Hanseatic League was ruled by a body of merchants from the cities. The league monopolized trade among member cities and influenced trade throughout Europe during its existence.

Han Wudi (Wu-ti) (140–87 B.C.E.)
Posthumous temple name of an energetic ruler commonly known as Emperor Wu of the **Han** dynasty of China whose name aptly means the "martial emperor." Wudi's main concerns were the threat to the empire's security posed by the **Xiongnu** tribes on the northern frontier and the need to consolidate control internally before attacking the Xiongnu. He launched a series of successful campaigns that removed the Xiongnu from the grasslands near China and brought military power deep into **Central Asia**. In 111 B.C.E. he conquered Annam (northern Vietnam), and 109–108 B.C.E. his forces invaded Korea and established Chinese rule over the northern part of the peninsula, thus bringing both areas into the Chinese cultural sphere.

Hapsburgs. *See* Habsburgs

Harappa
One of the major cities of ancient Indus culture, located on the **Indus River**. The name *Harappan* is used for the entire civilization although **Mohenjo-Daro** and Kalibangan were important cities. Harappa and other Indus cities were planned, with a grid pattern and wells; piped water, bathrooms, and waste drains for many houses; and civic granaries. Harappa, with as many as 35,000 inhabitants in the period 2500–1800 B.C.E., was surrounded by a brick wall more than 40 feet (12 m) thick. Harappan writing has not been deciphered.

Harappan Civilization
Society located in the **Indus River** valley named after **Harappa**, one of its two chief cities (the other was Mohenjo-Daro). Cities appeared in the Indus valley after

3000 B.C.E., and by 2600 a complex, urban society emerged. Harappan society embraced most of what is now Pakistan and parts of western India, an area much greater than its contemporary **Egyptian** and **Mesopotamian** civilizations. It was an agricultural civilization based on raising wheat, barley, and other crops and also engaged in domestic and foreign trade with **Mesopotamia** and elsewhere. Harappan cities were mainly constructed of brick and had one of the most sophisticated water and sewage systems of the premodern world. The inhabitants were most likely **Dravidian** speaking, but because their script has never been deciphered our knowledge of the Harappan civilization is limited. Its collapse around 1500 B.C.E. was once believed to have been the result of **Aryan** invasions, but historians now question this view and suspect ecological crises as the possible cause. Judging by such evidence as art motifs, some elements of **Harappan** culture appear to have been incorporated into later Indian civilization.

Hara Takeshi (Hara Kei) (1856–1921)
Japanese prime minister (1918–1921) and leader of the Seiyukai Party. Hara Takeshi, as a member of the lower house of the Diet, was called the first commoner to become prime minister, although he came from a **bushi** family background. He was considered a reformer who supported stronger parliamentary government and opposed a military intervention in Siberia, but he also suppressed the independence movement in Korea. He was assassinated while in office.

Harem (Harim) (from Arabic *haram*, meaning "forbidden")
Private quarters of multiple wives and concubines of wealthy or royal men. Harems existed in many cultures but spread with Islamic expansion due to the

Muslim practice of secluding and veiling women. Harems were often places of intense scheming, sometimes influencing royal politics. Large harems were common in Arab countries until the mid-twentieth century; today only rulers or the most conservative or immensely wealthy Muslims continue the practice.

Hargreaves, James (c. 1722–1778)
English inventor of the spinning jenny (1770). The jenny enabling one person to spin many different threads at one time. This, along with the flying shuttle, increased cloth production dramatically. When steam power was later added to the loom and the jenny the **Industrial Revolution** took off.

Harsha (606–647)
North Indian ruler who restored much of the **Gupta empire**. He converted to and promoted **Buddhism** and hosted pilgrims, most famously the Chinese pilgrim **Xuanzang**. His reign was celebrated by the poet Bana. Shortly after he died Harsha's empire disintegrated.

Harun al-Rashid
Muslim caliph who ruled in **Baghdad** from 786 to 809 during the height of the **Abbasid caliphate**'s power. His reign is in many ways idealized by **Muslims** for its expanse and general tranquility that led to a cultural and scientific fluorescence. Harun al-Rashid is remembered for the opulence of his court; institutional and bureaucratic innovations; and his vigorous recruitment and lavish patronage of intellectuals and scientists, which led to advances in many areas including paper making, optometry, and irrigation.

Harvard University
The oldest and one of the most prestigious American institutions of higher learning.

Founded in 1636 in Cambridge, Massachusetts, and named for John Harvard, the college was originally under church sponsorship. The university has produced many distinguished graduates who have influenced U.S. history and world events.

Harvey, William (1578–1657)
English anatomist who first discovered that blood circulates through the body. Previously, it was believed that blood flowed in one direction, much like the sap of plants. Harvey performed experiments that proved that the amount of blood pumped by the heart in one hour was more than all the blood in an animal's body. Therefore, the blood was being circulated. This was one of the most important discoveries in medicine during the **scientific revolution**. Harvey's quantifiable methods set a standard for research in biology.

Hashimite (Hashemite)
Arab descendants of the prophet **Muhammad** who founded the twentieth-century Hashimite dynasty. The Hashimites descended through Muhammad's daughter Fatima and eventually became emirs of **Mecca**, and in the twentieth century one, Husayn ibn Ali, became king of Hejaz. His sons became the kings of Iraq and Jordan, the modern Hashimite dynasty.

Hastings, Battle of (1066)
Battle in which Normans defeated Anglo-Saxons. In 1066 the new king, Harold II of England, had two competitors, both claimants to the throne of England: Harold Hardrada, king of Norway, and William, duke of Normandy. Hardrada invaded England in the north, and Harold was forced to rush an army to meet him. Harold, surprisingly, won at Stamford Bridge on September 25, only to hear three days later that William had invaded to the south at Hastings. Harold's army marched south 240 miles (386 km) to Hastings, where, exhausted and depleted, they gained the tactical advantage by taking the high ground. The Battle of Hastings was won by the Normans because Harold was killed by a random arrow fired in a high arc that went through his eye into his brain, not because the Norman military was superior to the Anglo-Saxons. The battle cleared the way for the Norman conquest of England and the crowning of William I.

Hatshepsut (c. 1540–1480 B.C.E.)
Queen of the ancient **Egyptian civilization** who ruled in her own right. Hatshepsut, the daughter of King Thutmose I, married her half brother Thutmose II. When her husband and her other brother both died, her husband's son by another wife, Thutmose III, succeeded to the throne as a minor. Hatshepsut became regent for the boy and then had herself crowned as pharaoh. With the help of good advisors she brought about expansion of the economy and trade and administrative innovations. Hatshepsut ruled for twenty years and was succeeded by Thutmose III.

Hattusha
The ancient capital of the **Hittites**, in modern-day Turkey. The Hittites were an ancient **Indo-European**-speaking people who established powerful kingdoms in western Asia in the **Fertile Crescent**. The Hittites moved into Anatolia (the Asian part of modern-day Turkey) around 2700 B.C.E., rose to great power around 1700 B.C.E., and disappeared by 1190 B.C.E.

Hausa States
Region of west African savanna states. Between the Niger River and Lake Chad, roughly in the southern region of modern Niger and northern Nigeria, the Hausa states first arose around 1300 as petty kingdoms or **city-states** of urban Hausa-speaking peoples. The flowering of the

region came first by 1650, as a major trade crossroad neighboring the **Songhay**, and later as the region became **Muslim**. By the early nineteenth century the Sokoto caliphate from the north came to dominate the Hausa states.

Hawkins, Sir John (1532–1595)

English admiral who revolutionized the English navy that met the **Spanish Armada** in 1588. Hawkins convinced the navy to build longer, faster, more seaworthy ship that were more heavily gunned with longer-range **cannons**. Hawkins also helped demonstrate the profitability of the slave-based Triangle Trade between Europe, Africa, and the Americas in his 1562 voyage.

Haydn, Franz Joseph (1732–1809)

Austrian music composer. Sometimes called "the father of the symphony," Haydn developed the symphony into a longer form, his later ones consisting of four movements, and expanded the orchestra into one similar to the modern symphony orchestra. Haydn composed more than 100 symphonies as well as more than 80 string quartets, operas, and choral pieces. He was a friend of **Wolfgang Amadeus Mozart**. Haydn's early and later works are in the classical style, while his middle works are often Romantic. Although most renowned during his lifetime for his instrumental pieces, today Haydn is known for his oratorios *The Creation* (1798) and *The Seasons* (1801).

Heavenly Mountains. *See* Tianshan (T'ien-shan)

Hebrew Covenant

Any one of several covenants, or binding agreements, that, according to the **Bible**, **Yahweh** (God) made with **Israel**. (1) The covenant with **Abraham**, recorded in Genesis, in which God promised Abraham a son, many descendants, and the land of Israel. (2) The covenant with Israel, communicated through Moses, by which earthly and spiritual blessings were guaranteed if Israel obeyed the moral and ceremonial laws revealed at Mount Sinai (found in the books of **Exodus**, Leviticus, and Deuteronomy). (3) The covenant with David, promising a continuous succession of descendants to sit upon his throne, again with obedience as a condition (2 Samuel 7). (4) The New Covenant, given through the prophets Jeremiah and Ezekiel, promising the Jews restoration to the land of Israel after the **Babylonian Captivity** and inner renewal of individuals. Each of the covenants follows a particular form that emphasizes the sovereign action of God.

Hebrews, Early

Nomadic people descended from the patriarch **Abraham**, according to the Hebrew **Bible**. Hebrew tradition tells of the Hebrews' subsequent bondage in Egypt after their migration from **Mesopotamia** to **Ancient Palestine** (and subdivision into twelve tribes), and of being led to freedom by Moses. They eventually conquered much of Palestine. The tribes were united into a kingdom under David (c. 1000 B.C.E.).

Hebrew Temple

One of three structures erected in **Jerusalem** on Mount Moriah for the worship of the God of **Israel**. The first, constructed by King **Solomon** circa 950 B.C.E., was destroyed by the Babylonians in 586 B.C.E. The temple was rebuilt circa 515 B.C.E., after the Jews returned from their **Babylonian Captivity**. The third and grandest temple was begun by King Herod the Great (37–4 B.C.E.) and was completed only in 64 C.E. One of the seven wonders of the ancient world, Herod's temple included a large temple area (26 acres, or

10.5 hectares), surrounded by high walls. Inside, and also enclosed by walls, were the Court of the Gentiles, separated by a wall from the Court of Women; the Court of Israel, accessible only to Jewish men; the Court of the Priests; and the temple proper. This last was divided into the Holy Place and, behind a thick curtain, the Holy of Holies, into which only the high priest could go, and that only once a year. The entire complex was leveled by the **Romans** in 70 C.E.

Hegel, Georg Wilhelm Friedrich (1770–1831)

German philosopher known for his study of all knowledge laid out as a dialectic (dialogue) between civilizations that explains all history. From Hegel, **Karl Marx** developed his theory of class, or economic dialectic, to explain all history.

Hegira (Hejira, Hijrah). *See* Hijra

Heian Period

Period of Japanese history from 794 C.E., when the imperial capital was moved to Heian (Kyoto) from Nara, to 1192 C.E., when rule by the imperial court was brought to an effective end. During the Heian period the imperial bureaucracy, created in the seventh and eighth centuries and modeled in part on the imperial government of China, gradually declined, and most of the countryside came under the control of monasteries or capital aristocrats. In the capital, however, the imperial court supported a sophisticated elite that sponsored splendid Buddhist temples and created a rich body of literature. Among the characteristics of Heian society was the relatively high status of women and their role in producing some of the world's earliest novels. The most famous was the *Tale of Genji* by **Murasaki Shikibu**, considered by many to be the greatest literary masterpiece in Japanese literature.

Heisenberg, Werner (1901–1976)

German physicist and author of the Heisenberg uncertainty principle. Heisenberg's mathematics helped provide the framework for Max Planck's theory of quantum mechanics. In 1927 Heisenberg suggested in his uncertainty principle that there is indeterminacy—that randomness is an intrinsic part of nature. This upsets classical physics, where given enough evidence future behavior should be predictable. The Heisenberg uncertainty principle also states that nothing can be purely measured because the attempt to measure alters the measurement.

Hellenic Philosophy

Philosophy of the ancient Greeks. The Greeks, in addition to their supernatural cosmology (Greek mythology), examined the world around them empirically, gathering data from the evidence in nature, such as the movement of the heavenly bodies or the physics on earth. The Greeks were the first to create a natural philosophy from the evidence in a fashion that today is known as science.

Hellenistic Greece. *See* Greece, Hellenistic

Helots

People conquered by the ancient Spartans and used as a servile labor force. In addition to the perioeci, who were not slaves but were dominated by the Spartans, the Helots provided the productive forces that enabled the citizens of **Sparta** themselves to be free for military service by the sixth century B.C.E. The Helots, even though they outnumbered the Spartans, had no civil rights and could be executed without trial by the Spartans.

Henry, Patrick (1736–1799)
American orator and prominent political figure during the **American Revolution**. Henry is famous for his "Give me liberty or give me death!" speech on March 23, 1775, as well as for being a delegate to the First **Continental Congress**. He also led the movement for a bill of rights during the Constitutional Convention.

Henry, Prince, "the Navigator"
(1394–1460)
Portuguese supporter of exploration in the **Age of Exploration**. Henry was the third son of King **John I** of Portugal. He became interested in the wider world, set up a center for studying navigation, and supported numerous trips of exploration down the west coast of Africa until his death in 1460. These trips set the foundation for further trips that eventually led to **Bartolomeu Dias** rounding the tip of Africa, **Vasco Da Gama** sailing to India, and even **Christopher Columbus** sailing to the New World.

Henry II (1133–1189)
Plantagenet king of England (1154–1189) and of numerous European territories. Henry II was a European ruler rather than merely an English king, but he was one of England's greatest monarchs. He strengthened England's government, revived justice (creating something like the modern court system), increased taxation, and conquered Ireland. Henry II married **Eleanor of Aquitaine**, a powerful women in her own right. Henry II is best known for his conflict with and murder of **Thomas Becket**, a onetime friend of Henry's made archbishop of Canterbury. Henry II's sons were **Richard I** and **John I**.

Henry IV (1553–1610)
King of France and founder of the **Bourbon** dynasty also known as Henry of

Navarre. Henry was king of Navarre and a **Huguenot** (Protestant) until he became king of France, but although he became Catholic he protected religious freedom with the **Edict of Nantes** in 1598. Henry was assassinated by a Catholic.

Henry VIII (1491–1547)
King of England (1509–1547). The second son of Henry VII, he ascended the throne and married his dead brother's widow, **Catherine of Aragon**. Henry wrote a treatise defending the **Roman Catholic Church** against **Martin Luther**'s reforms. Henry divorced Catherine to gain a male heir (Catherine's only surviving child was **Mary I**) and married Anne Boleyn against the wishes of his friend the chancellor **Sir Thomas More**, who was beheaded in 1535. Anne produced **Elizabeth I**. Henry broke from the Catholic Church, becoming head of the Church of England to gain the divorce and to facilitate the confiscation of church property and lands (1536–1539). Henry later had Anne executed for infidelity and married Jane Seymour, who died giving birth to a son, Edward VI. Henry then married Anne of Cleves, but he divorced her and married Catherine Howard; had Catherine Howard executed for infidelity; and married Catherine Parr, who survived him. During his reign a major transformation of government took place under the direction of Thomas Cromwell.

Heresy
Religious view or doctrine judged inconsistent with that held by a church, especially the **Roman Catholic Church**.
See also Albigensians; Arianism; Reformation

Herodotus (c. 484–425 B.C.E.)
Ancient Greek historian and author of *The Histories* (c. 446 B.C.E.). Cicero called him "the father of history." Herodotus traveled

widely, including trips to Egypt, the Black Sea, and Africa. He gathered histories of these lands and of Greece, which he referred to as "research" or "inquiry," which in Greek is *historia* giving us the modern meaning of the term *history*.

Herzl, Theodor (1860–1904)

Hungarian-born Viennese journalist and founder of modern Zionism. In 1878 Herzl's family moved to Vienna, where Herzl earned a doctorate in law and worked as a lawyer in Vienna and Salzburg. He left law and became a correspondent in Paris for a Viennese newspaper. In Paris he observed the **anti-Semitism** of the **Dreyfus Affair** in 1895. Herzl was convinced that the only solution to anti-Semitism was the establishment of a Jewish state. He considered Palestine and Argentina as locations. He published *The Jewish State* (1896) and with the support of other Jews founded the Zionist movement. The first Zionist Congress was held in Basel, Switzerland, in 1897 and created the World Zionist Organization with Herzl as its president. Herzl died before his dream of a Jewish state was realized, but in 1949 his remains were transferred to Israel.

Hidalgo, Father Miguel (1753–1811)

Mexican leader of a revolutionary movement against Spain, regarded as the father of Mexican independence. His following was a social revolt, mainly of indigenous peoples. Though the uprising against the upper classes of Mexico was eventually unsuccessful (due to hesitation on Hidalgo's part upon reaching the capital city), the date that Hidalgo called for the uprising to begin, September 16, 1810, is commemorated as Mexico's Independence Day. After Hidalgo's attempt at revolution failed, he and his followers were moving north to regroup when all of the leadership were caught and executed as traitors.

Hideyoshi (1536–1598)

Japanese feudal lord and warrior who continued the work of **Oda Nobunaga** in unifying the country between 1582 and 1591. Hideyoshi, of a humble background, rose up through the ranks as an able soldier and earned a reputation for ruthlessness and effectiveness. Distrustful of the political influence of Buddhist monks, he encouraged Catholic missionary activities but later persecuted many Christian converts whose loyalty he suspected. In 1592 he launched an invasion of Korea, perhaps as a prelude to an invasion of China. The invasion ended in failure, and the troops were withdrawn after his death in 1598. His work at unifying Japan was consolidated after his death by one of his commanders, **Tokugawa** Ieyasu.

Hideyoshi Invasions

Japanese invasions of Korea. In 1592 **Hideyoshi** launched an invasion of Korea, perhaps as a prelude to an invasion of China. The invasion ended in failure due to Chinese intervention and Korean resistance, including the naval victories of Admiral **Yi Sun-sin**. Japanese troops withdrew after Hideyoshi's death in 1598. The invasions brought a great loss of life and vast destruction to Korea, leaving a legacy of bitterness and suspicion toward the Japanese. Historians still debate whether his motives were megalomania or simply a desire to rid himself of the many soldiers he no longer needed once he had completed the unification of the country.

Hieroglyphics

Literally, "sacred carvings"—characters in the picture writings of the ancient **Egyptian civilization** or other cultures. Hieroglyphic symbols represent the object they depict or as symbols to denote certain sounds. The Egyptian hieroglyphics developed, possibly coming from Sumeria, around 2900 B.C.E. Not until the discovery of the **Rosetta stone** in 1799 was it possible to decipher much of the Egyptian hieroglyphics.

High Renaissance

The culmination of **Renaissance** artistic features of realism, classicism, harmony, and balance in the works of **Leonardo da Vinci**, Donato Bramante, **Michelangelo**, **Raphael**, Giorgione, and **Titian**, working roughly from 1485 to 1520 (later for Michelangelo and Titian). In music, the High Renaissance produced Josquin des Prés, while **Niccolò Machiavelli**'s *The Prince* set a new direction in political analysis comparable to scientific perspective in painting.

Hijra

Escape of **Muhammad** from **Mecca** to **Medina** in 622. This event became known as the Hijra ("migration"), the date of which became the first day of the first year of the **Muslim** calendar.

Himiko (Japanese for "Sun Princess") (third century)

Aged virgin woman recognized by the Wei dynasty as queen of the Wa (Japan) after she had sent a tributary embassy to China. Reputed to be a shaman who ruled through sorcery and possibly matriarchy, she was succeeded by a thirteen-year-old girl (Iyo) after her death and after a man had been repudiated by the warrior clans (*uji*). She was buried with pomp in a large, keyhole-shaped tomb (*kofun*).

Himmler, Heinrich (1900–1945)

German *Nazi* political leader and chief of the **SS** (1929–1945). Himmler turned **Adolf Hitler**'s personal bodyguard into the SS and made it a powerful and influential organization. In 1936 he became the head of the secret police (Gestapo), and from 1941 he oversaw the systematic extermination of Jews and others. In 1944, during **World War II**, he became commander in chief of the German home forces. In 1945 he was captured by the British, but he committed suicide before he could be put on trial.

Hindenburg, Paul von (1847–1934)

German soldier and statesman. During **World War I** Hindenburg was commander of the German army. From 1925 until his death he was president of Germany. In that capacity, but against his own wishes, he appointed **Adolf Hitler** as chancellor of Germany in 1933.

Hinduism

Term of nineteenth-century British origin used to describe a group of complex and varied yet related religious beliefs and practices of south Asia. Hinduism emerged in the second and first millennia B.C.E. out of a combination of **Aryan** and pre-Aryan religions. The earliest sacred texts of Hinduism are the **Vedas**, which date to before 700 B.C.E. The basic concepts adhered to by almost all Hindus are *samsara*, the law of reincarnation; *atman*, the individual soul; and **Brahman**, the universal soul. They were spelled out in the **Upanishads**, composed around 700–500 B.C.E. Hindus seek to escape the cycle of life and to achieve a spiritual liberation by uniting their atman with the brahman. Traditionally a tolerant faith, Hinduism incorporated a variety of religious practices, thereby developing a highly variegated religion whose adherents worshiped one or more of thousands of deities. The most commonly recognized are **Brahma**, **Vishnu**, and **Shiva**, including various incarnations, or avatars, of Vishnu such as Krishna and Rama. Hindus generally adhered to the caste system as a matter of religious duty, recognizing the high social status of the **Brahmins**. Both **Buddhism** and **Jainism** grew out of Hinduism to become generally recognized as separate faiths. A number of converts to Hinduism were made in Southeast Asia, but for the most part Hinduism was not a missionary religion. From the twelfth century onward its dominance in India was challenged by **Islam**, but it has remained the faith of the majority of the Indian subcontinent to the present. In recent years a more militant form of Hinduism has appeared in India and has become a political force in that country.

Hippias (r. 527–510)
Tyrant of ancient **Athens**. After a period of severe strife in Athens the tyrant **Peisistratus** (c. 600–527 C.E.) took control. At Peisistratus's death, his son Hippias took over. After Hippias's rule a period of civil war broke out, followed by the first establishment of democracy, led by Cleisthenes.

Hippodrome
Roman stadium for horse-and-chariot races. Many cities had hippodromes, but the one in **Constantinople**, completed by Constantine in 330, was the most famous. Organizations, in Constantinople known as the Blues and the Greens, provided the charioteers and other entertainers for the populous. Even the emperors often attended. The Hippodrome, along with **Hagia Sophia** and the palace, were the centers of **Byzantine** life. The Hippodrome existed in the city that would become **Istanbul** into the nineteenth century.

Hiratsuka Raicho (1886–1971)
Japanese feminist author and social critic. After graduating from college she entered the Narumi Women's English School, where she founded *Seito*, a feminist journal, as well as the *Seito-sha* ("Bluestocking Association") in 1911. As editor of *Seito*

she started a movement for the emancipation of women with Yosano Akiko and Ito Noe. With Ichikawa Fusae she founded the New Women's Society, and after **World War II** she founded the Federation of Japan Women's Organization (*Fudanren*), in 1953.

Hirohito (1901–1989) (posthumously, Showa)
Emperor of Japan from 1926 to 1989, and the longest reigning Japanese emperor. He was appointed regent in 1921 to his mentally incompetent father, the Taisho emperor, and succeeded to the throne in 1926. His early reign saw the expansion of Japanese military aggression abroad, including the invasions of **Manchuria** in 1931 and China in 1937 and the attack on U.S. and British forces in the Pacific in 1941. After **World War II** General **Douglas MacArthur** decided to maintain Hirohito on the throne, although he was required to renounce his divine status. He was generally absolved of any responsibility for World War II as a figurehead ruler. Recent research, however, suggests that he played an active role in supporting the military during the Chinese invasion and World War II.

Hiroshige (Ando Hiroshige) (1797–1858)
One of the last and greatest of Japan's woodblock artists principally famous for his city scenes and his landscape series *Fifty-Three Post Stations on the Tokaido*. Along with his older contemporary Katsushika Hokusai (1760–1849), he combined Western concepts of perspective with Japanese color and line to produce paintings that had a great influence on European art in the late nineteenth century, although neither artist was fully appreciated by their contemporaries in Japan.

Hiroshima

Japanese city in southern Kyûshû that became famous for being the site of the first use of nuclear weapons. On August 6, 1945, the United States dropped an atomic bomb on Hiroshima. Estimates of the death toll vary, but approximately one-third of the city's 300,000 residents died in the attack. A second bomb was dropped on Nagasaki three days later. The two attacks contributed to the surrender of Japan to the **Allies** on August 15, 1945.

Hispaniola

Large island in the West Indies, divided into two nations, the Republic of Haiti in the west and the Dominican Republic in the east. Before **Christopher Columbus** set foot on it on his first voyage to the Americas in 1492, Hispaniola was inhabited by the Arawaks, an **Amerindian** people. The Spanish eventually wiped them out, however, and populated the island with African slaves. The slaves rebelled in the late eighteenth century, and the island became independent as the Republic of Haiti in 1804. The Dominican Republic came into being in 1843 after another revolt.

Hitler, Adolf (1889–1945)

Chancellor and führer of the German Reich and head of the **Nazi** (National Socialist) party. In prison in 1924, Hitler dictated his autobiography, *Mein Kampf*, in which he espoused his ideas of the inequality of the races, the superiority of the "**Aryan**" race, and the Jew as enemies of the state. **Paul von Hindenburg** reluctantly appointed Hitler chancellor in 1933. Hitler consolidated his power, eliminated all opponents, and began rearming Germany against the **Versailles Treaty**. He reoccupied the Rhineland in 1936, pushed through the **Anschluss** with Austria in 1938, and invaded Czechoslovakia in 1939. When Hitler's Germany invaded Poland in 1939, **World War II** began. It is believed that Hitler committed suicide in 1945 when the war was clearly lost.

Hittites

Ancient Indo-European-speaking people who established powerful kingdoms in western Asia in the **Fertile Crescent**. The Hittites moved into Anatolia (the Asian part of modern-day Turkey) around 2700 B.C.E., rose to great power around 1700 B.C.E., and disappeared by 1190 B.C.E. Around 1600 B.C.E. the Hittites sacked **Babylon**. Although the Hittites were primarily agrarian, they also traded throughout western Asia.

Hobbes, Thomas (1588–1679)

English philosopher most noted for his work *The Leviathan* (1651), in which he stated that "without restraint, the life of man is solitary, poor, nasty, brutish, and short." Because he had lived through the **English Civil War** Hobbes believed that humans need a controlled state led by a monarchy.

Ho Chi Minh (1890–1969)

Vietnamese revolutionary and statesman. Born Nguyen That Thanh, he adopted the pen name Ngyuen Ai Quoc ("Ngyuyen the Patriot") and, later, Ho Chi Minh ("He Who Enlightens"). In 1917 he moved to France, where he became active in leftist politics. In 1930 he was a founder of the Vietnamese Communist Party. A leader of the movement for independence from France, he founded the **Viet Minh** guerilla movement to fight the Japanese forces that were occupying Indochina. In 1945 after the Japanese surrender, he proclaimed the Democratic Republic of Vietnam. When the French returned, he fought a successful guerilla campaign that led to their recognition of Viet Minh control over North Vietnam at the 1954 **Geneva Conference**.

Determined to see the reunification and communization of all Vietnam, Ho supported the **Viet Cong** in South Vietnam and in the 1960s began sending North Vietnamese troops in large numbers to fight the South Vietnamese and U.S. forces, subordinating economic development to his goal of reunification. After his death in 1969 his followers continued the war with the United States and the Saigon regime until reunification was completed in 1975. They then renamed Saigon Ho Chi Minh City.

Hohenstaufen

Aristocratic German family that held the throne as Holy Roman Emperors 1138–1254 (except for 1208–1212). **Frederick I, "Barbarossa"** (1152–1190) was a Hohenstaufen. The family competed for power with the Welf (or Guelf) family. This became the famous Guelf and Ghibelline competing Italian parties of the High **Middle Ages.** The name *Ghibelline* comes from Weibelungen, one of the Hohenstaufen castles.

Hojo

Branch of the powerful Japanese warrior Taira family. Its members serving as regents for puppet **shoguns** were the effective rulers of Japan from 1219 to 1333, during the **Kamakura** period. After **Minamoto Yoritimo**'s death, power fell to his wife Masako and her Hojo family. The Hojo regency marked an extreme in the Japanese tendency of indirect rule because they were only regents to puppet shoguns who in turn were supposedly ruling on behalf of puppet emperors. The Hojo regents refused to pay tribute to **Khubilai Khan** and executed his envoys, bringing about two **Mongol** invasions of Japan. The invasions failed, but the Hojo were unable to reward their **vassals**, leading to discontent that brought about their

downfall when many rallied to Go-Daigo's efforts to restore imperial rule. In 1333 a vassal, Ashikaga Takauji, took power.

Hojo Masako (1157–1225)

Japanese woman known as "the Nun-Shogun." Widow of the shogun **Minamoto Yoritomo** who became a Buddhist nun and served as a power behind the throne for her sons, she briefly placed her father, Hojo Tokimasa, under house arrest and led a coalition to put down an attempted imperial restoration in 1221.

Hokkaido

Northernmost of the four main islands of Japan. Until the late nineteenth century it was a frontier region of Japan inhabited by the aboriginal Ainu people. From the 1870s the Japanese government rapidly developed the island in order to secure the northern boundaries of the country and to expand agricultural production.

Holocaust

Literally, a sacrificial offering, the whole of which is consumed by fire. The term *Holocaust* is often used to refer to the murder of more than 6 million Jews as well as gypsies and others by the German **Nazis** during **World War II**, many of them by fire. **Adolf Hitler** gave orders for what he called the Final Solution in early 1941.

Holy Roman Empire

Political institution originated in 800 when **Charlemagne** was crowned emperor of the Romans by the **pope**. The name *Holy Roman Empire* was first used in 1254. German princes elected the Holy Roman Emperor, yet he was crowned by the pope. This provided the emperors with a paternalistic attitude toward all of Christendom in the West and a position of leadership in Europe, although by the fifteenth century the Holy Roman Empire was largely

German in political affairs. The title of Holy Roman Emperor existed until its abolition by **Napoléon Bonaparte** in 1806.

Homer (c. 700s B.C.E.)
Ancient Greek author of the *Iliad* and the *Odyssey*. The dating of Homer and his two epic poems is very rough, but a date of somewhere in the eighth century B.C.E. is most probable. Authorship of the *Iliad* and the *Odyssey* has been questioned, but tradition and most evidence favors a single author named Homer. The *Iliad* deals with the Trojan War, Achilles, and Hector, while the *Odyssey* deals with Odysseus's return from the Trojan War.

Homo Erectus ("upright man")
Hominid primate distinguished by a bipedal, erect stance, believed by some to be the direct ancestor of **Homo sapiens**. Homo erectus had a smaller brain than Homo sapiens. Homo erectus was preceded by Australopithecus. There is some doubt whether Homo erectus is a direct ancestor of Homo sapiens. Homo erectus ranged over much of the earth 1.6 million to 250,000 years ago, with fossils found in Africa, Asia, and Europe, yet extinction may have occurred as recently as 28,000 years ago.

Homo Sapiens ("thinking man")
Bipedal, erect primate distinguished by a highly developed brain. Homo sapiens have the ability to reason, produce language, and manipulate tools. Through language Homo sapiens can share accumulated and transient knowledge.

Hong Kong
Former British crown colony consisting of a small peninsula and some islands, including Hong Kong Island, on the south coast of China's Guangzhou province. In 1842 China ceded the island of Hong Kong to Britain as a result of the **Opium War**. More territory was added in 1860, and in 1898 the adjacent New Territories were leased for ninety-nine years. The colony emerged after **World War II** as a major financial and industrial center. In the 1984 Sino-British Declaration, Britain agreed to return Hong Kong to China following the expiration of the New Territories lease in 1997. China has maintained Hong Kong's separate economic system and some political autonomy in what it calls "one country, two systems."

Hongwu (1328–1398)
Ming dynasty founder born Zhu Yuanzhang who reigned as Hongwu (1368–1398). Born to a poor peasant family, he was orphaned at sixteen, became a monk, joined a rebel gang, and led a rebel army against the **Yuan dynasty (Mongol Empire)**. Hongwu established a capital at Nanjing in 1356 and drove the Mongols out of China twelve years later, freeing China from non-Chinese rule. Hongwu was an able ruler but ruthless. In 1380 he executed his prime minister and governed directly. While he resumed the **civil service examinations** and built institutions that successfully laid the foundations for the Ming state, he also executed thousands in bloody purges and instituted the practice of publicly beating officials, consolidating autocratic trends in Chinese imperial rule that had been underway since the **Song**. He left a legacy of despotism and cruelty.

Hong Xiuquan (1814–1864)
Founder of the Taiping ("Great Peace") religious sect and leader of the **Taiping Rebellion** (1850–1864). Hong had failed several times to pass the Chinese **civil service examinations** when he encountered Christian missionary activity in southern China. Influenced by Christian as well as

traditional Chinese religious and philosophical ideas, he saw himself as a messiah for a new religious and political order. He quickly gained a number of followers by promising a utopian society. His followers seized Nanjing, which they made their capital, and attempted to create a new dynasty. After initial military success the Taiping army began to lose. Nanjing was put under siege from which Hong believed God would save him. He turned leadership of the rebellion over to others and committed suicide in 1864. Hong's Taiping Rebellion is estimated to have cost 20 million lives and contributed to the decline of the **Qing dynasty**.

Hoover, Herbert C. (1874–1964)

Thirty-first president of the United States. A highly successful mining engineer, Hoover headed relief programs during **World War I** and was later named U.S. food administrator. Following service as secretary of commerce under Warren G. Harding and Calvin Coolidge, Hoover was elected president in 1928. His administration was soon overwhelmed by the economic collapse following the stock market crash of October 1929. Hoover's firm belief in the limited functions of the federal government crippled his ability to effectively confront the **Great Depression**. While he supported efforts at recovery of the private sector, his reluctance to provide adequate relief for the unemployed led to the rapid decline of his reputation. He was defeated by **Franklin D. Roosevelt** in 1932.

Hopi

Group of Pueblo **Amerindians** in Arizona. Their origin myth has them climbing up through four underground chambers and living in many locations. Archaeologists suggest that they did in fact occupy various locations. The Hopi, a farming and herding people, were relatively peaceful. There are approximately 6,000 Hopi still living in typical pueblo dwellings.

Hoplites

Military soldiers of ancient Greece who developed by the seventh century B.C.E. Hoplites were not aristocratic (as soldiers of **Mycenaean Greece** in the *Illiad* and *Odyssey* were), but because they bought their own equipment they were usually well-to-do. Hoplites not only revolutionized military tactics by fighting as an organized, tightly formed block called a phalanx, but the importance of this nonaristocratic class put pressure on the political structure that eventually brought popular reforms and, eventually, even **democracy**.

Horace (65–8 B.C.E.)

Roman Latin poet and satirist, second in fame only to **Virgil**. Horace gained **Octavian**'s favor and became one of the popular poets of the Roman upper classes. His poetry dealt with the delights and pleasures of life, although in later life he wrote more on good company and philosophy. His works include *Satires* (30 B.C.E.) and *Epistles* (20 B.C.E.).

Houphouét-Boigny, Félix (1905–1993)

First president of Ivory Coast (1960–1993). Educated in the French colonial system, from the dominant ethnic group, and with high social status, Houphouét-Boigny, a doctor by training, worked to end the colonial institution of forced labor and other inequities. He held numerous political positions, including prime minister and president of an independent Ivory Coast. He was one of the most influential political leaders in Africa and built Ivory Coast into one of the most prosperous African countries. Economic decline took a toll starting in the 1980s, but Houphouét-Boigny was reelected to a five-year term in 1990. He died in office in 1993.

House of Commons

In the United Kingdom, the lower chamber of **Parliament**. The House of Commons originated in the **Middle Ages** when commoners were invited to Parliament in the late thirteenth century because of the wealth that they controlled. In the fourteenth century the House of Commons became an integral part of Parliament, along with the **House of Lords** and the king. By the seventeenth century the House of Commons was powerful enough to abolish the House of Lords from 1649 to 1660. The House of Commons increased its power over finances and legislation through the centuries. With the **Act of Union** of 1707, Scotland sent members to the House of Commons. The **Reform Bill of 1832** reduced the role of the House of Lords and the monarchy in relation to the House of Commons. Renowned prime ministers such as William Pitt, Robert Peel, **William Gladstone** and **Benjamin Disraeli** extended the power of the House of Commons in the eighteenth and nineteenth centuries. There are currently 659 members of the House of Commons, elected from constituencies, and the dominant parties are Labour, **Conservative** (**Tory**), and Liberal Democrat. The leader of the party commanding a majority in the House of Commons is asked by the monarch to become prime minister.

House of Lords

In the United Kingdom, the upper chamber of **Parliament**. The House of Lords originated in the **Middle Ages** as a gathering of the barons and clergy (only the archbishops, bishops, and abbots) of the realm of England to consult with the king. This gathering was called Parliament (from the French for "to speak"), and no commoners were invited. With the establishment of a **House of Commons**, the barons, predominantly hereditary lords, and the clergy became known as the House of Lords, and together the two houses of Parliament presented bills to the king to be made into law. Over time, more control of finances and, eventually, of legislation for England fell to the House of Commons, although the House of Lords maintained veto power and delaying power into the twentieth century. The House of Lords was abolished from 1649 to 1660 during the English Republic. The **Acts of Union** (of England with Scotland in 1707 and with Ireland in 1800) incorporated Scottish and Irish lords. From the **Reform Bill of 1832** onward, the power of the House of Lords declined. In 1999 the House of Lords was radically restructured, with hereditary lords nearly banished and appointed lords replacing them.

Hsia Dynasty. *See* Xia

Huainanzi (*Huai-nan-tzu*)

Chinese classic text of the second century B.C.E. compiled under the direction of a nobleman of the same name. It contains a basic cosmology of **yin-yang** that came to be regarded as authoritative by most Daoist philosophers. It also incorporates many beliefs and practices of popular religion, such as the search for immortality, thus helping to incorporate concepts from folk religion into **Daoism**.

Huang Kung-wang (1269–1354)

Yuan dynasty Chinese master of landscape painting. His most famous work, *Dwelling in the Fuchun Mountains*, painted in his old age, has been one of the most admired and copied paintings in China. He also authored an influential treatise on painting.

Huguenots

French Calvinist **Protestants** of the sixteenth and seventeenth centuries. (Origins and meaning of the word are uncertain, but it was in use by the 1520s.) From the 1550s **Calvinism** spread through France and was organized on a federated or regional plan (without a top-heavy structure). By 1562 their numbers had increased, so Catholics, under the Duc de Guise, attacked and killed many Huguenots, beginning the **Wars of Religion**. Civil war between Huguenots and Catholics continued until 1598, when the **Edict of Nantes** declared Huguenots legal. Their numbers further increased until 1685, when the treaty was revoked and Huguenots were persecuted, driving many of them to leave for England, the Netherlands, Switzerland, and even America and South Africa. Since Huguenots were often crafters, the exodus was welcome in all those lands.

Huitzilopochtli

Aztec god of war and the sun. When the Aztecs, or Mexica, arrived in the Valley of Mexico around 1200 they brought their tribal god Huitzilopochtli with them, but with the fifteenth-century Aztec conquest of the Valley of Mexico Huitzilopochtli was elevated above the nature gods, and human sacrifices to him were emphasized.

Hukbalahap

Peasant resistance movement in the Philippines. It began during **World War II** as the Anti-Japanese People's Army but was directed as much at the rich Filipino landlords as it was against the Japanese. Based in central Luzon and led by Luis Taruc, the "Huks," who were denied representation in parliament, led a rebellion against Manila that was crushed with U.S. support by the Philippine government between 1950 and 1954.

Humanism

Philosophy developed during the **Italian Renaissance** emphasizing the worth and ability of the individual. Humanism is often seen as beginning with the poetry of **Petrarch** (b. 1304). This intellectual movement was based on the study of the Greek and Roman texts that were the foundation of the educational goals of *studia humanitatis* ("humanistic studies"). Although humanism was concerned largely with secular ideas and had a great influence on the politics of the Italian **city-states** (civic humanism), many humanists such as **Niccolò Machiavelli** and **Desiderius Erasmus** were devout Christians.

Humayun

Second **Mughal** emperor who ruled most of northern India 1530–1540 and 1555–1556. He lost his throne to an Afghan, Sher Shah, in 1540. After years of exile, mainly in Iran, he regained power in 1555, reestablishing the Mughal Empire, but he died the following year.

Hume, David (1711–1776)

Scottish philosopher and historian during the Scottish **Enlightenment**. Hume influenced the modern philosophical schools of skepticism and empiricism. He wrote about morality, politics, and natural religion and emphasized knowledge through experience. He described forceful experience as perception and lesser experience as beliefs. Hume argued that the existence of God could not be proven and remained an agnostic throughout his life. Hume's works include *A Treatise of Human Nature* (1739), *Philosophical Essays Concerning Human Understanding* (1748), and *History of Great Britain* (1754, 1756), a publication that made him wealthy.

Hundred Days Reform (1898)

Chinese imperial reforms directed toward political, administrative, and educational institutions in 1898. Defeat in the **Sino-Japanese War** (1894–1895) prompted the young emperor Guangxu to heed the progressive suggestions of Confucian scholar **Kang Youwei**. The emperor's Hundred Days Reform encouraged some Western-style changes to compete with Japan and the West. Guangxu's aunt, the **Empress Dowager** (**Ci Xi**), the real power at the court, repealed the reforms in an anti-Western reaction as a threat to her power and to the ways of rich conservative Chinese. She used her military influence to imprison the emperor and kill leading reformers. Kang Youwei escaped abroad.

Hundred Flowers Movement (1956–1957)
Movement launched by **Mao Zedong** to allow constructive self-criticism of the Chinese Communist government. It drew its name from a classical Chinese phrase meaning "let a hundred flowers bloom, let a hundred schools of thought contend." With official encouragement, a number of Chinese intellectuals and others began to express criticism of the **Chinese Communist Party** and state institutions. Mao responded to this criticism with an antirightist campaign that sent many of the nation's educated people to remote rural areas.

Hundred Years War (1337–1453)
War between England and France. A long but not continuous series of wars that were initially dynastic conflicts between Edward III, king of England, and Philip VI, king of France, over feudal jurisdictions. England won many of the battles (**Crécy** in 1346, **Poitiers** in 1356, and **Agincourt** in 1415), partly because of the use of a new weapon, the **longbow**, but France won the war. England had approximately one-third the resources of men and wealth of France. By the fifteenth century France had gained the advantage, including the inspiration of **Joan of Arc**. In 1453 the French had taken nearly all English landholdings on the Continent. The Hundred

Years War resulted in the growth of bureaucracy and administrations in both countries as well as increased royal power and the creation of **nationalism**.

Hungarian Revolt (1956)
Revolt against the **Union of Soviet Socialist Republic**'s control of Hungary during the **Cold War**. After **Joseph Stalin**'s death Soviet-controlled Eastern bloc nations such as East Germany, Poland, and **Yugoslavia** began to push for reforms. Concessions given to others and repression within Hungary led to demonstrations in Budapest, the Hungarian capital. The Soviets moved in tanks to control the demonstrations, and a full-scale revolt broke out. France, Britain, and the United States hinted that help would come, but they were distracted by the **Suez Crisis**. The Soviets crushed the revolt, executing more than 2,000 people. More than 200,000 Hungarians fled to Western Europe and the United States. The crushing of the Hungarian Revolt sent a signal to other Eastern European countries not to push reforms too far.

Hungarians. *See* Magyars

Huns
Central Asian people, probably Turkic speaking, who moved westward in the fourth century and by the fifth century, under the leadership of **Attila**, pushed Germanic groups such as the **Goths** (both Visigoths and Ostrogoths), Franks, and Vandals into the **Roman Empire**. The Huns were aggressive and vicious yet great warriors, and they were nearly unstoppable. They established no state or political structure, and at Attila's death their influence disappeared.

Hus, Jan (John Huss) (c. 1372–1415)
Czech preacher, theologian, and precursor of the **Reformation**. Hus preached against

corruption of the clergy in the **Roman Catholic Church** and questioned the power of the clergy. At the Council of Constance, Hus was condemned and burned for **heresy**. Many Czechs considered Hus a martyr, rebelled from the Church, and established a Hussite church, which incorporated reforms in the Articles of Prague (1420) such as granting of both elements (wine and bread) at communion, punishment of clergy for sins, freedom of preaching, and an end to worldly power by clergy. The Hussites fought and won several battles against armies of the **Holy Roman Empire**. In many ways the Hussite church foreshadowed the Reformation of **Martin Luther** in the sixteenth century.

Husayn (Hussein) (c. 635–680)

Grandson of **Muhammad** and heir to leadership for the **Shia Muslims**. Husayn was the son of **Ali**, the son-in-law of Muhammad. While some Muslims elected **caliphs** and became known as **Sunni** Muslims, others wanted a direct family line and became known as Shias. Husayn and a small band of followers were defeated at Karbala by a vastly superior force sent from Damascus by the **Umayyad caliph** Yazid in 680. That event is commemorated annually by Shias during the first ten days of the month of Muharram and provides a foundation for the Shia ethos of martyrdom.

Huss, John. See Hus, Jan (John Huss)

Hussein, Abdullah ibn. See Abdullah ibn Hussein

Hussein, Saddam (1937–)

Iraqi president (1979–2003), prime minister, and head of Iraq's armed forces. Hussein took part in the 1968 coup that returned the Ba'ath Socialist Party to power. He used his position of power to suppress opposition, including torture and executions and created a towering personality cult. He built up the military and tried to build weapons of mass destruction. After the 1990 invasion of Kuwait and the 1991 **Iraq War** the United States and its coalition thought that Hussein would be toppled, but he survived and rebuilt his military. In 2003 the United States and Britain, deeming Hussein a threat, invaded Iraq and overthrew his government. Weapons of mass destruction were never found. In 2004 Hussein was captured and held for trial.

Hussite Wars. See Hus, Jan (John Huss)

Hyderabad

City in the **Deccan plateau** region of India and capital of Andhra Pradesh state. It was founded in 1591 as a new capital for the Golconda kingdom, incorporated into the **Mughal empire**, and in the eighteenth century became the capital of a kingdom of Muslim rulers who called themselves Nizam. Under the **British Raj** it was the largest of the autonomous princely states. In 1948 the Hyderabad kingdom came under Indian control, and in 1956 in response to popular regional movements it was broken up into three parts along linguistic lines.

Hyksos

Semitic Asians who ruled the **Egyptian civilization** as the fifteenth dynasty (c. 1630–1521 B.C.E.). The Hyksos migrated into Egypt in the eighteenth century B.C.E., introducing the horse and chariot and superior weapons. An old theory was that the Hyksos were the Hebrews, but modern analysis does not support this. Although foreign, the Hyksos became thoroughly Egyptianized. After their dynasty the pharaoh-queen **Hatshepsut** denounced the Hyksos as illegitimate.

Iberian Peninsula
The geographic region of southwestern Europe below the Pyrenees Mountains, modern-day Spain and Portugal. The Greeks called its inhabitants Iberians. The Iberian Peninsula has been divided into many different political units throughout history. It was part of the **Roman Empire**, was conquered by **Islam** in 711 C.E., and was reconquered by Christians during the course of the eighth to fifteenth centuries. It became important during the **Age of Exploration** of the fifteenth and sixteenth centuries.

Ibn Battutah (1304–1368)
Widely traveled Muslim legal scholar. In 1325 Ibn Battutah left his home in Tangier (part of modern-day Morocco) at the age of twenty-one to begin travels that took twenty-nine years and covered approximately 73,000 miles and more than forty countries including **Russia**, India, China, Spain, and large regions of Africa and the **Middle East**. He left a journal known as *Travels of Ibn Battutah*, which is an important source of knowledge of Afro-Eurasia in the fourteenth century. Given his preference for the company of other scholars and for the society of Muslim elites, Ibn Battutah's views of local cultures beyond the walls of the Muslim courts are generally unfavorable. He was the most widely traveled person in the **Middle Ages** that we know of today, far surpassing **Marco Polo**.

Ibn Khaldun (1332–1406)
Tunisian Arab historian, scholar, and diplomat. Ibn Khaldun wrote an autobiography; a history of **Muslim** North Africa; and his masterpiece, the *Muqaddimah* ("Introduction"). In 1400, in a besieged Damascus, he was rescued by **Timur** because of his renown as a historian. Ibn Khaldun created a type of nonreligious history that remained a standard for centuries.

Ichikawa Fusae (1893–1981)
Japanese feminist and politician who led a campaign for women's social equality. In 1924 she founded the Fusen Kakutoku Domie ("Woman's Suffrage League"), succeeding in gaining the rights to organize and to attend political meetings. After **World War II** she joined with the U.S. occupation reformers in proposing the enfranchisement of women within the new Japanese constitution. She was elected five times to the Diet, Japan's parliament.

I Ching (*Yijing*)
Chinese classic of divination usually translated as *Book of Changes* or "Classic of Changes". Probably compiled during the **Warring States period** (475–221 B.C.E.), it was attributed to Wen Wang, father of the founder of the Zhou dynasty. The *I Ching* presents ideas on the nature of the world and on ethics that have had a great influence on **Confucianism** and **Daoism**. It became regarded as one of the five Confucian classics and is still widely read in East Asia today.

Ife

City in southwestern Nigeria. From at least the eleventh century it was the capital of a powerful kingdom of the same name. The Ife craftspeople produced a wonderfully humanistic copper and brass art as early as the thirteenth century. From the sixteenth century onward the culture went into decline, and **Oyo** replaced it as the most important **Yoruba** state.

Iliad

Greek epic poem about Achilles in the Trojan War written by **Homer** in the eighth century B.C.E. The *Iliad* is a poem of 15,693 lines in dactylic hexameter. In it, Achilles is offended by **Agamemnon**, so he withdraws his troops from the Achaean (Greek) force that is besieging Troy and asks the gods to show them how much they need Achilles and how wrong Agamemnon was. The battle goes back and forth, but when the Greek Patroclus is killed and the Greeks are about to lose the battle and their ships, Achilles returns, turns the battle in favor of the Greeks, and kills Hector of Troy. The poem ends with both Patroclus and Hector receiving proper burial.

Imam

Arabic for "before you" or "in front of"; an honorific title indicating leadership within **Islam**. The titles of **Muslim** leaders imam and **caliph** ("successor") are nearly interchangeable, and both words are found in the **Quran**. The word *imam* contains more of the sense of "example." For **Sunni Muslims**, *imam* refers to any Muslim who leads the congregational prayer. For Shias, *imam* has the more specific meaning of the descendant of the Prophet, who is the sole legitimate leader of the Muslim community.

IMF. *See* International Monetary Fund (IMF)

Imhotep

Ancient Egyptian chief advisor, architect, and scholar under King Djoser, later deified by classical Greeks and Romans as the god of medicine. Imhotep was elevated to demigod status when he had been dead only 100 years, suggesting that his medical expertise was more than mere fable. Imhotep is seen as initiating the Old Kingdom (2686–2160) as the architect of the step pyramid in Memphis, the first such structure to be built in Egypt.

Imperial City

Inner city of the Chinese capital **Beijing** containing the imperial court and offices of officialdom during the **Ming** and **Qing** dynasties. It was surrounded by a 6.5 mile (10 km) wall. Within the Imperial City was the Forbidden City, surrounded by another wall and a moat containing the imperial palaces. The huge scale of the Imperial and Forbidden cities symbolized the grandeur and power of the empire.

Imperial Rome. *See* Roman Empire

Imperium

The essence of kingship that remained in the **Roman Republic**. After kingship was abolished and the Roman Republic was established, its two **consuls** functioned somewhat as monarchs except that they were two, they served for only one year, and they were elected. The essence of authority that they held for that year was "imperium," in the sense of their being a special caste of human as Rome's rulers.

Impressionism

Artistic movement of Europe of the late nineteenth century. The term *impressionism* was coined in 1874 in reference to a painting by Claude Monet (1840–1926). In impressionist painting, artists covered their canvas with flat patches of color to create an impression of the true image, rather than trying to compete with the representational accuracy of photography. Along with Monet, some other impressionists are Camille Pissarro (1830–1903), Auguste Renoir (1841–1919), and Edgar Degas (1834–1917).

Inca Civilization (c. 1440–1532)

South American civilization of Peru, Ecuador, and Chile. The Incas controlled mostly mountainous regions and built terraced population centers with temples, palaces, aqueducts, and suspension bridges at sites such as Machu Picchu and the capital of Cuzco. The Inca expanded dramatically under Pachacutec and his son Topu Inca. Pachacutec expanded the Inca civilization by conquest, but also by skillful threats and claims of divine intervention. Both he and his son were great warriors and administrators. They also built more than 20,000 miles (32,000 km) of roads for transmission of messages and the military. The Incas had no writing system as we know it, but their *quipa* (a complex set of colored, knotted strings attached to rods) was an effective method of communicating information. They organized the country into districts and had an army of 200,000 men. When Francisco Pizarro arrived in 1532 with only a few hundred men but steel weapons, gunpowder, and horses, he easily defeated the Incas.

Indian Ocean

Third in size of the world's four oceans. Historically, the Indian Ocean has served as a major sea route for trade among the Indian subcontinent, Southeast Asia, the Middle East, and East Africa. In ancient times mariners learned to take advantages of the seasonal monsoon winds to make long-distance voyages. No other ocean served as a major conduit for commerce before the sixteenth century.

Indians. *See* Amerindians

Indo-Chinese War

Conflict between India and China in 1962 over their disputed 2,640-mile (4,250-km) border in isolated areas of the Himalayas. Disputes over the poorly surveyed border were aggravated by India's grant of asylum to the Dalai Lama and his supporters who were fleeing Tibet following an unsuccessful rebellion there. Chinese forces won a swift victory, occupying parts of the disputed boundary and humiliating India's prime minister, Jawaharlal Nehru. Tense relations between China and India were eased in 2003 when the two nations came to a de facto agreement on their border.

Indo-European

Language group probably originating in the Pontic-Caspian steppe, roughly modern-day Ukraine and adjacent parts of Russia. The Proto-Indo-European-speaking population expanded and fragmented some time around 4000 B.C.E., dividing into Anatolian, Indo-Iranian, and Greek languages by 3000 B.C.E. These languages eventually divided again, into the following language families or individual languages: Italic (Latin and the later Romance languages, including Italian, French, and Spanish); Germanic (including German and English); Armenian; Tocharian; Celtic; Balto-Slavic; and Albanian.

Indo-Pakistan Wars

Three conflicts between India and Pakistan, in 1947–1948, 1965, and 1971. The first conflict, an undeclared war over the disputed territory of Kashmir, broke out shortly after Partition in 1947 and ended with a cease-fire on January 1, 1949. The second also arose from the dispute over Kashmir, by then an Indian state with a Muslim majority that was claimed by Pakistan. Accusing Pakistan of supporting Muslim separatists, India attacked it on September 1, 1965. A cease-fire was arranged three weeks later. In the third conflict, in December 1971, India intervened in a separatist war in East Pakistan and won a clear military victory over Pakistan. The war resulted in the creation of an independent Bangladesh. India and Pakistan came close to conflict in 2001 over Pakistan's continued support of Muslim separatists in Kashmir.

Indra
Chief of the gods in the **Vedic** religion of the **Aryans**. A warrior god associated with lightning bolts, Indra played only a minor role in later **Hinduism**. Indra also appears in the mythology of **Buddhism** and **Jainism**.

Indulgence
In Catholic theology, a decrease in penance or forgiveness of sin granted by a priest for good work done by the sinner. An indulgence would lessen the sinner's time spent in purgatory. The **Roman Catholic Church** sold indulgences in the late **Middle Ages** (1300–1500) on the grounds that the "gift" of money was a good work in its use by the church. In reality, indulgences raised money for the church. This was viewed as a corruption by sixteenth-century reformers because it allowed the rich to escape punishment for sins. **Martin Luther** attacked the sale of indulgences in his **Ninety-five Theses** (1517); it became a major point in the start of the **Reformation**.

Indus. *See* Harappan Civilization; Indus River

Indus River
1,800-mile (2,900-km) river that begins in the Himalayas and flows into the Arabian Sea. The area drained by the Indus and its four major tributaries has been one of the world's major agricultural areas since at least the third millennium B.C.E. and was home to the ancient **Harappan civilization**, also known as the Indus Valley civilization. The Indus River is in the western part of the Indian subcontinent, and influences there from western Eurasia and **Central Asia** have often been marked. The name comes from the Sanskrit *sindhu*, meaning "river." The modern name *India* is derived from it.

Industrialization
The process of change from an agricultural economy to one based on the production of manufactured goods and services. Most scholars consider industrialization to have first taken hold with the **Industrial Revolution** that started in Britain in the eighteenth century and then began in the United States and continental Europe in the first half of the nineteenth century. Industrialization occurred later in eastern Europe, Asia, Latin America, and Africa. Industrialization is often equated with modernization and is accompanied by a shift from a largely rural society to one where much of the population is concentrated in urban centers. It also results in generally higher standards of living and complex changes in social and cultural patterns.

Industrial Revolution
The transformation of first Britain and then other societies from agrarian to industrial-based economies in the eighteenth and nineteenth centuries. A number of breakthroughs in the production of goods and services occurred: the use of coal as fuel; the harnessing of steam power; improvements in transportation such as canals, sealed roads, steamships, and railroads; and improvements in agriculture.

All of these together greatly increased productivity. The Industrial Revolution first occurred in Britain around the middle of the eighteenth century with developments such as the usable steam engine, invented by **James Watt** in 1769, and it spread to other western and central European countries and the United States in the first half of the nineteenth century. A second Industrial Revolution took place after 1870 in which steel, chemical, and a variety other industries replaced textiles as the dominant industry; petroleum replaced coal as the most important energy source; and the electric generator and the internal combustion engine replaced the steam engine as the key mechanical device. Germany and the United States replaced Britain as the leading industrial innovators during the second Industrial Revolution.

Indus Valley. *See* Harappan Civilization; Indus River

Infanticide

The conscious decision to kill children, often used in civilizations to reduce numbers of certain ethnic groups or one gender. In China, the killing of newborn infants was a common method of birth control, as it was in many other societies before the twentieth century. It has also been used as a method of eliminating deformed or ill babies. After the introduction of China's one-child policy in 1978, the preference for male children led to a rise in female infanticide.

Inner Mongolia

A region of grassland in northern China, part of a large plateau that becomes increasingly arid in the north. Inner Mongolia came to be distinguished from Outer Mongolia (now the country of Mongolia) as being a part of the Chinese state. Since

1949 it has been the Inner Mongolia Autonomous Republic, with an area of 454,000 square miles (1,177,500 sq km). The region formerly was ethnically Mongolian, but after 1949 the Chinese government encouraged settlement by ethnic Chinese, who soon became the majority. Traditionally, the area was contested between the Chinese empire and **Central Asian** nomadic peoples.

Innocent III (c. 1160–1216)

Pope (1198–1216) whose term brought the medieval **papacy** to the pinnacle of its power. Innocent III oversaw the Fourth **Crusade**, led a crusade against the **Albigensians**, and legitimized the practice of itinerant preaching by **Saint Francis of Assisi** and Saint Dominic and their followers. He made efforts at expansion in much of Europe and strongly protected Catholic doctrine from **heresy**.

See also Dominicans (Black Friars)

Inoue Kaoru (1835–1915)

One of the seven senior councillors (**genro**) who led **Meiji Japan** from 1868 until his death in 1909. Inoue cooperated with his boyhood friend **Ito Hirobumi** in a quixotic attack on the British legation in 1862, then went abroad with Ito to study in England. He returned to help lead his native Choshu in the **Meiji Restoration**. He served in various ministries and was influential in the new land tax scheme of 1873. Long foreign minister, he also served as minister to Okinawa and Korea and, near the end of his life, as special advisor to the emperor during the **Russo-Japanese War** of 1904–1905.

Inquisition

Special court of examination of **Christian** beliefs in the **Middle Ages**, and a general term for the persecution of variant beliefs in Christian Europe. The term *Inquisition* was used to refer to the "inquiring" into the beliefs of a person to determine if they were orthodox or heretical. Pope Gregory IX in 1233 established a court for the purpose of eradicating the Waldensian and **Albigensian** heresies. Originally, the punishment for **heresy** was excommunication, but later, when heresy was a crime against the state, it was death. The courts of inquisition were usually run by **Dominicans** or **Franciscans**. The **Spanish Inquisition**, which was authorized by Pope Sixtus in 1478 and persecuted **Muslims** and **Jews,** was distinct and separate from the medieval court of inquisition.

Institutes of the Christian Religion

Expansive work by **John Calvin** defining **Reformation** theology in the sixteenth century. The treatise was first published in Latin in 1536, then revised and eventually translated into French by Calvin, with the final content appearing in 1559. Extremely influential to French writing style and thought (it was the first work of its kind published in French as well as in Latin), Calvin's *Institutes* stressed the sovereign and redemptive roles of God and humankind's utter dependence on God's saving grace. The *Institutes* provided **Calvinists** clear guidance on the organization of the church.

International Monetary Fund (IMF)

Economic institution based in Washington DC proposed at **Bretton Woods** in 1944 and established in 1945 as part of the post–**World War II** effort to promote international prosperity and economic stability. Strongly influenced by **John Maynard Keynes**, the purpose of the IMF is to stabilize exchange rates, encourage international monetary cooperation, and eliminate foreign-exchange restrictions. As part of this effort it makes loans to assist countries with balance-of-payments difficulties. In 1986 the IMF established a "structural adjustment facility" to provide assistance to low-income countries. The IMF has been praised for keeping the international economic order stable. However, IMF loan-restructuring requirements have resulted in pressures on the governments of economically troubled countries to make painful cuts in social services that hurt their poorest citizens.

Investiture Controversy

Conflict between the **Roman Catholic Church** and secular authorities over who has the authority to appoint (invest) bishops and abbots. Bishops and abbots carried great power and influence within the church and as secular leaders at the time, so appointments were important. In 1075 Pope Gregory VII was challenged by **Henry IV** of Germany. The issue was tentatively settled by the **Concordat of Worms** in 1122, giving the church authority over its affairs and secular rulers authority over theirs—a modest separation of church and state.

Ionians

Greek civilization of the Ionian region along the west coast of **Asia Minor**. Exposed to attack by Lydia and the **Persian Empire**, Ionians attempted to free themselves from Persian control in the 490s B.C.E., leading to war between Persia and Athens when Athens came to the aid of the Ionians.

See also Croesus; Persian Wars

Ionic Order

Architectural order of design in ancient Greece. The Ionic Order followed the **Doric Order** and preceded the **Corinthian Order**. Ionic is characterized by a capital with a volute, or winding, design and a column standing on a complex base.

Iqbal, Mohammad (1877–1938)

Indian, poet, philosopher, and political leader. In 1930, while serving as president of the **Muslim League**, he proposed the creation of a separate **Muslim** state in the predominantly **Islamic** northwestern region of India. This idea led to the creation of Pakistan.

IRA. *See* Irish Republican Army (IRA)

Iran-Contra Affair (1986)
U.S. political scandal involving the illegal sale of missiles to Iran by the presidential administration of **Ronald Reagan** to secure the release of hostages in Lebanon. The hostages were held by groups friendly to Iran, and the U.S. National Security Council felt that the sale of missiles to Iran might influence their release. Some of the $48 million proceeds from the sale was diverted to the Contras, a U.S.-backed Nicaraguan rebel group fighting to overthrow the Marxist **Sandanista** government of Nicaragua. The U.S. Congress had banned the sale of arms to Iran and to the Contras. Congressional hearings and interrogations of Lieutenant Colonel Oliver North, the intermediary of the arms-for-hostages deal, were inconclusive as to who had originated or authorized the deal.

Iran Hostage Crisis (1979–1981)
Conflict between Iran and the United States. When the shah of Iran was overthrown in the Iranian Islamic Revolution, the United States was accused of supporting the shah and of complicity in his crimes against the Iranian people. Students participating in the revolution stormed the U.S. embassy and took sixty-six hostages on November 4, 1979. The hostages were moved to various locations and held until January 20, 1981, despite all the efforts of the United States and President **Jimmy Carter**. An attempted rescue by the U.S. military ended in complete failure. The release of the hostages was finally negotiated, but only after weakening Carter's status so severely that he lost the presidency to **Ronald Reagan**. The hostages were released early in Reagan's first term.

Iran-Iraq War (1980–1988)
Border conflict turned into a major extended war. Iraqi president **Saddam Hussein** negotiated a deal granting land to Iran in return for a halt in Iranian support for Iraqi Kurds, then backed out of the deal. Iraqi troops attacked a disputed region and then invaded Iranian oilfields. Iran retaliated, and the war gradually expanded to include attacks by air and on shipping in the Persian Gulf. The West, especially the United States, supplied Iraq while Iran's war materials ran low. In 1988 the **United Nations** negotiated a cease-fire between Iran and Iraq, and the countries reached a complete peace agreement in August of that year. No land was gained by either side, but an estimated 1.5 million lives were lost.

Iraq War (1991)
U.N.-led conflict with Iraq in response to Iraq's invasion of Kuwait. Iraq invaded Kuwait in 1990 to gain control of Kuwaiti oilfields and declared Kuwait a province of Iraq. The **United Nations** responded by imposing economic sanctions and gave an ultimatum to Iraq to leave or suffer military retaliation. A coalition of U.N. forces from twenty-nine countries, primarily the United States, invaded Kuwait in 1991. After a fierce air strike using high-technology electronically guided bombs, Operation Desert Storm launched a massive land invasion and pushed Iraqi forces out of Kuwait and well into Iraq. A "no-fly zone" was established in northern Iraq after **Saddam Hussein** ordered the massacre of thousands of Iraqi Kurds, and another no-fly zone was set up over southern Iraq to protect Kuwait.

Iraq War (2003–)
Invasion of Iraq led by the United States and Britain. Weapons inspectors from the **United Nations** had searched Iraq since the 1991 **Iraq War** looking for chemical, biological, and nuclear weapons, finding and destroying just a few. When the inspectors were prohibited from continuing their search, the United States gave Iraq an ultimatum: allow the inspections and provide evidence on the weapons, or be invaded. Iraqi president **Saddam Hussein** balked, and U.S. and British forces invaded quickly, driving all the way to the capital, Baghdad. Hussein escaped capture until 2004, and guerrilla resistance continued even after his capture as the United States attempted to rebuild Iraq's infrastructure. An interim Iraqi government was installed in June 2004.

Irish Potato Famine. *See* Potato Famine

Irish Republican Army (IRA)
Terrorist organization committed to the unification of Ireland. As **nationalism** spread to Ireland in the late nineteenth century, independence movements such as **Sinn Fein** moved from peaceful to militant means to gain their ends. In 1919 Sinn Fein created the Irish Republican Army. When the Irish Free State was established and Northern Ireland, which had been **Protestant** since the seventeenth century, remained part of the United Kingdom, the IRA took it upon itself to unify Ireland by force with killings and bombings. In the 1950s violence increased. In 1969 the IRA split into the Official IRA, which abandoned violence, and the Provisional IRA, which stepped up the terrorism. In the 1990s peace initiatives increased, but did not entirely stop, the violence. According to the 1998 Good Friday Agreement, the IRA was to turn in its arms, but it did not fully comply. In 2001 the IRA agreed to disarmament, however, the process came to a standstill again in 2002. Attempts to persuade the IRA to disarm in 2004 collapsed until July 2005, when the IRA declared that its campaign of violence was over and that it would disarm. In September 2005 the IRA claimed that most of their weapons had been collected and destroyed. The collection was verified, although the destruction was not.

Iron Age
Period of history when iron came into widespread use. The technique of making usable iron tools and weapons may have developed in the Caucasus or Anatolia regions before 1500 B.C.E. This was important because iron deposits were widespread and iron was more durable and cheaper to produce than bronze. By 1200 B.C.E. iron technology had spread throughout southwestern Asia, and eventually into Europe. Over the next millennium iron production became common from China to East Africa.

Iroquois
Amerindians who spoke Iroquoian and formed the Iroquois Confederacy. The Iroquois, living in what would become New York, Pennsylvania, Ontario, and Quebec, included the Cayuga, Cherokee, Huron, Mohawk, Oneida, Onondaga, Seneca, and Tuscarora tribes. They were primarily sedentary agriculturalists living in family units in longhouses. The Iroquois Confederacy (also called the **League of Iroquois** or the Five [later, Six] Nations) was an organization of tribes that worked effectively from the late sixteenth century through the eighteenth century. The Iroquois never numbered more than approximately 12,000 people with a maximum fighting force of only 2,000, yet they were able to thwart the advance of the French and English for more than a century.

Iroquois, League of

Confederation of five (later, six) **Amerindian** tribes in upper New York State. Composed of the Cayuga, Mohawk, Oneida, Onondaga, Seneca, and eventually the Tuscarora tribes, the League of Iroquois played a strategic role in the hostilities between England and France in the eighteenth century, despite the fact that the league was originally founded to foster peace among the Iroquois tribes.

Isabella I of Castile (1451–1504)

Monarch of Castile, wife of **Ferdinand of Aragon**, and patron of **Christopher Columbus**. Isabella married Ferdinand in 1469; became queen of Castile in 1474 (Ferdinand became king of Aragon in 1479, uniting Aragon and Castile); and then added Grenada and Navarre. Isabella encouraged the **Spanish Inquisition** starting in 1484. Her support for Columbus led to his trip westward across the Atlantic in 1492. Isabella and Ferdinand's daughter Catherine married King **Henry VIII** of England, who bore a daughter who would become Queen **Mary I**, "Bloody Mary."

Isaiah (eighth century B.C.E.)

Early Hebrew prophet (actually, the conflation of two prophets of this name) who preached a message of repentance and redemption. Israel was overrun by **Assyria**, and Isaiah prophesized that Judah, the southern kingdom of the Jews, would be saved only if the Jewish people repented their sins and were redeemed by God. This concept of forgiveness became an essential feature of the Jewish religion.

Isfahan Mosque

Royal mosque of Isfahan, Iran. It was the crowning architectural achievement of **Safavid** ruler Shah Abbas I (r. 1586–1628 C.E.). The mosque was constructed during the first third of the seventeenth century as part of a large complex of buildings organized as a rectangle. The mosque sits at the southern, short side of the grounds and looks north across a 1,640 × 492 foot (500 × 150 m) courtyard. The magnificent structure is built of approximately 18 million bricks and 500,000 decorative tiles that overwhelm and awe visitors. The royal mosque set the stylistic standard for future mosques in Isfahan and Iran.

Isis

Ancient Egyptian goddess of the dead, curer of the ill, and wife of **Osiris**. Osiris was god of the underworld and of the dead and resurrected king. Isis and Osiris produced Horus, the god of the living king. Isis was also viewed as the mother goddess, hence she was the goddess of protection. By Greco-Roman times Isis was the most important Egyptian goddess.

Islam (Arabic for "submission")

Religion founded in the seventh century in Arabia whose followers are known as **Muslims** ("submitters"). Muslim beliefs and practices are derived from the **Quran** (revealed to Muhammad through the angel Gabriel), from Islamic jurisprudence, and from the customs of Arab and other cultures. Islam is a monotheistic religion in the tradition of **Judaism** and **Christianity** and accepts **Abraham**, Moses, and **Jesus** as great prophets. The central concept of Islam is leading a life in accord with God's will. That includes the Five Pillars of the Islamic faith: (1) Allah is the one and only god and Muhammad is his Prophet; (2) all must pray five times daily, facing Mecca; (3) all must fast from sunrise to sunset during the holy month of **Ramadan**; (4) all must contribute alms for the weak and poor; and (5) those who are able must undertake at least one pilgrimage to Mecca.

Islamic Fundamentalism

Movement begun with the **Muslim Brotherhood** in the early twentieth century. The 1979 Iranian revolution in many ways brought the phenomenon to the attention of the global community. Islamic fundamentalism combines an appreciation for precedent, whether collective or personal, with practical mechanisms for dealing with contemporary economic, social, and political circumstances. It combines visions of the past and the future. Expressions of it punctuate Islamic history and often affect interactions with other world religions, particularly **Hinduism**, **Judaism**, and **Christianity**.

Islamic Salvation Front (Front Islamique du Salut; FIS)

Algerian Islamist movement that emerged in the 1980s. In 1992 the FIS was prevented from winning legislative elections in Algeria because the government canceled the second round of elections. Algeria moved from civilian rule to military control, the president was removed, and FIS forbidden. In 1997 Algeria introduced a new constitution that banned religious political parties. The front stepped up its use of violence, but in 2000 a negotiated settlement in a government amnesty program led to the surrender of the front's army along with the armies of other militant groups.

Ismail, Shah (r. 1487–1524)

Founder of the **Safavid dynasty** that ruled Iran from 1501 to 1722. The Safavids started as a **Sufi** religious order active in northwestern Iran and eastern Anatolia during the thirteenth and fourteenth centuries. In the fifteenth century the movement assumed messianic overtones and a more militant character. The Safavids declared **Shia** allegiances, and Shah Ismail (1487–1524) proclaimed himself to be the hidden **imam**, or Mahdi, and the reincarnation of **Ali**. He combined the characteristics of messiah and statesman, or spiritual and temporal power, and called for absolute, unqualified obedience from both the Sufi religious orders and the prominent Qizilbash tribal military forces. In 1501 Ismail occupied Tabriz and proclaimed himself shah, or king. Within a generation he had established control over nearly all of Iran. The Safavid dynasty is best known for converting the vast majority of the inhabitants of Iran to Shia Islam.

Israel

A Middle Eastern republic located at the eastern end of the Mediterranean Sea in what used to be called Palestine. The State of Israel was created by the **United Nations** on May 14, 1948, with **David Ben-Gurion** as its first prime minister. It was created as a homeland for the Jewish people in the region that the **Bible** claimed God had promised to the people of Israel. The majority of Israel's population was originally composed of immigrants and survivors of the **Holocaust** and **anti-Semitism**. Since its creation in 1948 Israel has been a site of virtually constant conflict. Hostile relations with the surrounding Arab world triggered a series of wars in the second half of the twentieth century. The **Arab-Israeli Wars**, the Six-Day War, and the **Iraq War** of 1991 are only a few of the violent conflicts Israel has participated in since its founding.

Issus, Battle of

Battle in which **Alexander the Great** defeated Darius III of Persia in 333 B.C.E. Alexander's army broke through the Persian army on the right and threatened the center, whereupon the Persians fled.

Istanbul

Great port city of Turkey and capital of the **Ottoman Empire**. Originally named Byzantium, the city was renamed **Constantinople** by Emperor Constantine in 330 C.E. as he made it the second capital of the **Roman Empire**. Constantinople was the capital of the **Byzantine Empire** throughout the **Middle Ages**. In 1453 the **Ottoman Turks** under **Mehmet II** conquered Constantinople, enlarged it, and renamed it Istanbul. It remained the capital of Turkey until 1923.

Isthmus of Panama. *See* Panama, Isthmus of; Panama Canal

Itagaki Taisuke (1837–1919)
Japanese loyalist from Tosa and councillor of state in 1869. He helped launch a campaign for elective prefectural assemblies. Itagaki founded the Risshisha (Society of Independence) in 1877 and set up the Jiyuto (Liberal) party, a forerunner of the Seiyukai party, in 1881. He was home minister under **Ito Hirobumi**, and in 1898 he and **Okuma Shigenobu** merged parties to form the Kenseito (Constitutional party).

Italian City-States
Eleventh-century independent cities in Italy that rose to become powerful political forces in the late **Middle Ages** and **Renaissance**. Under the leadership of a new middle class who made their wealth via banking and trade, unlike the feudal system, which existed during the Middle Ages, in which power and wealth were based on landownership, power in the **city-states** was tied to the control of trade and banking. There was often warfare among the cities as they tried to expand their power geographically. City-states such as **Florence**, Pisa, **Venice**, and Siena became very competitive with one another as they vied for wealth. They became centers of cultural achievement and were a major component of the development of the Renaissance in Italy.

Italian Renaissance
(fourteenth to sixteenth centuries)
Historical period of renewed interest in ancient Greece and **Rome**. The Italian Renaissance (*Renaissance* is French for "rebirth") began in the fourteenth century in the urban centers of northern Italy, where the merchant class dominated trade around the Mediterranean Sea. Demands for educated children of the merchant class led to the study of classical Latin and Greek literature and a renewed interest in the classical age. The revival of interest in classical culture exploded in a watershed of artistic and intellectual productivity that displayed stylistic qualities very different from those of the **Middle Ages**. There was a new appreciation of earthly pleasures and the abilities of the individual to do great things, known as **humanism**. Italian Renaissance artists and writers became famous for their creative genius. They include **Sandro Botticelli, Filippo Brunelleschi, Donatello, Leonardo da Vinci, Niccolò Machiavelli, Michelangelo,** and **Raphael**. The Italian Renaissance spread to the rest of Europe by the sixteenth century.

Ito Hirobumi (1841–1909)
First prime minister and the major architect of the modern Japanese state. A young **bushi** of the Chosho clan in western Japan, he became one of the key Japanese figures after the **Meiji Restoration** (1868). Having traveled abroad, he promoted Westernization and played an important role in creating Japan's modern monetary and banking system. Later, he was the principal author of the 1889 constitution that created a parliamentary system of government with powers reserved for the emperor and his advisors. Serving four times as prime minister, he created the Seiyukai (Friends of Constitutional Government) political party in 1901 after accepting the need for

active political parties. From 1905 to 1909 he served as the first resident-general of Korea, which had become a Japanese protectorate in the **Russo-Japanese War**. Although a moderating influence among Japanese imperialists, he was assassinated by a Korean nationalist shortly after resigning his post. Ito came to be regarded as one of Japan's greatest modern leaders despite the controversy over his support of imperialist policies.

Ito Noe (1895–1923)

Japanese anarchist, social critic, author, and feminist. After graduating from Ueno Girl's High School she joined the Seitosha (Bluestocking Society) in 1912; wrote social criticism in the society's literary organ, *Seito*; and translated the writings of Emma Goldman. She lived and worked with anarchist Osugi Sakae, with whom she was arrested during the chaos of the Great Kanto earthquake of 1923. She and her nephew were abducted and killed by an army lieutenant in the Amakasu Incident.

Itzamná

Most important **Maya** deity. Itzamná ("lizard house" or "iguana house") was the ruler of heaven, day, and night and encompassed or encased the earth. This god, according to the Maya, also gave humans writing, the calendar, and medicine.

Ivan III, "the Great" (1440–1505)

Grand prince of Moscow (1462–1505) and founder of the modern Russian state. Ivan consolidated **Russia**, expanded its boundaries, expelled the **Mongols** and the Hanseatic merchants, drove the Lithuanians west, and moved the church administration from **Kiev** (the former capital of Russia) to Moscow. Ivan married the niece of the last **Byzantine** emperor and claimed to be the successor of the Roman Caesars when **Constantinople** fell in 1453.

Ivan IV, "the Terrible" (1533–1584)

First tsar of Russia (1547–1584). He was unpredictable, autocratic, and "awe-inspiring" (the literal translation of his nickname). Ivan expanded Russian territory and ruthlessly pushed through laws and reforms to extend his power. He murdered his own son and heir, Ivan, and although he was succeeded by another son, Fyodor, the power vacuum created by Ivan IV's death was filled by a favorite—and nearly as ruthless a magnate—Boris Godunov. His reign saw large steps taken to centralize the Russian political administration system and to strengthen the monarchy.

Iwakura Tomomi (1825–1883)

Japanese court noble who supported the **Meiji Restoration** and became a minister of state (1871–1883). In 1871 he headed a mission to Europe and the United States that failed to secure abolition of the Unequal Treaties (a series of treaties imposed on China and Japan by the United States and Britain—the United States continued to maintain extraterritorial rights in Japan until 1911), but brought back much useful information on foreign institutions and technology. He returned to Japan in 1873 to forestall the threat of war with Korea. From 1873 until his death, Iwakura, a conservative, was a leader of Japan's moderate political forces.

Jacquerie (1358)

French peasant revolt. Named *jacquerie* for the nobility's habit of calling all peasants Jacque, the revolt resulted from the devastation of the countryside by English troops during the **Hundred Years War**, the **Black Death**, and French demands for taxation to pay for the war. The peasants destroyed castles and killed nobility, but within a month the revolt had been crushed and the participants massacred.

Jainism

Indian religion founded in the sixth century B.C.E. by Vardhamana **Mahavira**, a senior contemporary of **Siddhartha Gautama**, the Buddha. Jainism teaches its followers to achieve spiritual liberation through following a strict moral code based on asceticism and *ahimsa*—the principle of avoiding injury to living things. Jains were divided into two main sects: the Svetambara ("white-clad"), named for the white cloth of their monks, and Digambara ("sky-clad"), after the monks' practice of sometimes going naked. The austere lifestyle and restrictive diet limited the religion's mass appeal so that Jains were never more than a small minority in India, but they had great influence on Indian culture. In modern times many have been wealthy merchants and financiers.

James I and VI (1566–1625)

King of England and Scotland, the first of the Stuart line of monarchs in England. James VI, king of Scotland since 1567, succeeded **Elizabeth I** as James I, monarch of England, in 1603. As king of England he angered the **Puritans** by insisting, "No bishop, no king," and he alienated **Parliament** by tactless negotiations, insisting on the power of the monarchy.

James II (1633–1701)

King of England from 1685 to 1688; deposed in favor of William III and Mary II in the **Glorious Revolution**. As the duke of York and brother of **Charles II**, James was known as an effective leader, but as king he tried unsuccessfully to rule as an absolute monarch, ignoring **Parliament**. This caused members of Parliament to invite **William of Orange** and his wife Mary to replace James. James tried to regain his throne by leading forces in Ireland against William but eventually fled to France, where he remained until his death.

Janissaries (1360s–1826) (Turkish for "new force")

Elite military corps introduced by Murad I, sultan of the **Ottoman Turks**. Members were conscripted from the non-**Muslim**, mostly **Christian** population, converted to **Islam**, and trained as infantry. The Janissaries were noted for their loyalty to the sultan and to their individual unit, making them especially disciplined and effective fighters. Advances in **gunpowder** in the fourteenth century made the Janissaries even more effective as bodyguards of the sultan. In 1826 the corps revolted against the sultan and was disbanded.

Japan, Occupation of

The U.S. occupation of Japan at the end of **World War II**. Following the surrender of Japan on September 1, 1945, the country came under Allied, principally U.S., military control until 1952. General **Douglas MacArthur** served as head of the occupation as supreme commander of the Allied Powers (SCAP). Although technically backed by the eleven-nation Far Eastern Commission and the Four-Power Council (Britain, the United States, China, and the Soviet Union), the occupation was completely dominated by the U.S. military. It governed Japan indirectly, maintaining a parliament and a Japanese cabinet that directed the bureaucracy. A number of purges were conducted in the early years and a few Japanese officials were tried in the Tokyo War Crimes Tribunal; nine were executed. Land reform was carried out; the emperor was forced to renounce his divinity; images and writings glorifying war and ultranationalist messages were removed from films, textbooks, and popular literature; the *zaibatsu* were broken up; and in 1947 the occupation authorities drew up a "Peace Constitution" for Japan that made the country more democratic and prohibited it from maintaining military forces. At first, communists and other leftist dissidents were free to organize labor and promote their views, but, alarmed at their increasing influence, the U.S. forces carried out a "Red Purge" in 1949–1950 and reinstated many conservatives in the government. The occupation had mixed results but overall was regarded by both Americans and Japanese as laying the successful foundation for a postwar democratic Japan.

Japan Inc.

Term for the strong links among business, the central bureaucracy, and the dominant Liberal Democratic Party in Japan from the 1950s through the 1990s. The Japanese government under the Liberal Democratic Party, formed in 1955 from the merger of the two conservative Liberal and Democratic Parties, pursued policies of actively promoting economic growth through government aid and cooperation with the large business conglomerates (*keiretsu*). The emphasis was on expanding the export market share while foreign policy and other areas were given less attention. The policies contributed to Japan's rise as an economic superpower, although its aggressive export policy caused trade friction with the United States, Europe, and other countries.

Jati

Caste group in India. There are four major castes, or **varnas**: **Brahmins**, **Kshatriyas**, **Vaishyas**, and **Shudras**, broad universal groupings. Within each varna are subcastes or "jati." Vaishyas, for instance, would include farmers, merchants, traders, and craftsmen. Within this varna would be jatis of bakers or metalworkers. Each jati is characterized by endogamy (marriage within the group) and by social interaction only within the jati. The origins of jatis are not clear, but they appear to have been in existence since at least the first millennium of the common era. Some anthropologists believe the jatis came with the invasion of **Aryans** into the Indian subcontinent.

Jayavarman

The name of two great Cambodian rulers. Jayavarman II (d. 850) was the founder of the Khmer (Cambodian) empire. Jayavarman VII (r. 1181–c. 1215), ruling from **Angkor**, expanded the empire to its greatest extent, covering much of what is now Thailand and southern Vietnam as well as Cambodia. He added many buildings to the Angkor area, including the Angkor Thom temple.

Jefferson, Thomas (1743–1826)
Third president of the United States, first Secretary of State under **George Washington**, vice president under **John Adams**, and main author of the **Declaration of Independence** (1776). Jefferson was a delegate to the **Continental Congress** (1775–1776), and after his two terms as president became the leader of the Democratic-Republican Party. He contributed much to the political philosophy of his day and made the **Louisiana Purchase** (1803), which more than doubled the territory of the United States. Jefferson also initiated the **Lewis and Clark expedition** to explore that new purchase.

Jericho
Town in the Palestinian West Bank near the Dead Sea and one of the oldest settlements in the world, dating from around 9000 B.C.E. **Neolithic** Jericho provides evidence of the development of civilization with both town life and agriculture between 9000 and 3000 B.C.E. Excavations show that the town was abandoned and resettled several times. In the book of Joshua, the **Bible** tells of the Israelites conquering Jericho, the first city they overcame after their crossing into Canaan. It is also mentioned several other times in the **Old** and **New Testaments**.

Jerusalem
Ancient city in **Palestine**, made the capital of **Israel** by King David circa 1000 B.C.E.; now capital of the modern state of Israel (though contested by the Palestinians). The Semitic name *Jerusalem* means "city of peace." Throughout history countless armies have besieged, plundered, and destroyed parts or all of Jerusalem, including the armies of **Babylon** in 586 B.C.E. and **Rome** in 70 and 130 C.E. The present walls were built in 1540. The city became a center for Christian pilgrims during the fourth century C.E. and has remained one ever since because of its intimate connection with the last days of **Jesus**'s earthly career. After the capture of Jerusalem in 637 C.E., Jerusalem became a holy site for **Muslims**. An effort by Europeans to recapture the city to make it safe again for Christian **pilgrims** began the era of the **Crusades**. The city was divided until 1967, when Israel occupied all of it, leaving only the area of the **Dome of the Rock** under **Muslim** control.

Jesuits. *See* Society of Jesus (Jesuits)

Jesus Christ. *See* Jesus of Nazareth

Jesus of Nazareth (c. 4 B.C.E.–30 C.E.)
Central figure of **Christianity**. The name *Jesus Christ* is a combination of the name *Jesus of Nazareth* and the term *christ*, Greek for "anointed." Non-Christian and Christian sources tell of a man with disciples who performed healings and who was condemned to death by **Pontius Pilate**. Christian sources add much more: that Jesus was born in Bethlehem; that his ministry began with Jesus's baptism and was directed toward the tribes of Israel; and that he admitted to being the Christ, predicted his own death, and established his disciples under a new covenant or contract with God. He proclaimed the imminent coming of the Kingdom of God and the need for people who were to participate in it to cleanse themselves spiritually and live lives of ethical purity as laid out in his **Sermon on the Mount**. According to Christian sources Jesus was found guilty of political charges, crucified, and buried,

and on the third day he rose from the tomb and appeared to his followers. His followers hold Jesus Christ to be the Son of God, one with God, and the Holy Spirit—together known as the Trinity.

Jewish Diaspora
Dispersion of the Jews from **Palestine** after the **Babylonian Captivity** of 586 B.C.E. When Babylon conquered the Kingdom of **Judah**, the Jewish population was deported into slavery throughout the **Middle East**. Although allowed to return in 538 B.C.E., Jews had become a significant part of the population in many cities and countries. They had spread throughout the Middle East, Europe, and even to India and China. More Jews lived outside Palestine than within it. That has continued to be true to the present day, when, only about 4 million of the estimated 14 million Jews in the world reside in Israel. Some Jews argue that the diaspora must be overcome and Jews regathered in Israel, while others argue that the Jewish religion can be maintained anywhere.

Jews, Expulsion from Spain of the (1492)
Order for the Jews of Spain to leave or convert. In 1462 the Cortes (parliament) of Spain restricted the interaction of Jews with Christians, but as late as 1490 Jews were promised protection of their rights if they would help to overthrow the **Muslims** of Granada. Both **Ferdinand of Aragon** and **Isabella I of Castile** restricted the rights of Jews in their respective countries. Several months after the expulsion of the Muslims from Granada in March 1492, an edict expelling Jews was issued. Jews were given until July to leave Spain and were allowed to take property except gold, silver, or money. It is estimated that 200,000 of them left Spain, many for Portugal and others for Holland, Genoa, and Morocco.

It was not legal for Jews to set foot on Spanish soil until the edict was repealed in 1858.

Jiang Jieshi. *See* Chiang Kai-shek

Jiang Qing (1914–1991)
Third wife of **Mao Zedong** who became a formidable political influence in China during the rule of her husband, especially during the **Great Proletarian Cultural Revolution**. She became associated with the radical wing of the **Chinese Communist Party** and sponsored revolutionary-inspired operas and other cultural performances. After Mao's death in 1976 she was placed under arrest and tried as one of the so-called **Gang of Four** accused of involvement in the arrest and torture of thousands of political opponents. She hanged herself in prison.

Jiang Zemin (1926–)
Chinese communist leader who became general secretary of the **Chinese Communist Party** in 1992 and president of the People's Republic of China from 1993, stepping down from those posts in 2003. He was considered an economic reformer but was a political conservative who carried on the policies of **Deng Xiaoping**, promoting economic growth and foreign trade and investment while cracking down on political dissent.

Jihad
Arabic word meaning "struggle" or "striving," found in the **Quran**. It is used throughout the **Muslim** world in three forms. First, to individual Muslims *jihad* means the constant struggle to adhere to the "straight path" of **Islam**. Second, every Muslim community must strive to adhere purely to the tenets of Islam. Finally, Muslims everywhere are obliged to defend Islam against the aggressions of enemies of the faith.

Jinnah, Muhammad Ali (1876–1948)
Indian political leader and founder of Pakistan. He worked toward ensuring that **Muslims** would have adequate representation in an independent India, but, becoming disillusioned with the **Indian National Congress**, he assumed leadership of the **Muslim League** in 1913. In 1940 he led his party into supporting an independent Pakistan state for Muslims. After working in the negotiations for the partition of India, he served as Pakistan's first governor-general (1947–1948) and as resident of its constituent assembly.

Jizya (Jizyah)
Tribute tax paid by non-Muslims instituted by the Arabs during the time of the **Umayyad** and **Abbasid caliphates**. Although intended and serving as an important source of revenue for the caliphates, it also served as an incentive for many to convert to **Islam** to avoid its burden. Many **Muslim** governments after the Abbasid caliphate fell continued to levy this tax.

Joan of Arc (c. 1412–1431)
French mystic and heroine who inspired the French army during the **Hundred Years War**. Joan of Arc, known as the Maid of Orleans, as a young girl heard the voices of Saint Catherine and Saint Margaret, who told her that Charles should be crowned king and lead the army to victory. Joan never led the armies herself, but she rode with them in men's clothing and armor. She was captured by the Burgundians, turned over to the English, tried, convicted of heresy, and burned at the stake. Joan of Arc was canonized (made a saint) in 1920.

John of Salisbury (c. 1120–1180)
Medieval scholar, secretary of **Thomas Becket**, and bishop of Chartres. John studied under **Peter Abelard**; was employed at the archbishopric of Canterbury; was sent on missions to Rome, where he wrote about the papal court; and was in the cathedral at Canterbury when Becket was assassinated. He became bishop of Chartres in 1176.

John I (1166–1216)
King of England (1199–1216). John gained the throne under dispute, with some barons preferring his nephew Arthur. John antagonized the **Roman Catholic Church** by refusing to acknowledge Stephen Langton as archbishop of Canterbury. This action, along with John's failure to defeat the French in battle and his attempts to force financial penalties upon the aristocracy, finally provoked the barons into revolt. Civil war broke out, and John was forced to sign the document known as the **Magna Carta** ("Great Charter") in 1215. John has gone down in history as one of the most unpopular kings.

John Paul II (born Karol Wojtyla) (1920–2005)
Roman Catholic bishop of Rome (**pope**) 1978–2005. John Paul, of Poland, was the first non-Italian pope in 455 years. He campaigned against political oppression worldwide, first against communism in his native Poland and later by traveling more widely and speaking out more than any previous pope. John Paul also attempted to build bridges with other branches of Christianity and with other world religions, notably **Judaism** and **Islam**. He was conservative in his theology and resisted reforms beyond Vatican II (1962–1965), especially on the issues of ordination of women, marriage of the clergy, birth control, and homosexuality, and yet he was vocal in his insistence on individual human rights.

Johnson, Lyndon Baines (1909–1973)
Thirty-sixth president of the United States
(1963–1969). A teacher, congressional
aide, and Texas head of the National Youth
Administration, Johnson was elected to
the U.S. House of Representatives in 1937.
He won a **U.S. Senate** seat from Texas
in 1948, having lost a previous election, in
1941. Becoming Senate majority leader in
1955, Johnson was among the most powerful members of the Senate before losing
a bid for the 1960 presidential nomination
to **John F. Kennedy**, then accepting the
vice-presidential nomination. Becoming
president on Kennedy's assassination on
November 22, 1963, Johnson received
praise for the manner in which he guided
the nation through the tragedy and was
overwhelmingly elected in 1964. As president Johnson championed civil rights,
gaining passage of the **Civil Rights Act of
1964** and the Voting Rights Act of 1965.
His Great Society program of social reform
sought to "complete" the liberal reform
agenda of the New Deal/Fair Deal. While
Johnson achieved many successes, such as
Medicare and Medicaid, a number of his
programs were inadequately planned and
funded. The Great Society, and Johnson's
administration as a whole, suffered from
his growing commitment to the **Vietnam
War**. Johnson expanded U.S. involvement
with the Tonkin Gulf Resolution (1964) and
the introduction of combat troops and
bombing campaigns against North Vietnam (1965). Yet American troop increases
were matched by North Vietnam and the
Viet Cong, and Johnson was determined
to "limit" the war to avoid direct involvement by China or the Soviet Union. By
1968 the war was stalemated despite the
presence of U.S. personnel in South
Vietnam numbering more than 500,000,
and public opposition to the war was
mounting, especially after the Tet offensive that January. Facing a challenge to his
renomination by antiwar candidates
Eugene McCarthy and **Robert F. Kennedy**, Johnson withdrew from the race on
March 31, 1968, and he retired at the end
of his term.

Jomon
Japanese Neolithic culture that emerged
as early as 8500 B.C.E. and dominated the
Japanese archipelago until it was replaced
by the **Yayoi** culture in the late first millennium B.C.E. The name *Jomon*, meaning
"cord pattern," is derived from the characteristic pottery of the period. Taking advantage of the rich abundance of seafood and
edible plants, the Jomon, although a non-
agricultural people, developed an elaborate
culture with a rich pottery tradition.

Joseph II (1741–1790)
Austrian Holy Roman Emperor (1765–
1790). Joseph first co-ruled with his
mother, **Maria Theresa** (1765–1780), before ruling solely. He was known as an
"enlightened despot" because he autocrat-
ically attempted to bring to the **Habsburg**
territories administrative, legal, and economic reforms. He granted toleration to
Jews and **Protestants** in 1781 and abolished serfdom. He was truly concerned for
the general welfare of his people.

Juárez, Benito (1806–1872)
Mexican national hero and Mexico's only
indigenous president. Juárez led a revolution in 1855 to overthrow General
Antonio López de Santa Anna, who had
seized control of the government in 1853.
As minister of justice in the new government, Juárez implemented reforms that
were eventually included in the 1857
Mexican constitution. He is known for de-
creasing the power of the **Roman Catholic
Church** and rich landlords in order to help
Mexico became a constitutional democracy. His presidency was interrupted by

the installation (by French forces) of the Austrian archduke Maximilian in 1864 as emperor of Mexico, but he had the archduke executed in 1867 and returned to office. He achieved reelection in 1867 and 1871, although the 1871 election was contested.

Judaea (Judea)

The name, successively, of a province of the **Persian**, Ptolemaic, and **Seleucid** empires; a Jewish kingdom; and a **Roman** province. Judaea occupied the same land as its predecessor, the Kingdom of **Judah**. Because most of those whom the Persian king **Cyrus the Great** allowed to return from the **Babylonian Captivity** were from the tribe of Judah, the land was named after them and the people called Jews. **Jerusalem** was always its religious, if not political, capital. Conquered by the Roman general **Pompey the Great** in 63 B.C.E., Judaea was ruled thereafter either by Roman officials or by puppet kings like Herod the Great. Two revolts, in 70 and 130 C.E., brought devastating Roman repression and ended the independent existence of Judaea.

Judah

Southernmost of the three divisions of ancient **Palestine**. During the ninth century B.C.E. the twelve Hebrew tribes in Palestine split to follow different leaders, precipitated by the death of King **Solomon**, who had consolidated royal power and strengthened central government. Two of the tribes settled in southern Palestine with their capital at **Jerusalem**, as the Kingdom of Judah. The other divisions were Galilee, in the north, and Samaria, in the center. Judah became a tributary state of **Assyria**. With the rise of **Babylon** under the Chaldeans, Judah was conquered in 587 B.C.E. and the Hebrews were deported to Babylon (in the **Babylonian Captivity**). Under

the Persians of **Cyrus the Great**, the Hebrews were allowed to return in 515 B.C.E. and rebuild Jerusalem. Judah later came under the authority of **Alexander the Great**, then the Ptolemies, and then the **Seleucids**. Opposition to the Seleucids led to the rise of the Jewish Maccabees, who reestablished Judah as **Judaea**. In 63 B.C.E. the Romans conquered the region, and they installed Herod the Great as king of Judaea in 37 B.C.E. A Jewish revolt in 66 C.E. led to the Roman destruction of Jerusalem in 70 C.E.

Judaism

The religion of the Jews, as distinct from that of the Hebrew **Bible**, from which it derives and to which it adds. Though some elements of Judaism appear during the Babylonian exile (597–532 B.C.E.), its main features flower after the destruction of **Jerusalem** and the **Hebrew Temple** by the **Romans** in 70 C.E. With no access to their temple, Jews in **Babylonia** began to center their religion around the **Torah** (Pentateuch), which they saw as mostly instruction for all aspects of living. The synagogue replaced the Temple as the primary place of worship, and teaching by rabbis replaced sacrifice as the central act of worship. Explanations of the Torah and other parts of the Hebrew Bible were compiled into the Targum and various commentaries. Judaism stresses the uniqueness of God; the special status of the Jews; and the necessity of obedience to God's revealed will, especially keeping the Sabbath. In medieval Europe Judaism split into two major branches, **Ashkenazic** and **Sephardic**. Mysticism also developed. Later developments include changes arising as a result of the eighteenth-century **Enlightenment**; nineteenth-century reform movements; and, in response to **anti-Semitism**, Zionism. Modern Judaism is made up of four major groups of Jews: Orthodox,

Reformed, Conservative, and Liberal. Judaism is found worldwide, with its greatest concentrations in Israel and the United States.

Julian Calendar
Calendar year devised in 46 B.C.E. by order of **Julius Caesar**. The Roman calendar diverged from the solar year by three months. The Julian calendar divided the year into twelve months of thirty or thirty-one days each, except for February, with twenty-nine days (every four years February had thirty). The Julian calendar went into effect January 1, 45 B.C.E. The Julian calendar of $365^{1}/_{4}$ days was eleven minutes and fourteen seconds off from the solar calendar annually, which meant that by the sixteenth century the Julian calendar was off by ten days. Pope Gregory had the calendar corrected in 1582 as the Gregorian calendar.

Julio-Claudian Dynasty (14–68 C.E.)
Dynasty of Roman emperors, referring to the first four successors of **Octavian: Tiberius**, Caligula, Claudius I, and **Nero**. Although not of a direct bloodline, the emperors were all closely related, if only by adoption.

Julius Caesar. *See* Caesar, Julius

Julius II (1443–1513)
Catholic **pope** who restored the power of the **papacy** and began the construction of the present Church of Saint Peter's in Rome (1506). Julius removed foreign interference in the papacy. He engaged Donato Bramante, **Raphael**, and **Michelangelo** to work on Saint Peter's.

Junks
Chinese sailing vessels with up to five masts. Junks, which were used from at least **Tang** times, had many features—such as compartmentalized bulkhead construction and many square sails of linen-and-bamboo strips—that made them sturdy and maneuverable. Some were large and capable of long sea voyages carrying merchant cargos from Chinese ports to Southeast Asia. Their potential for long-distance voyages was demonstrated in the early fifteenth century by Chinese admirable **Zheng He**, who navigated as far as East Africa. Before **Christopher Columbus**'s time, Zheng He had built 400-foot-long junks (Columbus's *Santa María* was 60 feet long). Many of the technical features of junks spread across Eurasia and eventually influenced the development of the ocean-going vessels in Europe that made the European **Age of Discovery** possible.

Jurchen (in Chinese, Ruzhen)
Tungusic peoples of northeast Asia who established the Jin state (1115–1234) who ruled most of northern China. Originally hunters and farmers, the Jurchens adapted elements of Chinese culture but remained ethnically distinct. They continued to be a threat to their Chinese and Korean neighbors after their state was conquered by the **Mongol empire**. In the sixteenth century a group of Jurchen tribes were unified to create the **Manchu** nation that conquered and ruled all of China as the **Qing** dynasty (1644–1911).

Justinian (Justinian the Great) (483–565)
Most famous of all emperors of the Eastern Roman Empire, or **Byzantine Empire**. Justinian ruled from 527 to 565, when the **Roman Empire** was in decline, especially in the west, and determined to rebuild it. With his general, Belisarius, Justinian defeated the **Vandals** in North Africa and the Ostrogoths in Italy and restored the empire there by 552. Most of Justinian's conquests were short-lived additions to

the empire. His most important contribution was the codification of Roman laws in the **Corpus Juris Civilis** (Body of Civil Law), which remained the basis of law in the Byzantine Empire until its collapse in 1453 and is the basis of the legal systems of continental Europe even today.

Justinian Law. *See* Corpus Juris Civilis; Justinian (Justinian the Great)

K

Ka'aba (Kabah)
Holy shrine of **Islam** in **Mecca**, Saudi Arabia. The Ka'aba was the focus of pre-Islamic pagan religion in Arabia with a massive black cube filled with idols and a black meteorite embedded in the exterior wall. According to **Muslim** tradition, **Abraham** built the original Ka'aba as a monument to the One God, but idolators later took it over. **Muhammad** cleansed the Ka'aba of its pagan idols in 630 and made it the center of the Islamic faith. One of the Five Pillars of Islam is for Muslims to go on a pilgrimage to Mecca at least once in their lifetime. There they circle the Ka'aba seven times, kiss the black stone, drink from the well of Zam Zam, and perform other sacred rites.

Kabir (1440–1518)
Indian poet and mystic who drew upon **Hinduism** and **Islam** to teach a new spiritual path. His disciples established **Sikhism**, whose followers are called Sikhs.

Kaempfer, Engelbert (1651–1716)
German traveler and naturalist. Kaempfer sailed to Batavia in Indonesia and to Japan, where he stayed from 1690 to 1692. Upon his return to Germany he wrote a history of Japan and about the geology, botany, and zoology of Japan at a time when other Europeans were not allowed in the country.

Kaifeng
Chinese city in Henan province. In the fourth century B.C.E. the city, then known

as Daliang, was the capital of the state of Wei. With the opening of the **Grand Canal** under the **Sui** it became a great commercial center known as Kaifeng. It was the imperial capital of the northern **Song** dynasty (960–1127) and became one of the largest cities in the world. It declined after its capture by the **Jurchens** in 1127 but continued to be a regional center.

Kailasantha
Hindu temple at Ellora in the **Deccan plateau** of India, created for the Rashtrakuta ruler Krishna I in the eighth century. Excavated downward out of living rock (solid rock in its place of origin) to a depth of 100 feet (30.5 m), it is regarded as one of the masterpieces of Hindu art.

Kalidasa (fl. late fourth century)
Indian poet and dramatist regarded by many as India's greatest literary figure. Seven of his **Sanskrit** works have survived (some scholars recognize only six as definitely attributable to him) and are regarded as classics. Little is known about Kalidasa. Although even his caste and regional origin are uncertain, he is associated with the courts of **Chandragupta II** (c. 375–415) and Kumara Gupta I (415–454). His best-known work is *Cloud Messenger* (*Meghaduta*), one of the most popular poems written in Sanskrit.

Kamakura
City southwest of Tokyo, Japan, that served as the headquarters of the **Kamakura**

shogunate (1192–1333). Established by **Minamoto Yoritomo**, it was Japan's first shogunate in a period when control of land tenure (*shoen*) was shared between court aristocrats and local warriors (although the system is often called "feudal," it was not). During most of the Kamakura shogunate effective rule was in the hands not of the **shoguns** but of the **Hojo**, regents to the shoguns. During this period the **bushi** emerged as the dominant social class; **Zen** Buddhism, patronized by the bushi, began to flourish; and two invasions by the **Mongol empire** were repulsed. A revolt by Emperor Go-Daigo in 1333 brought the Kamakura shogunate to an end.

Kamasutra

Indian classic text of love attributed to the sage Vatsyayana and written in the early first millennium C.E., possibly during the **Gupta empire**. The *Kamasutra* (Sanskrit for "Classic of Love") is a textbook giving detailed instructions on erotic technique and aphrodisiac recipes and charms. The work recognized the erotic and passionate needs of women as well as men and represents a sophisticated view toward sexual relations in ancient India. It was often used as a marriage manual. The Indian interest in the erotic side of life is also revealed in contemporary painting and sculpture.

Kami

Term for the various spirits and deities worshiped by the Japanese people. Most kami represented natural forces such as mountains, unusual rocks, foxes, and so forth. Exceptional individuals could also become kami. Kami worship led to the formation of the native Japanese religion of **Shinto**. Belief in kami continued long after the introduction of **Buddhism** from Korea in the sixth century. In the nineteenth and twentieth centuries the belief that Japan

was a special land divinely protected by its kami was promoted by ultranationalists.

Kamikaze

Term meaning "divine wind" in Japanese and originally used for the typhoons that forced the withdrawal of **Mongol empire** forces from Japan in 1274 and 1281, perhaps sparing the land from Mongol conquest. In the nineteenth century, the term was used by Japanese nationalists as a sign that Japan was a special "land of the gods." It was used in **World War II** to describe the suicide aircraft used as a desperate measure to halt the advance of the Allied forces across the Pacific in 1944–1945.

Kana (Katakana)

Japanese syllabary system first used in the early tenth century to phonetically write Japanese words. The kana were derived from modified and simplified Chinese characters. Eventually two of forms of kana came into use: *hiragana*, used to write Chinese and Japanese words, and *katagana*. The latter has been used in modern times to write words derived from Western languages. In premodern times kana was used by women and was sometimes called "lady's writing," but later it came to be used alongside Chinese characters in the mixed-script system of modern Japanese.

Kanagawa, Treaty of

Treaty between the United States and Japan in 1854 forcing Japan to open ports for the resupply of U.S. ships following **Commodore Matthew Perry**'s arrival in Japan. Using **gunboat diplomacy**, the treaty opened two ports to American vessels and permitted the United States to post a consul in the country to protect American interests. The Treaty of Kanagawa was followed in 1858 by the so-called Harris Treaty, which formally established trade and diplomatic relations, and by similar treaties with other Western powers, ending Japan's period of isolation and setting in motion a series of events that led to the **Meiji Restoration** of 1868. Kanagawa is known today as Yokohama.

Kanchipuram (Kanchi)

Town in northern Tamil Nadu state in India also known as Conjeeveram, considered in modern times as one of the seven major sacred cities of **Hinduism** for its many temples. It served as the capital of the **Pallava** dynasty of southern India from the fourth to the ninth century.

Kangxi (K'ang-hsi) (1654–1722)

Reign of the **Qing** (**Manchu**) emperor of China from 1662 to 1722. An able ruler, Hsüan-yeh extended the Qing empire to Outer Mongolia and Taiwan. He eliminated the last **Ming** loyalist threats to Manchu rule; brought a final end to the nomad threat from Mongolia; and opened diplomatic relations with Russia, which the Chinese empire now bordered. He was famous for his frequent inspection trips around the empire and his patronage of literature and scholarship. Although the Manchu rulers of the Qing dynasty were considered by many Chinese as barbarian outsiders, his skillful rule and patronage of Chinese culture did much to lessen resentment over their rule.

Kang Youwei (K'ang Yu-wei) (1858–1927)

Chinese philosopher and political figure who used his interpretation of **Confucius** as a reformer as a precedent to argue that China needed to respond to the challenge of Western imperialism by carrying reforms that promoted modernization. In 1898 the emperor Guangxu agreed to let Kang implement the creation of Western-style institutions in the **Hundred Days Reform**, but he was soon ousted by conservatives and went into exile in Japan.

After the establishment of the Republic of China in 1912, Kang devoted his efforts to restoring the monarchy in China.

Kanishka (r. c. first or second century C.E.)

Great king of the **Kushan kingdom**, which ruled northwestern India and part of **Central Asia**. He is believed to have reigned sometime between 78 and 144 C.E. (some scholars suggest a later date). Kanishka is best known as a patron of **Buddhism** and convened the fourth great Buddhist council, important for marking the beginnings of **Mahayana Buddhism**. His court attracted many writers and scholars including Ashvaghosa, whose *Buddha Charita* is one of the earliest examples of classical **Sanskrit** poetic literature.

Kant, Immanuel (1724–1804)

German philosopher whose ideas heavily influenced subsequent philosophy of reason. Kant did extensive writing in the areas of the theory of knowledge, ethics, and aesthetics, and he questioned pure reason, replacing it with human instinctual reason. The schools of thought of Kantianism, idealism, and even transcendentalism are closely drawn from his ideas, which challenged some of the views of the **Enlightenment**.

Kashmir

Region in the northern Indian subcontinent disputed between India and Pakistan. Kashmir was ruled by **Hindus** and **Muslims** and then was annexed by the **Sikhs** in 1819. Under the **British Raj** Kashmir was ruled by a Hindu maharaja although the majority of its population was Muslim. After 1947 the Hindu ruler elected to join India, and most of Kashmir was incorporated into the Indian state of Jammu-Kashmir, while Pakistan held a small, western portion. The disputed border and

Pakistan's support for Muslim separatists led to the **Indo-Pakistan wars** of 1948–1949 and 1965 and contributed to the 1981 war. Since 1989 Kashmir has seen violent fighting between Muslims seeking either independence or union with Pakistan, and Indian forces. Pakistan's support for these groups has kept relations with India tense, with occasional military clashes along the cease-fire line agreed to by Pakistan and India in 1972 and which divides Kashmir between the two powers.

Kaunda, Kenneth (1924–)
Zambian statesman and first president of Zambia (1964–1991). He was a member of the **African National Congress** and became its president in 1959. The leader of a nonviolence movement, Kaunda was imprisoned by the British in 1959 until January 1960. In 1964, at Zambia's independence, he was elected as the country's first president. Progressively concerned with opposition, in 1972 he made Zambia a one-party state. After several reelections he legalized opposition parties, in 1990. In 1991 he was defeated by Frederick Chiluba, and in 1992 he stepped down from office. In 1997 Kaunda was put under house arrest by Chiluba for allegedly inciting a coup, and in 1999 there was an assassination attempt on him. He lives in Zambia in retirement with his wife.

Kautilya (fl. fourth century B.C.E.)
Brahmin prime minister of **Chandragupta Maurya** credited with the authorship of the *Arthashastra* (Science of Material Gain), a textbook on statecraft. He advised the young Chandragupta Maurya, who established the **Maurya empire**, and is regarded by some scholars as the genius behind the ruler's military and political successes. The *Arthashastra* gives ruthless but realistic advice somewhat similar to that of **Niccolò Machiavelli**'s *Prince*. Most

scholars now date at least parts of the work after Kautilya's lifetime. but it is thought to reflect his views.

Kemal, Mustafa (Kemal Pasha). *See* Atatürk, Kemal (Kemal Pasha)

Kempis, Thomas à (1379–1471)
Medieval monk, priest, and author of *Of the Imitation of Christ* (c. 1441). Thomas is an example of the devout, pietistic flowering of **Christianity** in the late **Middle Ages**. His writing influenced the Brethren of the Common Life, with whom **Desiderius Erasmus** trained. *Imitation* was intended as an introduction to the devout life, but it gained wide appeal in Europe as many people questioned the clergy and church structure, but not religion.

Kennedy, John F. (1917–1963)
Thirty-fifth president of the United States. A naval hero during **World War II**, member of Congress, and U.S. senator from Massachusetts, Kennedy was elected president in 1960, narrowly defeating **Richard M. Nixon** in a campaign that featured the first televised debates. He was the first Catholic to serve as president. Kennedy's legislative accomplishments were few, though he came to be an important supporter of the civil rights movement and the space program. **Cold War** issues dominated his presidency, including the failed invasion of Cuba at the **Bay of Pigs**; the Berlin Crisis of 1961, leading to construction of the **Berlin Wall**; and the **Cuban Missile Crisis**, in which he compelled the Soviet Union to withdraw nuclear-armed missiles from Cuba. Kennedy was assassinated by Lee Harvey Oswald in Dallas, Texas, on November 22, 1963.

Kennedy, Robert F. (1925–1968)
Attorney general of the United States and senator from New York. A younger

brother of **John F. Kennedy**, Robert Kennedy served on Senate committee staffs before managing his brother's presidential campaign in 1960. He served as attorney general in the Kennedy administration, focusing on organized crime and civil rights. Following his brother's assassination, Kennedy won election to the Senate from New York. Running for president as a liberal, antiwar Democrat in 1968, he was assassinated by Sirhan on June 5, 1968, just after winning the California Democratic primary.

Kent State
Anti-**Vietnam War** protest at Kent State University that ended with the shooting of student protesters by members of the Ohio National Guard. President **Richard M. Nixon**'s April 1970 announcement of the invasion of neutral Cambodia prompted intensified antiwar protests on numerous college campuses. In response to civil disorder on the Kent State campus, National Guard troops were dispatched to the university. On May 4, 1970, 2,000 students took part in a banned rally, which the troops attempted to break up. Without warning twenty-eight guardsmen fired on the crowd, killing four students and wounding nine others. The shootings prompted student protests on an unprecedented scale across the country.

Kenyatta, Jomo (c. 1894–1978)
Kenyan statesman, first prime minister of Kenya (1963–1964), and that country's first president (1964–1978). Born in what was then British East Africa, Kenyatta was active in the politics of independence from the late 1920s. He helped to organize the fifth **Pan-African Congress** in Manchester, England, with **W. E. B. Du Bois**. Imprisoned on charges of involvement with the **Mau Mau** insurrection, Kenyatta was nonetheless chosen as prime minister of a

newly independent Kenya and a year later, as its president. Kenyatta maintained a pro-Western and pro-British policy until his death, making Kenya one of the most stable African countries.

Kepler, Johannes (1571–1630)
Mathematician and a major figure in the **scientific revolution**. Kepler proved that the universe could be mathematically understood. He discovered three basic mathematical laws of planetary motion. The first law is that planets move in an ellipse. The second is that there is a force emanating from the sun (**Isaac Newton** later proved this as gravity) that moves planets in a mathematically explainable rate; that is, "a line from the sun to a planet sweeps out equal areas in equal times." The third is that there is a mathematical relationship between a planet's distance from the sun and its rate of revolution around the sun.

Keynes, John Maynard (1883–1946)
British economist. His most important work is *The General Theory of Employment, Interest, and Money* (1935). Keynes proposed a government-planned economy and recommended that governments invest by deficit spending in order to restart the economy. His views strongly influenced President **Franklin D. Roosevelt** in the United States. In 1942 Keynes received a seat in the House of Lords. He led the British committee at the **Bretton Woods Conference** in 1944 and was influential in the establishment of the **International Monetary Fund**. His economic views held sway in Britain and the United States until the **Margaret Thatcher** and **Ronald Reagan** eras.

KGB (*Komitet Gosudarstvennoy Bezopasnost*) (1953–1991)
Committee for State Security of the **Union of Soviet Socialist Republics**. One of the

Soviet Union's two secret police forces, responsible for both internal and external security. The KGB was renowned and feared for its espionage, surveillance, and subversion. With the breakup of the Soviet Union in 1991 the offices and records (those that were not destroyed) of the KGB were opened for the first time.

Khajuraho

Capital of the Chandella rulers of central India from the ninth to eleventh centuries, famous for its **Hindu** temples. They are best known for the sensual and sexually explicit nature of their sculptures. Preserved from **Muslim** destruction by their remoteness, the temples of Khajuraho have preserved much of the rich artistic heritage of medieval India.

Khayyam, Omar. *See Rubaiyat*

Khazars

Turkic tribal peoples who created a state in the seventh and eighth centuries that stretched from the Caucasus Mountains to the lower Volga River. Originally part of the Turkic federation, the Khazars broke free in the early seventh century and in 727 established a capital, Itil, on the lower Volga. Around 740 the ruling elite converted to **Judaism**. A few scholars believe many eastern European Jews are partially descended from these converted Khazars. The Khazars fought a series of inconclusive wars against Arabs in the **Caucasus** region in the early eighth century that prevented the expansion of **Islam** into southeastern Europe. In 965 a prince of Kiev, Syatoslav, defeated the Khazars; thereafter they ceased to be a power in the region.

Khilafat Movement

Indian **Muslim** movement that arose in reaction to the treatment of the **Ottoman** sultan and **caliph** at the end of **World** War I. The movement began in 1919 under the leadership of brothers Muhammad and Shaukat Ali. It became a political movement in alliance with the **Indian National Congress**, directed at the British. It was important in mobilizing anti-British sentiment among Indian Muslims. When **Kemal Atatürk** abolished the **caliphate** in 1924 the movement collapsed. **Mohandas K. Gandhi** extended his support but withdrew it when the movement became violent. This caused bitterness between **Hindus** and Muslims and contributed to the rise of Muslim nationalism that culminated with the establishment of Pakistan.

Khitan People

Altaic- (related to Mongolian or Turkic) speaking people who controlled much of **Manchuria** and northeastern China from the tenth to the early twelfth century. The Khitans destroyed the state of **Parhae** in the early tenth century and then established their own Liao dynasty based in southern Manchuria. They then forced first **Korea** and then **Song** China in the early eleventh century to pay them tribute. In the 1120s the Song allied with another **Central Asian** people, the **Jurchens**, to destroy the Liao state, whereupon the Jurchens replaced the Khitans as the rulers of Manchuria. Some Khitans established the Central Asian state of Kara-Khitai, which was destroyed by the Mongols in the thirteenth century.

Khmer Rouge

Cambodian communist movement that led a successful rebellion against the U.S.-backed Lon Nol regime from 1970 to 1975. The Khmer Rouge under their leader **Pol Pot** adhered to an extreme concept of revolution that sought to completely remake Cambodian society by destroying the country's urban middle class, its religious institutions, and most traditional and

Western-influenced sectors of society. After coming to power with the fall of Phnom Penh in April 1975, the Pol Pot government relocated almost the entire population of the capital to the countryside, where most perished under harsh conditions. Many thousands were executed in the "killing fields." Some historians estimate that the Khmer Rouge were responsible for the deaths of 2 million people, about a quarter of Cambodia's population. In late 1987 Vietnam, following border disputes, invaded Cambodia and installed a government under Heng Samrin. The Khmer Rouge retreated into the countryside and carried on a **guerrilla** war against the regime. Internally divided and reduced in numbers, the Khmer Rouge turned against Pol Pot in 1997.

Khoisan

Family of languages, known as click languages, spoken by non-**Bantu** peoples of southern Africa. Divided into North, Central, and South Khoisan languages, Khoisan is spoken mainly by Bushmen hunters and gatherers whose culture predates the Bantu. Khoisan languages are distinctive for their click sounds.

Khomeini, Ayatollah Ruhollah (1900–1989)

Iranian religious and political leader. Khomeini, a **Shia Muslim**, opposed Western influence in Iran under **Mohammad Reza Shah Pahlavi**. Khomeini was exiled to Turkey, then Iraq, and finally to France in the 1960s and 1970s. Khomeini was able to foment dissent toward the shah's government from his residence in Paris, and as Iran's government collapsed, Khomeini returned to Iran in 1979 and led the popular Islamic Revolution, which established a state of strict fundamentalist Muslim law with himself as virtual head of state. He supported the seizure of the U.S. embassy in Tehran (1979) and the holding of American hostages there until 1981, an event known as the **Iran hostage crisis**. Khomeini also led the country into the **Iran-Iraq War** (1980–1988).

Khrushchev, Nikita (1894–1971)

Soviet first secretary of the Communist Party of the Soviet Union (1953–1964) and premier of the Soviet Union (1958–1964). At **Joseph Stalin**'s death, in 1953, Khrushchev succeeded him as first secretary, and in 1956 he denounced Stalinism, moving the Soviet Union in a new direction. In 1956 he crushed the **Hungarian Revolt**, and in 1962 he attempted to move missiles into Cuba, embroiling the **Union of Soviet Socialist Republics** with the United States in the **Cuban Missile Crisis**. In a speech at the **United Nations**, Khrushchev drove home his anti-U.S. tirade by pounding on the lectern with his shoe. His failures against the United States, conflicts with China, and inability to improve the Soviet economy led to his removal in 1964. He died in retirement.

Khubilai Khan (1214–1294)

Mongol ruler and grandson of **Genghis Khan** who completed the Mongol conquest of China in 1279 and founded the **Yuan** dynasty. He established his capital at Khanbalikh (on the site of modern-day **Beijing**) and from there controlled a vast empire that included all of China and parts of **Central Asia**. Khubilai Khan employed Chinese officials and maintained much of the Chinese administrative structure. Although severe, he was a competent ruler. He employed many non-Chinese, mostly **Central Asian Muslims** and most famously **Marco Polo**, who left a positive description of his rule (although some historians now question whether Marco Polo really went to China). He launched military campaigns into Vietnam, Burma,

Java, and Japan, but the first two were only partly successful and the last two ended in failure. In 1281 Khubilai attempted a conquest of Japan, but his fleet of 4,500 ships and 150,000 men was, according to Japanese tradition, blown back by a **kamikaze** ("divine wind").

Khyber Pass

Mountain pass between Afghanistan and Pakistan. Control of the Khyber Pass, which is thirty-three miles long and as narrow as ten feet, has been contested for thousands of years. The pass has been traversed by armies from the invasion of the **Aryan** people into the **Indus River** basin in the sixth century B.C.E. to the British in the twentieth century.

Kiev

Capital of Ukraine and ancient capital of **Russia**. Founded in the ninth century by Oleg according to tradition, Kiev had Russia's first church and first bishop and was known as Holy Kiev for the great number of churches within the city. Kiev remained an important cultural center even after the capital of Russia was moved to Moscow. It became one of the largest and most important industrial cities of the Soviet Union.

Kim Dae Jung (1925–)

South Korean political opposition leader and president of South Korea (1998–2003). From the southeastern province of Cholla, a stronghold of antigovernment sentiment, Kim Dae Jung ran unsuccessfully for president again **Park Chung Hee** in 1971 and was then forced into exile. His kidnapping by Park's agents from a hotel in Japan in 1973 caused an international incident. Kim's return to Korea and rearrest in 1980 sparked a bloody uprising in Kwangju that year. Following the democratization of South Korea he was elected president in December 1997. His "sunshine policy" sought to reduce tensions between North and South Korea. Kim Dae Jung received the **Nobel Prize** for Peace in 2000 for this effort.

Kim Il Sung (born Kim Song-ju) (1912–1994)

North Korean communist leader. Kim fought the Japanese in the 1930s as a **guerrilla** fighter leading a small band that was forced to retreat to the Soviet Union during **World War II**. In 1945 he was returned to the Soviet-controlled northern half of Korea by the Soviet occupation forces. He established the Workers Party in 1946 and effectively ruled the northern half of the country from 1945 to 1948. When North Korea became independent as the Democratic People's Republic of Korea, he governed it through his position as head of the ruling Workers Party. Kim Il Sung persuaded the Soviets and the Chinese to support an invasion of South Korea in 1950 in an effort to reunite the country under his rule. After suffering defeat in the war he continued a hostile posture toward South Korea and its ally the United States while remaining an ally of both the Soviet Union and China, which provided economic support for his regime. At home, he established a thoroughly totalitarian state and an extreme cult of personality. He was praised as not only a political and military genius but a great thinker whose *juche* ("self-reliance") thought virtually supplanted Marxism-Leninism as the official ideology of the state. He groomed his son **Kim Jong Il** as his successor.

Kim Jong Il (1942–)

North Korean who succeeded his father, **Kim Il Sung**, as paramount leader of North Korea (the Democratic People's Republic of Korea) in 1994. Kim Jong Il was the son of Kim Il Sung by his second wife and was probably born in the Soviet

Union. Starting in the early 1970s the elder Kim began grooming his son to be his heir. Upon his father's death the "Dear Leader," as Kim Jong Il is called, assumed power and carried on his father's policies of highly centralized totalitarian control over his people and confrontation with the United States and South Korea. In 2000 he met with President **Kim Dae Jung** of South Korea, who visited him and began some small steps at increasing contact and cooperation between the two Koreas, but his missile program and his 2002 decision to openly resume the development of nuclear weapons created tensions with the United States, Japan, and the international community. In September 2005 North Korea announced that they would end their nuclear weapons program.

King, Martin Luther, Jr. (1929–1968)
Baptist minister at the forefront of the U.S. **civil rights movement** of the 1950s and 1960s. After **Rosa Parks**, an elderly African American woman, was arrested for refusing to give up her seat on a Montgomery, Alabama, bus on December 1, 1955, King organized a Montgomery bus boycott to place economic pressure on the bus system's practices. As a result segregation was outlawed on Montgomery buses. After the successful bus boycott King formed the Southern Christian Leadership Conference in 1957. Using **Mohandas K. Gandhi**'s idea of nonviolent resistance, so successful at Montgomery, King helped to organize protests throughout the South. Sit-ins occurred at white-only lunch counters, the first in Greensboro, North Carolina, in 1960. In 1963, while protesting civil rights violations in Birmingham, Alabama, King was jailed. From his cell King defended his policy of civil disobedience. He led a 250,000-person march for civil rights on Washington DC, giving his famous "I Have a Dream"

speech, broadening support for the 1964 **Civil Rights Act** and the 1965 Voting Rights Act. While in Memphis, Tennessee, supporting striking sanitation workers, King was shot and killed on his hotel's balcony on April 4, 1968, by James Earl Ray.

Kipchak
Central Asian nomadic group of mostly Turkic-speaking peoples that were a major military presence in the western Eurasian **steppe** from the eleventh century. Called Polovtsy by the Russians and Cumans by the Byzantines, the Kipchaks gained mastery over much of the area north of the Black Sea in the eleventh century, making direct contact between Kievan Russia and Byzantium difficult. They were defeated by the **Mongols** in 1237. Afterward, their territory and many of their people became absorbed into the **Golden Horde**. Others were sold as slaves, some becoming **Mamluk** slave warriors in Egypt.

Kirghiz
Speakers of a Turkic language who mostly reside in Kyrgyzstan, a landlocked Central Asian state bordered by Tajikistan, Uzbekistan, Kazakhstan, and China. Kyrgyzstan was colonized by Russia in 1864, became the Soviet Socialist Republic of Turkmen, and in 1991 joined the Commonwealth of Independent States. In the 1990s Kyrgyzstan had an estimated 4,851,000 residents, approximately 1,678,000 living in towns and roughly 3,144,00 in the countryside. Bishkek, in the north, is the capital city, but the southern part of Kyrgyzstan is more populous than the north. Kyrgyzstan, like other states in **Central Asia**, is a demographically fluid environment with the following breakdown in the 1990s: 64 percent Kirghiz; 13 percent Uzbek; 12 percent Russian; and the remainder Uighur, Tajik, Kazakh, Ukrainian, Tatar, German, and Jewish. The Kirghiz consider themselves

to be composed of forty tribes. The most notable groups of Kirghiz outside of Kyrgyzstan are those in China, where they are one of fifty-six ethnic groups recognized by the Chinese government, and in the Wakhan corridor of Afghanistan, where a community of approximately 30,000 Kirghiz was counted in 1979.

Kita Ikki (d. 1937)

Japanese political thinker and radical activist who contributed to the rise of ultra-nationalist violence in Japan in the 1930s. A member of the Kokuryokai (Black Dragon Society), an imperial group that sought to expand Japan's frontier to the Amur River, he abandoned his earlier socialism to accept a concept of Japan ruled by a selfless military in which the state would own all industry and the entire population would be dedicated to national greatness. He was executed in 1937 for his alleged involvement in the February 26, 1936, incident, in which a small group of radical soldiers attempted a coup.

Knight

Medieval cavalryman, heavily depended upon in warfare during the **Middle Ages**, who came to exemplify the chivalric code of honorable behavior in love and war. Knights were an integral part of **feudalism**, sometimes receiving dominion over **fiefs** of their own on the condition that they remain loyal to their feudal lord. As weaponry changed in the late Middle Ages and weapons using **gunpowder** became more important, knights declined in military importance, though they still fought at tournaments.

Knossus Culture. *See* Minoan Civilization

Koguryo

One of three states that contended for supremacy in Korea during the Three Kingdoms period (fourth century to 676 C.E.).

It emerged in the first century C.E. with its base in the Yalu River valley but eventually shifted its center southward with its capital at P'yongyang. A powerful state, at its peak Koguryo controlled most of Manchuria and northern Korea and defeated **Sui** and **Tang** dynasty attempts to subdue it. It succumbed to a joint **Silla**-Tang invasion in 660.

Kokutai

Japanese theory of government and society (often translated as "national polity") that was used from the **Meiji** period to **World War II** to describe the basic and unique character of the Japanese state. Always vague, it combined traditional Japanese values, especially Confucian loyalty to the ruler and filial piety, with more modern ideas of emperor worship and racial and cultural **nationalism**. After 1945 the idea of kokutai was associated with the ultra-nationalism and militarism that was discredited by Japan's defeat in World War II, and it is no longer part of mainstream Japanese political thought or rhetoric.

Kongo

African kingdom of the fourteenth to seventeenth centuries, located in west-central Africa on the Congo River. In the fourteenth century the Bakongo established a power kingdom as a confederation of several smaller units in central Africa, known as the Kingdom of Kongo. The Portuguese came in contact with the Kingdom of Kongo in 1482 and established a close diplomatic relationship with its kings. The kings converted to Christianity, but in 1665 slaving led the Portuguese to go to war with Kongo, defeat it, and decapitate its king, and the Kingdom of Kongo disintegrated.

Konoye Fumimaro (1891–1945)

Called the last of the Japanese **Fujiwara** noble family. Long a liberal politician, he became a proponent of imperial expansion when he became Japan's prime minister in 1937. He was in that position several times, including at the beginning of the **Sino-Japanese War** (1931–1945) as it expanded from **Manchuria** to war with China (also known as **World War II**). He concluded an alliance with the **Axis Powers** in 1940 and founded the Imperial Rule Assistance Association to replace Japan's political parties. He was slated to stand trial as a war criminal following **World War II**, but he committed suicide in December 1945.

Koran. *See* Quran (Qur'an or Koran)

Korean War (1950–1953)
Conflict that began June 25, 1950, when North Korea under **Kim Il Sung** invaded South Korea in a bid to reunify the country. The intervention of the United States, which entered under the banner of the **United Nations,** resulted in the defeat of North Korea. A number of other nations, such as Britain and Turkey, sent small numbers of forces under the UN flag. After General **Douglas MacArthur**'s Inchon landing in September 1950, U.S., South Korean, and other UN forces swiftly moved north of the thirty-eighth parallel, which divides the two countries, but they were stopped and driven back by China, which sent troops to defend North Korea in November. By early 1951 the war was at a stalemate along the border, and in July 1953 a cease-fire took place after truce talks began at **Panmunjom.** A demilitarized zone (DMZ) separating the two Koreas was established. The cessation of hostilities was only a truce, and the Koreas remained technically at war. U.S. troops continue to be stationed along the DMZ to reinforce South Korean forces. The conflict resulted in massive bombing of North Korea; widespread destruction throughout the Korean peninsula;

and the deaths of 4 million Koreans, mostly civilians, and 33,000 U.S. troops and perhaps 150,000 Chinese troops.

Koryo
Name of the Korean state from 935 to 1392, and sometimes the name of the dynasty that ruled it. Wang Kon reunified Korea and married into the former ruling Kyongju Kim dynasty. He renamed it from **Silla** to Koryo, a name derived from the ancient tribal state and people of northern Korea. Koryo's nearly five centuries saw the introduction of Chinese-style **civil service examinations**, the transition from a warrior to a civil aristocracy, and the growth in popularity of **Zen** ("Son") **Buddhism**. After a series of destructive **Mongol** invasions, the state became a Mongol **vassal** (1270–1356) and then regained full independence. In the late fourteenth century General Yi Song-gye seized power and established the new Yi dynasty. He renamed the state **Choson** but carried on many of institutions of Koryo. Koryo is still used as a name for Korea. The English name *Korea* is derived from it.

Kowtow (Ketou)
Chinese court protocol, an act of supplication originally used in religious ceremonies and adopted by the **Ming** and **Qing** emperors as the appropriate way to approach their imperial presence. All foreign and domestic visitors of the emperor were required to kneel and knock their heads on the floor three times as a sign of respect for the emperor. In 1793 the British representative Viscount George Macartney refused to kowtow, and the requirement was abolished for Western diplomats after the **Opium War**.

Koxinga (1624–1662)
Western name for the pirate Zheng Chenggong, who fought the newly established

Qing (**Manchu**) rulers of China from his base in Taiwan. Born to a Chinese father and a Japanese mother, Koxinga remained loyal to the **Ming** dynasty after its fall in 1644 and led a resistance to the Manchus. Initially fighting along the southern Chinese coast and leading troops along the lower **Yangzi River**, he went on to capture Taiwan from the Dutch in 1661. Koxinga died a year later, but his son continued the Ming loyalist resistance until Qing forces invaded and conquered Taiwan in 1683, incorporating the island into the Chinese empire.

Krupp, Alfred (1812–1887)
German industrialist, armaments maker, and driving force in German steel and **industrialization**. He was the son of Friedrich Krupp (1787–1826), who founded iron- and steelworks at Essen. Alfred Krupp invested in steam power to produce high-quality steel. By the 1870s Krupp's steelworks were among the largest in Europe. Krupp steel **cannons** helped **Prussia** defeat France in 1871 in the Franco-Prussian War, and his steelworks also built many German armaments in **World War I** and **World War II**.

Kshatriya
Second highest of the four **varna** status groups in **Hinduism**. The Kshatriyas were generally rulers and warriors, and they rank below the **Brahmin** priestly group in the caste system. Many subgroups of various socioeconomic statuses exist within the Kshatriya. Most of India's rulers have been identified with this caste.

Kublai Khan. *See* Khubilai Khan

Ku Klux Klan (KKK)
White supremacist terrorist organization. Founded in 1866 in Pulaski, Tennessee, by disgruntled Confederate veterans of the **American Civil War**, the Ku Klux Klan (KKK) began as a social club. Deriving its name from the Greek word *kuklos* ("circle"), the KKK was noted for its secrecy, hooded costumes, and elaborate rituals. It quickly moved to a campaign of intimidation and violence directed against African Americans and supporters of radical Reconstruction (especially voters) in an effort to restore the prewar social order in the South. Crushed by federal action through the Force Acts in the early 1870s, the KKK reemerged in 1915 at Stone Mountain, Georgia. The second incarnation of the klan, which directed its ire (and violence) at immigrants, Catholics, and "immorality" in addition to African Americans, grew to include millions of members and extended its reach into the Midwest and the West, dominating politics in several states. The klan declined rapidly after 1925 amidst factional fighting, corruption, and the conviction of the Indiana Klan leader on charges of rape and murder. Small groups remained, and the Klan reemerged in a much more diffuse form after **World War II** in the South and the Midwest. While the third incarnation of the klan temporarily grew in strength in response to the **civil rights movement**, it remains faction-ridden and a marginalized part of the extreme political right.

Kuo. *See* Guo (Kuo)

Kush
Ancient African kingdom in **Nubia** along the upper Nile south of Egypt. Recent research suggests that the region may have preceded the **Egyptian civilization** as an agrarian region and a kingdom. Nubia, during the height of Egyptian power from 2700 B.C.E., became a tributary, sending goods to Egypt but also borrowing

extensively from Egyptian culture, including pyramids. With the decline of Egypt, circa 700 B.C.E., Nubia became the independent kingdom of Kush with its capital at Napata, later at **Meroë**. Kush acted as an intermediary between Egypt and central and east Africa and, later, for the **Roman Empire**. Kush reached its peak in the first century C.E. and was eventually conquered by **Axum**, in the fourth century C.E.

Kushan Kingdom

State established by descendants of the Yuezhi people of **Central Asia** who ruled over much of northwestern India, Afghanistan, and part of Turkestan from the first through third centuries C.E. Established by Kujula Kadphises, it reached its heights under **Kanishka** in the late first to early second century. The Kushans facilitated trade along the **Silk Roads** by imposing order along important routes. They also were patrons of **Buddhism** and the arts, contributing to the spread of **Mahayana Buddhism** into **Central Asia** and China and the development of the Gandhara school of art.

Kyoto

City in central Japan that served as the imperial capital from 794 to 1868. Established by Emperor Kammu as the capital, it was modeled on the **Tang** capital of **Xi'an**, with a grid pattern, and known as Heian. During the **Heian period** (794–1160) the city was the center of a rich culture with many splendid **Buddhist** temples. During the period of the **Ashikaga** shogunate (1339–1573) it again became an important center of culture, although it suffered greatly during the *Sengoku* Warring States period from 1467–1568 (named in reference to the Chinese **Warring States period**), when feudal warlords fought incessant wars among themselves. It lost its status as the home of the emperor in 1868 but has remained an important cultural center.

Kyûshû

Southernmost of the four main islands of Japan. Despite its modest size of 14,177 square miles (36,719 sq km), it has always had a sizable population. The name *Kyûshû* is derived from the nine provinces that existed on the island in ancient times.

Laissez-faire (French for "non-interfering") Economic policy of government non-interference. Governments had set economic policy or restrictions throughout much of history, including in ancient **Rome** and during the **Middle Ages**. In the eighteenth century Adam Smith (1723–1790) called for free trade as a better way to encourage the economy. This approach became more widespread in the nineteenth century and is known as laissez-faire economics.

Lamaism

Form of **Buddhism** practiced in Tibet and Mongolia. The name is derived from the term *lama* ("superior one"), given to the higher-ranking monks. Lamaism grew out of a fusion between **Mahayana Buddhism**, introduced to Tibet from India in the eighth century, and the indigenous animist Bon religion. In the fourteenth century the Yellow Hat sect replaced the Red Hat sect as dominant. As lamas assumed political as well as spiritual authority, Tibet became a theocracy ruled by the head of the Yellow Hat sect, the **Dalai Lama**. In the sixteenth and seventeenth centuries the eastern **Mongols** were converted to lamaistic Buddhism. In both Tibet and, later, Mongolia conversion to rule by lamas contributed to a decline in the people's tradition of raiding their Chinese and other neighbors in favor of more peaceful pursuits.

Land of the Morning Calm

Term for Korea derived from the literal translation of the Korean name for their country, **Choson**, which in turn is derived from the Chinese name *Chao Xian* ("morning freshness"). It refers to the geographic position of Korea, east of China and hence a "morning country." It was the official name for Korea under the Yi dynasty (1392–1910) and is used by North Korea as the name for Korea.

Lao Tzu. *See* Laozi (Lao-tzu)

Laozi (Lao-tzu)

Reputed founder of **Daoism**. Laozi is said to have been active around 500 B.C.E., a contemporary of Confucius, and the author of the Daoist classic the **Dao de Jing** (**Tao te Ching**). Most scholars regard Laozi, whose name means "Old Master," as a mythical person and date the *Dao de Jing* to the third century B.C.E.

Las Casas, Bartolomé de (1474–1566)

Spanish **Dominican** priest and critic of Spain's policies of conquest and exploitation in the New World. Las Casas was called "Apostle of the Indians" for his criticism of the **encomienda**, or slavery of the Indians, and the **Requerimiento**, the document read to the Indians before the Spanish made war on them. Las Casas wrote *Brief History of the Indies* (1539), arguing for the Indians' equality with Spaniards.

Latifundia

Large agricultural estates of the **Roman Empire**. Often carved out of conquered lands, latifundia were granted to upper-class Romans for their service in the military or politics. They were run as nearly self-sufficient communities with a wide range of economic activity and division of labor. By the third century C.E. the latifundium had become the agricultural unit of much of the western Roman Empire, and with the decline of the empire the latifundia played not only a major economic role but also a political and cultural role. They are sometimes claimed as the basis of the medieval manor.

Latin American Wars of Independence.
See Wars of Independence, Latin American

Latitude
Angular measurement of the earth on a meridian, now measured in degrees from the equator to the North Pole and to the South Pole. Navigators had some idea of latitude, as measured by the stars, before the fifteenth century, but in that century implements were devised to make calculations easier and more accurate. Europeans calculated latitude by altitude of the North Star. **Longitude** was much more difficult to reckon, and not until the mid-eighteenth century was it possible to do so accurately.

Latium
Ancient region of the Italian peninsula of the Latini people roughly bordered by the Tiber and Anio rivers to the northwest, the Apennine hills to the east, and Campania to the south. **Octavian** combined Latium and Campania to form the first region of Italy in the **Roman Empire**. Latium is a coastal plain inhabited by an ethnic group with a common name—the Latini—and language—Latin. This region, these people, and their language became the center of Roman culture when, in the fourth century, the Latini were defeated

and absorbed into the Roman state with full citizenship.

League of Arab States. *See* Arab League

League of Iroquois. *See* Iroquois, League of

League of Nations
International organization established in 1919 by the **Versailles Treaty** to maintain peace and security by arbitrating international disputes. First formulated by President **Woodrow Wilson** of the United States, the organization included the victors of **World War I**, except for the United States, and most neutral countries and was headquartered in Geneva, Switzerland. Germany joined in 1926 and the Soviet Union in 1934, but Germany and Japan withdrew in 1933 and Italy in 1936. The League of Nations proved ineffective in stopping the expansion and aggression of Japan, Germany, and Italy in the 1930s. In 1946 league functions were absorbed by the **United Nations**.

Leakey, Louis and Mary (1903–1972; 1913–1996)
British-Kenyan archaeologists and anthropologists. Leakey, his wife Mary, and their son Richard made key discoveries regarding human origins in the Olduvai Gorge of Kenya. In 1959 Mary Leakey found early primate fossils that turned out to be 1.75 million years old. In 1975 she found hominid footprints of two adults and a child that were 3.5 million years old.

Lebensraum
German word meaning "living space," used by the **Nazis** to refer to the need of the German people for more land in which to live. First introduced in the 1870s, the term and the principle behind it were used to justify Germany's aggressive

expansion prior to and during **World War II**, especially in eastern Europe.

Lee Kuan Yew (1923–)

Lawyer and political leader who served as prime minister of **Singapore** (1959–1990). During British colonial rule in the 1950s Lee created the People's Action Party. He led the negotiations that established Singapore as a self-governing state within the British Commonwealth in 1959, and in 1963 he led it into the Federation of Malaysia. When the Malaysian government expelled Singapore from the federation two years later, Lee concentrated on developing his **city-state** into a dynamic economic power. By the time he resigned in 1990 Singapore had the highest standard of living in Southeast Asia and educational and social services comparable to the western developed industrialized nations. He was widely admired for his skill as an administrator, his intellectual brilliance, and his outspoken views but was criticized for governing in a paternalistic and autocratic manner.

Legalism

One of the **One Hundred Schools** of classical Chinese philosophy that emphasized the need for the authority of the ruler and the power of the state to be asserted and strengthened in order to establish an orderly, peaceful society. A number of thinkers contributed to its development, most importantly **Han Feizi** (c. 280–233 B.C.E.). Legalist teachings about the need for strict laws, regulations, and punishments had an important influence on the **Qin** state and on subsequent Chinese political thought.

Legions

The Roman army's divisions. Legions consisted of between 3,000 and 6,000 men comprised of light and heavy infantry (velites and **hoplites**) and cavalry. These legions were well organized and trained and often fought in phalanx maniples, or waves of block formations. They enabled **Rome** to conquer much of the ancient world although they were at a disadvantage fighting against the loosely organized **Germanic tribes**.

Lenin, Vladimir Ilyich (1870–1924)

Russian revolutionary, originally surnamed Ulyanov. He studied law at Kazan and Saint Petersburg, founded the Fighting Alliance for the Liberation of the Working Class in Saint Petersburg, and participated in underground revolutionary activities for which he was exiled to Siberia (1897–1900). In exile Lenin wrote about **Marxism**. At the 1903 Russian Social Democratic Labor Party Second Congress Lenin caused a split into two factions, **Bolsheviks** and Mensheviks. He left Russia and remained abroad (except for the 1905 **Russian Revolution**) writing until 1917, when he returned from Zurich, Switzerland, to take leadership of the 1917 **Russian Revolution**. He garnered widespread support with slogans such as "All power to the Soviets" and led the Bolsheviks to control of the revolution in October 1917. He became head of the Soviet government, made peace with Germany, and defeated the White Russians (those opposed to the Communists) in the ensuing civil war. Lenin died in 1924; his body was embalmed and placed in the Kremlin, and Petrograd (Saint Petersburg) was renamed Leningrad until 1991, when the name was changed back to Saint Petersburg.

Leo I, Saint (Leo the Great) (c. 390–461)

Roman Catholic pope (440–461). Leo expanded and solidified the authority of the **papacy**. He successfully fought the Pelagian and Manichean heresies and in 451 reached an agreement between the western and eastern Christian churches on the relationship between God the Father and **Jesus** the Son. In 452 Leo encouraged **Attila** to leave Italy, and in 455 he saved **Rome** from the **Vandals**.

Leo IX, Saint (1002–1054)
Roman Catholic **pope** (1048–1054) and reformer. Leo reformed the issue of simony (buying church office) and enforced clerical celibacy. His interference in south Italy created conflict with the **Byzantine Empire**. His excommunication of the patriarch of Constantinople led to the schism of the **Roman Catholic Church** and the **Eastern Orthodox Church** in 1054.

Leonardo da Vinci. *See* Da Vinci, Leonardo

Lepanto, Battle of (1571)
Sea battle near Greece between the **Ottoman Turks** and the Holy League of **Venice**, Genoa, Spain, and the **papacy**. Lepanto was the last great naval confrontation fought primarily with galleys, rowed warships. Although it was first major defeat of the Ottomans by the Europeans, they did not take advantage of the victory and it had little effect, other than as a boost in confidence.

Leviathan. See Hobbes, Thomas

Lewis and Clark Expedition (1804–1806)
U.S. transcontinental expedition of exploration. After President **Thomas Jefferson** had the United States complete the **Louisiana Purchase** from France in 1803, more than doubling the size of the new country, Jefferson initiated the Lewis and Clark expedition to explore and document the territory. Meriwether Lewis and William Clark left Saint Louis in 1804 with the Corps of Discovery, sailing up the Missouri River to the Dakotas, where they wintered. From there they crossed Montana, Idaho, and the Continental Divide. In 1805 they traveled down the Snake and Columbia rivers, reaching the Pacific Ocean. They returned in 1806. The Lewis and Clark expedition opened up the Louisiana Territory to American settlement and established the United States as a country stretching from the Atlantic to the Pacific ocean.

Lexington, Battle of (1775)
First battle of the **American Revolution**. British troops secretly set out to destroy the stores of arms and ammunition held by colonial militia in Lexington, Massachusetts. The mission was detected by the Americans, who met the British troops on the town green on April 19, 1775. After being ordered by British major John Pitcairn to disperse, the colonists moved to obey until a shot rang out, followed by several volleys of fire. Debate remains as to which side fired the first shot.

Liang Chi-chao (1873–1929)
Disciple of **Kang Youwei**, with whom he worked in the summer of 1898 in the **Hundred Days Reform** in late **Qing** China. Liang lectured to the Qing emperor Kuang-hsu on educational and administrative reform before the **Empress Dowager (Ci Xi)** and **Yuan Shih-kai** brought an end to the reform efforts. He fled with Kang to Japan until after the 1911 revolution and then returned to China as a reformer, supporting Yuan Shi-kai against **Sun Yat-sen**'s **Guomintang**.

Liberalism
Political view that individual liberty is of utmost importance. Liberalism became a prominent belief in Britain in the nineteenth century; its greatest proponent was

John Stuart Mill in his work *On Liberty* (1859). Liberalism arose in opposition to the power of the state as **nationalism** spread in Europe but also came to be associated with free-market theory. Later in the nineteenth century liberalism attached to social reforms.

Liberal Party

British political party founded in 1859. The Liberal Party generally represented the middle class, labor, and the non–Church of England denominations. For much of the late nineteenth century **William Gladstone** led the party, and he was prime minister numerous times. The Liberal Party carried out many social and political reforms including instituting elementary education, child labor laws, and workplace safety laws. The Factory Act of 1874 established a maximum work week of fifty-six hours. The party was instrumental in moving toward Irish Home Rule. The Liberal Party was surpassed by the Labour Party in the 1920s and merged with the Social Democrats to form the Liberal Democratic Party in the 1980s.

Li Hongzhang (Li Hung-chang) (1823–1901)

Chinese statesman who formed the regional Anhui army that helped put down the **Taiping Rebellion**. Later he became one of the leaders of the Self-Strengthening Movement, an attempt to bolster the **Qing** dynasty by implementing cautious reforms. Li served for more than four decades as the official most responsible for foreign affairs, negotiating the Treaty of Shimonoseki with Japan in 1895 His reforms were intended to adopt certain western institutions, especially military, without making any fundamental social, economic, or political changes. His efforts were discredited by China's humiliating defeat in the **Sino-Japanese War** of 1894–1895, including the destruction of the modern Beiyang fleet, whose construction he had supervised.

Limpopo River

River 1,100 miles (1,800 km) long originating as the Crocodile River and flowing in an arch that forms the boundary of South Africa, Botswana, and Zimbabwe and then flows through Mozambique to the Indian Ocean.

Lin Biao (Lin Piao) (1908–1971)

Chinese military commander and communist leader. A participant in the **Long March**, he later led Chinese forces in the **Korean War** (1950–1953). **Mao Zedong** made him minister of defense in 1959 and designated him his successor in 1969. Lin supported Mao's radical policies during the **Great Proletarian Cultural Revolution** but was killed in a plane crash in Mongolia in 1971 following his alleged involvement in a coup attempt.

Lincoln, Abraham (1809–1865)

Sixteenth president of the United States (1861–1865). His election on an anti-slavery platform helped to precipitate the **American Civil War**. During the Civil War he asserted broad presidential powers to direct the war effort of the Union. On January 1, 1863, he issued the Emancipation Proclamation, redefining the war as a struggle to end slavery. His 1863 Gettysburg Address is widely regarded as a preeminent expression of U.S. political ideals. Lincoln was reelected in 1864 and was assassinated by John Wilkes Booth in 1865.

Linga

Hindu phallic symbol representing the god **Shiva**. Its frequent representation reflects the importance of fertility and reproduction in **Hinduism**.

Little Ice Age
Northern hemispheric cooling from c. 1300 to 1850 with the most dramatic cooling from 1550 to 1850. There is evidence of glacial expansion from several regions of the world, including from equatorial areas such as the Andes Mountains. The Little Ice Age, following the **Medieval Optimum**, caused shorter, wetter summers and longer, colder winters, reducing the growing season by as much as one month. It eliminated some agrarian regions and certain crops and caused frequent famines.

Liu Shaoqi (Liu Shao-ch'i) (1898–1974)
Chinese communist leader and China's head of state from 1959 to 1968. Liu became associated with efforts to move away from **Mao Zedong**'s radical policies of the **Great Leap Forward** to a more pragmatic approach to development. During the **Great Proletarian Cultural Revolution** he was denounced by Mao's supporters as the "number one capitalist roader," removed from office, and imprisoned. He died from maltreatment in prison and was posthumously rehabilitated in 1980 by **Deng Xiaoping**.

Livingstone, David (1813–1873)
Scottish missionary, explorer, and author on Africa. Employed by the London Missionary Society from 1841 to 1857, Livingstone began to extend his explorations into new regions of Africa, keeping detailed journals and carefully noting the geography. From 1858 to 1864 he led an expedition through Zambia and Tanzania, and after being "rescued" by journalist Henry Stanley in 1871 he continued on his way. Livingstone worked hard to legitimize the African people in the eyes of Europeans and to replace the slave trade with other mercantile trade. He discovered numerous lakes, rivers, and other geographic sites, although he failed to discover the source of the Nile River. His major impact was the expansion of European interest in Africa through his exploits and publications.

Livy (59 B.C.E.–17 C.E.)
Titus Livius, known as Livy, wrote the extensive *History of Rome* from the arrival of Aeneas and the founding of **Rome** through 9 C.E. Although some of his factual information is fanciful, the historical characters and episodes he describes offer the historian a window into Roman virtues like patriotism and piety. The work consisted of 142 books, many of which survive only in fragments. Livy was a favorite of the emperor **Octavian**.
    See also *Aeneid, The*

Li Yuan
Founder and first emperor of the **Tang** (618–627), one of China's greatest dynasties. With help from his fourth son, Li Shimin, he led a successful rebellion against the **Sui** dynasty in 617 and became emperor in 618 under the name Gaozu. In 626 he abdicated in favor of Li Shimin, who succeeded him as Taizong (r. 627–650).

Lizard House. *See* Itzamná

Locke, John (1632–1704)
English philosopher. Locke attempted to apply a scientific method, in the mode of his contemporary and friend **Isaac Newton**, to all knowledge. In his work *Essay Concerning Human Understanding* (1690), Locke proposed that the human mind is a *tabula rasa* ("blank slate") onto which our senses feed data from experience. If fed enough data, humans could find the order and consistency of the universe. Locke, in looking for the fundamentals of human institutions as Newton had found gravity to be a fundamental force

in the physical world, concluded that the unalienable rights of humankind are life, liberty, and property. Locke provided a foundation upon which the **Enlightenment** was built.

Loess

Silty or loamy soil, usually colored yellowish brown, that is deposited by the wind over much of China and elsewhere in the Northern Hemisphere. Its rich, easily worked loess has made this region of China an agriculturally productive one and contributed to the fact that it was the heartland of Chinese civilization. The soils wash into the **Yellow River** (Huang He) giving the river its characteristic color and name.

Longbow

In the **Middle Ages**, originally a hunting weapon used by woodsmen. In the wars of conquest in Wales the English discovered the effectiveness of the weapon. It was easy and quick to construct from readily available ash trees, rapid to fire compared to the **crossbow**, and very accurate. The use of large numbers of longbowmen in the **Hundred Years War** (1338–1453) enabled the outnumbered English to defeat the French at the battles of **Crécy**, **Poitiers**, and **Agincourt**.

Longitude

Measurement of the earth along an east-west line. Whereas **latitude** was calculated from the stars by the fifteenth century, longitude could not be accurately measured until 1759, when John Harrison built a timepiece that could accurately measure it, making navigation safer.

Long March (1934–1935)

Long, circuitous retreat of Chinese communists from the Jiangxi Soviet in southern China to Yanan in a remote region of the northwest. Forced by the **Guomin-**dang offensive to abandon their Jiangxi base, about 100,000 communists participated, but only 6,000 survivors completed the trip after traveling 6,000 miles (9,700 km) over rugged terrain by foot. During the march **Mao Zedong** became the leader of the **Chinese Communist Party**. The Long March became a symbol of determination for the communists, and many of its survivors became prominent leaders after the communists came to power in 1949.

Long Parliament (1640–1660)

English **Parliament** called by **Charles I** that continued to meet through the **English Civil War** (1642–1649), the execution of the king (1649), and the establishment of the Commonwealth. The Long Parliament no longer regarded itself as a temporary body to advise the monarch, but as the source of authority of the English government. This conflict with the king brought on the Civil War and the king's death. In 1648 the Parliament was purged, and the remnant was known as the Rump Parliament. In 1659 the Parliament was restored, and in 1660 it dissolved itself.

Longshan

Term for a Neolithic culture that flourished in the lower **Yellow River** (Huang He) valley from 2500 to 1700 B.C.E., named for a site in Shandong province in China. The Longshan culture, which replaced the earlier **Yangshao culture**, was an agricultural society based on the cultivation of millet and the raising of pigs and goats and is noted for its distinctive black pottery. It developed into the **Shang** civilization.

López, Francisco Solano (1827–1870)

Paraguayan dictator (1862–1870) who involved Paraguay in a devastating war (1862–1867). López was a military leader in Paraguay at the age of nineteen, appointed minister of war and vice president by his father, whom he succeeded to the presidency upon his death in 1862. The War of the Triple Alliance (Brazil, Argentina, and Uruguay), begun over border disputes, nearly destroyed Paraguay.

Lord-Vassal Relationship. *See* Feudalism

Louis IX, Saint (1214–1270)
King of France seen as the model of saintly kingship. Louis stabilized France especially in its relations with England, bringing great prestige to the Capetian dynasty; built Sainte-Chapelle in Paris to house relics; and led two **Crusades**. He died on the second Crusade, to Tunis.

Louis XIV (1638–1715)
Longest-reigning king of France (1643–1715). Louis became king as a child, while his mother was regent and **Jules Mazarin** chief minister. At Mazarin's death in 1661 Louis took the reins of government. He was able to maintain absolute rule by not calling the **Estates General** (parliament) and ignoring the **Parlement** (courts) and the aristocracy. Under Louis the French military expanded and many wars were fought, but after 1700 most ended in defeat. Louis revoked the **Edict of Nantes** and persecuted the **Huguenots** (**Protestants**), but he cultivated the arts at the court at the **Palace of Versailles.**

Louis XVI (1754–1793)
King of France at the outbreak of the **French Revolution** (1789). With pressure from the aristocracy to concede the power of the courts, pressure from the middle class to grant it some participation in government, and pressure from the lower classes to reduce taxation, Louis called the **Estates General** in 1789. As the revolution broke out Louis XVI was forcibly brought to Paris from the **Palace of Versailles.** He and his family tried to escape but were captured. In 1792 the monarchy was abolished, and in 1793 Louis was executed by **guillotine.**

Louisiana Purchase (1803)
Sale of the vast Louisiana province by France to the United States. France had held this territory, ranging from the Mississippi River to the Rocky Mountains and from the Gulf of Mexico to Canada, until 1763, when at the **Treaty of Paris** it was given to Spain. In 1800 France regained Louisiana, but **Napoléon Bonaparte** realized that he could not control it against an antagonistic United States and a naval blockade from Britain, with which France was at war. Louisiana was therefore worthless to France and valuable to America. France sold it to the United States for $15 million. In 1804 President **Thomas Jefferson** sent the **Lewis and Clark expedition** to explore the new territory.

Louis-Philippe (1773–1850)
King of France (1830–1848). Eldest son of the Duke of Orléans, at the outbreak of the **French Revolution** father and son took the surname of Égalité ("Equality") and renounced their titles and estates. After the restoration of the French monarchy, Louis-Philippe recovered his estates and was elected king (called the "Citizen King") in the wake of the 1830 revolution. By the revolution of 1848 his support had disappeared under pressure for greater reforms, and he abdicated the throne and escaped to England.

Loyola, Ignatius, Saint (1491–1556)
Founder of the **Society of Jesus** (Jesuits) and prominent **Catholic Reformation** leader. Originally a soldier, while recuperating from an injury Loyola experienced a revelation. He used his military training to live a regimented life committed to God.

Loyola wrote *The Spiritual Exercises* and as others followed he founded the Society of Jesus in 1540, committed to poverty, chastity, and obedience to the **pope**. The Jesuits became a powerful tool of the **Roman Catholic Church** and of the **papacy** in the fight against the **Protestants** in the **Reformation**. The Jesuits were effective in reconverting Protestants in Europe to Catholicism and in spreading Catholicism to Asia and Latin America.

Luddites

Movement of workers during the English **Industrial Revolution** who opposed the increasingly mechanized workplace. Workers led by Nedd Ludd broke stocking-frame machines in Nottingham in 1811 in hopes of saving manual jobs. This effort spread to other workers throughout England, who smashed machinery when wages were cut or as a means to demand a raise. Luddites comprised only a small minority of workers.

Luftwaffe

German air force established in 1935 in contravention of the **Versailles Treaty**. **Hermann Goering** headed the Luftwaffe and built it into a formidable war machine in **World War II**. However, in the **Battle of Britain** the Luftwaffe failed to overpower the British air corps and gain control of the English Channel for a German invasion. Germany's modern air force, also called the Luftwaffe, was reestablished in 1956.

Lumumba, Patrice (1925–1961)

Congolese political leader and first prime minister of independent **Zaïre** (1960–1961). Lumumba worked his way up through Belgian Congo society. He founded the Congolese National Movement, with Pan-African interests, and became an important leader in the independence movement.

His party won a sweeping victory in 1960 elections and was made prime minister. He worked with **Kwame Nkrumah** attempting to form a union of Ghana and Zaïre. Under enormous pressure from revolts, army mutinies, Belgium, and Belgian and **United Nations** intervention, Lumumba was arrested and murdered in 1961.

Luther, Martin (1483–1546)

German priest, monk, and university professor who challenged the contemporary views of the **Roman Catholic Church** on salvation. He argued that "justification [salvation] was by faith alone," meaning that humans did not have control over their own salvation, therefore all they could do was to believe. In 1517 Luther wrote **Ninety-five Theses**, or complaints against the Catholic Church, and sent them to the archbishop of Mainz, a powerful church official. The story later developed that he also posted them on the cathedral door at Wittenberg, though many historians now doubt that this happened. When ordered to recant some of his positions he refused and was excommunicated; when others followed him, the **Reformation** was under way. His movement stated that priests were not a special caste of humans, but that there was a "priesthood of all believers." He also put the church service in the vernacular (local language), allowed priests to marry, and tried to move religion to the purity of the early Christian church.

Lutheranism

Christian denomination established by **Martin Luther**. Luther intended only to reform Catholicism, but when he was excommunicated for his views others followed him. Lutheranism maintained an episcopal structure and allowed churches to reform at their own pace. It upholds the priesthood of all believers, the primacy of the **New Testament**, and the importance of all Christians reading the **Bible**. Lutheranism believes in consubstantiation—that the bread and wine of communion become the body and blood of Christ and at the same time are bread and wine. Lutheranism became widespread in parts of Germany as well as Scandinavia.

Lu Xun (1881–1936)

Pseudonym for Zhou Shuren, a writer and a founder of modern Chinese literature. Lu, trained as doctor, became one of China's most revered writers, whose short stories and other works presented sharp social criticism of China. He later became associated with the **Chinese Communist Party**.

Lycurgus

Quasi-historical figure from ancient **Sparta** who purportedly wrote a legal code known as the Lycurgus Constitution. The code of law was actually developed over a long period of time rather than by one individual, but the main framework probably dates from the seventh century B.C.E. It was the basis of Spartan law.

Maathai, Wangari (1940–)
Kenyan environmentalist, activist, and winner of the **Nobel Prize** for Peace in 2004. The first east African woman to hold a Ph.D. and the first African woman to win the Nobel Peace Prize, Maathai founded the Green Belt movement in Kenya in 1977, which has planted more than 10 million trees to prevent soil erosion, provide wildlife habitat, and provide firewood for cooking. Women planted most of them. In 2002 Maathai was elected to **Parliament** and accepted a position as visiting fellow at Yale University, and in 2003 she was appointed deputy minister of Environment and Natural Resources in Kenya. She continues to work for environmental and women's causes in Africa.

MacArthur, Douglas (1880–1964)
Controversial U.S. army general. When MacArthur retired from the army in 1937 he was one of America's best-known soldiers. He graduated at the top of his military academy class at West Point in 1903, served with distinction in France in **World War I**, and was chief of staff (the army's senior leadership position) during the **Hoover** and early **Roosevelt** administrations. In 1935 he became a military adviser to the Philippines. He retired but was recalled to active duty in 1941 and commanded Filipino and American forces in the unsuccessful defense of the Philippines during the early months of **World War II**. MacArthur escaped to Australia in 1942 and began the reconquest of Japanese-held islands in the southwest Pacific. He returned to the Philippines in October 1944. MacArthur's success in the Pacific led him to the post of military governor of a defeated Japan. He has been given high marks for his oversight of Japan's postwar democratization and demilitarization. North Korea's invasion of South Korea in 1950 caught MacArthur by surprise, but he responded with a daring counterattack at Inchon that sent the northern, communist forces reeling north. MacArthur disagreed with **Harry S Truman**'s decision to limit the war in Korea and was determined to defeat the communists, even if that meant carrying the war into China. MacArthur undermined the administration's attempts to achieve a cease-fire and publicly disparaged the president's policies. Truman ordered MacArthur relieved of command in 1951. MacArthur returned to the United States to a tumultuous public reception and declared that in war "there is no substitute for victory." MacArthur was considered as a Republican candidate for president but was too controversial and polarizing. He spent most of his remaining years in obscurity.

Machel, Graça (1946–)
Mozambican statesman and world-renowned spokesperson for children's and women's rights. The widow of the founding president of Mozambique, Samora Machel, who died mysteriously in a plane crash in 1986, Graça Machel became minister of Education and Culture

in Mozambique in 1975. She has campaigned for children's and women's rights and education and served in related positions for the United Nations. She has received numerous awards for her work. In 1998 Machel married South African president **Nelson Mandela**. She continues her work in Mozambique and for the **United Nations**.

Machiavelli, Niccolò (1469–1527)
Italian Renaissance humanist, political writer, and author of *The Prince* (1513). Machiavelli, of **Florence**, was one of the most influential authors of western political theory. In *The Prince* Machiavelli explored issues of morality in the politics of the Italian **city-state**, including the ideas that the end result of a political action justifies the means, and that it is not realistic to expect politicians to act based on moral principles when trying to maintain their authority. Machiavelli also published *The Art of War* (1520) and *Discourses on the First Ten Books of Livy* (1518), an example of how the **humanists** were interested in classical sources. Many of his ideas were formed during his political career as a diplomat of the Florentine Republic.

Machu Picchu
Inca city in the Andes Mountains of Peru. Machu Picchu was built on a flattened mountaintop with terraces, **aqueducts**, and suspension bridges. The most important temple at Machu Picchu was the Hitching Post of the Sun, built to be near the sun god, where priests tried to "tie" the sun to a stone to keep it from disappearing. Temples to the sun god were often covered in gold to reflect the sunlight. Impressive ruins remain.

Madero, Francisco (1873–1913)
Apostle of the **Mexican Revolution**, statesman, and president of Mexico (1911–1913). Madero led the Mexican Revolution in 1910 and overthrew dictator Porfirio Díaz. Madero was elected president in 1911 and ruled for two years until he was deposed by an insurrection and murdered two days later.

Madison, James (1751–1836)
Delegate to the **Continental Congress** during the **American Revolution**, major contributor to the **United States Constitution** (known as the "Father of the Constitution"), and fourth U.S. president. Madison's proposal of a three-branch government (an executive branch, a bicameral legislative branch with state representation based on population, and a judicial branch) was, for the most part, adopted into constitutional law. His political alliance with **Thomas Jefferson** brought about the Republican Party, with an emphasis on strong central government. Although his difficulties as president during the War of 1812 cost him popularity, he remained a successful politician and retired peacefully to his home, Montpelier, in Virginia.

Madras (Chennai)
Capital and largest city in the southern Indian state of Tamil Nadu. It was a fishing village until the British **East India Company** established a factory and fortress there in 1639. It grew into an important commercial and administrative center. In the 1990s the city's name was officially changed to Chennai.

Magellan, Ferdinand (b. c. 1480–1521)
Portuguese explorer for Spain. Born to a minor noble family and raised in the household of King John II of Portugal, he participated in trips to India for Portugal and moved to Spain, where he was fitted with five ships and 250 crew. Magellan set sail September 20, 1519, and reached the

South American coast in December. Bad weather, disease, and crew revolts slowed the progress, but after sailing through the strait that would come to be called the **Strait of Magellan**, the remnants of the fleet were the first to sail westward all the way to East Asia. En route the crew endured by eating rats and leather. In April 1521 Magellan was killed by an island tribe. The mission command was taken over by Juan Sebastián de Elcano, who brought the flagship *Victoria* back to Spain in September 1522 with only eighteen survivors aboard but who was thus the first sailor to circumnavigate the globe. This proved that the entire world could be sailed in any direction.

Magistrate (China)

Chinese official heading a local unit of government. From at least **Tang** dynasty times the Chinese countryside was governed by the local magistrate, a civil servant who possessed administrative, police, and judicial powers. By late imperial times most owed their position to success in highly competitive **civil service examinations**, giving them great prestige. By mid **Qing** times the country magistrate administered, on average, about 250,000 people. Although magistrates were aided by a staff of clerks and the informal assistance of local gentry, the fact that China ruled so many people with so few officials has been viewed as a remarkable achievement.

Magistrate (Rome)

Roman official. From the formation of the **Roman Republic**, the government was run by magistrates. There were thirty-one magistrates, elected annually by all citizens. Their role was to keep the peace, collect taxes, and administer the law. Selected from the magistrates were quaestors, **praetors**, and eventually **consuls**—all considered magistrates. Their numbers increased over time as the republic and, later, the empire expanded.

Magna Carta (Latin for "Great Charter") (1215)

Document forced upon King **John I** of England in 1215 by his barons. It was signed on the island of Runnymeade in the Thames River outside London. Often seen as an early document of human or civil rights, it was originally written to force the king to abide by ancient rights of the nobility and therefore was more traditional than innovative. However, it was one of the first documents limiting the power of the monarchy and providing for courts and protections of a free citizenry, the church, and the merchant class. Over time it came to be seen as the origin of the English **Parliament**, court structure, and legal protections of the common person.

Magyars

People who settled in the Hungarian plain, known today as Hungarians. The Magyars are a Finno-Ugric-speaking people. Migrating from western Siberia in the fifth century C.E., they moved to the region north of the Caspian Sea and then westward through Ukraine and by the ninth century into Hungary. In the ninth and tenth centuries the Magyars were feared throughout eastern Europe and the **Byzantine Empire**. In 1000 the **pope** crowned Stephen as the first king of Magyars. He introduced Christianity. Surrounded by **Slavs**, Germans, and Romanians, the Magyars have maintained a strong ethnic and cultural sensibility with indigenous art, music, and literature.

Mahabharata

Along with the **Ramayana** one of the two great **Sanskrit** epics of India and, with 100,000 couplets, one of the world's longest. Its central narrative relates the struggle for power between two groups of cousins, the Kauravas and the Pandavas. The *Mahabharata* is important for establishing much of the mythology of **Hinduism**. One section of the epic, the ***Bhagavad Gita***, stands on its own as one of the most important works in the Hindu tradition explicating the nature of dharma (duty). Although set in very ancient times, it was probably completed in its present form about 400 C.E.

Maharaja

Term meaning "great ruler," used in India by Hindu kings and princes from the early centuries C.E. Originally referring to great kings and lords, it became commonly used by petty princes. The feminine form is maharani.

Mahavira (c. 540–468 B.C.E.)

Sanskrit title meaning "Great Hero," used for Vardhamana, an important teacher in the Jain religious tradition. An older contemporary of **Siddhartha Gautama**, the **Buddha**, he is considered in **Jainism** to have been the last of the twenty-four Tirthankaras ("Ford-Makers"), saints who developed the faith. Mahavira's teachings emphasize the need for asceticism and the practice of ahimsa, or non-injury to living things, and had great influence on Indian thought.

Mahayana Buddhism

Form of **Buddhism** meaning "the Greater Vehicle" to distinguish itself from **Theravada Buddhism**, "the Lesser Vehicle." It was formulated in northern India between the third century B.C.E. and the first century C.E. It differs from Theravada Buddhism (also called Hinayana Buddhism) in that it supplements the Pali-language canon with texts written in **Sanskrit**, most notably the *Lotus Sutra*. Central to its beliefs are the concept of the **bodhisattva**, the enlightened being who remains on earth to assist his or her fellows to achieve salvation. Mahayana Buddhism developed into many different sects, often focusing on a particular sutra (sacred text). It spread to **Central Asia** and to China, Korea, Japan, and Vietnam, becoming the principal form of Buddhism practiced in the latter lands.

Mahdist Revolution (1882–1885)

Sudanese revolt and creation of a Mahdist state (1885–1898). Muhammad Ahmad of Dongola, a Sudanese religious leader, proclaimed himself Mahdi ("Divinely Guided One") and led a **jihad** against the Egyptian colonial government. After a number of victories the Mahdists took the capital, Khartoum. Five months later the Mahdi died and was succeeded by a khalifa ("successor"). The Mahdist state survived revolts, war with Ethiopia, and famine only to be reconquered by the British in 1898 and see the khalifa killed in 1899. The Mahdist movement, however, has survived as a political party in Sudan, headed by the great-grandson of the Mahdi.

Mahmud of Ghazni (969–1030)

Muslim ruler of the Ghaznavid dynasty, which controlled Afghanistan and parts of Turkestan. Mahmud is most famous for the seventeen raids, by mostly Turkic forces, he led into India that in the name of **Islam** that looted and destroyed many **Hindu** and **Jain** temples.

Majapahit

Empire based in Java that flourished from 1293 to the later fifteenth century. At its peak under Hayam Waruk (1350–1389), it exercised some control—or at least influence—over much of the **Malay Peninsula**, Sumatra, Borneo, Sulawesi, Bali, and other islands. Majapahit's rulers were **Hindus**. Its greatness is extolled in the epic poem *Nagarakertagama* (1365).

Although its direct control was limited primarily to Java, some later Indonesian nationalist saw Majapahit as a precursor of the modern Indonesia.

Maji Maji (1905–1907)

Rebellion in German East Africa. Twenty or more small ethnic groups in southeastern Tanganyika (present-day Tanzania) rebelled against German colonialism, taxation, and enforced cotton agriculture. Because of the tribal or ethnic differences there a united front was never organized against the Germans. German reprisals, however, spread the rebellion. By 1907 it was quashed. The Maji Maji rebellion has become a part of Tanzanian memory, exemplifying the common people united.

Malacca

Malayan port along the Strait of Malacca that links the Indian and Pacific oceans. It was founded in 1402 by a Hindu prince from **Srivijaya** who converted to **Islam** and ruled as Iskandar Shah. Malacca became an important trading port for the medieval **spice trade** and was a center for the spread of Islam throughout the region until its capture by the Portuguese in 1511. Its importance as a trading center declined after it passed to Dutch control in 1641.

Malay Peninsula

Long peninsula extending southeasterly 700 miles (about 1,100 km) from the Asian mainland to Cape Balai, the southernmost point in Asia. It is also known as the Kra Peninsula, after the narrow isthmus located in Thailand. Historically, the Malay Peninsula has been a crossroads for trade between the Pacific and Indian oceans. A number of ports along the peninsula such as **Malacca** and, more recently, **Singapore** have been of strategic and economic importance. Today the peninsula is divided between Thailand and Malaysia.

Mali

Kingdom of the western Sudan region of Africa founded in the thirteenth century, also known as the Mandinka empire. Established by Sundjata Keïta (c. 1205–1255), it became the dominant empire in western Africa after the decline of the empire of **Ghana** and was the largest African empire in the **Middle Ages** and one of the greatest empires in precolonial Africa. The kingdom of Mali was built on gold, which was sent to the north across the **trans-Saharan trade** routes. The emperor **Mansa Musa** brought the kingdom to its greatest heights, controlling an area more than 1,200 miles (1,900 km) wide. He was renowned for his pilgrimage to **Mecca** in 1324, when the great wealth he spread had an unsettling effect on the economy of **Cairo** as he passed through. The Mali city of **Timbuktu** was an important intellectual and commercial center. By the mid-fourteenth century Mali became the target of military campaigns by groups around it, weakened, and was replaced by the **Songhay** empire in the fifteenth century.

Mamallapuram

Town (also called Mahabalipuram) in the southern Indian state of Tamil Nadu that served as a religious center for the **Pallava** dynasty in the seventh and eighth centuries. Its many surviving temples and monuments preserve the rich artistic and architectural tradition of medieval southern India.

Mameluke. *See* Mamluk (Mameluke)

Mamluk (Mameluke)

Slave soldiers in **Muslim** armies, and the name of two Egyptian dynasties. From the ninth century, Islamic armies trained special units of soldiers made up of boys captured in war and often used them to guard the sultan. In the thirteenth and fourteenth centuries, the Mamluks usurped power in Egypt and over much of the **Middle East** as a special ruling class. They were highly organized with a civil service and extensive international trade. In 1517 the Turks overthrew the Mamluks, but they regained power in the eighteenth century only to be defeated by **Napoléon Bonaparte**. The Mamluk dynasty was finally abolished in 1811.

Manchuria

Area of northeastern China north of Korea, roughly stretching from the Yellow Sea to the Amur River along the Russian border. A transition zone between the humid, agriculturally rich lands of East Asia and the **Central Asian steppe**, historically it has been the home of militarily formidable Central Asian peoples such as the **Khitans**, the **Jurchens**, and the **Manchus**. When the Manchus conquered China and established the **Qing** dynasty, Manchuria became a part of China. In the nineteenth century a huge migration of Chinese into the relatively sparsely populated region began, and by the twentieth century Manchuria was becoming an integral part of China. Attracted by its agricultural and mineral riches, Japan occupied the region, which it ruled through the puppet Manchukuo state from 1931 to 1945.

Manchus

People from northeast Asia who conquered China in the seventeenth century and established the **Qing** dynasty (1644–1911). The Manchus were of the same ethnic origins as the **Jurchens**, who had established the Jin state in northern China. They were united by Nurhachi (1559–1626), who took the title emperor in 1616. His son Abahai adapted the name *Qing* ("Pure") for his dynasty. The Manchus, despite their subsistence lifestyle, had adopted much of Chinese culture before their conquest of China. During their rule of China they sought to maintain their separate identity, but despite their efforts the Manchus gradually assimilated into Chinese culture.

Mandela, Nelson (1918–)

Antiapartheid leader and president of South Africa (1994–1999). He studied law, joined the **African National Congress (ANC)**, and founded the ANC Youth League. When the Afrikaner National Party came to power in 1948 it institutionalized racism and apartheid, and Mandela and the ANC began vigorous action against the government. In 1959 the ANC was outlawed. After peaceful demonstrators were massacred by the government in 1960, Mandela came to believe that violent action was necessary to break the government. In 1964 he was sentenced to life imprisonment. The struggle against apartheid grew in the 1970s and 1980s, and in 1988 the government began negotiating with Mandela. Afrikaner president F. W. de Klerk unbanned the ANC and released Mandela in 1990. De Klerk and Mandela shared the **Nobel Prize** for Peace in 1993. In 1994 the first democratic elections were held, and Mandela was elected president of South Africa. In 1999 he retired from public life.

Manichaeism

Religious belief developed by Mani (d. c. 276) that the universe is composed of two contending forces: good (light, spirit) and evil (darkness, material). Mani, a Persian, drew from his study of **Buddhism, Zoroastrianism**, and **Christianity**. He believed that the object of humankind is to release the light, stolen by Satan, that exists in each human. This can be accomplished by following a course of asceticism. Manichaeism was strong during the third century, became the official religion of the ninth-century Uighur state, and declined with the growth of Christianity. Elements of it were still prominent in groups such as the Cathari and the Albigenses in the twelfth and thirteenth centuries and survived in southeastern China into the seventeenth century. **Marco Polo** mistook Manichaeans for Christians.

Manila Galleon

A type of Spanish ship that sailed annually from Acapulco, Mexico, to Manila, in the Philippines. From 1573 to 1815 the Manila Galleons were the chief link between the Spanish colony in the Philippines and Spain. They provided basic goods for the Spanish community in the Philippines and large quantities of Mexican silver that was traded for Chinese goods. Until the eighteenth century, when Britain and other Western countries began to trade directly with China, the vessels were an important source of the silver used in East Asia for currency and stimulated trade throughout the region.

Manioc

Plant (also known as cassava) native to tropical areas of the Americas. Its leaves and shoots can be eaten, but its roots are a major source of carbohydrates. It produces large amounts of food, even in poor soil. With the discovery of the Americas, manioc was taken to Africa, where it has become a staple food in parts of central Africa. It is eaten in North America mainly as tapioca.

Mannerism

Style in art in the period between the **High Renaissance** and the **baroque**. Mannerism flourished from 1520 to 1600 with aesthetic ideals of grace, refinement, elegance, and sometimes bizarre exaggerations. Among the most famous artists of mannerism are Pontormo (1494–1556), Parmigianino (1503–1540), Bronzino (1503–1572), Tintoretto (1518–1594), and El Greco (1541–1614). Parmigianino's *The Madonna with the Long Neck* (c. 1535) and Bronzino's *Allegory of Venus* (c. 1546) are excellent examples of mannerism.

Manorialism

Medieval economic institution that integrated with the political-military structure known as **feudalism**. In return for a vassal's commitment to fight for a lord, the vassal was usually granted a **fief**, or land. This land was held by the lord and rented out to peasants (**serfs**, when bound in manorialism) who worked it, paying both in kind (goods produced) and in work (obligations to cultivate the lord's portions of land on the manor). Each manor was a nearly complete economic unit producing most of the food and goods required by its occupants. Land in manorialism was worked as large common fields divided into strips cultivated by each serf family in two-field or three-field **crop rotation**.

Mansa Musa (r. c. 1312–1337)

Emperor of ancient **Mali**. The kingdom of Mali reached its greatest extent under Mansa Musa, but his reign is known for the fact that he made a pilgrimage to **Mecca** in 1324. When he reached Cairo that year he dazzled its inhabitants with his enormous retinue, numbering more than 10,000, and by his gifts of gold. According to tradition his visit to Cairo created economic inflation by the influx of gold. He returned to Mali with an Arab architect, who designed numerous buildings in **Gao** and **Timbuktu**. A patron of learning and the arts, Mansa Musa built libraries and gathered scholars and poets.

Manumission

Term for freeing a person from slavery. The laws and practices regarding manumission were as varied as those governing slavery. In many societies slavery was a punishment for crime or the result of capture in war, and in many of them the children of slaves received manumission. In other societies slavery was strictly hereditary, and manumission was difficult or impossible. Slaves in many societies could buy their freedom. Some religions, such as **Islam**, recommended but did not require manumission of the descendants of slaves. In the American South manumission was difficult: South Carolina, Mississippi, Maryland, Alabama, and Arkansas passed laws in the nineteenth century prohibiting it. In the century after the **French Revolution** (1789–1815) most nations manumitted all slaves.

Maoism

Political ideology based on the theories and practices of **Mao Zedong**. Based on Marxism-Leninism, Maoism differed in seeing peasants as well as urban workers as a revolutionary class. Maoism also emphasized military strategy through **guerrilla** tactics, living off the land with the support of the rural population, and economic and social development by mass mobilization of the population, substituting revolutionary zeal and physical labor for technology when necessary. It also called for a continuous struggle against capitalist forces from without and capitalist tendencies from within. Although largely discredited in China after Mao's death in 1976, Maoist-inspired insurgencies continue today in several countries, including Peru and Nepal.

Maori Wars (1843–1847, 1860–1872)

Wars by the Maori people of New Zealand in an attempt to stop the occupation of New Zealand by British settlers. Demands for land by settlers forced the Maori into armed resistance, but modern weapons and the continuous flow of new settlers wore them down, and the Maori were driven to North Island. A peace treaty was reached in 1881.

Mao Zedong (Mao Tse-tung) (1893–1976)

Chinese revolutionary and communist leader who established the **People's Republic of China** in 1949. Mao Zedong came from a peasant family in Hunan province in central China, moved to **Beijing**, and became a founding member of the **Chinese Communist Party** (CCP) in 1921. He quarreled with the communist leadership by emphasizing a peasant-led communist movement instead of one that relied on urban workers. During the **Long March** of 1934–1935, when the Chinese communists were forced to flee to Yenan in the remote northwest, he was elected chairman of the party. He turned the CCP into a peasant-based mass movement and defeated the **Guomindang** (Nationalist Party). From 1949 to his death he ruled China as a dictator, developing a personality cult and placing emphasis on revolutionary zeal rather than technical expertise in transforming China. He remained hostile to Western countries and, after 1960, to the Soviet Union as well. His two attempts to return to the revolutionary ideals of the years prior to coming to power, the **Great Leap Forward** (1958–1962) and the **Great Proletarian Cultural Revolution** (1966–1976) plunged the country into turmoil and resulted in the death of millions, mainly from starvation. After his death Mao's policies were modified by his successors, who turned to international investment, trade, technical training, and private ownership of farms and industries. The ruling CCP continues to revere Mao as the state founder and as a great revolutionary while criticizing his personality cult and economic policies.

Maratha Wars (1774–1782, 1803–1805, 1817–1818)

Three wars between the Marathas of India and the troops of the British **East India Company**. In the eighteenth century the Marathas were a confederacy of Maratha-speaking warriors of the **Deccan plateau** of **Hindu** religious background who fought the **Mughals** and established control over parts of central and northern India. Their attempt to revive a great Hindu empire in India suffered a setback when they were defeated by Afghans at the battle of Panipat in 1761. They remained an important power until they were subdued by the British. In the second war the British army was led by Sir Arthur Wellesley (later Duke of Wellington). The wars made Britain the dominant power in the Indian subcontinent by 1818.

Marathon, Battle of (490 B.C.E.)

Greek battle against the Persian army under King **Darius** I. Darius ordered his generals to enslave the Athenians. The Persians landed at Marathon, in Greece, but the Athenians rushed to Marathon and held a narrow mountain pass, pinning the Persians. The Persians lost the confrontation even though they greatly outnumbered the Greeks. An Athenian courier, Pheidippides, ran 26 miles and 385 yards to warn **Athens**. The loss enraged the Persians further and set up their return in 480 B.C.E.

Marconi, Guglielmo (1874–1937)

Italian inventor of the wireless telegraph. Others had experimented with the idea of transmitting electrical signals, but Marconi was the first to devise the practical means of doing so. In 1896 he took out a patent in England for a wireless telegraphy machine. In 1901 he was the first to trans-

mit and receive signals across the Atlantic Ocean. Marconi invented other devices and was awarded the **Nobel Prize** for Physics in 1909.

Marco Polo. *See* Polo, Marco

Marcos, Ferdinand (1917–1989)

Philippines president (1965–1986). Entering the Philippine Congress in 1949, he became Senate leader in 1963 and was elected president of the Philippines in 1965. Initially a reformer, he ruled in an increasingly dictatorial style, declaring martial law in 1972. Although he lifted marital law in 1981, he continued to act ruthlessly. After the assassination of opposition leader Benigno S. Aquino Jr. in 1983, opposition to Marcos intensified, and he was forced into exile in Hawaii after a popularly supported military revolt took place in 1986. Ferdinand Marcos and his former beauty-queen wife, Imelda, left behind a legacy of corruption and abuse of power that damaged the Philippines' reputation for democratic government.

Maria Theresa (1717–1780)

Archduchess of Austria and queen of Hungary and Bohemia (1740–1780), wife and empress of **Holy Roman Emperor Francis I**, and mother of Holy Roman Emperor **Joseph II**. Although a very capable ruler, her accession as archduchess and queen led to the War of the Austrian Succession (1740–1748), followed by the **Seven Years' War** (1756–1763) and the War of the Bavarian Succession (1778–1779). These wars reduced Austria's power and influence, affecting its performance later, in the **Napoleonic Wars**.

Mark Antony. *See* Antony, Mark

Marrakech (Marrakesh)

Moroccan city founded in the ninth century that was a major commercial center at the northern end of the **trans-Saharan trade** routes in premodern Africa and is a large city in modern Morocco. Marrakech was renowned for its grand red-sandstone architecture, including the Great Gate at Marrakech. Goods such as gold and ivory from the south, particularly **Ghana** and **Mali**, made its way to the Mediterranean shore overland through Marrakech via camel caravans.

Marshall Plan (1948–1951)
U.S.-sponsored economic plan to aid Europe in its recovery after **World War II**, named for George C. Marshall, U.S. Secretary of State (1947–1949). Originally termed the European Economic Recovery Plan, the Marshall plan was proposed in 1947 by Marshall and implemented in 1948 to restore political, economic, and social stability to seventeen European nations. With it, the United States hoped to create an environment in which democracy could survive.

Martel, Charles (714–741)
Carolingian mayor of Francia (eastern France and western Germany), military leader, and grandfather of **Charlemagne**. Charles Martel ("Charles the Hammer") was renowned for his victory in 732 over the **Muslims** at the **Battle of Tours**, where a Frankish army routed the Muslim army and drove the Muslims out of France across the Pyrenees.

Martin V
Pope (1417–1431) elected by the Council of Constance, ending the **Great Schism**. After the division between French and Italian cardinals resulted in the election of two and three popes (1378–1417), the Council of Constance (1414–1418) accepted the resignation of one, deposed the other two, and elected Martin V as pope, healing the divisions that had damaged the **Roman Catholic Church**.

Marx, Karl (1818–1883)
German political and economic theorist and coauthor of *The Communist Manifesto* (1848). Marx and Friedrich Engels (1820–1895) wrote the *Manifesto* as a party program for the Communist League, a European workers' organization. Marx became the founder of modern communism. He lived in England from 1849, where he wrote *Das Kapital* in three volumes (1867, 1885, 1894), the latter two completed by Engels.

Marxism
Political and economic theory espoused by **Karl Marx** (1818–1883) and Friedrich Engels (1820–1895). Marx and Engels wrote *The Communist Manifesto* (1848) as a theoretical and practical party program for the Communist League, a workers' organization in Europe. Marxism claims that all of history can be explained by a theory of clashes of economic classes in a dialectical structure (that a thesis comes into conflict with an antithesis, out of which arises a synthesis that become the new thesis). Ultimately, there would be just two classes—the bourgeoisie and the proletariat. The clash between these two would be a revolution that would result in a classless society where property was owned by all—**communism**. Marxism called for this revolution by encouraging workers (the proletariat) to rise up against the owners of capitalist industry (the bourgeoisie).

Mary, Queen of Scots (1542–1587)
Queen of Scotland and heir to the English throne as granddaughter of **Henry VIII**'s sister Margaret. Mary was betrothed to the future Edward VI of England, but the marriage was blocked and she married the heir to the French throne, Francis. She was the daughter of James V of Scotland and the mother of the future **James I and VI**.

Mary was constantly involved in intrigues, marriages, and affairs, and **Elizabeth I** of England had her confined and then executed because of Mary's involvement in Catholic conspiracies against Elizabeth.

Mary, Virgin. *See* Virgin Mary

Mary I (1516–1558)
Queen of England and Ireland (1553–1558). Mary was the eldest daughter of **Henry VIII** with his first wife, **Catherine of Aragon**. Mary became queen after her younger half brother, Edward VI, died. She was a devout Catholic (Edward was a devout **Protestant**) who married the future **Philip II** of Spain (1554) and tried to return England to Catholicism. Philip left her to return to Spain after only one year, and Mary remained childless, but her connections with Philip and Spain turned many English against her. Between 1555 and 1558 nearly 300 Protestants were executed, hence her sobriquet Bloody Mary.

Masaccio (1401–1428)
Italian early **Renaissance** painter. Tommaso di Giovanni di Simone Guidi (known most commonly as Masaccio) was one of the first artists to apply rules of three-dimensional perspective and classical naturalism to his painting, as seen in his *Holy Trinity with the Virgin, St. John, and Two Donors* (1425). Masaccio died at age twenty-seven.

Masada
Ancient fortress in southeastern Israel, site of the last holdout of the Jews (71–73 C.E.) after the destruction of **Jerusalem** by **Rome** in 70 C.E. The fortress was built by Herod the Great and originally contained palaces as well as military fortifications. Masada was accessed by a single well-defended entrance, but the Romans constructed a second route up the cliffs.

Ending the Jewish-Roman struggle, the Jews ultimately opted to kill one another rather than be subjected to torture and butchery by the Romans.

Mass
Term for the entire service in the **Roman Catholic** and High Anglican churches. The word *mass* originally referred to the Eucharist, or Lord's Supper, in the service and came from a word at the end of the service to "dismiss." Since the fourth century *mass* has referred to the entire service in churches where the priest participates in the sacrifice of the body and blood of Christ—transubstantiation.

Massachusetts Bay Colony
English Puritan religious settlement founded in 1630 under Governor John Winthrop. King **Charles I** chartered the group of about 1,000 as the Massachusetts Bay Company in 1629. The settlement, one of the original permanent colonies in Massachusetts, merged in 1691 with Plymouth Colony due to a growing severance between the colony and England. The settlers created a theocratic government that only allowed church members to vote. The colony was allowed to settle and trade between the Charles and Merrimack rivers in New England, and Puritan stockholders were allowed to control the colony in America instead of England.

Mau Mau
Term for both a **guerrilla** group and an uprising in Kenya in the 1950s. The Mau Mau uprising (1952–1956) was an anticolonial, mainly agrarian, guerrilla movement against British control of Kenya. The term *Mau Mau* was used by the British and not by the freedom fighters themselves, who went under various titles. The British accused the Mau Mau of being communists, but they did not advocate

communism or socialism. Between 1952 and 1956 at least 12,000 Africans were killed, but Kenya became independent nonetheless in 1963.

Maurya Empire (c. 325–185 B.C.E.)
First Indian empire to rule over most of the Indian subcontinent. It was founded by **Chandragupta Maurya** (r. c. 325–297), who overthrew the Magadha kingdom of northeastern India. The empire reached its peak under **Ashoka** (c. 265–238), who renounced militarism and promoted **Buddhism**. Much of our knowledge of the empire comes from the account of **Megasthenes**, a Greek envoy to Chandragupta's court, and from inscriptions on pillars erected throughout the empire by Ashoka. The empire was important in creating a legacy of political unity in India and in helping to establish Buddhism as a major religion.

Maxwell, James (1831–1879)
Scottish physicist renowned for his electromagnetic theory. Maxwell is considered one of the most important physicists of all time and strongly influenced twentieth-century physics. His understanding of electromagnetic radiation paved the way for **Albert Einstein**'s Special Theory of Relativity and for quantum theory. Maxwell's ideas are also integral to modern theories of atomic and molecular structure.

Mayan Calendar
Complex dating system of the ancient Mayan civilization. It was the most accurate known calendar system until the Gregorian system of the sixteenth century. The year included 360 days, plus 5 "nameless" days, considered very unlucky and therefore observed by the Maya with sacrifices and fasting. The year was also divided

into a system of months and weeks, beginning on different days and thus adding to the calendar's complexity.

Mayan Civilization (c. 400 B.C.E.–1300 C.E.)
Mesoamerican civilization in the Yucatán Peninsula, Guatemala, and Honduras. The Maya were cultural heirs to the **Olmec** civilization and contemporaries of **Teotihuacán** in central Mexico. The Maya reached their peak in the fourth to eighth centuries C.E. and had a sophisticated writing system and advanced mathematics (in some areas they were ahead of any mathematics in Africa, Asia, or Europe). They cultivated maize, yams, **manioc**, and **cacao**; cacao was used to make a **chocolate** drink for the upper classes. The Maya had numerous urban centers with populations as large as 100,000 people, but Mayan civilization was only centrally administered circa the ninth to eleventh centuries. Their separate kingdoms constantly fought one another. Human sacrifice by decapitation was practiced to appease the gods.

May Fourth Movement
Chinese nationalist movement that began May 4, 1919, in **Beijing** with a student protest against the decision at the **Paris Peace Conference** to give former German possessions in Shandong province to Japan rather than returning them to China. The protest spread to other cities and led to a reexamination of Chinese culture and society and is often considered to be the birth of modern Chinese **nationalism**.

Mazarin, Jules, Cardinal (1602–1661)
French diplomat and minister under Louis XIII and Queen Regent Anne of Austria (mother of **Louis XIV**). A protégé of **Cardinal Richelieu**, Mazarin became first minister to Louis XIII in 1642 and remained in that post after Louis's death.

Blamed for the civil disturbances known as the **Frond**, Mazarin negotiated the **Treaty of Westphalia** (1648).

McAdam, John Loudon (1756–1836)

Scottish inventor of a system of road making known as "macadamizing" or building "macadam roads." Prior to McAdam roads were unimproved paths. He recommended packing crushed stone on them. This made British roads much more effective and cut travel time between destinations dramatically. Later, tar was added to the gravel and the result became known as "tarmac" roads.

McCormick, Cyrus Hall (1809–1884)

American inventor of the mechanical reaper (1831). The reaping machine was able to harvest a quantity of grain from the new open lands of the U.S. prairies that would have taken the work of many laborers. The mechanical reaper was the first major step forward in mechanizing agriculture and the opening of the vast U.S. farmlands.

Mecca

Holy city of **Islam** and birthplace of **Muhammad**. Mecca is located in western Saudi Arabia in a region known as the Hejaz. In pre-Islamic times the town was a commercial center on caravan routes, and it also benefited economically from its cult association. Mecca was the focus of pre-Islamic pagan religion in Arabia because of its shrine, the **Ka'aba**, a massive black cube. Muhammad cleansed the Ka'aba of its pagan idols and made it the center of the Islamic faith. One of the Five Pillars of **Islam** is that Muslims who are able to must make a pilgrimage to Mecca at least once in their lifetime. After the rise of Islam Mecca's significance was as a holy city and pilgrimage destination.

Medici (fourteenth to eighteenth centuries)

Italian family of merchants and bankers who rose to take control of the government in **Florence**. Florence, a republic in the fourteenth century, was dominated by the Medicis in the fifteenth, when they made themselves princes. They continued to be a presence in Italian politics until the eighteenth century, when there were no more Medici male heirs. Most notable in terms of their political influence, patronage of the arts, and ability to consolidate power were Lorenzo the Magnificent (1449–1492) and Cosimo I (1519–1574). The dynasty also produced two popes, Leo X and Clement VII, as well as two queens of France, Catherine de Médicis and Marie de Médicis.

Medieval Era. *See* Middle Ages

Medieval Optimum

Climatic period of warmer weather that reached its optimum 900–1000 C.E. The Medieval Optimum made it possible for some cultures, such as the **Vikings**, to expand and for many European feudal fiefdoms, such as England and France, to coalesce into states. The Medieval Optimum was followed by the **Little Ice Age**.

Medina

City to which **Muhammad** and his supporters retreated in 622, from their persecution in **Mecca**, to form the first **Muslim** community. The city was first known as **Yathrib** and was a political capital of Arabia. After Muhammad began receiving his revelations from God, according to Muslim tradition, he started to preach to the Meccans, but he and his followers were attacked for his criticism of contemporary society. The retreat to Medina, known as the **Hijra**, marks the start of the official calendar of Islam, for it was in Medina that

Muhammad formed the first Muslim community (the **Umma**). Medina is a pilgrimage destination today.

Megasthenes (c. 340–282 B.C.E.)
Greek historian. The **Hellenistic Greek** king Seleucus I sent Megasthenes as ambassador to the court of **Chandragupta Maurya** in India. He traveled through Afghanistan, Pakistan, the **Indus** valley, Tibet, and to the **Ganges River** and reported on his journey and observations of Indian culture and religious practices and the caste system. Megasthenes' history provided the basis of Western knowledge of India, although little of it has survived.

Mehmet II (1432–1481)
Seventh **Ottoman** sultan (1444–1446, 1451–1481). Known as Mehmet the Conqueror largely because of his conquest of **Constantinople**, which he expanded and renamed **Istanbul**. He is remembered for his territorial conquests in southeastern Europe and southwestern Asia and for his construction of palaces, including **Topkapi**, and a compendium of new law codes. With Mehmet's conquest of former **Abbasid** territory, the Ottomans inherited the mantle of **Muslim** world leadership, a global position articulated locally in part via emergent forms of artistic and cultural production, refinement of military institutions, comparatively liberal religious and social policies, and increasing economic vitality.

Meiji Constitution
Constitution of Japan implemented in stages from 1885 to 1889 and replaced by the U.S.-prepared constitution of 1947. Primarily the work of Japanese statesman **Ito Hirobumi**, it was modeled to a large extent on the 1871 constitution of imperial Germany. It combined a European-style peerage, a parliament with a house of peers and a lower house of elected representatives, a cabinet and privy council, and an emperor who held ultimate power. It also made the army and navy accountable directly to the emperor and thus independent of the parliament. The parliament of 1889, created under the constitution, was the first such elected body in Asia. In practice, the system gave ultimate power to a few statesmen close to the emperor, but it proved ineffective in checking adventurism by a somewhat autonomous military and its supporters in the 1930s and was replaced by a more democratic constitution after **World War II**.

Meiji Japan
Period of the Meiji emperor (1868–1912) created by a crisis in 1854, when the U.S. navy forced itself upon Japan, bringing down the **Tokugawa** government, the **bushi**, and the shogunate. In 1867 the emperor died and a new, fifteen-year-old emperor took the name Meiji, which gave the era its name. In 1868 the imperial seat was moved to a new capital at Tokyo (formerly **Edo**) from the old capital of **Kyoto**, and a new government was formed that moved Japan rapidly into the nineteenth-century world of **industrialization** with a modern military. This revolution changed the whole shape and direction of Japanese society to compete with the modern world. Meiji Japan was a period of brilliance, excitement, an outpouring of creative energies, and enlightenment.
See also Shogun

Meiji Restoration
Term for the revolution that ended the **Tokugawa** shogunate in 1868 and restored rule by imperial authority. Led by mostly younger **bushi** from the western outer **daimyos** of Japan, the Meiji Restoration was a response to the challenge imposed by

Western imperialism to Japanese sovereignty following the "opening" of Japan by **Commodore Matthew Perry** in 1854. The leaders of the new government claimed to be restoring the ancient direct rule by the Japanese emperor, but in reality Mutsuhito, who reigned as the Meiji emperor (1868–1912), was more of a puppet they used to wield their own power and to carry out sweeping reforms of Japanese society. These reforms were aimed at modernizing and westernizing society to establish a "strong military, rich country" that would preserve Japanese independence and catch up with the West. They included inviting Western experts to help create a modern conscript army and a modern navy, carry out land reforms, establish modern industry and banking, and create a Western-inspired constitution with an elected parliament. That the Meiji Restoration largely succeeded in its goals is exemplified by Japan's victory in the **Russo-Japanese War** of 1904–1905, after which Japan was accepted by Western nations as one of the great powers.

Mekong River
Longest river in Southeast Asia, flowing 2,700 miles (4,300 km). It begins in eastern Tibet and forms the border between Burma and Laos and between Laos and Thailand, then flows through Cambodia and Vietnam, emptying into the South China Sea south of Ho Chi Minh City (the former Saigon). The river is navigable for much of its course and drains a large area of Thailand, Laos, Cambodia, and southern Vietnam. It was historically important as a means of transportation and a source of water for irrigation.

Menander (c. 342–291 B.C.E.)
Ancient Greek Athenian comic poet. Educated under Theophrastus, Menander was noted for his refined wit and observation.

He wrote 105 comedies, none of which remains in its entirety.

Mencius (Mengzi) (371–289 B.C.E.)
Chinese philosopher whose book *Mengzi* (*Book of Mencius*) is one of the major works of **Confucianism**. Central to Mencius's teachings is the fundamental goodness and perfectibility of each person. He also helped to establish the idea that the ruler governed with the Mandate of Heaven, that is, with cosmic moral authority, as long as he was moral, but if he failed to govern with benevolence the people had the right to rebel. Their rebellion would be a sign that the ruler had lost the Mandate of Heaven.

Menelik II (1844–1913)
King of Shoa (1865–1889) and emperor of Ethiopia (1889–1913). Menelik expanded the empire, modernized the country, and in 1896 at the Battle of Adwa (Adua) defeated an Italian invasion force. The victory ensured the full sovereignty and independence of Ethiopia. Menelik modernized the country's educational system and much of its infrastructure, such as telephone and railroads, and built the new capital city of Addis Ababa.

Menes
First king of a united Egypt around 3100 B.C.E. Little is known of Menes, but he established the first Egyptian royal dynasty and united Egypt as a kingdom of Upper and Lower Egypt with a crown signifying both.

Menkaure (c. 2552–2504 B.C.E.)
Fifth king of the Fourth Dynasty of the Old Kingdom of ancient Egypt. Menkaure supervised the building of the third and smallest of the **Pyramids of Giza** and was traditionally remembered for being pious and just.

Mennonites

A Christian group, known as **Anabaptists,** that is neither Catholic nor **Protestant.** The Anabaptists first appeared is numerous places around Europe in the 1520s and 1530s during the **Reformation**, and they picked up the name *Mennonite* from Menno Simons (1496–1561), one of their leaders. They believe in following the **New Testament** thoroughly, including adult baptism, separation from the state, and nonviolence. The Mennonites were persecuted for their views on baptism and their democratic ways. There are approximately 1 million Mennonites worldwide in the twenty-first century.

Mercantilism

Economic system of modified capitalism beneficial to the state. In the sixteenth to eighteenth centuries European states encouraged overseas commercial activity in their colonies, especially to gain access to cheap raw materials that could be shipped back to the home country to be manufactured, with the finished product sold back to the colony. The object was to maximize the accumulation of gold or silver in the home country. Mercantilism assumed a finite economy of which each country was anxious to grab as large a piece as possible to gain advantage over other European countries.

Meroë

Capital of the kingdom of **Kush** from the sixth century B.C.E. onward. Originally the Kushite capital was at Napata, but it was moved, historians believe, for defensive purposes and to take advantage of better agriculture and the convergence of several trade routes and the Nile at Meroë. The city developed from indigenous culture but also was influenced by Egyptian culture, including the use of pyramids. It gradually absorbed elements of other cultures such as those of **Hellenistic Greece** and Persia. As the Kushite kingdom declined in the second century C.E., Meroë declined. It was abandoned in the fourth century.

Merovingians

Frankish dynastic family of the fifth to eighth centuries. The Merovingians ruled a region of northeastern France. Named for Mérovée (d. 458), whose grandson Clovis converted to Christianity circa 500. The Merovingians were good warriors but ineffective administrators, and by the seventh century power was held by the "mayors" of the palace. In the eighth century the mayoral family of **Charles Martel** gained virtual control of the dynasty. His son Pépin became king of the Franks in 751 and was the father of **Charlemagne**, whose Carolingian dynasty replaced the Merovingians.

Mesa Verde

National park in Colorado founded to preserve ancient Native American cliff structures. Mesa Verde (Spanish for "green table"), named for the greenery that covers the plateau, is the site of many pueblo ruins. Some of these dwellings, up to thirteen centuries old, were fashioned directly under cliffs. Mesa Verde was originally inhabited by Basket Weavers (about 100–700 C.E.), ancestors of the Pueblo Indians who made it their home from roughly 700 to 1276 C.E., when a severe drought forced them to abandon the location.

Mesoamerica (Greek for "Middle America")

Term referring to Mexico and Central America. Mesoamerica was the region of the Americas first populated with agrarian cultures around 5000 B.C.E. growing maize, beans, pumpkins, squash, chili peppers, and **cacao**; farther south they grew manioc and potatoes. Mesoamerica was the location of numerous fully sedentary peoples with complex **city-states** such as the **Olmecs**, **Maya**, **Toltecs**, and **Aztecs** as well as the people of **Teotihuacán**.

Mesopotamia

Greek term meaning "land between the rivers" given to the area between the **Tigris** and the **Euphrates**. It was one of the cradles of civilization. Between 5000 and 3000 B.C.E. its peoples developed organized systems of agriculture, administration, and urban life; specialized crafts including pottery and metallurgy; and even writing. The civilization of **Sumer** was one of the earliest in Mesopotamia, with the great city of **Ur**. **Akkadian** and **Babylonian** civilizations developed there in the third millennium B.C.E.

Messiah. See Handel, George Frederick

Mestizos

People of mixed race. The term is used in Mexico, Central America, and South America to mean a person of combined European and Native American descent.

Metamorphoses. See Ovid

Methodism

Christian Protestant denomination founded by **John Wesley** (1703–1791) in the eighteenth century. Originally part of the Anglican Church, Methodism stressed personal piety and relationship to God. After Wesley's death the movement split from the Anglicans to form a separate denomination. Growth was dramatic in England, Wales, and the United States in the nineteenth century. Methodism played an important role in the American **abolitionist** movement.

Metternich, Prince of (Klemens Wenzel Nepomuk Lothar Metternich) (1773–1859)

Austrian diplomat. In 1809 he was appointed foreign minister (1809–1848), and he played a prominent role in the **Congress of Vienna** (1814–1815) after the Napoleonic Wars. He was the most influential spokesman for conservatism in Europe in the mid-nineteenth century and worked to suppress liberal and national movements. When the revolution of 1848 overturned his government, he fled to England, although he returned to Austria in 1851.

Mexican Revolution (1910–1920)

Armed overthrow of the Mexican dictatorial regime of Porfirio Díaz and establishment of a liberal democracy. **Francisco Madero** led a movement for democracy, while **Pancho Villa**, a bandit with a reputation of taking from the rich and giving to the poor, began a **guerrilla** war against the government, and **Emiliano Zapata**, leader of an agrarian reform movement to distribute land to the people, also led a peasant army. Together these three brought about a full-scale revolution demanding democracy, land reform, and labor rights for the working class. The United States got involved in trying to influence the revolution and protect oil interests in Mexico. **Venustiano Carranza** called a convention that framed a new constitution in 1917, and Carranza became president. In 1920 Carranza was murdered, Álvaro Obregón assumed the presidency, and stability came to Mexico.

Mfecane (Nguni for "the crushing")

Militant and traditionally based process of state formation of the **Zulus** of South Africa in the early nineteenth century. The Zulus had created a powerful nation by the time Europeans appeared in number in the nineteenth century, and they put up a tremendous struggle against the Europeans. In 1966 John Omer-Cooper published a history outlining the greatness of the Zulu led by **Shaka Zulu**. This revised the study of African history by deemphasizing the importance of Europeans and increasing the importance of native Africans, at a time when many African countries were gaining independence but **apartheid** was growing in South Africa.

Michelangelo (1475–1564)
Primarily a sculptor and also a brilliant painter, architect, and engineer of the **Renaissance**. Michelangelo di Lodovico Buonarroti Simoni was the greatest influence on the High Renaissance and the most famous of all Renaissance artists, known as a solitary genius. Michelangelo's sculpture *Pietà* (1500) established a new height for classical realism infused with emotion, as did his *David* (1501–1504) and *Moses* (1513–1515). His most famous painting was the **Sistine Chapel** ceiling at Saint Peter's Cathedral in Rome, and his most renowned architecture Saint Peter's (1546–1564) itself.

Middle Ages
In Europe, the period from the fall of the **Roman Empire** (approximately 500 C.E.) until around 1500 C.E. Known as the Middle Ages (the Latin term *medieval* means "middle ages"), it was named in the **Renaissance** as the period in the middle, between the "important" eras of the Greeks and Romans and the Renaissance (meaning "rebirth"). The Middle Ages is often divided into early **Middle Ages** (500–1000), High Middle Ages (1000–1300), and late Middle Ages (1300–1500). Institutions of the Middle Ages include **feudalism**, **manorialism**, the **Roman Catholic Church**, **guilds**, **monasteries and convents**, and **universities**. The High Middle Ages was a period of economic growth and cultural vitality that saw the establishment of universities, new cities, and large cathedrals. The late Middle Ages was a period of relative decline, with population loss due to famine and plague, major wars, and peasant revolts.

Middle East
Geopolitical construct first used in print by the American admiral Alfred Thayer Mahan in an essay that appeared in the September 1902 issue of the *National Review*, published in London. The terms *Near East* and *Levant* are European geographical references that predate Middle East. *Middle East* as a term became increasingly more commonplace between the two world wars. The meaning has shifted but always subsumes a variety of cultural and political units and geographic regions, depending on the user's perspective, in any era. Its geographic centrality has made the Middle East a crossroads and source of many innovations in world history. The Middle East is often inappropriately equated with the **Muslim** world as a whole. The most populous Muslim countries are outside the Middle East, while Israel is not Muslim and Turkey has a secular government. Generally agreed boundaries for the region in 2005 are Egypt in the West, Yemen in the South, Iran in the East, and Turkey in the North. The Maghreb (North Africa), as part of the Middle East, is debated by scholars.

Middle Kingdom
Name commonly used by the Chinese for their country (in Chinese, *Zhongguo*). This term, in use since ancient times, implies that China is the country in the center of the world. Because ancient China was not surrounded by other advanced states, the Chinese considered themselves to be the

sole center of higher culture including literacy, higher art and literature, agriculture, and handicrafts, and, most importantly, the Middle Kingdom was the home of the sages who taught people how to live an ethical and civilized life. The peoples surrounding China were considered barbarians lacking proper culture, government, or ethical teachings. The Chinese emperors from at least **Zhou** times (1028–221 B.C.E.) claimed to be not merely the rulers of the Chinese state but the rulers of all civilized humanity, the sole intermediary between heaven and earth. Thus China was in the center—the "middle"—of the world.

Middle Path

Also known as the **Eightfold Path**, one of the basic teachings of **Buddhism**. The Eightfold Path, taught by **Siddhartha Gautama** (the Buddha) and sometimes called the Noble Eightfold Path, requires right belief, right resolve, right speech, right behavior, right livelihood, right effort, right contemplation, and right meditation. Often called the Middle Path because it avoids the extremes of asceticism and luxurious, sensual life and instead teaches moderation and balance.

Milan, Edict of (313)

Law legalizing Christianity in the **Roman Empire**. Emperor Constantine converted Roman policy toward Christians by officially tolerating the religion and according Christian clergy protection and exemptions from public duty. It was not until 391, under Emperor **Theodosius I**, that Christianity became the official religion of Rome.

Milton, John (1608–1674)

English writer and exponent of **Protestantism** and the parliamentary cause in the **English Civil War**. The dominant English writer of the seventeenth century, Milton is best known for his epic poems *Paradise Lost* (1667, 1674) and *Paradise Regained* (1671).

Minamoto Yoritomo (1147–1199)

Japanese military leader, the first to assume the title **shogun**, and founder of the **Kamakura** shogunate (1192–1333). He was a member of the Minamoto family, the principal rival to the Taira family that dominated Japan from 1160. Minamoto Yoritomo's father was killed by the Taira, who removed his family from power. With the help of his brother Minamoto Yoshitsune, who would become a legendary tragic hero in Japanese culture, Yoritomo defeated the Taira, annihilating their forces at Danno-ura in 1185. Yoritomo then killed his brother Yoshitsune and all other possible rivals and assumed complete power that year. He created the title *sei-itai-shogun* ("great barbarian-subduing general"), or shogun, in 1192. This is often considered as the beginning of Japan's feudal period, when military hegemons and their **bushi** followers ruled Japan.

Ming (1368–1644)

Chinese dynasty that saw the expulsion of the **Mongols** from China and an economic and cultural flowering. Founded by peasant-born Zhu Yuanzhang (r. 1368–1398), the Ming maintained some of the practices of their Mongol predecessors, such as the **civil service examination** system, and restored the earlier bureaucratic and cultural institutions and the **tributary system** with China's neighbors. While agriculture flourished and China resumed its place as the world's largest and most prosperous society, the Ming period, although dynamic, was also characterized by ideological rigidity and political conservatism. The **Great Wall** was built in its present form, and contact with outsiders was more limited. Literature, especially novels and **Neo-Confucian** philosophy, flourished. The dynasty was conquered by the **Manchus** in the mid-seventeenth century.

Ming Hongwu. *See* Hongwu

Minoan Civilization
Bronze Age civilization on Crete (c. 3500–1100 B.C.E.) based around the Palace of Minos and named for the legendary king Minos. Occupied from Neolithic times, the Knossus (Cnossus) cultural remains reveal a spectacular complex of buildings. The Minoan civilization was innovative, with complex economic and social organization and its own script. The civilization was overrun by the **Mycenaean** Greeks, although the palace complex was not destroyed until later by an earthquake.

Mississippian Culture
Prehistoric interrelated **Amerindian** cultures in the central and southeastern regions of North America. From around 700 C.E. until the arrival of Europeans, the Mississippian Culture flourished with large populations based on maize, bean, and squash cultivation, especially along rivers. Although each village was autonomous, alliances were constantly in flux and wars common. One of the peculiar features of the Mississippian culture, which did not exist in the preceding Hopewell culture, was the creation of huge, pyramidal, flat-topped earthen **burial mounds**, several of which still exist.

Missouri Compromise (1820–1821)
Solution to a congressional conflict between slave states and free states over the admission of Missouri to the United States of America. The answer came when Maine, a proposed free state, requested admission; this kept the number of slave and free states balanced should Missouri,

a slave state, be admitted. Henry Clay negotiated an agreement delineating that the remaining territory of the Louisiana Purchase would be free north of 36°30', the southern border of Missouri. The compromise was sufficient for a time, but tension between North and South remained. The compromise was repealed by the Kansas-Nebraska Act in 1854.

Mita
A system of Andean labor groups of the sixteenth century, similar to the **Aztec** calpulli. The mita was used by the elite to organize the commoners to gather tribute, to organize labor, or to build public projects. The work was not to exceed two weeks in length, and the system was not supposed to be used more than three or four times annually, but these restrictions were often ignored. The system remained in effect into the nineteenth century.

Mithra. *See* Mithraism

Mithraism
Ancient Persian religion based on Mithra, the god of light. Popular in the Roman Empire in the second and third centuries, Mithraism placed emphasis on courage and honor and was spread primarily among the soldiers. Mithraism had baptism and communion, similar to Christianity with which it competed in those centuries.

Mixtec
Mesoamerican civilization of central Mexico in the mountains of Oaxaca, and an Indian population in that region of modern Mexico. The Mixtec civilization thrived from the ninth to the fourteenth century C.E. They formed a loose confederation and came into contact with the **Zapotec** civilization.

Mobutu, Sese Seko (1930–1997)
Zairian president. After military training in the Belgian Congo and journalism training in Belgium, Mobutu joined **Patrice Lumumba** as army chief of staff of the nationalist forces. He then led a coup that removed Lumumba and appointed an interim government. In 1965 Mobutu seized power with the aid of the army, established a single political party, and was repeatedly elected to seven-year terms as president of the Congo (renamed Zaïre in 1971). Mobutu became notorious for misrule, and by the 1990s rioting and, finally, a full revolt in 1996 brought him down. He fled to Gabon in 1997 and died that year from cancer.

Moche. *See* Mochica

Mochica
Ancient Peruvian civilization from the first to the eighth century C.E. On the northern coast of Peru the Mochica were the dominant culture, building numerous urban centers and huge temples to the sun and moon in pyramidal and terraced-platform designs. The Mochica had extensive irrigation systems and farmed maize, beans, and other crops. It is not known why they disappeared.

Moctezuma II (r. 1502–1520)
Monarch of the triple alliance of the Aztecs at the time of arrival of the Spaniards in 1519. Believing an Aztec tradition that the god Quetzalcóatl would return to reclaim his lost kingdom, Moctezuma mistook the Spanish **conquistador Hernando Cortés** for Quetzalcóatl and, after attempts to appease him with gifts, invited him into the well-defended capital, **Tenochtitlán**. Cortés took Moctezuma hostage, although a revolt by the Aztec people drove Cortés out. He returned with enemies of the Aztecs and captured the capital. Moctezuma was eventually stoned to death by his own people.

Modern Devotion Movement (in Latin, "Devotio Moderna")
Christian religious movement originating in the Low Countries in the late **Middle Ages**. Its simplicity and piety made it attractive to people disconcerted with the **Roman Catholic Church**'s emphasis on wealth and display. The Modern Devotion movement also gave greater equality and autonomy to women. The most famous group of the Modern Devotion movement was the Brethren of the Common Life, and its most famous product was **Desiderius Erasmus**.

Modernization
Term for the political, economic, social, and institutional changes that occurred first in western Europe and North America as a result of the **Industrial Revolution**, the **Enlightenment**, and the development of modern science. Modernization is often equated with **westernization**, but most historians make a distinction between the two. Some historians see the process of modernization as having started in east Asian countries, particularly Japan, independently from western Europe.

Moguls. *See* Mughals (Moguls)

Mohammed. *See* Muhammad

Mohenjo-Daro
City of an ancient Indus culture located on the **Indus River**. Mohenjo-Daro, a name given to the city by modern archaeologists, which is Sanskrit for "City of the Dead." Like **Harappa**, it was a major planned city with a grid pattern; wells, piped water, bathrooms, and drains for many houses;

civic granaries; and thick brick surrounding walls. Mohenjo-Daro was at its height from 2500 to 1800 B.C.E.

Molière, Jean-Baptiste (1622–1673)

French playwright born Jean-Baptiste Poquelin. Considered the greatest French writer of dramatic comedy, Molière attacked hypocrisy, vice, and injustice. He is sometimes compared to **Shakespeare** for the development of his characters. Among his most famous plays are *Tartuffe* (1664), *The Misanthrope* (1666), and *The Bourgeois Gentleman* (1670).

Molly Maguires

Secret Irish antilandlord organization, and later a secret U.S. organization of miners in eastern Pennsylvania. Originally, in the early and mid-nineteenth century, the Molly Maguires were a grassroots organization protesting the abuses of landlords in Ireland. Taking its name from that organization, the American Molly Maguires, composed primarily of Irish-American miners, protested ill treatment by mine owners in the period 1865–1875. They were crushed by repressive measures and prosecutions.

Mombasa

Kenya's second-largest city and the largest port in east Africa. **Ibn Battutah** sailed to Mombasa in 1331, and **Vasco da Gama** followed him in 1498. By the fifteenth century it had become the most important trading center in East Africa. In the sixteenth century the Portuguese built a large fort there. In the nineteenth century the British used Mombasa as the capital of East Africa. It became a tourist center in the twentieth century.

Mon

A Southeast Asian people forming a small ethnic minority in Burma and Thailand. The Mon established a number of small states in the late first millennium C.E., such as Dvaravati, Thaton, and Haripunjaya, that were strongly influenced by Indian culture and were probably the first literate societies in that region. These states were absorbed by the Burman and Thai peoples in the eleventh and twelfth centuries.

Monasteries and Convents

Communities of Christians or Buddhists living under religious vows, usually as a single gender. In the early centuries of Christianity, individual believers sometimes went off into the wilderness, such as the desert, to live a life of isolation to contemplate God. This would be true monasticism (meaning "alone"), but these individuals often attracted followers and whole communities of **monks** developed. By the sixth century orders of monks and nuns lived in monasteries or convents following sets of rules such as those of **Saint Benedict**. Monasteries and convents were very successful in the **Middle Ages** because of their communal life of shared property and work. Monasteries and convents were often repositories of knowledge, with libraries and learned individuals resident, and often they had the most advanced economies and living conditions. Monasteries and convents often owned large amounts of farmland and had **serfs** to work it. Because they owned land, monasteries and convents sometimes had **feudal** obligations of supplying warriors to their lord.

Mongol Empire

Empire founded by **Genghis Khan** early in the thirteenth century. A group of **steppe** nomads of the region of modern Mongolia, the Mongols were excellent horsemen and skilled archers. Genghis Khan unified the Mongols and created an empire stretching from **Manchuria** to the Black

Sea. His successors under Ogodei Khan and Mongke Khan continued his conquests, bringing Russia under their rule in 1241 and advancing into central Europe as far as Hungary, Poland, and Bulgaria; conquering Iran and Iraq in 1258; completing the conquest of China; and subduing Korea. **Khubilai Khan** was one of the greatest of these conquerors. Although they brought almost all of **Central Asia** under their rule, the Mongols began to suffer some setbacks at the empire's farthest reaches. In 1260 they were defeated by the **Mamluks** of Egypt at Ain Jalut, preventing them from completing the conquest of the **Middle East**. Two sea-based invasions of Japan in 1274 and 1281 ended in failure, and expeditions to Burma in 1287 and a very ambitious sea-based invasion of Java in 1291 led to some initial successes but proved logistically impossible to support. Karakoram in Mongolia served as the first capital, but Khubilai Khan moved the capital to Khanbalikh, on the site of what is now Beijing. After 1300 the various regional khanates became fully independent from the emperors in Khanbalikh, and Mongol unity came to an end. In 1368 the Mongols were driven out of China, and in 1372 a Chinese army burned Karakoram. The Mongol empire created what historians sometimes call the *Pax Mongolica*, or a great peace across Eurasia, which facilitated transregional trade and cultural contact.

Monks

People who remove themselves from the everyday world to devote themselves to asceticism or contemplating God. A Latin term, *monk* originally was interpreted to simply mean alone. Some groups of monks form communities, known as **monasteries**, where they hold no private property. There are monks in **Christianity** and in **Buddhism**. Because monks have committed their lives to their religion, they are often highly admired in their society. In the **Middle Ages** Christian monks were among the few educated people and played a very important role in society.

Monotheism

Belief in one god. Most ancient societies were polytheistic (believing in many gods). The Egyptians flirted with monotheism in the fourteenth century B.C.E., but the first prominent monotheistic religion was **Judaism** as it developed from the thirteenth to the sixth century B.C.E.

Monroe, James (1758–1831)

Fifth U.S. president (1817–1825) and author of the **Monroe Doctrine**. Monroe was elected after the War of 1812, the last president of the Revolutionary War generation. He presided over the so-called Era of Good Feelings. Peace was established with Great Britain, a treaty was signed with Spain (1819) allowing the United States to expand to the Pacific Ocean, and in 1823 President Monroe gave a speech stating the Monroe Doctrine—that the New World and Old World should not interfere in each other's affairs.

Monroe Doctrine (1823)

U.S. diplomatic policy delivered to Congress by President James Monroe stating three points—noncolonization, two spheres, and nonintervention. First proposed by **John Quincy Adams**, the Monroe Doctrine claims that the Western Hemisphere is no longer open for European colonization, the United States will not become involved in European wars, and the European powers are not to become militarily or forcefully involved in the Americas. This policy effectively separated the Old World of Europe and the New World of the United States until the beginning of **World War I**. It represented the American quest for independence, sovereignty, and separation from Europe.

Monte Alban
Zapotec site in present-day Oaxaca, Mexico. From the eighth century B.C.E. to the fourth century C.E., the site of the complex society contained pyramids, plazas, ball courts, and tombs, all typical of the Zapotec and other **Mesoamerican** civilizations. At present the site has extensive ruins.

Montesquieu, Charles-Louis de Secondat, Baron de la Brède et de (1689–1755)
French political philosopher during the **Enlightenment**. He was best known in his day for *Persian Letters* (1721), a satire of French life. His modern reputation rests mainly on *Spirit of the Laws* (1748), an Enlightenment treatise proposing government with separation of executive, legislative, and judicial powers modeled on the British government. His ideas were well known by the American founding fathers as well as by the leaders of the **French Revolution**.

Montezuma. *See* Moctezuma II

Montgomery, Alabama
Site of a boycott of the city bus system by African Americans to protest segregation in bus seating. Prompted by the arrest of **Rosa Parks** for refusing to give up her seat to a white passenger in December 1955, the successful boycott brought to national prominence the Reverend **Martin Luther King Jr.** as a leader of the **civil rights movement** and began an era of protest by African Americans.

More, Sir Thomas (1478–1535)
English diplomat, lord chancellor of England, and writer. In 1529 More was the first layperson to become lord chancellor.

He resigned in 1532 over his refusal to acknowledge King **Henry VIII** as head of the church in England and was beheaded for refusing to accept Henry's divorce from **Catherine of Aragon** and marriage to Anne Boleyn. More composed *Utopia* in 1516, in which he criticized contemporary European society. He was canonized 400 years after his death.

Mormons
Members of the Church of **Jesus Christ** of Latter-day Saints. The Mormons were founded by Joseph Smith in Palmyra, New York. He had revelations from God and was visited by God, Jesus, and the angel Moroni who in 1823 gave Smith golden tablets from which he translated *The Book of Mormon*. Mormons claim to be Christians and believe that the Bible is the word of God, but not a complete record of God. The Mormons settled in Illinois but, because of persecution, made a great migration to Utah in 1846, settling what would become Salt Lake City. In the later nineteenth century many Mormons practiced polygamy, but in 1890, under pressure from the U.S. government, the church banned the practice.

Morse, Samuel F. B. (1791–1872)
American developer of the telegraph and inventor of the International Morse Code. Morse became interested in the electric telegraph in 1832 and demonstrated a version of it in 1837. After numerous improvements he sent a message between Baltimore and the U.S. Capitol in Washington DC, in 1844. Within a decade the telegraph, using Morse's code, was being used throughout the United States and Europe.

Mozart, Wolfgang Amadeus (1756–1791)
Austrian musician and composer. Mozart composed more than 600 works even

though he died before his thirty-sixth birthday. Working primarily in his native Salzburg and in Vienna, Mozart began to compose at age five and performed for the empress at age six. Among his most famous works are the operas *The Marriage of Figaro* (1786), *Don Giovanni* (1787), and *The Magic Flute* (1791); his *Requiem* (1791); and the piano piece *Eine kleine Nachtmusik* (1787).

Mughals (Moguls)

Muslim dynasty of **Central Asian** origins that invaded India in 1526 under **Babur** and by the end of the seventeenth century had extended its rule over all of the subcontinent except the extreme south. Mughal rulers included **Humayun, Akbar,** Jahangir, Shah Jahan, and **Aurangzeb.** Under the Mughals, Persian and Indian artistic influences combined to produce a distinctive Indo-Muslim style in miniature painting and architecture that is highly admired in the world today. The most famous of the Mughals' many architectural monuments, fortress, palaces, and mosques is the **Taj Mahal.** The early rulers tolerated the **Hinduism** of the majority of their subjects but the Muslim zeal of Aurangzeb (r. 1658–1707) led to Hindu revolts that weakened the empire. Internal disintegration and pressure from the Marathas brought on decline throughout the eighteenth and nineteenth centuries until the dynasty was abolished by the British in 1858 following the **Sepoy Mutiny.**

Muhammad (c. 570–632)

Prophet of **Islam.** From a merchant family of **Mecca,** in Arabia, and orphaned by age six, Muhammad married a wealthy woman and became a merchant. With some knowledge of **Judaism** and **Christianity,** he had a profound spiritual experience around 610. His series of visions or revelations were recorded after his death as the **Quran** (Arabic for "recitation"). His sayings were recorded as the **Hadith.** Both the Quran and the Hadith express how to follow the straight path. After some resistance, Muhammad's message spread throughout Arabia and, within 100 years of his death, all the way from India to Spain. The fundamentals of his message were that there is one god, Allah, and that the righteous will be rewarded and the wicked punished, hence leading a life in accord with God's will. The believers of this religion are called **Muslims.**

Muhammad I Askia (d. 1538)

King of the **Songhay** empire. Muhammad I Askia usurped the throne and militarily expanded the west African empire of the Niger River region, which had replaced the empire of **Mali.** The emperors of the Songhay were always **Muslim,** although the entire population was not. The Songhay empire was the last of the great African grasslands empires.

Muhammad Reza Shah Pahlavi (1919–1980)

Ruler of Iran (1941–1979). After his father, Reza Shah Pahlavi, was forced into exile, Muhammad Reza Shah Pahlavi gained the throne. In the 1950s he struggled for control of the country with Muhammad Mosaddeq, but with the covert assistance of the United States the shah gained supreme power, denationalizing the petroleum companies and increasing oil production. He introduced reforms and rapid economic development in Iran but coupled these actions with severe repression. His rule came to an end in 1979 during a revolution led by the Islamic clergy. He was overthrown after the return of **Ayatollah Ruhollah Khomeini.** The shah was exiled to several countries before going to the United States for medical treatment for cancer. His residing in the United States led to the taking of American hostages in the **Iran hostage crisis**. The shah left the United States and was granted asylum in Egypt, where he died.

Mukden Incident (September 18, 1931)
Japanese incident in China that sparked a Japanese invasion. Japanese forces set off an explosion on the South Manchurian Railway, which was under Japanese control, and then accused the Chinese of being responsible for it. In response, Japan seized the city of Mukden (Shenyang) in **Manchuria**. The action was carried out by members of the Japanese Guandong army, apparently without consultation with the government in Tokyo. The Japanese military used this incident as an excuse to occupy all of Manchuria, setting up the puppet Manchukuo state the following year. The incident marked the beginning of the Japanese expansion into China in the 1930s that led to **World War II**.

Munich "Beer Hall" Putsch (1923)
Abortive attempt by a rising **Adolf Hitler** and the **Nazis** to overthrow the German government. In a beer hall in Munich the Nazis called for a rebellion to overthrow the **Weimar Republic** of Germany. Hitler made a passionate speech that gained him recognition and led to a march by several thousand Nazis the next day. A riot ensued, and Hitler was arrested and imprisoned for nine months, during which he dictated the first part of his famous manifesto *Mein Kampf* (1925).

Munich Pact (1938)
Agreement between Germany, Britain, France, and Italy that Czechoslovakia would be divided with the western part, **Sudetenland**, handed over to **Adolf Hitler**'s Germany as appeasement. Hitler

had been pressing for the unification of all German peoples. With the **Anschluss**, or annexation of Austria, it became clear that he was serious. Hitler threatened war and then promised peace only if the Sudetenland (a region of predominantly German-speaking Czechs) was incorporated into Germany. The region was the most industrialized part of Czechoslovakia. Representatives of the other nations, especially Britain's Prime Minister **Neville Chamberlain**, agreed to the pact to avoid war. Chamberlain returned to Britain proclaiming "peace for our time." Five months later German troops marched into the rest of Czechoslovakia, and Britain and the other nations knew that they had been taken: Germany was now the strongest nation in Europe.

Muong
Ethnic minority group in Vietnam who speak a Mon-Khmer language. The Muong live in hilly or mountainous areas, subsisting on wet rice agriculture. The rugged areas they live in have helped them maintain their own culture. The Muong have often rebelled against Vietnamese political authority. During the **Vietnam War** many supported the U.S. forces in their resistance to communist Vietnamese control.

Murasaki Shikibu (fl. c. 1000)
Author of the Japanese classic novel *Tale of Genji*. She was a lady-in-waiting at the court of **Heian**, Japan, but little is known about her life other than what we can glean from her novel, finished around 1000 C.E. A massive work, it depicts the court life of Japan at that time, providing valuable insights into the culture and social customs of the elite. The work is considered Japan's greatest literary masterpiece and has often been called the world's first novel.

Muromachi Period. *See* Ashikaga

Muslim (Arabic for "one who has submitted to God")
A follower of the religion of **Islam** as laid out in the **Quran** and the **Hadith** (traditions of the Prophet) and Islamic law (**sharia**). The religion recognizes **Muhammad** as the last of the great prophets of God who set creation on the straight path. A Muslim is supposed to live in accordance with the will of God. There are five acts of faith (called Five Pillars): acknowledging one God and Muhammad as his Prophet, praying five times a day, fasting during the month of Ramadan, giving alms to the poor, and undertaking a pilgrimage to Mecca.

Muslim Brotherhood
Islamic movement in Egypt founded in 1928. Started among workers of the **Suez Canal** zone by schoolteacher Hasan al-Banna, its original goal was to reform Islamic society by eliminating Western influences. Moving to Cairo, the Muslim Brotherhood became more radical and more middle class, with its mission to turn Egypt into a theocratic Islamic state. The brotherhood was abolished in 1954 by **Gamal Abdel Nasser** by publicly hanging several members.

Muslim League
Indian political party founded in 1906 as the All-India Muslim League to represent Muslims who felt increasingly threatened by the rise of a Hindu-dominated **nationalist** movement. In 1916 the Muslim League worked out an agreement with the **Indian National Congress** for separate electorates and reserved seats in Muslim minority provinces. In 1940, under its charismatic leader **Mohammad Ali Jinnah**, it called for the creation of a separate Muslim state of Pakistan. The league's importance ended after Pakistan's independence in 1947.

Mussolini, Benito (1883–1945)
Italian founder of **fascism** and leader of Italy during **World War II**. Mussolini, from a revolutionary socialist background, founded the fascist movement in 1919 as a mixture of **nationalism**, **socialism**, and militarism. In 1922 Mussolini's Blackshirts, paramilitary groups, marched on Rome, and Mussolini was made prime minister. In 1925 he seized complete power and became dictator. He was known as *Il Duce* ("The Leader"). Mussolini annexed Abyssinia in 1936 to avenge an Italian humiliation in 1896 and joined Germany as one of the **Axis Powers** in World War II. Mussolini was executed by Italian communists in 1945, just before the end of the war.

Mutapa. *See* Mwenemutapa (Mutapa)

Mutsu Munemitsu (1844–1896)
Japanese foreign minister who with Prime Minister Ito Hirobumi engineered the revision of the Unequal Treaties (1894), the **Sino-Japanese War** (1894–1895), and weathered the Triple Intervention (1895). Born into a **Tokugawa**-related **daimyo** house, he became a loyalist allied with **Sakamoto Ryoma**. He served in the early **Meiji** government but was convicted of treason in the Seinan Incident (1877) and served four years in prison. Rehabilitated by his friends **Ito Hirobumi** and **Inoue Kaoru**, he served in various capacities, including minister to the United States, where he negotiated the first equal treaty with a Western nation (Mexico) in 1888.

Mwenemutapa (Mutapa)
State (1450–1884) established in the northern part of present-day Zimbabwe. After the decline of the **Great Zimbabwe**,

a Bantu-speaking people known as the Mwenemutapa, of southeastern Africa, settled south of the Zambezi River. They brought iron-working skills and agriculture with them. Because of gold and trade in the region, Mwenemutapa developed a centralized state with a military and government. Mwenemutapa was trading with Swahili traders by the fifteenth century and with Portuguese traders during the sixteenth century. By the middle of the seventeenth century the Portuguese had turned the rulers of Mwenemutapa into mere puppets.

Mycenaean. *See* Greece, Mycenaean

Mythology

A collection of fables or stories used to explain some practice, belief, natural phenomenon, or institution that may have a historical basis but whose origins are forgotten. Mythology is often used to explain a culture's religion, religious beliefs, or religious rites.

Nabataea

Kingdom of ancient Jordan. The Nabataeas were a people who entered the region of modern-day Jordan during the seventh century B.C.E. and formed a kingdom in the second century B.C.E., during the time of the **Seleucids** and the **Ptolemies**. The kingdom of Nabataea was conquered, along with much of the Palestinian region, by the Romans in 63 B.C.E., although the Romans left Nabataea as a buffer state until 106 C.E., when it was fully absorbed into the **Roman Empire**.

Nadir Shah (1688–1747)

Iranian military and political leader. Nadir had already established a strong military reputation by 1719 when Ghilzai Afghans from the Kandahar region invaded Iran and laid siege to the **Safavid dynasty**'s capital city, Isfahan. By 1722 the Afghans had deposed the Safavids and were imposing harsh conditions on the population. In 1729 Nadir helped drive the Afghans out of Iran. In 1736 he removed the Safavid rulers and then embarked on a series of military campaigns that generated one of the last great nomadic empires of conquest, which stretched from **Baghdad** to **Delhi**. The last years of his life were marked by paranoia and outbursts of extreme violence. Nadir was assassinated in 1747.

NAFTA. *See* North American Free Trade Agreement (NAFTA)

Nagasaki

Japanese city in the southern island of **Kyûshû** that served under the **Tokugawa** as Japan's window on the outside world. From the early seventeenth century the shoguns closed Japan to foreigners except for a single trading settlement on the island of Deshima in Nagasaki harbor, at which the Dutch and Chinese were allowed to trade. On August 9, 1945, Nagasaki was the target of the second **atomic bomb** dropped by U.S. forces, three days after the first one was dropped on **Hiroshima**. Approximately 40,000 people were killed immediately and many thousands died later, contributing to Japan's surrender to the **Allies** on August 15, 1945.

Nanjing, Treaty of (1842)

Treaty between China and Britain that concluded the **Opium War**. The first of the Unequal Treaties that Western nations and, later, Japan imposed on China, it ceded **Hong Kong** to Britain and opened the ports of **Shanghai**, Guangzhou (**Canton**), Xiamen (Amoy), Fuzhou (Foochow), and Ningbo (Ningpo) to British merchants. The treaty also imposed a $21 million indemnity to compensate the British for opium the Chinese seized at Canton and the cost of the war, which the British started. It marked the beginning of the treaty system and led to foreign economic penetration of China. A U.S. treaty of 1844 established the principle of extraterritoriality for Americans in China.

Nanking, Rape of (1937)
Sack and pillage of the Chinese capital city of Nanking (Nanjing) during the second **Sino-Japanese War**. After the city was conquered Japanese troops were turned loose, and between 40,000 and 300,000 civilians were slaughtered, many of the women after having been raped first.

Nantes, Edict of (1598)
Edict ending decades of religious wars in France between Catholics and **Protestants**. The proclamation by King **Henry IV** allowed French Protestants, known as **Huguenots**, freedom of worship in seventy-five towns and granted them equal rights to Catholics. The edict was revoked in 1685 by **Louis XIV**.

Napoléon Bonaparte (1769–1821)
French general, consul, and emperor. Born in Corsica, Napoléon rose to general by age twenty-six during the **French Revolution** and won numerous campaigns. His attempt to conquer Egypt to interfere with British access to India was thwarted by a brilliant naval battle (1798) commanded by the British admiral Horatio Nelson. Napoléon returned to Europe, overthrew the French government of the Directory, and established himself as consul, supreme ruler of France. He reformed the French legal and educational systems and in 1804 had himself crowned emperor of the French. He led France into a series of wars, known as the Napoleonic Wars, against Prussia, Austria, Britain, and Russia. After many victories Napoléon began to lose, and in 1814 he abdicated the throne and was banished to the island of Elba (1814). In 1815 he returned to France and raised an army, but he was finally defeated at the **Battle of Waterloo** (1815) and was exiled to the island of Saint Helena in the Atlantic.

Nasser, Gamal Abdel (1918–1970)
Egyptian prime minister (1954–1956, 1967–1970) and president (1956–1970). Nasser led a revolt that overthrew King Farouk in 1952 and encouraged **nationalism** and economic growth. Nasser was the most influential leader in the Arab world of his day. He presided over Egypt's seizure of the **Suez Canal** in 1956, its close relations with the Soviet Union, and the six-day **Arab-Israeli War** in 1967. After Egypt's defeat in the 1967 war Nasser resigned, but the **National Assembly** refused to accept his resignation.

National Assembly
French political body formed in 1789 when the **Estates General** met and the Third Estate was dissatisfied with its role in the body. The Third Estate represented most of the French people, while the clergy and the aristocracy represented very few. The Third Estate declared itself the National Assembly representing the French people on June 17, 1789. When locked out of the Estates General chambers, the National Assembly—now joined by most of the clergy and some aristocracy—moved across the street to a tennis court where the members took an oath not to disband until a constitution had been drawn up. On July 7 the body changed its name to Constituent National Assembly, and from that point it is often referred to as the Constituent Assembly, or simply the Constituent. The Constituent Assembly was dissolved on September 30, 1791, and replaced with the National Constituent Assembly, which was in turn replaced by the Convention on September 21, 1792.

Nationalism
Sense of identity among a group of people who consider themselves as belonging to a nation. A nation is a community that shares a common heritage and whose

members believe they share a common destiny. This community may be based on any or all of the following: a shared experience of membership in a state, the use of a common written and/or spoken language, shared customs, a common religion, and a belief in a common ancestry. Historians regard nationalism as a modern phenomenon emerging in the eighteenth century in Europe and the Americas, forged by the **French Revolution** and the **American Revolution**, and in the nineteenth and twentieth centuries in Asia and Africa. Probably no other type of identity has been more powerful in generating conflicts and struggles, and in shaping international politics in the nineteenth, twentieth, and twenty-first centuries. One characteristic of nationalism is the importance placed on the state. Nationalists generally feel that each nation should have a state as its political embodiment and that each state should be a nation.

Nation-State

Concept predominant in the nineteenth century of a political unit of a people. A nation-state is composed primarily of one people (or at least a perception of being one people) and ruled by that people. Developed out of the **French Revolution** and the **Napoleonic Wars**, political units comprising a single people—defined by language, ethnicity, customs, religion, history, or geographic territory—formed in Europe, replacing small principalities containing part of a people such as Hanover, Baden, or **Venice** and putting pressure on the old dynastic empires such as the **Ottoman Empire** or the **Austro-Hungarian Empire**. By the end of the nineteenth century new nation-states had come into being, such as Belgium, Germany, Italy, and Greece, and the nation-state was regarded by most peoples as the ideal sovereign political unit.

Native Americans. *See* Amerindians

NATO. *See* North Atlantic Treaty Organization (NATO)

Natural Law

Theory in Western culture, first articulated in Hellenic times, that there is a rational system that governs the universe. Natural law helped to provide a basis for Western science because it implied that the forces of nature were rational, comprehensible, and to some extent predictable. The concept of natural law was also interpreted by many as meaning that there is a universal system of justice that is derived from nature, not from any particular government or society. The latter interpretation laid some of the intellectual foundations of the ideals of the **Enlightenment**.

Navajo

Amerindian tribe that settled in the region that is now the southwestern United States, probably between 900 and 1200 C.E., near the Pueblos, and absorbed many Pueblo traditions, including maize cultivation and weaving. The Navajo are distinctive for speaking Apachean, an Athabascan language that is different from most Amerindian languages. In 1863 the Navajo were forcibly moved to reservations. Today most Navajo live on reservations in Arizona, New Mexico, and Utah.

Navarre, Henry of. *See* Henry IV

Nazca

Ancient Mesoamerican culture (200 B.C.E.–600 C.E.) in the area that is now Peru. There is substantial pottery from this culture, including multicolored images of people, animals, and plants. The Nazca also produced large images on the coastal plain, known as the Nazca lines, by stripping away the topsoil to expose the underlying sand. The purpose of these lines is not certain but is presumed to have been religious.

Nazi

Name for an individual member of the National Socialist German Workers' Party (*Nationalsozialistische Deutsche Arbeiterpartei*). Founded in 1919 and taken over by **Adolf Hitler** in 1921, the Nazi Party took control of Germany in 1933. The Nazis believed in **fascism**, or subordination of the individual to the state, and opposed **democracy** and **communism**. Soon after Hitler came to power in 1933, all other parties were outlawed and any opposition was crushed. The Nazis declared their belief in a pure **Aryan** race and in **anti-Semitism**. The Nazi beliefs were laid out in Hitler's *Mein Kampf* (1925). The Nazi Party ruled Germany throughout **World War II** until Germany's defeat in 1945. The Nazi Party has been outlawed in Germany but appears occasionally among extreme right-wing movements elsewhere.

Nebuchadnezzar II (Nebuchadrezzar II) (c. 630–562 B.C.E.)

King of **Babylon** (605–562 B.C.E.). A great warrior, he became king after he defeated Egypt at the Battle of Carchemish (605 B.C.E.). After his third successful attack on **Jerusalem** he destroyed the city, including the **Hebrew Temple**, and carried its leading citizens into the **Babylonian Captivity**. He expanded the empire through conquests and enhanced the grandeur of his capital, Babylon. Legend holds that he built the beautiful Hanging Gardens for his wife. Nebuchadnezzar appears in several important passages of the Hebrew Bible (in Jeremiah, Ezekiel, and Daniel and in later chapters of Kings and Chronicles).

Negritude

Intellectual movement of postcolonial Africa that rejects the political, social, moral, and artistic domination of the West. Originating with the French-speaking black intellectuals of Africa and coined by **Léopold Senghor**, the term *negritude* referred primarily to writing and other arts but has come to emphasize black experience and consciousness in all fields and in all countries of the world. Negritude was adopted by some French Caribbean intellectuals, notably Aimee Cesaire.

Nehru, Jawaharlal (1889–1964)

Major leader of India's independence movement and India's first prime minister (1947–1964). The son of a prominent politician, Motilal Nehru, Jawaharlal Nehru became an associate of **Mohandas K. Gandhi** in the **Indian National Congress**, participating in nonviolent noncooperation campaigns against British rule. However, he differed with Gandhi's vision of India as a nation of self-sufficient villages, advocating instead the need for **industrialization**. As prime minister he sought to develop India through a series of five-year plans and by protecting indigenous manufacturers from foreign competition. Nehru steered India toward political neutrality in the **cold war** and won recognition as a respected statesman. But India remained poor, and its conflicts with its neighbors Pakistan and China were unresolved. Two years after his death his only child, **Indira Gandhi**, succeeded him as leader of the Congress Party and as prime minister.

Neo-Confucianism

Modern term for the school of Confucian thought that emerged during the **Song** dynasty period in China, culminating in the interpretations of **Zhu Xi** (1130–1200). Neo-Confucianism was an ethical philosophy that taught that each individual should strive to pursue a virtuous life. This involved carefully and sincerely carrying out one's social obligations and serving family and society. It was also a political philosophy that emphasized the duty of rulers to act as moral exemplars and to attend to the needs of the people in order to create a harmonious society. Influenced by **Buddhism** and, to a lesser extent, **Daoism**, Neo-Confucian thinkers gave a metaphysical foundation to this teaching, emphasizing the interconnectedness of all things and humanity's place in the greater cosmos. They also reinterpreted the idea of sagehood as something closer to the Buddhist concept of enlightenment and encouraged meditation as part of moral training. Neo-Confucianism became the dominant school of thought in China from the fourteenth century because it was the state ideology that served as the basis for the **civil service examinations**. It was the officially promoted school of thought in Korea during the Yi dynasty and in **Tokugawa** Japan.

Neoliberalism

Market-opening policies that most Latin America countries have put into place since the mid-1980s, such as the **North American Free Trade Agreement** (NAFTA). Although neoliberalism is intended to expand national economies, many people at the lower end of the economic scale have felt threatened by it. The 1994 **Zapatista uprising** in Mexico was partly caused by neoliberalism.

Neolithic Age

Literally "new Stone Age," a term for the period of human history that began about 12,000 years ago, named for the polished stone tools that characterized cultures of this time. The Neolithic age saw the transition to agriculture; the rapid expansion of human populations; and the development of pottery, weaving, and larger, more complex societies that eventually led to the rise of civilizations.

Neoplatonism

Modern term for **Plotinus**'s renewal of ancient philosophy, including Plato's, in the third century C.E. Plotinus, a Greek-speaking Egyptian within the **Roman Empire**, created a school in Rome and became the center of an intellectual circle studying the philosophies of **Plato, Aristotle**, Pythagoras, and the Stoics and even some eastern mysticism. Neoplatonism became almost a religion among its adherents by the end of the third century. It dominated much of the ancient Western world until the sixth century and influenced Byzantine, Islamic, medieval (**Saint Augustine of Hippo**), and **Renaissance** philosophy. **Giovanni Pico della Mirandola** was a key Neoplatonist of the Renaissance. This blend of ancient philosophies was often the only form in which Plato and other Greek philosophers were known until the Renaissance.

Nerchinsk, Treaty of (1689)

Treaty between Russia and China. Signed in the city of Nerchinsk, Russia, this seventeenth-century treaty was the first between China and a Western country. The treaty determined the Russo-Chinese border.

Nero (Nero Claudius Caesar) (37–68)

Roman emperor (54–68). Nero came to the throne after the suspicious death of Claudius and the poisoning of Claudius's son Britannicus. His first years as emperor were successful. Some hailed his era as a **golden age**. Always controlled by a domineering mother, Nero's murder of her freed his artistic passions and desires for athletic displays such as **gladiator** games. He forced his advisor Seneca to commit suicide and later executed his own wife, Octavia. These actions undermined Nero's support from the propertied classes, but he remained highly popular with the masses.

A fire that devastated **Rome** (64) further strained the economy. During Nero's reign Britain revolted under **Boudicca** (60) and **Palestine** revolted (66). Nero rebuilt Rome after the fire in a glorious fashion.

Nevsky, Alexander, Saint (c. 1220–1263) Prince of Novgorod (1236–1252), prince of **Kiev** (1246–1252), and grand prince of Vladimir (1252–1263). Alexander led Russian forces against Swedes in the Battle of Neva (1240)—giving him the name Nevsky—and against German Teutonic Knights at Lake Peipus (1242), stopping the eastward expansion of both. In 1246, after the death of their father, Alexander and his brother Andrew, who was grand prince of Vladimir, traveled to the **Mongol empire**'s great khan and collaborated with him. In 1252, after Andrew conspired against the Mongols, Alexander had the Mongols depose Andrew, and Alexander was made grand prince. He continued to collaborate with the Mongols, helping them to impose taxes but negotiating where possible, restoring Russia by building fortifications and churches. At his death in 1263 Russia disintegrated into feudal principalities. **Joseph Stalin** declared Nevsky a national hero during Russia's **World War II** defense against Germany, commemorating Nevsky's thirteenth-century defense.

New Imperialism
Term for the rapid expansion of European imperialism in the second half of the nineteenth and the early twentieth centuries. During this period the major European powers including Britain, France, Germany, Belgium, and Italy partitioned almost all of Africa into colonies and expanded their colonial holdings in Asia and the Pacific. In some areas, such as Persia and parts of China, Western nations defined spheres of influence where they held some indirect control. Largely directed by the major European powers, especially Britain, France, and Russia, the United States and Japan also participated in colonial acquisitions during this time. This accelerated expansion of European rule is sometimes attributed to the demands for markets, raw materials, and areas of investment driven by their industrializing economies and to nationalist rivalries. The strongest reason for the New Imperialism was the belief that these factors would make a country stronger, and individuals who participated in colonialism richer.

Ne Win, U (1911–2002)
Burmese general and autocratic ruler who served as prime minister (1958–1962) and led a coup in 1962 against the U Nu government. He then proclaimed the Socialist Republic of the Union of Burma and made the country a one-party state under the Burma Socialist Programme Party. His long rule of Burma was one of economic stagnation, political repression, and isolation, with little trade and limited contact with other nations. Once one of the most prosperous nations in Southeast Asia, Burma became one of the poorest under Ne Win. He stepped down from most posts in 1988 but continued to wield power behind the scenes. He was put under house arrest in 2002 and died that year.

New Model Army
English Civil War military organization developed in 1644. The New Model Army was well disciplined, well financed, and commanded by men who had been promoted on their merit rather than their aristocratic blood. The first commander was Thomas Fairfax, with his second in command **Oliver Cromwell**, who turned out to be a brilliant commander. The New

Model Army fought with professionalism but also with religious zeal and defeated the royalist army of **Charles I**. During the republic (1653–1660), the New Model Army played an influential role.

New Testament. *See* Bible

Newton, Isaac (1642–1727)
Founder of modern science with his explanation of gravity in the *Mathematical Principles of Natural Philosophy* (1687). Newton's publication was one of the most influential works of all time. It was the culmination of scientific experiments, observations, and mathematical reasoning of the **scientific revolution** from **Nicolaus Copernicus** through **Tycho Brahe, Johannes Kepler, Galileo, William Gilbert**, and **René Descartes**. Newton's explanation of gravity tied together many branches of physical science and proved that there is one set of laws of the physical universe, not two, as in the rejected Aristotelian view. Newton proved that mathematical rules could explain the functions of the physical universe.

Ngyuyen Van Thieu (1923–)
South Vietnamese president (1967–1975). He participated in the overthrow of the Ngo Dinh Diem government in 1963 to become one of the military strongmen that ran South Vietnam. He 1967 he was elected its president. Despite opposition to his dictatorial methods, he was supported by the United States because he vigorously pursued the war against the **Viet Cong** and North Vietnam. He fled to Taiwan in April 1975 when communist forces overran South Vietnam.

Nicholas II (1868–1918)
Last Russian tsar (1895–1917). Nicholas tried to expand Russia's influence with an alliance with France in 1895 and expansionism in Asia that led to the disastrous **Russo-Japanese War** (1904–1905) and a **Russian Revolution** in 1905. Nicholas was forced to allow the creation of the Duma (parliament). During **World War I** Russia fought with the **Triple Entente** against Germany, but Nicholas's personal command of the army left Tsarina Alexandra and Rasputin in charge of the government. Huge military losses led to the outbreak of the Russian Revolution in 1917. Nicholas, his wife Alexandra, and their children were killed by the **Bolsheviks** during the Russian Revolution.

Nile Valley
Fertile valley several miles wide along the Nile River, which flows for thousands of miles from the heart of Africa north to the Mediterranean Sea. Annually, the Nile floods its banks in autumn and deposits silt that creates a region of rich soil and abundant harvests. The river also provides a means of transportation. This region supported one of the earliest civilizations, extending from the cataracts of Nubia and upper Egypt north to the mouth of the Nile delta, which was first united around 3100 B.C.E.

Ninety-five Theses (1517)
Document of complaints against the **Roman Catholic Church** written by **Martin Luther** that sparked the **Reformation**. The document's real name the, "Disputation on the Power and Efficacy of Indulgences," dealt with the abuse of indulgences—the absolution of guilt and penalty for sins committed—and their sale. The sale of indulgences had become a major source of income for the church and led to many abuses. The Ninety-five Theses so challenged the church that Luther was ordered to recant them. His refusal brought on a break with the Catholic

Church and the beginning the Reformation rejecting much of the church's structure and theology.

Nineveh
Largest city and sometime capital of ancient **Assyria**. One of the oldest cities in the world, Ninevah lay on the banks of the **Tigris River**, across from the modern-day city of Mosul, **Iraq**. Great rulers of Assyria who reigned in Ninevah included Tiglath-pileser I; Shalmaneser III; Esar-haddon and his son Asher-bani-pal; Sargon II, who captured Samaria, capital of the Northern Kingdom of **Israel** in 722 B.C.E.; and **Sennacherib**. The city features prominently in the books 2 Chronicles, Jonah, and Nahum of the Hebrew **Bible**. A very large city with magnificent buildings, lush gardens, and high walls, Ninevah was destroyed in 612 B.C.E. by Nabopolassar of **Babylon**.

Nirvana
Term used in both **Hinduism** and **Buddhism** for a state of freedom from the cycle of births and rebirths. In Buddhism, nirvana (Sanskrit for "nonexistence") is the major goal of the Eightfold Path. Although viewed as a transcendent state in which one is merged with the universal, it has been interpreted as a kind of paradise by some sects of Buddhism.

Nixon, Richard M. (1913–1994)
Thirty-seventh president of the United States (1969–1974). He served as U.S. vice president under President **Dwight D. Eisenhower** and then served as president himself. During his first term Nixon was successful in building foreign relations; in 1972 he helped to establish diplomatic relations with China with the first visit to China by an American president and later that year also paid a state visit to the **Union of Soviet Socialist Republics**, signing ten agreements, including **SALT I**. In 1973 he pulled the United States out of the **Vietnam War**. Nixon signed a treaty with **Leonid Brezhnev**, the leader of the USSR, to limit nuclear weapons. Nixon's second term was overwhelmed by the Watergate scandal, which stemmed from illegal activities by Nixon and his aides related to the burglary and wiretapping of the national headquarters of the Democratic Party at the Watergate complex in Washington DC. In 1974 he was forced to resign from the presidency.

Nkrumah, Kwame (1909–1972)
Pan-African leader and first prime minister and first president of Ghana. Nkrumah was educated in the British Gold Coast, the United States, and Britain. He became interested in Pan-African affairs and wrote about fighting colonialism. Upon returning to Gold Coast he helped organize civil disobedience. In 1952 he became prime minister of Gold Coast and led the nation to its independence in 1957 as Ghana. Nkrumah then began to act upon his Pan-Africanist ideals. He supported other independence movements and envisioned a united Africa. In 1960 Nkrumah was elected as the first president of Ghana. In 1966, while traveling in an effort to end the **Vietnam War**, a coup toppled his government. Nkrumah settled in Guinea, where he died of cancer in 1972.

No
Japanese form of drama developed in the fifteenth century. The highly stylized and symbolic form of drama evolved out of earlier simple plays in the court of the **Ashikaga shogun** Yoshimitsu by Kan'ami (1333–1384) and his son Seami (1363–1443). It is performed on an almost bare stage by an elaborately costumed chief actor and his assistant. Although a secular

art form, like **Zen** Buddhism No characterizes the refined and disciplined spirit of the aesthetics of feudal Japan.

Nobel, Alfred Bernhard (1833–1896)
Swedish chemist, engineer, inventor of dynamite, and founder of the **Nobel Prize**. Nobel found a way of making nitroglycerin safer to work with in the form of dynamite (1862) and invented a more powerful explosive, blasting gelatin (1876). He used the immense fortune these inventions earned him to establish the Nobel Foundation, which awards Nobel Prizes.

Nobel Prize
An award from the Nobel Foundation established by **Alfred B. Nobel** from money made from his invention of explosive devices. Nobel Prizes are given to individuals who have made major contributions in the fields of physics, chemistry, medicine, literature, or the establishment of peace. The first prizes were awarded in 1901.

Nobilis
Name for the Roman aristocracy by the third century B.C.E. The Roman aristocracy was originally known as **patricians** and the lower classes were known as **plebeians**. The classes were hereditary and people were forbidden to marry outside their class. They completely dominated the government of the **Roman Republic**. During the fifth and fourth centuries B.C.E. a "struggle of the orders" led to reforms in the government and a blurring of class lines, with the upper class known as the nobilis (Latin for "well-known" or "noticeable") and the lower class as commoners.

Nobility
The upper class or the aristocracy. The term *nobility* comes from the Latin term *nobilis* ("well-known" or "noticeable"). In the **Roman Republic** nobility was mostly

hereditary, although there was some fluidity in the classes. A person could rise into the nobility. In medieval Europe and in some other societies throughout history, nobility has been synonymous with aristocracy and rigidly hereditary.

Nok Culture
Ancient **Iron Age** culture of Nigeria. Nok artifacts from 500 B.C.E. to 200 C.E. include clay figurines of animals and human beings, iron and stone tools, and other ornaments. The Nok culture was based on farming and trading. Anthropologists believe that iron working spread from the Nok culture to other parts of sub-Saharan Africa.

Nome
Administrative division of ancient Egypt. By the time of the Egyptian Old Kingdom (c. 2575–2130 B.C.E.) the country was divided into nomes. Nome divisions were used in Egypt until the **Muslim** conquests of the seventh century C.E.

Norman Conquest (1066)
Conquest of **Anglo-Saxon England** by **William of Normandy** and the Normans. The descent of the crown of England, held by Edward the Confessor, was contested by Harold Godwinson, earl of Essex; Harold Hardrada of Norway; and William, duke of Normandy. When Edward died in 1066 the Anglo-Saxon Witan (Great Council) elected Harold Godwinson king. Harold Hardrada invaded England in the north, but was defeated by King Harold in a hard-fought battle. William declared his right to the throne and invaded from the south with an army of 5,000, landing near Hastings. Harold immediately marched his army south and attacked the Normans. Only a chance arrow killing King Harold won the day for the Normans. William marched on to London and was crowned

King William I. The Normans spent several years consolidating their conquest of England, using their administrative acumen to build a strong foundation.

Normandy Campaign (1944)

World War II campaign by the **Allies** to invade the European continent. On D-day, June 6, 1944, British, U.S., and Canadian forces landed on five beaches on the Normandy coast of France. Allied bombing of the coast prevented a German build-up, and diversions confused the German command about where the invasion might take place. Paratroopers landed to cut communications and rail lines while massive deployments of troops were landed by ship. German forces put up very stiff resistance, but the Normandy campaign was successful at establishing a foothold on the Continent for Allied forces to gain entry and pour in. From Normandy, General Omar Bradley's U.S. First Army broke out and swept across France.

Normans

Vikings who settled in northwestern France during the ninth and tenth centuries C.E. Their strong, centralized feudal society expanded into England with the **Norman Conquest**, when **William of Normandy** defeated the Anglo-Saxon king of England, Harold, at the **Battle of Hastings** in 1066. Then, in 1130, the Norman king Robert II founded a Norman kingdom in Sicily. The Normans assimilated quickly into the societies they conquered, bringing architectural and military innovations.

Norsemen. *See* Normans; Vikings

North American Free Trade Agreement (NAFTA)

Economic agreement permitting free trade among Canada, Mexico, and the United States signed in 1992, which took effect in 1994. It removes all tariffs between member countries. NAFTA increased trade among these countries, but opponents ague that it helps large businesses and hurts small businesses.

North Atlantic Treaty Organization (NATO)

Defensive organization of European and North American countries. NATO was formed in 1949 to defend the North Atlantic against the threat of the **Union of Soviet Socialist Republics** (USSR). With the collapse of the USSR in 1991, NATO began to work with Russia, and in 1999 the Czech Republic, Hungary, and Poland joined the organization. The only aggressive actions taken by NATO to date are the bombing of Serb military positions in **Bosnia-Herzegovina** in 1995 and the bombing of Serbia itself in 1999 in an attempt to end genocide in the Kosovo region.

Northern Renaissance

Sixteenth-century flowering of **humanism** among Christian intellectuals and artists in northern Europe. Although the **Renaissance** first blossomed in the **city-states** of northern Italy during the early fourteenth century, its focus would later shift northward, especially once Italy came under **Habsburg** domination in the first half of the sixteenth century. Emphasis on the abilities of the individual and looking back to original sources, such as the classics and the **Bible**, brought on creative work in many fields. The Northern Renaissance's focus was more religious and less classical or secular than the Italian Renaissance's. Artists like **Albrecht Dürer** traveled to Italy and brought the intellectual and artistic flavor of the Renaissance to northern Europe.

Northmen. *See* Normans; Vikings

Northumbria. *See* Anglo-Saxon England

Notre Dame Cathedral
Gothic church in Paris built 1163–c. 1250. Notre Dame demonstrates the Gothic features of a long axis, a double ambulatory of the choir, pointed arches, groin vaults, clerestory windows, large rose windows, and flying buttresses. Notre Dame Cathedral dominated old Paris and stood as a symbol of medieval France.

Nubia
Region of the upper **Nile Valley** south of the Nile River's second cataract. Recent research suggests that Nubia may be the source of agriculture and even of kingship exported to Egypt. During the height of the **Egyptian civilization**'s power from 3100 to 1085 B.C.E., Nubia acted as a tributary and intermediary for trade with central and east Africa, sending ivory, ebony, frankincense, and leopard skins. With the **Kush** invasion and the subsequent decline of Egypt in the eighth century B.C.E., Nubia became the independent kingdom of Kush circa 500 B.C.E. Kush was conquered by **Axum** in the fourth century C.E.

Nuclear Disarmament
Movement to eliminate the use of nuclear weapons. Immediately upon the creation and use of nuclear weapons during **World War II**, some people worked to stop the building of nuclear weapons. **Albert Einstein**, **Albert Schweitzer**, and Bertrand Russell pushed for nuclear disarmament. The 1963 Nuclear Test Ban Treaty was an international ban on testing nuclear weapons. In 1968 the Soviet Union, the United Kingdom, and the United States signed the Treaty on the Non-Proliferation of Nuclear Weapons (commonly known as the Non-Proliferation Treaty or NPT), which was endorsed by fifty-nine additional countries. Throughout the 1990s the United States and **Russia** each reduced their stockpiles of nuclear weapons.

Nuclear Test Ban Treaty (1963). *See* Nuclear Disarmament

Nürnberg Trials (Nuremberg)
(1945–1946)
International trials held in Nürnberg, Germany, of **Axis** leaders and organizations responsible for crimes of **World War II**. The International Military Tribunal indicted **Nazis** for fours crimes: (1) crimes against peace in violation of international treaties and agreements; (2) crimes against humanity such as exterminations, deportations, and genocide; (3) war crimes in violation of the laws of war; and (4) a common plan to commit the previous three crimes. If an organization was found guilty of crimes, individuals could be tried as members of the organization. Ten leaders were executed, two committed suicide, and Rudolf Hess was sentenced to life in prison. Several, including **Adolf Hitler** and **Martin Bormann**, were sentenced in absentia.

Nyerere, Julius (1922–1999)
First prime minister of independent Tanganyika (1962–1964) and first president of Tanzania (1964–1985). Educated in Uganda and Scotland, after returning to Tanganyika Nyerere was active in the independence movement throughout the 1950s. He formed the Tanganyika African National Union (1954) calling for peaceful change and social and racial equality. After Tanganyika's independence in 1961, he was made prime minister, then president.

After he negotiated a union with Zanzibar in 1964, he was made president of the new state of Tanzania, a position he held until his retirement in 1985. In 1967 he presented the **Arusha Declaration**, proposing the creation of a socialist, egalitarian society where land would be collectively farmed. Nyerere was an active spokesperson for African affairs throughout the 1960s and 1970s.

O

OAS. *See* Organization of American States (OAS)

OAU (Organization of African Unity)
Organization to promote African unity formed in 1963. As **African decolonization** swept across the continent, thirty-two newly independent, mostly northern African states formed the OAU to facilitate cooperation. In 2000 the OAU became the African Union with fifty-three states.

Oaxaca
Center of several **Mesoamerican** civilizations in southern Mexico. **Mixtec** and **Zapotec** cultures from the eighth century B.C.E. through the fourth century C.E. were among the greatest of Mesoamerican civilizations. Oaxaca became an Aztec garrison in the fifteenth century and was conquered by Spain in 1521. It lies in a fertile valley more than 5,000 feet (1,500 m) above sea level. Extensive ruins exist.

Octavian, Julius Caesar (63 B.C.E.–14 C.E.)
Roman general and emperor. Octavian was **Julius Caesar**'s grandnephew and adopted son. At Caesar's murder Octavian raised an army, became **consul**, allied with **Mark Antony** and Lepidus to form the Second Triumvirate ruling the **Roman Republic,** and eliminated Caesar's assassins. By 31 B.C.E. Octavian had defeated all opposition, including Antony and **Cleopatra** at the **Battle of Actium**. Octavian returned to Rome where in 27 B.C.E. he was given the honorific title *Augustus* ("Re-

vered One"), by which he was thereafter known. Augustus became the **princeps** and gained the Senate title imperator (emperor of the entire Roman world), from that time there was no longer a true Roman Republic, but the **Roman Empire**. Under Augustus's guidance, **Livy, Virgil,** and **Horace** wrote about the history and power of Rome as Augustus pushed for a return to traditional Roman morals and virtues.

October Revolution (1917). *See* Russian Revolution

Oda Nobunaga (1534–1582)
Japanese warlord who emerged in the power struggles of the late **Ashikaga** period as the dominant military ruler assisted by the use of muskets, which had been recently introduced to Japan by the Portuguese. In 1568 he entered **Kyoto,** and in 1573 he ousted the last Ashikaga **shogun.** Oda carried out "sword hunts" to disarm the non-**bushi** population and began surveys of land for tax purposes. His efforts to end the chaos of Japan and to establish a central state were cut short by his suicide after he was wounded in an attempted assassination, but they were continued by one of his generals, **Hideyoshi.**

Odyssey
Greek poem about Odysseus's return home from the **Trojan War** written by **Homer** in the eighth century B.C.E. An epic poem of over 12,000 lines, the *Odyssey* first

covers the adventures of Telemachus (Odysseus's son); then Odysseus's adventures during travel and at homecoming after ten years away at the Trojan War; and also the rescue of Odysseus's wife, Penelope, from the voracious suitors who wished to marry her.

Oedipus the King. See Sophocles

O'Higgins, Bernardo (1778–1842)
Chilean revolutionary and statesman. O'Higgins was a leader of the revolutionary campaign against Spain and the first "supreme director" (head of state) of Chile, from 1817 to 1823. O'Higgins joined **José de San Martin** in their successful effort toward Chilean independence from Spain and went on to become the first national leader in North or South America to eradicate black slavery.

Oil Crisis
Worldwide economic crisis created by the 1973 **Arab-Israeli War**. In 1973 **OPEC** (the Organization of Petroleum Exporting Countries) raised oil prices by 70 percent and then by 130 percent and refused sales to Western countries that had supported Israel in the Arab-Israeli War. The rise in petroleum prices created a severe gasoline shortage in the United States, forcing customers to wait in long lines for fuel, and produced an enormous rise in the price of all products manufactured from petroleum or using oil for energy. The airline industry suffered because of severe increases in the cost of jet fuel. Between 1973 and 1980 the price of oil increased tenfold, creating a second oil crisis in 1979. The 1970s oil crises realigned the power of Western manufacturing countries and third world oil-producing countries and exposed the vulnerability of Western oil-consuming countries, especially the United States and western European countries.

Oil Embargo. *See* Oil Crisis

Okubo Toshimichi (1830–1878)
Japanese politician influential in introducing Western ideas to Japan. Born in Satsuma, he became a **Meiji** loyalist and helped to bring down the **Tokugawa bakufu** in 1867. He was very important in the disestablishment of the old feudal regime and was the major figure in suppressing the movement to invade Korea in 1873. In 1874 he became home minister and sponsored a military expedition to Taiwan. After a rebellion in Satsuma in 1877, he was assassinated by a fellow clansman of Satsuma for having sided with the government against his boyhood friend **Saigo Takmori.**

Okuma Shigenobu (1838–1922)
Early supporter of the Japanese emperor from Hizen. As finance minister in 1876, Okuma's scheme for commuting annual **bushi** stipends saved the government millions. He was ousted from government in 1881, allegedly for embarrassing the government over a land scheme in Jokkaido but actually for proposing a British-style parliamentary democracy. He founded a reform party called the Kaishinto in 1882. While serving as foreign minister, he was attacked by a bomb-wielding terrorist (he lost a leg) for his attempt to reach a mixed court compromise to revise the Unequal Treaties in 1889. He again served as foreign minister in 1896 and 1897. In 1898 he and **Itagaki Taisuke** merged their parties to form the Kenseito (Constitutional Party), and Okuma served for a brief period as prime minister. During his second term as prime minister (1914–1916) Japan entered **World War I** on the Allied side, presenting China with the Twenty-One Demands.

Old Testament. *See* Bible

Olmec Civilization (c. 1200 B.C.E.–400 B.C.E.)

Mesoamerican civilization on the Gulf of Mexico. The name Olmec ("rubber people") is taken from the rubber trees of the region. The Olmec people constructed huge ceremonial centers with pyramids, temples, altars, and palaces. The civilization stretched from present-day Mexico City to El Salvador. The people had a rich agriculture of beans, maize, chili peppers, squash, and tomatoes and produced decorative objects from jade and obsidian and colossal head carvings from rock. Olmec traditions of maize cultivation and construction of ceremonial centers became the basis of later Mesoamerican civilizations such as that at Teotihuacán and the Maya.

Olympic Games

Name for an ancient and a modern athletic competition. From 776 B.C.E. until 393 C.E. the ancient Olympic Games were held every four years in Olympia, Greece. They were primarily held in honor of the god Zeus. The athletes were any male citizens in the Greek empire. In the beginning the games only lasted one day, with one event, the stadion, but they eventually grew to last five days with ten events and were pan-Hellenic. The games ended in 393 because the Roman emperor Theodosius I ended all functioning idol worship sanctuaries. The modern Olympic Games began in 1896 in Athens, Greece. Their goal was to promote friendship and understanding among nations. The International Olympic Committee organizes the games, setting the program, choosing the host city, and determining the definition of "amateur athlete." The first winter Olympic Games were held in 1924 in France.

One Hundred Schools

Chinese term describing the rethinking of society in the Eastern Zhou period (771–256 B.C.E.). China went through a tumultuous era, feudalism evolved, and stability was lost. In attempts to stem the confusion numerous philosophers developed schools of thought such as legalism, Daoism, Confucianism, Moism, and naturalism, known as the One Hundred Schools.

Onin War (1467–1477)

Conflict between two major groups of feudal families in fifteenth-century Japan. The war began with a succession dispute in the Ashikaga shogunate. Two major great families, the Hosokawa and the Yamana, then jockeyed for power. The war led to the destruction of Kyoto and the further weakening of declining central authority in late medieval Japan and to nearly a century of civil war until Oda Nobunaga, Hideyoshi, and Tokugawa Ieyasu reunited the country.

OPEC (Organization of Petroleum Exporting Countries)

International organization established in 1960 to coordinate member oil policies and sales. Its founding members, Iran, Iraq, Kuwait, Saudi Arabia, and Venezuela, have been joined by Algeria, Indonesia, Libya, Nigeria, Qatar, and the United Arab Emirates. In 1973 OPEC raised oil prices 70 percent and then 130 percent and refused oil sales to Western countries that had supported Israel in the 1973 Arab-Israeli War. Between 1973 and 1980 the price of oil increased tenfold. OPEC's influence has been reduced by increased production of petroleum in non-OPEC countries.

Opium War (1839–1842)

War between China and Britain that began with Chinese attempts to stop the importation of opium. In 1839, when Chinese officials confiscated British opium at the port of Guangzhou (Canton), Britain sent warships and defeated the Chinese, forcing the **Qing** government to open some of its ports to British trade under the **Treaty of Nanjing** in 1842. Attempts to restrict foreign trade by the Qing led to a second conflict with Britain and France (1858–1860), resulting in another humiliating defeat for the Chinese and the opening of more ports.

Optimates

Roman term indicating the "best men." The Greeks and Romans used words for *good,* such as "optimus," to denote men of high birth and good social standing. The Optimates were people elected to office and to the Senate and of high moral excellence. For the Romans, office, class, and moral quality were synonymous.

Oracles

Greek form of divination. There were fixed oracle sites around mainland Greece and Asia Minor. Several were healing oracles. Most questions asked the oracles related to what sacrifices would gain divine favor; however, a wide range of questions was asked, such as whether one's wife would conceive or whether a marriage was wise. Frequently the responses were provided by a priest or priestess who spoke in the person of a god, such as at the Oracle of Apollo or the Oracle of Delphi.

Organization of African Unity. *See* OAU (Organization of African Unity)

Organization of American States (OAS)

A regional organization originally founded in 1890 to promote commerce between the countries of the Americas, given its current name and a more political purpose in 1948. The main objectives of the organization, whose membership has grown to thirty-five members from Canada to Argentina, were to promote democracy and economic integration, to peacefully re- solve disputes among members, to defend its members' national sovereignty, and to act as a forum for inter-American discussions. During the **cold war**, under the leadership of the United States, it served as an anti-Communist organization, suspending Cuba's membership in 1962.

Organization of Petroleum Exporting Countries. *See* OPEC (Organization of Petroleum Exporting Countries)

Osaka

City on the main Japanese island of Honshu that since the seventeenth century has been second in size after Tokyo. During the **Tokugawa shogunate** (1603–1868) it became a great commercial center and the home of a vigorous *ukiyo* ("floating world") cultural life supported by the rising class of townspeople. It is famous for its sixteenth-century castle.

Osiris

Ancient Egyptian god of fertility and of the dead and resurrected king. Osiris was viewed as father of Horus, the god of the living king, and wife of **Isis**, mourner and searcher for the dead. In later Egyptian mythology Osiris became ruler of the underworld and the dead and of renewal of life through descendants.

Osman I (1258–1326)

Founder of the **Ottoman Empire.** In the 1280s Osman I established a state, which he declared independent from the **Seljuks** in 1299. He assumed the title of sultan and began a state that would eventually turn into an empire lasting until after **World War I.**

Ostracism

Ancient Athenian method of banishment. In the fifth century B.C.E. citizenship was narrowly defined as being born of free citizen stock. Each year the citizens were asked if an ostracism should take place, and if they voted yes it was held in the **agora**. Each citizen who wished to vote wrote on a fragment of pottery (*ostrakon*) the name of the citizen he wanted banished. If there was a total of as least 6,000 votes, the man with the largest number of votes was ostracized. He had ten days to leave **Athens** and had to remain in exile for ten years. He did not forfeit citizenship or property, and at the end of the ten years he could return to Athens.

Ostrogoths. *See* Goths

Ottoman Empire
Empire of Ottoman Turks extending from the fourteenth century to the end of **World War I**. **Osman I** founded a state in the Anatolian peninsula (the Asian part of modern-day Turkey) in the 1280s, declaring Turkish independence from the **Seljuks** in 1299. The Ottomans expanded into Europe in 1345 and conquered Constantinople in 1453. By 1566 the empire reached its greatest size under **Suleyman I**, extending to North Africa and into central Europe. From the fifteenth to seventeenth centuries the Ottoman Empire was a center of high culture and many intellectual achievements. It was still powerful in the seventeenth century, but by the eighteenth century it began to decline. It decreased in size and lost in several confrontations with Russia. The nineteenth century saw Britain, Austria, France, and Prussia propping up the Ottoman Empire to maintain a balance of power in the region and to keep Russia from extending its influence into the Black Sea and the Mediterranean. The **Crimean War** (1854–1856) was fought for this purpose. By the early twentieth century most of the European territories had been lost by the Ottomans in the expansion of **nationalism**,

and a group known as the **Young Turks** was pushing for reforms within Turkey. In 1914 the outbreak of World War I brought in the Ottoman Empire on the side of Germany, but with the end of the war the allies occupied **Istanbul**, and in 1920 the Treaty of Sèvres cut the empire to pieces. In 1922 the sultanate was abolished, and in 1923 the Republic of Turkey was established.

Ottoman Turks
Turkish-speaking people from the eastern **steppes** who moved into the Anatolian peninsula and were ruled by the Ottoman dynasty (beginning with **Osman I**, who ruled in 1281–1326). Largely **Muslim** when they arrived, the Ottomans became the center of the Muslim world. They were set back temporarily in 1402 when defeated by the **Mongol** conqueror **Timur**. The Ottoman Turks conquered the **Byzantine Empire** and **Constantinople** in 1453 and turned Constantinople into their capital as **Istanbul**. The Ottoman Turks produced a brilliant, long-lived empire that, at its peak, ruled territories from Budapest to the Persian Gulf, and from the Caspian Sea to Algeria.

Otto I, "the Great" (912–973)
Duke of Saxony, German king (936–973), and Holy Roman Emperor (962–973). Otto consolidated Germany by reducing the power of his feudal **vassals** and by military conquest eastward, including of the Hungarians. He continued a German tradition since the time of **Charlemagne** of supporting the **Roman Catholic Church** and using the church's influence to bolster his own governance, extending his influence into Italy.

Ovid (full name Publius Ovidius Naso) (43 B.C.E.–17 C.E.)
Roman poet known for *The Metamorphoses* (8 C.E.), a panorama of the Greek and

Roman myths and a masterpiece of literature. It was the first attempt to bring together all Greek myths in one cohesive whole. Ovid was a renowned poet and honored and patronized by the Roman emperor **Octavian** until the emperor banished Ovid for encouraging Octavian's daughter, Julia, in a life of lasciviousness (which Julia performed well even before her relationship with Ovid).

Oxford University
One of the oldest universities in the world. Founded some time before 1180, Oxford was renowned for its education in theology and in the humanities. At present there are thirty-nine colleges within the university, and it is still renowned for the humanities.

Oyo
Region of southwestern Nigeria. Oyo was the capital of the Kingdom of Oyo in the seventeenth and eighteenth centuries. The people of Oyo, the Yoruba, were town dwellers noted for their cavalry. The Kingdom of Oyo controlled some of the trade routes that supplied slaves to Europeans in the seventeenth and eighteenth centuries. Oyo defeated its rival Dahomey, but in the nineteenth century the kingdom was broken up into a number of smaller states and in 1888 they came under British protection.

P

Pachacutec (Pachacuti) (c. 1418–1471)
Inca emperor (1438–1471). He dramatically expanded the Inca empire in southern Peru and then to the north and into Ecuador, creating the vast influence of the Incas. Pachacutec was reputed to be a mighty warrior and also a great administrator. Much of his expansion was by gaining submission of provinces by skillful threats and claims of divine intervention. He invented a state religion based on the worship of a creator god, Viracocha and is reputed to have designed the Inca capital of Cuzco. His son **Topu Inca** continued the conquests and expansion of the Inca.

Pacific, War of the
Conflict between Chile, Peru, and Bolivia (1879–1884) over control of the Atacama Desert region and its rich nitrate deposits. Following increased tensions over the ill-defined boundaries in the area, Chile attacked first Bolivia then Peru. Chile emerged victorious, annexing Bolivia's coastline and forcing Peru to surrender its southernmost province. The war gave Chile control of the mineral region, led to an occupation of parts of southern Peru that did not end until 1929, and left Bolivia a landlocked country.

Paekche Kingdom
Kingdom in the southwestern part of the Korean Peninsula that was one of three states that competed for supremacy during Korea's Three Kingdoms Period (fourth century to 676). Paekche developed a refined Buddhist culture. In the sixth century Paekche sent missionaries to Japan, where they introduced **Buddhism** and literacy. Until its conquest by **Silla** in 660, Paekche continued to have close relations with and a strong cultural influence on the emerging Japanese state.

Pagan
City in the dry plains of central Burma (Myanmar) that was the capital of the ethnic Burman kingdom of Pagan. The city and kingdoms declined after a **Mongol** invasion in 1287. Today it is famous for its many Buddhist temples reflecting the prosperity and high culture of the state.

Pahlavi. *See* Muhammad Reza Shah Pahlavi

Palenque
Maya city in present-day Chiapas, Mexico. Named after a modern neighboring village, Palenque was constructed from 600 to 900 C.E. Its buildings were smooth plastered, unlike most limestone Maya construction. The city contained a palace, a watchtower, and temples. Extensive ruins remain.

Paleo-Indians
North American peoples of the **Paleolithic Age**. Like all Paleolithic people, they were hunters and gatherers. There is evidence from 9000 B.C.E. of hunters making fluted-stone projectile points attached to shafts of ivory and wood, used to hunt mammoths, mastodons, camels, and ground sloths.

The Paleo-Indians also made grinding implements and ate a variety of foods according to their environment. They made baskets and nets and lived in caves and rock shelters. They had domesticated the dog very early, and some historians believe that they brought the dog with them from Asia and that it enabled them to survive in their new environment.

Paleolithic Age

Ancient period of human cultural development characterized by the making of chipped stone tools. Early study of mankind is divided into the Paleolithic (Old Stone Age) and the **Neolithic** (New Stone Age) eras. Most of human history belongs to the Paleolithic period, named after the characteristic stone tools found by archaeologists. It was a time when humans lived in small bands and subsisted by hunting and foraging for edible products. Homo erectus and **Homo sapiens** existed in the Paleolithic age. The Paleolithic ended about 10,000 years ago with the development of polished stone tools and the beginnings of agriculture.

Palestine, Ancient

Middle East region along the Mediterranean Sea. The territory was about 150 miles (240 km) long and, in the south, 55 miles (90 km) wide. The eastern coast of the Mediterranean forms its western border, the Jordan Valley its eastern limit. The Negev (a desert region) of the Sinai Peninsula marks the southern end, while the hills of Galilee lie in the north. Situated between the **Nile Valley** and **Mesopotamia**, Palestine (**meaning "Land of the Philistines"**) was the most convenient route for merchants and armies from the beginning of recorded history. Some of the oldest cities in the world are found there, including Jericho, Hebron, and **Jerusalem**, usually located where ample

water supplies were available. The great powers—**Egypt**, **Assyria**, **Babylonia**, **Hellenistic Greece**, and the **Roman Empire**—contended constantly for control of Palestine, which saw many crucial battles, including several near Megiddo in the north (the source of the name **Armageddon**).

Palestinian Authority

Governing body of the Palestinian autonomous regions of the West Bank and Gaza Strip, established in 1994. As part of a peace agreement between Israel and the **Palestinian Liberation Organization**, the territories were to be gradually handed over to government by the Palestinian Authority. In 1996 Palestinian Authority elections were held and **Yasser Arafat** won the presidency decisively. In 2005 the Israeli military oversaw the withdrawal of Jewish settlers in Gaza, although the complete withdrawal of Israel from Palestinian territories has not been completed because of continued violence on both sides.

Palestinian Liberation Organization (PLO)

Political organization established in 1964 to press for the creation of a Palestinian homeland. Palestine was under British mandate after **World War I**, and the Peel Commission recommended the creation of a Jewish state and a Palestinian state. In 1947 the **United Nations** also recommended the creation of two states. With the creation of the state of Israel in 1948 and a war with surrounding Arab states, the recommendation to create a Palestinian state was dropped and **Palestinians** were dispersed among a number of countries, especially Jordan. In the 1960s, 1970s, and 1980s **guerrilla** warfare against Israel was organized by the PLO. In 1994 the PLO, in negotiations with Israel, agreed to the formation of an autonomous state under the governance of the **Palestinian Authority**. **Yasser Arafat**, the long-time head of the PLO was elected president of the Palestinian Authority. He died in 2004 and was succeeded by Mahmoud Abbas.

Palestinians

Arab population attached historically and/or physically to Palestine, a territory construed to encompass Israel and Israeli-occupied territories, areas under the control of the **Palestinian Authority**, and parts of Jordan. There are approximately 10 million Palestinians, a large minority of whom are Christian. Nearly 5 million Palestinians live in the West Bank, the Gaza Strip, and Israel proper. There are nearly 4 million more Palestinians concentrated in surrounding states: almost 3 million in Jordan, more than 400,000 in Syria and Lebanon, and about 70,000 in Egypt. There are well over 500,000 Palestinians in other Arab nations and slightly fewer throughout the rest of the world.

Pallavas

South Indian Hindu dynasty that flourished from the fourth to the ninth century. From their capital of Pallavapur on the Bay of Bengal they traded with parts of Southeast Asia, contributing to the spread of Indian culture in that region. They were patrons of the arts and of Hindu religion, their most famous legacy being the temples of **Mamallapuram** (Mahabalipuram).

Pan-African Congresses

A series of meetings to focus on African interests. The impetus for these gatherings came from African Americans, West Indians, and Africans. **W. E. B. Du Bois** was the driving force behind the congresses in 1900, 1919, 1921, 1923, 1927, and 1945. The 1945 Pan-African Congress in Manchester, England, was the first to focus on African independence and self-government. The 1963 Pan-African Congress in Ethiopia led to the creation of the Organization of African Unity (**OAU**), which in 2000 became the African Union (AU).

Panama, Isthmus of

Narrowest land connecting the American continents. In 1513 Spanish explorers led by **Vasco Núñez de Balboa** were the first Europeans to reach the west coast of the isthmus and the Pacific Ocean, and they established a settlement there. The land was claimed by the Spanish and fought over by the English and the Scottish in the seventeenth century because it provided a short route to the west coast of North America. Later, the French, British, and Americans planned to build a canal across the isthmus, and the United States eventually completed its construction.

Panama Canal

Canal cutting across Central America at the Isthmus of Panama from the Atlantic to the Pacific ocean. The canal is nearly 51 miles (82 km) long, with three sets of locks, and it shortened the ocean voyage from New York to San Francisco by almost 8,000 miles (13,000 km). Because of its strategic location it was carved out of a Colombian province at the behest of the United States. It was begun by the French and completed by the United States between 1904 and 1914. The Panama Canal was administered by the United States until 1999, when it was turned over to Panama.

Pan-Arab Movement

Political orientation that calls for all Arabs to be politically organized within one single nation, not as many separate states. The ideology took shape in the late Ottoman period with Abdul Hamid II's 1876 constitution and gained strength in the

Arab provinces of the **Ottoman Empire** after the **Young Turks** seized power in 1908. The Hashemite clan from the Hijaz generated tangible expressions of a pan-Arab orientation between the World Wars. After **World War II** and before the War on Terror pan-Arabism was championed by **Gamal Abdel Nasser** in Egypt, Hafez Assad in Syria, and **Saddam Hussein** in Iraq. The Arab League, consisting of twenty-two member states, remains an institutional repository of pan-Arabism.

Panhellenism

The belief that what the Greeks held in common, such as language, history, customs, and religion, was more important than what separated them. The Greeks viewed people other than Greeks as "barbarians," or those who spoke "barbar" (i.e., not Greek). The Greeks called themselves Hellenes and saw their culture as united even though the region was never politically united. Panhellenism existed from earlier times, but it became prominent with the **Persian War** in the fifth century B.C.E. The threat from the outside made clear what distinguished being Greek. Panhellenic games were open to all Greeks.

Panini

Indian grammarian and author of *Ashtadhyayi* (Eight Chapters) the classic of **Sanskrit** grammar in the fourth century B.C.E. Panini's grammar was the most scientific study of a language until the development of modern linguistics in the nineteenth century. The work was important in stabilizing the classical form of Sanskrit, the most important language of scholarship, literature, and religious texts in the Indian subcontinent.

Panmunjom

Truce village along the demilitarized zone (DMZ) that separates North and South Korea. It was the scene of protracted negotiations that led to the cessation of hostilities in the **Korean War** in July 1953.

Pao-chia System. *See* Baojia

Papacy (the Pope) (Latin for "father")
Office of the bishop of **Rome**, the supreme pontiff of the **Roman Catholic Church**. The papacy claimed its primacy from Jesus's granting of authority to the apostle Peter. The papacy of Gregory I (590–604) increased in power and prestige. During the eighth century the papacy struck an arrangement with **Charlemagne**'s monarchy to support each other. By the tenth century the papacy had become a secular power, and in the eleventh century a long process of conflict with monarchies over who held the power to install bishops and abbots began. The Church of Saint Peter in Rome, as the seat of the bishop of Rome, has held great importance throughout the history of the papacy.

Paper

Writing material developed in China in the later **Han** dynasty period. The earliest reference dates to 105, when a process of making paper from mulberry trees and fibers was recorded. By the **Tang** dynasty paper making was becoming common, which, along with the simultaneous invention of printing, led to an expansion of reading materials and the growth of literacy. Paper making spread to Korea at least by the eighth century, and the oldest extant example dates from 751. At about the same time the technique of paper making arrived in the **Middle East**. Paper was being produced in Europe by the fourteenth century.

Papyrus

Writing material manufactured by the ancient **Egyptian civilization**. Produced since at least 3000 B.C.E., papyrus is made from a marsh plant that grows in the swamps along the Nile River. It became the most widely used writing material in the Greco-Roman world. It was made by slicing the inner pith of the plant into strips and placing strips first in one direction and then perpendicularly. They were then pressed, and the plant's natural juices acted as glue. When dry the papyrus was smoothed with a stone. Sheets could be connected to one another to form a roll or scroll. In Europe, where the plant did not grow, **parchment** made of animal skins became the standard writing material.

Parchment

Writing material used throughout Europe in the **Middle Ages** and named for the city of **Pergamum**. Parchment was made from the skins of sheep and goats or even rabbit, deer, or pig. The skin was washed, dipped in water mixed with lime to remove the fat and hair, stretched, scraped, and dried. Finally it was finished with a pumice stone. Fine parchment is very durable. If kept dry and away from vermin, it can last indefinitely. It makes a very smooth and even surface for writing (unlike **papyrus**). Parchment can be written on both sides and therefore works better as codices (books) than as scrolls.

Parhae

Manchurian state created in the early eighth century following the collapse of the northern Korean state of **Koguryo**. Parhae at its peak was a powerful state with a mixed Korean and Manchurian tribal population; extended from northern Korea to the Amur River; and played an important role in the power struggles among **Silla** Korea, **Tang** China, and **Heian** Japan. It collapsed in the early tenth century under pressure from the **Khitans**. Some twentieth-century Koreans regarded

Parhae as a Korean state and from this basis claimed most of **Manchuria** as part of historic Korea.

Pariahs

People outside the caste system of **Hinduism**. This lowest social grouping was often called untouchables because its members were considered unclean and therefore "untouchable" by people in the caste system. Theoretically, the pariahs were outside the caste system. The term *pariah* is derived from "Paraiyan," the name for a caste of laborers in southern India, but came to be applied to all outcastes. In the twentieth century reforms sought to end the stigma toward the group, which **Mohandas K. Gandhi** later renamed *harijans* ("children of god"). The Republic of India has developed programs to help them advance socially, but discrimination remains.

Paris, Congress of (1856)

Conference to end the Crimean War. Britain, Austria, Russia, Turkey, and Sardinia were present. Russia conceded territories in the Balkans. The Black Sea and the Danube River were supposed to be neutral and open. Turkey was propped up by the Western powers, although the decline of the **Ottoman Empire** continued.

Paris, Treaty of (1763) (also known as Peace of Paris)

Treaty ending the **Seven Years' War**. In the treaty signed by Britain, France, and Spain, Britain gained all of Canada and the American territory between the Allegheny Mountains and the Mississippi River (except New Orleans) from France and received Florida from Spain, while Spain received New Orleans and Louisiana from France and Cuba and the Philippines from Britain. France received Guadeloupe, Martinique, and Saint Lucia, and a much reduced role in India. The Treaty of Paris established the predominance of Britain over France as of 1763 and thereby removed Britain's only impediment to overseas domination.

Paris, Treaty of (1783) (also known as Peace of Paris)
Treaty between the United States and Britain ending the **American Revolution**. Negotiated by **John Adams**, John Jay, and **Benjamin Franklin** on the American side, the treaty recognized the independence of the United States but failed to settle the frontier, leading to continued conflicts and, eventually, the War of 1812.

Paris Peace Conference (1919–1920)
Meeting of the leaders of thirty-two states at the end of **World War I**. Negotiations were dominated by the five major powers responsible for the defeat of the Central powers: Britain, France, Italy, Japan, and the United States. Five treaties emerged from the Paris Peace Conference, the first and most important known as the **Versailles Treaty**.

Park Chung Hee (1917–1979)
South Korean general and leader 1961–1979. Park was a schoolteacher who served as a young officer in the Japanese army during **World War II** and as an officer in the South Korean army during the **Korean War**. In 1961 he led a military coup, and he was then elected president in 1963. He continued an increasingly authoritarian rule, assuming dictatorial power in 1972. Under Park, South Korea pursued a policy of rapid economic growth leading to the "Miracle on the Han," in which South Korea achieved the world's fastest rate of economic growth. Despite his success in directing South Korea's transformation from a poverty-stricken, largely agricultural society to a major exporter of industrial goods and in greatly increasing the standard of living, many Koreans tired of his authoritarian policies, including suppression of labor unions and political dissent. Following increasing unrest and riots he was assassinated by the head of his own huge security organization, the Agency for National Security Planning (ANSP), commonly referred to as the "KCIA," in October 1979.

Parks, Rosa (1913–2005)
Montgomery, Alabama, seamstress and National Association for the Advancement of Colored People (NAACP) activist. Her arrest in December 1955 for refusing to give up her seat on a city bus to a white passenger in violation of the city's policy of segregation in bus seating led to a boycott of the bus system by black passengers. The thirteen-month boycott, along with a successful federal court suit brought by local civil rights leaders, led to an end to the policy of segregation on city buses. Among those leading the boycott under the auspices of the Montgomery Improvement Association was the Reverend **Martin Luther King Jr.**, a local Baptist minister. His involvement in the boycott marked King's emergence as a national leader of the modern **civil rights movement**. Through her action Parks achieved a legendary status in the movement. She later moved to Detroit, where she continued her involvement in issues of civil rights.

Parlement
The French court system in the *ancien régime*, abolished in the **French Revolution**. Having originated as the Parlement of Paris, it had become a series of provincial courts. One of the sparks leading to the French Revolution was the aristocracy's pressure to gain control of the Parlements

and the Parlements' opposition to the monarchy.

Parliament

Originally an English consultative body to the king composed of nobles and the upper clergy of bishops and abbots. By the end of the thirteenth century the king occasionally invited wealthy commoners to the meetings because they paid much of the taxes. Over time they became a regular component as the **House of Commons**, and the clergy and nobility became the **House of Lords**. Parliament remained a court of the king, meeting and acting at his will, until the **English Civil War** and the **Glorious Revolution** of the late seventeenth century. Parliament is the legislative and executive body of the United Kingdom today. Parliaments or Parliament-like bodies have spread throughout much of the world.

Parthenon

Temple of Athena built on the Acropolis in Athens. The word *parthenon* means "virgin," in reference to Athena. Begun in 447 B.C.E., in the time of Pericles, the **Doric Order** temple was dedicated in 438 B.C.E. Work on a previous temple on the site was destroyed in the **Persian War** of 480–479 B.C.E. The Parthenon was built as an offering for Athenian success in the war. The temple originally housed a gold-and-ivory statue of Athena designed by Phidias. The Parthenon was basically intact until 1687, when a Turkish **gunpowder** magazine stored in it was exploded by besieging Venetians.

Pascal, Blaise (1623–1662)

French mathematician, physicist, and philosopher. Pascal laid the foundation for the modern theory of probability and developed Pascal's principle of pressure in fluids. He also wrote a work of Christian apologetics known as *Pensées*.

Pataliputra

Ancient capital of the Magadha kingdom and of the **Maurya empire** located on the site of modern-day Patna in Bihar state of eastern India. It also served as the capital of the **Gupta empire** and was a great center of learning. **Buddhist** pilgrims from as far away as China visited and studied at its **monasteries**. It declined in the seventh century.

Patrician (Roman)

Aristocratic ruling class of the **Roman Republic**. The patricians expelled the kings of **Rome** around 500 B.C.E. and set up a republic consisting of three parts: two chief magistrates, known as **consuls**, selected from the patricians for one year; the Senate, composed of life-term patricians selected by the consuls; and the assembly of the common people, or **plebeians**. The assembly was controlled by the patricians, as was the priesthood. Patricians were hereditary and forbidden to marry commoners. Gradually over the fifth and fourth centuries B.C.E., class lines blurred and patricians were replaced by **nobilis**, or **nobility**.

Patton, George S. (1885–1945)

U.S. Army general in **World War II**. Patton was a West Point graduate who was the first American officer assigned to tanks in **World War I**. In World War II he commanded an armored corps in the invasion of North Africa, the Seventh Army in the invasion of Sicily, and the Third Army in France and Germany. A skilled and aggressive leader, Patton's most significant action was the relief of Bastogne, Belgium, during the **Battle of the Bulge**. Colorful and controversial, he was reprimanded for slapping two soldiers suffering from combat fatigue, whom he accused of cowardice. Patton died following an automobile accident in Germany in December 1945.

Paul the Apostle (Saul of Tarsus)
(c. 10–67)
Jewish Roman convert to Christianity who played a critical role in developing the Christian church. Originally an enemy of Christianity, following his conversion Paul became the strongest advocate of the religion, traveling tirelessly around the **Roman Empire** to establish churches and meet with and encourage groups of Christians in **Asia Minor** and Greece. His correspondence with these churches comprises the biblical books of Paul's Letter to the Romans, First and Second Letters to the Corinthians, Letter to the Galatians, Letter to the Ephesians, Letter to the Philippians, Letter to the Colossians, First and Second Letters to the Thessalonians, First and Second Letters to Timothy, Letter to Titus, Letter to Philemon, and Letter to Hebrews.

Pax Romana ("Roman Peace") (14 –180)
Period of relative peace and prosperity throughout the **Roman Empire**. The Pax Romana was a concept of international stability made possible by the power of the empire. At **Octavian**'s (Augustus's) death in 14 C.E. a series of corrupt emperors, the **Julio-Claudians**, were followed by the five "good emperors" who ruled until 180 C.E. As a concept the Pax Romana went far beyond 180 C.E. and influenced even the German emperors from the fifth to the ninth centuries, the British Empire of the nineteenth century, and U.S. international diplomacy of the twentieth and twenty-first centuries.

Peace Constitution
Popular name for the 1947 Japanese constitution drawn up by the U.S. occupation forces and ratified by the Japanese parliament. The name is derived from Article 9 of the constitution, which prohibited Japan from possessing armed forces. The constitution stripped the emperor of all powers, making him a symbol of the state and people, and provided a more democratic government that the previous **Meiji constitution**. The constitution is still in effect although Article 9 was reinterpreted during the **Korean War** to permit Japan to maintain a national "Self-Defense Force."

Peace of Augsburg. *See* Augsburg, Peace of

Peace of Paris (1763). *See* Paris, Treaty of (1763)

Peace of Westphalia. *See* Westphalia, Treaty of

Pearl Harbor
Port on the island of Oahu, Hawaii. Japan's carrier aircraft surprise attack on the U.S. Navy's Pacific Fleet at Pearl Harbor early on the morning of December 7, 1941, led to the United States' entry into **World War II.**

Peasants' Revolt, English. *See* English Peasants' Revolt

Peasants' War (1524–1525)
Rebellion across southern and central Germany. The largest revolt of medieval or early modern Europe. Difficult conditions led to disaffection, but the **Reformation** provided justification because it claimed that all people were important in God's eyes and discrimination of peasants as serfs was unacceptable. The *Twelve Articles* (1525), laid out by the leaders of the Peasants' War, stated that no Christian man or woman should be held in bondage. Participants in the Peasants' War expected **Martin Luther** to come to their aid, but instead, after initial sympathy, he denounced the rebellion.

Peisistratus (c. 600–527 C.E.)
Tyrant of ancient **Athens**. After a period of severe strife Peisistratus came to power as a tyrant, reduced the authority of the aristocracy, and stabilized the economy. At Peisistratus's death his son **Hippias** ruled Athens (527–510 C.E.).

Peking. *See* Beijing

Peloponnesian League
Oldest and longest Greek alliance. The ancient name was "Spartans and Their Allies," and it existed in the sixth century B.C.E. Its allies swore to have similar friends and allies as **Sparta**, although the alliance never bound members to be friends except during a league war with an outside force. Members could even go to war with one another. Sparta always commanded the armies and appointed officers. After the **Peloponnesian War** ended in the defeat of **Athens**, the league tended to become a Spartan empire. It disintegrated in the 370s.

Peloponnesian War (431–404 B.C.E.)
War between the poleis of **Athens** and **Sparta**. Sparta had been the dominant **polis** until the end of the **Persian Wars** in 479 B.C.E., when Athens came to the fore in Greek leadership. Tension between the two always existed, but it burst into full-scale war in 431 B.C.E. Most of the Greek poleis sided with one or the other. Athens was led by **Pericles** until his death in 429 B.C.E. It suffered a series of devastating defeats including the destruction of its fleet in 405 B.C.E. In 404 B.C.E. Athens was conquered and the Athenian government overthrown by a group later known as the Thirty Tyrants. Although Sparta had won, all the Greek states had been so weakened that they were overrun by Macedonia in 338 B.C.E.

People's Liberation Army
Chinese army founded by the **Chinese Communist Party** in 1927 as the armed wing of the communist movement. Having survived the **Long March**, the People's Liberation Army waged a **guerrilla** war against the **Guomindang** and, during **World War II**, the Japanese. It became the armed forces of China with the creation of the **Peoples' Republic of China** in 1949. Under **Lin Biao**, who became its commander in 1959, it became very active in Chinese politics. After Lin's fall in 1971 following an alleged coup attempt, its role in politics was reduced. After 1979 the Chinese leadership reduced its sized and attempted to make it more professional and technically equipped.

People's Republic of China (PRC)
Name of the Chinese communist state first proclaimed in **Beijing** on October 1, 1949, by revolutionary leader **Mao Zedong**. The PRC ended more than a century of weak central governments and regional warlords in China. Initially, the communist leaders of the PRC were successful in accomplishing their goals of making China unified, stable, and fully independent. The attempts to create a new society based on the socialist ideas of Marxism-Leninism as interpreted by Mao were less successful in transforming China into a modern industrial society and were modified after Mao's death in 1976. In the 1980s China opened its markets to international trade and investment and established a mixed socialist-capitalist economy while retaining an authoritarian political system under the Chinese Communist Party. This led to a rapid growth in the Chinese economy and the emergence of China as a major economic and military power.

Pergamum
Ancient Attalid capital city in the area that today is Turkey. Important in the fourth,

third, and second centuries B.C.E., the city was enlarged and beautified by the Attalid kings, especially Eumenes II, who transformed it into a **Hellenistic Greek** cultural capital modeled after **Athens**. It was an intellectual center with a great library where Romans went to study after the empire was taken over by **Rome** in 133 B.C.E. Pergamum was renowned for its library and for the development of **parchment**, named for the city. It is famous as one of the few archaeologically excavated cities of the Hellenistic period outside Macedonia.

Pericles (c. 495–429 B.C.E.)

Athenian political leader and general. Although an aristocrat, he was a strong supporter of Athenian **democracy**. Pericles came to prominence in **Athens** in the 460s B.C.E. and led the more aggressive foreign policy of the 450s B.C.E. He introduced pay for jurors, limited citizenship to men with both an Athenian mother and an Athenian father, and proposed an assembly or league of all Greece that was blocked by Sparta. Pericles commanded the expedition to quell a revolt in Euboea and encouraged the building program of Athens in the 440s and 430s B.C.E., including the **Parthenon**. He was elected general annually and held leadership of Athens, including direction of the **Peloponnesian War**, until the hardship of the war diminished his popularity. He continued to be elected to office until his death from the plague in 429 B.C.E.

Periplus

Earliest written account of East Africa. Believed to have been written by a Greek living in Egypt in the second half of the first century C.E., the Periplus remained the standard of knowledge of this region for Greeks and Romans for hundreds of years, describing products shipped into and out of the area.

Perón, Eva (1919–1952)

Argentine political figure and wife of president **Juan Perón**. Eva Perón was affectionately known by some groups as Evita but was hated by opposing factions. She became her husband's liaison between the working classes and the government and organized the women's section of the Peronist Party. She sought the vice presidency in 1951 but was prevented by the military. She died the next year.

Perón, Juan (1895–1974)

President of Argentina (1946–1955, 1973–1974). As a soldier he participated in the fascist coup in 1943, and he was elected president in 1946. Perón, a charismatic politician, sought policies that promoted labor and **nationalism** and founded the Peronist Party. His second wife, **Eva Perón**, aided these pursuits. Juan Perón was removed from office by the military in 1955, having been adversely affected by his excommunication from the **Roman Catholic Church**, grief over Eva's death in 1952, and dealings with labor unrest and economic problems. He returned to Argentina in 1973 and, still with much support from the labor movement, was reelected to the presidency. Perón made his third wife, Isabel Perón, his vice president. He died in office in 1974.

Perry, Commodore Matthew Calbraith (1794–1858)

U.S. naval officer in command of an expedition of four ships that landed near Edo, Japan, in 1853 with a letter from President Millard Fillmore ordering the opening of Japan to U.S. trade.

Persepolis

Archaeological site in southeastern Iran. It represents the high point of architectural grandeur achieved by the **Achaemenids** (c. 550–330 B.C.E.) in Iran. Persepolis is the palace and tomb complex for **Xerxes I**, **Darius I** ("the Great"), and other ancient Persian kings. The buildings comprising Persepolis are elevated between 30 and 60 feet (9 and 18 m) above ground level on an artificial terrace. The location was chosen by **Cyrus the Great**, whose tomb is in nearby Persepolis proper at Pasargadae. Achaemenid architecture was influenced by the Greeks and the Egyptians and evolved into a monumental style in which relief sculpture was used as an adjunct to massive architectural complexes such as Persepolis.

Persian Empire
Sixth to fifth century B.C.E. empire stretching from Greece to India and from Egypt to the Caspian and Aral seas. An alliance of Persians, Medes, and Scythians sacked **Nineveh** in 612 B.C.E., ending the Assyrian Empire. In 550 B.C.E. **Cyrus the Great** conquered the Medes and expanded the Persian Empire into Lydia and the Greek cities on the Anatolian (Turkish) coast. Cyrus then conquered eastward as far as western India and southward to the city of **Babylon** by 539 B.C.E. Cyrus's son Cambyses conquered Egypt in 525. Under **Darius I** ("the Great") (522–486 B.C.E.) Persia began nearly two centuries of peaceful rule. Although the empire expanded, attempts by both Darius and his successor **Xerxes I** to conquer Greece were thwarted. The Persian Empire survived until conquered by **Alexander the Great** by 326 B.C.E.

Persian Wars (490–479 B.C.E.)
Conflict between the Persian Empire and the Greek **poleis**, especially **Athens**. A revolt against the Persians by the Greek Ionians brought Athens into the conflict. Persia under King **Darius I** ("the Great") (522–486 B.C.E.) responded by attacking Athens but was stopped at the **Battle of Marathon** in 490 B.C.E. The Persians returned in 480 B.C.E. under King **Xerxes I** with an army of 150,000 and destroyed Athens but were defeated in the naval **Battle of Salamis** and the land **Battle of Plataea**. The Athenian victory was astonishing, considering the lopsided numbers not in their favor. Victory convinced the Athenians that humans could accomplish anything if they worked together and used their intelligence. Thus began the **classical Greek** period.

Peter I, "the Great" (1672–1725)
Russian tsar (1682–1725) and reformer. Peter expanded Russia, defeating the Tatars to gain access to the Black Sea, and expanded into the Baltic region, annexing Estonia and Latvia. His reforms and modernization of the military and the government brought Russia into the modern world with greater association with Europe. In 1703 he made Saint Petersburg his capital.

Petrarch (full name Francesco Petrarca) (1304–1374)
Italian Renaissance poet and scholar who produced secular literature and is credited with being the first **humanist**. He wrote in both Latin, producing *Africa* (1341), about the famed Roman general Scipio Africanus, and Italian, with works such as *Canzoniere* (1342). Petrarch described the world around him based on the inspiration of Laura, his muse, as well as the influence of classical Greek and Latin texts. He wrote love poetry in sonnet form that was later imitated by other writers including **William Shakespeare**.

Pharisees
One of several prominent groups of Jewish leaders in the first century C.E., along with the **Sadducees**, who dominated the **Hebrew Temple** and priesthood, and the

scribes, who were experts in the Hebrew scriptures. They were laymen who stressed the study of the **Torah** and of a mass of oral traditions that sought to interpret and apply it to daily life. Unlike the Sadducees, they were close to, and popular among, the masses; they accepted not only the Pentateuch but also the Prophets and the Writings as scripture; they believed in bodily resurrection after death; and they largely supported revolution against Roman domination. Most of the Pharisees opposed **Jesus** and his followers, though some, notably **Paul the Apostle** (Saul of Tarsus), became **Christians**.

Philip II (Macedonia) (382–336 B.C.E.)
Macedonian king and builder of the Macedonian empire. Philip II transformed a weak Macedonian kingdom into the dominant power in the Greek world. Using his great infantry and cavalry he conquered the entire region from the Black Sea to the Peloponnese of Greece. He also exploited the gold from Thracian mines to pay for large mercenary armies. Philip planned to attack Persia, but his life was ended by an assassin and that project was left to his son, **Alexander III**.

Philip II (Spain) (1527–1598)
Spanish king (1556–1598) and ruler of the Netherlands, Milan, Naples, Spanish America, and Portugal after 1580, and husband of **Mary I** of England (1554–1558). From his court at Madrid Philip II ruled an empire unequaled and generally unchallenged in Europe. This was Spain's **golden age**. Philip created a centralized government without an Estates General by administering through paid agents. His massive palace, the Escorial, took two decades to build (1563–1584). Philip's ardent Catholic zeal created problems for Spain in the Netherlands with the **Dutch Revolt** (1568–1648) and with England,

leading to the destruction of the **Spanish Armada** in 1588.

Philip II (Philip Augustus) (1165–1223)
French medieval monarch (r. 1180–1223). Philip Augustus, a Capetian, fought the English and reduced their influence on the continent. He also defeated the Count of **Flanders** and the Duke of **Burgundy**, expanding the royal domain. He consolidated and expanded royal authority in France by creating paid administrators and relying less on the aristocracy. He also increased the royal revenues to pay for expanded government and for fortifying Paris.

Philip IV, "the Fair" (1268–1314)
King of France (1285–1314). Philip's struggle with the Catholic **papacy** in Rome was resolved when the papal court moved to Avignon, France (1309–1378) in the so-called **Babylonian Captivity**. He increased his royal powers by reducing the power of many of his barons and confiscated property from Jews. His three sons succeeded him as kings of France Louis X, Philip V, and Charles IV.

Philosophes
Name for the social and political philosophers, mainly French, of the eighteenth-century **Enlightenment**. The philosophes searched for the fundamentals of social institutions as the natural philosophers had done for the physical universe. They wrote about the nature of laws, natural law, and the best design for government. The philosophes included **Montesquieu**, Condorcet, Diderot, **Voltaire**, and Maupertuis.

Phoenicians
Ancient people who settled on the eastern coast of the Mediterranean Sea. Divided into several kingdoms at different times, the Phoenicians became known as great

international traders from the cities of Tyre, Sidon, and Byblos and established the country of Phoenicia by the ninth century B.C.E. They established trading centers elsewhere around the Mediterranean, the most famous of which was **Carthage**, on the north coast of Africa. From this location the Phoenicians dominated trade in the western Mediterranean. The term *Punic* for the wars between Rome and Carthage comes from the name *Phoenician*.

Physiocrat

Member of an eighteenth-century French school of economics. The physiocrats believed in a natural economy wherein government should never interfere. As part of the **Enlightenment** belief in natural law, the physiocrats argued against the contemporary mercantilist belief that nations should regulate trade to increase the national wealth. They rationalized economics, although their ideas about the sources of wealth consisting of the products of the soil were not generally accepted.

Pico della Mirandola, Giovanni (1463–1494)

Italian Renaissance philosopher. Pico della Mirandola settled in Florence in 1484, where Marsilio Ficino encouraged him to study **Neoplatonism**. Fluent in many languages, he studied philosophy in Padua, Paris, and Ferrara. Admired for his intellectual pursuits as well as his good personality, the Neoplatonist pursued a quest for "complete wisdom." Some of his writings, such as *Conclusions in Every Kind of Science* (1486), which attempted to reconcile Greek philosophy, **Judaism**, and **Christianity**, were declared heretical by Pope Innocent VIII. In this work he argued for three categories of "things": supercelestial (God); celestial (planets and stars); and terrestrial (the earth) where humans had the freedom and power to

shape their own destiny. In *The Dignity of Man* he proclaimed the unlimited potential of human beings to accomplish great things, one of the foundations of the Renaissance. At the end of his life Pico della Mirandola became enamored with the teachings of **Savonarola**, the fiery Florentine preacher, and he was preparing to take the orders of a **Dominican** monk when he died in 1494.

Pilate, Pontius

Roman governor of **Judaea** (26–36 C.E.) during the reign of the emperor **Tiberius**. Strongly anti-Semitic like his powerful patron Sejanus, Pilate repeatedly outraged the religious sensitivities of the Jews under his rule: he brought Roman army standards, with their pagan symbols, into **Jerusalem**; used **Hebrew Temple** funds to finance an aqueduct; and minted coins with Roman religious emblems. Known for his pride, cruelty, and corrupt government, Pilate was eventually removed after he slaughtered some Samaritans. His ordering the crucifixion of **Jesus**, whom he acknowledged to be innocent, fits his character. His fear of being reported to **Tiberius** may reflect the vulnerability of his position in Rome after the fall of Sejanus from power.

Pilgrims

Name applied to **Puritans** in England and America in the seventeenth century. Seeing themselves on a religious journey in life, Puritans called themselves Pilgrims. The most famous treatise of Puritanism is John Bunyan's *The Pilgrim's Progress* (1684). Pilgrims believed in **Calvinism**, including predestination—meaning that God decrees who will be saved (the elect) and who will be damned (the reprobate). They looked for signs of election in themselves and others and lived cleanly and worked hard to show that they had God's favor. As Puritans they believed that the church in England in the seventeenth century had not reformed enough and needed to be "purified," hence that name. Some Puritans felt the church in England could not be reformed and emigrated to America.

Pinochet, Augusto (1915–)
Chilean general and president of Chile (1974–1990). Pinochet became commander of the Chilean military in 1973 and led a coup that toppled and killed Marxist president **Salvador Allende.** Pinochet headed a four-man junta that imposed a brutal repression, abolished political parties, suppressed civil liberties, banned unions, and dissolved Congress.

Pisa, Council of. *See* Council of Pisa

Pisistratus. *See* Peisistratus

Pitt, William, the Elder (First Earl of Chatham, Viscount Pitt of Burton-Pysent) (1708–1778)
British statesman and leader of the British government during the **Seven Years' War** and after. Virtually prime minister (1756–1761, 1766–1768), Pitt maneuvered Britain to victories over the French in North America, the Caribbean, and India, often with creative use of the British navy. Pitt was father of **William Pitt the Younger.**

Pitt, William, the Younger (1759–1806)
British prime minister (1783–1801, 1804–1806) during the **French Revolution** and the Napoleonic Wars. Pitt, who was prime minister at age twenty-four, introduced financial reforms; championed the ending of the slave trade; strengthened the British military, especially the navy; solidified the office of prime minister and the role of Parliament; and reformed the governance of India. Pitt led Britain into war with

France in 1793. After his return to office in 1804 and the resumption of hostilities with Napoleonic France, Pitt died in office.

Pizarro, Francisco (c. 1478–1541)
Spanish conquistador and conqueror of the Incas of Peru. In 1532 Pizarro, three brothers, and a handful of other Spanish soldiers encountered the **Inca civilization** during a war between two brothers for emperor of the Incas. Pizarro intervened, held captive the successful Inca, and used him as a puppet to gain control of the empire and its enormous wealth for himself. Pizarro then executed the emperor, withstood an Inca rebellion, proceeded to distribute the lands as he wished, and set up a new capital at Lima. Pizarro was assassinated by a rival Spaniard in Lima in 1541.

Plague. *See* Black Death

Plains of Abraham
Site of the French and Indian War (1754–1763) battle in 1759 in North America between French and British troops that decided the future of Canada in favor of Britain. In the French and Indian War (1754–1763) the Marquis de Montcalm, who took control of French forces in 1756, attacked the British at Fort Oswego and Fort William Henry and seized both. In 1758 the British captured several French forts, and in 1759 they captured Forts Niagara and Ticonderoga. British general James Wolfe besieged the city of Quebec, defended by Montcalm. Wolfe stormed the Plains of Abraham above the city. Both leaders were killed in the battle, but the victory for Britain secured British control of Canada.

Plantagenet
Line of fourteen English kings starting with Henry II in 1154 and continuing

through Richard III in 1485. The Planta-genets (the name comes from Geoffrey of Anjou's emblem, the yellow broom flower, *planta genista*) are usually divided into the names of the related families: Anjou, Lancaster, and York.

Plassey, Battle of (1757)

Battle in India between the British and the local Indian ruler of Bengal. In the Battle of Plassey, part of the **Seven Years' War**, Robert Clive of the British **East India Company** led a force of British and Indian troops to victory over Nawab Siraj ud-Daula on June 23, 1757. This effectively left the entire Indian subcontinent open to British supremacy.

Plataea, Battle of (479 B.C.E.)

Victorious Greek land battle against the Persians that followed the **Battle of Salamis**. The Persians under King **Xerxes I** arrived in Greece with 150,000 men. With a sizable Greek army of combined Athenian and Spartan troops, Greece defeated the Persians at Plataea, northwest of Attica. The Persians did not return to Greece, and this opened Greece to a period of great flowering known as "classical Greece."

Plato (c. 427–347 B.C.E.)

Ancient Greek philosopher. Plato, along with **Socrates** and **Aristotle**, helped shape Western intellectual traditions. Plato lived in Athens during a time of great turmoil, conflict, and war and was discouraged by the actions of the state, especially when the Athenians executed his mentor, Socrates, in 399 B.C.E. Plato attempted to find a solution to the ills of society through philosophy and believed that philosophers would need to be the rulers of the state. In the fourth century B.C.E. Plato founded the Academy in Athens, the prototype of the university. Plato wrote numerous philosophical treatises (unlike Socrates, who

wrote none) and is best known for ***The Republic***, in which he defines "justice" and the state and describes the role of philosophers as leaders of society.

Platonic Philosophy

Philosophy sometimes called realism and sometimes idealism that presents a universe of "ideas," or the essences of all things existing from eternity to eternity. Platonic philosophy is the world of "being," in which nothing ever changes because everything in it is perfect. Things existing in our world are reflections of those ideas; they come and go and are in the less exalted—less real—world of "becoming." For example, the idea of justice is perfect and unchanging; just men and just laws may approximate the idea of justice but only imperfectly; apart from that they come and go as just men die and just laws are repealed, ignored, or replaced. The perfect **city-state** exists only in the world of ideas; Sparta may reflect it more than Athens but still has its imperfections and will deteriorate like anything else in the world of becoming. The political implications are that only philosophic people who study and know the world of ideas should have authority over other people. Class positions should be determined by abilities, but nonphilosophic types should never have any control of a city-state's destiny. The Christian church held Platonic philosophy in high regard as an example of God's mind.

Plautus (fl. 205–184 B.C.E.)

Roman playwright, author of some of the earliest Latin works to survive complete. Some scholars have attributed more than 100 plays to Plautus, and at least 21 are known to be by him. His plays, often adaptations of Greek comedies, were performed throughout the time of the **Roman**

Empire and were revived in the **Renaissance** when twelve plays were rediscovered in Germany in 1429.

Plebeians
Commoners in the **Roman Republic**. The name *plebeians* ("plebs") was given to the masses as opposed to the **patricians**. When the patricians, or aristocrats, expelled the kings of **Rome** around 500 B.C.E., they formed a republic completely dominated by the patricians. The plebeians had an assembly, but it too was controlled by the patricians until the plebeians formed their own assembly, known as the Tribal Assembly; its representatives were known as tribunes. This assembly of plebeians would draw up resolutions, known as **plebiscites**. Patricians and plebeians were forbidden to marry based on the laws of the **Twelve Tables**. Over several centuries the lines blurred, and the classes became the **nobilis**, or **nobility**, and commoners.

Plebiscite
Assembly of the **plebeians**, or plebs, the common people of Rome. From as early as 449 B.C.E., decisions of the plebiscites were recognized as legally binding within the **Roman Republic** as long as they also received sanction from the patrician senators. At the time of the Conflict of the Orders in the fifth and fourth centuries, the plebiscites became recognized as a lower court, or body of the government. By 287 B.C.E. the plebiscites, dominated by the wealthier plebeians, gained political equality with the patricians.

Pliny the Elder (23–79)
Roman equestrian, author of *Natural History*, historian, and uncle of **Pliny the Younger**. *Natural History* is an encyclopedia of all knowledge of animals, vegetables, and minerals, but with much other knowledge also incorporated. Pliny the Elder also wrote a history of the German wars with Rome and other works, all of which have been lost. His writings were always meant to be practical and concrete, rather than philosophical. He died leading a rescue near Pompeii during the eruption of Vesuvius.

Pliny the Younger (c. 61–112)
Roman senator, **consul**, author, and nephew of **Pliny the Elder**. He published ten books of literary letters on the social, domestic, judicial, and political affairs of Rome, himself, and his friends. Pliny the Younger also wrote in other fields of literature. His letters give the only eyewitness account of the eruption of Vesuvius, in which his uncle died. He was a close friend of the emperor **Trajan**.

PLO. *See* Palestinian Liberation Organization (PLO)

Plotinus (205–269)
Neoplatonist philosopher. Probably born in the Egypt of the **Roman Empire** and Greek speaking, Plotinus became a teacher and the center of a circle of intellectuals in Rome. His essays, written originally for teaching, cover the whole of ancient philosophy, logic, ethics, and aesthetics. **Neoplatonism** combined the philosophies of **Plato**, **Aristotle**, Pythagoras, and **Stoicism** and became a philosophy and religion followed by much of the ancient Western world from the third century until the sixth century. It strongly influenced both medieval and **Renaissance** Europe.

Plough. *See* Plow

Plow
Agricultural implement used to break up soil for planting and cultivating. The plow is the most important agricultural tool

ever developed. Originally replacing digging sticks, the scratch plow was an implement that could be pulled or pushed through soil. By **Roman** times light plows were drawn by oxen. By the High **Middle Ages** the heavy wheeled plow drawn by oxen (and later, by horses) made it possible to break up the thick soils of northern Europe using a moldboard, which turned over the slice of earth cut by the plowshare. Plows made it possible to cultivate the great prairies of America.

Plutarch (c. 45–125)

Greek historian of the early Roman period. Plutarch lived at Chaeronea and traveled through Greece, Egypt, and Italy. Best remembered for his *Parallel Lives*, which contained fifty biographies of Greek and Roman political and military leaders. It focused on the virtues and vices of these great leaders using mostly anecdotal and some historical evidence. Plutarch was most interested in questions of their morality. Although Greek, Plutarch accepted Roman rule because he believed in Roman leaders' strength and achievements.

Poitiers, Battle of (1356)

Hundred Years War battle between England and France. A severely outnumbered English army under King Edward III's son, Edward, "the Black Prince," routed the French army by using dismounted knights and archers with **longbows**. French king John the Good was captured and would have signed a treaty ending the war, but he died in prison in London, having returned there to make up for unpaid ransom, in 1364.

Polis (plural: poleis)

Ancient Greek political unit or state. The polis, such as **Athens**, **Sparta**, Corinth, or Thebes, was not defined by territory but as a people acting in concert. The polis was not dominated by a city (a **city-state**); urban and rural regions were equal politically. The polis was an exclusive community, and in the fifth century B.C.E. Athens restricted citizenship to children of existing citizens. Most poleis were dominated by an aristocracy until **democracy** was established in Athens in 508 B.C.E.

Polo, Marco (1254–1324)

Venetian merchant who traveled to **Mongol** China. Marco Polo's father, Niccolò, and his uncle Maffeo traveled and traded throughout Mongol lands from 1260 to 1269 and met **Khubilai Khan**. The Polos were also charged as papal representatives to make contact with Christians and to bring the Mongols to Christ. When they returned to China from **Venice** in 1271 they took seventeen-year-old Marco. The great khan liked Marco and, while allowing the Polos to continue their trading, sent him on numerous diplomatic missions. After seventeen years in China the Polos were granted leave to return to Venice. They returned by sea via Sumatra, Ceylon, India, and Arabia and arrived home in 1295. Most remarkable about Marco Polo is not that he traveled to China, as other merchants did, but that he wrote a book about his travels that, in copy, was widely read and has survived. The story influenced late medieval and early modern Europe and, especially, the **Age of Exploration**.

Pol Pot (1925–1998)

Cambodian leader and head of the **Khmer Rouge** communist movement. A mediocre student, in 1949 he went to France to study radio engineering, became an anti-French activist and a communist, and returned to Cambodia in 1953 to become a **guerrilla** leader. Around 1975 he changed his name from Saloth Sar to Pol Pot. As prime minister of Cambodia from 1976 to

1979 he carried out a ruthless "reconstruction" of the country that led to an estimated 1.7 million deaths. Following a Vietnamese invasion in 1979 he fled with other Khmer Rouge leaders into the jungle to wage a guerrilla war against the Vietnamese-installed regime. He was removed from leadership by his colleagues in the late 1990s. In 1998 he died, reportedly of a heart attack, and his body was burned.

Polybius (c. 200–118 B.C.E.)

Greek historian of **Rome**'s rise to power and the Mediterranean world. Son of a prominent Athenian, Polybius was deemed unfriendly to Rome after its conquest of Greece and was deported to Rome, where he became friendly with Scipio and accompanied him to Spain and Africa. He observed the destruction of **Carthage** and traveled again to the eastern Mediterranean. His forty-volume *Universal History*, only part of which survives, chronicles Rome's rise to dominance from 220 to 146 B.C.E.

Polynesian Culture

The culture of the islands of the South Pacific Ocean known as Polynesia. Polynesia includes the Hawaiian Islands, French Polynesia, the Cook Islands, the Samoan Islands, and numerous others. The islands were populated over centuries, from the fourth century B.C.E. through the sixth century C.E., by seafaring peoples from the west. The islands generally are devoid of edible indigenous plants or animals, so most of these were transported in. Traditions included their own mythology of the origins of the earth and of peopling the islands.

Polytheism

Term for religions that have more than one deity. Christians, Muslims, and Jews have often made the dichotomy between polytheism and **monotheism** fundamental in their thinking, but in reality the complexity and diversity of religious beliefs sometimes defies such simple categories. Many Hindus, for example, believe in many gods yet also in the universal Brahman. To many non-Christians the Christian belief in the Holy Trinity, in Satan, and in saints appears polytheistic, while adherents of other religious faiths see various gods as manifestations of a universal cosmic spiritual energy or force.

Pompeii

Roman city destroyed by the eruption of Mount Vesuvius in 79 C.E. Pompeii became a prominent Campania seaside town in Augustan **Rome**. An earthquake in 62 C.E. had damaged the city, and it was being repaired in opulent fashion. It was completely destroyed by the eruption, buried under deep ash. The site was rediscovered in 1748. Systematic study of Pompeii began in 1861, and in the 1950s careful excavation and conservation of the well-preserved city began. Approximately four-fifths of Pompeii has been archaeologically excavated. Artworks; everyday objects; and even people, animals, and food have been discovered, providing the best-known Roman city.

Pompey the Great (106–48 B.C.E.)

Roman general and part of the First Triumvirate with **Julius Caesar** and Crassus. In 59 B.C.E. Pompey, Caesar, and Crassus formed the triumvirate, and Pompey married Caesar's daughter Julia, but after Pompey quarreled with Caesar civil war broke out in **Rome**. Pompey was defeated at the Battle of Pharsalus in 48 B.C.E., fled to Egypt, and was stabbed to death as he arrived there. Pompey did not want to destroy the Republic, but he bent its rules severely to benefit himself.

Pope

Latin colloquial word for "father" used for the bishop of Rome. Originally the term *pope* was used for any bishop and even for abbots, from around the third century. In the fifth century the bishops of Rome claimed primacy among all Christian bishops based on the Petrine Doctrine (which states that Peter was the first bishop of Rome). The term's use to designate the bishop of Rome probably began in the eleventh century. That Rome was the imperial capital helped to solidify the claim.

Popol Vuh

Maya book of mythology and cosmology. Written in Quiché (Guatemalan Maya language) with Spanish letters by a Maya author around 1555, after the Spanish conquest, the Popol Vuh tells of the creation of the human race, the origins of the gods, and the history of the Quiché people. The original, now lost, was copied and translated in the eighteenth century.

Populares. *See* Optimates

Population Explosion

Term used to describe the rapid increase in the world's population since 1500 C.E., especially in the twentieth century. According to a widely but not universally accepted estimate, the world's population rose from 400 to 600 million between 1500 and 1700 (50 percent in two centuries) a historically sharp increase. The population grew another 50 percent in the one century from 1700 to 1800. In the next century it grew more than 66 percent. In the twentieth century it grew nearly 400 percent, from 1.6 billion to 6.1 billion people, with the sharpest growth in the developing countries of Asia, Africa, and Latin America. A number of reasons such as improvements in food production and distribution and medicine help account for this increase in human numbers. The lowering death rate is more contributory than the rising birthrate. At the start of the twenty-first century the rate of population growth appeared to be slowing, but it was still increasing at a historically high rate.

Port Arthur

Western name for the Chinese port city of Lüshun in Liaoning Province in southern **Manchuria**. Because of its strategic location at the tip of the Liaoning Peninsula at the entrance of the Gulf of Bohai and its excellent year-round ice-free harbor, Port Arthur attracted the attention of imperialist powers in the late nineteenth century. It was also the base for China's modern Beiyang fleet. China ceded it to Japan in the Treaty of Shimonoseki in 1895, but Japan was forced by several European powers to withdraw. Russia then acquired control of Port Arthur in 1898 but lost it to Japan in the **Russo-Japanese War** in 1905. At the end of **World War II** it was acquired by the Soviet Union, but Moscow returned it to Chinese sovereignty in 1954.

Portolan (plural: portolani)

Sailing charts used during the **Middle Ages** and the **Age of Exploration**. Maps were academic schemes of the general layout of the world or a region and gave relative positions of countries or seas, but maps were useless for actual travel. A portolan was a useful chart drawn by a sea captain or navigator to show the actual course, describing the waters, the winds, the flotsam, and coastlines.

Poseidon

Greek god of the sea, of earthquakes, and of horses. Poseidon created storms and calms at sea and monstrous figures that opposed **Odysseus** such as the Cyclops. In art Poseidon is indistinguishable from **Zeus** unless accompanied by specific attributes.

Poseidon was worshipped widely in Greece and even in **Athens** contended with the goddess **Athena** for loyalty.

Potato Famine (1845–1848)

Irish failure of the country's entire potato crop that caused widespread hardship and migration out of Ireland. The potato (indigenous to South America) was introduced to Ireland by 1600 and by the eighteenth century had come to predominate as a food source. The Irish population doubled because of the good calorie source. An average laborer ate 10–20 pounds (4.5–9 kg) a day. From 1845 to 1848 potato blight ruined the entire crop. Public works, price controls, and food supplies from Britain did little to stop the suffering. Almost 1 million Irish died from starvation and disease. More than 1.5 million fled to England, Scotland, the United States, Canada, and Australia.

Potosí

Bolivian city where vast silver deposits were discovered in 1545. With the discovery Spain shifted its emphasis in the **New World** from confiscating gold to mining silver. **Charles V** made Potosí an imperial town, and from 1545 to 1800 the Spanish crown collected one-fifth the vast value of silver in taxes. In the seventeenth century Potosí was probably the third-largest city in the Americas. Bullion fleets loaded with silver sailed from the New World to Spain or the Spanish Netherlands.

Potsdam Conference (1945)

Allied peace settlement conference of **World War II**. Held in Potsdam, Germany, outside Berlin, the conference was attended by President **Harry S Truman** of the United States, Prime Minister **Winston Churchill** (replaced by **Clement Attlee**, who became prime minister during the conference), and Premier **Joseph Stalin** of the Soviet Union. The major concerns were not to write a peace treaty but to formulate an immediate administration for defeated Germany and to define the role of the Soviet Union in Eastern Europe. Germany was divided into zones of occupation controlled by the United States, the Soviet Union, Britain, and France.

Po Valley

Italy's major river valley, the region where most of the country's population is settled. The Po River begins in the Alps and flows southeasterly across northern Italy before emptying in to the Adriatic Sea south of Venice. The Po Valley is very fertile and its farms produce olives, vegetables, wheat, citrus fruits, and grapes for wine. The city of Milan became rich and politically powerful in this location during the **Renaissance** because it was located at the intersection of trade routes between the Alpine passes and Italy's coastal cities.

Praetor

An official of the **Roman Republic**. Originally praetors were the two magistrates chosen annually to serve as heads of state. In the fourth century B.C.E. that role was termed **consul** and a third praetor was added as a lesser official supporting the consuls and acting as chief magistrate and president of the Senate in their absence. A praetor could also act as a general, leading armies. In the third century B.C.E. the number of praetors was increased from one to two and later to four, six, and eight. Under **Julius Caesar** their number was increased to sixteen.

Prakrit Language

Name for the everyday languages of ancient India, which were related to but differed from the classical language **Sanskrit**.

The most important of the Prakrit languages was Pali, which became the religious language of **Buddhism** because most of the sacred texts were composed in it.

Presbyter

Term derived from the Greek word for "elder," as an official of the Christian church. In the Catholic Church, presbyters received their authority from bishops. In the **Reformation, Calvinist** churches were administered by a council of presbyters, and in Scotland the Calvinist church became known as the Presbyterian Church.

Prester John

Legendary ruler of a Christian kingdom originally believed to have been located in Asia and later, in Africa. He was first mentioned in 1145, but in 1165 a mysterious letter appeared in Europe addressed to various kings from Prester John and claiming him to be king of the Indies and guardian of the tomb of Saint Thomas. Many theories arose as to his origins and location. By the fifteenth century the belief that he was a king in Ethiopia encouraged exploration, because Europeans believed that they could circumvent the Muslim world and link up with Prester John's Christian civilization.

PRI (Partido Revolucionario Institucional)

Spanish for "Institutional Revolutionary Party," the political party that ruled Mexico from its founding in 1929 to 2000, and the abbreviation by which it is known. The party was founded by Plutarco Elías Calles to stabilize Mexico after two decades of conflict. Its name is derived from the fact that it sought to institutionalize the new power structure created by the **Mexican Revolution** as well as consolidate some of the revolution's important achievements, such as land reforms. Under the PRI Mexico was in practice a one-party state for six decades. The party leader served as Mexico's president for a six-year term with extensive powers. By custom each president named his successor, who then faced little opposition in the national election. Through an elaborate system of patronage administered by labor and peasant organizations, business groups, and local governments, the PRI provided Mexico's longest period of political stability and moderate economic growth. Criticized for its corruption and pressured by people in Mexico and the United States seeking democratic reform, the PRI lost its monopoly of power in the 2000 elections, when opposition leader Vicente Fox was elected president and the PRI lost its majority in the National Congress.

Prince, The. *See* Machiavelli, Niccolò

Prince Henry. *See* Henry, Prince, "the Navigator"

Princeps

Title meaning "first citizen," given to emperors of the **Roman Empire**. From the rule of **Octavian** (Augustus), the emperors were titled "princeps" as a cover for the fact that they ruled as dictators rather than as merely the first of all the citizens of Rome. Use of the term designates the shift from the **Roman Republic** to the Roman Empire.

Princeton, Battle of (1777)

Victorious American colonial battle. The **Battle of Trenton** was the first clearly successful campaign by the **Continental Army** under **George Washington** against British troops during the **American Revolution**. After the victory in Trenton, Washington boldly decided to quietly break camp during the night of January 3, 1977, escaping **Charles Cornwallis**'s forces. His army drove back the three British regiments it met in Princeton, New Jersey, and continued to Morristown, New Jersey, where it quartered for the winter and out of range of the British troops at New Brunswick, New Jersey. This gave Washington a good defensive position as the war continued.

Printing Press

Machine using movable type to print words. Movable type, first invented in the 1040s in China, was reinvented in Europe by **Johannes Gutenberg** with funding from Johann Fust and help from Gutenberg's son-in-law Peter Schöffer around 1450 in Mainz, Germany. Printing with cast movable type required plentiful printing material (**paper** became widespread in Europe in the early 1400s), oil-based ink, and pressing equipment (borrowed from the paper-making process). Printing initially attempted to replicate handwriting and its use was limited, but it soon spread across Europe and was used for all fields of study. It dramatically increased the number of books and printed material. By 1500 printing presses had produced around 6 million books.

Prophets

The term *prophet* is Greek for "one who speaks for another." The Hebrew prophets thought of themselves as spokesmen for God. Throughout Hebrew history, and especially from the eighth to sixth centuries B.C.E., a series of Hebrew prophets including **Isaiah**, Jeremiah, Ezekiel, and **Amos** counseled and rebuked the Hebrew people for not observing ethical monotheism and affirmed the special destiny of the Jews, all the while claiming the universality of the beliefs.

Protestant

An adherent to the Christian churches that broke from the **Roman Catholic Church** in the sixteenth-century **Reformation** or to other reformed churches that have formed since then. The term *Protestant* was first applied in 1529, to people who protested the actions of German princes who tried to suppress the reform movement. Protestants believed they were adhering to the principles of the first-century Christian church and following the **Bible** with a simplified service, emphasis on teaching in the sermon rather than on the mass, a priesthood of all believers rather than of a special caste, and services in the vernacular (the local language) rather than Latin. Protestants believed that all Christians should be able to read the Bible and interpret it, so they emphasized literacy and translated the Bible into the vernacular. Because administration, interpretation, and doctrine were not centralized, Protestants broke into numerous denominations such as **Lutherans; Calvinists** (Presbyterians); Anglicans; and, later, Congregationalists, Baptists, and **Methodists**.

Protestant Work Ethic. *See* Weber, Max

Prussia

Former German kingdom. Originally (in the **Middle Ages**) a region east of the Vistula River with its capital at Königsberg, Prussia was incorporated into the northern German principality of **Brandenburg** with its capital at Berlin in 1618. The Kingdom of Prussia was proclaimed in 1701 and grew under **Frederick the Great** to become a major European power. During the **French Revolution** Prussia fought against France and was one of the few German countries to survive. After the **Franco-Prussian War** of 1870–1871 Prussia became the nucleus of a united Germany with its capital at Berlin. Prussia's monarchy ended with **World War I**.

Ptolemaic Universe

The universe as described by **Ptolemy** in the *Almagest* (c. 150). Aristotle had described the universe as geocentric (earth centered), with the other heavenly bodies moving around the earth. Ptolemy elaborated and mathematized this universe. He established mathematical explanations and computations for it. His model had nine concentric spheres around the earth, each sphere containing heavenly bodies progressing outward to the final sphere containing the stars. The Ptolemaic universe was accepted until 1543 when **Copernicus** questioned the necessity of the elaborate mathematics used to explain retrograde motion in it.

Ptolemy (B.C.E.)

Name of the Macedonian kings of Egypt and Cyprus. Ptolemy I (367–282 B.C.E.) had served **Alexander the Great** as general. At Alexander's death he took Alexander's body to Memphis, Egypt, and set himself up as ruler. He also wrote a history of Alexander. His son, Ptolemy II (308–246 B.C.E.), ruled jointly with his father until the latter's death in 282 B.C.E., when he succeeded the throne. There were Ptolemies through Ptolemy XIV (c. 59–44 B.C.E.).

Ptolemy (fl. 146–170)

Greek/Egyptian scientist and mathematician. Working at **Alexandria**, Egypt, Ptolemy wrote many of the definitive works on astronomy, mathematics, geography, and harmonics used for the next 1,400 years. His astronomical elaborations on **Aristotle**, the *Almagest* (c. 150) created the **Ptolemaic universe**, which stood as the standard view until **Nicolaus Copernicus** in 1543. It has the earth at the center and a series of concentric spheres circling it and containing all the other heavenly bodies. Ptolemy's *Geography* also became the standard work on its subject. It contains lists of places by **longitude** and **latitude**, and was one of the first works to locate places that way.

Pueblo. *See* Anasazi

Punic Wars (264–146 B.C.E.)

War between **Rome** and **Carthage** that is divided into three waves of conflict. The First Punic War (264–241 B.C.E.) pitted Rome (headed by an alliance of Greek city-states) against Hamilcar Barca in what started as a trade dispute. The Second Punic War (218–201 B.C.E.) was initiated by a harsh treaty imposed on Carthage by Rome after the first conflict. The Carthaginian general **Hannibal** was defeated by Rome; Carthage was stripped of all of its land except a small territory in North Africa; and Rome dominated the Mediterranean Sea. When the Third Punic War (149–146 B.C.E.) erupted Carthage was too weak to be a real threat, and Rome besieged and completely destroyed it.

Punjab

Area in south Asia now divided between India and Pakistan and watered by the **Indus River** and four of its tributaries. An agriculturally rich land, the Punjab has played an important role in history as the home of a number of political and cultural centers from **Harappan** times to the present. In 1799 Ranjit Singh created a **Sikh** kingdom in the Punjab that was defeated in the Sikh Wars of the early nineteenth century (1845–1846, 1848–1849) by the British, who then incorporated it into their empire. In 1947 it was partitioned, with the predominantly Sikh and Hindu eastern regions becoming part of India and the predominantly **Muslim** western region becoming part of Pakistan. A Sikh separatist movement in the Indian portion of Punjab has resulted in occasional violence.

Purdah

Set of practices involving female veiling and seclusion in **Muslim** societies. In varying degrees this practice is followed throughout the Islamic world. In some dialects the word *purdah* is used for both the clothing and the practice. Between the **Nile** and the **Indus** rivers terms for the clothing and practices associated with purdah also include *hijab*, *chador*, and *burqa*.

Pure Land

Popular form of **Mahayana Buddhism** found primarily in eastern Asia. It is based on three **Sanskrit** scriptures. Followers believe in the rebirth of the **Buddha**'s paradise, called *Sukhavati* ("Pure Land"). Those who stay faithful and follow the scriptures and show devotion will remain in the Pure Land upon death, where they will be free from pain and want until they reach their own enlightenment. Women must first attain masculinity through rebirth before they are allowed to reach Sukhavati.

Puritans

English and American Protestant believers in **Calvinism** in the seventeenth century. Puritans believed, like Lutherans, in justification (salvation) by faith, not by works, and in the priesthood of all believers. But as Calvinists they also believed in predestination—that God decrees who will be saved (the elect) and who will be damned (the reprobate). Puritans believed that the church in England in the seventeenth century had not reformed enough and needed to be "purified," hence their name. They looked for signs of election in themselves and others and lived cleanly and worked hard to show that they had God's favor. Seeing themselves on a religious journey in life, Puritans called themselves **Pilgrims**. The most famous treatise of Puritanism is John Bunyan's *The Pilgrim's Progress*

(1684). In the **English Civil War** (1642–1649) the Puritans sided against the king.

P'yongyang

Capital of the Democratic People's Republic of Korea (North Korea). Located in the Taedong Valley, P'yongyang is an ancient city, the probable site of the ancient Old **Choson** kingdom of the third to second centuries B.C.E. It was the largest city in the northern part of the country during the Yi dynasty and became the North Korean capital with that country's founding in 1948.

Pyramid of the Sun

Massive pyramid of **Teotihuacán**, a **Mesoamerican** city. Teotihuacán was the capital of a kingdom for nearly 1,000 years (third century B.C.E.–c. 800 C.E.). The city had a population of as many as 150,000 with temples and palaces along a main thoroughfare dominated by the Pyramid of the Sun, a ceremonial center more than 200 feet (60 m) high, the largest structure of its type in the Western Hemisphere. Its base measures 720 by 760 feet. At the opposite end of the city are the Pyramid of the Moon and the Temple of **Quetzalcóatl**. The purpose of the pyramid is unknown.

Pyramids of Giza (Egypt)

Three Egyptian pyramids built for kings of the fourth dynasty (c. 2575–2465). The first and largest, the Great Pyramid, was built for Khufu, the second king of the fourth dynasty. The second was built for Khafre, the fourth king, and the third for Menkaure, the fifth king. The Great Pyramid was originally 481 feet (147 m) high and measured 756 feet (230 m) on each side. It was constructed with great precision, is oriented to the cardinal points of the compass, and contains burial chambers for the king and queen. The three Pyramids of Giza are surrounded by minor pyramids.

Q

Qianlong (Ch'ien-lung) (1710–1799)
Name for the long-reigning **Qing** (Manchu) emperor of China (1736–1796) whose given name was Hongli. Under his rule China reached its greatest territorial extent, absorbing much of Turkestan (now **Xingjiang** province). Qianlong also carried out successful military campaigns in Annam, Burma, and Nepal. A patron of the arts and scholarship, he presided over a prosperous period of Chinese history. Qianlong's reign was also characterized by strict censorship, corruption, rebellions by the White Lotus Society, and China's rejection of Britain's efforts to expand trade when it sent the McCartney mission in 1793. Not wanting to rule longer than his illustrious Manchu predecessor **Kangxi**, Qianlong abdicated in favor of his son in 1796 but continued to be the real power at court until his death.

Qin (221–206 B.C.E.)
Ancient Chinese state and a dynasty. Qin was a state on the frontier of Chinese civilization during the **Warring States period**. Under a series of ambitious and able rulers it defeated its rivals and unified China in 221, creating the first Chinese empire under **Qin Shi Huangdi**, who established the short-lived Qin dynasty. Qin Shi Huangdi created a highly centralized and regulated state guided by the philosophy of legalism, which emphasized the need to govern strictly and harshly. He also completed the first great defensive wall. The harshness of his rule earned him resentment and a reputation for cruelty, and the dynasty did not long survive his death. Despite the criticisms of later Chinese historians, the Qin laid the foundations for the Chinese empire, one of the most enduring in history.

See also Great Wall

Qing (1644–1911)
Chinese dynasty also known as the Manchu dynasty after the seminomadic northeast Asian people who established it by defeating and conquering the **Ming**. Despite their nomadic origins the Qing rulers became great patrons of Chinese culture, which flourished under their reigns. Under two outstanding emperors. **Kangxi** (r. 1662–1722) and **Qianlong** (r. 1736–1796). The Chinese empire reached its greatest geographic extent, absorbing Tibet, **Xingjiang**, all of Mongolia, and parts of what is now Siberia. China's population grew rapidly, reaching 450 million in 1850 while maintaining a fairly high degree of prosperity. But the empire went into decline from the time of the Opium Wars (1839–1842) as it failed to meet the challenge of Western imperialism.

Qingdao (Tsingtao)
Port and industrial city on the southern coast of the Shandong Peninsula. It was established as a treaty port in the 1880s and came under German control in 1898 under a ninety-nine-year lease. The Japanese occupied it during **World War I** and returned it to Chinese sovereignty in 1922.

Qin Shi Huangdi (c. 259–210 B.C.E.)
Literally meaning "Qin First Emperor," the title assumed by King Zheng of the **Qin** dynasty when he unified China in 221 B.C.E. Zheng came to the throne of Qin in 247 during the **Warring States period** and completed the conquest of China that had been begun by his predecessors. An energetic ruler, he created a highly centralized empire, building a series of roads leading his capital of Xianyang and constructing a series of fortifications on the northern **steppe** frontier. He established a uniform system of measurements, enacted strict and detailed rules with severe punishments, and appointed his officials based on talent rather than heredity. Qin Shi Huangdi sought to impose order on intellectual life by limiting teachings to practical subjects and burning books of all schools of thought except for those by legalist philosophers. Despite his sweeping reforms and vigorous rule, he governed primarily by fear. His dynasty collapsed soon after his death in 210 B.C.E. His burial site near Xianyang included thousands of life-size models of his armed forces known as the **Terra-Cotta Army**.

See also Great Wall

Qiu Jin (1875–1907)
Chinese feminist and revolutionary whose execution in 1907 made her a patriotic martyr. In 1904 Qiu Jin left her husband to study in Japan, where she became involved with radical Chinese political groups. She joined the Tongmenghui (Revolutionary Alliance) and was active in other groups. She campaigned against the practices of child marriage and the **foot binding** of women and joined in efforts to overthrow the **Qing** government, which she regarded as weak and ineffective in dealing with threats to China. In 1907 she was implicated in an antigovernment uprising and was executed, becoming an inspiration for generations of Chinese women.

Quetzalcóatl
Feathered serpent deity of ancient **Meso-american** civilizations. Quetzalcóatl first appeared in the **Teotihuacán** civilization (third–eighth centuries C.E.) as an earth and water god. In the city of Teotihuacán, the Temple of Quetzalcóatl was built in the form of a shortened pyramid, painted red, and decorated with heads of the god. Beneath the temple were graves of people ritually sacrificed. In the later **Toltec** culture, Quetzalcóatl became the god of the morning and evening stars—of birth and death. In **Aztec** civilization, Quetzalcóatl was the official title of the high priest, the deity of the priests, the inventor of the calendar, and the god of learning and was also associated with the planet Venus. The Aztec capital **Tenochtitlán** had a Temple of Quetzalcóatl. Quetzalcóatl's calendar spawned the belief that Quetzalcóatl would return in the year Ce Acatl, which coincided with the year that **Hernando Cortés** landed, convincing **Moctezuma** that the Spaniards were divine.

Quezon, Manuel Luis (1878–1944)
Filipino statesman. He served with **Emilio Aguinaldo** in the Philippine war for independence from Spain (1896–1898) and the United States (1898–1901). He became one of the most prominent political leaders in the Philippines under U.S. colonial rule and was elected the first president of the transitional Philippine Commonwealth in 1935. Forced into exile by the Japanese in 1942, he headed the Philippine government in exile in the United States until his death.

Quinine
Antibacterial substance effective against malaria especially when used as a

prophylactic (for protection). Made from cinchona bark, found in South America, the extract known as quinine was made commercially by 1830. It was taken by Europeans as they entered malarial regions such as in Africa, enabling them to conquer Africa in the nineteenth century without enormous loss of life. Because quinine tastes bitter it was sometimes taken with gin and the lime juice that was given to British sailors and hence is the source of the drink gin and tonic.

Quipu

Inca accounting device. This long rope with forty-eight secondary cords and numerous tertiary cords attached to the secondary cords had knots marking units of tens and hundreds. It enabled agencies to do complex accounting, similar to checkered tables used in medieval England. Each area of Incan government had its own color quipu. The quipus were often kept as permanent records of accounting.

Quran (Qur'an or Koran) (means "recitation")

The holy book of **Islam**. According to **Muslim** belief, the Quran is revelations received as a series of visions by **Muhammad**. He experienced a spiritual awakening and received revelations from 610 to 632 that he understood as messages communicated from God ("Allah" in Arabic) through the angel Gabriel, who instructed Muhammad to spread the message to others. Muslims regard it as inerrant and immutably preserved. Originally these revelations were transmitted orally, but after Muhammad's death in 632 his followers wrote them down as the Quran during the 650s. The Quran explains God and God's relationship to the world and is the primary authority for the Islamic religion.

R

Rabelais, François (1494–1553)
French **Renaissance** author and satirist interested in **humanist** philosophy. His witty book *Pantagruel* (1532) looked at medieval scholastic learning, and *Gargantua* (1534) offered a commentary of what it meant to acquire a humanist education. He believed people had the right to be free and that they should enjoy life on earth and that people were inherently good. Rabelais attacked the prejudices of scholastic learning and celebrated earthly life of pleasure, free will, and folly. Among the notable features of his work are his extraordinary use of language and his often ribald humor.

Rabin, Yitzhak (1922–1995)
Israeli general, prime minister of Israel (1974–1977, 1992–1995), and **Nobel Prize** winner. He was commander of the Israeli forces in the **Arab-Israeli War of 1967**, and as prime minister in 1992 he signed a peace accord with the **Palestinian Liberation Organization** and **Yasser Arafat**. Rabin and Arafat were awarded the **Nobel Prize** for Peace in 1994. In 1995 Rabin was assassinated by a Jewish right-wing extremist.

Railroads (British for Railways)
Mechanized transport on iron or steel rails. The first public steam railroad was the Stockton to Darlington Railway, which opened in England in 1825. Railroads existed before that time as wagons run on boards or rails in mines. Stationary steam engines were used to pull wagons up inclines, and in 1804 a steam engine was attached as a locomotive to draw the wagons. Passengers were first moved around 1806. The Stockton to Darlington locomotive was called the Locomotion and was designed by George Stephenson, maker of the Rocket, which ran on the Liverpool and Manchester Railway. The first U.S. railroad was the Baltimore and Ohio Railroad, opened in 1830. Railroads opened the interiors of large lands such as the United States, Africa, and Australia in the mid-nineteenth century. The United States was spanned by railroads when the Union Pacific and Central Pacific joined at Promontory, Utah, in 1869.

Raj. *See* British Raj

Raja
Sanskrit term for "ruler," an **Indo-European** word related to the Latin term *rex*. Princes and petty rulers in India were called rajas, and rulers of major states were known as *maharajas* ("great rulers").

Rajasthani Art
Distinctive style of realistic painting developed during the sixteenth and seventeenth centuries in the princely states of Rajasthan in western India. Rajasthani painting continued until the nineteenth century. It evolved from manuscript illustrations, blending Persian and India traditions. Rajasthani art was contemporary with **Mughal** painting but differs in its bolder

use of color and its rendering of land-scapes.

Rajputs

Members of a class of warriors and land-owners in central and northern India, probably of **Central Asian** descent. From the ninth to the sixteenth century they dominated much of Rajasthan. Their fortresses were conquered by the **Mughals**, who allowed them some autonomy. Some of their chiefs, such as the rulers of Jodhpur, Jaipur, and Udaipur, managed to retain some autonomy under British rule. The name *Rajput* survives as a sub-caste in modern India.

Ralegh, Sir Walter. *See* Raleigh, Sir Walter

Raleigh, Sir Walter (c. 1552–1618)

English soldier, explorer, writer, and entrepreneur. As a favorite of Queen **Elizabeth I**, Raleigh was granted land in Ireland, where he planted the new crops of potato and tobacco from the New World. He was knighted in 1585. Raleigh became interested in the New World and traveled there on several expeditions, exploring the southeastern coast of North America. He tried to establish a colony in what is now North Carolina and named the region Virginia after Elizabeth, "the Virgin Queen." His first attempt (1585) was abandoned while the second (1587) disappeared mysteriously and is known as the Lost Colony. Raleigh lost favor with the queen, and at her death the new king, **James I**, charged Raleigh with treason and had him imprisoned. After twelve years he was released and took part in another expedition (1616), to South America. Upon his return Raleigh was sentenced to death for disobeying orders and was beheaded.

Ramadan

Ninth month of the **Muslim** calendar specified by the Five Pillars of Islam as a month of fasting. Muslims are required (though some are excused) to abstain from food, drink, and sex during the daylight hours of Ramadan. Muslims believe that on the twenty-seventh of Ramadan, the "Night of Power," **Muhammad** ascended briefly to heaven.

Ramayana

One of the two great epics of India and a major source of Hindu mythology. The *Ramayana* is attributed to the sage Valmiki and was written in **Sanskrit** perhaps around 300 B.C.E. It tells the story of the hero Rama of Ayodhya, his wife Sita, and her abduction by the Ravana, the demon-king of Lanka (Sri Lanka). The epic has been immensely popular in India and in Southeast Asia, where it has been the source of many dances, plays, and artistic works.

Raphael (1485–1520) (full name Raphaello Sanzio)

Italian Renaissance painter and student of Perugino. Raphael synthesized the greatness of **Leonardo da Vinci** and **Michelangelo** in his paintings and became the most important painter of the **High Renaissance**. His painting *The School of Athens* (1510–1511) is a culmination of the period, merging realism and idealism with the balance and harmony of body and spirit.

Re. *See* Amon-Re

Reagan, Ronald (1911–2004)

The fortieth president of the United States (1981–1989). A Hollywood movie actor, Reagan became governor of California and then president of the United States. A conservative Republican and a hard-liner against **communism**, Reagan increased military spending and reduced social services spending. The national debt increased tremendously during his terms.

He was a strong ally of **Margaret Thatcher** of Britain. Pressure on the Soviet Union through the **arms race** eventually helped to collapse the Eastern bloc communist countries.

Realism
Artistic movement of nineteenth-century Europe. Reacting to both the emphasis on feeling and imagination of Romanticism and the overly cerebral neoclassicism, realism dealt with the realities of a world of science and of revolutions. Realism expressed truth and sincerity and relied on direct experience. Gustave Courbet (1819–1877) and Édouard Manet (1832–1883) are among the painters of realism.

Red Fort (Lal Qila)
Fortress in Old Delhi, India, built in the mid-seventeenth century by the **Mughal** emperor Shah Jahan. The name is derived from the Persian word for the red sandstone used to construct it. It and another Red Fort in Agra, India, remain as symbols of the power of the Mughal rulers.

Red Guards
Organized groups of young supporters of the radical policies of **Mao Zedong** during the **Great Proletarian Cultural Revolution** (1966–1976). Students from secondary schools and universities arose after instigation by Mao and formed bands. They attacked Mao opponents and so-called revisionist and reactionary elements in the **Chinese Communist Party** as well as adult authority in general throughout society. These attacks resulted in large-scale destruction of property and thousands of deaths. In many cities Red Guards coalesced into rival factions that fought one another. They were disbanded in the 1970s and many members were sent to the countryside for "reeducation."

Red River
The principal river of northern Vietnam, called Song Hong in Vietnamese. In its basin lies the capital Hanoi. On its 750-mile (1,200-km) journey from southwestern China to the **Gulf of Tonkin** it deposits a rich alluvium that has made the Red River basin one of Vietnam's two "rice baskets." The other is the Mekong Delta.

Reformation
Religious, political, and social reform movement of sixteenth-century Europe. There had been many reforms of the Christian church since its origins, but the Reformation of the sixteenth century was different. Corruption within the church and growing pressures from social change outside it led to the German **Martin Luther**'s stand. Luther, in his Ninety-five Theses of 1517, called for reforms of the church administration and liturgy. When ordered to recant his statements, Luther refused and was excommunicated. Many followers agreed with Luther, and the split from the **Roman Catholic Church** began. Those who followed Luther were originally called Reformers, after 1529 Protestants, and later Lutherans. Other Reformers such as **Huldrych Zwingli** were working in Switzerland. In 1525 the **Anabaptists** in Switzerland and the Netherlands pushed the Reformation to more radical levels. In 1541 **John Calvin** began a second generation of reform, later called **Calvinism**. Calvinism spread through Switzerland, France, the Netherlands, Scotland, and England. Large numbers of Catholics left the church and followed the Reformation movement across Europe as different denominations of Protestants. In the middle of the sixteenth century the Catholics responded in the **Catholic Reformation**, which involved reforms in the **papacy**; the foundation of new religious

orders such as the **Society of Jesus**, or Jesuits; and a churchwide meeting called the **Council of Trent** in 1545.

Reform Bill of 1832

British law of extensive reforms. In Britain in the early nineteenth century pressure had increased from the rising middle class to expand the franchise (voting rights), eliminate **rotten boroughs** (towns that had disappeared but were still allowed to elect two members of Parliament), and bring other reforms. The Reform Bill extended the franchise to some of the middle class but the working class was bitterly disappointed. Not until 1928 could all men and women over twenty-one vote.

Relics

Objects venerated by religious people because of their association with a holy person. A relic could be a piece of bone or cloth or another object from a holy person declared a saint. Relics became common in the **Roman Catholic Church** by the ninth century, when **Carolingian** churches were constructed in such a way as to display them. They became important to the Catholic Church as a means for the people to focus on something tangible to think about living a holy life like the saint's. Relics also became a source of money for the church as venerators put money in collection boxes for relics.

Religion

An organized system of faith and worship of the supernatural found in every society. Religions have played a fundamental role in defining the beliefs and values of most cultures. In many societies, such as **Islam**, medieval Europe, Hindu India, or Thailand, a particular religious system has been central to almost every aspect of life. In other societies, such as China, Korea or Japan, secular belief systems such as

Confucianism or a tradition of religious pluralism has prevailed. But in every society religion has been an important aspect of culture.

Rembrandt (1606–1669)

Painter from Leyden, the Netherlands. Rembrandt made his career in Amsterdam at the height of Dutch art. His paintings incorporate an intense realism with religiosity and emotion. Rembrandt preferred **Old Testament** themes such as *The Binding of Samson* (1636), although his most famous painting today is *The Night Watch* (1642).

Renaissance (French for "rebirth")

Rebirth of classical views on the capability of humans. The term is applied to a movement in European history from the fourteenth century through the sixteenth century in which there was intellectual and artistic renewed interest (a rebirth) in the thinking and arts of the classical era of ancient **Greece** and **Rome**. The idea of rebirth was developed by art historian Giorgio Vasarii (1511–1574). The Greeks and Romans believed that humans are capable of accomplishing great things. In comparison with the medieval Christian view that humans were created by God to glorify God and that otherwise they are mere dust, the Renaissance view was that humans are creators and capable of greatness. This belief in human accomplishment and emulation of the classical arts led to a tremendous outburst in creativity in Italy in the arts and literature, especially in **Florence**, **Venice**, and Rome. The Renaissance reached its peak in the **High Renaissance** around 1500 with artists such as **Michelangelo**, **Leonardo da Vinci**, and **Raphael**.

Renaissance Architecture

Building design looking back to ancient Greece and Rome for inspiration. In their architecture, fifteenth-century Italian **Renaissance** masters like **Filippo Brunelleschi** and **Leone Battista Alberti** sought to use light, perspective, and other elements of the natural world. Renaissance design tended to be simple in its use of materials and geometric patterns (unlike the previous Gothic style, which was very ornate). These stylistic devices spread across Europe in the sixteenth century and influenced the baroque style of the seventeenth century.

Renaissance Art

Painting and sculpture developed in fourteenth-century Italy with a style that looked to classical **Rome** and Greece for inspiration over a period of two centuries. **Renaissance** art was preceded by the Gothic art of the **Middle Ages**. Milestones of Renaissance art include **Masaccio**'s use of linear perspective in the *Holy Trinity* (1425), which used foreshortening to give the illusion of depth; **Botticelli**'s *The Birth of Venus* (c. 1480), which dealt with a classical subject; Perugino's *Delivery of the Keys* (1482), with its perspective, harmony, and balance; and **Michelangelo**'s *Pietà* (c. 1500), expressing naturalism and emotion. There was an increased interest in secular subject matter although great religious works were produced as well. The **High Renaissance** of the late fifteenth century boasts such artists as **Leonardo da Vinci**, **Raphael**, and Michelangelo. Renaissance art developed into mannerism, which displays exaggerated emotions, in the sixteenth century.

Renaissance Florence

Fifteenth-century (*Quattrocento*) center of **Renaissance** artistic and intellectual achievement. During this **golden age** the **city-state** of **Florence** was financially well off due to its wealthy class of merchants (the major industry was textiles) and bankers. Although Florence came to be dominated by wealthy families like the **Medicis,** the Pazzis, and the Strozzis, Florence prided itself on its republican sentiment. Renaissance Florence produced or attracted many of the great painters, sculptors, architects, and writers of the fifteenth and sixteenth centuries. Florence was eventually overrun by the more powerful states of France and the **Holy Roman Empire.**

Renaissance Literature

Intellectual humanist movement that emerged during the **Renaissance** fostering a flowering of vernacular literature (written in the local language rather than Latin). One of the pioneers of vernacular literature, although medieval, was **Dante Alighieri**, considered the father of the Italian language, who completed *The Divine Comedy* in 1321. He helped pave the way for future authors including Marsilio Ficino, **Petrarch**, **Giovanni Boccaccio**, **François Rabelais**, **Miguel de Cervantes**, and **William Shakespeare**. With the advent of printing in the mid-fifteenth century more secular and religious literature was produced and made easily accessible.

Repartimiento

Tribute and labor system of Spanish colonial America. Natives had to provide tribute or give a certain amount of time throughout the year to the Spanish for work on farms, in mines, or at other sites. The repartimiento was a reform in 1550 of the **encomienda**, which had given native Americans to Spaniards as forced labor.

Republic, The (c. 379 B.C.E.)

Plato's treatise on government. Written as a dialogue in which **Socrates** questions his students, *The Republic* is a discussion on the nature of justice and the state and the role of the philosopher as leader of the state. Plato lived in **Athens** during a time of great turmoil and he was disgusted with the leadership of the **polis** and critical of **democracy**. In *The Republic* Plato uses his famous cave analogy, in which he describes average people as living in a cave and seeing only shadows of reality while philosophers are like people on the outside who see reality and have the responsibility to interpret it to the rest.

Republic of China

Official name of the central government of mainland China from January 1, 1912, to the establishment of the **People's Republic of China** on October 1, 1949. The Republic of China was proclaimed following the collapse of the **Qing** dynasty in late 1911. Its capital was Nanjing (Nanking), although a wartime capital existed in Chongqing (Chungking) from 1939 to 1945. From 1928 the central government was controlled by the **Guomindang** (Nationalist Party), which fled to Taiwan in 1949. The government of Taiwan since 1949 has continued to call itself the Republic of China, implying that it represents all of China, not just the island province.

Requerimiento

Spanish document read to **Amerindians** in the New World before making war on them. As early as 1493 the Requerimiento required that natives acknowledge the supremacy of the **Roman Catholic Church** and the sovereignty of the Spanish monarch on pain of war and slavery. In the sixteenth century most **conquistadors** took the Requerimiento lightly and did not read it or quickly stated it before attacking. The document absolved the Spaniards of responsibility for their actions. **Bartolomé de Las Casas** thought it laughable and fought against the brutal treatment of the Indians.

Restif de la Bretonne, Nicolas Edmé (1734–1806)

French novelist who published more than 250 novels of detailed **realism** featuring low-life characters or bawdy situations. Many were based on his own life.

Revolutionary War. *See* American Revolution

Rhee, Syngman (Yi Song-man) (1875–1965)

Korean nationalist leader and South Korean president (1948–1960). Rhee attended an American mission school and as a young man became a member of the reform group in the late Yi dynasty. Fleeing to the United States in 1899, he graduated with a doctoral degree in political science from Princeton University and became one of the principal exiled nationalist leaders during the Japanese colonial rule of Korea (1910–1945) living in Hawaii and Washington DC. In 1945 he returned to Korea and was elected as the first president of the Republic of Korea (South Korea) by the National Assembly in 1948. He led South Korea's resistance to North Korea's invasion during the **Korean War** (1950–1953). Increasing dissatisfaction with Rhee's authoritarian rule led to a student led uprising in 1960 and his second exile to Hawaii.

Rhodes, Cecil (1853–1902)

English imperialist, capitalist, prime minister of Cape Colony, conqueror of **Rhodesia** (present-day Zimbabwe and Zambia), and founder of the Rhodes Scholarships. Born to a poor family, by age thirty-six Rhodes had made a fortune in diamonds and gold in South Africa. He was elected to the parliament of Cape Colony and made its prime minister (1890–1896). From 1890 to 1897 he used his wealth to gain control of Rhodesia and beyond. He founded the Rhodes Scholarships to establish connections between English-speaking nations and **Oxford University**.

Rhodesia

African colony founded by the conquests of the Briton **Cecil Rhodes** in the nineteenth century that became a country in 1964. It has been named Southern Rhodesia (1890–1964), Rhodesia (1964–1978), Zimbabwe-Rhodesia (1978–1979), and Zimbabwe (since 1980). British rule ended in 1970 when Rhodesia declared itself independent and a republic, but under white rule. Britain imposed sanctions on Rhodesia, and violence between blacks and whites increased. In 1980 Rhodesia became Zimbabwe with black majority rule.

Ricci, Matteo (1552–1610)

Italian Jesuit missionary who sought to convert the Chinese to Christianity. The Jesuits were aware of the Chinese people's pride in their culture, so they attempted to draw parallels between Confucianism and Christianity to encourage conversion. Ricci shared scientific knowledge and technology such as clocks with Chinese officials in an attempt to win the favor of the intelligentsia. Each culture learned from the other and was impressed with and curious about aspects of the other's civilizations. Ricci adopted Chinese dress and customs and brought information about the Chinese, including their more advanced printing methods, back to Europe.

Richard I, "the Lionhearted" (1157–1199)

King of England (1189–1199). Richard spent less than a year of his ten-year reign in England, but his military success, crusading bravado, and effective advisors who ran England made him very popular. He was one of the leaders of the Third Crusade, winning a victory against the famous Muslim leader **Saladin** but failing to take **Jerusalem**. On his way home Richard was captured and held captive in Austria for fourteen months. Later, fighting to regain lost territory in France, he was wounded and died. Richard was succeeded by his brother, **John I**.

Richelieu, Cardinal Armand Jean du Plessis (1585–1642)

French cleric and royal advisor. Richelieu was the architect of French royal absolutism. He served as the chief minister of Louis XIII (1624–1642) and with the philosophy of "reason of state" sought to increase the power of the central bureaucracy, taking power from local and noble control in the process. His decision to enter the **Thirty Years' War** (1618–1648) as an opponent of Spain to cripple the **Habsburgs**, who had dominated France, led to French superiority on the Continent. After Richelieu's death and the death of Louis XIII, **Louis XIV** and his chief minister **Jules Mazarin**, a protégé of Richelieu's, continued to develop the power of absolute government along Richelieu's design.

Rifle

Rifling, or boring of a gun-barrel with spiraling grooves. First done in the sixteenth century, rifling became common only in the eighteenth century. Spiral grooving spins the ball (later, the oblong bullet) and gives it a truer trajectory. Rifles were slow to load, hence were used for hunting, not warfare, until the nineteenth century. In the nineteenth century percussion caps, smokeless powder, oblong bullets, and breechloading made rifles increasingly effective at longer ranges and more rapid firing.

Rigveda

Oldest and most sacred of the **Vedas** of ancient India. Consisting of 1,028 hymns for use at sacrifices by the **Aryans** to their gods, the Rigveda was probably composed between 1500 and 900 B.C.E. It is revered by Hindus, making it perhaps the oldest sacred text in the world as well as a major source on the religion and culture of ancient India.

Rites of Zhou (Zhou Li)

Ancient Chinese ritual text attributed to Zhou Gong (the duke of Zhou) in the twelfth century but probably compiled about 300 B.C.E. It deals with government, the military, and education and was incorporated into the Confucian canon as an authoritative text and guide for philosophers and policy makers.

River Valley Civilizations

Early civilizations, such as those of **Egypt**, **Mesopotamia**, the **Indus** Valley, and the early **Chinese** civilization of the Yellow River basin, that appeared in river valleys. The rich, easily worked alluvial soils and the ease of communication and transportation that rivers provide facilitated large concentrations of farming communities and the growth of more complex societies. The need to control the river from flooding and to build irrigation canals, reservoirs, and dikes all encouraged large-scale organization and the growth of states.

Rizal, José (1861–1896)

Filipino **nationalist** and novelist. After studying medicine in Spain Rizal became a novelist. His writings were a vehicle for expressing Philippine nationalist sentiments. The Spanish exiled him to Mindanao after he formed the Liga Filipina, a reform society. The Spanish colonial authorities executed him in 1896, falsely accusing him of involvement in a nationalist uprising that occurred that year. He has become the most revered nationalist figure in the Philippines.

Robert I, the Bruce (Robert Bruce) (1274–1329)

King of Scotland (1306–1329). As a Scottish aristocrat, Robert the Bruce resisted English occupation. As king, Bruce won a major victory over the English at the Battle of Bannockburn in 1314. In 1328 a treaty with the English established Bruce's title as king and Scotland's independence. Bruce was able to consolidate Scottish government and at his death transferred a relatively stable country to his son David II.

Robespierre, Maximilien (1758–1794)

French revolutionary during the **French Revolution** and architect of the Terror. Robespierre was elected to the **Estates General** in 1789 and became a leader of the radical Jacobins in the **National Convention**. On the **Committee of Public Safety** Robespierre helped to hunt and destroy enemies of the revolution. This effort became so widespread it was known as the Terror. The Terror centralized authority in the hands of the revolutionary government and eliminated opposition. When members of the Committee of Public Safety denounced Robespierre himself as an enemy of the revolution, he was arrested and executed.

Rockefeller, John D. (1839–1937)

American business owner and philanthropist who dominated the U.S. oil industry in the late nineteenth and early twentieth centuries. Originally a bookkeeper, Rockefeller entered the oil business in 1863 as a partner in a Cleveland, Ohio, oil refinery and established Standard Oil Company of Ohio in 1867. A skilled business organizer and ruthless competitor, Rockefeller pioneered the use of the trust in 1881 to establish a near monopoly in the petroleum industry, becoming a target of antitrust activists in the process. When Ohio outlawed the Standard Oil Trust in 1892 Rockefeller reorganized his business as a holding company, Standard Oil of New Jersey, which survived until broken up in a U.S. Supreme Court decision in 1911. Rockefeller remained a major force in the petroleum industry but no longer dominated it. One of America's wealthiest men, he spent his later years supporting a number of philanthropic causes.

Roman Architecture

Architectural style of the **Roman Republic** and **Roman Empire**. Initially influenced by Italic and Etruscan styles, Greek architecture was also incorporated when the Roman Republic began to expand at the end of the third century B.C.E. The Romans utilized mud brick and local stone (such as tufa and limestone) with marble façades. The **arch** and the vault defined Roman design, which manifested itself differently across the empire depending on local influences. One of the most influential Roman architectural legacies was the development of poured concrete, which enabled the creation of such monuments as the Pantheon (c. 118–28 C.E.), whose dome spanned 142 feet (43 m).

Roman Catholic Church

Christian church developed in the postapostolic era, hierarchically structured, and claiming a continuous administrative existence from Saint Peter. The name *Roman Catholic* has been in use since the **Reformation** to distinguish the church from **Protestantism**. The term *catholic* has been in use since the early centuries of the church, meaning "universal" and, later, "orthodox." The Roman Catholic Church's theology is centered around the sacraments—earthly manifestations of God's grace and seven in number, and also in belief in the church as a divinely commissioned institution and in the church's role in mediating salvation. The church

evolved in the first century after **Jesus**'s death and by the fifth century was elaborately structured. During the **Middle Ages** the Roman Catholic Church became the only European-wide administrative structure following the form of the **Roman Empire**, with dioceses (districts) administered from the major cities by **bishops** who answered to the **pope** (the bishop of Rome). In 1054 the eastern churches refused to acknowledge the supremacy of the Roman pope and split to become the **Eastern Orthodox Church**. In the sixteenth century corruption within the Roman Catholic Church led to the **Reformation** and a splintering into numerous Protestant denominations. Over the centuries the Roman Catholic Church has reformed through numerous councils and is continuously evolving.

Romance of the Three Kingdoms

Chinese novel attributed in its present form to Le Guanzhong, a fourteenth-century writer of novels and drama. Written in a simple literary style, it is based on the wars of the Three Kingdoms period of the third century C.E. It has remained one of the most popular works of fiction in East Asia.

Roman Empire (27 B.C.E.–c. 476 C.E. in the west; 27 B.C.E.–1453 C.E. in the east)

Vast empire of the Mediterranean world and continuation of the **Roman Republic**. The Roman Empire was known for its conquests, unified laws, technology, effective administration, and stability, especially in the period 14–180 C.E., known as the **Pax Romana** ("Roman Peace"). Roman civilization spans a period from 500 B.C.E., when the Republic was founded, to 1453 C.E., when the Eastern Roman Empire, known as the **Byzantine Empire**, fell to the Ottomans. Even though the Roman Republic built an empire of multiple peoples ruled centrally, it became the Roman Empire after Octavian defeated all opposition and returned to Rome in 27 B.C.E. to be made **princeps** ("first citizen") and given the title Augustus. Even though the Senate and the rest of the administration still existed, Augustus and his successors ruled as emperors. Imperial Rome maintained stability abroad by powerful armies and good diplomacy and at home by a good judicial system, adequate food supplies, and entertainment for the common people. Roman technology included the effective use of the **arch** for the construction of large buildings and **aqueducts** to bring water to the cities. The Roman Empire was divided into two administrative units in 375 C.E., and as the western half crumbled under Germanic invasions, the eastern half continued.

Romanesque Architecture

Medieval architectural style of the eleventh and twelfth centuries distinguished by rounded arches, thick vaulting, heavy walls, columns, and piers. The name *Romanesque* was taken from its "Roman"-like appearance with repetitive arches reflective of Roman **basilicas**. Romanesque church architecture normally has an enlarged eastern choir and a nave divided into units with columns and piers. Pisa Cathedral in Italy and Durham Cathedral in England are two distant and differing examples of Romanesque.

Roman Law

Collective codified (written) laws. At the foundation of the **Roman Republic** (509 B.C.E.), law was based on custom and existed in an oral tradition. When it was codified in the **Twelve Tables**, the **plebeians** were no longer entirely at the mercy of upper-class interpretation of the laws. When **Octavian** rose to power, the republic came under the domination of the emperor, who enacted many of the laws, which the Senate ratified as a matter of course. The Justinian Code (534 C.E.) consolidated past laws and jury decisions to comprise a system of civil law. The legal system in ancient Rome, which continued to develop during the empire, served as the foundation of laws across western Europe and in the later European colonies.

Roman Religion

Myths of ancient Rome illustrating Roman religion as a mix of Greek, indigenous, and Indo-European ideas. These **polytheistic** myths were used to illustrate legal and moral lessons like civic virtue. It was during the **Pax Romana** that **Christianity** developed within the **Roman Empire**.

Roman Republic (c. 500–27 B.C.E.)

State that began in the Italian peninsula and grew to dominate the entire Mediterranean world. The Roman Republic was renowned for its mixed constitution—a combination of monarchy, oligarchy, and democracy—and for its effective army. Around 500 B.C.E. the **patricians** of Rome expelled their kings and set up a republic consisting of three parts: two chief magistrates, known as **consuls**, selected from the patricians for one year; the **Senate**, composed of life-term patricians selected by the consuls; and the assembly of the common people, called **plebeians**. The plebeians formed their own assembly, known as the Tribal Assembly; its representatives were called Tribunes. This structure was modified in the third century B.C.E., creating more social mobility and proved successful. The Roman Republic began to expand in the third century B.C.E. and by the first century B.C.E. controlled most of the Mediterranean world. From 133 to 31 B.C.E. the Roman Republic was rocked by unrest and civil war. **Julius Caesar** became virtual dictator of the republic in 47 B.C.E., and after Caesar's murder in 44 B.C.E. his grandnephew and adopted son **Octavian** came to power, In 27 B.C.E. he became **princeps** and was given the title Augustus. The Roman Republic at this point became the **Roman Empire**.

Romanticism

Artistic and intellectual movement of the late eighteenth and early nineteenth centuries that emphasized emotional, mystical, natural, and supernatural interests over the cerebral, the orderly, and the utilitarian. The Romantics reacted to the **Enlightenment**, the **Industrial Revolution**, and the **French Revolution**, all of which seemed to deny the emotional side of humankind. The Romantics tried to reintegrate these elements through the use of poetry, paintings, novels, music, and other arts. Some of the famous proponents of Romanticism were poet and painter William Blake, poet William Wordsworth, novelist Mary Shelley, and musical composer Richard Wagner.

Rome

Name of a city, a republic, and an empire. Rome was originally the city, later associated with the surrounding territory. With the establishment of the **Roman Republic** the name *Rome* came to designate the empire that was gradually built up by the Republic. With the accession of **Octavian** as Augustus, Rome became the **Roman Empire**. The empire disintegrated in the west in the third, fourth, and fifth centuries, and although it survived in the east, it became known as the **Byzantine Empire** and was no longer known as Rome.

Rome, Decline of

Long and gradual process of disintegration of the **Roman Empire**. The fall of the Roman Empire was propagated by fiscal and class conflict during the third century

C.E. In a fifty-year period there were about fifty claimants to the throne. Following a series of tyrannical and inadequate emperors as well as waves of attacks by the **Germanic tribes** on the northern border of the empire, the Roman Empire was divided into eastern and western portions in the fourth century. While the western Roman Empire lasted until the Turks conquered **Constantinople** in 1453, the eastern empire began to fall when the Visigoths overran the Italian peninsula in 410 C.E. and when the city of Rome was sacked again in 476 C.E.

Roosevelt, Franklin D. (1882–1945)

Thirty-second president of the United States. After serving as a New York state senator and assistant secretary of the navy under President **Woodrow Wilson**, Franklin D. Roosevelt (often called FDR) was the Democratic Party's nominee for vice president in 1920. Shortly after losing that election Roosevelt was stricken with polio, which left his legs paralyzed. Elected governor of New York in 1928, he defeated **Herbert C. Hoover** in the presidential election of 1932 with a pledge to vigorously fight the effects of the **Great Depression**. His New Deal reform program brought relief to the unemployed, addressed structural problems in industry and agriculture, implemented programs of planned development in particularly distressed areas of the country, provided support for the rights of organized labor, and established structural safety nets to ensure against a future economic collapse of similar scale. In the process Roosevelt fundamentally altered the relationship of the federal government to the American people and greatly increased its scope and power. While the New Deal did not end the Great Depression, it did enable the nation to survive the crisis. The economy recovered with the **World War II** mobilization. Reelected in 1936, 1940, and 1944, FDR is the only U.S. president elected to more than two terms. During World War II he played a major role in the development of **Allied** strategy, authorized development of the **atomic bomb**, and sought diplomatic arrangements to ensure the postwar peace. Toward these ends, he met with **Winston Churchill** and **Joseph Stalin** at Tehran, Iran (1943), and Yalta, Ukraine (1945), in addition to holding numerous other conferences with Churchill alone.

Roosevelt, Theodore (1858–1919)
Twenty-sixth president of the United States. Following a career as a New York state legislator, cattle rancher, civil service commissioner, New York City police commissioner, assistant secretary of the navy, and soldier in the **Spanish-American War**, Theodore Roosevelt was elected governor of New York as a Republican in 1898. In 1900 he was elected U.S. vice president under William McKinley, and he became president upon McKinley's assassination in 1901. Roosevelt was elected president in 1904. As president he championed the cause of progressive reform and considerably expanded the power of the presidency. Among his domestic achievements were passage of the Pure Food and Drug Act and the Meat Inspection Act, moderate support of organized labor through his Square Deal program, railroad regulation, and efforts to regulate business trusts and break up those that resisted compliance (called trust-busting). In foreign policy, Roosevelt secured the rights to build the **Panama Canal** and began its construction, negotiated peace between Russia and Japan in 1905 (for which he won the **Nobel Prize** for Peace), and proclaimed the Roosevelt Corollary to the **Monroe Doctrine** to forestall European intervention in the Caribbean. After leaving office in 1909 he traveled to Africa and Europe, but growing dissatisfied with his chosen successor, William Howard Taft, Roosevelt again ran for president in 1912 as the candidate of the Progressive ("Bull Moose") Party. With the Republican vote split between Taft and Roosevelt, the election was won by Democrat Woodrow Wilson.

Rosetta Stone (c. 197–196 B.C.E.)
Stone tablet with the same events described in Greek, Egyptian, and **hieroglyphics** that enabled scholars to solve the mystery of hieroglyphics. Discovered by the French when Napoléon invaded Egypt in 1799, the parallel texts finally made it possible in the nineteenth century to decipher ancient Egyptian hieroglyphics, opening up the world of Egyptology.

Rotten Boroughs
English towns with few or no residents that still sent two members to Parliament. Certain towns in England had been specified in the **Middle Ages** as Royal Boroughs, meaning they sent members to **Parliament**. By the late eighteenth century some of them had declined to few or no residents, while new industrial towns had grown up but had no voting power. In the **Reform Bill of 1832** more than fifty rotten boroughs were abolished while more individuals in the industrial towns were enfranchised.

Rousseau, Jean-Jacques (1712–1778)
French philosopher of the **Enlightenment**. Swiss-born Rousseau criticized the existing social order, the *ancien régime* ("old order"), in France but believed in the innate goodness of humans, which he described as the "noble savage," an individual unaffected by demands of society. In this vein Rousseau laid out a new educational concept for the natural man in *Émile* (1762). And yet Rousseau proposed in *The*

Social Contract (1762) that humans accept social contracts to maintain order and that there is a "general will" that forces all individuals in society to abide by the rules of the social contract.

Royal Air Force (RAF)

Air force of the United Kingdom. The RAF, originally part of the army, became famous during **World War II** in the **Battle of Britain**. Against overwhelming numbers the RAF held off the German **Luftwaffe** (air force) and thwarted Germany's plan to invade Britain. **Winston Churchill**, referring to the RAF pilots, said, "Never in the field of human conflict, was so much owed by so many to so few."

Royal Commentaries of the Inca

Vast account of the **Inca** written by Garcilaso de la Vega, son of an Inca mother and Spanish noble father. The Royal Commentaries became the most widely read source on the Inca during the Spanish colonial period. It, along with the view of the Pizarro brothers, and the history of **Bartolomé de Las Casas**, provided the Europeans with their knowledge of the Incas.

Rubaiyat

A quatrain of verse poetry. The most famous Rubaiyat was written by Persian poet and mathematician Omar Khayyám (d. 1123 C.E.), who wrote his Rubaiyat during the final year of his life. Other Persian literati, such as Rumi and Hafez, also wrote Rubaiyat. The *Rubaiyat* of Omar Khayyám is among the few Persian masterpieces translated into most major languages, including English, French, German, Italian, Russian, Chinese, Hindi, Arabic, and Urdu. In 1859 Edward J. Fitzgerald completed perhaps the most famous translation of the *Rubaiyat* from Persian into English.

Rubens, Peter Paul (1577–1640)

Flemish painter of the northern **baroque** period. Rubens, an ardent Catholic during the **Reformation**, studied painting in Italy. He created huge paintings (many of them with religious themes) full of color, movement, and great emotion. Rubens also wrote humanist commentaries on classical Latin texts but is known for paintings such as *The Raising of the Cross* (1609–1610) and *Battle of the Amazons* (c. 1618).

Rumi, Jalal al-Din al- (1207–1273)

Islamic scholar and poet. Rumi was born in northern Afghanistan, and he died in southwestern Turkey. An Islamic scholar and a follower of Tasawwuf, or **Sufism**, Rumi is most famous for his poetry, particularly his mystical "Mathnawi." The Mevleviyya order of Sufis (sometimes known as the whirling dervishes) consider him their founder. Rumi remains influential for modern Muslim intellectuals, and his writings have been translated into many languages.

Rump Parliament

Remnant of the English **Parliament** after the **English Civil War**. A Parliament was called by King Charles I in 1640. It remained in existence against the king's wishes throughout the English Civil War (1642–1649), called into existence the **New Model Army**, and called for the execution of the king (1649). The remnant (seventy-eight members of Parliament), known as the Rump Parliament, still sat in 1653 when **Oliver Cromwell** said, "Be gone you rogues. You have sate long enough." Six years later it was recalled to end the commonwealth, dissolve itself, and allow for the **Restoration** of the monarchy in 1660.

Runnymeade. *See* Magna Carta

Rus

Swedish **Vikings** who penetrated Russia in the mid-eighth century. The Finnish term

Rus gave the name *Russia* to the area conquered or influenced by the Rus.

Russia

Region of the vast eastern European plain settled by the Slavs in the third century C.E. The region was overrun numerous times by tribes including **Goths, Huns, Avars, Bulgars, Magyars, Khazars,** and **Vikings** who were known as the **Rus** and who gave their name to the territory. Semilegendary figure, Rurik established the first Russian principality at Novgorod in 862 and soon after that Kiev, which became the center of Russia. Russia became Christian under Vladimir, prince of Kiev, in 989. Kiev was destroyed by the Mongols in 1240, and most of Russia was conquered. A slow recovery left the leadership in Moscow because of its location. **Alexander Nevsky**'s son became the first prince of Moscow. **Ivan III** (r. 1462–1505), grand prince of Moscow, consolidated the Russian state; drove the Mongols, **Hanseatic** merchants, and Lithuanians out; moved the church's center to Moscow; and married the niece of the last Byzantine emperor. **Ivan IV** became the first **tsar** of Russia (r. 1547–1584).

Russian Orthodox Church

Eastern Orthodox Church in **Russia.** Russia became Christian in 989, and when the eastern and western Christian churches split in 1054 Russia's churches remained in the Eastern Orthodox tradition. However, the patriarch of **Constantinople** does not claim authority over the Russian Orthodox Church. The Russian Orthodox Church recognizes seven major sacraments, like the **Roman Catholic Church,** but does not recognize the authority of the **pope.**

Russian Revolution (1905)

Revolt of factory workers, the military, and some peasants against the government of Tsar **Nicholas II.** Russia's defeat in the **Russo-Japanese War** brought on heavy taxation and discontent with the government. Many believed that the tsar was being poorly advised, and they marched in a peaceful demonstration in Saint Petersburg. When troops fired upon the demonstrators, leaders of the people were outraged and a council, or soviet, of workers was formed. The revolt subsided when the tsar promised reforms, but the government became increasingly harsh and oppressive instead.

Russian Revolution (October Revolution) (1917)

Overthrow of the tsarist government in Russia and establishment first of a republic and then of a union of soviets. Russia suffered from massive discontent caused by **World War I,** little relief for the poverty-stricken serfs who had been emancipated in 1861, and the pressures of rapid **industrialization,** putting many stresses on the rigid, absolutist state of **Tsar Nicholas II.** The first phase of the revolution erupted during food shortages in Saint Petersburg in March 1917. The tsarist regime was toppled and a new provisional republican government was established. When this government continued Russia's involvement in World War I and did not deal adequately with land reform and food shortages, the moderate soviets, headed by Lavr Georgiyevich Kornilov, came to control the government that July. The second, radical phase of the revolution unfolded when **Vladimir Lenin** led the successful **Bolshevik Revolution** on October 24–25, 1917 (new style calendar November 6–7).

Russo-Japanese War (1904–1905)

Conflict between Russia and Japan over control of Korea and **Manchuria.** After years of tensions between the rival expansionary powers, Japan launched an attack on the Russian forces when Russia reneged on an agreement to withdraw its forces from southern Manchuria. After Japanese forces won victories in Manchuria and sank the Russian fleet at Tsushima, Japan, the United States brokered a peace (the Treaty of Portsmouth) that in effect left Japan in control of Korea. The war, the first major victory of a non-Western nation over a Western power, greatly contributed to international recognition of Japan as a rising, modernizing country with the strongest military force in the Pacific. All of this weakened the tsarist regime of Russia and led to the loss of independence for Korea. Japan's victory over a European nation inspired anti-imperialist movements in other parts of Asia.

Rwanda Massacres (1994)
Genocide, warfare, and humanitarian disaster in the African country of Rwanda. Rwanda's majority ethnic group is Hutu and the country also has a large minority Tutsi population. In 1959–1960 the Hutus came to power, driving 200,000 Tutsis into exile. In 1994 the sons of the exiled Tutsis returned to massacre Hutus. A genocidal civil war ensued, with an estimated 500,000 Hutus and 500,000 Tutsis killed or lost to disease. Another 2 million people, almost a third of the total population, left the country for neighboring Congo, Tanzania, and Burundi.

Ryoanji Temple
Zen temple in Kyoto, Japan, famous for its rock garden. Consisting of a flat, rectangular surface of raked white sand with fifteen scattered rocks, the garden is said to represent the ocean with islands protruding above its surface. Created in the fifteenth century, the garden expresses the severe, simple aesthetics of medieval Japan.

S

Sadat, Anwar el- (1918–1981)
Egyptian president (1970–1981) and winner of the **Nobel Prize** for Peace (1978). A military officer, Sadat supported **Gamal Abdel Nasser**'s rise to power in the 1950s. He became acting president upon Nasser's death and was elected president in 1970. He promoted reforms in the economy and political structure and in 1972 expelled the Soviet Union's advisors and technicians. Sadat led Egypt and Syria to an invasion of Israel, the 1973 **Arab-Israeli War**, in which Egypt retook some territory in the Sinai. After the war Sadat began to work toward peace with Israel, traveling to Jerusalem in 1977. In 1978, with U.S. president **Jimmy Carter** as mediator, Sadat and Israeli prime minister **Menachem Begin** negotiated a peace agreement called the Camp David Accords. Sadat and Begin were awarded the **Nobel Prize** for Peace for this effort. In 1979 Egypt and Israel signed a peace treaty. Sadat's reputation in Egypt deteriorated, and he was assassinated by **Muslim** extremists in 1981.

Sadducees
Jewish priestly sect that controlled the second **Hebrew Temple** until its destruction in 70 C.E. The Sadducees were wealthy and powerful in Jerusalem for two centuries prior to the destruction of the temple but were in constant conflict with the **Pharisees**. The Sadducees followed the **Torah** purely and gave little weight to postbiblical traditions.

Sadi (1213–1291)
Persian poet from the city of Shiraz, considered one of the masters of classical Persian literature. His best-known works are *Bustan* (*The Orchard*) and *Gulistan* (*The Rose Garden*). His works contain many aphorisms and humorous reflections that deal with moral virtues, the absurdity of human existence, and Sufi ideals and concepts of **Sufism**.

Safavid Dynasty (1501–1722)
Islamic dynasty in Iran. The Safavids became noteworthy as an Islamic Sufi order active in eastern Anatolia and northwestern Iran during the thirteenth-century demise of **Seljuk** rule. The founder of the dynasty, **Shah Ismail**, had earlier declared his allegiance to **Shia Islam**. The Safavids are known for converting most Iranians to Shiism. Shah Abbas Safavid (1588–1629) greatly expanded the capital city of Isfahan through various means including mercantilist ventures involving the export of state-monopolized Iranian silk.

Sahara Trade
Trans–Sahara Desert trade predominantly running north–south. The Sahara Desert divides Africa into north Africa, which is a Mediterranean region, and sub-Saharan Africa. Trade between these two regions has crossed the Sahara for thousands of years, although the introduction of the camel in the first centuries of the common era made regular and extended trade possible, with gold, ivory, spices, and slaves

moving north to the Mediterranean coast, and horses, textiles, and paper going south. East–west trade generally ran north or south of the desert, never straight across it.

Saigo Takamori (1828–1877)
Japanese revolutionary, an early opponent of the **Tokugawa shogunate**. He was exiled (1859–1864) but returned to train **bushi** (samurai) warriors in the Satsuma region. In 1867 his troops supported the emperor in the **Meiji Restoration** and led the development of a conscription army for the government. He resigned from the Meiji government when his advocacy of war with Korea in 1873 was rejected. He returned to his home in Kagoshima and opened a school for military training. In 1877 some of his students began a revolt against the government. Saigo took leadership of the revolt, which lasted for six months. When his ex-bushi army was defeated by conscripted peasant imperial troops and he was mortally wounded, he had a faithful warrior behead him.

Sailendra (Shailendra)
Dynasty that flourished in Java from around the mid-eighth to the mid-ninth century. Based in the agriculturally rich island of Java, it held some influence, if not direct rule, over much of Southeast Asia. In the ninth century it relocated to Palembang in Sumatra. It left many monuments, the most famous of them the great Buddhist temple of **Borobodur**.

Saint Bartholomew's Day Massacre (1572)
French slaughter of **Protestants**. On August 24, 1572, Catholics throughout France killed thousands of French Protestants, called **Huguenots**. A religious war had been raging since 1562 in France, but fear of a Huguenot takeover of govern-

ment led to the assassination of leading Huguenots and killings all over France.

Saint Bernard Pass
Actually, two passes across the Swiss Alps, the Great Saint Bernard Pass and the Little Saint Bernard Pass. The passes were used as Roman military roads. In the **Middle Ages** the roads were watched over by the Augustinian monks of Saint Bernard. The monks and their large dogs saved the lives of wayfarers and provided a hospice for all travelers.

Saint Lawrence Seaway
System of river, canals, and locks that provide a deep waterway from Lake Superior to the Atlantic Ocean. The Saint Lawrence Seaway extends 186 miles (299 km) from Montreal, Canada, to Lake Ontario. Canada and the United States began its construction in 1954 and the seaway opened in 1959. Altogether the seaway enables ships to travel more than 2,300 miles (3,700 km) inland from the Atlantic. The seaway opened the Great Lakes region of Canada and the United States to enormous economic development and connected the interior to the rest of the world via ocean shipping.

Saint Peter's (Rome)
Roman Catholic church of the bishop of Rome (the **pope**). Saint Peter's became the most important church in Christianity because Rome was the center of the **Roman Empire**. The original church, allegedly built over the grave of Saint Peter, was built in 324. The new Saint Peter's, started in 1506 during the **papacy** of **Julius II**, was designed by Donato Bramante but not completed for more than 120 years. **Michelangelo** became its architect in 1546 and continued in that role until his death in 1564. It is built in a **High Renaissance** style.

Sakamoto Ryoma (1835–1867)
Japanese revolutionary who fled his native Tosa at the age of twenty-eight. In 1866 he succeeded in forming an alliance between the two traditional province enemies of Satsuma and Choshu to help overthrow the **Tokugawa Bakufu**. In 1867 he formulated the Eight-Point Program for the modernization of Japan, a political guideline for the new government and cabinet. Only one month later, on November 15, 1867, he was assassinated in Kyoto at the age of thirty-three.

Saladin (c. 1138–1193)
Sultan of Egypt and Syria, **Muslim** hero of the **Crusades**, and founder of the Ayyubid dynasty. Saladin reconquered **Jerusalem** from the western Christian crusaders in 1187 by uniting Muslim forces and employing new military techniques. He led Muslim forces against the Third Crusade and **Richard I**. Saladin was defeated by the Christians in 1191 but withdrew primarily because the crusaders had fought to a draw and the Christian leader Richard I had left the **Middle East**.

Salamis, Battle of (480 B.C.E.)
Turning point in the Greek war with Persia. The Persian king **Xerxes I** invaded Greece with 1,200 ships and 150,000 men while Athens assembled a navy of 380 ships and 9,000 men. The land war was given up for lost, but Athenian Themistocles planned the battle, tricking Xerxes into thinking that the Greek navy was in disarray. Xerxes attacked in the narrow Salamis channel and the Greeks won a decisive victory, consequently enabling the Greek land force to win the **Battle of Plataea** the following year. These victories encouraged the great flowering of Greek culture known as **classical Greece**.

SALT I (Strategic Arms Limitations Treaty)
Negotiated by President **Richard M. Nixon** of the United States and President **Leonid Brezhnev** of the **Union of Soviet Socialist Republics** in 1972. It limited the manufacture of certain types of nuclear missiles.

Samarkand
City of modern Uzbekistan and the capital of **Timur**'s Turkic empire in the fourteenth century. Originally founded as early as the sixth century B.C.E., it was conquered by **Alexander the Great** in 329 B.C.E. By the sixth century C.E., it was the most important of the **Sogdian Silk Road** cities. The Arabs conquered it in the eighth century C.E. and it has been a **Muslim** city since then. The **Mongols** destroyed it in the thirteenth century. Rebuilt, it became Timur's capital, and under his grandson **Ulugh Beg** it reached heights of art and culture. Samarkand was a major stop on the route between Asia and the **Middle East** and Europe. Today it is the second-largest city in Uzbekistan.

Samnite Wars
Series of wars between the Latins and the Samnites, southern neighbors of **Rome**, 343–90 B.C.E. The Samnites defeated the Latins of Rome several times. During the **Punic Wars** the Samnites allied with **Hannibal**, but finally in 90 B.C.E. the Samnites were defeated for the last time and absorbed into the **Roman Republic**.

Samori. *See* Touré, Samori

Samudragupta (r. c. 335–375)
Indian emperor of the **Gupta empire**. He extended the empire of his father, **Chandra Gupta**, to bring most of northern India under his control. His reign marks part of what later historians have called the

"Gupta golden age," when the arts and sciences in India flourished.

Samurai. *See* Bushi

San. *See* Khoisan

Sandinista
A member of the Sandinista National Liberation Front, a Nicaraguan **guerrilla** group founded in 1962. Named for César Augusto Sandino, a hero of resistance against the U.S. occupation (1927–1933), the Sandinistas were formed to resist the tyranny of the Somoza family, gaining support primarily from the landless peasantry. The Sandinistas clashed with the National Guard until 1967, when a full civil war broke out (1967–1979). The Sandinistas overthrew President Anastasio Debayle Somoza in 1979 and ruled Nicaragua under Daniel Ortega from 1979 to 1990, breaking up the country's large estates and distributing land to the peasants. Resistance to the Sandinistas, known as the Contras, arose from the dispossessed landowners and was supported by the United States. In 1990 elections replaced the Sandinistas with a coalition heavily funded by the United States.

San Martín, José de (1778–1850)
Argentine hero of South American independence movements against Spain. With San Martín's aid, Argentina, Chile, and Peru were liberated from Spanish rule. He worked with **Bernardo O'Higgins** in the liberation of Chile. He was appointed protector of Peru but turned over his power to **Simón Bolívar** in 1822. San Martín spent the remainder of his life in exile in Europe.

Sanskrit
Classical language of India in which many classics of Hindu religion and Indian literature were written. The language appeared in the second millennium B.C.E. and reached its classical form in the grammar by **Panini** about 400 B.C.E. No longer spoken in India, Sanskrit continued to be the primary language of scholarship as well as of much Indian literature until recent times. It is still an official language of the Republic of India.

Santa María
The flagship of **Christopher Columbus**'s voyage to the New World in 1492. The *Santa María* was a nao, a typical fifteenth-century cargo ship not renowned for its handling ability but bigger than the *Niña* or the *Pinta*. A three-masted, square and lateen-sailed ship, it measured about 108 tons, was about 60 feet (18.3 m) long and 20 feet (6 m) wide and carried a crew of forty. Columbus was its captain until it ran aground and sank on Haiti on Christmas Eve 1492.

Sartre, Jean-Paul (1905–1980)
French existential philosopher, novelist, and playwright. The central concepts of his philosophy are freedom and action. His works include *Being and Nothingness* (1943), on individual freedom and the responsibilities of choices that humans make. In 1964 Sartre was awarded the **Nobel Prize** for literature but turned it down on the grounds of the award being **bourgeois**. Sartre was a longtime friend of **Simone de Beauvoir** and in a bitter feud with **Albert Camus**.

Sasanids (224–651)
Mesopotamian dynasty that overthrew the Parthians (224) and ruled Persia and Babylonia. Claiming descent from the Persian **Achaemenids**, the Sasanids created a sophisticated cosmopolitan culture with their capital at Ctesiphon. Trade extended to the east and west, and under Shapur I (239–272) the Sasanid empire expanded

militarily, even defeating **Roman** armies. The Sasanids revived **Zoroastrianism**, which became the state religion. From the end of Shapur's reign until 651 the Sasanids existed precariously between the **Roman** and **Byzantine empires** in the west and the Kushan empire in the east. In 651 **Islam** overran the Sasanids.

Sassanians. *See* Sasanids

Sati (Suttee)

Hindi term meaning "virtuous woman" and used by Westerners to refer to the practice in which a widow immolated herself on her husband's funeral pyre. Of ancient origin, the custom was idealized in India as a sign of wifely virtue. Sati was abolished by the British in the nineteenth century.

Satori

Japanese term for enlightenment taught by **Buddhism**. The concept of satori became popular in medieval Japan during the **Kamakura** period. The two major sects of **Zen** established during that period—Rinzai and Soto—differed on whether satori could be achieved suddenly, as Rinzai taught, or only gradually through a long process of meditation, as Soto taught.

Satrap

Governor of provinces in the empire of the **Achaemenids. Darius I**, in the sixth century B.C.E., divided the empire into provinces called satrapies. Each satrap was tax collector, judge, and army commander of his province. The role of satrap continued long after Darius I and was used by **Alexander the Great.**

Satyagraha

The policy of civil disobedience developed by **Mohandas K. Gandhi** in South Africa and later employed in India against British rule. Meaning "truth-force" in Hindi, satyagraha involved using passive resistance and adhering to ethical conduct in struggle. The technique was effective in undermining British rule in India and was adopted by other groups such as activists in the **civil rights movement** in the United States.

Saul of Tarsus. *See* Paul the Apostle (Saul of Tarsus)

Savannah Region

Term for an area of the tropics characterized by tall grasses and scattered trees. Savannahs are found in South America and parts of Asia, but the most extensive regions of savannah are in Africa. Savannah covers most of west Africa and a considerable portion of central, southern, and east Africa. The savannah region of Africa saw some of the most important historic states, such as **Oyo, Mali, Songhay**, and the **Great Zimbabwe.**

Savonarola, Girolamo (1452–1498)

Italian Renaissance preacher and reformer. A **Dominican** monk, Savonarola began preaching in Renaissance **Florence** in 1482, denouncing immorality and vanity within and outside the **Roman Catholic Church**, angering church authorities. He also claimed to have apocalyptic visions. In 1494 and 1495 Savonarola had gained virtual control of Florence as it became a republic, angering the secular authorities. Refusing an order in 1495 by the **pope** to go to Rome for questioning, Savonarola was excommunicated in 1497 and burned at the stake in 1498.

Saxons

Germanic tribe that invaded Britain in the fourth century C.E. The Saxons, settled in lower Denmark and Germany, began to invade Britain in the late fourth century, and by 410 the Romans left Britain to the invading Saxons, Angles, Picts, and Irish as well as the native Celts. On the Continent, **Charlemagne** conquered the Saxons after repeated attempts during the eighth century.

Schlieffen Plan

German plan for **World War I** named for Count Schlieffen, a field marshal. The plan called for a German attack on France through Belgium, the defeat of France within six weeks by cutting Paris off from the sea, and holding off Russia with secondary forces until the main German army could be removed from France to attack. The Schlieffen Plan was premised on the knowledge that Belgium was lightly defended and that Russia would take a long time to mobilize its army.

Scholasticism

Medieval merger of philosophy and theology. From the ninth to the fourteenth century medieval scholars worked to justify the differences between Greco-Roman philosophy and Judaeo-Christian theology. **Thomas Aquinas** in the thirteenth century effectively succeeded, in what became known as scholasticism. Scholasticism fits Aristotelian logic into Christian theology. In scholasticism, conclusions are predetermined. Because God created all, all must have a purpose, and the purpose of all is to glorify God. Therefore the natural world is merely to glorify God and humankind's role is to determine how. Scholasticism presupposed divine authority and regarded the purpose of logic as finding a way to fit any knowledge into the divine plan. Knowledge and faith became one.

Schweitzer, Albert (1875–1965)

German humanitarian, theologian, philanthropist, missionary doctor, organist, and prolific writer. Schweitzer won the **Nobel Prize** for Peace in 1952 for his work building a fellowship of all nations. Most of Schweitzer's work was in sub-Saharan Africa, where he became a symbol of the Western world's humanitarian care for the third world.

Scientific Revolution

Revolution in the knowledge and understanding of the physical world that took place in Europe in the sixteenth and seventeenth centuries. The scientific revolution was built upon earlier knowledge accumulated across Africa, Europe, and Asia. It is associated with the discoveries and ideas of **Nicolaus Copernicus** (1473–1543), **Johannes Kepler** (1571–1630), and **Galileo** (1564–1642) and culminated in the mathematics and physical laws of **Isaac Newton** (1642–1727). The scientific revolution saw the development of the scientific method; laid the foundations for modern study of biology, physics, chemistry, and astronomy; and affected all areas of Western thought.

Scottish National Party (SNP)

Scottish political party formed in 1934 whose platform is Scottish independence. In the 1970s the SNP became powerful, electing eleven members to the United Kingdom's **Parliament**. In the 1990s the SNP gained support that influenced the Labour Party to grant Scotland its own parliament in 1999. The SNP was initially not in favor of the Parliament as a distraction from independence, but now they see it as a means to independence.

Scriptoria

Writing centers in **monasteries and convents** in Europe during the **Middle Ages**. Monasteries required texts for religious services, and copying them was necessary. By the Carolingian era scriptoria were major sources for building up the holdings of libraries at court and in the monasteries. Often copyists reproduced the text and illuminators added images if the text was a valuable one.

Selassie, Haile (1892–1975)

Emperor of Ethiopia (1930–1974) and statesman born Tafari Makonnen. Haile Selassie was a prominent figure in African and world affairs. Exiled during the Italian occupation of Ethiopia (1936–1941), restored by the **Allies**, and deposed by Marxist military officers in 1974, Selassie was assassinated a year later. Before 1930 he was known as Ras ("Chief") Tafari, from which the Rastafarians take their name.

Seleucids

Members of a Hellenistic empire founded by one of **Alexander the Great**'s generals, Seleucus I. Between 312 and 364 B.C.E. the Seleucids ruled much of the **Middle East**, from Thrace in Europe to the edges of India, the remains of Alexander's Macedonian empire, with its capital at Antioch. The Seleucid kingdom became a major center of Hellenistic culture. In 188 B.C.E. the Seleucids negotiated a peace with Rome, but in 64 B.C.E. Pompey annexed Syria, dissolving the Seleucid empire.

Selim I (1465–1521)

Ottoman Turk ruler (1512–1520). His accession to the Ottoman throne was marked by the forced deposition and murder of his father and Selim's killing of his brothers and nephews. Selim extended Ottoman territory in the **Middle East** by conquering Syria, **Palestine**, Egypt, **Mecca**, and **Medina**. With control over Islam's two holiest cities, Selim assumed the titled **caliph** from the defunct **Abbasid caliphate**. He was an ardent **Sunni Muslim** who undertook many campaigns in Anatolia to purge his realm of **Shia** Muslims, and his greatest accomplishment in this regard was his convincing defeat of the Shia **Safavids** in the 1514 Battle of Chaldiran.

Selim III (1761–1808)

Ottoman sultan (1789–1807) who Westernized the **Ottoman Empire**. An accomplished composer and poet, he was influenced by Western culture. When he became sultan, he established a committee of reformers, heavily influenced by the **French Revolution**. He instituted governmental, military, land, tax, educational, and social reforms. Selim also established embassies in most European capitals. He was impressed by **Napoléon Bonaparte** and was persuaded to support France, declaring war on Great Britain and Russia during the Napoleonic Wars.

Seljuks

A Turkish people who ruled much of the **Muslim** heartland (1037–c. 1300), pushed back the European crusaders from the Middle East, and reunited the Muslim world from Afghanistan to the Mediterranean. The center of their empire was Rum, in Asia Minor. The Seljuks eventually fell to the **Mongols** and were overcome by internal disintegration and the rise of the **Ottoman Turks**, who gained control of Asia Minor.

Senate, Roman

The legislative body of the **Roman Republic**. Composed of approximately 300 senior statesmen of Rome, usually former magistrates. Senators were chosen for life by the censors. The Roman Senate dealt with internal laws and foreign affairs. The two highest magistrates—the **consuls**—executed the legislation of the Senate. With the transformation to the **Roman Empire** the Senate continued to exist and legislate (in fact, it was enlarged), but the emperor held absolute power.

Senate, United States

The upper house of the U.S. Congress. The Senate and the House of Representatives constitute the two chambers of Congress, the legislative branch of the U.S. government. The Senate is composed of two senators elected from each state, or 100 members, for six-year terms. For a law to be enacted both the Senate and the House of Representatives must pass it; it is then sent to the U.S. president to be signed.

Sendero Luminoso (Spanish for "Shining Path")

Peruvian revolutionary communist organization. Founded in 1970, the avowedly **Maoist** Sendero Luminoso used **guerrilla** tactics and terrorism to advance its revolution, whose goal was the replacement of Peru's moderate government with an ultraleftist one. Founder Abimael Guzmán, a university professor, used young intellectuals to arm and train indigenous peoples in the mountains. They moved from remote regions of the Andes to commit bombings and assassinations in the cities. In 1992 Guzmán was arrested and sentenced to life imprisonment, but the group has continued to commit terrorist acts. In 2003 it was estimated that 70,000 people had been killed by the Sendero Luminoso and government forces opposing it.

Seneca the Elder (c. 50 B.C.E.–40 C.E.)

Roman writer of rhetoric and a history of **Rome**. His history, from the civil wars almost to his death, is now lost. Seneca also wrote works of witty sayings for his sons.

Seneca the Younger (c. 4 B.C.E.–65 C.E.)

Roman writer, statesman, and tutor to **Nero**. Prominent during Nero's reign, Seneca wrote numerous works including works on ethics for Nero as well as other prose works, letters, poetry, plays, and speeches. The bulk of his prose was philosophical and is an important source for our understanding of **Stoicism**.

Senghor, Léopold (1906–2001)

Senegalese poet, philosopher, and the first president of Senegal (1960–1981). Educated in contemporary literature at the prestigious École Normale Supérieure in Paris, drafted into the French army in **World War II**, and elected to the French National Assembly, Senghor was thoroughly European and African in his culture. He was the first African elected to the Académie Française. He was also influenced by the writings of **W. E. B. Du Bois** and by the **Pan-African Congresses**. He became one of the founders of **negritude**—focusing on Africanness rather than Europeanness. Senghor spent his last years writing poetry and developing a theory of converging civilizations.

Sennacherib (c. 730–681 B.C.E.)

King of **Assyria** (c. 705–681 B.C.E.). He made **Nineveh** his capital and turned it into a magnificent city with a new palace, canals, aqueducts, and a city wall with fifteen spectacular gates. Sennacherib appears in the **Old Testament**.

Sephardim

Jews of or descended from the Jews of Spain and Portugal. Jews who were expelled from Spain and Portugal, especially in 1492, dispersed across Europe, but in their largest numbers moved to the Netherlands; England; and, in the seventeenth and eighteenth centuries, on to the New World. The Sephardim had Spanish language and culture and remained separate from the **Ashkenazic Jews** of eastern Europe. Some Sephardim were well educated and wealthy at the time of their expulsion and maintained their status for generations, even into the twenty-first century.

Sepoy Mutiny (1857–1858)

Widespread mutiny in India against the British by sepoys, Indian troops employed by the British **East India Company**. The rebellion started when it was rumored that the new cartridges being introduced, which soldiers had to bite before loading them into their new Enfield rifles, were lubricated with pig and cow grease, thus violating both **Muslim** and **Hindu** religious prohibitions (the rumor was partly true). Although few Indian princes other than the **Mughal** emperor joined the mutineers, the sepoys seized control of **Delhi** and other areas, briefly challenging British control over India. The Sepoy Mutiny represented Indian dissatisfaction with the British overlords but also acted as a turning point. After crushing the rebellion, the British government took direct control of India from the East India Company and ended the last remnant of the Mughal empire.

Serf

Medieval European peasant who was bound contractually to a lord to work parts of the lord's land. A serf was not a slave because a serf was not owned by the lord, but a written or verbal contract bound the serf to the lord for a certain number of years, and the serf owed payment in cash or kind (goods) and had a work obligation whereby the serf worked a specified number of days each week, month, or year. If no work obligation was involved, the person was a free peasant, not a serf. In return for the payment and work the lord provided land to work and protection. Often the contract was for long terms, such as ninety-nine years. Consequently, serfs rarely fulfilled the contract and when they died an heir would have to pay a penalty for breaking the contract before the heir could enter into another contract to work the same land. In medieval Europe most of the population was serfs. Serfdom began in the eighth or ninth century and became the norm in the tenth. As the population increased from the eleventh to the thirteenth century, serfdom's obligations became more severe— a matter of supply (limited land) and demand (rising population). Serfdom declined in western Europe beginning in the fourteenth century but was reinforced in eastern Europe beginning in the sixteenth century. Serfs in Russia were not freed until the nineteenth century.

Sermon on the Mount

Discourse by **Jesus** containing the essence of his ethical teachings (in the Bible, Matthew 5–7). In it Jesus teaches his disciples about the Kingdom of God and fulfillment of the laws of righteousness according to **Judaism**. The Beatitudes are a section of the sermon in which Jesus lays out the precepts of the Kingdom of God in simple but consoling fashion: "Blessed are the peacemakers. . . ." The Sermon on the Mount is the most quoted and influential text of the Bible, having influenced even non-Christians such as **Mohandas K. Gandhi**. The sermon sets Christians into three groups: those who follow God, those who do not, and those who pretend to follow.

Seven Years' War (1754–1763)

War between Britain and France with Prussia allied with Britain and Austria and Spain allied with France. The war actually lasted nine years but was not formally declared until 1756. It was fought in Europe, North America (where it was known as the French and Indian War), the Caribbean, India, and the Philippines. For the first four years France was successful in Europe, the Mediterranean, and North America, but starting in 1759 Britain had victories under the political leadership of **William Pitt the Elder** and by Prussian forces on several fronts. By 1760 Britain controlled all of North America and by 1762, most of the Caribbean. The **Treaty of Paris** of 1763 ended the Seven Years' War, with Britain predominant over France on all fronts including India, where France's role effectively ended.

Sforza, Francesco (1401–1466)
Renaissance ruler of Milan and part of the powerful Sforza family. The Sforza dukes of Milan (1450–1494), who came to power after the last Visconti ruler died, were part of a tight interweaving of politics and religion during the Renaissance and the **Reformation**. They used their political influence on the **Roman Catholic Church** and used the church to influence politics. Francesco used his military power, asserted when Milan was besieged by Venetians in the mid-fifteenth century, to become the Milanese head of state. He was very successful in continuing the Viscontis' program of making Milan a strong centralized state. He devised a system of taxation that generated an enormous amount of revenue, which the government used to fortify its military.

Shah of Iran. *See* Muhammad Reza Shah Pahlavi

Shaka Zulu (c. 1790–1828)
Zulu king (1816–1828) and mythologized figure in Zulu tradition. Shaka, son of a Zulu chief, became leader of the federated military under organizer and military innovator **Dingiswayo**. When Dingiswayo was murdered by a rival, Shaka took control, consolidated the confederation, and assumed the Zulu kingship. Under Shaka's

leadership the Zulus rapidly became a formidable power in south Africa.

Shakespeare, William (1564–1616)
English playwright and poet during the reign of Queen **Elizabeth I** (r. 1558–1603). Shakespeare was a prolific writer of comedies, histories, romances, and tragedies including *Midsummer Night's Dream* (1595), *Henry VI* (1590–1592), *Romeo and Juliet* (1595), and *Hamlet* (1601–1602). He also acted and penned many sonnets, which stand as a testament to his skillful, beautiful use of the English language. His influential works are renowned for their intense portrayals of human emotion and the interconnectedness of life. Shakespeare's plays were originally performed in London's Globe Theater, built in 1599.

Shamans
Northeast Asian religious figures who in a number of societies play an important role in mediating between the spiritual realm and the day-to-day world. Among Koreans, as well as some Manchurian, Siberian, and Central Asian peoples, shamans are believed to have the power to cross into the spiritual world, sometimes leaving their bodies to do so. In Korea, shamanism was often supported by the state, but this practice declined during the Choson dynasty (1392–1910). Many modern Koreans continue to visit shamanist shrines to seek the aid of professional shamans in dealing with malevolent spirits. Forms of shamanism were also practiced in parts of China and Japan. The term is also used more generally to include **Amerindian** figures who can communicate with spirits.

Shang (1766–1122 B.C.E.)
Earliest historical Chinese dynasty, centered in the **Yellow River** valley of the northern Chinese plains. Although the

traditional dates are 1766–1122 B.C.E., historians now estimate that the dates are more likely circa 1600–1045 B.C.E. Shang seems to have been organized as a **city-state** with satellite cities. During its last two centuries the capital was at the modern-day city of Anyang. Shang saw the beginnings of a recognizable Chinese civilization with the use of early forms of Chinese characters; ancestor worship; and powerful, semisacred kingship. Shang culture was noted for the practice of interpreting cracks made in bones and tortoise shells for divination, the creation of superb and often huge bronze vessels, large tombs, and the practice of human sacrifice.

Shanghai

China's largest commercial and industrial city, located on the Huangpu River near the mouth of the **Yangzi River**. Shanghai was one of the first treaty ports, opened to Westerners in 1842 after the **Opium War**. It became China's most important trading and industrial center and its most Westernized city. Many of China's modern movements, from the **Chinese Communist Party** to the film industry, began in Shanghai. It became a truly international city with a large foreign community in the first half of the twentieth century. Much of Shanghai until the 1930s was under the administration of foreign nations who administered various areas known as "concessions." Shanghai went into a period of decline when the communists came to power in 1949 and it was replaced by **Hong Kong** as an international commercial city, but with a shift in policy toward international trade and investment after 1980 the city regained it status as the country's leading business center.

Shankara (c. 788–820)

South Indian philosopher and one of the formulators of the Vedanta ("End of the Vedas"), the most important of the six systems of Hindu thought. Through his commentaries on the *Brahma Sutras* and the **Upanishads** he developed his doctrine that emphasized the eternal, unchanging reality of Brahman, which he interpreted in a way that resembled the Buddhist concept of **nirvana**.

Sharia

Revealed or canonical **Islamic** law addressing many subjects and based on a number of primary sources including the **Quran**, the **Hadith**, the Sunna, *qiyas* (analogy), and *ijma* (consensus of juridical opinion). The sharia contains both prescriptions and proscriptions on behaviors ranging from obligatory (performance is rewarded; omission is punished) to recommended (performance is rewarded; omission is not punished) to indifferent (neither punished nor rewarded) to undesirable (disapproved but not punished) and finally to prohibited (punished; with degrees of punishment depending on the severity of the sin, measured as either grave, venal, or trespass). There are a variety of sharia-based legal schools and traditions within and between **Sunni** Islam (including Hanafi, Maliki, Shafi, and Hanbali) and **Shia** Islam (Akbari, Usuli). In many Islamic settings sharia-based legal frameworks are often modified, redefined, augmented, and bypassed, with individual decrees forming separate bodies of civil, criminal, and commercial case law and legal codes. The relationship among the sharia and other legal frames of reference is a key index of social and political life in most **Muslim** societies.

Sheba, Queen of

Traditional queen of a land in southwestern Arabia or across the Red Sea in Ethiopia. The **Old Testament** and Islamic traditions speak of the Queen of Sheba and claim that she visited the court of **Solomon** (r. c. 974–937 B.C.E.). Ethiopian tradition has Sheba bearing a son by Solomon, Menilek I, who was the founder of the **Solomonic dynasty**, which according to tradition continued almost uninterrupted through **Haile Selassie** in the twentieth century.

Sheikh

Word often used by non-Arabic speakers to refer to a man with high status. It can refer to an influential elder, a tribal leader, or a religious authority figure, whether a mullah member of the Ulama (a community of learned men) or a Sufi spiritual guide. Sheikhs in Arabic-speaking regions are similar to khans in the Turkish-speaking world or rish safids in Persian-speaking communities.

Shia Muslims (also Shi'a, Shi'i, or Shiite) Minority branch of **Muslims** who believe that the leader of **Islam** should be a direct descendant of **Muhammad**. At his death in 632 C.E., Muhammad left no instructions for his succession and no sons. Some of his followers selected **Abu Bakr** as **caliph** ("successor"); they followers became known as **Sunni** ("people of tradition") Muslims. Others thought that Muhammad did not intend that approach and that only an heir to Muhammad should lead. They became known as *shias* ("partisans") of Ali, or Shia Muslims. While only 10 percent of Muslims are Shias, they constitute a majority in Iran and Iraq, although Sunnis controlled the Iraqi government until the U.S. invasion of 2003. Shia Islam includes several varieties with varying beliefs.

Shiite Muslims. *See* Shia Muslims

Shining Path. *See* Sendero Luminoso

Shinto

Japanese indigenous religion literally meaning "the way of the gods." Having its origins in prehistoric times, Shinto recognizes varied spirits called **kami** that represent forces of nature, especially those that inspire awe, such as prominent mountains or rocks, and the ancestors of individuals who also inspire awe, such as great warriors. Unlike **Buddhism**, which since the sixth century has coexisted with it, Shinto has no official scriptures or well-defined doctrine and little in the way of ethical teachings. Its mythology as recorded in the Kojiki (Record of Ancient Matters) and the Nihon Shoki (Chronicles of Japan) in the eighth century focus on the sun goddess **Amaterasu** and on the imperial line as her descendants. After the **Meiji Restoration** Shinto was made the state religion and became associated with the cult of the emperor and ultranationalism. It ceased to be the state religion in 1945, although it remains one of the forms of religious expression in Japan.

Shiva

One of the principle Hindu gods, often regarded with **Brahma** and **Vishnu** as the main deities of **Hinduism**. Shiva is known as the destroyer because his role is to destroy the world, but he also creates life and represents both asceticism and sensuality. His consort is Parvati, who also appears as Durga and Kali. Shaivite cult was very popular in medieval India and Southeast Asia and inspired many great temples and art. Shiva is often represented by a linga (phallus).

Shoen

Aristocratic, tax-free autonomous estates or manors in Japan from the eighth to the fifteenth century. The shoen, which began as grants to **Shinto** shrines, **Buddhist** temples, or members of the imperial family, undermined the central government of **Heian** Japan by essentially giving economic and political power to the shoens' owners and led to the rise of the provincial military class. The **Kamakura bakufu** appointed stewards to gain control over the shoen. They disappeared when rural villages became self-governing units owing loyalty to a feudal lord who divided them into fiefs.

Shogun

Military hegemons who were the effective rulers of Japan during its feudal period from the late twelfth to the nineteenth century. Their governments were called shogunates, or **bakufu** ("tent government"). The term was coined in 1192 by **Minamoto Yoritomo**, who took the title *sei-i tai-shogun* ("great barbarian-subduing general"), a term previously given to generals who had led successful campaigns against the native Ainu peoples of northern Japan. The shoguns never abolished the imperial court but, rather, created the parallel government known as the bakufu that held real power while the emperors continued to reign ceremoniously in **Kyoto**. There were three shogunates. The **Kamakura** shogunate founded by Minamoto Yoritomo ruled from a town south of modern-day Tokyo until 1333; the **Ashikaga** (also called Muromachi) shogunate ruled from Kyoto from 1339 to 1573; and the last and most powerful, the **Tokugawa** Shogunate, ruled from **Edo** (modern-day Tokyo) from 1603 to 1868, when the shogunate was abolished in the **Meiji Restoration**.

Shotoku Taishi (574–622)

Japanese prince who as regent for Empress Suiko carried out reforms that helped to transform the government of the **Yamato** state from a clan society to a centralized administration modeled on China. He sent the first recorded ambassador to China in 607; brought Chinese artists and crafters to Japan; and adopted Chinese laws, bureaucratic institutions, and the Chinese calendar. He also promoted both **Buddhism** and **Confucianism**. His reforms were continued by his successors.

Shudras

Fourth and lowest of the four **varnas**, the major social groupings in India's caste system. A distinction was traditionally made between the upper three castes of **Brahmins, Kshatriyas**, and **Vaishyas**, who were "twice-born," and the Shudras, who were much lower in the religious and social system of **Hinduism**. Most were originally farmers and laborers. Some historians believe the Shudras are descendants of indigenous peoples conquered by the ancient Aryans.

Siam

Former name for Thailand. The name *Siam* is derived from the Siamese Thai ethnic group that lives in the center of the country. Because there are many other ethnic groups, such as the Lao Thai of the northeast, the government changed the name in 1939 to *Muong Thai* ("Land of the Thais"). The name *Thai* itself means "free." After briefly being changed back to Siam in 1945, the country has been called Thailand.

Siddhartha Gautama (c. 480–400 B.C.E.)

Historical founder of **Buddhism** best known as the Buddha (**Sanskrit** for "the enlightened one"). According to later recorded tradition, Siddhartha Gautama was the son of a prince who left a protected environment to seek the meaning of existence. At the age of thirty-five he experienced enlightenment while meditating under a bodhi tree. He then devoted his life to helping others seek enlightenment and thereby began a line of teaching that evolved into Buddhism. He gave sermons in the eastern Gangetic Plain of India and attracted a number of disciples. Siddhartha taught his fundamental truth: that all life is full of suffering, which is caused by desire, and the way to end desire is to follow the **Eightfold Path** of views, aspirations, speech, conduct, livelihood, effort, mindfulness, and meditation. He accepted the Hindu belief in the cycle of births and rebirths but taught that those who achieved enlightenment could escape this cycle. Although Siddhartha made no claims of divinity, his followers later made him an object of reverence.

Sidon

Ancient **Phoenician** city from the third millennium B.C.E., in the area that is modern-day Lebanon. Mentioned in **Homer** and the **Old Testament**, Sidon was an important Mediterranean port city of the empires of **Assyria, Babylonia, Persia, Alexander the Great**, the **Seleucids**, the **Ptolemies**, and the **Romans**.

Sigismund (1368–1437)

Holy Roman Emperor and king of Bohemia and Hungary. Sigismund forced Pope John XXIII to call the Council of Constance in 1414. There the **Great Schism** was ended by the election of Pope Martin V. The council also ordered the burning of **John Hus**. Following Hus's death the Hussites rebelled within the **Holy Roman Empire**.

Sihanouk, Norodom (1922–)

King of Cambodia (1941–1955, 1993–). Sihanouk helped to gain independence for Cambodia in 1953. He abdicated the throne in 1955 to serve first as prime minister and then as head of state. He tried to maintain neutrality for Cambodia, but was overthrown in a military coup led by pro–U.S. general Lon Nol. He briefly returned to Cambodia when the **Khmer Rouge** regime came to power in 1975 but soon returned to exile. Sihanouk was restored as king in 1993.

Sikhism

A monotheistic religion founded in the **Punjab** region of India in the fifteenth century by Guru Nanak. Sikhism combines the **Islamic** belief in one universal, omnipotent god with the Hindu concepts of karma and reincarnation. It also shares with **Hinduism** a concern with achieving liberation from the cycle of birth and rebirths, a liberation called *mukti*, which is similar to *moksha*. Sikhism, however, rejects the Hindu notion of caste, believing instead in the equality of all humanity. The doctrines are written in the holy book the Adi Granth. Nanak was the first of ten gurus; the last guru, Gobind Singh, created the *khalsa*, a brotherhood of soldier-saints in 1699. In the early nineteenth century Ranjit Singh established a powerful Sikh kingdom in the Punjab, but it was defeated and annexed by the British in 1849. The Sikhs have remained a small but active minority in the economic and political life of modern India. A separatist movement that arose in India in the late twentieth century resulted in violent clashes with Indian government authorities.

Silk Roads

A series of interconnecting trade routes between China and India and China and Persia that ran through the Gobi Desert and **Samarkand**, eventually reaching Mediterranean ports and Italy. The Silk Roads functioned as an intercultural highway of trade and ideas from ancient times, as early as the third century B.C.E. Much of the European trade to Asia was superseded by sea travel in the sixteenth century, although trans-Eurasian trade continued. Trade from China to India and Persia existed centuries before trade with Europe played any role. Silk from China to

Europe was only one of thousands of trade goods, including spices, that moved along the Silk Roads. The name was coined by German geographer Ferdinand Paul Wilhelm Freiherr in the 1870s.

Silla

Classical Korean state and one of the Three Kingdoms. Along with **Paekche** and **Koguryo**, Silla competed for dominance in the Korean peninsula from the fourth to the seventh century until Korea was unified in 676. Silla, located in the southeastern part of the peninsula, was by tradition founded in 57 B.C.E. but only appears in historical records beginning in the fourth century C.E. The last of the Three Kingdoms to adopt **Buddhism**, Silla conquered its two rivals with the help of **Tang** China. During the united Silla period (676–935) Korea was a prosperous, culturally sophisticated aristocratic state ruled by the Kim royal family. Its capital, Kyongju, was among the largest cities in Asia. After a brief period of disunity Korea was reunited under a new dynasty and renamed **Koryo** although its elite viewed themselves as legitimate successors to Silla.

Silver Trade

Historical worldwide trade in silver. Much of the silver ended up in the **Middle East** and Asia, where Europeans traded it for textiles, spices, and other goods. The silver trade increased with the flow of silver bullion from the New World in the sixteenth and seventeenth centuries. With the discovery of the New World large quantities of gold and silver were found in Mexico, but soon incredibly rich silver mines were located in places such as **Potosí**, a Bolivian city where vast silver deposits were discovered in 1545. With that discovery Spain shifted its emphasis in the New World from the confiscation of gold to silver mining. **Charles V** made Potosí an imperial town, and from 1545 to 1800 the Spanish crown collected one-fifth the vast value of the silver in taxes. Bullion fleets loaded with silver sailed from the New World to Spain or the Spanish Netherlands, and English pirates, sometimes funded by the monarch, raided the Spanish silver fleets. Silver was also shipped from Acapulco to the Spanish colony of the Philippines to be traded for Asian goods. The silver trade caused inflation throughout Eurasia in the sixteenth and seventeenth centuries.

Sima Qian (Ssu-ma Ch'ien) (c. 145–185 B.C.E.)

Chinese historian and official at the court of emperor **Han Wudi**. His great history *Shi Ji* (Historical Records) provided a model for the official histories followed by Chinese scholars for the next two millennia. Few if any historians have been more influential. His history traces China from mythical times to the **Han dynasty**. It includes essays on various topics and biographies of prominent people, generals, and statesmen as well as poets. It also contains annals and descriptions of foreign peoples. A strong moral tone of praise and blame pervades the work. Sima Qian was castrated by Wudi for defending a general who had surrendered to the **Xiongnu**.

Sinan (1489–1588)

Ottoman architect who designed the Sehzade Mosque in Istanbul, Turkey, for **Süleyman I**. Sinan worked as chief architect for the **Ottoman Empire** at its height and designed more than 200 mosques, palaces, public baths, and schools as well as numerous other buildings. His most famous designs were two mosques built for Süleyman in **Istanbul**. He completed the Sehzade Mosque in 1548, modeled after **Hagia Sophia**, a sixth-century Byzantine church.

Singapore

City and sovereign state on an island at the southern tip of the **Malay Peninsula**. As a small village called Tumasik it was acquired by the British **East India Company** in 1819. Singapore developed into a major port, and its strategic location at the point where the Indian and Pacific oceans meet made it useful as a British naval port. The city became part of Malaysia in 1963, but the Malaysian government expelled it in 1965, partly out of fears that its predominantly Chinese population would threaten the ethnic Malay political domination of Malaysia. Under President **Lee Kuan Yew** Singapore prospered to become one of the richest nations per capita in Asia, a center for trade and industry, and one of the so-called four tigers of the Pacific Rim. Although ruled by a parliamentary government, Singapore has been called a "nanny state" by critics for its efficient but intrusive and authoritarian government.

Sinitic Language

One of the three main branches of the Sino-Tibetan language family, the other two being Tibetic and Burmic. The Sinitic languages include Mandarin Chinese (or Northern Chinese), the official language of China, with more than 800 million speakers, and the other Chinese languages mostly spoken in southern China such as Cantonese, Hunanese, Wu (spoken in the Shanghai area), and Min (spoken in Fujian province of China and Taiwan). Although the spoken languages of China differ considerably, the written language is the same. Since 1949 Mandarin has been universally taught in China and is spoken by most people.

Sinn Fein

Meaning "We Ourselves," an Irish **nationalist** organization founded in 1905. During the twentieth century Sinn Fein (pronounced "shin fane") became progressively more radical as an arm of the provisional **Irish Republican Army** and was at the center of much violence in Northern Ireland. By the 1980s it gained political legitimacy within Northern Ireland, and in the late 1990s it was brought into the peace process between the United Kingdom and people vying for Northern Ireland's unification with the Republic of Ireland.

Sino-Japanese War (1894–1895)

Conflict between China and Japan over influence in Korea. Both countries used the pretext of aiding the Korean government in putting down a rebellion to send troops into the country. Japan attacked the Chinese forces, drove them out of Korea, and sank the newly built Chinese Northern (Beiyang) Fleet. In the Treaty of Shimonoseki the Chinese were forced to abandon their suzerainty over Korea under the former **tributary system** and surrender territory to Japan, most notably Taiwan, and to give Japan commercial concessions. The war demonstrated the success of Japan's modernization efforts following the **Meiji Restoration** and the failure of China's Self-Strengthening Movement.

Sino-Japanese War (1931–1945)

Japanese invasion of China. Japan had been extending its influence into China since the late nineteenth century and especially since **World War I**. Japanese forces took **Manchuria** in 1931. In 1937 Japan invaded China directly, destroying **Nanking**. Chinese armies under **Chiang Kai-shek** and Chinese Communists both fought the Japanese. After the Japanese attack on the United States at **Pearl Harbor** the Sino-Japanese War became part of **World War II**.

Sino-Vietnamese

Ruling class of Vietnam. After its independence from China in the tenth century the

Vietnamese state and its officials borrowed, often enthusiastically, from China, so that Vietnam became known as the "Lesser Dragon." The ruling class learned and wrote in Chinese (although they developed their own script in the fifteenth century); adopted Chinese styles in art, music, and literature; and adopted a variety political and social customs from their northern neighbors. Nonetheless, the Sino-Vietnamese remained quite distinct from the Chinese in many ways, such as in their language and the higher social status of Vietnamese women.

Sistine Chapel

Chapel of the Vatican in Rome most noted for its ceiling painted by **Michelangelo**. He painted the ceiling at the height of his career (1508–1512) and did it alone. He made more than 200 preliminary drawings and decided on majestic **Old Testament** scenes and figures with prophets and sibyls, all foretelling the coming of **Jesus** Christ. The commission was unusual because Michelangelo was primarily an architect and sculptor, but he was forced, under protest, to accept it.

Slave Coast

Region of west Africa from Ghana to Nigeria where many slaves originated in the period 1650–1850. Slaves were taken from other regions of Africa, but the enormous **Slave Trade** of this period was transporting them primarily to the Americas and Caribbean. Western sub-Saharan Africa from Senegal to Cameroon provided most of the slaves, with the Slave Coast the most active location.

Slave Trade. *See* Atlantic Slave Trade

Slavs

Most numerous ethnic and linguistic group in Europe. The Slavs originated in

Asia and migrated into eastern Europe. They speak Slavic, an **Indo-European** language. Slavs are divided into East Slavs (Belarussians, Russians, and Ukrainians), West Slavs (Czechs, Poles, Slovaks, and Wens), and South Slavs (Croats, Macedonians, Serbs, and Slovenes). The Belarussians, Macedonians, Russians, some Serbs, and Ukrainians use the Cyrillic alphabet and generally belong to the **Eastern Orthodox Church**, while the Croats, Czechs, Poles, some Serbs, Slovaks, Slovenes, and Wens use the Latin alphabet and generally belong to the **Roman Catholic Church**.

Social Contract, The. *See* Rousseau, Jean-Jacques

Social Darwinism

Nineteenth-century belief, originally espoused by Herbert Spencer, of social evolution. Before **Charles Darwin**'s theory of evolution (1859), Spencer wrote *Principles of Psychology* (1855). Social Darwinism claims that the best-fitted humans survive and rise to the top, in a process of natural selection. Therefore, people at the top of the social and economic scale deserve to be there for they are biologically most fit. Social Darwinism can be used to support conservatism and to justify inequality and even racism by stating that existing conditions are simply natural selection at work.

Socialism

Theory of society that advocates social, political, and economic equality and the state direction of economic activity in order to achieve that equality. Many of the original socialists believed that these ends required the abolition of all private property. Socialism first emerged as a major school of thought in the early nineteenth century, and by the end of that century most Western nations had political parties committed to achieving a socialist society.

Among the most influential of the many schools of socialism was that founded by **Karl Marx**. In the twentieth century socialism largely split into Marxists, who advocated revolution and sought to establish one-party communist states, and social democrats, who sought to achieve gradual reform that would lead to a democratic social welfare state.

Society of Jesus (Jesuits)

Christian religious order founded by **Ignatius Loyola** in 1540. Loyola was a soldier, but when he was recuperating after being wounded, he had a vision of a Christian brotherhood organized on militaristic lines. The Society of Jesus was established by the **papacy** in 1540, and Loyola was elected the first superior general. The society played a large part in the **Council of Trent** (1545–1563), which reinvigorated the **Roman Catholic Church**. Jesuits were sent as the front line of attack against the **Protestant Reformation** and as missionaries to convert the indigenous peoples in newly discovered areas of the Americas and Asia.

Socrates (469–399 B.C.E.)

Ancient Greek philosopher. Along with **Plato** and **Aristotle**, Socrates shaped the intellectual tradition of the West. He left no written treatises, but as the educator (although he claimed not to be a teacher) of men such as Plato, he left an indelible mark. Socrates lived in **Athens** during the pinnacle of its greatness after winning the second **Persian War** (480–479 B.C.E.), when Athens became the leader of Greek society. Socrates believed that the unexplored life is not worth living and that goodness is knowledge, and he implored humans to recognize that they are responsible for their own ignorance or wisdom and therefore for their own moral attitudes. We know of Socrates' philosophy primarily through Plato's dialogues in which Socrates questions his students.

Sogdiana

Name for the **Transoxiana** region, land between the Oxus (Amu Darya) and Syr Darya rivers in western **Turkestan**, during the time when it was inhabited by an Iranian-speaking people called the Sogdians. With a homeland in a strategic center the **Silk Road**, the Sogdians were active in trade during the first millennium C.E., forming a merchant diaspora that extended from Persia to China. Sogdiana became a center for **Manichaeism**, which the Sogdians introduced farther east, including to the Uighurs in the eighth century. The Sogdians helped to extend civilization to the peoples of the **steppe**. After the eighth century Sogdiana became increasingly Turkish and Islamic.

Solomon (r. c. 974–937 B.C.E.)

King of Israel and son of King David. Based on the Hebrew **Old Testament**, Solomon, meaning "peaceful," was proclaimed successor to his father and became a very successful king of Israel, providing a peaceful forty-year reign. Solomon married a daughter of the Egyptian pharaoh. Commercial activity during his reign was extensive, and **Jerusalem** became a transformed city of wealth and luxury. Devoted to **Yahweh**, Solomon built a grand temple in Jerusalem. The *Odes of Solomon* and the *Psalms of Solomon*, both ascribed incorrectly to Solomon, were written between the first century B.C.E. and the first century C.E.

Solomonic Dynasty (c. 990 B.C.E.–1974 C.E.)

Ethiopian dynastic line, according to tradition descended from King **Solomon** and the **Queen of Sheba**. **Haile Selassie**, who became emperor of Ethiopia in 1930 and was deposed in 1974, claimed to be the last of an almost continuous line from Solomon, broken by the Zagwe dynasty of the twelfth to thirteenth centuries and Tewodros II (1855–1868). Some scholars trace the Solomonic dynasty back to 1270.

Solon (fl. 600–560 B.C.E.)

Athenian politician and reformer. In the sixth century B.C.E. **Athens** slipped into conflict between the aristocracy and the commoners. Solon attempted to achieve a compromise between the privileged and the unprivileged. He established reforms wherein all debts were canceled and slavery for indebtedness was abolished. Solon organized the Athenians into property classes in which members of the top two classes could hold major political offices and the others could either hold office or, at least, attend the Assembly. He also compiled a new law code in which all free men were equal under the law.

Song (960–1279)

Chinese dynasty that saw a brilliant cultural flowering and important technical and commercial developments. Founded by Zhao Kuangyin (known posthumously as **Song Taizu**), the Song ended a half century of disunity. Despite an enormous professional army, Song leaders were unable to achieve decisive military advantages over their northern neighbors. In 1127 one of these groups, the **Jurchens**, conquered the northern half of China and created the Jin dynasty. The Song moved their capital from Kaifeng in the north to Hangzhou in the south, inaugurating a period known as the Southern Song (1127–1279). During the Song an extensive system of canals and other transportation improvements encouraged a flourishing internal trade and many prosperous cities. Improvements in silk, lacquer, and ceramic industries; expansion of iron and steel production;

agricultural improvements; and a sophisticated banking system including the use of paper money have led modern historians to describe this period as a "Song Commercial Revolution." China reached the highest level of material culture in the world. **Buddhism** lost state sponsorship and **Confucianism** underwent a revival in a form called **Neo-Confucianism**. The Southern Song ended with conquest by the **Mongols** in 1279.

Songhay

West African empire (1464–1591) of the Niger River region that superseded the empire of **Mali**. The Songhay had their capital at **Gao** and their major intellectual and commercial center at **Timbuktu**. They built an elaborate government, had an army and navy, and controlled much of the **trans-Saharan trade** from the gold and ivory coasts to north Africa and the Mediterranean. Gao at its peak had about 75,000 residents. The emperors of the Songhay were **Muslim**, although the entire population was not. Timbuktu had a Muslim **university**. The Songhay empire was the last of the great African **savannah** empires.

Song of Roland

Epic poem written in Old French circa 1100 C.E. about the Battle of Roncesvalles of 778. Known also by the French title *Chanson de Roland*, the poem is of a type called **Chanson de geste** or ("song [praise] of heroic deeds"). *Song of Roland* embodies the heroic elements of the High **Middle Ages**, with Roland, nephew and baron of **Charlemagne**, asked to defend the rear against the Muslims as Charlemagne's army left Spain. The treason of Roland's stepfather and fellow baron sets up a monumental battle, the death of Roland and the vengeance of Charlemagne. *Song of Roland* was written (by an unknown author) to encourage bravery and valor in the newly begun **Crusades** (1095) and to establish a clear sense of good versus evil in the fight with the Muslims.

Song Mei-ling (Song Meiling) (1895–2003)

Wife of **Guomindang** leader Chiang Kai-shek, sister of financier and Guomindang official T. V. Soong and **Song Qingling**, the wife of Chinese nationalist leader **Sun Yat-sen**, and wife of Guomindang leader **Chiang Kai-shek**. Educated in the United States, Song Mei-ling married Chiang Kai-shek and played an active role in foreign policy, especially in cultivating U.S. support for her husband's regime.

Song Qingling (Soong Ch'ing-ling) (1890–1981)

Second wife of Chinese revolutionary **Sun Yat-sen** and prominent Chinese leader. She came from a wealthy Christian family in **Shanghai**. Song Qingling's brother, T. V. Soong, was an important official in the **Guomindang** government of China before 1949, and her sister, **Song Mei-ling**, was the wife of Guomindang leader **Chiang Kai-shek**. Unlike her siblings, she later supported the communists and held high posts in the **People's Republic of China**.

Song Taizu

Posthumous name of Zhao Kuangyin (r. 960–976), who usurped the throne of the Later **Zhou** state and North China in 960 and established the **Song** dynasty (960–1279). Over the next few years he continued the reunification of China and brought an end to the period of disunity that accompanied the fall of the **Tang**. Following Zhao's death, his younger brother finished unification by 979.

Sophists

Ancient Greek wandering professors. In the fifth century B.C.E. numerous individuals traveled around the Greek world giving lectures. They did not constitute a particular school of thought, although they spread Greek ideas of philosophy, mathematics, science, and geography throughout the wider Greek world and eastern Mediterranean. They were sometimes viewed with suspicion because they did not teach religion or a particular morality.

Sophocles (c. 496–413 B.C.E.)

Ancient Greek playwright and one of the three major authors of Greek tragedy along with **Euripedes** and **Aeschylus**. Sophocles wrote approximately 125 plays of which 8 survive, including *Antigone* (c. 441 B.C.E.) and *Oedipus the King* (c. 429 B.C.E.). Both plays deal with the Oedipus story. In *Antigone*, the daughter of Oedipus, Antigone, is forced to decide whether to follow tradition and the gods and bury her brother or obey the law laid down by her uncle, Creon, the new king. Antigone is heroic and performs the burial even though it brings her live burial and suicide. *Oedipus the King* relates the discovery by Oedipus that he killed his father and married his mother. This tragic realization causes Oedipus to gouge out his own eyes and curse his sons.

Soviet Union. *See* Union of Soviet Socialist Republics (USSR)

Spanish-American War

1898 conflict between the United States and Spain. The United States had considered acquiring Cuba in the early nineteenth century. By the late nineteenth century, as Britain, France, Germany, Belgium, and Italy conquered territories and built empires in Africa and Asia, the United States used the opportunity of

Spanish misrule in Cuba to intervene. As riots broke out in Havana the United States sent the battleship *Maine* into the harbor, where it mysteriously blew up. "Remember the Maine" became the slogan for war with a decrepit Spain. The United States acquired Guam, Puerto Rico, and the Philippines from the war.

Spanish Armada

Spanish fleet sent against England. In 1588 **Philip II** of Spain sent a fleet, under the command of the Duke of Medina-Sidonia, of 130 ships and nearly 30,000 men into the English Channel to clear the way for the Spanish army in the Netherlands to be ferried across it for an invasion of England. The Spanish planned to overthrow the Protestant queen **Elizabeth I**. The English navy, redesigned by **Sir John Hawkins** and commanded by Charles Howard (Second Baron Howard of Effingham), Sir Francis Drake, Martin Frobisher, and Hawkins, routed the armada using faster, more maneuverable, and better-armed ships. Spain lost forty-four ships in battle and in the flight, which necessitated sailing entirely around the British Isles. The defeat of the armada destroyed Spain's chance of defeating Protestantism militarily and established England as a major naval power.

Spanish Civil War (1936–1939)

Civil war in Spain between Republicans and Nationalists that gained much international attention because democratic versus fascist ideologies were involved. When the Spanish Republic was elected in 1931 the monarch left Spain. By 1936 the military, monarchists, **nationalists**, and the **Roman Catholic Church** allied, feeling that the Republican government was not maintaining order. A civil war broke out, with great bloodshed and terror used by both sides. The Soviet Union supported the Republicans, hoping for a communist

revolution, and sent advisors and aid. Nazi Germany and Italy supported the Nationalists and sent military aid. Men around the world volunteered to fight for each side. Americans fought for the republic as the Abraham Lincoln Brigade. The Spanish Civil War was won by the Nationalists and General Francisco Franco, but ultimately Spain was ruined financially and spiritually and did not fully recover for more than thirty years. Franco ruled as a dictator until his death in 1975.

Spanish Inquisition

Persecution of Muslims, Jews, heretics, and converts by Christian authorities in Spain in the fifteenth and sixteenth centuries. Separate from the papal **inquisition**, the Spanish Inquisition was created by Pope Sixtus IV in 1478 at the request of **Ferdinand of Aragon** and **Isabella I** to enforce uniformity of Christian belief, especially among Muslims and Jews who chose to convert rather than leave Spain. The Spanish Inquisition was originally directed by the inquisitor general, Dominican monk Tomás de Torquemada.

Spanish Netherlands

Low Countries, including modern-day Belgium, Luxembourg, and the Netherlands, that were part of the **Habsburg** holdings and transferred to the Spanish Habsburgs with **Philip II**. As gold and silver poured into Spain from the New World, much of it went to the Spanish Netherlands, Spain's industrial heartland. When the northernmost of these provinces broke away as the **United Provinces** in the Dutch Revolt, the southern provinces remained united with Spain in the Union of Arras (1579) and also remained **Catholic**.

Sparta

Polis in Laconia in ancient Greece. By the eighth century B.C.E. Sparta conquered the surrounding people, enslaving one group as **Helots** and controlling another as *perioeci*, both of whom provided most of the labor and production for the Spartans, enabling them to become purely focused on their military. The Spartans became the supreme land force in Greece. At age seven boys were sent away for military training until age twenty, when they became soldiers. At thirty they joined the Assembly and had full legal privileges. Sparta fought with **Athens** against Persia in the **Persian Wars** (490–479 B.C.E.) but against Athens in the **Peloponnesian War** (431–404 B.C.E.). Sparta was victorious yet shattered and never fully recovered.

Spartacus (c. 109–71 B.C.E.)

Roman slave (born in Thrace) and gladiator who led a revolt against Rome in 73 B.C.E. At the height of the rebellion Spartacus led thousands of rebel slave warriors and routed two Roman legions. After two years Spartacus was defeated by Roman armies led by Crassus and crucified.

Spice Trade

Trade in spices from eastern Asia and the Moluccas (Spice Islands in Indonesia) to India, the **Middle East**, and eventually Europe. Spices used in food preparation, medicine, and religious ceremonies have been traded from the East to the West for thousands of years. In Europe in the early **Middle Ages**, the spices went through **Axum** in the area that is modern-day Ethiopia. After the rise of **Islam** in the eighth century, the spice trade from India westward was controlled by **Muslim** traders. Goods from the Moluccas went to **Malacca** in Malaysia, where Muslim or Indian traders transported the spices to the Malabar Coast of western India. From there, the spices were shipped either to the Persian Gulf and onward to Beirut, Lebanon, or Aleppo, Syria, via the **Euphrates River**, or

through the Red Sea and overland to Alexandria, Egypt. Venetian merchants bought the spices at these three sites and transported them to Europe. The Venetian monopoly on spices shipped to Europe was only broken in 1498, when the Portuguese discovered a route around Africa to India.

Spitfire

British aircraft made famous in the **Battle of Britain**. The Spitfire was first developed in 1936, with the first production airplanes delivered in 1938. By 1939, the year that **World War II** began, Britain had 182 Spitfires. The early versions of the plane could fly at 350 miles per hour and carried eight guns. In the Battle of Britain the Spitfire and the Hurricane proved themselves equal or superior to the best fighter planes of Germany and built the reputation of having saved Britain.

Sputnik

First spacecraft to orbit the earth. *Sputnik I*, an unmanned satellite, was launched by rocket in October 1957 by the **Union of Soviet Socialist Republics** and orbited the earth sending back radio signals. The accomplishment startled the United States and began a space rivalry between the two superpowers. Within a month the Soviets had sent up *Sputnik II* with a live dog aboard. The Americans countered with a space program that had to come from behind, but while the Soviets went for size and power the United States built small, efficient craft for accumulation of data.

Srivijaya

Maritime state of southern Sumatra containing the port of Palembang. Srivijaya dominated the Malacca Strait from the late seventh to the eleventh century. Taking advantage of its location on the waterways linking the Indian and Pacific oceans, Srivijaya flourished as a center of both commerce and **Buddhism**. It declined in the ninth century, revived in the tenth when it created a commercial empire that controlled much of Malaya and what is now western Indonesia, and then declined again in the eleventh century and eventually disappeared.

SS (Schutzstaffel)

Elite corps of the German **Nazi** Party. The term *Schutzstaffel* is German for "protective echelon." The black-uniformed corps was formed by **Adolf Hitler** in 1925 as a bodyguard. From 1929 to 1945 the SS was headed by **Heinrich Himmler**. By the time the Nazi Party gained control of Germany in 1933 the SS comprised more than 50,000 men selected for their "racial purity" and physical perfection. By 1939 there were 250,000 SS, divided into the Allgemeine SS (police and the Gestapo) and the Waffen SS (Hitler's bodyguard, concentration camp administrators, and elite combat troops). The SS used death's-head and lightning-shaped "SS" symbols to create an image of superiority and invincibility. Its members were trained for absolute obedience and loyalty. The **Nürnberg Trials** declared the SS a criminal organization in 1946.

Stalin, Joseph (1879–1953)

Absolute ruler of the **Union of Soviet Socialist Republics** and the leader of world communism from 1927 until his death in 1953. He is credited with transforming the USSR from an agricultural society into an industrialized world superpower. Born Joseph Vissarionovich Dzhugashvili, Stalin grew up in Gori, Georgia. He joined the Bolsheviks in 1903. He rose through the party ranks until 1913, when he was banished to Siberia. He remained there until 1917. It was during this time that he adopted his public name, Stalin, meaning "man of steel." He continued to rise through the party until he achieved the rank of general secretary. Upon **Vladimir Ilyich Lenin**'s death, Stalin proceeded to eliminate all opposition, most notably that of Leon Trotsky, and he secured his power by 1927. Through a series of Five-Year Plans, Stalin attempted to collectivize agriculture and create a powerful, industrial state. Stalin followed many of the views of **Karl Marx** and Lenin, but added a policy of police terror to accelerate the industrialization process. He defeated the German army during **World War II**. Stalin's rule was characterized by a sharp decrease in civil liberties and the use of fear and violence to secure his power. During the "purges," he banished and executed millions of people, fearing that they were a threat to his position. After his death Stalin was embalmed and placed in Lenin's mausoleum. His body was later moved to a nondescript grave near the Kremlin.

Stalingrad, Battle of (1942–1943)

World War II major battle in the Soviet Union. The German invasion of the Soviet Union was directed toward Stalingrad in August 1942. The German Sixth Army penetrated the city, but in the winter the Soviets countered with six armies. By January 1943 the German army was surrounded and it surrendered. Extensive bombing by the German **Luftwaffe**, heavy bombardment, and house-to-house fighting made the Battle of Stalingrad one of the deadliest of World War II. The German defeat ended its eastern front. The Soviet Union continually requested that the **Allies** open a western front during the Battle of Stalingrad to draw German forces away from the Soviet Union.

Stamp Act of 1765

British law that inspired American colonial resistance. Passed by the British **Parliament** in March 1765, this act approving taxes on public documents reflected an effort to rationalize British colonial administration and to defray the costs of colonial defense. In formulating the taxes, Parliament challenged the autonomy and legitimacy of colonial self-government, sparking the beginning of a protracted period of debate over the nature and limits of British sovereignty and ultimately leading to colonial assertions of independence in 1776.

States General. *See* Estates General (States General)

States System
System in which political units claim sovereignty over their internal affairs and the right to participate in international affairs with other states with at least some degree of diplomatic and political equality. The states system in which global politics were viewed as the interaction of sovereign states emerged in the sixteenth through nineteenth centuries, based on the European state system that was established during that period. Gradually a body of international law was created to establish rules governing legal claims and conduct among states. The number of recognized sovereign states grew rapidly after the two world wars with the collapse of the major colonial empires. By the beginning of the twenty-first century nearly 200 political units were widely recognized as independent states. Most are members of the **United Nations**.

Steam Engine. *See* Watt, James

Stein, Gertrude (1874–1946)
American author and influence on the intellectual scene of Europe in the first half of the twentieth century. Stein moved to Paris in 1903; befriended Ernest Hemingway, Pablo Picasso, Henri Matisse, and many others; and influenced many of the American writers, in particular. Her best-known work is *Three Lives* (1908).

Steinem, Gloria (1936–)
American writer and leader of the **feminist movement**. Steinem campaigned for women's rights in politics, education, employment, and social life. In 1971 Steinem helped found the National Women's Political Caucus and the Women's Action Alliance. She founded *Ms.* magazine in 1972 as a publication for and by women.

Steppe
A type of climatic and vegetational zone found in several locations worldwide. The term is frequently used for the grassland belt that lies in the center of Eurasia from **Manchuria** to Hungary, bordered in the north by boreal forests and in the south by deserts, mountains, and better-watered agricultural lands. The steppe supported pastoral nomad populations that upon achieving mastery of the horse and bow in the first millennium B.C.E. became major threats to the settled agricultural societies on their borders. Besides raiding, the highly mobile peoples of the steppe raised horses, sheep, goats, cattle, and camels and engaged in and often promoted trade. As traders they often helped to facilitate **cross-cultural encounters**. The steppe peoples formed a number of formidable warrior confederations such as the Xiongnu, the Hunnic, the Turkic, and—most famously—the **Mongol empire**. With the rise of armies equipped with firearms and artillery from the sixteenth to the eighteenth century, the steppe peoples lost their military advantage.

Stevenson, Robert Louis (1850–1894)
Scottish author of novels and poems. In the late nineteenth century Stevenson was among the most popular writers as author

of *Treasure Island* (1883), *Kidnapped* (1886), *The Strange Case of Dr. Jekyll and Mr. Hyde* (1886), and many others novels. Stevenson, a sickly child, wrote adventure, romance, and fantasy stories beloved of adults and children alike. His somewhat predictable melodrama is now out of style.

Stoicism

Ancient Greek philosophical movement founded by Zeno in **Athens** in 313 B.C.E. Zeno's school of philosophy comprised logic, physics, and ethics in a holistic approach. Stoicism appeals to nature and reason. It argues that humans should live according to reason because they are reasonable, and this enables humans to understand the natural world around them. These reasonable people form a community of reason.

Stonehenge

Ancient stone monument in England built around 1500 B.C.E. for unknown purpose. Their positions allow the stones to function as an accurate astronomical calendar capable of predicting seasonal changes such as the summer solstice and even some eclipses. There is evidence of an altar, but its purpose is unknown. Stonehenge was one of numerous monolithic ceremonial or burial centers of western Europe.

Stowe, Harriet Beecher (1811–1896)

Abolitionist author of *Uncle Tom's Cabin* (1852). Stowe was from an intellectual Connecticut family and moved to Cincinnati where she became interested in the abolition of slavery. *Uncle Tom's Cabin* contributed powerfully to the abolitionist movement and hence to the onset of the **American Civil War.**

Strait of Magellan

Waterway of 350 miles through the southern tip of South America. **Ferdinand Magellan** left Europe in 1519 with five ships, sailed to South America, and in October 1520 sailed his remaining three ships through a channel that led to the Pacific Ocean, later to bear the name Strait of Magellan. To its north is Patagonia, while on its south lie **Tierra del Fuego** ("Land of Fire") and Cape Horn.

Strait of Malacca

Body of water connecting the Andaman Sea of the Indian Ocean with the South China Sea. The straits are about 500 miles (800 km) long and narrow to only 40 miles (64 km) separating the **Malay Peninsula** from the Indonesian island of Sumatra. Since at least the first millennium B.C.E. it has been a strategic trade link between the Indian Ocean and the China Sea. A number of important states such as **Srivijaya** and **Malacca** emerged to monitor and control that trade. The Portuguese, the Dutch, and lastly the British established a naval presence there. The British established **Singapore** near the entrance to the strait as its main naval base and trading center in Southeast Asia in the early nineteenth century. The strait remains strategically important today.

Strozzi, Alessandra (1407–1471)

Influential **Italian Renaissance** woman. Born in **Florence** to the small but elite Macinghi family, Alessandra married Matteo Strozzi and entered a family of vast wealth traceable to the tenth century. A political enemy of the Medicis, Matteo Strozzi was exiled in 1434 to Pesaro. When he and three of their children died in 1435, Alessandra returned to Florence to raise her five surviving children. In a collection of seventy-three letters written to her sons living in exile, Alessandra Strozzi expresses how she dedicated herself to establishing financial security for her children through marriage negotiations and by encouraging business endeavors to secure family preservation and financial success. She dedicated herself to supporting the future of her family until her death in 1471.

Stupa

Mound or monument commemorating the Buddha's death. Based on funerary mounds, or tumuli, the design of early stupas maintained the hemispherical shape of a mound. An early and classic example is the Great Stupa of Sanchi, built in the second or first century B.C.E. The form spread with **Buddhism**, evolving into the multistoried pagoda designs of China, Korea, and Japan.

Sudetenland

Region of western Czechoslovakia adjacent to and ceded to Germany just prior to **World War II**. The Sudetenland, part of the traditional region of Bohemia but granted to Czechoslovakia after **World War I**, was German in language and culture. As **Adolf Hitler** expanded Germany for "living space," he negotiated the concession of the Sudetenland to Germany in the **Munich Pact** of 1938. Prime Minister **Neville Chamberlain** of Britain returned from the Munich conference hailing a compromise that would bring "peace in our time." Granting the Sudetenland to Germany gave away Czechoslovakia's defenses and most of its industry in an attempt to appease Hitler. In 1993 Czechoslovakia separated into the Czech Republic and Slovakia.

Suez Canal

Man-made 100-mile canal connecting the Mediterranean Sea and the Red Sea. The Suez Canal, designed by Ferdinand-Marie de Lesseps, was begun in 1859 and completed in 1869. Although built by France, Britain gained the most because the canal shortened the route from Britain to British India by 6,000 miles (9,700 km). In 1888,

by international convention, the canal was open to all nations. During **World War I** and **World War II** Britain used troops to keep the canal open to its allies. In 1956 Egypt claimed control of the Suez Canal—a point of contention in the **Arab-Israeli wars**.

Suez Crisis (1956)

International crisis over control of the **Suez Canal** precipitated by Egypt's claim to control the canal, which had been open to all nations by international convention. Egypt's premier **Gamal Abdel Nasser** nationalized the Suez Canal to remove outside influence and to raise funds to build the **Aswan Dam** on the Nile River when both the United States and the Soviet Union withdrew their support. Israel, Britain, and France invaded to open the canal, but the United States condemned the invasion. The Suez Crisis diverted attention and resources from a possible response to the Soviet crushing of the **Hungarian Revolt**, also in 1956.

Sufism

Mystical tradition of **Islam**. Sufism developed as an alternative to the strict orthodox Islam that seemed removed from emotional connections with God. Sufism strives for a personal connection with God through revelation, often through poetry, music, or dance—or even what is beyond the senses. It was known as the *tariqua* ("path"). Sufis, through their networks or brotherhoods, became masters of conversion. Sufism helped to introduce Islam to all Muslim frontier regions including sub-Saharan Africa, India, and inner Eurasia and spread rapidly in the nineteenth century.

Sugar Trade

Important international trade in the sixteenth to eighteenth centuries. Sugar has been refined from sugarcane since at least Roman times. Sugar came from North Africa or northwest Asia in the **Middle Ages**, and sugar production was brought to Spain by Muslims. With the discovery of the New World sugarcane was grown in the Caribbean, where it became the most important export and a highly valued commodity in Europe. Britain, France, and Spain fought naval battles during the seventeenth and eighteenth centuries to control the sugar trade.

Suharto (1921–)

Indonesian general and president (1967–1998). Suharto crushed a communist coup attempt in 1965 and afterward assumed great powers. He became president in 1967 and governed the state as a dictator until he was forced to resign in 1998 following widespread riots that resulted from a 1997–1998 collapse of Indonesia's economy. Under his rule Indonesia opened its economy to foreign investment, adding manufactured goods to its exports of petroleum and timber to stimulate economic growth. His regime, however, was also marked by widespread corruption and political repression. The suddenness and scale of the economic collapse also suggested that he failed to provide the social institutions and infrastructure needed to emulate the sustained development of some of the other Pacific Rim states such as Taiwan and South Korea.

Sui

Chinese dynasty (581–618) that ended nearly three centuries of disunity. It was a short-lived dynasty of two emperors, **Sui Wendi** and **Sui Yangdi**, who established their capital at **Xi'an** in western China. The Sui rulers restored the **Great Wall**, reconstructed and expanded the **Grand Canal**, and launched campaigns against China's neighbors. Yangdi suffered defeats in his campaigns against the Korean state of **Koguryo** that, along with peasant unrest, led to the overthrow of the Sui and its replacement by the **Tang** dynasty. Sui achievements in restoring a unified empire were long lasting. China never again experienced a long period of disunity.

Sui Wendi (541–604)

Posthumous temple name for Yang Jian, a general of mixed Chinese and Xianbei descent who founded the **Sui** dynasty (r. 581–604). While acting as regent, Wendi usurped the throne from the boy emperor of the Northern **Zhou** dynasty in 581. He completed the conquest of southern China in 589, thereby reunifying China after nearly three centuries of division. He promoted **Buddhism**, sought the support of **Confucian** scholars, and created a self-supporting militia system. His dynasty came to an end only fourteen years after his death in 604, but many of its institutions were inherited by the **Tang** dynasty.

Sui Yangdi (569–618)

Posthumous temple name of Yang Guang, the second emperor of the **Sui** dynasty (604–618). Yangdi built the **Grand Canal** linking the **Yellow River** valley with the productive **Yangzi River** delta and constructed a new capital at Luoyang. The strain on the population through heavy taxation and labor service to support his enormous projects and his unsuccessful military campaigns against the northern Korean state of **Koguryo** led to rebellion and the collapse of the dynasty.

Sukarno (1901–1970)

Charismatic Indonesian independence leader and president (1945–1967). A prominent member of the Indonesian Nationalist Party in the 1920s and 1930s, Sukarno became the leader of a **nationalist** movement under the Japanese occupation of the Dutch East Indies. In 1945 he declared himself president of the Republic of Indonesia and led a war of resistance to the reestablishment of Dutch rule from 1945 to 1949, a conflict referred to as the Indonesian Revolution. From 1949 to 1967 he was president of independent Indonesia. His presidency was characterized by flamboyance; his attempts to play a role as a leader of the third world, such as by hosting the Bandung Conference in 1955; and by economic stagnation and widespread poverty. He sought support from Indonesian communists, but after their failed coup attempt in 1965 he lost effective power and was forced to resign two years later.

Sukhothai

City and capital of a kingdom that ruled much of Thailand from the thirteenth to the fifteenth century. Located in north-central Thailand, Sukhothai was the first independent ethnically Thai state in the fertile Chao Phraya River basin that became the heartland of Thailand. Under Ramkhangaeng (r. c. 1279–1298) it established control over an area from Laos to the Malay Peninsula. After the establishment of **Ayudhya** in 1351 Sukhothai declined, and it was abandoned at the end of the fifteenth century.

Suleyman I, "the Magnificent" (1494–1566)

Ottoman **caliph** (1520–1566). Also known as Suleyman the Lawgiver. His conquests include large acquisitions in the Balkans, eastern Europe, and the Mediterranean Sea and all of North Africa and the Middle East (except Iran), including the Red Sea and Persian Gulf. The **Ottoman Empire** reached its greatest expanse under Suleyman. He is known as the Lawgiver because he augmented the **sharia**-based legal framework with a series of *firmans* (decrees) that were organized into legal codes called *kanun*. Europeans depicted Suleyman as a threatening menace, but inside the Ottoman Empire he was known as a fair ruler who fought corruption and as a great patron of artists, philosophers, poets, musicians, intellectuals, and scientists.

Sumer

Mesopotamian civilization first developed around 4000 B.C.E. that gave the world the wheel, the **plow**, the calendar, a system of numbers, and the clock. The Sumerians had a writing system of cuneiform symbols, irrigation, and an organized administration that enabled them to produce cities, the most important of which was **Ur**, constructed of sun-dried bricks. In the center of Ur (and other Sumerian cities) was a **ziggurat** ("pinnacle"), an artificial mountain of layers topped by a temple. Religion in Sumer was composed of deities as manifestations of nature, such as the sun, the moon, lightning, rain, and changing seasons, but the religion provided little guidance or comfort; rather, it brought the people demands of action and threats of punishment. The great Sumerian poem *The Epic of Gilgamesh* is the story of the king of Uruk and explains much of their mythology.

Sunni Muslims

Majority branch of **Muslims** who follow the *Sunna*, ("trodden path"), which includes the **Quran** (Koran), the **Hadith** (sayings of **Muhammad**), and belief in the chain of **caliphs** as leaders of **Islam**. Muhammad, at his death in 632 C.E., left no instructions for his succession and no sons. Some of his followers selected **Abu Bakr** as caliph ("successor"); they became known as Sunni Muslims. Others thought that Muhammad did not intend that approach and that only an heir to Muhammad should lead. They became known as *shias* ("partisans") of Ali, or **Shia** Muslims. Sunnis constitute 90 percent of Muslims in the world, but conflict remains between Shia and Sunni in places such as Iran and Iraq.

Sun Yat-sen (1866–1925)

Chinese revolutionary and statesman who founded the **Guomindang** (Nationalist Party). Receiving a Western education in **Hong Kong** and Hawaii, Sun sought to overthrow the **Qing** dynasty and create a modern state in China that would be strong and prosperous. He established the Tongmenghui (United League), a revolutionary organization, in 1905, which after the 1911 revolution was reorganized as the Guomindang. Sun's political philosophy was summed up in the three People's Principles, which emphasized nationalism, democracy, and people's livelihood (prosperity). Following the suppression of the Guomindang by the new republican government in **Beijing**, Sun made his headquarters in his native Guangdong province in southern China and sought Russian help in political organization and military training. After his death the party established control over most of China. He is revered as a nationalist patriot today in both the **People's Republic of China** and Taiwan.

Sunzi (Sun-tzu) (fl. early fourth century)

Reputed author of the Chinese classic of war and military strategy *Bing Fa* (*Art of War*). He stressed the importance of taking political factors into consideration in war and having a good knowledge of the enemy. His strategy was to use deception and avoid conflict until conditions favored the attacker. His ideas had a great influence on Chinese and, more recently, Western military strategists.

Surat

City in the western Indian state of Gujarat that was a major port in the sixteenth and seventeenth centuries. In 1612 the British **East India Company** established its first trading settlement in India at Surat.

Surrealism

Artistic movement of the first half of the twentieth century. Surrealism attempted to bypass the conscious and express the workings of the artist's mind directly on the canvas. Among the leading surrealists were Salvador Dalí (1904–1989), Frida Kahlo (1907–1954), Joan Miró (1893–1983), and Paul Klee (1879–1940).

Susa

Capital of the **Achaemenid** empire of **Darius I**. Located in Iran, the site of Susa has been extensively excavated, with extremely valuable finds including the **Code of Hammurabi** of **Babylon** and the palace of Darius I.

Suttee. *See* Sati (Suttee)

Swahili

African mercantile people living along the southeastern coast of Africa. The term *swahili* means "people of the coast" in Arabic. Their language, Kiswahili, is **Bantu** but has incorporated many Arabic words. Because of their location, the Swahili have long been intermediaries for trade, including during the **Atlantic slave trade** between Africa and America. They are predominantly urban, mercantile, and sometimes maritime. The Swahili civilization was at its height in the twelfth to sixteenth centuries, with a high level of sophistication. The Swahili language is important today.

Syracuse

Coastal town in Sicily important in Greek civilization. Founded in 734 B.C.E. as a trading base by Corinth, Syracuse became the center of its own empire in the fifth and fourth centuries B.C.E. In the third century Syracuse allied with Rome, and then with Carthage. Rome captured the city in 211 B.C.E., although the famous mathematician and inventor **Archimedes** helped design its defenses.

Tacitus, P. Cornelius (c. 55–120)
Roman historian, governor, senator, and **consul**. Tacitus's first literary works were *Agricola*, the biography of a governor of Roman Britain, and *Germania*, about the Germanic peoples moving into the Roman Empire in the first century (both 97 and 98). His *Histories* (c. 104–112) covers the years from 68 to 96, and *Annals* (c. 112–120), the years from 14 to 68. Tacitus's histories are fascinating albeit remarkably biased and uneven.

Tagalog
Language and culture of central Luzon in the Philippines. Because it was the language of Manila and the Philippine language with the largest number of speakers, Tagolog became the basis of Filipino, the national language of the Philippines. Since independence Filipino has been taught in all the country's schools.

Tagore, Rabindranath (1861–1941)
Indian Bengali poet, composer, playwright, painter, and winner of the **Nobel Prize** for Literature in 1913. Tagore wrote in the local Bengali language, freeing literature from its dependence on the traditional **Sanskrit** literature of India. His work *Gitanjali* (1910) won him great acclaim and the Nobel Prize. He worked to introduce Indian arts to the West and Western arts to India. He traveled widely in Europe and the United States and became a spokesman for Indian independence.

Taika
Reforms carried out in Japan over several decades after a prince, the future Emperor Tenji (r. 668–671), and a supporter of Fujiwara Kamatari came to power. The Taika ("Great Change") reforms introduced institutions and practices that continued the process of creating a centralized bureaucratic state on the Chinese model that had been started by **Shotoku Taishi**.

Taiping Rebellion (1850–1864)
Rebellion against the **Qing** dynasty by the Taipings, a religious and political group founded and led by **Hong Xiuquan**. The Taipings drew upon Christianity as well as **Confucianism** and Chinese secret society traditions to proclaim a new vision of society. The rebellion was crushed by Qing forces with some help from Westerners employed by the Qing, and the rebel capital of Nanjing was captured in 1864. At the rebellion's peak the Taipings controlled large regions of central and southern China. The rebellion, which seriously threatened the Qing, cost millions of lives—some estimate 20 million—making it one of the most costly conflicts in history in terms of human life.

Taj Mahal
Memorial complex in the Indian city of Agra built by the fifth **Mughal** emperor Shah Jahan (r. 1628–1658) to honor his favorite wife, Mumtaz Mahal, who died in childbirth. It is regarded as one of the finest examples of the blend of Persian,

Islamic, and Indian forms that characterized Mughal architecture.

Tale of Genji. *See Genji, Tale of*

Talmud
Jewish text of religious and ethical teachings. After the **Jewish diaspora** a cohesive Jewish community did not exist. To provide guidance to widely scattered Jews, rabbinical teachings on the **Torah** were collected along with legal judgments, religious duties, and other aspects of Jewish life. By the middle of the fourth century B.C.E. this compilation of writings, known as the *Talmud*, provided a practical guide for daily conduct.

Tamerlane. *See* Timur (Timur Leng, "Timur the Lame" or Tamerlane)

Tang (618–907)
Chinese dynasty noted for its military strength, economic prosperity, and cultural achievements. The Tang dynasty was established by **Li Yuan**, titled Gaozu, who made his capital at Chang'an, which became perhaps the largest city in the world at that time. The Tang further developed the **civil service examinations**, which proved highly effective in recruiting men of talent to serve the imperial bureaucracy, and expanded their empire into the **Xingjiang** region and the Pamirs, mountains of **Central Asia**. Under the Tang, **Buddhism** flourished, the printing press was invented, great works of art were created, and Chinese poetry enjoyed perhaps its greatest period. The Tang encouraged trade along the **Silk Roads** and the sea routes with Southeast Asia. After the **An Lushan** rebellion (755–763) the dynasty went into a period of decline.

Tang Taixang (Li Shimin) (600–649)
Posthumous name of Li Shimin, who assisted his father, **Li Yuan**, in founding the Tang dynasty and who reigned (626–649) after forcing his father to abdicate. Regarded as one of China's greatest emperors, Tang Taixang secured the empire by defeating the eastern Turks and strengthened the state by expanding the **civil service examination** system and establishing more state-supported schools to train officials.

Tangut
A Tibetan people of the northwestern borderlands of China who established the Chinese-influenced state of Xi Xia (Hsi Hsia) in Gansu and Inner Mongolia. The Tanguts had an economy based on irrigated agriculture, pastoralism, and trade along the **Silk Roads**. Originally a tributary people of China, they proclaimed their independence from **Song** China in 1038. **Buddhism** was their state religion, and Xi Xia was important as a center of Buddhism, as is evidenced by the caves at Dunhuang, a great repository of Buddhist paintings and manuscripts. The state was destroyed by the **Mongols** in 1227.

Tang Xuanzang (684–762)
Emperor (r. 712–56) of **Tang** China famed as a great patron of scholarship, literature, and the arts. His reign marks a high point in Chinese culture during which two of China's greatest poets, Li Bo and Du Fu, and two of its great painters, Wu Daozi and Wang Wei, flourished. In his later years Tang Xuanzang fell under the influence of corrupt and untrustworthy courtiers and officials including a concubine, Lady Yang, and a general, **An Lushan**, who led a rebellion in 755.

Tantras
Scriptures of the tantric sects of India who worshiped goddesses with magical ceremonies. Tantras focus on Shakti, the personification of female fertility and creative

energy. **Hindu** and Buddhist Tantras were written from the seventh century. Tantric **Buddhism** spread to Tibet and China from the ninth century.

Tantrism

Esoteric form of Indian religious thought and practice based on **Sanskrit** treatises known as **Tantras** that contain secret teachings involving physical and psychological techniques and practices. There was tantric **Hinduism** and **Jainism**, but tantric **Buddhism** is best known, for its influence on **Mahayana Buddhism**. Tantric Buddhism emerged in the sixth century and flourished through the eleventh and twelfth centuries. It was also known as Vajrayana Buddhism ("Way of the Thunderbolt") and Mantrayana Buddhism ("Way of the Mantra"), the latter named for the practice of repeatedly reciting an incantation called a mantra.

Taoism. *See* Daoism (Taoism)

Tea Ceremony

Aesthetic ritual originally derived from the Chinese **Zen Buddhist** monks' practice of drinking tea in honor of their first patriarch, Bodhidharma. In Japan it emerged in the fifteenth century as a method of hosting guests while quietly appreciating the beauty found in simple and everyday things. It was further refined by the tea master Sen Rikyu, who served in the court of the warlord **Hideyoshi**. Tea ceremony influenced the development of Japanese art, especially raku pottery.

Temple Mount. *See* Hebrew Temple

Temple of Jerusalem. *See* Hebrew Temple

Tenno ("Heavenly Emperor")

Term for the Japanese emperor. The Japanese imperial line of the Yamato clan claimed descent from the legendary Jimmu Tenno, who supposedly ascended to the throne in 660 B.C.E. By the ninth century the emperors were largely figureheads, with the real power in the hands of various officials, but they continued their sacerdotal and ceremonial functions to the nineteenth century. With the **Meiji Restoration** an elaborate ideology known as *tennosei* was created, which claimed that all ultimate authority was in the hands of the emperor—although in practice emperors continued to be largely ceremonial rulers. Japanese ultranationalists also claimed that the semidivine status of the emperors made them and made the Japanese people they ruled unique and special. In 1945, under the U.S. occupation authorities, Emperor **Hirohito** was forced to renounce his sacred status, but the monarchy was maintained.

Tenochtitlán

Capital city of the **Mesoamerican Aztec** civilization. Tenochtitlán was built in Lake **Texcoco** in the Valley of Mexico at the site of modern-day Mexico City. At its peak, with a population of around 250,000, it became the capital of a vast, tribute-paying empire, although the power of the central government was limited beyond Tenochtitlán itself. At the center of the city was the sacred precinct with huge pyramids dedicated to gods, on top of which human sacrifices were made. In 1521 **Hernando Cortés** was invited into Tenochtitlán by the monarch **Moctezuma** and took Moctezuma hostage. When the people revolted Cortés was driven from the city, but he returned leading enemies of the Aztecs and conquered and destroyed Tenochtitlán.

Teotihuacán

First metropolis of **Mesoamerica**. Teotihuacán was the capital of a kingdom for nearly 1,000 years from the third century B.C.E. to c. 800 C.E. The city had a population of as many as 150,000 and a main thoroughfare lined with temples and palaces. It was dominated by the **Pyramid of the Sun**, a massive ceremonial center more than 200 feet (60 m) high, and the Pyramid of the Moon. The entire city was laid out on a north–south, east–west grid plan. The people traded products including cacao, food, obsidian, and rubber over a vast region. The language of Teotihuacán is unknown. Teotihuacán was in many ways heir to the **Olmec civilization**, as is the contemporary **Maya civilization**.

Teresa of Ávila, Saint (born Teresa de Cepeda y Ahumada) (1515–1582)
Spanish nun, mystic, and author. In 1555 she had a religious awakening and began a remarkable career. She led a reform of the Carmelite order to restore its austerity and contemplative nature. She founded reformed **monasteries and convents** throughout Spain and greatly influenced King **Philip II**. Her writings include *The Way of Perfection* (1583) and *The Interior Castle* (1588), both published after her death.

Terra-Cotta Army
Life-size clay figures buried to guard the huge underground tomb of third-century B.C.E. Chinese emperor **Qin Shi Huangdi** (r. 247–210 B.C.E.). They were discovered in excavations in 1974. Each figure's face has a realistic representation of a genuine individual. The scale of the clay army reflects the power and grandiose nature of China's first emperor. So far about 7,000 figures have been found.

Tet Offensive (1968)
Battle offensive launched January 29 through February 25, 1968, by North Vietnam and its **Viet Cong** allies against U.S. and South Vietnamese forces during the **Vietnam War**. The surprise attack was timed for the Vietnamese Lunar New Year holiday (Tet). The communists hoped to spark a popular uprising against the South Vietnamese government. The offensive was a military failure that resulted in heavy communist loses, but it served to damage American and South Vietnamese morale. Many view it as a turning point in the war that eventually led to the U.S. withdrawal of all forces from Vietnam in 1973.

Texas Rangers
Policing force in Texas organized in the 1830s. Originally a militia for the protection of settlers against Indians, during the Texas war for independence and the period of the Republic of Texas the Texas Rangers were the border patrol. Noted for their marksmanship and discipline, they established law and order in the Wild West. They merged with the state police in 1935.

Texcoco
Lake and **city-state** in central Mexico. Important **Mesoamerican** cities were built on the lake. Originally one of five lakes, Texcoco, the largest, was the site of a city built by the Nahuatl tribe, who moved into the Valley of Mexico after the collapse of the **Toltec civilization**. The city was destroyed in 1428, but when the **Aztecs** gained ascendancy they built their capital, **Tenochtitlán**, in Texcoco, connected to the mainland by long causeways. This provided the Aztec with security. At the center of the city was the sacred precinct with huge pyramids dedicated to gods, on top of which human sacrifices were made. **Hernando Cortés** was invited into Tenochtitlán by the monarch Moctezuma in 1521 and destroyed it. Texcoco the city-state was part of the "Triple Alliance," with the Aztecs or Mexica from Tenochtitlán

being by far the most powerful of the three.

Thatcher, Margaret (1925–)

British prime minister (1979–1990). Thatcher became Conservative Party leader in 1975 and in 1979 was the first woman elected as Britain's prime minister. She emphasized free trade, privatization of previously nationalized industries, lowering of the top tax rates, suppression of labor unions, and anticommunism. Her resolve in maintaining her policies won her the epithet "the Iron Lady." In 1982, after Argentina invaded the Falkland Islands, Thatcher responded with the **Falklands War**, which successfully retook the islands for Britain. She was the longest-serving British prime minister of the twentieth century. She resigned as prime minister in 1990, gave up her seat in **Parliament** in 1992, and was created a life peer, Baroness Thatcher of Kesteven, in that same year.

Theodoric (454–526)

King of the Ostrogoths (471–526) and king of Italy (493–526). Theodoric, who spent ten years in captivity in **Constantinople**, threatened to invade the **Byzantine Empire** but was persuaded to invade Italy instead, conquering nearly all of it, settling his capital at Ravenna, and declaring himself king. He began the merger of Roman and Germanic cultures.

Theodosius I, "the Great"

Roman emperor (r. 379–395) who decreed **Christianity** the official religion of the **Roman Empire**. Christianity was declared legal by the **Edict of Milan** in 313, but after conflict and persecution Theodosius banned all pagan practices and declared Christianity the only legal religion of Rome.

Theravada Buddhism

Major form of **Buddhism** dominant in Sri Lanka, Burma (Myanmar), Thailand, Laos, and Cambodia. The name *Theravada* means "Way of the Elders" in Pali, and Theravada belongs to the branch of Buddhism sometimes called Hinayana ("the Lesser Vehicle") to distinguish it from **Mahayana** ("the Greater Vehicle"). Mahayana is predominant in East Asia. The Theravada school originated in northern India, flourished in Sri Lanka, and from there spread to Burma and Thailand in the eleventh to thirteenth centuries. It places emphasis on laypersons serving a period of their lives as monks and does not worship **bodhisattvas** or spiritual manifestations of the Buddha.

Thermidorian Reaction

French Revolution swing to the right following the execution of **Maximilien Robespierre**. Tired of the Terror and following Robespierre's execution in 1794, the National Convention began to debate a new constitution, but in 1795 the National Convention was replaced by a five-member Directory and two legislative councils that ruled France until **Napoléon Bonaparte** ousted the Directory and made himself First Consul in 1799.

Third World

Term used for the developing countries of the world. The third world includes most of Africa, Asia, and Latin America. The term originated in French (*le tiers monde*) and was originally employed in a classification system used by the **United Nations** (UN) to distinguish among the developed capitalist countries (the first world), the developed communist countries (the second world), and the remaining underdeveloped countries (the third world). The third world emerged as a distinct entity in international politics following the process

328 THIRTY YEARS' WAR

of decolonization that brought independence to a large group of African and Asian countries in the 1950s and 1960s. Their historical experience of imperialism and common problems, such as poverty and underdevelopment, shared with countries of Latin America, led them to act as a bloc in international forums, particularly the UN.

Thirty Years' War (1618–1648)
European series of wars begun as a religious war but turned into a political and territorial war. In 1618 the Thirty Years' War began as hostility within the German states between **Protestants** and Catholics in Bohemia when a Protestant church was destroyed and the Protestants rebelled and elected a Protestant king. The Catholic Holy Roman Emperor crushed the rebellion in Bohemia, but other Protestant states rebelled. Catholic forces under General **Albrecht von Wallenstein** defeated the Danish Protestants. Soon Swedish Protestants under King **Gustavus II** entered the war, partly for Protestantism and partly for political aggrandizement. Gustavus built the best army in Europe and defeated the Catholic forces. In the Battle of Lützen (1632) Gustavus's army defeated Wallenstein's army, but Gustavus was killed. The emperor, fearing Wallenstein's power, arrested him, and Wallenstein was assassinated trying to escape. With the **Habsburg** Catholic forces unstopped, Catholic France, directed by **Cardinal Richelieu**, entered on the side of the Protestants to block the Habsburgs. Swedish Protestant and French Catholic armies repeatedly defeated the Catholic Habsburgs. In 1648 the **Peace of Westphalia** ended the war, giving France Alsace and Lorraine, giving Sweden territories, and protecting **Calvinism** and **Lutheranism**. Europe suffered horribly from the war, with possibly millions of deaths. Germany was left in a terrible state from which it would take nearly 200 years to recover.

Thucydides (c. 455–400 B.C.E.)
Ancient Greek historian. Considered the greatest Greek historian, Thucydides was born in **Athens**. As a general in the **Peloponnesian War** he was unsuccessful, and upon banishment he wrote a history of the events. His history was based on documents and evidence and provides an impartial analysis of the causes and course of the war. Thucydides wrote his history for "those who desire an exact knowledge of the past as a key to the future, which in all probability will repeat or resemble the past."

Tianshan (T'ien-shan)
Mountain range extending 1,500 miles that forms the boundary between northwestern China and Kyrgyzstan and runs east–west through most of Kyrgyzstan. The name *Tianshan* means "Heavenly Mountains." The range is one of the highest in the world; its tallest peak reaches over 24,406 feet (7,439 m). The range is the reputed home of several important **Central Asian** peoples. Its fertile valleys have always attracted pastoral nomadic peoples. The western **Turks** had their base in the area.

Tiberius (42 B.C.E.–37 C.E.)
Roman emperor, general, and successor to **Octavian**. Tiberius was the chosen successor to Octavian, who was also his stepfather and father-in-law. He was a successful general who ruled (14–37 C.E.) with a heavy hand as emperor. Increasingly tyrannical, Tiberius made many enemies and executed many opponents. He retired to Capri in 26, and when he died in 37 **Rome** rejoiced.

Tiber River
Italian river 252 miles (405 km) long and originating in the **Apennines**, traveling

through central Italy, and emptying into the Mediterranean Sea just west of Rome at Ostia. The Tiber River played an important role in Roman history.

Tibet

Region of high mountains and arid plateaus now incorporated into China but independent for most of its history. Historically, farming in the 1,000-mile (1,600-km) -long great valley in the south supported most of Tibet's population. In the north, nomads raided surrounding territory. The Yarlung dynasty created a Tibetan empire (620–842) that became a powerful military rival to **Tang** China. Tibet became a Buddhist state mixing **Buddhism** with its native Bon religion. This gave rise to **Lamaism**, which eventually penetrated every aspect of Tibetan life. By the sixteenth century Tibet was a Lamaistic theocracy. In the eighteenth century Tibet recognized the suzerainty of the **Manchu** emperors of the **Qing** dynasty, but **Dalai Lamas** retained control over internal administration and many aspects of foreign policy, especially relating to south Asia. Tibet was largely autonomous in the twentieth century until China's communist government asserted direct control in 1959, causing its ruler, the Dalai Lama, to flee to India. Civil unrest over Chinese rule has continued to plague Tibet since it became a Chinese province in 1965.

Tierra del Fuego

Land at the extreme southern tip of South America. Named Tierra del Fuego ("Land of Fires") by **Ferdinand Magellan** in 1520 when he sailed through the waterway later named for him, the **Strait of Magellan**. The land to the south of the strait had hundreds of indigenous signal fires burning each night throughout Magellan's passage, although his crew saw no people. This led to great fear and suspicion of the region.

Tigris River

River originating in the mountains of Turkey and flowing 1,180 miles (1,900 km) to the Persian Gulf. The **Tigris** and **Euphrates** rivers begin in the same Turkish mountains, the Tigris to the east of the Euphrates, and travel parallel courses only 250 miles (400 km) apart at the widest and 30 (50) at the narrowest, near Baghdad, joining together approximately 50 miles (80 km) before the gulf. The region between the two is known as **Mesopotamia** ("land between the rivers"). The Tigris and the Euphrates enabled the development of some of the earliest civilizations in the world. For thousands of years the rivers were tapped for irrigation, and the cultures of **Sumer**, **Babylonia**, **Assyria** arose there.

Timbuktu

Intellectual and commercial center of the **Mali** and **Songhay** empires of Africa between the thirteenth and eighteenth centuries. Timbuktu had an Islamic university with courses in theology, law, and literature. The Sankore Mosque was a major center of learning. Commercially, Timbuktu was on the **trans-Saharan trade** routes that moved gold and ivory from the south to the north and, ultimately, to the Mediterranean world.

Timur (Timur Leng, "Timur the Lame," or Tamerlane) (1336–1405)

Steppe leader who, claiming the status of son-in-law of **Genghis Khan** through his marriage to a woman of descent from **Genghis Khan**, created a short-lived empire over a large territory in Asia. Establishing himself as ruler of most of **Turkestan**, he then used Turkestan as a base to launch destructive campaigns from 1380 to 1402 against Persia, the **Golden Horde** that governed the Russian steppes, the sultanate of Delhi, and the **Mamluks** of Egypt and

Syria, and the **Ottoman Turks** in Anatolia. He was preparing for an invasion of China when he died in 1405. A skilled military commander noted for his brutality, Timur never established a stable administrative structure and much of his empire collapsed with his death. Timur brought artisans to add splendor to his capital, **Samarkand**, and patronized the arts, but his main legacy was one of terror and brutality. His grandson **Ulugh Beg** was able to raise the dynasty founded by Timur to heights of art and culture.

Titian (c. 1488–1576) (full name Tiziano Vecellio)
Renaissance painter from **Venice**, a contemporary of **Leonardo da Vinci**, **Michelangelo**, and **Raphael**. Titian painted in a sensuous style that was unsurpassed, with works such as *Bacchanal* (c. 1518). Unusual in its pagan subject, the painting is lush and rich in color and sensuous form. Titian was a brilliant portraitist, as seen in *Man with a Glove* (c. 1520) and *Pope Paul III and His Grandson* (1546).

Tokugawa
Japanese family that served as **shoguns** during the Tokugawa shogunate (1603–1868). The founder of the shogunate was Tokugawa Ieyasu (1543–1616), a warlord allied with **Hideyoshi**. He defeated the **daimyo** loyal to Hideyoshi's son and successor at Sekigahara in 1600 and established his capital at **Edo**. Under the Tokugawa rulers Japan enjoyed two-and-a-half centuries of peace and stability. The economy grew, commerce flourished, a vigorous commercial middle class emerged, and the arts flowered. Society was frozen into rigid classes of **bushi**, peasants, artisans, and merchants. The Tokugawa rulers were suspicious of **Christianity** with its foreign links and loyalties and relentlessly persecuted it. They also limited

contact between Japan and the outside world, a policy that has been called *sakoku* ("closed country"). Diplomatic relations and carefully regulated trade with China and the Dutch was permitted at **Nagasaki** and some trade was carried out indirectly with China through Okinawa, but otherwise Japan remained a world apart under the Tokugawa. The shogunate ended with the **Meiji Restoration** in 1868, which took place following the forcible opening of Japanese ports by Westerners.

Toltec Civilization (c. 900–1200)
Mesoamerican civilization that ruled central Mexico in the period between the **Maya** and the **Aztec** civilizations. The name *Toltec* means "urbanite" or "cultured people." The Toltec were a warring people who practiced human sacrifice on a large scale. They worshiped a pantheon of gods; the war gods were of primary importance. Their capital was at Tula. The Toltecs moved into the Yucatán and influenced the Maya. The impressive Maya ruins at Chichén Itzá have many similarities to the Toltec capital of Tula.

Tonkin (Tongking)
The northern region of Vietnam containing the fertile **Red River** valley and the capital, Hanoi. During the French rule of Indochina, the name Tonkin was given to this region by the French but not used by the Vietnamese. It is also a name for the body of water that lies east of northern Vietnam and south of China, the Gulf of Tonkin.

Topkapi Palace
Ottoman royal palace. Upon his conquest of **Constantinople** in 1453, the Ottoman sultan **Mehmet II** commissioned the building of the palace complex that later came to be known as Topkapi Saray. It is situated on a hill overlooking both the Sea of Marmara and the Bosporus Strait. Upon

completion of its first phase of construction the palace covered 75,000 square feet (7,000 square meters) and was surrounded by fortified walls 4,600 feet (1,400 meters) in length. The compound is next to **Hagia Sophia**, a church that the Ottomans converted into a mosque. From the time of Mehmet II until its last royal Ottoman occupant, Abdul Mejid (r. 1839–1860), the palace grew steadily to form a citylike complex of buildings and annexes.

Topu Inca (c. 1435–1493)

Inca emperor (r. 1471–1493). Son of **Pachacutec**, who expanded the Inca empire by conquest and using skillful threats and claims of divine intervention, Topu continued the expansion, mainly by conquest. The vast empire stretched from the border of modern-day Ecuador and Colombia in the north to central Chile and northwestern Argentina in the south, with a population of perhaps 9–12 million by the time of Topu's death. In his last years Topu traveled across his empire establishing local administration.

Torah

Law in the Jewish religion. The Torah, containing the five books of Moses—Genesis, Exodus, Leviticus, Numbers, and Deuteronomy—lays out the religious and moral requirements of **Judaism** in both prescriptions and prohibitions (both seen in the Ten Commandments). The Torah provides guidance to the individual and for the individual's relationship to society. The laws protect the weak, poor, and downtrodden—a great innovation over most other religions or law codes, which protected property or the social hierarchy.

Tordesillas, Treaty of (1494)

Agreement between Portugal and Spain to divide up newly discovered territories. A treaty was drawn up by Pope Alexander VI in 1493 to settle disputes by both countries over new discoveries, but it was revised at Tordesillas in 1494. The new treaty drew a line from pole to polewest of Greenwich, England (46° 37' W in modern terms). All newly discovered lands west of this line were given to Spain, and those east of the line went to Portugal. This was a diplomatic victory for Portugal because it kept control of the trade route to India and gained Brazil, probably unknown in 1494. Both countries hoped to get the Moluccas in the East Indies. Spain initially won the Moluccas, but in 1529 the Treaty of Saragossa gave the Moluccas to Portugal.

Tories (America)

British loyalists in the American colonies. During the **American Revolution** approximately one-third of the colonists remained loyal to Great Britain and the crown and were known as Tories, but their actions were punished by imprisonment and confiscation of property. Some Tories moved to Canada, back to Britain, or even joined the British army.

Tories (England)

Members of an English political party formed in the seventeenth century. They supported King **James II** and monarchical rights. Tories took their name from Irish outlaws who killed English settlers. After the **Glorious Revolution** of 1688 the Tory Party continued to favor monarchy, the divine right of kings, and the Church of England. It became known as the Conservative Party in the nineteenth century.

Touré, Samori (1830–1900)

Muslim military leader and state builder in Guinea. Touré trained local warriors into a military and declared himself king of Malinka, a territory that now comprises Guinea and parts of Mali and Ivory Coast. As the French began to colonize the west coast of Africa, Touré fought them and created one of the most powerful states, resisting French conquest for more than seventeen years. His military tactics are generally recognized as superior to those of the French, but his armaments were inferior. In 1898 the French finally captured Touré and deported him to Gabon, completing their conquest of west Africa. Touré died in Gabon.

Tours, Battle of (732)
Frankish (Carolingian) victory over a **Muslim** army. **Charles Martel** (**Charlemagne**'s grandfather) routed the Muslim army and drove the Muslims out of France across the Pyrenees into Spain. **Islam** had expanded from its origins 100 years earlier to reach deeply into Europe. The Frankish victory was later extolled as more dramatic than it really was, though it established the Franks as a major power in eighth-century Europe.

Toussaint L'Ouverture, François Dominique (c. 1744–1803)
Haitian revolutionary leader. Inspired by the **French Revolution**, Toussaint L'Ouverture led a slave revolt in Haiti in 1791. When Britain invaded Haiti in 1793 and allied with Spain, Toussaint organized the resistance. By 1795 Toussaint was governing the entire island, and when **Napoléon Bonaparte** sent forces to subdue him Toussaint again resisted. He was captured and sent to France, where he died in a dungeon. In 1804 Haiti, under one of Toussaint's commanders, declared its independence making it the first liberated territory in the Caribbean or Latin America.

Toyotomi Hideyoshi. *See* Hideyoshi

Trail of Tears
Enforced exile of Amerindians of the United States from southeastern states to Oklahoma. As settlers moved to Georgia, Alabama, Mississippi, Florida, and Louisiana in the 1830s, the U.S. authorities moved Cherokee, Seminole, Creek, Cochtaw, and Chickasaw tribes out of the region westward to Oklahoma. The suffering and high death toll along the way became known as the Trail of Tears.

Trajan (c. 53–117)
Roman general and emperor (98–117). A distinguished general, Trajan was adopted by Emperor Nerva to succeed him. After his effective reign provided needed stability for the **Roman Empire**, Trajan in turn adopted **Hadrian** to succeed him. Many public works were constructed during the reign of Trajan.

Transalpine. *See* Gaul

Transoxiana (also called Sogdiana)
Central Asian land between the Amu Darya River (the ancient Oxus River) and the Syr Darya River, now part of Uzbekistan and southwestern Kazakhstan. Transoxiana in ancient times was a very important crossroads of trade, religion, and ideas between East and West. The most important city was **Samarkand**. Along with **Bactria** to the east, Transoxiana was part of the Achaemenian empire of **Cyrus the Great** in the sixth century B.C.E., part of the empire of **Alexander the Great** in the fourth century B.C.E., and part of the **Seleucid** empire in the third century B.C.E. The region had a strong **Buddhist** influence until the coming of **Islam** in the seventh century C.E. It was invaded by **Genghis Khan** in 1219 and by **Timur** in the fourteenth century.

Trans-Saharan Trade
Trade between the Mediterranean Sea and the Sudan region of Africa south of the Sahara Desert. The Sahara Desert has

come and gone throughout time. It appeared in its present form by about 3000 B.C.E., dividing North Africa and the Mediterranean region from west Africa. Around the first century C.E. the camel, which was already in use along the southern rim of the Sahara, spread to North Africa, making trade across the desert possible. Nomadic tribes moved the trade between northern and sub-Saharan Africa in small quantities during Roman times, but after the rise of **Islam** in the seventh century several major trade routes appeared. The western route from Morocco through Mauritania led to ancient **Ghana** between the Senegal and Niger rivers. A central route began in northern Algeria and ran almost directly south through **Timbuktu** and on to the region of modern-day Ghana. An eastern route from Tripoli in Libya led through Niger, west of Lake Chad, and south to the Niger River. These remained the principle trade routes until the twentieth century. Along these routes southward moved horses, salt, cloth, metalwork, and Islam. Northward moved gold, ivory, slaves, goat hides, senna, and cola nuts. Ancient Ghana became known as the land of gold, and gold drove much of the trade and, later, the European interest in sub-Saharan Africa.

Treaty of Nerchinsk. *See* Nerchinsk, Treaty of

Treaty of Paris. *See* Paris, Treaty of

Treaty of Tordesillas. *See* Tordesillas, Treaty of

Treaty of Westphalia. *See* Westphalia, Treaty of

Treaty Ports
Chinese ports that were opened to foreign trade and residency as a result of treaties signed with Western powers in the nineteenth century. Starting with the **Treaty of Nanjing** (Nanking) in 1842 between China and Britain at the end of the **Opium War,** China was forced to open certain ports to Westerners. Foreigners living in these ports were largely governed by the laws of their own countries. The treaty port became a symbol of the weakness of China and its gradual loss of sovereignty to foreigners. China regained full control over these ports by 1943. The term *treaty ports* is also used for similar ports in Japan and Korea.

Treblinka. *See* Death Camps, German

Trent, Council of. *See* Council of Trent

Trenton, Battle of (1776)
The first clear success by the American troops under **George Washington** against the British army during the **American Revolution** on December 26, 1776. Washington made a daring crossing of the icy Delaware River on Christmas Day, 1776, and subsequently captured approximately 900 Hessian soldiers in the pay of the British. This led to a boost in confidence throughout the colonies and a similarly successful operation in the **Battle of Princeton** several days later.

Tributary System
Term for China's way of conducting foreign affairs in premodern times. The Chinese emperor regarded himself as the "celestial emperor"—the mediator between heaven and earth and the ruler of civilization. The Chinese empire was seen as the center of civilization and other lands were theoretically subordinate to the emperor. Rulers of states outside the empire were ranked in a hierarchy in which those who adhered closest to Chinese cultural norms were highest. These rulers paid tribute to the emperor, who confirmed

their authority and gave them "gifts." In reality these were often merely trade missions, but foreign trade was simply regarded as tribute. Korea, Vietnam, and several states along China's northern and western borders and in Southeast Asia—and occasionally Japan—accepted this system as a means to maintain good relations with China or secure trade with it. The tributary system ran into conflict with Western ideas of foreign relations in the nineteenth century.

Triple Alliance

Nineteenth-century agreement between Germany, **Austria-Hungary**, and Italy. After the formation of Germany and Italy and the Franco-Prussian War of 1870–1871, France felt threatened and Germany was a new power in Europe. Germany had allied with Russia and Austria-Hungary in the Three Emperors League, but Russia and Austria-Hungary were at odds over the Balkans. Germany formed an alliance with Austria-Hungary in 1879, and the two powers signed a treaty with Italy in 1882, forming the Triple Alliance. Serbia and Romania joined this bloc in 1882 and 1883. This threatened France into forming its own alliances, which became the **Triple Entente**. These alliances formed rigid adversarial blocs that created the conditions for **World War I**.

Triple Entente

Agreement between Britain, France, and Russia to counter the **Triple Alliance**. France, fearing Germany after the Franco-Prussian War of 1870–1871 and any alliance Germany may have made, formed an alliance with Russia in 1894. Britain signed the Entente Cordiale with France in 1904 and an entente with Russia in 1907, thus forming the Triple Entente. These alliances formed a rigid adversarial blocs that created the conditions for **World War I**.

Trojan War

Legendary war described in **Homer's** *Iliad*. The date of the Trojan War is believed to have been in the thirteenth century B.C.E., toward the end of the Greek **Mycenaean age**, or about 450 years before the writing of the *Iliad* in approximately 750 B.C.E. Excavations by Heinrich Schliemann (fl. 1822–1890) and others at Troy have turned up interesting finds from the thirteenth century, but there is still no proof that these are remnants of the legendary city of Troy from the Trojan War.

Truman, Harry S (1884–1972)

Thirty-third president of the United States (1945–1953). An artillery officer during **World War I** and later an unsuccessful businessman, Truman was elected to the **United States Senate** from Missouri and became **Franklin D. Roosevelt**'s unexpected candidate for vice president in the 1944 election. Roosevelt's untimely death in 1945 put Truman in the White House. Truman authorized dropping the **atomic bombs** on **Hiroshima** and **Nagasaki** that ended **World War II**. He ended racial segregation in the armed forces and federally funded schools. In 1947 Truman established what became known as the Truman Doctrine—that the United States should aid any country threatened by the Soviet Union or communism. In 1948 Truman's administration introduced the **Marshall Plan** to rebuild war-ravaged Europe. In 1949 Truman helped establish the **North Atlantic Treaty Organization** (NATO). Truman engaged the United States in the **Korean War** and then differences of strategy led to his removing **Douglas MacArthur** from military command.

Trung Sisters

Leaders of a first-century C.E. Vietnamese rebellion against the Chinese **Han dynasty**. Trung Trac and her sister Trung

Nhi drove the Chinese out of much of Vietnam but were defeated and executed in 43. The Chinese continued to rule Vietnam until the eleventh century. The sisters became Vietnamese national heroes and symbols of the high social status of Southeast Asian women.

Tupac Amaru II (born José Gabriel Condorcanqui) (c. 1742–1781)
Peruvian revolutionary. A mestizo who claimed royal descent from the last **Inca** ruler, Tupac Amaru, he led an Amerindian rebellion in 1780 against Spanish rule in Peru that spread to Bolivia and Argentina. The revolt began as an alliance of Peruvian-born whites, mestizos, and indigenous people but became primarily an indigenous movement against the power structure. Tupac and his family were captured in 1781 and taken to **Cuzco**, where Tupac witnessed the execution of his family. He was then mutilated, drawn and quartered, and beheaded. The revolt continued for some time until the insurgents were granted pardons. It frightened the Peruvian and Bolivian elites, who became wary of indigenous participation in independence movements.

Turkestan
Region of **Central Asia** that extends from the Caspian Sea to the Altai Mountains, bordering the taiga forest belt of Siberia and the **steppe** belt to the north and Afghanistan and Tibet to the south. It includes the modern states of Kazakhstan, Uzbekistan, Turkmenistan, Kyrgyzstan, and Tajikistan and **Xingjiang** province of China. Much of Turkestan is desert or semidesert grassland, but it also contains mountains, fertile river valleys, and oases. Historically Turkestan has been a great crossroads with many flourishing trading centers such as Bukhara and **Samarkand**, major cities on the **Silk Roads**. It was also the home or headquarters of many great Central Asian empires such as that of **Timur**. The easternmost region became part of the **Qing** empire in the eighteenth century and Xingjiang province of China in the twentieth, and most of Turkestan was conquered by Russia in the nineteenth century. With the collapse of the Soviet Union in 1991 the formerly Russian-ruled regions became five independent states.

Turks
Central Asian Turkic-speaking peoples, originally nomads from the Altai Mountains between **Turkestan** and Mongolia. In the mid-sixth century the Turks created a large empire that stretched from Mongolia to the Caspian Sea. The empire collapsed but various Turk groups formed important components in the armies of many **steppe** empires, including that of the **Mongols**. From the ninth century many Turks converted to **Islam** and served as soldiers for Middle Eastern rulers. In the eleventh century under the **Seljuks** they gained control of much of Iraq, Syria, and parts of Anatolia. At the end of the thirteenth century the Osmanli Turks created a state that became the **Ottoman Empire** that ruled most of the **Middle East**, North Africa, and the Balkans by the sixteenth century. Most people in the modern states of Turkey, Azerbaijan, Kazakhstan, Uzbekistan, Turkmenistan, and Kyrgyzstan regard themselves as Turks, not in a nationalistic way, but because they speak Turkic.

Tutankhamon (r. c. 1347–1338 B.C.E.)
Ancient Egyptian boy-pharaoh who restored the **Egyptian civilization**'s capital and religion. Tutankhamon's predecessor, **Amenhotep IV**, attempted to change the religion of Egypt from worship of **Amon-Re** to Aton and moved the capital from Thebes to the new city of **Akhenaton**.

Tutankhamon returned the government to Thebes and restored the old religion. Tutankhamon is known primarily for his tomb, discovered in 1922 unlooted in the Valley of the Kings. His mummified body was inside a coffin of gold and surrounded by jewels and weapons.

Tutu, Desmond (1931–)

South African clergyman, opponent of **apartheid**, and 1984 winner of the **Nobel Prize** for Peace. As secretary-general of the South African Council of Churches, Tutu became a spokesman for the rights of black South Africans and against apartheid. He called for economic sanctions against the government and emphasized nonviolence. He was awarded the Nobel Prize for Peace for his efforts. In 1985 he became bishop and in 1986 archbishop of Cape Town. In 1996 he became archbishop emeritus. South African president **Nelson Mandela** appointed Tutu head of the Truth and Reconciliation Committee to investigate human rights abuses during apartheid.

Twelve Tables (451–450 B.C.E.)

Roman laws, originally an oral tradition, codified (written down). A commission of ten legal experts addressed the issues of redresses for wrongs, paternal power, and property rights as **Rome's patricians** (the upper class) and **plebeians** (the common people) struggled for legal rights and political influence. The customary laws were inscribed onto twelve stone tables and put on display in the Roman Forum for all citizens to read. Although they would soon become antiquated, a precedent was set that all free citizens had a right to protection under the law.

Tycho. *See* Brahe, Tycho

Tydings-McDuffie Act

Act passed by the United States Congress and signed by President **Franklin D. Roosevelt** in 1934 that laid out the process for the independence of the Philippines. Under its provisions, the Philippines became autonomous in 1935 with an elected president and a congress, while the United States continued to handle defense, foreign affairs, and monetary matters. Full independence came on July 4, 1946.

Tyranny. *See* Tyrant

Tyrant

Greek word for the rule as monarch by a usurper in a troubled time. A tyrant could be benevolent or malevolent but ruled with strong influence over an existing government. During the civil war in **Athens**, **Peisistratus** and his son **Hippias** ruled as tyrants. Tyrants would take over a government because of dissatisfaction, and then dissatisfaction with the tyrant would lead to the downfall of tyranny.

U

Ultra

British **World War II** campaign to break the German naval U-boat codes. By the capture of an **Enigma** machine and painstaking work on codes at the secret Bletchley Park facility, the British cracked the first code in 1941 only to have the Germans alter the Enigma in 1942 so that Bletchley Park had to recrack it. With the code cracked, U-boat positions were known, so transport ships could avoid them and attack ships could sink them. Ultra helped the **Allies** win the **Battle of the Atlantic**.

Ulugh Beg (1393–1449)

Grandson of **Timur** and patron of the arts and intellectual matters. He raised the dynasty founded by Timur to cultural heights and made the city of **Samarkand** an intellectual and artistic center, establishing a madrassa (center of higher Islamic religious learning) there. Ulugh Beg was a poet, historian, mathematician, and astronomer. With the use of an observatory he had constructed in Samarkand, he even corrected some of the famous second-century astronomer **Ptolemy**'s calculations. After his father's death in 1447 Ulugh Beg was ineffective at ruling, and his son had him killed.

Umar (c. 581–644)

Second **caliph** of Islam (634–644). Umar, an ardent supporter of **Muhammad**, followed **Abu Bakr** as caliph. Under Umar Islam began its major conquests and the administration of the conquered lands, created the **Muslim** calendar, and established Islamic law.

Umayyad Caliphate (661–750)

Dynasty of **caliphs** (successors) who ruled most of the new Islamic world from their capital at **Damascus**. The Umayyad was a period of expansion and conflict with the **Byzantine Empire**. By the eighth century Islam had spread throughout the **Middle East**, across North Africa, and through the Iberian Peninsula (Spain and Portugal). The extravagant court absorbed great amounts of money, and discontent eventually brought it down after a revolt of several years by the **Abbasid caliphate**. A member of the Umayyads founded the Caliphate of Córdoba in Spain.

Umma

Arabic for "community." The **Quran** uses the word *umma* many times in different contexts, but the umma is the **Muslim** community or those who follow Islamic values.

Underground Railroad

System for helping African American slaves to freedom before the **American Civil War**. Escaped southern slaves were secretly helped to reach places of safety along routes planned to bring them to freedom in northern states or Canada. It had no formal organization, and much of the help was provided by free African Americans and slaves who used systems such as directions provided in the designs of quilts that were hung on the front porches of houses. Harriet "Moses" Tubman was one of the most famous African Americans to provide assistance, helping around 300 slaves escape. Northern **abolitionists** provided minimal assistance. Estimates of the number of slaves freed by the Underground Railroad range from 40,000 to 100,000.

Union, Act of (1707)

Union of the Kingdoms of England and Scotland into the Kingdom of Great Britain during Queen Anne's reign. Since 1603 the two countries had shared the same monarch, but Scotland had its own parliament, laws, a separate church (Presbyterian), and a formidable army. In forming the union Scotland lost its independent government but maintained its separate church and laws. However, within fifty years Scotland's economic and intellectual growth had catapulted it into the Scottish **Enlightenment**. The new flag of Great Britain, the Union Jack, combined the flags of England and Scotland. Ireland was added in a separate Act of Union in 1801.

Union of Soviet Socialist Republics (USSR) (1917–1991)

Eurasian empire comprised of fifteen Soviet republics, the largest of which was Russia, with the capital at Moscow. The USSR, also known as the Soviet Union, was the largest country in the world and, during its greatest period (1946–1991), it was one of the two world superpowers, along with the United States. The Communist Party ruled the USSR, and from 1946 to 1991 the United States and the USSR were rivals and often enemies. The USSR came into being at the **Russian Revolution** of 1917 out of the old, tsarist Russia. Some important leaders of the USSR were **Vladimir Ilyich Lenin, Joseph Stalin, Nikita Khrushchev, Leonid Brezhnev**, and Mikhail Gorbachev. The USSR attempted to compete with the United States in a nuclear arms, or atomic weapons, race, which by the 1980s economically weakened the country. After the **fall of the USSR** in 1991, many of the republics declaring themselves independent.

Union of Soviet Socialist Republics (USSR), Fall of the

Collapse of the Soviet Union. In March 1985, after the deaths of the previous two leaders within three years, the Soviet Union selected Mikhail Gorbachev to serve as general secretary of the Communist Party. Gorbachev was the youngest member of the Politburo, the chief committee of the Communist Party. Convinced that the USSR was headed toward economic ruin, Gorbachev enacted the policies of *perestroika* (restructuring of the economy) and *glasnost* (openness toward discussion). In 1989 Soviet citizens were allowed to voice views contrary to those of Soviet Communist Party leaders. Gorbachev also allowed for the creation of the 2,250-seat National Congress of People's Deputies; 1,500 seats were to be filled by the vote of the people. Despite Gorbachev's best intentions, however, he soon found the USSR on the brink of collapse. Reforms threw the Soviet Union into turmoil, and in 1991 individual Soviet republics began to emerge as free states. States such as Latvia and Lithuania, which had been seized by **Joseph Stalin** in 1940, demanded and received their independence. On January 1, 1992, the communist hammer-and-sickle flag was lowered for the final time, officially ending the existence of the USSR.

United Arab Republic (1958–1971)

Attempt by Egyptian president **Gamal Abdel Nasser** to establish Egyptian leadership in the Arab world. In 1958 Egypt and Syria combined to form the United Arab Republic, but it never worked smoothly and did not provide a model for the rest of the Arab world as expected. In 1961 the union was dissolved although Egypt continued to use the name United Arab Republic until 1971.

United Kingdom of Great Britain and Northern Ireland

Official name of the united countries of England, Scotland, Northern Ireland, and Wales. Great Britain includes England, Scotland, and Wales. Wales was absorbed by England in the thirteenth century. Scotland united with England in the **Act of Union** of 1707, and Ireland united in the Act of Union of 1801. After the major part of Ireland became independent in 1924, Northern Ireland became a part of the United Kingdom of Great Britain and Northern Ireland.

United Nations Organization

International organization established in 1945 by twenty-six allied powers in an effort to provide a more effective successor to the **League of Nations** in peacefully resolving international conflicts. The organization consists of the United Nations General Assembly and the Security Council. The five major **Allied** powers—the United States, the Soviet Union (later, its successor Russia), Britain, France, and China—were made permanent members of the Security Council and given veto power over decisions by the General Assembly. Eventually almost all sovereign nations joined; its membership reached 185 in its first half century. The United Nations proved less effective than many of its promoters hoped. However, a number of organizations operating under the United Nations or associated with it, such as the United Nations Educational, Scientific,

and Cultural Organization (UNESCO), the International Atomic Energy Agency (IAEA), the World Health Organization (WHO), the United Nations Conference of Trade and Development (UNCTAD), and the Office of the United Nations High Commissioner for Refugees (UNHCR) carry on important humanitarian, monitoring, and conflict-resolution work.

United Provinces (1581–1795)

Low Countries northern provinces that split from the southern provinces to form the United Provinces in the Union of Utrecht (1579) and the Oath of Abjuration (1581). Originally part of the **Habsburg** holdings under **Philip II** of Spain that included modern-day Belgium, Luxembourg, and the Netherlands, the northern provinces rebelled in the Dutch Revolt (1559–1648) and formed the United Provinces, also known as the **Dutch Republic**. The United Provinces were predominantly **Calvinist**, while the southern **Spanish Netherlands** remained Catholic. With major commercial cities such as Amsterdam and Haarlem and great fleets of ships, the United Provinces became a major European power in the seventeenth century known, a period known as the Dutch "Golden Age." The United Provinces of the Netherlands lasted until 1795 when it was conquered by France during the **French Revolution**.

United States Constitution

American document drafted and proposed by the Philadelphia Convention of 1787 and ratified in 1788. The United States Constitution provides for republican government premised on separation of powers, federalism, and strong respect for individual rights. It is the longest-lived national constitution in existence today and has established a vigorous national government.

Universities

Corporations of masters and students for higher education. Muslim madrassas (mosque schools) preceded the development of universities in Europe in the **Middle Ages**. Some historians claim that universities did not exist elsewhere before the medieval institutions of the twelfth and thirteenth centuries, although others argue that the madrassas of the **Middle East**, such as Cairo's Al-Azhar, were the models for early European universities; **Timubuktu** had three universities in the twelfth century with a student population of 25,000. In both instances they were schools of higher learning, but with narrow religious focus. European universities taught the seven liberal arts—grammar, logic, rhetoric, geometry, arithmetic, astronomy, and music—as well as the professional subjects of medicine, law, and theology. Of the European universities, Salerno had an institution of higher learning specializing in medicine in the ninth century, and Bologna had one specializing in canon and civil law by the end of the eleventh century. Paris had a university specializing in theology by the mid-twelfth century and **Oxford**, by the end of the twelfth century. Following them were Cambridge (1209), Salamanca (1218), Montpellier (1220), Padua (1222), Florence (1321), Heidelberg (1386), St Andrews (1410), and Louvain (1425). Oxford and Paris united their individual colleges as universities early in the thirteenth century, and Cambridge did so soon after.

Untouchables. *See* Pariahs

Upanishads

Group of Hindu sacred texts believed to have been compiled between 800 and 300 B.C.E. The 108 known Upanishads (**Sanskrit** for "Sessions") present the earliest formulations of many of the basic concepts of **Hinduism**, such as the individual soul, the universal **Brahman**, and reincarnation. They are among the most revered texts in the Hindu tradition.

Ur

City of ancient **Sumer** in **Mesopotamia**. Southeast of **Babylon** on the **Euphrates River** (though the site is now in desert, not on the river), Ur was occupied from the fifth millennium to the fourth century B.C.E. In the mid-third millennium B.C.E. Ur was ruled by the **Akkadians**, but by the late third millennium there was a separate Empire of Ur. Ur was an important city in a lush fertile region. It became the capital of Sumer and was an important city under the Chaldean kings of Babylon. Ur was first excavated in the early twentieth century by British and American archaeologists.

Urban II (1042–1099)

Roman Catholic **pope** (1088–1099) who called for the First **Crusade**. Urban II called the Council of Clermont in 1095 and proclaimed a crusade to free the Holy Land that eventually reached **Jerusalem** in 1099.

Urban VI (1318–1389)

Roman Catholic pope (1378–1389) whose actions precipitated the **Great Schism** wherein two different popes were elected at once, ruling from 1378 to 1415. One pope was located in Rome while another was located in Avignon, France. In 1409 a council met to resolve the situation, and its members elected yet a third pope. Eventually a council accepted the resignation of one pope, deposed the other two, and elected a new pope in 1415.

Urbino, Duchy of (family name Montefeltro)

Powerful patrons of **Renaissance** art. During the Renaissance Urbino was an Italian center of art and architecture as well as the capital of a duchy controlled by the Montefeltro family from 1444 to 1508. The dukes of Urbino were patrons of artists like Piero della Francesca (who painted Federigo da Montefeltro and his wife, Battista Sforza, over the background of the central Italian principality) and literary figures such as Castiglione (whose setting for *The Book of the Courtier* was the court of Guidobaldo da Montefeltro).

Uruk

Ancient **Mesopotamian** city in the region that is now Iraq. One of the great cities of Sumer along with **Ur**, Uruk had walls six miles in circumference, built by Gilgamesh, according to the legendary *Epic of Gilgamesh*. The earliest settlement of Uruk dates to 5000 B.C.E. In the mid-third millennium it was ruled by the **Akkadians**, and later, as part of the Empire of Ur, Uruk was probably at its height.

Usman dan Fodio (1754–1817)

Islamic mystic and founder of the **Fulani**-based Sokoto caliphate in northwestern Nigeria. Usman dan Fodio, a **Muslim** scholar and a teacher, began to gather a large following, a community of believers. It became a rebellion against social and economic injustices. In 1804 he was declared an **imam**, and, preaching religious reform, he raised millenarian hopes among the people, who through a **jihad** formed their own state. Soon after he retired from politics to teach.

Utopia. See More, Sir Thomas

Uzbeks

Turkic group who emerged in the eleventh to fifteenth centuries from a mingling of Turkic, Mongolian, and Iranian peoples. In the early sixteenth century under Shaybani Khan, the Uzbeks created one of the last **steppe** empires, covering much of **Turkestan**. Further conquests were checked by their defeat by the **Safavid** Persians. Today Uzbeks are the majority ethnic group of Uzbekistan and form minorities in several other **Central Asian** states.

V

Vaishya

The third ranked of the four **varnas**, the major social groups of India's **Hindu** caste system. According to the ancient Code of Manu, their duty was to tend cattle and they may originally have been cattle herders. Later, the Vaishyas were primarily a mercantile class.

Valois

French royal family from Philip VI (1328) to the death of Henry II (1589). At Henry II's death the crown passed to the **Bourbon** family.

Vandals

Germanic tribe that entered the **Roman Empire** in the second century C.E. Constantine granted them lands on the banks of the Danube River. In 406 the Vandals moved through Gaul, devastating lands as they moved, and settled in Spain and North Africa, from which they attacked throughout the Mediterranean region by sea. In 455 they plundered the city of **Rome**. The Vandal kingdom in Africa declined by the sixth century.

Van Eyck, Jan (c. 1395–1441)

Netherlandish painter of the **Northern Renaissance**. Van Eyck found patronage in the court of John III of Holland (r. 1419–1425) and Philip the Good of Bruges (r. 1419–1467). Born in the Netherlands, by the end of his life Van Eyck was famous across Europe. He utilized oil paint (new to painters) to create paintings of extraordinary detail, not only of human figures but of architectural details and landscapes. His innovative use of color and light to create realism can be seen in *The Arnolfini Wedding* (1434).

Vargas, Getúlio (1883–1954)

President of Brazil (1930–1945, 1951–1954) whose revolutionary policies so changed the established order that his country was launched into the forefront of modern Latin American nations. Under Vargas's leadership, the balance of power in Brazil shifted from the individual states to the central government, and from the wealthy landowners to the middle and lower classes in urban areas. Vargas's most important accomplishments were modernizing the economy and industrializing the nation. Under pressure to resign, Vargas committed suicide in 1954.

Varna

The four basic delineations of caste in **Hindu** society consisting of, in order of social ranking: **Brahmins**, a priestly class; **Kshatriyas**, a class of warriors and rulers; **Vaishyas**, a class of cattle owners and merchants; and **Shudras**, a class of farmers and laborers. The term *varna* is derived from the **Sanskrit** word for "color," and it is theorized that it grew from an effort to make a distinction between the dominant light-skinned Aryan groups and the dark-skinned non-Aryan peoples of ancient India. Varna along with **jati** (regional subgroupings) form the caste system of India.

Adhering to the rules for each varna was a religious and—in early times—a legal duty. These rules no longer have any legal recognition, but they still influence social relations and conduct in India.

Varuna
In the Vedic period of India (1500–900 B.C.E.), the **Aryan** god who ruled the sky and water and personified authority. He later declined in importance in **Hindu** religion.

Vassal
In the feudal relationship, the subordinate person holding lands from a superior lord. Usually the vassal would hold lands from the lord and owe homage and allegiance to the lord, normally in the form of military service. A vassal might in turn be a lord to someone else who would be his vassal. Within the feudal structure a hierarchy of lords and vassals provided the military, legal, and social structure of the aristocracy.

Vedas
Most sacred and authoritative texts of **Hinduism**. They are the earliest **Sanskrit** scriptures, dating from as early as 1500 B.C.E. There are four basic collections consisting of hymns, sacrificial rites, chants, and occult formulas and spells. The oldest and most revered is the **Rigveda**, a collection of 1,028 hymns. They provide the earliest decipherable written record of the culture of ancient India.

Vedic
Indo-Aryan (Hindu) cultural term meaning "knowledge." The term *Vedic* often refers to the Indo-Aryan or early Indian philosophy that is the basis of **Hinduism**.

Venice
Powerful Italian medieval and **Renaissance** commercial city on the Adriatic Sea. During the **Middle Ages** the **city-state** of Venice was instrumental in conquering **Constantinople** during the Fourth **Crusade** (1204), and Venetian merchants such as **Marco Polo** traveled to China in the thirteenth century. This helped Venice into the strategic position of controlling east–west commerce. The Venetian Republic (run by a senate and the Council of Ten) grew in commercial and political power, defeating Genoa in 1380 and further securing its power as a seafaring power. During the Renaissance Venice played an important role, if lesser than Florence's. **Titian** was one of the great Venetian artists. Once the Portuguese had sailed all the way to the Far East (1498), Venice went into a decline. It gradually lost much of its territory to the Turks during the sixteenth century.

Versailles, Palace of
French palace built for **Louis XIV**, begun in 1669. Designed by Louis Le Vau, Jules Hardouin-Mansart, Charles Lebrun, and Antoine Coysevox, Versailles was meant to draw the aristocracy to the king's palace, where they could be controlled. The palace was completed in 1685. It is one of the finest examples of **baroque** architecture in France.

Versailles Treaty (1919)
Treaty that emerged from the **Paris Peace Conference** between Germany and the Allied powers at the end of **World War I**. Of the Allied powers (Britain, France, Italy, Japan, and the United States), only the United States refused to ratify the treaty, due to objections of the U.S. Congress. Germany signed the treaty under protest. The Versailles Treaty's main terms included the surrender of all German colonies; the return of Alsace-Lorraine to France; ceding lands to Belgium, Lithuania, Czechoslovakia, and Poland; German

reparations to Britain and France; German acceptance of guilt for causing the war; limitation of Germany's army to 100,000 men; and limitations on Germany's navy. Each of the Central powers countries received separate treaties.

Vesalius, Andreas (1514–1564)

Anatomist and author of *On the Fabric of the Human Body* (1543). Vesalius learned anatomy, like all anatomists of his day, from the great Roman author **Galen**. But Vesalius did not merely copy Galen blindly; he actually performed dissections on human bodies and questioned Galen's text. Vesalius saw that the great blood vessels originated from the heart, not from the liver, as in Galen's work. Vesalius established one of the foundation blocks of the **scientific revolution**—observation. His book was published in the same year as **Nicolaus Copernicus**'s *On the Revolution of the Heavenly Bodies*. Together Vesalius and Copernicus began the movement of science by the use of observation and mathematics.

Vespucci, Amerigo (1451–1512)

Italian explorer in the **Age of Exploration** for whom America is named. Vespucci made four sailing voyages to the New World for Spain, and his published descriptions were so widely read that his name, Amerigo, was adopted for the new continents. Vespucci was the first to refer to South America as the "New World."

Vezir/Wazir

Word used in **Islamic**, particularly Turko-Persian, contexts in reference to a high-ranking deputy to a ruler, such as a prime minister, or to another member of the bureaucratic or ministerial elite.

Vichy

Government of France established in 1940 under the authority of **Nazi** Germany during **World War II**. Northern France was conquered, occupied, and administered by German forces. Southern France was allowed to maintain its own government at Vichy, although only as a puppet of Germany. Run by Marshal Philippe Pétain in collaboration with **Adolf Hitler**, a new constitution was created. Vichy France was never recognized by the **Allies**, and after the Allied liberation of France in 1944 the Vichy government moved to Germany, where it collapsed along with Germany in 1945.

Victoria, Queen (1819–1901)

Queen of Great Britain (1837–1901) and Empress of India (1876–). Granddaughter of **George III** and married to Prince Albert of Saxe-Coburg-Gotha, Victoria (Alexandrina Victoria) had four sons and five daughters with Albert who married into several of the royal families of Europe. Victoria was related to the royal families of Belgium, Denmark, Germany, Greece, Norway, Romania, Russia, and Sweden. As queen she had great legislative influence and worked effectively with several prime ministers, especially Viscount Melbourne (William Lamb) and **Benjamin Disraeli**. She disliked intensely Prime Minister **William Gladstone**. During her reign Britain reached its greatest heights of power and prosperity, with an empire doubled in size upon which "the sun never set." Also during her reign the middle class gained expanded voting rights and the working class gained worker protections. At the 1861 death of Prince Albert, who had advised Victoria immensely, Victoria withdrew from the public until her golden (1887) and diamond (1897) jubilees. She died in 1901 in the sixty-fourth year of her reign survived by forty grandchildren and thirty-seven great-grandchildren and succeeded by her eldest son, Edward VII.

Vienna, Congress of (1814–1815)

Meeting and agreement reached at Vienna, Austria, by Austria, Britain, Prussia, Russia, and France as to the disposition of the empire left by the defeat of **Napoléon Bonaparte**. Spain, Portugal, and Sweden were also involved in the negotiations. The Congress of Vienna settled the frontiers of all territories north of the Alps because the Napoleonic Wars had disturbed previously existing boundaries and governments. The prominent individuals at the Congress were Fürst von Metternich from Austria, Viscount Castlereagh of Britain, Prince von Hardenberg of **Prussia**, Alexander I of Russia, and from France, Prince Talleyrand. The final treaty, signed June 19, 1815, was the most comprehensive treaty Europe had ever created, realigning territories and creating new states, and it lasted for more than forty years. However, the idea of **nationalism** and self-determination of inhabitants was ignored, and that would become the undoing of the work of the Congress of Vienna in the second half of the nineteenth century.

Viet Cong

South Vietnam–based **communist guerrilla** organization that fought the South Vietnamese government and its U.S. allies. Founded as the National Front for the Liberation of South Vietnam in 1960, it was called the Viet Cong by its opponents. Directed and supplied by North Vietnam, the Viet Cong waged an effective campaign that, with the help of North Vietnamese troops, led to the communist takeover of South Vietnam in 1975.

Viet Minh

Vietnamese **communist guerrilla** movement founded in 1941 by **Ho Chi Minh** and other members of the Indo-Chinese Communist Party for the purpose of expelling the French and Japanese from Vietnam. Initially it had support from the United States. At the end of **World War II**, Ho Chi Minh proclaimed the Democratic Republic of Vietnam and directed the Viet Minh against French efforts to regain control over the country. Following the Viet Minh victory at **Dien Bien Phu** in 1954, the French ceded independence to Vietnam, which was partitioned into North Vietnam and South Vietnam.

Vietnam War

War for the unification of Vietnam waged by North Vietnam and its **Viet Cong** allies in South Vietnam against the government of Saigon and its U.S. allies. The war had no clear starting point, but **guerrilla** fighting in South Vietnam took place after the creation of the Viet Cong in 1960. The United States sent advisors to assist the South Vietnamese, and in 1964 President **Lyndon B. Johnson** was given congressional approval in the Tonkin Gulf Resolution to expand U.S. military action against the communists. By 1967 there were 400,000 U.S. troops in South Vietnam. The war, however, proved politically divisive in the United States. After North Vietnam and the Viet Cong launched the **Tet Offensive** moral in South Vietnam and the United States declined, eventually leading to the withdrawal of U.S. forces in 1973 and the fall of Saigon to the communist forces in April 1975. Vietnam was reunified under the Hanoi government in 1976.

Vijayanagar

City in south India founded in 1336 as the capital of a powerful **Hindu** empire of the same name, which is **Sanskrit** for "City of Victory." The empire reached its peak under Krishna Deva Raya (r. 1509–1529), but succumbed to attacks by the **Muslim** kingdoms of Bijapur, Ahmadnagar, and Golconda. The city was destroyed in 1565 although the empire continued for some time afterward. It prevented the Muslims from extending their rule over the southernmost part of India.

Vikings

Seafaring Scandinavian peoples who raided, traded, and settled across much of Europe and the North Atlantic between the eighth and the eleventh century. Swedes settled in what is today Russia; Danes conquered lands in England and France (Normandy, taken from North men); Norwegians set up kingdoms in Scotland and Ireland; Eric the Red colonized Iceland and set up settlements in Greenland; and **Leif Eiriksson** set up a community in North America circa 1000. The Vikings were seeking wealth and new land due to rapid population growth in their homelands. Their trade went as far as Byzantium (now **Istanbul**) and the **Muslim Middle East**. During the tenth century power was consolidated into larger, more powerful kingdoms.

Villa, Pancho (1878–1923)

Mexican revolutionary who fought for labor and land reform. The struggle for reform led to taking up arms against the corrupt Porfirio Díaz regime, which favored large landowners and industrialists. This turned into the Mexican Revolution (1910–1920). Villa fought alongside **Francisco Madero** (1873–1913) and **Venustiano Carranza** (1859–1920), but in 1914 Villa broke from Carranza and allied with **Emiliano Zapata** (1879–1919). Villa invaded the United States in 1916 but was driven back into Mexico by the U.S. Army. Villa helped to overthrow Carranza in 1920 and was assassinated in 1923.

Vínland

Land, likely in Newfoundland, Canada, discovered by **Leif Eiriksson** around 1000 C.E. According to sagas, Leif named it Vínland for the wild grape vines, hence "wine land." Leif also claimed that there was wild grain growing there. Modern research has discovered a Norse trade settlement in this region dated to 1000 C.E. There is substantial proof of Norse settlements in North America.

Virgil (Vergil) (full name Publius Vergilius) (70–19 B.C.E.)

Roman poet. Famous in his own day, Virgil remains widely read today and is best remembered for the *Georgics* (36–29 B.C.E.), an instructional guide to farming, and *The Aeneid* (26–19 B.C.E.), which was promoted by the emperor Augustus (**Octavian**) as a national epic glorifying the **Roman Empire**.

Virgin Mary

Mother of **Jesus of Nazareth** resulting from a miraculous conception according to **Christianity**. Jesus was conceived in Mary by the power of the Holy Spirit. Catholicism also claims for Mary perpetual virginity, immaculate conception (was born and lived without original sin), and assumption into heaven. Worship of Mary as Mother of God became popular from the fifth century onward. Mary has been the subject of much art, music, and literature. Her humility and obedience to the message of God have made her a model of the Christian life, particularly for women. Mary is a saint in the **Roman Catholic Church**.

Visconti

Italian family who controlled the duchy of Milan and all of Lombardy (1277–1447). The first Visconti Duke of Milan was Archbishop Ottone Visconti (1207–1295). The lordship became hereditary in 1349. The Viscontis sought to centralize the power of the state and wanted to expand their power through Tuscany and Umbria while preventing **Venice** from expanding in mainland Italy. After the last Visconti ruler of Milan, Filippo Maria Visconti, died in 1447 the Viscontis were succeeded by the **Sforza** family.

Vishnu

One of the principal deities of **Hinduism**, regarded as the preserver of the world and its moral order. Vishnu is worshiped in his various incarnations, or avatars, the most popular being Rama and Krishna his seventh and eighth incarnations, respectively.

Visigoths. *See* Goths

Vladimir I, Saint (956–1015)

Grand Duke of **Kiev** (978–1015) who established the **Eastern Orthodox Church** in Russia. Vladimir converted to Christianity, married the sister of the Byzantine emperor, and brought the Eastern Orthodox Church to Kiev. He became the patron saint of Russia.

Voltaire (1694–1778)

French **Enlightenment** writer, author of *Candide* (1759). Voltaire (born François-Marie Arouet) wrote voluminously, producing plays, poems, novels, histories, and essays. He was considered one of the greatest wits of his age. Voltaire worked for Louis XV and for King Frederick of Prussia. *Candide* shocked its audience and religious authorities, and yet it became a best seller for its humor, irreverence, and emphasis on limits and suffering—contrary to the traditions of the Enlightenment.

Vo Nguyen Giap (1912–)

Vietnamese general and political leader. Giap, a member of the Communist Party, led **Viet Minh** forces against the Japanese and captured Hanoi in 1945. Under the political leadership of **Ho Chi Minh** Giap commanded forces against the French, winning a decisive victory at **Dien Bien Phu** in 1954. He later used successful **guerrilla** tactics against South Vietnamese and U.S. forces in the **Vietnam War**. Giap planned the **Tet Offensive**, which resulted in heavy losses but proved effective in undermining U.S. and South Vietnamese morale.

Vuh. *See* Popol Vuh

W

Wahhabism
Central Arabian expression of the prevalent eighteenth-century theme of rural Islamic revivalism. Muhammad Abd al-Wahhab (1703–1792) labeled **Sufism**, for its veneration of saints, as **polytheism** and its practitioners as apostates. Wahhab insisted that the **Quran** and the **Hadith** were the only reliable sources for comprehending divine will, and he denounced unthinking adherence to any inherited practice. He believed that responsibility lies with individual **Muslims** to obey divine commands contained in the Quran and the Hadith. The Wahhabi message of self-generated purification is adhered to in parts of **Islam**. Wahhabism forms the ideological basis of the modern state of Saudi Arabia and has been exported from there to other locales such as Chechnya, Afghanistan, India, and the Philippines.

Wallenstein, Albrecht von (1583–1634)
German general of the **Thirty Years' War**. Born in Bohemia and a convert to Catholicism, Wallenstein became the leading commander of the forces of the **Holy Roman Empire** to crush the **Protestant** revolt. He defeated the Bohemian and Danish armies but was in turn defeated by the elite Swedish army under King **Gustavus II**, although Gustavus was killed. The emperor, Ferdinand II, feared that Wallenstein had intrigued with Gustavus and had him arrested. Trying to escape, Wallenstein was assassinated.

Walpole, Horace (1717–1797)
English author and wit, son of **Robert Walpole**, a prime minister. Walpole wrote voluminous correspondence as well as literature including the gothic novel *The Castle of Otranto* (1764). Walpole also served in **Parliament** (1741–1768), like his father.

Walpole, Robert (1676–1745)
English statesman and prime minister (not yet an official title). As first lord of the treasury and chancellor of the exchequer, from 1721 until his resignation in 1742, Walpole was the most powerful man in Britain.

Wang Anshi (1021–86)
Chinese scholar and statesman who carried out reform efforts during the **Song** dynasty. Serving as chief councilor (1070–1073), Wang Anshi sought to encourage economic development and strengthen the state by promoting reforms that stabilized prices, reduced land taxes, provided low-interest loans to help farmers, and reorganized the military and police forces. Opponents of his reforms forced him to resign and reversed most of his new measures, but he remained a figure of controversy.

Wang Jingwei (Wang Ching-wei) (1883–1944)
Early Chinese supporter of **Sun Yat-sen** who was arrested and sentenced to life imprisonment in 1910 for attempting to assassinate the regent of China. Released in

1912, Wang studied in France until 1917, when he became personal assistant to Sun until Sun's death in 1925. He formed an uneasy truce with **Chiang Kai-shek** to lead the **Guomindang**. He served as president of the Nationalist Party (1932–1938) with Chiang Kai-shek as head of the military, but broke with Chiang in 1938, advocating peace with Japan and continuing the struggle against the communists. From 1940 to his death he was premier of the Japanese puppet government of China at Nanjing.

Wang Mang

Founder of the short-lived Chinese Xin dynasty (9–25 C.E.). He used his position as regent to usurp the throne of the **Han** rulers, dividing the Han dynasty into the Former Han (206 B.C.E.–9 C.E.) and the Later Han (25–220 C.E.). He attempted to implement idealistic policies based on **Confucianism**, such as equally distributing the land. These measures were impossible to enforce and turned the wealthy landholders against Wang Mang. He was killed in 23 C.E., but it was two more years until order was restored and the Han dynasty continued.

Warlords

Chinese regional military commanders who during the years following the 1911 collapse of the **Qing** dynasty took on much of the effective control of China. Peak years of warlord control over China were 1916–1928. After 1928 the **Guomindang** gradually established control over most of China, although regional warlords often maintained effective power over areas of the country as subordinate commanders to the central Guomindang authority, especially in remote western parts of the country, until the 1940s.

Warring States Period

Period of Chinese history from 403 to 221 B.C.E. when between ten and twelve states competed for power in China. Although there was a nominal **Zhou** king, he ruled only a small territory. Eventually one of the states, the **Qin**, unified seven major states and several minor ones into China, bringing the era of competing states to an end. The Warring States period saw philosophy and literature flourish. Among the great philosophers of the period were **Mencius**, associated with **Confucianism**; **Zhuangzi**, a major teacher of **Daoism**; and **Han Feizi**, the legalist thinker. The Japanese, in reference to this period, named the era 1467–1568 C.E. "The Warring States Period."

Wars of Independence, Latin American (1808–1826)

Movement that gained independence for Latin American countries from Spanish or Portuguese control. Latin American countries were governed by officials from Spain or Portugal. Creoles, individuals born in the Americas of Spanish or Portuguese ancestry, resented administrative control from abroad. Inspired by the **Enlightenment** and emboldened by Napoleonic invasions of Spain and Portugal, creoles such as **Simón Bolívar** and **Bernardo O'Higgins** took part in revolts and uprisings between 1808 and 1825 that brought independence to most colonies in Latin America.

Wars of Religion. *See* French Wars of Religion

Washington, George (1752–1799)

Commander in chief of the **Continental Army** during the **American Revolution** and first U.S. president (1789–1797). Washington, a rich landowner in Virginia, distinguished himself militarily by fighting for the British in the French and Indian War. The Second **Continental Congress** appointed him commander in chief of the colonial forces, both for his proven military ability and because as a southerner he could bring some of the southern states, less inclined to rebellion, into the colonial cause. Delegates to the Constitutional Convention unanimously voted Washington to be the first president of the United States, a position he occupied for eight years. Despite offers to stay in leadership of the country—and even to become king—Washington stepped down after his two terms were up, retiring to his estate, Mount Vernon. This established a precedent for future presidents to avoid seeking a third term. Washington's contributions as a general and as the first executive of the United States led Americans to begin calling him "the Father of Our Country."

Waterloo, Battle of (1815)

Decisive battle ending **Napoléon Bonaparte**'s reign. Napoléon had been defeated and exiled to the island of Elba in 1814, but he escaped and regathered his army in 1815. Near the Belgian town of Waterloo, on June 18, 1815, the French forces met the combined British, Dutch, Belgian, and German armies commanded by the British general Arthur Wellesley, the Duke of Wellington. The main **Prussian** force under Field Marshal Gebhard von Blücher was delayed, and the French army attacked the center of the British until the Prussians arrived and attacked the French flank, allowing Wellington to advance and route the French. Napoléon was defeated, abdicated, and was exiled to the island of Saint Helena in the South Atlantic for the rest of his life.

Watermills

Water-powered mills, probably developed in China or the **Middle East** and common in Europe in the **Middle Ages**. The Romans had watermills, but they were not widespread. By the early Middle Ages horizontal and vertical mills—both undershot (water flowing under the wheel to turn it) and overshot (water led through a millrace to the top of the wheel)—existed. Watermills became an important source of power to grind grain, full cloth, saw wood, and hammer iron.

Watt, James (1736–1819)

Scottish inventor of the steam engine. Watts altered a Newcomen atmospheric engine into the much more usable steam engine by 1769. The steam engine was initially used to power pumps in mines, but in 1782 Watts invented a rotary steam engine with a far wider application: ability to turn a shaft and drive machinery. By 1800 Watt's firm had built hundreds of steam engines. The **Industrial Revolution** was driven by steam power.

Watteau, Jean-Antoine (1684–1721)

French painter of the rococo period. Watteau broke from the **baroque** style of his predecessors. His was a style of light subject matter and bright and peaceful settings with a touch of eighteenth-century frivolity but with classical elements. One of his best-known paintings is *A Pilgrimage for Cythera* (1717).

WAVES (1942–1972)

Program established during **World War II** as a women's component of the United States Navy. The WAVES (Women Accepted for Volunteer Emergency Service) provided women in the navy with a more formal status than was accorded the 11,000 "yeomen (female)" who served in **World War I**. Serving in noncombat positions at shore installations primarily in the continental United States, the WAVES reached a peak strength of 86,000 in 1944. In 1972 the WAVES program was terminated as women were integrated into the regular navy.

Wayang

Javanese classical puppet drama form in which puppets are manipulated behind a translucent screen. The term is derived from the Javanese word for "shadow." Possibly of south Indian origin, wayang developed into a high art form used to dramatize the Hindu epics *Ramayana* and *Mahabharata* and other mythical stories. Some forms of wayang use wooden puppets or even live actors.

Weber, Max (1864–1920)

German sociologist and political economist best known for *The Protestant Ethic and the Spirit of Capitalism* (1904–1905). Published in English translation in 1930, the work made the argument that **Protestant** religion, in particular **Calvinism**, created an atmosphere of hard work and pursuit of wealth as a sign of one's election (salvation) within predestination and thereby fueled the development of **capitalism**. Protestantism fostered a spirit of discipline and rigor that enabled people to successfully acquire wealth.

Weimar Republic

German republic established in 1919. The national assembly met in Weimar and wrote a new constitution providing two legislative houses and a president. Weak from the start, the Weimar government never gained the support of all the population, and especially not of the military. When the worldwide depression hit in 1929 Germany suffered severely, and the Weimar Republic was ineffective in responding. Increasingly groups formed with the intent to overthrow the republic. In the confusion the National Socialist German Workers' Party (**Nazi** Party) gained control in 1933 and overthrew the constitution.

Wergild

Payment in Anglo-Saxon societies made by a murderer or maimer to the relatives of the victim. Apparently common in early **Germanic tribes**, the *wergild* ("man-price") was an amount fixed by the age, gender, and status of the victim and delivered as recompense to the victim's relatives for any damages done.

Wesley, John (1703–1791)

English minister and founder of the Methodist Church. Son of a Church of England minister, John Wesley and his brother Charles led an evangelical revival movement within the church based on discipline, or method—hence the name *Methodist.* Wesley worked as a missionary in Georgia (1735–1738) and from 1739 to 1744 built a church organization. The Anglican Church shut Wesley out, but he continued to preach in fields and streets. In 1744 the first conference of Methodist ministers met, although Wesley remained loyal to the Church of England. He ordained Thomas Coke and Francis Asbury to lead the Methodist Episcopal Church in America. Wesley became an influential leader of the **abolitionist** movement with his *Notes on Slavery* (1774).

Westernization

Term used to describe the process by which non-Western societies adopt Western (European and U.S.) values, institutions, or technology. Some degree of Westernization took place in many Asian and African lands the nineteenth and twentieth centuries as a result of European and American global dominance. It often took place as the result of European imperialism, but it has also occurred voluntarily, both as a result of the need to compete with Western nations politically, economically, and militarily and simply due to the appeal of aspects of Western culture. It has seldom resulted in the complete rejection of a non-Western society's cultural heritage.

Westminster

English region in a western suburb of London, seat of the British government. William II first built his palace in Westminster circa 1090, and by 1160 courts were meeting in Westminster. By the thirteenth century Westminster was considered the major site of the English courts, including **Parliament**'s **House of Lords** and, later, the **House of Commons**. Today Westminster is the seat of most branches of government of the United Kingdom.

Westminster Abbey

English monastic and royal church in **Westminster**, London. Westminster Abbey was rebuilt starting in 1245 in the **Gothic** style. Because a royal palace and the courts resided in Westminster, Westminster Abbey became a royal church, and many of Britain's monarchs have been crowned, married, and buried there. Many other British notables are buried in Westminster Abbey.

Westphalia, Peace of. *See* Westphalia, Treaty of

Westphalia, Treaty of (1648)

Treaty ending the **Thirty Years' War** (1618–1648). The Treaty of Westphalia established independent states in Switzerland, the United Provinces (the Netherlands), and the German states, thereby blocking the **Holy Roman Empire** from becoming a unified Catholic kingdom and the **Habsburgs** from making the entire Netherlands Catholic. The treaty ended the war, giving France Alsace and Lorraine, giving Sweden German territories, and protecting **Calvinism** and **Lutheranism**.

Whitby, Synod of (664)

Ecclesiastical (church) council to determine the proper date for Easter. The Scottish and Irish calculation of when Easter should be differed from the Roman calculation used at Canterbury. The outcome of the synod was to use the dating system of Rome, and nearly all English churches followed suit. Although important, the Synod of Whitby was not the major confrontation of the Roman church and the Irish church, as Saint Bede and subsequent historians have claimed.

White Lotus Rebellion (1796–1804)

Uprising by a loose network of Chinese Buddhists against the **Qing** (**Manchu**) dynasty. Although the rebellion was put down, it weakened the Qing and is regarded by some historians as the beginning of the decline of that dynasty. White Lotus was a popular form of **Buddhism** with a millenarian expectation of future catastrophe that can be traced back to the eleventh or twelfth century. It led uprisings against the **Yuan** (**Mongol**) dynasty in the mid-fourteenth century.

William of Normandy (William I or William the Conqueror) (1027–1087)

Duke of Normandy and king of England (1066–1087). Second cousin to the English king Edward the Confessor, William was purportedly promised the English throne by both Edward and Harold Godwinson, Edward's successor to the throne. William invaded England to take the throne in 1066, defeated King Harold, and was declared King William I of England. He ordered a survey—the Domesday Book—of all property for taxation and created a well-organized and efficient government. William spent much of his later life on the Continent fighting the king of France. He was wounded and died there.

William I, "the Silent" (William of Orange) (1533–1584)

Founder of the **United Provinces** of the Netherlands. William was Duke of

Orange and Count of Nassau-Dillenburg. Loyal statesman for Emperor Charles V and King **Philip II** of Spain, made stadholder, William provided leadership for the Dutch Revolt against Spain and Philip II and rallied the Dutch provinces to unify and fight. He became a **Calvinist** in 1573. William was assassinated by a royalist sympathizer in 1584.

Wilson, Woodrow (1856–1924)

Twenty-eighth president of the United States (1913–1921). Following an academic career including president of Princeton University, Wilson was elected governor of New Jersey in 1910 as a Democrat, won the presidency in 1912, and was re-elected in 1916. A progressive reformer, he established the Federal Reserve System and the Federal Trade Commission. His domestic agenda was soon overtaken by diplomatic crises with Mexico and, more significantly, the beginning of **World War I.** Declaring U.S. neutrality, Wilson sought to keep the United States at peace while mediating an end to the conflict. Repeated violations of the United States' neutral rights on the high seas by German submarines, and the resultant deaths of numerous Americans, led to the United States' entry into the war on the allied side in April 1917. Wilson promoted a nonvindictive peace, based on his Fourteen Points, at the **Paris Peace Conference** and the resulting **Versailles Treaty.** While he obtained Allied consent to the creation of the **League of Nations,** designed to preserve the peace, he could not prevent the inclusion of harsh terms against Germany in other areas. Republican Party opposition to the League of Nations led the U.S. Congress to reject the treaty.

Windmills

Machines using wind as a source of power, used in Europe from the **Middle Ages.**

Possibly brought to Europe from the **Middle East** during the **Crusades,** the earliest known reference to windmills is from a Persian document from 644 C.E. Persian millwrights were sent by **Genghis Khan** to China, where windmills were used in irrigation. The windmill began to appear in Europe in the twelfth century and became common by the fourteenth century. Windmills, like watermills, were used for a wide variety of jobs such as grinding grain, crushing olives or mustard seed, fulling cloth, and sawing wood. Although widespread, they were most effective in the Netherlands and eastern England where the land was flat and the winds regularly blew off the oceans.

Witchcraft

The exercise of supernatural powers by certain humans. Beliefs in witchcraft are found in most of the world's cultures and often involve the control of nature and communication with a spirit world. Such beliefs declined with the acceptance of a more secular worldview in the modern era, though the late twentieth century saw a small revival of nature-oriented witchcraft as part of the development of esoteric New Age belief systems.

Witch Craze

Name often given to the upsurge in prosecutions for **witchcraft** in Europe and, to a lesser degree, British North America, in the fifteenth to seventeenth centuries. Accusations of witchcraft were not common in the **Middle Ages,** but in the fifteenth century the idea spread among learned clergy and officials that witches were people in league with the devil, not simply people who used magic to do bad deeds. This distinction made witchcraft much more serious, and hundreds of thousands of people were accused, with probably more than 50,000 people executed. About

80 percent of them were women because women were regarded as the weaker sex and so more likely to give in to the devil's temptations. The witch craze declined as people in positions of power no longer believed that the devil would bother to work through human agents.

Wollstonecraft, Mary. *See* Godwin, Mary Wollstonecraft

Woman's Suffrage

The right of women to participate in political life that inspired movements in major Western and some non-Western nations in the nineteenth and early twentieth centuries. Encouraged by the ideals of equality and **democracy**, woman's suffrage was advocated as early as the late eighteenth century by the British writer **Mary Wollstonecraft Godwin**. Women gained the right to vote at the national level first in New Zealand, in 1893, but it was only after **World War I** that most Western nations granted women suffrage, including Britain in 1918, Germany in 1919, the United States in 1920, and France in 1944. At the start of the twenty-first century women in some **Muslim** countries, such as Saudi Arabia, still did not have the right to take part in politics.

World Bank

Institution and agency of the United Nations based in Washington DC that was created after the **Bretton Woods Conference** in 1944 to promote international economic prosperity and stability. It consists of the International Bank for Reconstruction and Development (IBRD), established in 1945, and the International Development Association, established in 1960. Member nations contribute money to the World Bank, which then lends it to developing countries to aid in economic development projects. A special fund was established in 1977 for assistance to the poorest countries.

World System

Concept first developed by the French scholar Ferdinand Braudel and systematized by U.S. political-social scientist Immanuel Wallerstein. It argues that the central theme of modern world history since 1500 has been the creation of a world economic system centered in western Europe. Most political, cultural, and economic developments have been shaped by this world system. It is the central story of history, along with shifts in the core, semiperiphery, and periphery. Some world historians have modified it by seeing smaller "world-systems" existing before 1500, such as an Islamic world trading/cultural/political system between 1000 and 1500. One scholar, Andre Frank, traces world systems back 5,000 years. A central theme of world history, some historians maintain, is the creation and impact of the world system or world systems.

World War I

War between the Allied forces (France, Britain, Russia, Japan, Serbia, and Italy) and the Central powers (Germany, **Austria-Hungary**, the **Ottoman Empire**, and Bulgaria). It began in the summer of 1914 and concluded after an Allied victory with an armistice on November 11, 1918, and the **Versailles Treaty** in 1919, which resulted from the **Paris Peace Conference**. A number of countries joined the Allies later in the war, most importantly the United States in 1917. The war was sparked by **nationalist** rivalries in the Balkans. The fundamental causes of the conflict include colonial and nationalist rivalries among the European powers and fear of Germany's growing military might and imperialist ambitions. The war saw the overthrow of the German and Russian monarchies, the disintegration of the Austro-Hungarian and Ottoman empires, the creation of several new states in Europe based on the principle of national self-determination, and the emergence of the United States as a world power.

World War II
War fought between the **Allies** (Britain, France, and from 1941 the Soviet Union and the United States) and the **Axis Powers** (Germany, Italy, and Japan). The war began separately in Asia with Japan's invasion of China in 1937 and in Europe with Germany's invasion of Poland in 1939. It ended with Allied victories in Europe in May 1945 and in Asia in August of that year. The principal cause of the war was the expansionist policies of the militaristic, ultranationalist regimes of Germany, Italy, and Japan in the 1930s. It was the largest conflict in world history in scale; an estimated 15 million military personnel and 35 to 40 million civilians died. The racist nature of the Axis states resulted in atrocities unprecedented in modern times, such as the **Rape of Nanking** and, most notably, the **Holocaust**. World War II saw policies of **Nazi** Germany, Fascist Italy, and imperialist Japan discredited and the emergence of the United States and the Soviet Union as the world's two principal powers, and it contributed to the disintegration of the European colonial empires and the creation of the **United Nations Organization**.

Worms, Concordat of (1122)
Settlement of the first Lateran Council that officially ended the **Investiture Controversy**, a conflict between the **Roman Catholic Church** and secular rulers over who had the right to name (invest) regional church officials such as bishops and abbots.

Worms, Diet of (1521)
Meeting of Christian clergy and between Holy Roman Emperor **Charles V** and **Martin Luther** to discuss Luther's teachings. It was held in Worms, Germany. Luther took a stand for reforms in the church, and his teachings were formally condemned in the **Edict of Worms**.

Worms, Edict of (1521)
Condemnation by Holy Roman Emperor **Charles V** of **Martin Luther**'s beliefs. Charles V called a meeting in the German city of Worms, the **Diet of Worms**, where the proclamation called the Edict of Worms was issued. It placed Luther outside the law (meaning that anyone who harmed him would not be punished) and prohibited dissemination of his teachings. The Edict of Worms established the confrontation between many of the states of Europe and the rising **Protestantism**.

Wright, Richard (1908–1960)
African American writer best known for his novel *Native Son* (1940). Born to poor, illiterate Mississippi sharecropper parents, Wright is one of the best-known African American writers and the first powerful interpreter and representative of the African American experience. His writing deals with individuals alienated by repressive, materialist American society.

Wright, Wilbur and Orville
(1867–1912, 1871–1948)
The first men to fly in a motor-driven, heavier-than-air machine. On December 17, 1903, at Kill Devil Hill near Kitty Hawk, North Carolina, Orville Wright flew an airplane the brothers had constructed for twelve seconds, traveling 120 feet (37 m). Later Wilbur stayed aloft for fifty-nine seconds, flying 852 feet (260 m). The airplane had a wingspan of 40 feet (12 m) and a twelve-horsepower engine.

Wudi. *See* Han Wudi (Wu-ti) (Emperor Wu)

Wu Zhao (Wu Chao) (c. 627–705)
Second wife of **Tang** emperor Gaozong (r. 650–683) and China's only woman to found a dynasty. An imperial concubine, she became the power behind the throne late in her husband's reign and under the reigns of two sons. In 690 she took the unprecedented step of seizing control of the throne and established a short-lived **Zhou** dynasty ruling as emperor (not empress). Later Chinese historians condemned her as a wicked tyrant and an example of the danger of women in power. Modern scholars see her as an able if ruthless ruler.

Xavier, Saint Francis (1506–1552)
Spanish Jesuit missionary to the Far East. Francis helped **Ignatius Loyola** found the **Society of Jesus** in 1540. In that year he was sent by King John III of Portugal to India to spread **Christianity**. He preached in India, Malacca, and Japan, converting tens of thousands. While trying to gain admission to the Chinese mainland he died. He was declared a saint in 1622.

Xenophon (c. 435–354 B.C.E.)
Ancient Greek historian, philosopher, and general. Born in **Athens**, Xenophon studied with **Socrates**. He commanded an army under the Persian prince Cyrus and wrote a history of the campaign. He also wrote a history of Greece as a continuation of the history of **Thucydides** and a work about Socrates that explains Socrates' philosophy.

Xerxes I, "the Great" (r. 486–465 B.C.E.)
King of ancient Persia and invader of **Athens**. Xerxes succeeded **Darius I**, added Egypt to the Persian empire, and invaded Greece (480 B.C.E.) with an army of 150,000 and a navy of 700 ships. At the Battle of Thermopylae a Greek force of 9,000 held the Persians for two days, allowing the Athenian navy time to outmaneuver the Persian navy and destroy it at the **Battle of Salamis**. Xerxes withdrew, and his army was defeated at the **Battle of Plataea** in 479 B.C.E.

Xia (traditional dates 2200–1766 B.C.E.)
Chinese dynasty, traditionally the first dynasty founded by the son of Yu, one of China's mythical cultural heroes. Supposedly the dynasty ruled much of the **Yellow River** basin, but many modern scholars believe that the dynasty was a later invention in order to give greater antiquity to the centralized Chinese state. Some scholars connect archaeological evidence to the legendary Xia.

Xi'an (Hsi-an)
Chinese city and capital of the **Qin** dynasty in northwestern China. An ancient city, Xi'an served as the capital of the former **Han** dynasty and was renamed Chang'an. Later it became the imperial capital again under the **Tang**. Under the Tang Chang'an was perhaps the world's largest and wealthiest city. Under the **Ming** it was given the its present name of Xi'an ("Western Peace") and has remained an important regional center.

Xi'an Incident (1936)
Kidnapping of Chinese **Guomindang** leader **Chiang Kai-shek** by one of his military commanders, Zhang Xueliang. Chiang was forced to agree to an alliance between the Guomindang and the communists against the Japanese. It marked a temporary truce between the two groups and an official hardening of resistance to Japanese efforts to dominate China.

Xingjiang (Hsin-chiang)
Large Chinese territory in the northeastern part of the country, a region also called eastern **Turkestan**. Traditionally the arid

region was the home to thriving oasis communities that served as posts along the **Silk Road**. In the mid-eighteenth century it was brought under Chinese control by the **Qing** dynasty. With a majority non-Chinese, mostly Uighur- and other Turkic-speaking **Muslim** population, Xingjiang was the source of many rebellions in the nineteenth century and fell under the influence of the Soviet Union in the second quarter of the twentieth century until the Communists consolidated their control over it in 1950.

Xiongnu (Hsiung-nu)

The first nomadic confederation to organize the tribes of the **steppe** on a large scale to confront China. They were a **Central Asian** nomadic group that posed a military threat to the states of China from the fifth century B.C.E. to the fifth century C.E. The unifier of the Xiongnu was Maodun (209 B.C.E.). They became increasingly well organized, prompting the states of northern China to erected a system of wall fortifications. The emperor **Han Wudi** (r. 140–87 B.C.E.) launched a vigorous campaign against them that included expanding Chinese control into **Manchuria** and northern Korea to outflank them in the east, and expeditions to **Turkestan** to find allies against them in the west. Eventually the Xiongnu confederacy split and became less of a threat to China. In the fourth century other Central Asian peoples overran northern China.

See also Great Wall

Xuanzang (Hsuan-tsang) (602–664)

Chinese **Buddhist** scholar and pilgrim famous for his travel and study in India. In 629 Xuanzang journeyed to India via **Central Asia** and studied at the famous monastery of Nalanda in the eastern Gangetic Plain. While in India he attracted many Buddhist followers and the patronage of the Indian ruler Harsha. Returning to China in 645, he brought back many Buddhist texts. His *Records of the Western Region of the Great Tang Dynasty* provides important information on India, and his life was the basis of the popular Chinese novel *Journey to the West*.

Xunzi (Hsun-tzu) (c. 300–237 B.C.E.)

Important Chinese philosopher noted for his opposition to the **Confucian** and **Mencian** idea that human nature is fundamentally good. Xunzi taught that education and strict rules of order and propriety are needed to control human emotions that lead to immoral behavior. His ideas had some influence on **legalism**.

Yahweh

Hebrew for "god." The **Early Hebrews** originally worshipped many gods, but according to their scriptures, around 1750 B.C.E. **Abraham** came to an understanding that there was but one god, Yahweh, a name which probably meant "causes to be." By Moses's time, circa 1300 B.C.E., Yahweh was seen as the one and only creator and sustainer god. The Hebrews were required to follow Yahweh's ethical standards and laws.

Yamagata Aritomo (1838–1922)

Japanese general and statesman who served as one of the **genro,** or senior officials, during the **Meiji** period. He was a strong advocate of the modernization of the Japanese armed forces and the most important builder of the modern Japanese army. He served as prime minister (1889–1891 and 1898–1900). Yamagata also served as chief of staff during the **Russo-Japanese War.** He continued to be one of the most influential figures in Japanese politics to his death. Few leaders did more than Yamagata to shape the transformation of Japan into a modern industrial and military power in the late nineteenth and early twentieth centuries.

Yamato

Name for a clan in ancient Japan and for the earliest Japanese state its members helped to create that eventually unified most of the Japanese archipelago. The Yamato clan, associated with the sun goddess **Amaterasu**, emerged in the fifth or sixth century, although the exact chronology is not clear. In the sixth century the Yamato kings introduced **Buddhism, Confucianism,** and writing to Japan from Korean and in the seventh century the Yamato court opened diplomatic relations with the **Sui** dynasty and began to create a bureaucratic state modeled on China. The present imperial family of Japan is descended from the Yamato clan, making it the world's oldest royal family. The country of Japan was originally known as Yamato, although the Japanese state adopted the name *Nippon* from the Chinese (meaning "Land of the Rising Sun").

Yangban

Term for the Korean aristocracy prior to the twentieth century. Literally meaning "two sides," the term *yangban* refers to the civil and military officials who served the Korean state. It came into use during the **Koryo** period (935–1392) and gradually came to refer to the hereditary aristocracy who served as the state officials that dominated society. Economically, the yangban class was based on the ownership of land and slaves. Yangban prized learning and sought to demonstrate or renew their status by excelling in the **civil service examinations.** Besides serving the state and administering their estates, yangban—especially under the Yi dynasty (1392–1910)—wrote poetry, painted, pursued scholarship, and lived according to a strict code of **Confucianist** ethical norms. The status was legally abolished after 1894, but yangban families continued to serve as Korea's elite until the social upheavals that followed **World War II**.

Yang Guifei (Yang Kuei-fei)
Concubine of the **Tang** emperor Xuanzong (r. 712–756) and notorious Chinese beauty and political schemer. She is said to have used the emperor's infatuation with her to secure a position for her brother Yang Guozhong as his chief minister and to help an adventurer of Turkic origin, **An Lushan**, become influential at court. Xuanzong is said to have spent so much time with her that he neglected his duties, endangering the empire. An Lushan led a revolt in 755, forcing the emperor and his court to flee. The members of the court forced the emperor to execute Yang and her brother. The love affair between Yang Guifei and the emperor has long been a popular subject of Chinese literature and is used as a cautionary tale by Chinese moralists on the danger of women in positions of power.

Yangshao Culture (c. 4500–3000 B.C.E.)
Neolithic culture in the middle **Yellow River** valley named for a site in northern Henan province in China. Yangshao was based on agriculture, mainly millet, and produced red burnished pottery often painted with black designs. It later evolved into the **Longshan** culture, the latter ancestral to **Shang**, China's earliest civilization.

Yangzi River (Yangtze River or Chang Jiang)
River flowing 3,915 miles (6,300 km) that rises in the Kunlun Mountains of Tibet and flows across south-central China to the East China Sea. It is the third-longest river in the world and the longest in China.

The Yangzi and its tributaries drain China's most agriculturally productive area that since the twelfth century has been the country's principal granary. It is navigable for roughly 1,700 miles (2,700 km) facilitating commerce throughout the region. During the Southern **Song**, the **Ming**, and the **Qing** dynasties, the lower Yangzi became the most prosperous region of the country and was home to many of its scholars, artists, and political leaders. In recent years the government of China has attempted to control the river's flooding and harness its energy for electricity by building the controversial Three Gorges Dam, one of the largest construction projects ever attempted.

Yathrib
City in Arabia later known as **Medina**. After **Muhammad**'s escape to Yathrib from **Mecca** (622), the city became known as Medina ("Luminous City") and became one of **Islam**'s two holiest cities, along with Mecca.

Yayoi (c. 250 B.C.E.–250 C.E.)
Prehistoric culture of Japan subsequent to the **Jomon** culture. Some scholars believe the Yayoi people were newcomers into the Japanese archipelago, perhaps from Korea. Their culture arose on the southern Japanese island of **Kyûshû** near the Korea Strait and spread northeastward toward the Kanto Plain. The Yayoi culture was based on wet-paddy rice cultivation (of Chinese origin), but the people continued to hunt and collect seafood as the Jomon culture did.

Yellow River (Huang He)
River flowing approximately 2,900 miles (4,700 km) across China into the Yellow Sea. The Yellow River, which looks yellow because of **loess** silt in the water, and its tributaries the Wei, the Fen, and

the Wuding, form the heartland of Chinese civilization, with the first Chinese states having emerged there. The river is subject to frequent floods, earning it the nickname "China's sorrow." Since the first millennium B.C.E. Chinese governments have attempted to control the river through dikes and other hydraulic works but have never been entirely successful. The river has changed its course twenty-six times in the last 3,000 years.

Yi Dynasty. *See* Choson

Yin-Yang (literally "moon-sun")
Opposite but complementary principles that together make up the basic elements of life according to Chinese philosophy. In the third century B.C.E. yin-yang theory became a distinctive school of thought, but later its ideas were absorbed by other schools of thought and became part of the Chinese worldview. *Yin* is dark, passive, and female, and *yang* is bright, active, and male; yin represents earth and yang, heaven. The view of the world as consisting of compatible and necessarily complementary opposites, each containing a little of the other, contrasts with the sharper dualism that characterizes much of Western and Middle Eastern cosmology.

Yi Song-gye (1335–1392)
General who established the Yi dynasty that ruled Korea from 1392 to 1910, among the longest-ruling dynasties in world history. Yi, who came from the northeast frontier region and may have been of partly Manchurian tribal origin, was supported by a group of **Neo-Confucianist** reformers who wanted to reinvigorate the Korean state and implement sweeping social reforms in accordance to **Zhu Xi**'s interpretation of **Confucianism**. With their help Yi deposed the last Wang

king of the **Koryo** state and renamed the state **Choson** after an ancient Korean state. He abdicated after six years on the throne in favor of one of his sons.

Yi Sun-sin (1545–1597)
Korean admiral and national hero who fought the Japanese during the **Hideyoshi invasions** (1592–1598). While the Korean court remained largely unprepared, Yi, as commander of the navy in the southwestern Cholla province, began building a fleet when rumors of a planned Japanese invasion reached Korea. He implemented a number of military innovations, the most famous of which was the "turtle boat," the world's first iron-clad ship. Mounted with swiveling cannons, the turtle boats were highly effective in resisting Japanese cannon fire while ramming and destroying enemy ships. Yi's naval successes hindered Japan's ability to reinforce and supply its land forces, contributing to the war's stalemate and the eventual Japanese withdrawal from the peninsula. Yi was killed in battle during the last year of the war.

Yoga
One of the six orthodox schools of **Hinduism** best known for its physical exercise. The philosophy of yoga is expressed in its classic text the *Yoga-sutra*, by Patanjali (believed to have lived in the second century B.C.E.). The physical practices of yoga, of ancient origins, are intended to achieve spiritual liberation—a goal of all Hindus. In the modern era yoga has been practiced all over the world.

Yongle (Yung-le) (1359–1424)
Ming emperor of China (1402–1424) whose vigorous rule strengthened and extended the Chinese empire. Yongle is the name for his reign, and his own name was Zhu Di. He was the son of the first Ming ruler, the **Hongwu** emperor, and was a

capable general in the Ming army. After his father's death, the Yongle emperor used his military power to usurp the throne from his nephew after three years of civil war. He sponsored the voyages of **Zheng He** to Southeast Asia and the Indian Ocean, brought Japan into the **tributary system**, and launched campaigns in Annam (Vietnam) and in the Mongolian steppe. Concerned about new threats by the **Mongol Empire**, he moved the capital from Nanjing to **Beijing** in 1421 and restored the **Grand Canal** to supply it. This northward orientation of China resulted in a loss of interest in the southern voyages of Zheng He, which were also deemed too expensive.

Yongzheng (1678–1735)

Chinese imperial name (r. 1723–1735) of the second emperor of the **Qing** dynasty. The first three Qing emperors, including Yongzheng, saw the Chinese empire reach great power. The fourth son, named Yinzhen, of emperor **Kangxi** (r. 1662–1722), Yongzheng's administrative reforms enhanced the revenue of the state. He centralized control of the government by creating the Grand Council, with five or six members directly answerable to him, thus involving the emperor in the daily administration of government.

Yorktown

Site of the besiegement and final surrender of British troops to American and French forces at the end of the **American Revolution**. As September 1781 drew to a close, the British army under **Charles Cornwallis** found itself trapped between combined forces of American and French troops by land and French warships by sea. Cornwallis requested relief from the British navy, which arrived one week too late, on October 26, 1781. Cornwallis had surrendered to the colonials on October 19, 1781. The British formally recognized America as an independent nation in 1783.

Yoruba

People of southwestern Nigeria, Benin, and northern Togo. The Yoruba were originally from the **Oyo**, but by the nineteenth century came to include numerous distinct groups all of whom are descended from earlier kingdoms of that region. The Yoruba are urban people but with an agricultural economy.

Yosano Akiko (1878–1942)

Japanese poet, feminist, activist, and critic. Best known for passionately romantic verse, she wrote literary criticism for the *Seito* feminist journal. She and her husband, Yosano Tekkan, also a poet, published the literary journal *Myojo*, which introduced a number of poets of the new romantic movement to the literary public. A prominent pacifist and feminist, Yosano spoke out against the second **Sino-Japanese War** and the growing nationalistic fervor of the times. She later founded a women's college, the Bunka Gakuin.

Yoshida, Shigeru (1878–1967)

Post–**World War II** Japanese political leader and prime minister (1946–1947, 1948–1954) whose energetic leadership earned him the epithet "Wan Man [One-Man] Yoshida." A diplomat with pro-British and pro-American sentiments, he was distrusted by the militarists who dominated Japan in the 1930s and early 1940s. After Japan's defeat he became the chief architect of the postwar political system that emphasized supporting U.S. foreign policy, minimizing military expenditures, and concentrating on economic growth. He was staunchly anticommunist and pursued conservative, probusiness policies that would shape Japan's course of political and economic development for the next several decades.

Young Ireland

Irish **nationalist** movement of the 1840s. Inspired by **Young Italy** and Giuseppe Mazzini, Young Ireland called for a renewal of Irish and Celtic culture. In the midst of a series of revolutions in Europe in 1848, Young Ireland became increasingly militant and its members even attempted their own revolution, unsuccessfully.

Young Italy

Italian patriotic organization formed in 1831 by Giuseppe Mazzini. Young Italy was a primary mover in the Risorgimento, the **nationalist** unification movement that created the state of Italy out of smaller principalities.

Young Turks (Committee of Union and Progress [CUP])

Name for the **Ottoman nationalist** reform party that held the reins of the **Ottoman Empire** from 1908 to 1919. The three core Young Turk constituencies were the exile community, discontented civil servants and students, and a coalition of disaffected army officers. The first phase of the Young Turk period, from 1909 to 1913, saw a struggle for power between the CUP leadership and its mid and junior-level officer and civil servant base. The CUP gradually gained full control of government but by 1913 had devolved into a virtual military dictatorship under the triumvirate of Enver Pasa, Talat Pasa, and Cemal Pasa. The Young Turk/CUP era triggered debate over the politics of Arab, Turkish, and Islamic identities that lasted well after **World War I**.

Yuan (1260–1368)

Chinese dynasty also known as the **Mongol** Empire. The Mongol ruler **Khubilai Khan** (r. 1260–1294) inherited control over northern China, completed the conquest of the south, and took on the Chinese dynastic title *Yuan*. Under the Yuan the Mongols held the top posts in government and Chinese officials served at the lower levels. The Mongols, however, generally did not interfere with the cultural life of China, and the arts and letters flourished. The Yuan was China's golden age of drama. In the fourteenth century the Mongol military declined, and a series of Chinese revolts led to the expulsion of the Mongols from China in 1368.

Yuan Shih-kai (1859–1916)

President of China (1912–1916). A **warlord** in Shandong, Yuan was the resident general in Korea during the **Sino-Japanese War** (1894–1895). He supported the **Empress Dowager, Ci Xi,** against the reform movement (1898). As governor of Hebei he helped suppress the **Boxer Rebellion.** During the Republican Revolution of 1911 he procured a truce in which the **Qing** emperor abdicated on February 12, 1912. Through an assassination attempt and voting fraud, he managed to become president of the Republic of China in 1913. In 1914 he dissolved the parliament and on January 1, 1916, he assumed the title of emperor. A rebellion forced him almost immediately to restore the republic.

Yugoslavia (1929–1992)

Southeastern European country formed after **World War I**. Originally the Kingdom of the Serbs, Croats, and Slovenes, formed after the war out of the remains of **Austria-Hungary**, the country was ruled by Serbs and renamed Yugoslavia in 1929. Yugoslavia was overrun by the Germans in **World War II**. Marshal Tito and the communists, with aid from the Soviet Union, reunited the country after the war. After Tito's death in 1980 multiparty systems began to democratize and open Yugoslavia.

Independence movements in Croatia, Kosovo, and Slovenia led to Serbian oppression and warfare. Albanians were massacred in interracial warfare. In 1991 Croatia and Slovenia were recognized as independent, but ethnic cleansing in **Bosnia-Herzegovina** led to **United Nations** sanctions against Serbia and UN air strikes. In 1995 the Dayton Accord brought about a cease-fire. Serbia and Montenegro continued to claim to be Yugoslavia but without international recognition. Continued aggression against Kosovo by the Serbs brought on more air strikes in 1999. In 2003 an agreement was reached for Serbia and Montenegro to form a loose federation, with elections to decide their future in three years.

Yurt

Tentlike dwelling used by nomadic and seminomadic peoples along the eastern **steppe** of **Central Asia.** In constructing a yurt (also called ger), sheets of textiles, skins, or felt are placed over a frame of wooden poles and the floor is lined with furs or felt. A central hole in the roof allows smoke from a fire to escape.

Z

Zagwe

Dynastic name of twelfth- and thirteenth-century Ethiopian Christians. By tradition descended from the last kings of **Axum**, whom they deposed, the Zagwe controlled northern and central Ethiopia. They were known for their monolithic rock–hewn churches.

Zaibatsu

Japanese business conglomerates with their ownership concentrated in the hands of a single family. *Zaibatsu* emerged in the late nineteenth century with the rapid industrialization of **Meiji Japan**. Initially they were aided by the Meiji government, with which the founders had political links. By the early twentieth century four giants—Mitsubishi, Mitsui, Yasuda, and Sumitomo—controlled much of Japan's industry and wielded enormous political influence. After 1945 they were broken up by the U.S. occupation authorities for their contribution to Japan's militarist and expansionist efforts. Although no longer controlled by the original families, parts of the zaibatsu became parts of new postwar industrial groups known as *keiretsu*.

Zaïre

Former name (1971–1997) of the Democratic Republic of Congo.
See also Congo

Zanj (869–883)

Arabic name referring to the East African coast first mentioned by Jahiz of Basra in the ninth century C.E., known for the black slave rebellion against the **Abbasid caliphate**. East Africans (later known as Zanj) were brought into Iraq to drain the salt marshes. Led by Ali ibn Muhammad and joined by black Africans from the army and some locals, the slaves defeated an Abbasid army, gained control of southern Iraq, and established their own capital in the salt marshes. They won more military victories and expanded their territorial control through 878. From 879 onward the caliphate armies had more success against the Zanj, and by 883 the revolt was crushed.

Zanzibar

East African island and seaport. Zanzibar, now a part of Tanzania, was an important commercial center for the transfer of goods between Asia and Africa. In 1806 Syyid Said became Muslim sultan of Zanzibar and for fifty years controlled a vast commercial domain in East Africa. The British controlled Zanzibar in the late nineteenth century, and the United States also recognized its importance and established a consulate there in 1836.

Zapata, Emiliano (1879–1919)

Mexican revolutionary who fought for agrarian and land reforms. The Zapatistas (Nahuatl-speaking indigenous people and humble mestizos of the region of Morelos) rebelled against the corrupt Porfirio Díaz regime for perpetuating a system in which large landowners were favored to such an extent that by 1910 90 percent of Mexico's indigenous communities had lost their lands. The rallying cry became "Land and Liberty!" This movement became part of the **Mexican Revolution** (1910–1920). In 1911 Zapata joined **Francisco Madero's** democratic revolution, but when Madero dropped land reform Zapata broke with him and later joined forces with **Pancho Villa**. Zapata attacked large landowners and redistributed their land to the peasants. He was killed by revolutionary rival **Venustiano Carranza's** soldiers. Zapata's reputation in Mexico remains enormously influential.

Zapatista Uprising (1994)

Mexican armed revolt by indigenous peoples. Maya and Tzotzil natives from Chiapas, Mexico, rebelled against 500 years of oppression and against neoliberalism in a peasant-based antigovernment **guerrilla** conflict. They called themselves the Zapatista Army for National Liberation in the spirit of the early-twentieth-century revolutionary **Emiliano Zapata**, who fought for land reforms for indigenous peoples. By 1997 the Zapatistas had moved away from armed conflict and peacefully marched on Mexico City to demand government action.

Zapotec Civilization (c. 400 B.C.E.–300 C.E.)

Mesoamerican civilization of central Mexico near the modern-day city of Oaxaca. The Zapotec were a highlands people who built temples and pyramids on stone terraces on a 1,200-foot (366-m) mountain at **Monte Alban**, with the population living on terraces cut into the mountainsides. The Zapotec were influenced by the **Olmec** and had a pantheon of gods. Like most Mesoamerican civilizations, they practiced human sacrifice.

Zen

Sect of **Buddhism** derived from the **Sanskrit** term *dhyana* ("meditation"), pronounced "*chan*" in Chinese, "*son*" in Korean, and "*zen*" in Japanese. Associated with the missionary Bodhidharma, Zen became popular in **Tang** China. It became an important sect in Korea and Japan in the twelfth and thirteenth centuries, when it is was patronized by military rulers, although it had been introduced earlier in both countries. Zen adherents use various methods in addition to meditation, including paradoxical statements called koan, in order to achieve enlightenment. In Japan, Zen's emphasis on the aesthetics of simplicity and disciplined meditation influenced the arts and literature during **Kamakura** and **Ashikaga** times. Zen inspired both the **tea ceremony** and **No** drama.

Zeng Guofan (Tseng Kuo-fan) (1811–1872)

Chinese scholar, official, and military commander who helped to restore the **Qing** dynasty in the mid-nineteenth century. Zeng Guofan organized the Huainan army that contributed to the defeat of the **Taiping Rebellion**. Later he carried out reforms such as the establishment of the Jiangnan arsenal to produce Western arms and the introduction of schools to study Western languages and technology as part of the Self-Strengthening Movement. These reforms proved insufficient to enable China to withstand the challenge of Western imperialism or to save the Qing dynasty. Nonetheless, the **Guomindang** government in the 1930s made Zeng a symbol of Chinese patriotism and selfless service to the state.

Zeus

Greatest of the ancient Greek gods, ruler of Olympus, and father of gods and humans.

Later identified with the Roman god Jupiter, Zeus was the offspring of Cronus and Rhea, who devoured all their children except Zeus, who then overthrew Cronus. Zeus mated with countless goddesses and mortal women and produced legions of offspring.

Zhang Qian (Chang Ch'ien)
(d. 114 B.C.E.)
Chinese diplomat and explorer who helped to establish contact between the **Han** dynasty and western Eurasia. Sent by emperor **Han Wudi** in 138 B.C.E. to contact the Indo-European-speaking Yuezhi tribal peoples in **Central Asia**, he was captured by the **Xiongnu**, who detained him for ten years. During that time Zhang Qian married and had children before escaping to proceed westward again on his mission. He failed to convince the Yuezhi to unite in an alliance against the Xiongnu. On his return to China he was captured again by the Xiongnu and detained for another year. He made it back to China around 125 B.C.E. In a second trip (118–115 B.C.E.), he attempted to forge an alliance with the Wusun but also failed. His deputy traveled farther, to what is now Uzbekistan and Afghanistan. Zhang's expeditions promoted greater knowledge about the West in China and helped to establish the **Silk Roads**.

Zhang Xueliang (Chang Hsüeh-liang)
(1898–2001)
Chinese warlord, son of Chang Tso-lin, whom he succeeded after the latter was assassinated by Japan in 1928. In 1936 he kidnapped his nominal leader, **Chiang Kai-shek**, at Xi'an to compel cooperation between the **Guomindang** and the communists against Japan. Zhang then surrendered to Chiang and was tried and sentenced for his part in the affair; he was pardoned but kept in custody until 1962.

He went to Taiwan when the Guomindang regime fled there in 1949.

Zheng He (Cheng Ho) (1371–1433)
Chinese eunuch admiral of **Muslim** background who led seven maritime expeditions to Southeast Asia, India, Arabia, and the east coast of Africa (1405–1407, 1407–1409, 1409–1411, 1413–1415, 1417–1419, 1421–1422, 1431–1433). The purpose of these voyages is not clear, but they were probably part of the **Ming** dynasty's attempt to extend its influence and protect sea-lanes in Southeast Asia from pirates. The expeditions were huge; the first had 28,000 men in more than 300 ships. Some of Zheng He's ships were 400 feet (122 m) long (Christopher Columbus's *Santa María* measured 60 feet). Zheng He's expeditions established Chinese naval supremacy in the South China Sea and the Indian Ocean and displayed China's potential to create an overseas empire. The expeditions ran into opposition from members of court who found them too costly, and they were discontinued. Zheng He fell out of favor, was banished, and nearly all his documents were destroyed. China by the 1440s had ended most oceangoing trips.

Zhou (Chou) (c. 1045–256 B.C.E.)
Period in which the Zhou dynasty ruled at least nominally over most of northern and, later, central China. The Zhou were a warlike people from the Wei Valley who conquered **Shang** and established a new state under King Wu and his brother, the Duke of Zhou. The latter was honored by later Chinese as a great sage. The Zhou established a feudal system of government. After suffering defeat by a nomadic tribe in 771 B.C.E. the Zhou moved their capital from the Wei Valley, in northwestern China, to the more eastern city of Luoyang. The Zhou gradually lost control over most of China, but rulers of various states gave

the dynasty nominal allegiance until the Zhou were destroyed by **Qin** in 256 B.C.E. The Zhou period saw the emergence of the great schools of ancient philosophy including **Confucianism, Daoism,** and **legalism.** Conventionally, the period is divided into the Western Zhou (1045–771) and Eastern Zhou (771–256).

Zhou Enlai (Chou En-lai) (1898–1976) **Chinese Communist Party** leader. Zhou, born to a mandarin family, became a member of the Politburo of the Chinese Communist Party in 1927 and remained one until his death. He served as premier of the **People's Republic of China** from 1954 to 1976, functioning as head of administration and as China's chief diplomat. He played an important role in the Afro-Asian Bandung Conference in 1955 and in improving relations with Japan and the United States in the 1970s. He remains one of the most admired of modern Chinese leaders.

Zhuangzi (Chuang-tzu) (meaning "Master Zhuang") (d. 329 B.C.E.) Chinese philosopher and major interpreter of **Daoism.** He is principally known by the book named after and attributed to him (*Zhuangzi*), although the book is believed to have been compiled following his death, in the third century B.C.E. Zhuangzi's mysticism, relativism, and love of paradox greatly influenced Chinese literature, art, and thought.

Zhu Xi (Chu Hsi) (1130–1200) Chinese philosopher and a major formulator of **Neo-Confucianism.** Zhu devoted himself to a careful study of the Chinese classics. His commentaries on them stressed the importance of duty, ritual, responsibility to family and society, and the need to strive for individual moral perfection. His interpretations of the classics associated with **Confucianism** became

the basis for the Chinese **civil service examinations.** He also wrote a handbook on the rituals and ceremonies associated with marriage that influenced marital customs in China and Korea. Zhu's interlinear commentaries to the Confucian classics have been included in most editions since late imperial China.

Ziggurat
Mesopotamian pyramidal temple tower built in a stepped, terraced fashion. Ziggurats were constructed in **Mesopotamia** from about 2200 until 500 B.C.E. They were built with interiors of mud bricks and exteriors of baked brick; had no internal chambers; and were square or rectangular, with the stepped construction either as a spiral ramp or with external means of ascent, often unknown today. The terraces were landscaped, like the Hanging Gardens of **Babylon.** The Tower of Babel may have been the ziggurat of Marduk in Babylon. The largest existing ziggurat is in the ancient city of **Ur.**

Zimbabwe. *See* Great Zimbabwe

Zollverein
Customs agreement, especially that formed by various German states between 1819 and 1871, whereby toll charges were not collected on goods moving between those states. The Zollverein helped pave the way for the political unification of Germany in 1871.

Zoroaster. *See* Zoroastrianism

Zoroastrianism
Ancient religion of Iran. Zoroastrianism was founded by the Iranian Zoroaster in the sixth century B.C.E. Zoroaster believed in a supreme god who created light and darkness, often associated with good and evil; therefore Zoroastrianism has elements

of **monotheism** as well as **polytheism** and is dualistic. Zoroaster saw himself as a prophet sent to purify religion and believed that the end of the world and the Kingdom of Heaven were near. Zoroastrianism provides the individual with free choice in a struggle against evil, making it a moral religion, but one in which destiny ultimately is the most powerful force in the termination of a life. Zoroastrianism influenced **Judaism, Christianity,** and **Islam.**

Zulu War. *See* Anglo-Zulu War

Zwingli, Huldrych (1485–1531)
Swiss reformer. Baptized Ulrich, Zwingli was a humanist in the **Desiderius Eras-** mus tradition but followed many of **Martin Luther**'s ideas on reform of the **Roman Catholic Church**. As a priest in Zurich, Zwingli called for reforms of the mass in line with the New Testament. By 1525 the Zurich church was following many of his reforms, but the city magistrates forced him to slow the reform movement. Zwingli and Luther were never able to agree on the meaning of the rite of the Eucharist, hence the reformers, or **Protestants,** never unified. Some of Zwingli's followers adopted more radical reforms and became known as **Anabaptists** ("rebaptizers") for their belief in adult, rather than infant, baptism.

WEB SITES

General World History and World History Education Web Sites

Some Web sites listed here are for world history organizations. Some are teaching sites, and some provide vast documentation. All offer useful information and links to other sites. Just about every state in the United States has a Web site with information on specific state education requirements.

American Historical Association	http://www.historians.org/teaching/
Annenberg/CPB	http://www.learner.org/
Center for History and New Media: World History Matters	http://chnm.gmu.edu/worldhistorymatters/
Center for History and New Media: World History Sources	http://chnm.gmu.edu/worldhistorysources/
Choices Program, The	http://www.choices.edu/index.cfm
College Board AP Courses	http://apcentral.collegeboard.com
Films for the Humanities and Sciences	http://www.film.com/Films_Home/Index.cfm?S=1
General History from the University of Kansas	http://ukans.edu/history
History/Social Studies Web Site K–12	http://my.execps.com/~dboals/boals.html
H-Net Humanities and Social Sciences	http://www.h-net.msu.edu/~world/
Journal of World History	http://www.uhpress.hawaii.edu/journals/jwh/
National Center for History in the Schools	http://www.sscnet.ucla.edu/nchs/worldlinks.html
National Council for History Education	http://www.history.org/nche/
National Security Archive	http://www.hwu.edu/~nsarchiv/
Social Studies School Service	http://www.socialstudies.com
Spartacus Schoolnet	http://www.spartacus.schoolnet.co.uk
Stanford Program on International and Cross-Cultural Education	http://spice.stanford.edu/
World Area Studies Internet Resources	http://www.wcsu.ctstateu.edu/socialsci/area.html
World Art Treasures	http://www.bergerfoundation.ch/
World Factbook, The	http://www.odci.gov/cia/publications/factbook/
World History Association	http://www.thewha.org

| World History Connected | http://worldhistoryconnected.press.uiuc.edu/ |
| WWW Virtual Library | http://vlib.org/Home.html |

Specialty Web Sites

Every specialty has a multitude of Web sites. Many are good and informative, but beware of those produced by nonexperts. Links on reputable sites will usually take you to other reputable sites.

Africa Action	http://www.africaaction.org/index.php
African Research Central	http://www.africa-research.org/main.html
African Studies	http://www.africanstudies.org/
Ancient Greece	http://www.ancientgreece.com
Ancient Mesoamerican Civilizations	http://www.angelfire.com/ca/humanorigins/index.html
Ancient Mesopotamia	http://historylink101.com/ancient_mesopotamia.htm
Ancient World Cultures	http://eawc.evansville.edu/index.htm
British History	http://history.ac.uk/
British History	http://british-history.ac.uk/
Byzantine Studies	http://www.metmuseum.org/explore/Byzantium/byz_1.html
China Institute	http://www.chinainstitute.org/
Medieval History	http://www.fordham.edu/halsall/
Medieval History	http://labyrinth.georgetown.edu/
Oriental Institute	http://oi.uchicago.edu/OI/default.html
Silk Road	http://www.silk-road.com/toc/intro.html
Women in World History	http://www.womeninworldhistory.com/

BIBLIOGRAPHY

Selected World History Studies and Guides

Abu-Lughod, Janet L. *Before European Hegemony: The World System, A.D. 1250–1350.* 1989. Reprint, New York: Oxford University Press, 1991. Argues for a world economy before the rise of European domination.

Adams, Steven, Michael Adas, and Kevin Reilly. *Selected Course Outlines and Reading Lists from American Colleges and Universities: World History.* Princeton, NJ: Markus Weiner Publishers, 1998. Course outlines for different approaches to global history.

Bentley, Jerry. *Old World Encounters: Cross-Cultural Contacts and Exchanges in Pre-Modern Times.* New York: Oxford University Press, 1993. A study of interactions rather than one separating cultures.

Best, Antony, Jussi M. Hanhimäki, Joseph A. Maiolo, and Kirsten E. Schulze. *International History of the Twentieth Century.* London: Routledge, 2004. The twentieth century from a non-U.S. perspective.

Crosby, Alfred W. *Ecological Imperialism: The Biological Expansion of Europe, 900–1900.* Cambridge and New York: Cambridge University Press, 1993. A global view of historical impact on the environment.

Dunn, Ross, ed. *The New World History: A Teacher's Companion.* Boston: Bedford / St. Martin's, 2000. Essays by many of the great names in the teaching of world history.

Gamble, Clive. *Timewalkers: The Prehistory of Global Colonization.* Cambridge, MA: Harvard University Press, 1994. A thought-provoking work on the process of the spread of human civilization.

Journal of World History. The official journal of the World History Association.

Norton, Mary Beth, and Pamela Gerardi, eds. *The American Historical Association's Guide to Historical Literature.* 2 vols. New York: Oxford University Press, 1995. The American Historical Association's monumental guide by area and period.

Roupp, Heidi, ed. *Teaching World History: A Resource Book.* Armonk, NY: M.E. Sharpe, 1997. A useful guide for teachers.

Simmons, I. G. *Changing the Face of the Earth: Culture, Environment, and History.* Oxford: Blackwell, 1989. A geographic, multidisciplinary look at the impact of humans on the global ecosystem.

Selected World History Texts

Bentley, Jerry H., and Herbert F. Ziegler. *Traditions and Encounters: A Global Perspective on the Past.* Boston: McGraw-Hill, 2002.

Craig, Albert M., William A. Graham, Donald Kagan, Steven Ozment, and Frank M. Turner. *The Heritage of World Civilizations.* 2nd ed. Upper Saddle River, NJ: Prentice Hall, 2004.

Duiker, William, and Jackson J. Spielvogel. *The Essential World History.* Belmont, CA: Wadsworth Publishing, 2005.

Spodek, Howard. *The World's History.* 3rd ed. Upper Saddle River, NJ: Prentice Hall, 2006.

Stearns, Peter N., Michael Adas, Marc Jason Gilbert, and Stuart Schwartz. *World Civilizations: The Global Experience.* New York: Longman, 2003.

Selected World History Document Readers

Andrea, Alfred J., and James H. Overfield. *The Human Record: Sources of Global History.* Boston: Houghton Mifflin, 2004.

Riley, Philip F., Frank A. Gerome, Henry A. Myers, and Chong-Kun Yoon. *The Global Experience: Readings in World History.* 5th ed. Upper Saddle River, NJ: Prentice Hall, 2005.

INDEX

About the Author

JOHN J. BUTT is Professor of History at James Madison University, where he teaches Global History and British, Medieval, and Early Modern European History. His research interests include sixteenth and seventeenth-century developments in agriculture and botany. He is author of *Daily Life in the Age of Charlemagne* (2002). Dr. Butt is also Director of Honors Abroad at Oxford University, and the University of St Andrews.